THE CAMBRIDGE HISTORY OF

AFRICAN AND CARIBBEAN LITERATURE

*

This history offers new perspectives on African and Caribbean literature. It provides the general coverage and specific information expected of a major history. Chapters address the literature itself, the practices and conditions of its composition, and its complex relationship with African social and geopolitical history. The book provides an introduction to the entire body of productions that can be considered to comprise the field of African literature, defined both by imaginative expression in Africa itself and the black diaspora. It also accounts for the specific historical and cultural context in which this expression has been manifested in Africa and the Caribbean: the formal particularities of the literary corpus, both oral and written, that can be ascribed to the two areas, and the diversity of material and texts covered by the representative works. This magisterial history of African literature is an essential resource for specialists and students.

Professor F. Abiola Irele is Professor of Afro-American Studies and Romance Languages and Literatures at Harvard University. His publications include an annotated edition of *Selected Poems of Léopold Sédar Senghor* (1977), *The African Experience in Literature and Ideology* (1981; reprinted 1990), and an annotated edition of *Aimé Césaire's Cahier d'un retour au pays natal* (1994; second edition 1999), as well as numerous articles and reviews and a recent volume of essays, *The African Imagination* (2001). He is a contributing editor to the new *Norton Anthology of World Literature* and is currently editor of *Research in African Literatures*. He is general editor of the series *Cambridge Studies in African and Caribbean Literature.*

Simon Gikandi is Robert Hayden Professor of English Language and Literature at the University of Michigan, Ann Arbor. His books include *Reading the African Novel, Reading Chinua Achebe, Writing in Limbo: Modernism and Caribbean Literature, Maps of Englishness: Writing Identity in the Culture of Colonialism*, and *Ngugi wa Thiong'o*. He is the general editor of *The Encyclopedia of African Literature*.

THE CAMBRIDGE HISTORY OF AFRICAN AND CARIBBEAN LITERATURE

*

VOLUME 1

*

Edited by
F. ABIOLA IRELE
and
SIMON GIKANDI

PUBLISHED BY THE PRESS SYNDICATE OF THE UNIVERSITY OF CAMBRIDGE
The Pitt Building, Trumpington Street, Cambridge, United Kingdom

CAMBRIDGE UNIVERSITY PRESS
The Edinburgh Building, Cambridge CB2 2RU, UK
40 West 20th Street, New York, NY 10011-4211, USA
477 Williamstown Road, Port Melbourne, VIC 3207, Australia
Ruiz de Alarcón 13, 28014 Madrid, Spain
Dock House, The Waterfront, Cape Town 8001, South Africa

http://www.cambridge.org

First published 2004

Printed in the United Kingdom at the University Press, Cambridge

Typeface Dante MT 10.5/13 pt *System* LaTeX 2ε [TB]

A catalogue record for this book is available from the British Library

Library of Congress cataloging in publication data

Irele, Abiola.
The Cambridge history of African and Caribbean literature / edited by F. Abiola Irele and Simon Gikandi.
p. cm.
Includes bibliographical references and index.
ISBN 0 521 59434 0 (hardback)
1. Literature – Black authors – History and criticism. I. Gikandi, Simon II. Title.
PN841.174 2003
809′.8896 – dc21 2003046121

Volume 1 ISBN 0 521 83275 6
Only available as a two-volume set ISBN 0 521 59434 0 hardback

Contents

Contents

Volume 2

Notes on contributors

FARIDA ABU-HAIDAR is with the Institute of Linguists in London.

OUESSINA ALIDOU is a professor in the Department of Africana Studies of Rutgers University, Piscataway, New Jersey.

DAVID ATTWELL is Chair of the Department of English in the School of Language, Culture, and Communication of the University of Natal, Pietermaritzburg, South Africa.

KARIN BARBER is Professor of African Cultural Anthropology at the Centre of West African Studies, University of Birmingham, England.

ANN BIERSTEKER is a professor with African and African American Studies at Yale University.

ANTHONY CHENNELLS is a professor in the Department of English at the University of Zimbabwe, in Mount Pleasant, Harare.

AMPIE COETZEE is Senior Professor of Afrikaans Literature at the University of the Western Cape, Bellville (near Cape Town), South Africa.

J. MICHAEL DASH is Professor of French at New York University.

MOIRA FERGUSON is Professor of English at the University of Missouri-Kansas City.

PATRICIA GEESEY is Associate Professor of French at the University of North Florida.

SIMON GIKANDI is Professor of English Language and Literature at the University of Michigan in Ann Arbor.

LIZ GUNNER is a member of the Department of English at the University of Natal, Scottsville in South Africa.

RUSSELL G. HAMILTON is Professor Emeritus of Lusophone African, Brazilian, and Portuguese Literatures at Vanderbilt University.

F. ABIOLA IRELE is Professor of Afro-American Studies and Romance Languages and Literatures at Harvard University.

DAN IZEVBAYE is a professor in the Faculty of Arts at the University of Fort Hare in South Africa.

SYLVIE KANDÉ is an independent scholar residing in New York.

ADELE KING is Professor of French at Ball State University in Muncie, Indiana.

TEODROS KIROS is Professor of Philosophy at Suffolk University in Boston.

MILTON KRIEGER is with the Department of Liberal Studies of Western Washington University in Bellingham.

DANIEL P. KUNENE is a professor in the Department of African Languages and Literature at the University of Wisconsin, Madison.

ROBERT ERIC LIVINGSTON is Associate Director of the Institute for Collaborative Research and Public Humanities at the Ohio State University in Columbus.

BÉNÉDICTE MAUGUIÈRE is Professor of Francophone Studies at the University of Louisiana at Lafayette.

ALAMIN MAZRUI is a professor in the Department of African American and African Studies at the Ohio State University in Columbus.

MILDRED MORTIMER is Professor of French at the University of Colorado in Boulder.

LUPENGA MPHANDE is with the Department of African American and African Studies at the Ohio State University in Columbus.

NICK NESBITT is a professor in the Department of French at Miami University in Oxford, Ohio.

M'BARE N'GOM is Chair of the Department of Foreign Languages at Morgan State University in Baltimore.

ODE S. OGEDE is a professor in the Department of English at North Carolina Central University in Durham.

ISIDORE OKPEWHO is a professor in the Department of Afro-American and African Studies at the State University of New York-Binghamton.

TEJUMOLA OLANIYAN is with the Department of African Languages and Literature at the University of Wisconsin in Madison.

LIZABETH PARAVISINI-GEBERT is a professor in the Department of Hispanic Studies at Vassar College in Poughkeepsie, New York.

ATO QUAYSON is with the Department of English in Pembroke College, Cambridge.

ALAIN RICARD is with the Centre d'Etude d'Afrique Noire of the Universités de Bordeaux, France.

ELAINE SAVORY is Director of the Literature Program at the New School University, New York City.

FLORA VEIT-WILD is a member of the Philosophische Fakultät III, Asien- und Afrikawissenschaften of Humbolt-Universität zu Berlin.

KEITH Q. WARNER is Professor of French and Caribbean Studies at George Mason University, Fairfax, Virginia.

MAUREEN WARNER-LEWIS is Professor of African-Caribbean Language and Orature in the Department of Literatures in English, University of the West Indies, Mona, Jamaica.

SABRA WEBBER is an Associate Professor, with a joint appointment in the Departments of Near Eastern Languages and Cultures and Comparative Studies in the Humanities at the Ohio State University in Columbus.

DEREK WRIGHT is Professor of English at the University of Queensland in Brisbane, Australia.

KWESI YANKAH is a professor at the University of Ghana in Legon.

Preface

In her inaugural lecture as Professor of English at University College, Ibadan, Molly Mahood justified the formal study of English literature in an African university on the grounds that the English language was uniquely placed to play a significant role in the emergence of new national literatures in the African territories under British rule, as part of the process of their transformation into national entities that the colonial situation had inevitably set in motion. Invoking the precedent established in the early part of the twentieth century by the signal contribution of Irish writers to the renewal of English, Mahood envisioned a parallel development in which creative writers in Africa would function as effective bearers of an original imagination, rooted in the local culture, and forging out of the common experience a new and compelling expression in English. Her intimation of a literary renaissance in Africa based on English was further premised on a sociological observation that took account of the progressive rise of a national elite educated in a common language, that of the colonizer, and from whose ranks would arise not only the creative writers but also a new reading public, and in particular a cadre of informed critics, responding to their work in terms familiar to both writer and public and thus serving as the primary audience for the new literature. In her view, the university in Africa could thus be regarded as the enabling environment for the formation of a new literary culture, in what Stanley Fish was later to call "an interpretive community," for which the colonial language stood to function as the determining cohesive element (Mahood 1955).

The main point of Mahood's argument which has to do with the potential for the rise of a new literature in English was soon to be fully verified in the Nigerian context that was the immediate focus of her attention. Although Cyprian Ekwensi and Amos Tutuola were already published writers by the time she delivered her lecture, the significance of their work as harbingers of a new literary culture was to be heightened by the appearance in 1958 of Chinua Achebe's novel, *Things Fall Apart*, a work that has since established itself as one of the master texts of modern African literature. The fact that Achebe himself was an alumnus of Ibadan thus gave point and effect to Mahood's argument, for Achebe's achievement was soon to be mirrored in that of other alumni of Ibadan, notably Wole Soyinka, Christopher Okigbo, and John Pepper Clark, whose work began to appear in the immediate aftermath of Nigerian independence. With other writers who had no direct connection with the university but who began their careers in the early sixties, such as Gabriel Okara and Onuora Nzekwu, they represent the first generation in the full emergence of literature in English as a major component of Nigeria's cultural history in modern times.

It is of particular interest, fifty and more years since Molly Mahood's inaugural lecture, to evoke the Nigerian case, which has been in many ways emblematic of the cultural transitions that accompanied the political process on the African continent in the second half of the twentieth century, for similar developments were taking place in other parts of colonial Africa, with varying degrees of achievement and interest. The developments in which the European languages began to be employed effectively as means of the expression of African responses to the historical, social, and cultural implications of the colonial dispensation, for the representation of indigenous modes of life and the articulation of a new sense of identity, derived from the traditional, precolonial folkways and heritage of cultural values. This new literature of African assertion, in many ways the culmination of an earlier discourse going back to the eighteenth century concerned with exploring the historic encounter with Europe, helped to define a new historic profile of Africans and black people as part of the human community, a status they had been denied by an accumulated history of slavery, colonialism, racism. The writer assumed a prophetic role as the vanguard of the African revolution – the "voice of vision in his own time" as Wole Soyinka was later to proclaim – and literature an intense valuation as the mode of expression of a new consciousness. For reasons having to do with this thematic focus related to African self-definition, as well as its accessibility in the European languages, it is this tradition of African letters that has come to be regarded as the central reference in the general conception of African literature.

The emergence in the years after the Second World War of the African writer as a cultural icon also helped to direct attention to other areas of African imaginative life, in particular that represented by the oral tradition, obscured by the emphasis upon literacy as the mark of modernity. The oral texts that infused with life the institutional framework of precolonial African societies and cultures featured in western scholarship largely as ancillary documents in such disciplines as anthropology and ethnohistory. The emphasis on structure and orientation toward expressive values in literary scholarship occasioned by the so-called "oral-formulaic theory" associated with Parry and Lord helped to foster a renewed attention to African orality and a recognition of its purely literary articulations. Two major collections initiated in the sixties helped to provide the wealth of primary material on various aspects and genres of African oral literature that sustained this interest. These collections, the Oxford Library of African Literature and the "Classiques Africains" series in France have furnished the main reference texts on which scholarship on African oral literature continues to rely. The concern with the indigenous heritage of literature culminated in the rediscovery of the great oral epics, *Sundiata*, *Ozidi*, *Mwindo*, and others, a result that has been due as much to the diligent research of scholars as to the enterprise of both academic and trade publishers in Europe and America, which has enabled the texts to become available in workable editions. The collections, monographs, and detailed studies produced by African and European scholars have thus contributed immensely to our understanding of the modalities and procedures of African orality, so that the oral literature came to assume a new significance as elements of Africa's cultural capital. At the same time they presented theoretical and methodological interest for academic areas such as discourse analysis and performance theory (via the pioneering work of Victor Turner, 1967, on ritual) as well as for comparative poetics, for example, with respect to parallels between the modes of literary creation in Africa and in medieval Europe: parallels which have been pursued in the work of scholars like Jeff Opland (1983) and, in the later phase of his career, Paul Zumthor (1983; 1990).

The scholarly interest in African orality also drew attention to the considerable body of literature in the African languages that had come into existence as a consequence of the reduction of these languages to writing, one of the enduring effects of Christian evangelization. The ancient tradition of Ethiopian literature in Ge'ez, and modern works like Thomas Mofolo's *Shaka* in the Sotho language, and the series of Yoruba novels by D. O. Fagunwa, were thus able finally to receive the consideration they deserved. African-language literatures came to be regarded as a distinct province of the general landscape of imaginative life and literary activity on the African continent (Jahn 1961 and 1966; Gérard 1971 and 1981).

These were the circumstances that gave impetus to the academic study of African literature as a discipline, focused on the two modes of existence, oral and written, in which this literature has been manifested. We have endeavored in the present work to provide an account of the entire body of productions that can be considered to comprise this broad field as defined both by imaginative expression in African itself, and aspects of the continuum as represented by literature in the Caribbean and to some extent in North America. The work has been designed to take account of the specific historical and cultural context in which this expression has been shown in the two areas of human experience concerned by the project, the formal particularities of the literary corpus, both oral and written, that can be ascribed to the two areas and, in particular, the diversity of material covered by the representative texts.

This observation raises the question of delimitation of the field designated by the term "African literature." We are aware of the fact that the extensive scope and the heterogeneous character of the material covered by this history raise the problem of definition in an acute way. However, we have not attempted to provide an unqualified answer to the question as to what qualifies as African literature, either in terms of intrinsic features of theme and cultural reference, or of stylistic modes and formal conventions, and ultimately, of extrinsic factors related to conditions of production, performance and transmission of the texts, oral and written. The question of definition arises from the peculiar historical pressures that have attended the development of modern African expression, and their implications for the academic study of African literature. As Dan Izevbaye has shown, in the various efforts to define African literature, it has not been possible to apply the standard criteria such as language (as, for example, with French literature) or that of a unified territorial/national reference (as with the literature of England/Britain) (Izevbaye 1968). The political and ideological background to the emergence of modern African literature – pan-Africanism and African nationalism – has thus determined the recourse to the term now in common usage, which the present work has not only adopted but seeks to endorse in its reference to the entire field of imaginative expression in Africa.

In conformity with accepted practice, therefore, the term "African literature" has been taken here to mean the literature that has been produced on the African continent, whatever the specific provenance of the oral or written text and of the corpus being considered, and whatever the language of expression of the text in question, the particular modes it employs, or the conventions to which it conforms. Africa is viewed here in geopolitical terms, covering both the sub-Saharan regions habitually associated with black populations, as well as North Africa, including Egypt, inhabited today predominantly by Arab people. This explains the inclusion of literature in Arabic, despite the inevitable overlap with the Middle East. The project's working definition is especially important for literature by Africans of European descent, notably South Africans writing in English and Afrikaans, who are being located within the social and cultural history and the literary traditions of a continent with which they have often maintained an ambiguous relation in the past, but to which they have become aware of being irrevocably bound. In this perspective, Afrikaans is considered an African language, comparable to Ki-Swahili in its emergence on African soil as recognizably a new language, and in its development as a significant communicative and expressive medium.

The literary area defined by the geopolitical conception of Africa that underlies this work embraces a wide variety of languages, each serving to ground a cluster of literary forms. As already noted, imaginative expression in Africa can be identified in two broadly distinct modes: on one hand, that associated with an indigenous oral tradition, and on the other, that deriving from the conventions of the literate cultures with which the continent has been in contact for the best part of the preceding millennium. However, this primary division soon begins to yield a multiplicity of categories determined by the considerable range of languages and literary conventions to be found on the African continent. Given this diversity, a literary history of Africa, consisting of a coherent and linear narrative of its development over time, and valid for the entire continent, is neither feasible nor even meaningful. These considerations have compelled an approach that departs in important respects from the conventional literary histories, which typically consist in a progressive narration of distinctive periods and movements in the evolution of a national literature, with appropriate emphasis on the great figures and works that have determined this evolution. This work has therefore been conceived as essentially a comprehensive survey of the field, structured along generic lines as regards the oral tradition, and along linguistic/regional lines as regards the modern literature in both the African and European languages.

The term "African literature" has also been taken to refer, albeit in what may be considered a secondary sense, to the "colonial literature" produced by metropolitan European writers for whom Africa has served as the setting either for a complete cycle of works (Pierre Loti, Rider Haggard, Joyce Cary) or for single/specific works (as in the case of Joseph Conrad, Graham Greene, and Castro Soromenho). It needs to be stressed that the discourse of power either elaborated by this literature or implicit within it represents the principal symbolic channel of the colonial ideology, with which Africans and black people in the African diaspora have had to contend.

This prompts a consideration of the thematic and formal links between African literature and Caribbean literature, links that make it convenient to consider them together in a single project. The early forms of expression by blacks in the New World, either in the oral mode (the folktales, songs, and chants, as well as the textual content of ritual practices) or in the literate mode (as exemplified notably by the slave narratives) not only reflect an African response to the novel historical circumstances of Atlantic slavery; they also bear the stamp of a distinctive African sensibility. The slave narratives in particular mark the common origins of modern literary expression by blacks in Africa and the New World; they began as African texts, evolving later into a distinctly American genre (Woodard 1999; Andrews and Gates 2000). They represent the earliest texts in which the implications of the historic encounter between Africa and Europe are documented in factual terms and explored in imaginative terms, and inaugurate a modern awareness arising out of this encounter, an awareness that is bound to a new sense of the black racial community, defined as much by its objective situation of historical adversity as by the cultural continuities which bind the black populations of the African diaspora to the mother continent. The postulate of a fundamental African sensibility conditioned by common forms of social experience and cultural practice is strengthened by the evident vitality in the New World of African-derived forms of folklore and religious expression. This awareness informs such concepts as pan-Africanism and Negritude, and provides the keynote to the most significant literature by black writers in the twentieth century.

Despite its connection to Africa, literature in the Caribbean has developed along specific thematic and expressive channels related to the charged historical drama of the region and its complex racial and cultural composition. This makes it imperative to take account of the double reference of Caribbean literature: as both the reflection of a global African experience and as testimony to a process of collective self-fashioning in a new environment. Although unified by reference to a common experience (slavery and its colonial sequel), literature in the Caribbean exhibits some of the diversity remarked upon in the case of Africa, not least as regards the literary traditions associated with the three languages of expression in the region: English, French, and Spanish. It is thus important to stress the contribution of the Caribbean region to contemporary literary culture. Contemporary West Indian literature in English can be considered as one of the focal areas of literary modernism (Gikandi 1992). The award of the Nobel Prize to Derek Walcott in 1993 has been regarded not only as a consecration of the work of Walcott himself but of West Indian literature in general: of a literary renaissance represented by the work of such eminent figures as George Lamming, Wilson Harris, Edward Kamau Brathwaite, up to and including Lorna Goodison (perhaps the most eloquent poetic voice today in the region). It is also of interest to note the current revival of interest in the work of Jean Rhys, whose work and career appear to confirm the connection between European modernism and the perception of the Caribbean as an area of literary reference. This connection is even clearer in the French West Indies, where the work of Aimé Césaire, to whom we are indebted for the term "négritude," was hailed from the beginning by André Breton as an outstanding demonstration of the moral and aesthetic principles of the Surrealist movement. Edouard Glissant, Simone Schwarz-Bart, Maryse Condé, and, more recently, Patrick Chamoiseau (Prix Goncourt, 1992) have been able to sustain in their own work this innovative thrust of francophone Caribbean literature, within which we locate the Haitians: René Depestre, Jean Métellus, and Frankétienne. Finally, as regards the Caribbean, it needs to be recalled that Alejo Carpentier (the originator of the concept of "magic realism"), Nicolás Guillén and Pales Matos spearheaded a literary renaissance in Cuba that gave a powerful impulse to modern literature in other parts of the Spanish-speaking world.

As can be seen, apart from the cultural continuities they represent, a major point of interest is that both modern African literature in the European languages and Caribbean literature provide powerful testimonies to the colonial experience, which, thanks to the work of Immanuel Wallerstein, has come to be regarded as a crucial factor in the constitution of the present global system (1974). We might remark in passing that the discourse of modernity these literatures propose is central to Paul Gilroy's formulation of the concept of "The Black Atlantic" (Gilroy 1993). It is of interest at the same time to draw attention to the comparative perspective that African and Caribbean literatures provide on western canonical texts and the literary conventions associated with them, a perspective that illuminates the relation of these literatures to the various metropolitan traditions from which they derive not merely their language of expression and standard forms, but also, as J. P. Clark has averred, much of their fundamental creative impulse (Clark 1970). Conversely, there is a growing recognition of the impact of African and African-derived forms of expression on European modernism. Thus, along with writers from Latin America and other parts of the Third World (notably India, in the case of English), African and Caribbean writers have contributed in very important ways to the expansion of the expressive field of European languages. The dynamics of this "Euro-African intertextuality" (Irele 2001) may be said to lend further theoretical density to the concept of the "postcolonial," a concept that, since its inauguration by the work of Bill Ashcroft, Gareth Griffiths, and Helen Tiffin (1989) has stood in need of rigorous theoretical formulation and textual exemplification.

*

The remarks above serve to indicate the direction of the present work. We need to say a word of explanation concerning the structure of the book. We have designed the work as a succession of self-contained chapters focused on specific areas, with a bibliography of primary and secondary works provided at the end of each chapter. This arrangement involves the inevitable overlap between chapters; however, we do not consider this a serious problem, conscious of the fact that, confronted with such a large work, readers can be expected to go to topics in which they are interested.

The early chapters are devoted to an extensive overview of the oral tradition in Africa and the New World. This is followed by accounts of representative instances of the written literature in the African languages. The transition to modern experience signaled by literary and intellectual response to the encounter with Europe, in all its tragic dimensions, provides the keynote of the latter chapters, devoted largely to the literature in the European languages, marked by its engagement with the problems of racial emancipation and of decolonization both in Africa and the New World as well as with the aftermath in the post-independence period. Against this general background, the chapters have been organized as a series of surveys along linguistic and regional lines, in order to reflect the coherence they lend to the material and to allow in each case for a certain measure of chronological ordering in the presentations. These survey chapters are complemented by "thematic" chapters that take account of convergences across linguistic and regional categories. The very nature of the project dictates that the presentation in each area should incorporate a historical perspective wherever possible. This is especially the case with the modern literature, where the major thematic preoccupations that have attended the genesis and evolution of literature by black people require to be presented in close relation to the ideological and intellectual concerns by which African and Caribbean expression has been driven since the eighteenth century.

It is believed that the structure outlined above has the methodological advantage of focusing attention not only on the intrinsic aspects of the various bodies of texts and literary productions examined here, but also on the correlations between them. For example, the continuity that binds the oral tradition to modern expression in African literature has been convincingly demonstrated by Leroy Vail and Landeg White in their study *Power and the Praise Poem* (1991), a study that has the special merit of indicating the possibility of arriving at a unified vision of the entire field of African literature by proceeding from structural analysis of formal features to the conventions they enjoin and the apprehension of the world they entail.

As regards the extrinsic aspects, the particular problems that arise from the guiding conception of the project happen in fact to form an integral part of the history of the literature. We have highlighted a number of factors such as the colonial situation and the role of formative journals, in the rise of modern African literature. One other issue that pervades the volume is that of the question of language, which has constantly featured in discussions of African literature, and whose cultural dimension and implications for the creative process have been highlighted by the pronouncements of Ngugi wa Thiong'o and his shift from English to Gikuyu for his own creative work (Ngugi 1986). Another issue that arises from a consideration of the corpus is the question of "national" literatures in Africa being increasingly raised by African scholars, notably the Beninois critic Adrien Wanou, who has argued for the "territorial imperative" as a determining factor in the development of new literary traditions in contemporary Africa, a question that assumed prominence with the publication of Richard Bjornson's pioneering study of Cameroonian literature (1991).

This brings us to a final point regarding the character of this work as a reference. Although questions of value have not been be excluded (they are already implicit in the choice of authors and texts), contributors have had to bear in mind that the emphasis of the publication has had to be a factual account of the development of each aspect of the corpus, rather than on evaluative discussion of texts and works or critical appraisal of writers, a function we leave to the judgment of scholar critics and ultimately to history.

Bibliography

Andrews, William L., and Henry Louis Gates, Jr., eds. 2000. *Slave Narratives*. New York: Library of America.

Ashcroft, Bill, Gareth Griffiths, and Helen Tiffin. 1989. *The Empire Writes Back: Theory and Practice in Post-Colonial Literatures*. London: Routledge.

Bjornson, Richard. 1991. *The African Quest for Freedom and Identity*. Bloomington: Indiana University Press.

Clark, John Pepper. 1970. *The Example of Shakespeare*. London: Longman.

Gérard, Albert. 1971. "Black Africa." *Review of National Literatures* 2. 2.

1981. *African Language Literatures*. Washington, DC: Three Continents Press.

Gikandi, Simon. 1992. *Writing in Limbo: Modernism and Caribbean Literature*. Ithaca: Cornell University Press.

Gilroy, Paul. 1993. *The Black Atlantic: Modernity and Double Consciousness*. Cambridge, MA: Harvard University Press.

Irele, F. Abiola. 2001. *The African Imagination: Literature in Africa and the Black Diaspora*. New York: Oxford University Press.

Izevbaye, Dan. 1968. "Defining African Literature." *African Literature Today* 1.1.

Jahn, Janheinz. 1961. *Muntu*. London: Faber and Faber.

1966. *A History of Neo-African Literature*. London: Faber and Faber.

Mahood, Molly. 1955. "The Place of English in an African University." An Inaugural Lecture delivered at University College, Ibadan, on 7 November. Ibadan: Ibadan University Press.

Ngugi wa Thiong'o. 1986. *Decolonizing the Mind*. Oxford and London: James Currey/Heinemann.

Opland, Jeff. 1983. *Xhosa Oral Poetry: Aspects of a Black South African Tradition*. Cambridge: Cambridge University Press.

Turner, Victor. 1967. *The Forest of Symbols: Aspects of Ndembu Ritual*. Ithaca: Cornell University Press.

Vail, Leroy, and Landeg White. 1991. *Power and the Praise Poem: Southern African Voices in History*. Charlottesville: University Press of Virginia; Oxford: James Currey.

Wallerstein, Immanuel. 1974. *The Modern World System: Capitalist Agriculture and the Origins of the European World Economy in the Sixteenth Century*. New York: Academic Press.

Woodard, Helena. 1999. *African-British Writings in the Eighteenth Century: The Politics of Race and Reason*. Westport: Greenwood.

Zumthor, Paul. 1983. *Introduction à la poésie orale*. Paris: Seuil.

1990. *Oral Poetry: An Introduction*. Trans. Kathryn Murphy-Judy. Minneapolis: University of Minnesota Press.

Acknowledgments

We are grateful to Ruthmarie H. Mitsch, of the Ohio State University, for editorial assistance with this project, and to Anne Mischo, a graphic designer with the Ohio State University, for her preparation of maps for this volume. Adeline Koh at the University of Michigan provided assistance with the proofreading of the project.

Chronology

Cambridge History of African and Caribbean Literature

HISTORICAL AND POLITICAL EVENTS	LITERARY AND CULTURAL EVENTS
Trans-Saharan Trade (Antiquity)	
Egypt: Old Kingdom (2500 BCE)	
	Book of the Dead (c. 1500 BCE)
Egypt: Middle Kingdom (1900–1500 BCE)	
Egypt: New Kingdom (1500–1200 BCE)	
	Hymn of Akhenaten (c. 1375 BCE)
Kush, Meroe, Nubia	
Greek Conquest of Egypt (100 BCE)	
	Herodotus: *History* (c. 450 BCE)
	Aesop: *Fables*
	Apuleius: *The Golden Ass* (c. 155 BCE)
	Terence (195–159 BCE): *The Self-Tormentor*; *Woman of Andros*
	Periplus of the Erythrean Sea (100)
Introduction and Spread of Christianity in North Africa (200–350)	
	St. Augustine: *Confessions* (400)
Axum (100–700)	
	Development of Ge'ez script
Rise of Ghana (300–1200)	
Arab Conquest of North Africa (640–700)	
	Epic of Antara
Spread of Islam in West Africa (800–1000)	Arab Chronicles: Ibn Khaldun, Ibn Battuta, etc.
Zanji Empire and Swahili City States (10th century)	
Ozi Kingdom (10th – 13th century)	

HISTORICAL AND POLITICAL EVENTS	LITERARY AND CULTURAL EVENTS
Islam in East Africa (1000)	*Epic of Banu Hilal* Swahili – *utenzi* tradition; writing in Swahili-Arabic script
Rise of Mali (c. 1200)	
Chewa settle in Malawi (c. 1200–1400)	
Great Zimbabwe flourished (1200–1400)	
Rise of Kongo Kingdom (c. 1300)	*The Mwindo Epic*
Consolidation of Islamic Learning in West Africa (1400)	*Epic of Son-Jara*
Munhumutapa State flourishes (c. 1420–1720)	
Rise of Songhay (1495)	*Epic of Askia the Great*
Portuguese rule in East Africa (1498–1699)	Fumo Liyongo wa Bauri
	Leo Africanus (c. 1513)
Rise of Benin (c. 1400)	*The Ozidi Saga*
Zimbabwe (Monomotapa) (c. 1500)	African oral tradition enters West Atlantic (1560–1870)
Portuguese explorers on the West and Central African coasts (1450–1600); Portuguese attempt to consolidate power in Munhumutapa State (c. 1590–1690)	Hausa Literature in Arabic language; Joao de Barros: *Da Asia* (1552)
Atlantic Slave Trade (late 1500s – mid-19th century)	Camões: *Os Lusiades* (1572)
Dutch in South Africa (late 16th century); Dutch control of Cape of Good Hope (1652)	Joao dos Santos: *Ethiopia Oriental* (1609)
Lunda empire expands south from Southern Congo into Zambia (c. 1600–1700); Lovale settle in Northwest Zambia and Southern Congo (c. 1690); Changamire destroy Portuguese settlements in Northeast Zimbabwe (1690)	
British begin trafficking slaves (1620s); Royal Adventurers receive charter, authorizing slaves as supply source (1660s)	
Bemba consolidate their power in Northeastern Zambia under leadership of kings entitled Chitimukulu (c. 1700–1800)	
Ukawsaw Gronniosaw is born in Borno (1710–14?)	

HISTORICAL AND POLITICAL EVENTS	LITERARY AND CULTURAL EVENTS
Arab and Portuguese slave raids destabilize Malawian and Eastern Zambian societies (c. 1700–1890); Portuguese depose Munhumutapa Choika (1719)	
	Golden age of *utenzi* tradition; *Utendi wa Tambuka* (1728)
Increasing Omani influence in East Africa (1700s–1800s)	Ukawsaw Gronniosaw: *A Narrative of the Most Remarkable Particulars . . .* (1770)
Mazrui rule in Mombasa (1729–1837)	Phillis Wheatley: *Poems on Various Subjects, Religious and Moral* (1773)
British peace with the Maroons in Jamaica (1738)	Edward Long: *History of Jamaica* (1774)
Seven Years' War (1756–63)	
Bemba hegemony established in Northeastern Zambia (late 18th century)	Posthumous publication of Ignatius Sancho's *Letters* (1782)
	Quobna Ottobah Cugoano: *Thoughts and Sentiments on the Evils and Wicked Traffic of the Slavery and Commerce of the Human Species* (1787)
Haitian Revolution (1790–1804)	Olaudah Equiano: *The Interesting Narrative of Olaudah Equiano* (1789)
Rise of Chaka and Zulu (c. 1795); London Missionary Society (LMS) (1795)	Oral narratives of histories, myths, stories, poetries, epic tales and other traditions (Southern Africa)
Napoleon invades Egypt (1798)	
Aborigines Protection Society to abolish slavery, with William Wilberforce and Thomas Fowell Buxton at helm (1799)	Mungo Park: *Travels in the Interior Districts of Africa* (1799)
Islamic *Qadiriyya* Revivalism in Hausaland (1800)	Zulu *izibongo*
First Ngoni invasions into Zimbabwe (early 1800s)	Birth of *Ajami* literature in West African languages
Usman Dan Fodiyo, Jihad Wars in Hausaland – Rise of Sokoto Caliphate (1804–10)	*Al-Inkishafi* (1810s)
British wrench control of Cape of Good Hope from Dutch (1806); Dutch are traditionally farmers ("boers") while the British represent capitalism	Jihad *Ajami* literature in Hausa language
Abolition of Slave Trade: Britain and the US (1807). Congress of Vienna extends laws against slave trade to rest of Europe (1815). Abolition of slavery:	Ntsikana, Xhosa chief and oral poet, under the influence of Christianity, begins to compose hymns orally in the Xhosa musical rhythms and

HISTORICAL AND POLITICAL EVENTS	LITERARY AND CULTURAL EVENTS
England (1833), France (1848); Emancipation Proclamation, freeing slaves in US (1863)	idioms. His most famous hymn, "Ulo Thix' omkhulu" (You are the great God), in the form of a praise poem for God as a warrior to protect and preserve truth and goodness, is written down and translated into English, bringing together the oral and the written. The hymn is printed and published in 1828.
Egypt under British occupation (1822–1914)	
	John Bennie, sent by Glasgow Missionary Society (GMS) (1821), learns Xhosa, creates an orthography, and writes the first book in Xhosa in the form of a primary reader. A small booklet is printed (1824) containing an alphabet, prayers for going to bed, waking, beginning a meal, concluding a meal, the Ten Commandments, and the Lord's Prayer. GMS publishes "a systematic Vocabulary of the Kaffrarian language in two parts; to which is prefixed an Introduction to the Kaffrarian Grammar" (1926), published at Lovedale.
Founding of Fourah Bay College (1827)	
	Sigismund Wilhelm Koelle: *Polyglotta Africana* (1854)
French conquest of Algeria (1830); Algerian resistance to French invasion (1835–47); Ngoni under Zwangendaba cross the Zambezi (1835); other Ngoni groups move north of the Zambezi (late 1830s)	Setswana translation of the Gospel of St. Luke translated by Robert Moffat (1830) – "the first published Scripture translation in a South African Bantu language"
	London's Anti-Slavery Society publishes Mary Prince's *The History of Mary Prince, A West Indian Slave, Related by Herself* (1831)
Emancipation of slaves in Caribbean (1834–68)	
Emancipation of slaves of Southern Africa (1833), which becomes a major grievance of the Dutch, and one of	

HISTORICAL AND POLITICAL EVENTS	LITERARY AND CULTURAL EVENTS
the causes of "the Great Trek" (1836), which is the migration north by the Dutch who were till now confined to the Western Cape. This was to result in many wars and the loss of land and livestock to the Dutch trekkers, as well as personal freedom, whose consequences are still felt. Newspapers in African languages established by the missionaries begin to play an important role in stimulating interest in learning to read and write, but especially to read the Bible. These can be considered a mid-nineteenth-century phenomenon, spanning approximately the last two-thirds of this century. Some of the titles are: *Umshumayele Indaba* (Broadcaster of News) by the Wesleyan missionaries (1837); *Ikwezi* (Morning Star) in English and Xhosa, by the GMS (1844); *Indaba* (The News), by the GMS at the Lovedale Mission Press – bilingual, two-thirds in Xhosa and one-third in English; *The Kafir Express*, established by Dr. James Stewart (1870)	
	Thomas Fowell Buxton: *The African Slave Trade and Its Remedy* (1840)
Frederick Douglass escapes from slavery (1838), gives first anti-slavery lecture for William Lloyd Garrison's Anti-Slavery Society (1841)	
Indentured Indian labor arrives in Trinidad and Guyana (1845–1917)	Yoruba-language publications begin (1840s)
	Robert Moffat: *Missionary Labours and Scenes in Southern Africa* (1842)
Ngoni factions settle in Zambia and Malawi (1845–55)	French missionaries of the Paris Evangelical Mission Society (PEMS) arrive in Lesotho, pay respects to King Moshoeshoe, and are given site to establish their mission, which they name Morija. The mission becomes a thriving cultural center and the home of the newspaper *Leselinyana la Lesotho* and of the publishing house called Morija Sesuto Book Depot.

HISTORICAL AND POLITICAL EVENTS	LITERARY AND CULTURAL EVENTS
	Frederick Douglass: *Narrative of the Life of Frederick Douglass* (1845)
	Robert Knox: *The Races of Man* (1846)
	Gobineau: *Essai sur l'inégalité des races humaines* (1853–55); Frederick Douglass: *My Bondage and My Freedom* (1855)
	David Livingstone: *Missionary Travels and Researches* (1857)
	Utenzi wa Mwana Kupona (1858)
London Missionary Society establishes Matabele Mission (1859)	Regular reports and letters from agents of the LMS, and subsequently the Church of Scotland and Free Church of Scotland published in missionary magazines 1860–90. Some subsequently republished in the Oppenheimer Series 1945–50. Jesuit Zambezi Mission Letters 1879–89 republished in 1960s and 1970s. Harriet Wilson: *Our Nig* (1859)
	Richard Francis Burton: *Lake Regions of Central Africa* (1860)
Bemba increase their wealth by exchanging slaves and ivory for guns (c. 1860–90)	
	John Speke: *Discovery of the Source of the Nile* (1864)
	David and Charles Livingstone: *Narrative of an Expedition to the Zambesi and Its Tributaries* (1865)
Sufism in West Africa; founding of Touba, Senegal (1866)	Shaykh Bamba: *Masalik al-Jinan* (The Roads to Paradise)
Diamonds discovered in Griqualand and later where Kimberley now stands (1870); Lobengula confirmed as Ndebele king (1870)	
	H. M. Stanley: *How I Found Livingstone in Central Africa* (1872)
Death of Livingstone (1873)	
	H. M. Stanley: *Through the Dark Continent* (1878)
Tunisia becomes a French Protectorate (1881)	Suppression of *Ajami* literature in French-controlled Hausaland
French colonization in West Africa (late 1800s)	Swahili chronicles: *Habari za Mrima* (1880); Swahili as official language

HISTORICAL AND POLITICAL EVENTS	LITERARY AND CULTURAL EVENTS
British colonization in West Africa (late 1800s) Mahdi Rebellion in Sudan (1881)	F. C. Selous: *A Hunter's Wanderings in Africa* (1881) Latinization of Hausa alphabet Translation of English literature into Hausa language Olive Schreiner: *The Story of an African Farm* (1883)
Berlin Conference (Partition of Africa (1884–85))	H. M. Stanley: *The Congo and the Founding of Its Free State: A Story of Work and Exploration* (1885); H. Rider Haggard: *King Solomon's Mines* (1885)
German rule in Tanganyika (1885); British colonial rule in East Africa (1885) Gold discovered (1886): Transvaal declared a gold mining area Introduction of the *Pass System* to control movement in order to control availability of cheap labor, defining the relationship of the people and the police as a constantly and inevitably violent one, resulting in such events as the Sharpeville Massacre.	Writing in Swahili-Roman script; Swahili translations of English classics; Swahili historical chronicles
	Edward Wilmot Blyden: *Christianity, Islam and the Negro Race* (1887)
Lobengula grants concession to Charles Rudd, who works for Cecil Rhodes to mine metals and minerals in his territories (1888) Royal Charter granted to Cecil Rhodes's British South Africa Company on the strength of the Rudd Concession (1889)	
Boer War (1889–1902) Islamic Revivalist Movement in Nigeria (1890s) Frederick Lugard establishes depot of Imperial British East Africa Company at Dagoretti (1890); British protectorate in Malawi declared and northern and southern boundaries agreed with Germany and Portugal (1890); British South Africa Company forces occupy Mashonaland (1890)	H. M. Stanley: *In Darkest Africa* (1890)

HISTORICAL AND POLITICAL EVENTS	LITERARY AND CULTURAL EVENTS
British South Africa Company invades Ndebele kingdom. Lobengula escapes northwards and possibly dies (1893)	
Rhodesia becomes name for British South Africa Company territories (1895)	
Kenya Protectorate established (1895); remaining independent areas of East and Northeast Zambia brought under British Control (1895–99)	Enoch Sontonga composes "Nkosi sikelel' i Afrika" (God Bless Africa) (c. 1897), a choral piece that was sung at the first meeting of the African National Congress (ANC) in 1912 and at many of their political meetings and rallies and was to become the national anthem of South Africa and other southern African countries
Anglo-Boer War (1899–1902)	
Mauritania French Protectorate (1903)	
British Central Africa Protectorate renamed Nyasaland Protectorate (1907)	Swahili acquires nationalist role
Maji-Maji Rising in German East Africa (1908–12)	
Union of South Africa formed (1910), unifying whites against blacks	Thomas Mofolo: *Pitseng* (1910) Republican Cuba's journal *Bohemia* (1910–50s)
Morocco becomes a French Protectorate (1912)	
Libya under Italian occupation (1912–47)	
Formation of the African National Congress (1912), in recognition of the common oppression of all blacks and of the need for united action; The Natives Land Act passed in South Africa (1913), the first major land law legally disenfranchising the black from owning land Marcus Garvey founds Universal Negro Improvement Association in Jamaica (1914)	
First World War (1914–18); Egypt British Protectorate (1914–22); Native Associations formed in Nyasaland to press for more African control over economic, social, and political issues in the protectorate (1914–15)	Sol T. Plaatje: *Native Life in South Africa* (1915)

HISTORICAL AND POLITICAL EVENTS	LITERARY AND CULTURAL EVENTS
Members of the Ndebele royal family form the National Home Movement to recover land for the nation and petition George V (1915)	
Du Bois and Pan-African Conference, Paris (1919); Egyptian Nationalist uprising (1919)	
Kikuyu Association formed (1920)	Harlem Renaissance (c. 1921–29)
East African Association formed (1921)	René Maran: *Batouala* (1921)
Southern Rhodesia settlers vote to become a self-governing colony rather than a fifth province of South Africa when the British South Africa Company charter ends (1922)	
Rhodesia Bantu Voters' Association formed (1923)	
Kikuyu Central Association formed (1924)	New Testament of the Bible first published in Gikuyu (1926)
	Lamine Senghor's journal *La Voix des Nègres,* from Paris (1927); Jean Rhys: *The Left Bank and Other Stories* (1927)
Jomo Kenyatta travels to London as representative of the Kikuyu Central Association (1929)	*Muigwithania* first published (1928)
Creation of Zaria Translation Bureau in Nigeria (1930)	Thomas Mofolo: *Shaka* (1930)
Libyan Independence (1931)	
	C. L. R. James and associates' Trinidad journal *The Beacon* (1931–33, 1939)
African National Congress founded in Southern Rhodesia (1934)	Stanley Kiama Gathigira: *Miikarire ya Agikuyu* (1934)
Labor riots in anglophone Caribbean territories (1935–37)	L. S. Senghor and associates' emergence and the journal *L'Etudiant Noir* (1935)
Italian invasion of Abyssinia (1936)	Birth of Hausa fiction writing in Hausa language
	Leo Frobenius: *History of African Civilizations* (1936)
	Jomo Kenyatta: *Facing Mount Kenya* (1938)
	D. O. Fagunwa: *Ogboju Ode ninu Igbo Irunmale* (1938); C. L. R. James: *The Black Jacobins* (1938)
	Aimé Césaire: *Notebook of a Return to the Native Land* (1939)

HISTORICAL AND POLITICAL EVENTS	LITERARY AND CULTURAL EVENTS
Second World War (1939–45)	Aimé Césaire's Martinique journal *Tropiques* (1941–45)
Kikuyu Central Association banned (1940)	
	Albert Camus: *L'étranger (The Stranger)* (1942)
	Frank Collymore's Barbados journal *Bim*, with Derek Walcott's first poems in print (1942–90s)
Brazzaville Conference (1944); Kenya African Union founded (1944); Nyasaland African Congress holds first conference in which Hastings Banda is involved (1944)	Eric Williams: *Capitalism and Slavery* (1944)
Manchester Pan-African Conference (1945)	A. J. Seymour's British Guiana journal *Kyk-Over-Al* (1945–90s)
Pan-African Conference, Manchester (1946)	Edna Manley's Jamaica journal *Focus* (1946–60)
Jomo Kenyatta becomes Kenya African Union president (1947)	Alioune Diop and associates' founding of *Présence Africaine* (1947)
Arrival of the SS Empire Windrush in England (1948)	L. S. Senghor: *Chants d'ombre; Anthologie* (1948)
National Party comes to power in South Africa and institutes policy of Apartheid (1948)	Hausa nationalist literature
	Placide Tempels: *Bantu Philosophy* (1949)
	Mouloud Feraoun: *Le fils du pauvre* (1950)
	South Africa's journal *Drum*, a pioneer voice of culture and politics, continent-wide
	Doris Lessing: *The Grass Is Singing* (1950)
	Emergence of Agostinho Neto and the Angolan journal *Mensagem* (1951–52)
Declaration of public emergency in Kenya (1952)	Amos Tutuola: *The Palm Wine Drinkard* (1952); Samuel Selvon: *A Brighter Sun* (1952); Mohammed Dib: *La grande maison* (1952)
Mau-Mau War (1952–56)	
	Camara Laye: *The African Child* (1953); Phyllis Allfrey: *The Orchid House* (1953); George Lamming: *In the Castle of My Skin* (1953)
Algerian War of Independence (1954–62)	Cheik Anta Diop: *Nations nègres et culture* (1954)
	Nigerian journal *Odu* (1955–)

HISTORICAL AND POLITICAL EVENTS	LITERARY AND CULTURAL EVENTS
Bandung Conference (1956)	
Suez Crisis (1956)	Shaping of Swahili novel and play; Shaaban Robert (1909–62)
Morocco and Tunisia become independent (1956)	
Ghana Independence (1957)	Albert Memmi: *Le portrait du colonisé* (1957)
Hastings Banda assumes presidency of the Congress (1957)	Ulli Beier and Nigerian associates' journal *Black Orpheus* (1957–82)
Hastings Banda and other Congress leaders detained (1958)	
Loi Cadre, French African Colonies (1958)	First Congress of Black Writers, Paris (1956)
General de Gaulle and Referendum on "French Community" Independence of Guinea (1958)	Chinua Achebe: *Things Fall Apart* (1958)
Malawi Congress Party founded to replace banned Nyasaland African Congress with Orton Chirwa acting as leader until Banda's release (1959); ANC (SR) proscribed (1959)	Student journal from University College, Ibadan, *The Horn* (1958–64)
	Student journal from University College, Makerere, *Penpoint* (1958–late 1960s)
Castro seizes power in Cuba (1959)	
	Ballets Africains of Guinea (Fodeba Keita)
	Second Congress of Black Writers, Rome, 1959
1960: Year of African Independence: Nigeria, Somalia, Mauritania, and several other African countries	
National Democratic Party formed to replace ANC (SR) (1960); Banda released from Gwelo prison (1960)	Wole Soyinka: *A Dance of the Forests* (1960)
South Africa: Sharpeville Massacre (1960)	Revolutionary Cuba's journal *Casa de las Américas* (1960–)
Reign of Hassan II of Morocco (1961–99)	Frantz Fanon: *The Wretched of the Earth* (1961); V. S. Naipaul: *A House for Mr. Biswas* (1961)
War of Independence, Portuguese colonies (1961–74)	The journal *Transition/Ch'indaba*, started by Rajat Neogy, continued by Wole Soyinka (1961–)
Algerian Independence (1962); Independence in Trinidad/Tobago and Jamaica (1962)	Africa's Anglophone writers meet, with Ngugi attending, in Kampala (1962)

HISTORICAL AND POLITICAL EVENTS	LITERARY AND CULTURAL EVENTS
Founding of Organization of African Unity (1963); Kenya independence (1963)	Julius Nyerere translates Shakespeare (1963); Swahili nationalist literature; emergence of Swahili free verse
	Bernard Fonlon and associates' Cameroon journal *Abbia* (1963–82)
Zanzibar revolution (1964); Zambian independence with Kenneth Kaunda as Prime Minister and Malawian independence with Hastings Banda as Prime Minister (1964); Ian Smith becomes Rhodesian Prime Minister (1964); Nkomo and Mugabe in detention (1964–74)	
Fall of Kwame Nkrumah (1966); Malawi becomes a republic and one-party state with Banda as president (1966); Independence in Barbados (1966)	Dakar Arts Festival (1966); Chinua Achebe: *A Man of the People* (1966)
	Ahamdou Kourouma: *Les soleils des indépendances* (*The Suns of Independence*) (first published in Canada, 1968); Stanlake Samkange: *On Trial for My Country* (1966)
Nigerian Civil War (1967–70); *Ujamaa* (1967)	Olive Senior, Commonwealth Writers Prize (1967); David Rubadiri: *No Bride Price* (1967)
	Ayi Kwei Armah: *The Beautyful Ones Are Not Yet Born* (1968); Miguel Barnet: *Biographia de un Cimarron* translated into English as *Autobiography of a Runaway Slave* (1968)
	Yambo Ouologuem: *Bound to Violence* (1968)
	Samuel Selvon awarded Hummingbird Medal of the Order of the Trinity (for literature) by the government of Trinidad and Tobago (1969)
	Algiers Arts Festival (1969)
	Ahmadou Kourouma: *Les soleils des indépendances* (published in France, 1974)
Coup by Siyad Barre in Somalia (1969)	
Nigeria Oil Boom (1970); Hastings Banda declared president for life (1970); Black Power uprising in Trinidad (1970)	

HISTORICAL AND POLITICAL EVENTS	LITERARY AND CULTURAL EVENTS
	V. S. Naipual: Booker Prize for *In a Free State* (1971)
	Chinua Achebe's journal *Okike* (1972); Walter Rodney: *How Europe Underdeveloped Africa* (1972)
Kaunda established a one-party state in Zambia (1973); Bahamas independence (1973)	Ayi Kwei Armah: *Two Thousand Seasons* (1973); Kamau Brathwaite: *The Arrivants* (1973)
	Agostinho Neto: *Sacred Hope* (1974)
Soweto (1976)	Ngugi wa Thiong'o and Ngugi wa Mirii, with the Kamiriithu Cultural Center, develop and produce *Ngaahika Ndeenda (I Will Marry When I Want)* (1976)
Ogaden War between Ethiopia and Somalia (1976–77)	Hausa Boomtown literature; Hausa women's romance literature; Lagos Arts Festival (1977)
Independence in Dominica (1978)	Journal and publishing house *Staffrider*, superseding *Drum* for South Africa (1978–); Dambudzo Marechera: *House of Hunger* (1978)
	Mariam Bâ: *So Long a Letter* (1979); (Wins Noma Award for Publishing in Africa, 1980)
	Nuruddin Farah: *Variations on the Theme of an African Dictatorship (1979–83)*; *Sweet and Sour Milk* (1979)
Zimbabwean independence with Robert Mugabe as Prime Minister (1980)	Austin Clarke, Casa de las Américas Prize (1980)
	Nuruddin Farah: *Sardines* (1981)
	Jack Mapanje: *Of Chameleons and Gods* (1982); Frank Chipasula: *This Is the Time* (1982); Felix Mnthali: *When Sunset Comes to Sapitwa* (1982); Chenjerai Hove: *Up in Arms* (1982)
	J. M. Coetzee: Booker Prize for *The Life and Times of Michael K* (1983)
US invasion of Grenada (1983)	Nuruddin Farah: *Close Sesame* (1983); Jamaica Kincaid: *At the Bottom of the River* (1983)
	Senghor elected to the French Academy (1983)
	David Dabydeen: Commonwealth Poetry Prize (1984); Malawi Writer's Group anthology, *Namaluzi* (1984)

HISTORICAL AND POLITICAL EVENTS	LITERARY AND CULTURAL EVENTS
	Maryse Condé: Grand Prix Littéraire de la Femme for *Moi, Tituba* (1986)
	Wole Soyinka: Nobel Prize (1986)
	Tahar Ben Jelloun: Prix Goncourt for *La nuit sacrée* (1987)
	Naguib Mafouz: Nobel Prize (1988); the Qur'an first published in Gikuyu (1988); Tsitsi Dangarembga: *Nervous Conditions* (1988); Chenjerai Hove: *Bones* (1988)
	Chenjerai Hove: Noma Award (1989); Shimmer Chinodya: *Harvest of Thorns* (1989); Marlene Nourbese Philip: *She Tries Her Tongue* (1989)
Nelson Mandela released from jail as a political prisoner after 27 years (1990)	
Fall of Siyad Barre, Somali dictator (1991)	Nadine Gordimer: Nobel Prize (1991)
Somali Civil War (1991–93)	
Start of Algerian Civil War (1992)	Patrick Chamoiseau: Prix Goncourt for *Texaco* (1992)
	Ben Okri: Booker Prize for *The Famished Road* (1992)
	Henri Lopes: Grand Prix de la Francophonie de l'Académie Française (1993)
	Derek Walcott: Nobel Prize (1992); Caryl Phillips: *Crossing the River* (1993)
Nelson Mandela elected President of South Africa (1994)	Kamau Brathwaite: Neustadt Prize (1994)
	Caya Makhele: Grand Prix de la Nouvelle Francophone for "Les Travaux d'Ariane"
	Caryl Phillips: Lannan Literary Award (1994)
	Noma Award to work in Afrikaans (1995)
Execution of Ken Saro-Wiwa by Military Government in Nigeria (1995)	Dapo Adeniyi's Nigeria journal *Glendora Review* (1995–)
	Abdourahman Waberi: Grand Prix de l'Afrique noire for *Cahier Nomade* (1996)
	Calixthe Beyala: Grand Prix de l'Académie Française for *Les honneurs perdus* (1996)

HISTORICAL AND POLITICAL EVENTS	LITERARY AND CULTURAL EVENTS
	Calixthe Beyala judged guilty of plagiarism for sections of *Le petit prince de Belleville* (1996) Earl Lovelace: Commonwealth Writer's Prize for *Salt* (1997) Nuruddin Farah: Neustadt Prize (1998) J. M. Coetzee: Booker Prize for *Disgrace* (1999) Jackie Kay: Guardian Fiction Prize for *Trumpet* (1999) Tierno Monénembo: Prix Tropiques for *L'aîné des orphelins* (2000) Noma Award for Swahili work by Kimani Njogu and Rocha Chimerah (2000) Marie Ndiaye: Prix Fémina for *Rosie Carpe* (2001); Lorna Goodison: *Travelling Mercies* (2001); V. S. Naipaul: Nobel Prize (2001)

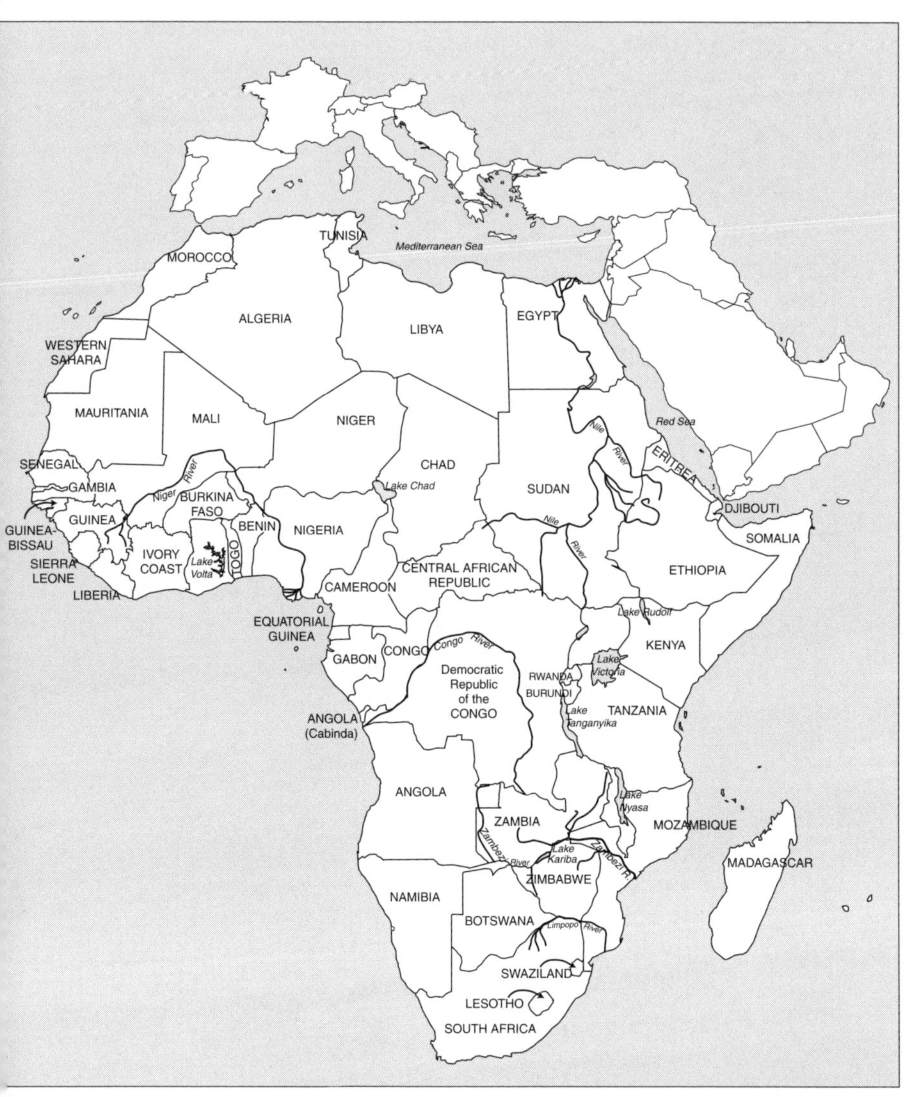

Map 1 Africa (physical and political)

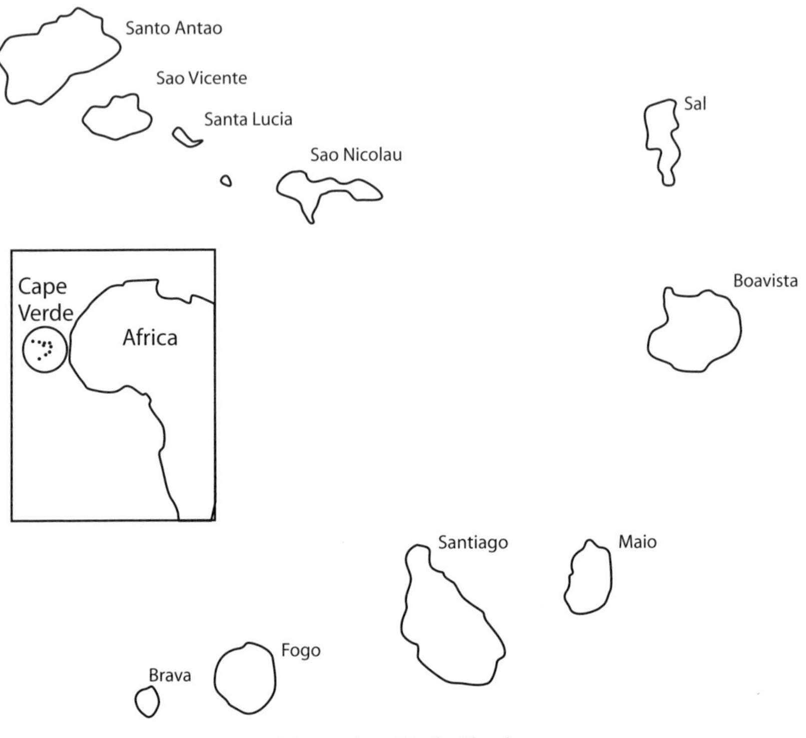

Map 2 Cape Verde Islands

Map 3 The Caribbean

Map 4 East and Central Africa

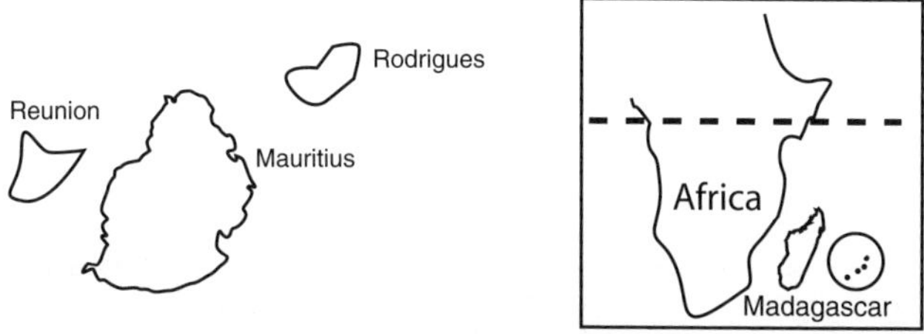

Map 5 Mauritius

Map 6 North Africa

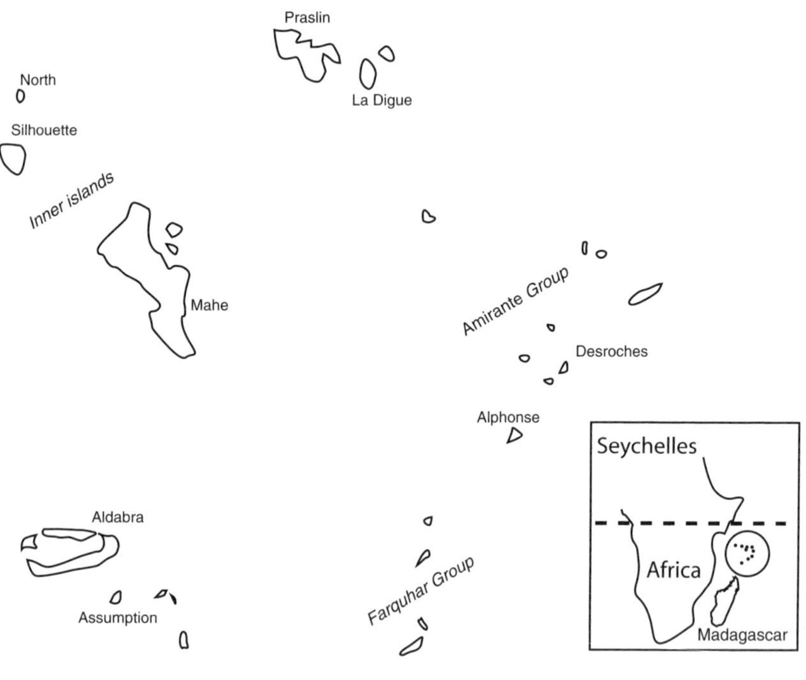

Map 7 Seychelles Islands

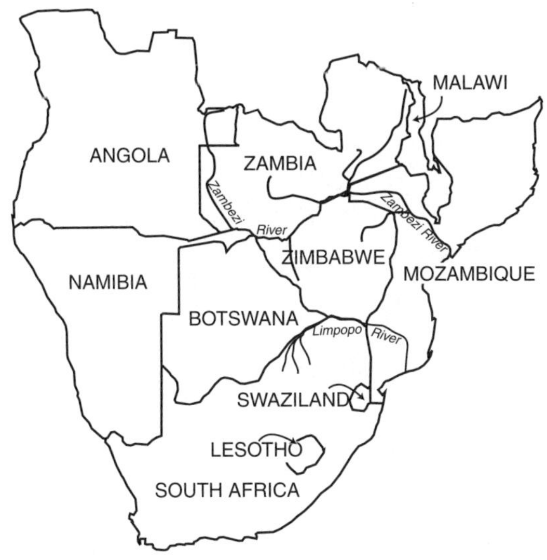

Map 8 Southern Africa

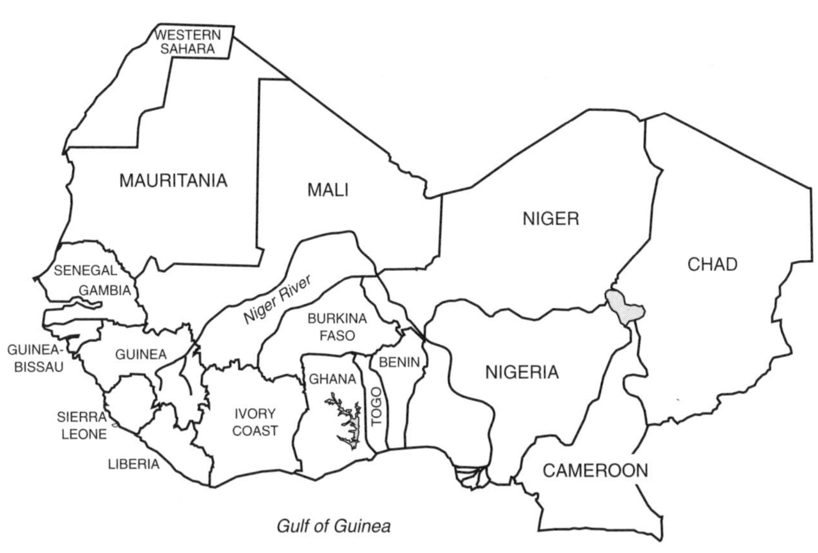

Map 9 West Africa

I

Africa and orality

LIZ GUNNER

The continent of Africa can be viewed as a site of enormous, long, and ongoing creativity in relation to orality as a vector for the production of social life, religious beliefs, and the constant constituting and reconstituting of society, ideology, and aesthetics. If it is language which has a crucial role in the production and reproduction of society, then in the case of orality it is often language combined with the performativity of the body, and enacted in both the public and the private space. If it is justifiable to call the African continent "the oral continent par excellence" we need to ask why this is so. What precisely might it mean and what conclusions could flow therefrom? Orality needs to be seen in the African context as the means by which societies of varying complexity regulated themselves, organized their present and their pasts, made formal spaces for philosophical reflections, pronounced on power, questioned and in some cases contested power, and generally paid homage to "the word," language, as the means by which humanity was made and constantly refashioned. Orality was the means by which Africa made its existence, its history long before the colonial and imperial presence of the west manifested itself. In this sense, orality needs to be seen not simply as "the absence of literacy" but as something self-constitutive, *sui generis*. The accepting of this proposition has consequences for an understanding of world culture: namely, it is neither possible nor accurate to take one model that valorizes the written word as the blueprint for how the human race has developed.

What we can learn from the African model is that orality, manifested as types of formal speech communication, in some circumstances coexisting with music in the form of song, or with instruments, and dance, generated an almost unimaginable range of genres that enabled and empowered social, political, and spiritual existence. In some instances a specific mode of orality encoded a state's history; this was the case with the form of *ubwwiiru*, the nineteenth-century Rwandan dynastic ritual code that the historians Joseph Rwabukumba and Alexis Kagame have turned into a written record and made part of a broader historical narrative (Feierman 1994; Rwabukumba and Mudandagizi 1974; Kagame 1975). In the west, the *oriki* (praise poetry) of the Yoruba interwove personal and public history and provided a poetic vehicle for the powerful as well as the ordinary citizen (Barber 1991; Babalola 1966; Yai 1994). Forms such as *oriki* recreated the past in the present; they made and, in the present, still "make possible the crossing from the world of the dead to the world of the living, making the past present again" (Barber 1991: 76). Thus they demonstrate the different kinds of historicity that an oral form can generate with very different conventions of interactivity from those governing a conventional historical printed text (Farias 1992; Vansina 1985; Opland 1974, 1987). History was often encapsulated in the elaborate dynastic poetry of a kingdom, composed and reproduced by specially trained bards and presenting a legitimizing, heroic view of past and present to the people at large. This was the case with the court poets of Rwanda. Alexis Kagame has meticulously documented this "specialized and learned artistic tradition" (Finnegan 1970: 87; Kagame 1951; Coupez and Kamanzi 1970), outlining the privileged position of the association of royal poets who were split between those who performed the works of others and those who composed new work. A "long and rigorous period of apprenticeship" by young members of the families of poets ensured mastery of existing poems and of the "vocabulary, imagery and subject-matter which formed the traditional basis of any future composition" (Finnegan 1970: 89). This genre of court poetry, plus the secret ritual texts, the *ubwwiiru*, and other genres from Rwanda are among the best documented on the continent and provide an indication of how orality could operate at the heart of the state. Poetry was, in a way, the heartbeat of royalty. As the increasingly beleaguered kings of the nineteenth-century kingdom of Rwanda fended off their hostile neighbors, and then had to contend with the incoming colonial powers of Germany and Belgium, the royal poetic tradition was also affected, and shifted, taking on first the patina of the colonial overlords' voice and then reflecting also the counterviews of a dissident group of poets who sought out "antidynastic histories in their own past" (Hertefelt 1964; Feierman 1994: 60).

I have mentioned the Rwandan case in some detail to demonstrate firstly a formidable example of poetry, politics, and power operating in a particular historical context in Africa, without the mediation of the written or printed word. What the Rwandan example also shows is that the set of cultural practices that the poetry embodied was not static. Rather it was dynamic, changing in response to the historical pressures of the time. There is no evidence that the genres of the Rwandan court have survived into the modern era (the monarchy was abolished in 1959) and only the meticulous scholarship of Rwandan and non-Rwandan scholars provides an archive from which we can attempt to reconfigure, in the interests of the history of both world and African culture, the vibrant voices of a past poetic tradition.

Some forms of orality now exist only in written, audio or visual archives, although brief, remembered snatches may remain, tantalizingly, in living discourse, encapsulating metonymically a vast unreachable hinterland of cultural knowledge. Like the Central African drums, two of them Kuba, and one Lele, described by the historian Jan Vansina, such fragments "impress onto their own society a silent discourse, and simultaneously, as loci of memory, recite silently their own past and that of the society that made them possible" (Mudimbe 1994: 68; Vansina 1984: 47). There are, however, oral genres that exist vigorously in the contemporary era, either as part of a new global culture, as part of the local, or as what the musicologist Thomas Turino in his study of Zimbabwean music has called the indigenous, namely, a line of culture that may be closer to performance genres not significantly altered by modernity (Turino 2000: 17–18). Part of this chapter will demonstrate the ways in which orality has been extended into various configurations of modernity, thus belying the argument for a purist orality that is beyond the grasp of the modern. Nor should we see orality in Africa in the new millennium as a residual state, battered by forms of modernity: songs, chants, a dance, a gesture with a fly whisk or a spear, used simply as a nostalgic resource by politicians seeking to evoke a distant idyllic past and so link themselves to it; rather we can see it as a mode of communicative action that has in the past been finely honed to fit a myriad of different social, ideological, and aesthetic needs in many different societies on the continent. In the present, forms of orality have in some cases powered the new technologies of mass communication by influencing their direction. The extensive presence of live performances and recordings of tied and freelance singers, and poets on Hausa television and radio stations in northern Nigeria is one example of this (Furniss 1996: 126–27). Literacy has impacted in various ways on oral modes of communication and has often produced brilliant hybrid forms (touched on below), but the book itself, in terms of written literature from the continent, has been profoundly influenced by orality. It could be argued that the directions taken by contemporary written African literature, have largely been shaped by the presence of a substantial and established body of rhetoric holding deep knowledge with which writers have often felt compelled to engage, even when moving from the African language/s in which the poetry or narrative is expressed, to writing in English, French, or Portuguese.

As the example of the Rwandan school of specialist poets demonstrates, one of the roles of oral forms in many parts of the continent has been to give verbal expression to the ordering of societies through the public recitation of genealogies and praises of rulers, often by highly skilled and specialist poets. In the Rwandan case the often esoteric poetry, full of archaisms and elaborate prosody, was not accessible to the majority of the kingdom's subjects even though they all (Tutsi, Hutu, and Twa) shared the same language, Kinyarwanda.[1] In other comparable forms of poetry, there was often a shared knowledge of the poetic skills, so that it was, in important ways, a more widely accessible form. Praise poetry in Shona and Zulu exemplify this more horizontal proliferation of both linked genres and poetic skills. Certainly the vast areas across which the form of praise poetry has been used, testify to the importance placed on the making of meaning and the place of dense, rich poetic language as carriers of public social values and ideologies.

The need for societies to have memory banks that act as mirrors and as a form of working archive led in many instances to the extensive use of oral poetry to formalize memory of the past, and to make the past comprehensible and accessible. Praise poetry, differently named, often with elaborate yet flexible prosodies, and existing in each instance in a particular hierarchy of genres, has its place in a number of very differently constituted societies covering a range of language groups across the continent. It is one of the most widespread forms of oral poetry that engaged with the attempt to provide public, active memorials through performance. It can be found in many sub-Saharan African societies and in some instances it has found a niche as an ongoing cultural practice in contemporary communities or in the modern state. A number of south and southern African societies still have considerable cultural capital held in praise poetry. In South Africa, Xhosa praise poets who supported figures opposed to the apartheid Nationalist government were on more than one occasion persecuted by the apartheid police (Opland 1998: 278–81) and in the postapartheid state former President Mandela is frequently accompanied on official business by his praise poet, Zolani Mkiva, who has also released a number of compact discs of his work, with musical backing. The praise poet has license to critique the object of his praise, but this is usually done sparingly. Praise poetry has often been constituted as history from above, for instance the *lithoko* of the Basotho (Damane and Saunders 1974; Kunene 1971), the court poetry of the old kingdom of Rwanda (Kagame 1951), Hausa praise poetry and song (Smith 1957, 1978; Gidley 1975; Muhammad 1979; Furniss 1996), and the royal and chiefly *izibongo* of the Zulu (Nyembezi 1958; Cope 1968; Gunner and Gwala 1991). Even here, the history of rulers is often rich with ambiguities and frequently contains the resistant voices of those groups that have been defeated, and the dissident voices of critics (Brown 1998: 94–95;

Hamilton 1998). It is the ability of praise poetry to absorb and reflect changes within the society it enunciates (Vail and White 1991) and also to provide a sense of the past in the present (Barber 1989: 20) that are among its most compelling qualities and ensure its place as one of the great genres of the continent. Nevertheless its continued existence is uncertain. Among the Basotho in the nineteenth century, the elaborate *lithoko* with their heroic ethos and elaborate imagery captured the exploits of King Mshweshwe and his sons as they battled to maintain their mountain kingdom against Boer attacks but the poetry also allowed for moments of reflexivity and for the inclusion of close observation of the natural world and of place which frequently became absorbed into the praise names themselves (Kunene 1971). This official poetry still flourishes on state occasions but now lacks the pervasive influence it once had, and it has been argued that a new genre "of the people," *lifela*, is more representative of modern Basotho national and transnational identity than the older *lithoko* (Coplan 1994). Shona praise poetry, once part of an assembly of spoken and sung genres (Hodza and Fortune 1979) in which clan praises had a particularly important role has largely fallen into disuse. Hodza and Fortune note that

> One of the most pleasing forms of love poetry, and, indeed, of praise poetry as a whole, arises out of the rhythmic use of praise names and their expansions, accompanied by variations in the imagery. (Hodza and Fortune 1979: 39)

Their beauty and intricacy, their deep engagement with the imagery of the natural world are very striking, as the following two examples illustrate, one from the poetry of love and courtship, and the other from the praises of a wife to her husband:

> You are my mother,
> One with loving embraces
> One with a neck as long as a giraffe's . . .
> My calabash, so light yet so capacious.
> Tasty paste that sticks to my gums,
> Ground nuts doubly ground.
> (Hodza and Fortune 1979: 39)

And

> (Tembo clan praises of endearment):
> Thank you Zebra;
> Zebra with a striped coat;
> One adorned with its own skin;
> One who gives delight . . .
> Thank you, Hornless wild beast;

Your sweetness lies at your base;
A stalk of sweet sorghum;
Male yet female in your love.
(Hodza and Fortune 1979: 163)

Even though such intimate eloquence has fallen out of fashion, new genres, as in the Basotho case, have emerged. During the war of liberation of the 1970s, in what was then Rhodesia, the rich and symbolic imagery of many of the popular songs, sold commercially on audiocassettes and even played on the radio station of the Smith government, often held hidden messages linked to the struggle. The ease with which urban audiences "read" such *chimurenga* (liberation) songs was in large part due to the way they "hugged the common cultural ground which they shared with their audiences" although the message was new (Pongweni 1997: 65). In his account of the new music that played so crucial a role as a conduit of comment and resistance, Alec Pongweni identifies three types of songs, already part of Shona cultural practice, that were utilized in *chimurenga* music: the narrative genre known as *ndgaringo*; another genre, *kudeketera,* which built on the repetition of small units; and the genre of work songs known as *jukwara*, which frequently made use of poetic license (Pongweni 1997: 66; 1982; Vambe 2000). The example of such Zimbabwean music, which was so knotted into accepted linguistic and musical forms but at the same time departed from them, shows orality as a dynamic force, operating as part of what Raymond Williams has termed "emergent culture" (Williams 1977). Important as its presence is, it cannot call back into active use the elaborate speech genres that were once part of the Shona language repertoire.

The multiplicity of expressive forms that African societies have produced is shown by its exploitation by those well outside the domains of public power. As Jean Derive has pointed out, the capacity for oral performance is not merely the "distinctive sign" of a given social condition, but is also a potential means of exerting pressure upon or transforming social conditions and power relations (James 1997: 468; Derive 1995). Thus those without power may nevertheless use a recognized art form to complain, and hope for change. Derive has recorded how Douala married women would make use of a sung and danced genre performed in public on the arrival of an important visitor, to record, obliquely but publicly, their anxieties and the problems they were experiencing as women, and often as women in a polygynous situation (Derive 1978). Although such a genre might not be seen by outsiders as prestigious, by those within Douala society the genre, known as *kurubi donkili*, was highly enough regarded to have produced its own famous composers (such as Nasara Kamagati) and to be valued as a means by which those without power, in this case women and particularly married women, could claim a space of free and public expression (Derive 1978). The potential of exerting pressure, even if not of transforming power relations, is held in such a genre. In carefully documented cases from other parts of the continent, such as Mozambique, we see how song, often with dance, can become a vehicle not only for critical comment by generations of the oppressed but how it can hold with a kind of shifting tenacity "a whole tradition of rejection" (Vail and White 1997: 63).

The ChiSena worksong, with the name of Paiva (a brutal overseer whose name then signifies successive exploitative figures and ultimately the system itself) recurring through the decades, became a means of inscribing in social memory the successive malpractices relating to land appropriation and labor misuse by the Portuguese, and more broadly the colonial system under which the people suffered (Vail and White 1997: 60). Once again, the dynamic nature of song is noted, as the "same" song appears in Luabo (rather than ChiSena) and is described as "a map of suffering which our children will have to know" (Vail and White 1997: 56). It then moves again to become a women's dance song that comments cogently, and with inserted improvised drama elaborating the main themes, on the harsh conditions and the frequent sexual assaults women had to suffer as they worked in the cotton plantations in the mid-1950s. What the body of "Paiva songs" shows is how an older song can, through a measure of "recontextualizing," as performance theorists term it (Bauman and Brigs 1990), move languages and genres and yet remain recognizably "the same." Only in the 1970s, after the withdrawal of the Portuguese from Mozambique, did new words become attached to the song that then contained not only the criticism so central to the earlier songs, but also triumph over the oppressive Paiva figure:

> Paiva is diabolical
> *Ay Ay*
> Now we have escaped.
> (Vail and White:
> 1997: 60)

As the two instances above show, the license for those without formal power to comment and criticize through song or poetry (and sometimes dance and song) is a crucial part of the way orality has operated in African societies. The powerful could listen and take note, but they could not strike back as the license given to the genres themselves provided protection. A popular song deeply critical of the early nineteenth-century Zulu king, Dingane, recorded by the musician and composer, Princess Magogo (d. 1989), a member of the Zulu royal house, had as its theme line: "Each day we are killed by Dingane" (Tracey 1974; Gunner 2002a).

In some instances the marginal voices produce not critical comment but long, semi-autobiographical finely crafted poetry that encapsulates some of the primary values of the larger community. Marginal people include the youth. Thus among the nomadic Fulani of West Africa, it is the young men who compose elaborate and intense poems, known as *jamooje nai*, for their cattle on the long and lonely journeys across the bare and forbidding savannah. Christiane Seydou points out that the poetry contains "their life, their soul"; in this genre that is individual and confessional yet exists within the clear parameters of a recognized form, their making of the poetry becomes the means by which they map and control, mentally, the harsh terrain through which they travel; and their mastery of the artistic resource offered by the poetry is displayed to the full community on their return to the river Niger in Mali (Seydou, 1991; Seydou, Biebuyck and Bekombo 1997).

What the African records and the ongoing production of culture in Africa make clear is that orality is not an amorphous, vaguely communal preliterate state awaiting redemption by various manifestations of modernity. It is rather a protean presence, changing, interacting, and producing a different kind of cultural equilibrium on the African continent, defining its own modernities through language (Benveniste 1966; Voloshinov 1986). The records of African performance genres show time and again that particular societies may produce precisely honed kinds of expressive art to fit the particular ambience of a specific culture. In a society that has for centuries been decimated by internecine wars, by slavery, and by disease, the specialist (male) Nzakara poets from the Central African Republic sing with stoic, sometimes satiric eloquence about death, the betrayal of women, and the impossible hardships of life (de Dampierre, 1963: 33). The production of the finest poetry by those who choose the art remains an austere obligation and a mark of high social value. Eric de Dampierre describes how a poet, accompanying himself on the harp, may use the accepted devices of his form – the known phrases, elliptical language, archaic words – and yet insert his own "voice" as a composer. In the instance of the Nzakara we see, again, performance as a cultural practice not linked to the reification of power but rather an expressive art form that is part of the ongoing making of meaning for both producers and listeners.

How oral material is transmitted between the generations, and what factors ensure that songs, chanted or spoken poetry, prayers, proverbs, narratives, and so on are passed on is clearly a central question, crucial to social reproduction. Whereas the genres such as praise poetry, which are largely situated in the public domain, enunciate history and power "from above" other genres situated in the expressive forms of subaltern groups such as women and youth are in many cases less accessible to outsiders and are given less rhetorical space. They are often, though, crucially important to social structure. Initiation songs provide an insight into the ways in which African societies have engaged with song and forms of dance as the key modes through which they approach the difficult process of the move to adulthood and the responsibilities that go with it. John Blacking's work on the initiation schools of the Venda in southern Africa, and in particular those for Venda girls, opens up a number of fascinating points in this regard (Blacking 1969). He points out that like the modern system of school education, initiation is designed to "indoctrinate," not educate in the true sense of the word, namely, to reveal and develop individual qualities and abilities. Within that caveat, he explores what values and knowledge were being taught. In Venda society, Blacking observes, what is stressed is "the overriding importance of being human," and he continues, "technical incompetence in human relations is never accepted" (Blacking 1969: 71). He emphasizes that for women in Venda society, nonattendance at *domba* would prevent them from having any real say in women's affairs and would isolate an individual from her peers in times of trouble. In traditional Venda society, women hold considerable power and almost undisputed authority in certain fields of religious duty, home management, marriage and divorce negotiations, the preparation of girls for marriage, and the control of young mothers. It is attendance at *domba* that regulates a woman's status and precise seniority among her peers for her whole life (Blacking 1969: 4).

Songs as well as dances have a central role in the educational process of initiation, and the exacting dances are practiced by novices both individually, with a teacher, and then communally in the evenings. The songs that make up the stage known as *vhusha* come from a variety of sources: some are composed by the graduates themselves, some are adaptations of beer songs, of children's songs, and so on. The teaching that is carried through both the songs and the dances seeks to redefine the novices' somatic knowledge as regards sexuality, pregnancy, childbirth, and the responsibilities of marriage. The compact and allusive songs thus hold and transmit cultural knowledge and social values through the intensive learning situation, which is both focused on the individual, when the novice learns with a single tutor, and the group, communal rehearsals where the skills are welded into a single whole.

In addition to the focus on the way in which novices may in some cases compose fresh songs or adapt existing songs, sometimes from other genres, Blacking also draws attention to the contrasting role of the specialist, or master of words, in another stage of the initiation process, namely, the learning of the regulations or *imilayo*. Here an interesting differentiation between popular and specialist knowledge and usage in relation to verse is evident: for the experts, the passing on of the "laws" is "primarily an exercise in memory and imagination" whereas for the average person the songs or fragments of songs become "passwords of a mutual aid society." Interestingly, Blacking takes his reader briefly into the densely poetic and value-laden map used by the masters of initiation with whom he worked most closely, and points to the pattern of a journey followed by many; for one master, this took the form of "the beginning, the river, the public meeting place, the drum, the fire, the council hut." The gap between the verbal skills of the specialists and the far more generalized knowledge of the initiates can be seen as illustrating a general characteristic of orality as it is (or has been) practiced in many African societies, namely, that of a deeply productive symbiosis between the specialist and the ordinary performer. The relevance of the performance and of attendance at *domba* for young Venda girls can be judged by the fact that it is seen as having a place in the construction of modern identities in the new millennium and in the new postapartheid nation.[2]

Resistant memory, which holds the history of a minority and ensures the maintenance of a community, has also found imaginative expression through song. The capacity of song to wrap itself round a point of great importance in the past and thus allow that moment or cluster of moments to live on in the collective memory is well illustrated by the songs of the Herero people now living in northern Botswana and forced to flee from South West Africa after conflict with the Germans in the early years of the twentieth century (Alnaes 1989). Kirsten Alnaes argues that the pain of the past is encountered through the images of "death, destruction, loss of land and loss of meaning and normality." She continues by showing how images of regeneration can exist alongside such confrontations with "the death-world" of past generations (1989: 293–94). Thus the songs and laments performed have the dual role of catharsis and revitalization and bind together a very different past and present. Alnaes also points out that such songs, often performed within the home, and in order to educate the postmigration generations into their past, function as reminders of the contrast between a secure present and a time of trauma in earlier, but relatively recent, history (1989: 293–94).

Current work on orality emphasizes its place in contemporary cultural practice in Africa and its often dialogic role with writing or print and with the electronic media. The hybrid forms to which I referred earlier have often been born of such synergies. The hymns from the AmaNazaretha church in South Africa founded by Isaiah Shembe in 1910 and composed by him were written down by scribes, copied in longhand into the personal notebooks of church members, or simply learnt by those without access to the tools of literacy – a pen, paper, and the knowledge of writing. Today they are both sung and in some instances used as dancing items in church worship. Their imagery and range of reference that are part of the power of their performance mean that the hymns carry the power not only to confirm a particular view or position, but also to transform it. Moreover, the words contain their force within the broader musical performance and this has its own role in evoking a broadly political consciousness (Blacking 1995: 201). Performers and listeners / audience are part of a fluid set of subjectivities that relate to the history of Christianity, Zulu and South African history, and an intersecting regional and national imaginary (Gunner 2002b; Muller 1999). It is this capacity to reshape while drawing on older energies that marks some of the genres of modern African orality and it is the composite power of the word, music, and the dance that is significant. Deborah James's comments on the modern South African migrant genre of *kiba* and its power to draw people together are also true of the AmaNazaretha hymns:

> The lyrics alone . . . cannot explain the strength of this new source of identification. But, in the broader performance context, lyrics combine with dance and music to embody a life and a specific view of morality which men and women labour migrants have created for themselves. (James 1997: 470)

The huge investment of cultural capital in a range of often intersecting oral genres and the active role of practitioners in constantly moving a genre forward and remaking it is an area of oral studies that is currently being emphasized in the work of scholars. The older model of freestanding oral genres, manifested in the often very fine collections of single or relatively few genres of "oral literature" from a particular African society such as those published by the pathbreaking Oxford Library of African Literature series in the late 1960s and the 1970s (for example Goody 1972; Cope 1968; Coupez and Kamanzi 1970; Morris 1964; Bin Ismail and Lienhardt 1968), has been superseded by theories of orality that embrace a far more interactive and interdependent sense of cultural practices and "text" (Hanks 1989). Thus Graham Furniss writes of contemporary Hausa literature that genres: oral, written, and those written first and then performed, are both genres in the conventional sense *and* are defined by their practitioners in relation to one another. He observes that

> the practitioners operate complex networks of borrowing, countering and redefinition which means that the genre is never an entirely fixed set of features even if the label appears to stay the same . . . some genres constitute the building blocks of others and may appear as performed events in their own right in one context and then, in another context, appear as constitutive elements in another genre . . . Similarly, the relation between genres may invoke the satirical subversion of a dominant form by another. (Furniss 1996: 16)

In the same way Karin Barber argues for the fluid, floating nature of genre boundaries and the way in which, in any number of cultures, recognized clusters of words migrate across genres and are redefined by their new context (Barber 1999: 21).

In an era of globalization, orality has not disappeared but has often adapted itself in its many different forms to become a vehicle for the expression of the fears and hopes of new generations of Africans. Thus, while it is true that, in some instances, genres of poetry or song and of narrative have not endured the erosion of the social base that sustained their performances and their producers, other genres have survived or grown. In two interesting instances from South Africa the social and economic pressures of the migrant labor system in the apartheid era have led to the emergence of new genres that retain a loose connection to their parent genre but maintain a certain independence as well. These can be seen in a double sense as "migrant" genres; thus the Sotho genre of *lifela*, fashioned by men moving between Lesotho and the mines of Johannesburg, grew both from young men's initiation songs and from the praise poetry of Basotho royalty and chiefs known as *lithoko* (Coplan 1994; Damane and Sanders 1974; Kunene 1971). Migrant or rebellious Basotho women, existing largely on the fringes of their male compatriots' social spaces, the border bars of Lesotho, and the shebeens of Johannesburg, made their own distinctive version of the genre and by so doing were able to create an identity for themselves as bold yet suffering women, enunciating a new version of what it meant to be a migrant (Coplan 1994). In another South African instance (already mentioned above), women moving between the rural areas of the north and Johannesburg worked first within a men's song and dance genre used in the hostels (*kiba*) and then moved the form into a more exclusively female domain. The name of the genre remained the same but it took on an additional and specifically female form and became a crucial vector for the making of modern identities for migrant women, one that embraced both modernity and a sense of rural belonging (James 1994; 1997; 1999).

In many cases the electronic media, namely, television and radio, have played an important role in enabling new genres to emerge, or adaptations of old genres to continue; the audiocassette has also been a key instrument of transmission (Fardon and Furniss 2000). The use of the audiocassette as well as the radio in the spread of Somali oral poetry has been particularly remarkable and in one memorable instance a certain popular poem, *Leexo*, sung over the airwaves while a key parliamentary debate was in progress in the capital, Mogadishu, toppled a government (Johnson 1995: 115–17). In general, the evidence from contemporary studies shows that many oral genres are resilient and adaptable to the intense changes that have accompanied modern technology, urban living, and often difficult and oppressive industrial conditions. Oral genres have provided a means of formalizing new experiences and in a number of societies, for instance in the case of the Somali genres of the *balwo* and *heello* mentioned above, and in the urban genre of *isicathamiya* in South Africa, they have provided powerful new cultural texts for people's lives (Johnson 1974; Andrzejewski and Lewis 1964; Erlmann 1991; 1996; Johnson 2001).

Part of the defining of an African or African modernities and the connection of this to orality has been the way in which new publics have been made through the use of the electronic media. Radio, still the most influential medium on the continent, is often a conduit for new hybrid forms of orality that sometimes have their own complicated genealogies of origin and command large audiences in the urban and rural areas of the continent, and sometimes globally. The form of *isicathamiya* that was heard on the Paul Simon album *Gracelands* with the Ladysmith Black Mambazo group is one such genre (Erlmann 1991; 1996). Its cultural appeal lies in a complex of words, music, and dance, but within South Africa its continuing vitality is partly generated by the way in which radio, in this case the Zulu-language radio station uKhozi, announces fixtures all over the country, plays the latest music, and conducts interviews with eminent choir leaders. The genre of *maskanda*, also from South Africa, has been traced back to the solo love songs of lonely young women (James 1999: 73) but is now a style in which men and women perform. *Maskanda* works with standard themes but keeps as one of its vital functions the power to criticize and comment on social conditions, inequalities and, when necessary, the foolish ways of the powerful. Even a majestic form such as the West African epic, and in particular the Mandinka epic of Sunjata, has found its place in the electronic media, in this case largely though the work of the singer Salif Keita.

Here too, however, some critics argue that the move to the electronic media has meant a diminution in terms of the subtleties, verbal richness, and the carefulness of the text when compared to those produced by master *griots/jali* such as the Gambian "master of the word" Bamba Suso (Diawara 1997; Suso and Kanute 1999).

The active presence in Africa of the epic genre is being increasingly recognized and documented by scholars, and the epics themselves are in some instances being re-formed by singers such as Salif Keita (Belcher 1999; Okpewho 1979; 1992; Johnson, Hale and Belcher 1997); the role of epic as a carrier of messages about history, and its place in the present, as well as its function in defining regional and transnational identities is constantly being debated. Yet a slighter, emergent genre like the South African freedom song, may have played its part, briefly, as a vehicle for national consciousness and run its course. Now rarely heard, except at trades union rallies, they were, from the 1950s onwards a staple part of African oppositional public discourse, carrying their melodies and words along broad streets, into the camps and the bush of Angola, into dingy halls and into the jails of the apartheid era. They often played a role, as Blacking has suggested (1995), in the creation of a new trans-ethnic imagined community, and in the construction of new personal and group identities.

The work of documenting and debating the role of African oral genres in mediating social relationships, cementing personal and social ties, and generally making sense of the world, is an ongoing one. New work sometimes focuses on a genre or cluster of genres that has had its own vibrant, hidden life in the market place of people's lives although not in the libraries of academia. Thus the genre of jocular poetry, the Borana genre known as *qoosaa-taapaa*, and sung in the villages of northern Kenya and the slums of Nairobi, has recently been studied and shown to play a key role in the articulation of male and age-set, as well as clan relations. It also allows women to speak out from their marginalized positions and, through this witty and entertaining form, make their views about the "vices" of men heard in public, and also, on occasion, their views on a particular political dispute (Wako 2002). Such forms, currently being brought to a wider audience, together with the often highly coded genres of Somali poetry (Andrzejewski and Lewis 1964; Andrzejewski and Andrzejewski 1993) commenting on love, honor, matters of philosophy and religion and, as in the case of the Dervish soldier/poet Maxamed Cabdille Xasan (c.1860–1921), on war against the colonialist, cannot be seen as part of what Abiola Irele has termed "the prison of the mythopoetic imagination" (Irele 1987:217) but rather as expressions of the diverse, modern world. It is in this world that African orality has its place.

Notes

1. See Hintjens 2001 for a chilling and finely argued account of early colonial complicity in the construction of ethnic rivalries in Rwanda and the state planning of the ethnic genocide in 1994.
2. Brief clips of the final, snake-like dance of all the initiates were shown on the South African Broadcasting Corporation national television in 2001 during one of the evening news relays.

Bibliography

Alnaes, Kirsten. 1989. "Living with the Past: The Songs of the Herero in Botswana." *Africa* 59.3: 267–99.

Andrzejewski, B. W., and Sheila Andrzejewski, trans. 1993. *An Anthology of Somali Poetry*. Bloomington: Indiana University Press.

Andrzejewski, B. W., and I. M. Lewis. 1964. *Somali Poetry: An Introduction*. Oxford: Clarendon Press.

Babalola, Adeboye. 1966. *The Content and Form of Yoruba "Ijala."* Oxford: Clarendon Press.

Barber, Karin. 1989. "Interpreting Oriki as History and as Literature." In *Discourse and its Disguises: The Interpretation of African Oral Texts*. Ed. K. Barber and P. de F. Moraes Farias. Birmingham: Centre of West African Studies, University of Birmingham: 13–23.

1991. *I Could Speak until Tomorrow: "Oriki," Women and the Past in a Yoruba Town*. Edinburgh and Washington, DC: Edinburgh University Press and Smithsonian Institute Press for the International Africa Institute.

1997. "Preliminary Notes on Audiences in Africa." *Africa* 67.3: 348–62.

1999. "Quotation in the Constitution of Yoruba Texts." *Research in African Literatures* 30.2: 17–41.

Bauman, Richard, and Charles L. Briggs. 1990. "Poetics and Performance as Critical Perspectives on Language and Social Life." *Annual Review of Anthropology* 19: 59–88.

Belcher, Stephen. 1999. *Epic Traditions of Africa*. Bloomington: Indiana University Press.

Benveniste, Emile. 1966. *Problèmes de linguistiques générales*. Paris: Gallimard.

Blacking, John. 1969. "Songs, Dances, Mimes and Symbolism of Venda Girls' Initiation Schools." *African Studies* 28.1: 3–36; 28.2: 69–118; 28.3: 149–200.

1995. *Music, Culture and Experience: Selected Papers of John Blacking*. Ed. and introd. Reginald Byron. Chicago: University of Chicago Press.

Brown, Duncan. 1998. *Voicing the Text: South African Oral Poetry and Performance*. Cape Town: Oxford University Press.

Cope, Trevor. 1968. *Izibongo: Zulu Praise Poems*. Oxford: Clarendon Press.

Coplan, David. 1994. *In the Time of Cannibals: The Word Music of South Africa's Basotho Migrants*. Chicago: University of Chicago Press.

Coupez, A., and Kamanzi, Th. 1970. *Littérature de cour au Rwanda*. Oxford: Clarendon Press.

Damane, M. and P. B. Sanders, eds. 1974. *Lithoko: Sotho Praise Poems*. Oxford: Clarendon Press.

De Dampierre, E. 1963. *Poètes Nzakara*. Paris: Julliard.

Derive, Jean. 1978. "Le chant de Kurubi a Kong." *Annales de l'Université d'Abidjan. Serie J: Traditions Orales* 2: 85–114.

1995. "The Function of Oral Art in the Regulation of Social Power in Dyula Society." In *Power, Marginality and African Oral Literature*. Ed. Graham Furniss and Liz Gunner. Cambridge: Cambridge University Press: 122–29.

Diawara, Mamadou. 1997. "Mande Oral Popular Culture Revisited by the Electronic Media." In *Readings in African Popular Culture*. Ed. Karin Barber. Oxford: James Currey in association with the African International Institute: 40–47. (Revised and translated from *Passages* 9, 1994.)

Erlmann, Veit. 1991. *African Stars: Studies in Black South African Performance*. Chicago: University of Chicago Press.

1996. *Nightsong: Performance, Power and Practice in South Africa*. Chicago: University of Chicago Press.

Fardon, Richard, and Graham Furniss, eds. 2000. *African Broadcast Cultures. Radio in Transition*. Oxford: James Currey.

Farias, P. de Moraes. 1992. "History and Consolation: Royal Yoruba Bards Comment on Their Craft." *History in Africa* 19: 263–97.

Feierman, Steven. 1994. "Africa in History. The End of Universal Narratives." In *Imperial Histories and Postcolonial Displacements*. Ed. Gyan Prakash. Princeton: Princeton University Press: 40–65.

Finnegan, Ruth. 1970. *Oral Literature in Africa*. Oxford: Clarendon Press.

1977. *Oral Poetry: Its Nature, Significance and Social Context*. Cambridge: Cambridge University Press.

Furniss, Graham. 1995. "The Power of Words and the Relationship between Hausa Genres." In *Power, Marginality and African Oral Literature*. Ed. G. Furniss and L. Gunner. Cambridge: Cambridge University Press: 130–46.

1996. *Poetry, Prose and Popular Culture in Hausa*. Edinburgh: Edinburgh University Press for the International Africa Institute, London.

Gidley, C. G. B. 1975. "'Roko': A Hausa Praise Crier's Account of his Craft." *African Language Studies* 16: 93–115.

Goody, Jack. 1972. *The Myth of the Bagre*. Oxford: Clarendon Press.

Görög-Karady, Veronika, with Catherine Bouillet and Tal Tamari. 1992. *Bibliographie annotée: littérature orale d'Afrique noire*. Paris: Conseil International de la Langue Française.

Gunner, Liz. 2002a. *The Man of Heaven and the Beautiful Ones of God. Writings from a South African Church*. Leiden: Brill.

2002b. "A Royal Woman, an Artist, and the Ambiguities of National Belonging: The Case of Princess Constance Magogo." *Kunapipi* 24.1–2: 205–23.

Gunner, Liz, and Mafika Gwala, eds. and trans. 1991. *"Musho!" Zulu Popular Praises*. East Lansing, Michigan: Michigan State University Press.

Hamilton, Carolyn. 1998. *Terrific Majesty: The Powers of Shaka Zulu and the Limits of Historical Invention*. Cambridge, MA: Harvard University Press.

Hanks, W. F. 1989. "Text and Textuality." *Annual Review of Anthropology* 18: 95–127.

Hasani bin Ismail. 1968. *The Medicine Man: Swifa ya Nguvumali*. Ed. and trans. Peter Lienhardt, Oxford: Clarendon Press.

Hertefelt, Marcel d', and A. Coupez. 1964. *La royauté sacrée de l'ancien Rwanda*. Tervuren: Musée royal de l'Afrique centrale.

Higgins, John, ed. 2001. *The Raymond Williams Reader*. Oxford: Blackwell.

Hintjens, Helen M. 2001. "When Identity Becomes a Knife: Reflecting on the Genocide in Rwanda." *Ethnicities* 1.1: 25–55.

Hodza, Aaron C., and G. Fortune. 1979. *Shona Praise Poetry*. Oxford: Clarendon Press.

Irele, Abiola. 1987. "In Praise of Alienation." In *Surreptitious Speech: Présence Africaine and the Politics of Otherness 1947–1987*. Ed. V. Y. Mudimbe. Chicago: University of Chicago Press: 201–26.

James, Deborah. 1994. "Basadi ba Baeng: Female Migrant Performance from the Northern Transvaal." In *Politics and Performance in Southern African Theatre, Poetry and Song*. Ed. Liz Gunner. Johannesburg: Witwatersrand University Press: 81–110.

1997. "'Music of Origin': Class, Social Category and the Performers and Audience of *Kiba*, a South African Genre." *Africa* 67.3: 454–75.

1999. *Songs of the Women Migrants: Performance and Identity in South Africa*. Johannesburg: Witwatersrand University Press in association with The International African Institute, London.

Johnson, John W. 1974. *Heelooy Heelleellooy: The Development of the Heello in Modern Somali Poetry*. Bloomington, Indiana: Research Center for the Language Sciences.

1995. "Power, Marginality and Somali Oral Poetry: Case Studies in the Dynamics of Tradition." In *Power, Marginality and African Oral Literature*. Ed. G. Furniss and L. Gunner. Cambridge: Cambridge University Press: 111–21.

Johnson, John W., and Fadigi Sisoko. [1986] 1992. *The Epic of SonJara, a West African Tradition: New Notes and translation by J. W. Johnson. Text by Fadigi Sisoko*. Bloomington: Indiana University Press.

Johnson, John W., Thomas A. Hale, and Stephen Belcher, eds. 1997. *Oral Epics from Africa: Vibrant Voices from a Vast Continent*. Bloomington: Indiana University Press.

Johnson, Simone L. 2001. "Defining the Migrant Experience: An Analysis of the Poetry and Performance of a South African Migrant Genre." MA diss. University of Natal, Pietermaritzburg.

Kagame, Alexis. 1951. "La poésie dynastique au Rwanda." Brussels: Institut Colonial Belge.

1975. *Un Abrégé de l'ethno-histoire du Rwanda*, vol. II. Butare: Editions Universitaires du Rwanda.

Kunene, D. P. 1971. *Heroic Poetry of the Basotho*. Oxford: Clarendon Press.

Morris, Henry F. 1964. *The Heroic Recitations of the Bahima of Ankole*. Oxford: Clarendon Press.

Mudimbe, V. Y. 1994. *The Idea of Africa*. Bloomington: Indiana University Press.

Muhammad, Dalhatu. 1979. "Interaction between the Oral and the Literate Traditions of Hausa Poetry." *Harsunan Nijeriya* 9: 85–90.

Muller, Carol. 1999. *Rituals of Fertility and the Sacrifice of Desire: Nazarite Women's Performance in South Africa*. Chicago: University of Chicago Press.

Nyembezi, C. L. S. 1948. "The Historical Background to the *Izibongo* of the Zulu Military Age." *African Studies* 7: 110–25 and 157–74.

1958. *Izibongo Zamakhosi*. Pietermaritzburg: Shuter and Shooter.

Okpewho, Isidore. 1979. *The Epic in Africa*. New York: Columbia University Press.

1992. *African Oral Literature: Backgrounds, Character and Continuity*. Bloomington: Indiana University Press.

Opland, Jeff. 1974. "Praise Poems as Historical Sources." In *Beyond the Cape Frontier: Studies in the History of the Transkei and the Ciskei*. Ed. Christopher Saunders and Robin Derricourt. London: Longman: 1–37.

1987. "The Bones of Mafanta: A Xhosa Oral Poet's Response to Context in South Africa." *Research in African Literatures* 18.1: 36–50.

1998. *Xhosa Poets and Poetry*. Cape Town: David Philip.

Pongweni, Alec. 1982. *Songs That Won the Liberation War*. Harare: The College Press.

1997. "The Chimurenga Songs of the Zimbabwean War of Liberation." In *Readings in African Popular Culture*. Ed. Karin Barber. Oxford: James Currey in association with the African International Institute: 63–72.

Rwabukumba, Joseph and Vincent Mudandagizi. 1974. "Les formes historiques de la dépendance personelle dans l'état rwandais." *Cahiers d'Etudes Africaines* 14.1.

Seydou, Christiane. 1991. *Bergers des mots*. Paris: Classiques Africains.

Seydou, Christiane, Brunhilde Biebuyck, and Manga Bekombo. 1997. *Voix d'Afrique*, vol. 1. *Poésie*. Paris: Classiques Africains.

Smith, M. G. 1957. "The Social Functions and Meaning of Hausa Praise-Singing." *Africa* 27.1: 26–43.

1978. *The Affairs of Daura: History and Change in a Hausa State 1800–1958*. Berkeley and Los Angeles: University of California Press.

Stein, Pippa. 1998. "Reconfiguring the Past and Present: Performing Literary Histories in a Johannesburg Classroom." *TESOL Quarterly* 32.3: 517–28.

Suso, Bamba, and Banna Kanute. 1999. *The Epic of Sunjata*. Trans. Gordon Innes with Bokari Sidibe, ed. and introd. Graham Furniss and Lucy Duran. London: Penguin.

Torino, Thomas. 2000. *Nationalists, Cosmopolitans and Popular Music in Zimbabwe*. Chicago: University of Chicago Press.

Tracey, Hugh. 1974. *The Zulu Songs of Princess Constance Magogo kaDinuzulu*. Music of Africa Series no. 37. Gallo SGALP 167.

Vail, Leroy, and Landeg White. 1991. *Power and the Praise Poem. Voices in Southern African History*. Oxford: James Currey.

1997. "Plantation Protest. The History of a Mozambican Song." In *Readings in African Popular Culture*. Ed. Karin Barber. Oxford: James Currey in association with the African International Institute: 54–62 (*Journal of Southern African Studies* 5.1 [1978]: 1–25).

Vambe, Maurice T. V. 2000. "Popular Songs and Social Realities in Post-Independence Zimbabwe." *African Studies Review* 43.2: 73–85.

Vansina, Jan. 1984. *Art History in Africa*. London: Longman.

1985. *Oral Tradition as History*. Oxford: James Currey.

2000. "Useful Anachronisms: The Rwandan Esoteric Code of Kingship." *History in Africa*: 415–21.

Voloshinov, V. N. [1929] 1986. *Marxism and the Philosophy of Language*. Trans. L. Matjeka and I. R. Titunik. Cambridge, MA: Harvard University Press.

Wako, Fugich. 2002. "*Qoosaa-taapaa* as an Oral Literary Genre among the Borana: Mediating Social Relationships in Joke and Play." PhD thesis. University of Witwatersrand, Johannesburg.

Williams, Raymond. 1977. *Marxism and Literature*. Oxford: Oxford University Press.

Yai, Olabiyi. 1994. "In Praise of Metonymy: The Concepts of 'Tradition' and 'Creativity' in the Transmission of Yoruba Artistry over Time and Space." In *The Yoruba Artist: New Theoretical Perspectives on African Arts*. Ed. Rowland Abiodun, Henry F. Drewal, and John Pemberton III. Washington, DC: Smithsonian: 107–15.

2

The folktale and its extensions

KWESI YANKAH

The folktale is the most important strand within the prose narrative complex in Africa. It is also the most widely studied. The distinctiveness of the folktale as a genre, however, is questionable due to its close textual affinities with other expressive genres such as myth, epic, dilemma tale, legend and proverb.

Even though local terminology often provides the best basis for resolving ambiguities in genre taxonomies (see Herskovits and Herskovits 1958), the folktale has sometimes posed a problem in Africa. In certain cultures, such as the Limba of Sierra Leone, the folktale and proverb do not have separate labels (Finnegan 1967: 28). Besides this, whenever the folktale has been cited in ongoing discourse for the purposes of persuasion, it has attracted the label "proverb" in certain cultures (see Yankah 1995: 88–93). The overlap between the proverb and tale should not be surprising, since they both convey moral lessons, and are mutually interactive in performance situations. Tales based on proverbs abound in Africa, and so do proverbs based on folktales. No doubt scholars who have compiled proverbs in Africa have often shown interest in the folktale (see Rattray 1916 and 1930; Dugaste 1975).

Dilemma tale

The dilemma tale constitutes a large class of folktales in Africa, but it has attracted very little attention partly because it does not appear to constitute a genre of its own. In the early twentieth century, dilemma tales sporadically appeared in folktale and legend compilations (see for example Hesler 1930; Cardinall 1931; Guillot 1946). In practice, they are hardly narrated independently, but emerge during the telling of riddles and folktales, with which they bear a close resemblance.

The dilemma tale is a narrative that ends in an unresolved puzzle and invites the audience to debate a solution. Without the concluding puzzle, it may appear as a folktale. Even though dominated by human characters, dilemma tales in Africa may also have animals as principal characters. A number of such tales involve the mother-in-law, where one has to choose between wife and mother-in-law in allocating scarce resources, for example providing a missing eye or ferrying kinsmen across a river. These conundrums are significant not necessarily as literary products, but as pointers to cultural values, which often guide participants in providing and debating answers. The first major independent compilation of dilemma tales in Africa was by William Bascom in the mid-seventies (Bascom 1975).

Myth

Myth, as a sacred narrative that explains the processes that have shaped the world, has not enjoyed unanimous recognition among scholars of the African narrative, partly because the criteria for its global definition are not fully evident in the potential examples from Africa (see Finnegan 1970: 361–67; Okpewho 1983 and 1992: 181–82). On one hand, there are several published collections of African narratives designated by their authors as myth, such as Cater G. Woodson's *African Myths*, Ulli Beier's *The Origin of Life and Death: African Creation Myths*, Jan Knappert's *Myths and Legends of the Congo*, and *African Mythology*, by Alice Werner. Even so, there is evidence to suggest that not all such authors were certain of the correct narrative category to which their collections should belong. In his introduction to *African Myths*, Woodson interchanges the terms folktale, myth, and legend (1928: ix). On the other hand, scholars like Hermann Baumann and Ruth Finnegan doubt the existence of myth in Africa, but for different reasons. To Baumann, the Negro is devoid of the gift of myth making (see Radin 1952: 2). To Finnegan, however, scholars of the African "myth" have not provided enough contextual information, for their collections to be truly classified as myth (1972: 361ff.).

Considered sacred, true, and authoritative, the myth uses divine and ancestral characters to explain the origins of natural phenomena and cultural institutions. Creation myths, clan/lineage myths (accounting for the groups' origins), myths associated with divination have all been recorded in various parts of Africa (see Abrahamsson 1951; Bascom 1969; Parrinder 1986). The extent to which such stories are considered true and authoritative, however, has not always been clarified.

The problem diminishes in cultures where separate indigenous labels exist for fictitious and belief narratives, such as in Dahomey (Herskovits and Herskovits 1958). Even here, as the Herskovitses point out, the distinction is sometimes blurred. The gap between myth and folktale is blurred further by trickster tales in Africa, which in places appear to combine the features of myth and folktale. Studying trickster figures among the Akan, Yoruba, Fon, and Ogo-Yurugu, for example, Robert D. Pelton observes that the most distinctive feature of the West African trickster is his association with divination (1980: 273). Combined with several cultural phenomena they generate in stories, tricksters would appear then to partly fulfill the criteria for spinning myths. Yet, the sacred traits of the trickster, even if relevant, may have diminished over time since trickster figures like Ananse are sources of sheer imaginative delight in the cultures in which they exist, and are considered to belong within the realm of the folktale (see Yankah 1983). Isidore Okpewho puts the entire myth controversy in a broad perspective, and treats the myth in Africa as a creative resource from which larger cultural values are derived (1983).

The folktale

Despite areas of overlap with other narrative forms, the folktale has a distinctive character of subsisting largely on play, fantasy, and aesthetic delight. The African folktale performer skillfully deploys literary, musical, linguistic, and dramatic devices to endow his imaginative narrative with an orchestral quality that compels co-participation by his audience. Because of its pervasiveness and popularity as a major source of entertainment in rural Africa, the folktale has arrested the attention of scholars and missionaries since the nineteenth century.

Its continued relevance in Africa is due partly to the unflagging dominance of the spoken word in Africa as well as the subtle and diverse manifestations of the folktale in contemporary life. What follows is an overview of important landmarks in the study of African folktale and a discussion of its nature and literary dynamics.

The collection of tales in Africa began in the mid-nineteenth century, as a sequel to trends in eighteenth-century Europe, where nationalism had fostered a recognition and respect for national literatures. A systematic collection of folksongs, tales, and myths had begun in Europe, through which treasures of past life could be rediscovered and preserved. If national literatures had been collected in Germany, Greece, Norway, and Russia, the same could be done in Africa, except that on the African continent, the collection of tales in the nineteenth century was done more out of colonial interest than nationalism.

In the second half of the nineteenth century, missionaries, anthropologists, and linguists began collecting large texts of folktales, riddles, proverbs, and customary practices. For the missionaries and linguists, these provided reliable data for the isolation of sound units and grammatical structures, crucial in determining the linguistic and literary maturity of "primitive mind," and the capacity of primitive languages to express thought (Finnegan 1970: 30). Missionaries also needed to understand the languages of colonial subjects, because such knowledge was valuable in the studying of the spontaneous use of language in folktales. Anthropologists collecting such texts also saw in them a means of accessing the mind of their native subjects, and determining residues of past and present modes of life. In any case, the close interaction between folktales and related verbal genres made it unproductive to collect the tales exclusively; they were collected and compiled together with art forms such as riddles and proverbs. Thus, Sigismund Koelle in 1854 wrote on *African Native Literature or Proverbs, Tales, Fables and Historical Fragments in the Kanuri or Bornu Language,* while Richard Burton about a decade later wrote on the wit and wisdom of West Africa, in which he compiled 2,268 proverbs and riddles and anecdotes from the Yoruba, Efik, Ga, Twi, and Ewe (Burton 1865). Other major tale collections in the nineteenth century include Bleek's 1864 compilation of Hottentot tales, and Lord Chatelain's work on Angolan folktales (1894).

Operating against a background of Darwin's theory of social evolution, which locates the "primitive" man at the lowest rung of the evolutionary ladder, where emphasis was supposedly more on communal than individual creativity, early scholars could not have unambiguously discerned esthetic merits in folktales from Africa. Ethnocentrism as well as miscomprehension of the African world led to a biased portrayal of the African tale as childlike. The comments of Henry Stanley in his collection of Central African narratives, in the early part of the twentieth century, attest to this. The very title Stanley gives to his compilation, *My Dark Companions and Their Strange Stories*, foreshadows its content. Consider the following remarks in his introduction:

> Many of the stories related were naturally of little value, having neither novelty nor originality; and in many cases . . . the stories were importations from Asia; while others were mere masks of low inclination. I therefore had often to sit out a lengthy tale which had not a single point in it. (Stanley 1906: 1)

Despite the streak of cultural arrogance here, a few scholars admitted the artistic worth of African folktales. In a preface to his collection of Hottentot tales, Bleek, for instance, boldly admits that the literary capacity of Africans "has been employed in almost the same direction as that which had been taken by our own earliest literatures . . ." (1864: xii–xiii).

Some scholars thus applied to their African collections the label "literature" as far back as the nineteenth century (see Koelle 1854, Burton 1865). It is partly based on this recognition that the American Folklore Society published Chatelain's *Folktales of Angola* in its very first memoir in 1894.

Since the beginning of the twentieth century, the African folktale has been studied by scholars of various academic persuasions, largely anthropology, folklore, and literature. Anthropologists like R. S. Rattray (1930), Tremearne (1913), Herskovits and Herskovits (1958), Evans-Pritchard (1967), Finnegan (1967) have made landmark studies of the Akan, Hausa, Dahomean, Zande, and Limba imaginative tales, bringing into focus various literary manifestations of the trickster in Africa. Particularly remarkable is Rattray's pioneering study of Akan folktales, where the stories, richly augmented with illustrations, are presented first in the original language (as told) before their translation into English. This way the linguistic and literary flavor of the stories is partly preserved.

One important discipline that has paid close attention to the African folktale is the discipline of folklore. Since the 1930s, folklore scholars in their search for the origin and distribution of tales circulating in Africa have utilized the discipline's unique tools, systematically to classify component units of African tales under crosscultural categories, called tale types and motif indexes, an approach developed by Anti Aarne and Stith Thompson. Inspired by diffusionist scholars, also known as the historic-geographic school, this approach to folktale studies sought to determine the original source and geographic distribution of folktales through a comparison of tale variants from different parts of the world.

Diffusionists

Since the 1930s, a number of such studies on the African folktale have been undertaken in unpublished doctoral dissertations in American universities. These include Mary Klipple's study of African folktales with foreign analogues (1938), Kenneth Clarke's motif index analysis of West African tales (1957), Ojo Arewa's classification of folktales of Northeastern Africa (1966), and Lambrecht's tale type analysis of Central Africa (1967). In the past two decades tale and motif index analyses have been done on Malagasy tales (Haring 1982) and verbal traditions in the Arab world (El-Shamy 1995).

The application of motif and tale type analysis in the study of African folktales extends beyond studies in America. In Europe, this has been adopted by the French school of African narrative scholars at the Centre National de la Recherche Scientifique (CNRS) later renamed Equipe de Recherche Associée (ERA). The group's membership consists of such linguists, oral literary scholars, and anthropologists as Geneviève Calame-Griaule, Gérard Dumestre, Veronika Görög-Karady, and Christiane Seydou. Having conducted fieldwork among several ethnic groups in West Africa (such as the Bambara, Fulani, Dogon, Shanga, Kru, Bete, and Zarma), the French school concentrates on the study of folktales, and has applied motif and tale type indexes for comparative purposes, apart from studying the folktale as a communicative process.

In 1981 and 1982, the French school organized two conferences in Britain and France, respectively, inviting other scholars from Britain. Proceedings of the 1981 symposium appear in Görög-Karady's edited volume, *Genres, Forms and Meanings: Essays in African Oral Literature*, which consists of ten essays on African oral narratives using comparative, literary, and anthropological approaches.

Formal approach

Closely related to the diffusionist-inspired use of tale type and motif indexes is the application of the formal (morphological) approach to the study of the African folktale. Developed by the Russian scholar Vladimir Propp in 1928, the morphological study seeks to identify the constituent motifs or building blocks of a tale and determine their relationship to the overall plot. Just as the grammarian studies the acceptable combination of words to form sentences, formalism is interested in the ordering of episodes to form a story.

In 1971, Alan Dundes applied Propp's formalism to the study of the trickster tales in Africa, and abstracted a characteristic pattern to which they appeared to conform. The tales, typically involving encounters between a smallish wily animal trickster and a bigger creature, revealed a recurrent pattern of the making and breaking of friendship. Dundes subsequently proposed the following sequence of functions, or "motifemes," as characteristic of African trickster tales: friendship, contract, violation, discovery, and end of friendship. Thus even though the trickster (say the hare) and his counterpart (the elephant, for example) initially find themselves wrapped in a bond of mutual trust, a series of incidents based on lust, selfishness, and insatiable greed on either side leads to a breach of faith, and eventual separation.

Almost at the same time as Dundes, Lee Haring (1972), using Propp's formalist approach, discerns in trickster tales told among people of African descent (in Africa, Jamaica, and USA) a formal pattern similar in essence to Alan Dundes's observations. The sequence of motifemes was:

(1) False friendship, where the trickster feigns friendship with another character;
(2) Contract, where the two agree somewhat to particular terms of a contract;
(3) Violation, where the trickster violates the contract;
(4) Trickery, where one character tricks the other;
(5) Deception, which is the result of trickery; and
(6) The trickster's escape or reward, which ends the tale.

Ten years after his study of trickster tales, Haring combines Propp's morphological approach and Aarne–Thompson's tale type and motif-index scheme in the study of Malagasy tales (Haring 1982), where he classifies over 800 Malagasy texts into seven formal categories.

Earlier on, Marion Kilson, following Dundes (1971) and Haring (1972), had applied the formal approach in the study of Mende tales (Kilson 1976).

Literary esthetics

Studies of the African folktale presented so far have been largely text-centered, expressing little or no interest in the tale's social and creative dynamics. Not all studies of the folktale have been so inclined. Operating on the premise that the folktale is a living, dynamic art form whose esthetic value is best realized in performance, other scholars from a wide range of disciplines (literature, folklore, anthropology, linguistics) have undertaken combined studies of text, context, and performance. Such studies include Ruth Finnegan's work on storytelling among the Limba of Sierra Leone (Finnegan 1967) and Dan Ben-Amos's study of storytelling in Benin (Ben-Amos 1972, 1975), where interest has been shown in the narrators, as well as their styles and techniques of narrative expression.

Since the seventies, an influential school has emerged in Wisconsin, led by Harold Scheub, which has combined the study of literary esthetics with structuralism, narrative technique, and performance in the study of the African folktale. In his analysis of *ntsomi* among the Xhosa, Scheub, for instance, discusses the narrative technique of manipulating core cliché, song, and dance in pushing a plot forward to its denouement. Particularly important is his repertoire study of artists and their creative techniques (Scheub 1972, 1975). Interest in literary esthetics and narrative techniques can also be seen in studies on the Haya (Seitel 1980), Kikuyu (Mwangi 1982), Tabwa (Cancel 1989), Yoruba (Sekoni 1990, 1994), and Ewe (Konrad 1994).

The summary review above shows the broad range of perspectives from which the African folktale has been studied. The following section attempts to tie together the salient features of the African folktale from the viewpoint of content, style, and mode of performance.

Content

Even though the tale is told largely for artistic ends, performers and audiences hardly lose sight of its moral, whether it advocates patience, punishes greed and selfishness, or merely explains the source of the crab's fatty shell. In any case, themes in the folktale may be conveyed by a stock of characters with stereotypical traits belonging to the human, animal, and supernatural realms. Human characters range from infant heroes to maidens, young suitors, kings, and old ladies. Tales involving animals and tricksters are, however, the most prevalent. Such stories may juxtapose the brute strength of big and ferocious beasts like the leopard, elephant, and wolf, with the fragility of small but wily animals, known for their intrigues and enormous capacity to outwit bigger opponents, including supernatural beings. Such wily creatures are often heroes, tricksters, and culture-bearers.

The summaries below exemplify such tales. From the Agni-Bona of Ivory Coast comes the following tale with an infant protagonist:

> A wicked king once decided to rear a python, to deter his subjects from interacting with him. Over time, Python devoured all animals and children that came its way; and yet it was impossible for anybody to report this to the king. A woman then gave birth to a child one morning. The baby was abandoned inside a pumpkin; beside the pumpkin was the knife used to cut the baby's umbilical cord. At noon, Python went on the prowl boasting of his insatiable appetite in song, to which the baby would reply from a distance, singing its plight as an abandoned child. Out of curiosity, Python went closer and closer wondering whose voice that was, and went to lie near the pumpkin. As Python attempted to seize the baby, the latter took the knife and thrust it into Python's mouth, killing it. Following Python's death the people got greater access to their king. That is why the king no longer raises pythons.
>
> (Galli 1983: 27–31)

The story depicts the oppressive rule of a tyrant, which is foiled by the courage of a newly born child, where efforts of adults had failed. One cannot miss the irony here of a fearsome destructive beast yielding to none but a harmless infant, who single-handedly becomes responsible for restoring order in a chaotic terrain. The theme above is not different from the following, narrated by the

Kiganda of Uganda, where evil forces, out to devour a girl, are frustrated by the instinctive impulses of juveniles:

> An only child called Nnambi lost both her mother and father. She therefore went to stay with her grandmother who did not like her. One day, the old lady went to look for vegetables, and found a certain animal called Wante. Wante asked her what she would give back in return for a meat offer. The old woman said she would offer her child for meat, and that the child would be available when she went to fetch water at the well. The child went to the well with her friends, and anytime the animal met them and asked, "Who among you is called Nnambi," all the children replied they were called Nnambi. The animal returned to complain to the old woman. The old woman said, the next time round, she would let the girl carry a water pot with a chipped rim, which would easily identify her. When the other children saw Nnambi's chipped pot, they said it was very beautiful. Out of envy, they took stones and broke the pot. (Nabasuta 1983: 66–67)

The trickster

The most prevalent stories in Africa are, however, trickster tales. Characterized by Radin as "creator and destroyer, giver and negator, he who dupes others and who is always duped himself" (1952: xxiii), the trickster appears in multiple forms in Africa, mostly as an animal, but occasionally as a human being or a deity.

In contemporary Egyptian culture, there are two trickster figures, both humans, who are believed to have existed in the past (El-Shamy 1980: 219–21). In Yoruba and Fon cultures the tricksters are deities. In several other parts of Africa the tricksters are animals. Among the Bantu, it is the little hare. The tortoise is the trickster in some parts of West Africa. Among the Ila of Zambia, hare and tortoise coexist as tricksters. The antelope, squirrel, weasel, and wren also occur as tricksters in other parts of Africa.

The spider, the best-known trickster in Africa, exists among the Limba of Sierra Leone, the Hausa of Nigeria, Gbaya of Cameroon, Sara of Chad, Luo, Azande of Sudan, and Ngbandi of Congo (Finnegan 1970: 315ff.). Among the Akan of Ghana and in parts of Ivory Coast, the spider is Ananse. The eminence of Ananse as a character in Akan and Ghanaian folktales in general is evident in the label *anansesem*, "matters of Ananse," which designates the folktale in general whether or not Ananse features. The impact of Ananse on Ghanaian cultures goes further. He appears in proverbs, songs, personal names, and Ghanaian idiomatic expression. When water simmers in the pot, it is Ananse bathing his children, according to the Akan. When the foot goes to sleep, or there is a feeling of prickly pins in it, "Ananse has tied the foot." At the Ghana Cultural Center in Accra, where the public is treated to cultural performances, the theater's auditorium has been named *Anansekrom*, the metropolis of Ananse – the home of unlimited humor, delight, and fantasy. Ananse indeed embodies the quintessence of esthetic pleasure. This delight is achieved through cunning, trickery, humor, and the outwitting of physically superior adversaries.

Significantly, Ananse was transported to the African diaspora during the transatlantic slave trade, where it exists in Jamaica, Surinam, Dominican Republic, Guyana, Trinidad, Grenada, the Bahamas, and the St. Vincent Islands under derived designations like B'Anansi, Boy Nasty, and Gulumbanasi. Besides the presence of Ananse in Caribbean tales, the name evokes associations of farce, fiction, and entertainment. In the St. Vincent Islands, "Anansi story" stands for all amusements displayed during wakes, whether these are tales of the spider, riddles, games, or the European *Märchen* (see Yankah 1989).

I present below summaries of two stories where the trickster pitches his wits against powerful opponents:

> God and Kweku Ananse are great friends. One day, Ananse asks God, "Which is more painful, injury or false accusation?" God says injury; Ananse says false accusation. In an argument that follows, God takes a knife and inflicts injury on Ananse. Ananse heals the wound, and secretly persuades other animals to dig a tunnel under the kitchen of God's mother-in-law (the mother of God's newest and most beautiful wife). Ananse arranges to sleep in God's house, and sneaks to defecate in the kitchen. As God's mother-in-law sweeps the kitchen, she discovers feces. Who could have done that, she wonders. Just then, she hears a chorus of voices from underneath singing, "God has defecated . . . God has defecated . . . God has defecated." The news spreads all over. As God is exposed, he feels so embarrassed he makes a suicide attempt. Ananse then reminds God of the riddle he posed earlier. Truly to be falsely accused is more painful than injuries. Ananse is proved right.

The above story is a clear explication of the making and breaking of friendship with which trickster tales in Africa have been characterized. Here the trickster enters the sacred realm, fraternizes with the Supreme Being, with the sole purpose of proving his superior wits over Him. In the final analysis, God's hallowed image is defiled by worldly follies and intrigues masterminded by a subordinate "colleague." To the trickster, duping and outwitting need not respect supernatural boundaries.

Indeed, in most instances where God occurs in Akan folktales, there is a conflicting interaction between Him and Ananse. Thus while in cases where God interacts with other characters His intervention is solicited to resolve crises, Ananse's interaction with God always leads to a breach of faith.

The deterioration of friendship above is not different from the following story recorded by Lee Haring among the Akamba of Kenya, in which Monkey, the trickster, fools Crocodile:

> The crocodile asked the monkey to visit him. The monkey asked the crocodile, "How shall I reach your home when I don't know how to swim?" The crocodile told the monkey to jump on his back. On the way, the crocodile felt hungry and asked the monkey, "Can you give me your heart? Because I am feeling hungry." The monkey told the crocodile, "This is what we are going to do: we are going to go back, because when we become friendly to somebody we leave our hearts at home." Now the monkey told the crocodile, "You see, I am very weak, I cannot be eaten. So we have to go back and I will get you my heart." The crocodile agreed that they should turn back. When they reached the shore, the monkey climbed into a mango tree and picked a mango. He threw it and said to the crocodile, "There is the heart." But the mango got into the water. (Haring 1972: 165–66)

Performance

The artistic merits of the folktale are only partly realized in text. While the literary ingredients of irony, metaphor, hyperbole, personification, etc. can be discerned in a tale text, it takes a good performer to optimally portray the folktale as an art form. Thus even though the trickster in Africa is considered the best embodiment of fun, trickery, humor, and fantasy, this can be realized only through the agency of performance. In the case of Ananse, for example, he cannot be depicted effectively outside the culture's perception of his stereotypical trait as an anomalous speaker: he whines. Similarly he cannot be well portrayed in the West Indies without lisping, stuttering, or speaking "Black English."

It takes a good performance to bring a tale to life; and for the researcher, not even the most ingenious techniques in translation and transcription can fully depict the stylistic and dramatic nuances of the folktale performance.

That the folktale is considered in Africa as a source of esthetic pleasure can be seen in the formulae that frame a performance. The opening and closing formulas invariably depict the absence of truth in the tale. The opening formula used by Haya of Tanzania, "See so that we may see" (Seitel 1980), chanted by the audience, places a responsibility on the teller to portray vividly an imaginative experience that fulfills the society's esthetic canons. The Gbaya of Cameroon open with a song by the narrator that enlists the audience's attention: "Listen to a tale"; and the audience responds with a phrase that establishes the tale's esthetic ideals: "a tale for laughter" (Noss 1977: 136). The Ashanti-Akan of Ghana use the introductory formula "we don't really mean it, we don't really mean it" (that the impending narration is true). Among the Fanti-Akan, the narrator's formula, "The tale is not meant to be believed," elicits the audience's response, "It is meant to be kept," once again emphasizing imaginative fantasy as the dominant esthetic. Indeed, among the Agni of Ivory Coast, the expression for telling a tale means "to lie" (Galli 1983: 22).

Even so, there are various levels of framing in folktale performance; for within the realm of fantasy, there is a notion of truth, which may be contested by the audience through playful interjections and dialogue with the narrator. The audience may inject reminders, request further explanation, or challenge an observation, to which the teller is obligated to react. In one narration I recorded among the Akan, the query "Did you see it with your own eyes?" was replied, "Yes with my own eyes, it's not a hearsay." To the question "Were you walking with them?" the raconteur said, "Yes, I was with them . . ."

Although participants are aware of the tale's world of fantasy, the narrators are also sensitive to their responsibility for boosting the telling with a measure of realism. So they co-operate in playing along, to sustain the dialog; if they renege, they violate the spirit of play and make-believe assumed in the opening formula.

In certain cultures, the performance is further boosted by the presence of an auxiliary performer, or intermediary, who receives the tale from the teller and passes it on to the wider audience. As in royal oratory (Yankah 1995: 19–24) and epic singing (Johnson 1986: 25), the respondent receives the narration in bits as it is told, and either repeats it literally or adjoins a phrase of assent. Such institutionalized mediations in tale telling are found among the Agni-Bona of Ivory Coast (Galli 1983), Mossi of Burkina Faso, Limba of Sierra Leone (Finnegan 1967), and the Nzema (Agovi 1973) and Dagare of Ghana. They also exist in certain traditions of storytelling among black Americans (Jones-Jackson 1987: 44).

In enacting the tale itself, the narrators rely on dramatic, literary, and linguistic devices, and indeed deploy every technique within their artistic reach. Even though they are instructing their audience about moral values, the esthetic factor is dominant, for the tale's plot may already be known. The story is appreciated, tasted, even "eaten" in some cultures if it is esthetically pleasing.

The storytellers' challenge is to use dramatic, linguistic, and literary techniques to enliven their narration. So they mime, growl like a leopard, whine like Ananse, and tiptoe their way to the kitchen of God's in-laws. Raconteurs indeed stretch every sinew to enact all roles in the plot single-handedly, and vividly portray a multisensory experience in word and action. Descriptive skills are inevitable here, and one important device narrators in Africa have used to good effect is descriptive adverbials, technically called "ideophones," which vividly depict multisensory experience: sound, smell, sensation, touch, color. Thus in jumping to snatch an orphan's food, an old lady in an Akan story strikes the meal with her buttocks, and the resultant sound was *hwan, hwom,* or *hwererere,* according to the narrator. In another section of the plot, when a benevolent crab bites the girl to cue her in solving the old woman's riddle, the resultant sound portraying the intense impact was *dwee* (see Yankah 1984, and also Noss 1972, 1977).

Song, dance, and music are indispensable in storytelling; and performances without these are considered drab. But one should distinguish here between the intranarrative song, which is an integral part of a tale's plot, sung by a character in the tale, and song spasmodically injected by the audience to arrest boredom.

The intranarrative song may be performed by a character in dramatic moments: as a dialogic device, to delay action, achieve a magical feat, or foreground emotion. Because of the importance of song in narration, a performer may apologize in advance if his tale has no song (Noss 1977: 138).

Even where there is no song in a tale's plot, any member of the audience, in certain cultures, may petition the narrator and lead a song, to arrest boredom. The *mmoguo* songs among the Akan are well known. Their very essence is discernible from the word's derivation. *Bo gu* means to reject, or shove aside. It marks moments in a narration where the privilege of authoritative diversion shifts into the hands of the audience. The song interjected may have no thematic relevance to the tale at hand; but like the plot-associated lyric, it is expected to compel total participation by petitioner, narrator, and the rest of the audience.

Songs in folktales have simple choruses, and lend themselves easily to communal involvement, drumming, and dancing. This compels total immersion by the entire congregation, who may provide background rhythm by clapping, or beating on improvised instruments. In certain cultures, the presence or absence of song in a story provides the basis for an ethnic taxonomy of narrative genres (Noss 1977: 138).

As the tale ends, the closing formula once again comes in to underscore the supremacy of the communal esthetic. The Akan say, "If my tale is sweet, if it is not sweet, take it back and forth." This is indeed a formulaic acknowledgment of the inherent hazards in exposing oneself to the evaluation of a critical audience, whose high expectations may have been upheld or disappointed.

It is not surprising that tale telling is depicted as a burden in parts of Africa; for after their turns, the narrators among the Gbaya set the "burden" under a tree (Noss 1977: 136), and among the Akan transfer the "burden" onto the head of a chosen performer (Yankah 1983: 12), who is challenged to equal or surpass the previous effort.

The folktale in Africa is a burden; but it is a burden gracefully borne by narrators and diffused to embrace the audience at large. As the Akan say, "When two people carry a load, it's no burden." The significance of the folktale may have slackened with the spread of literacy and urbanization in Africa; but it is still vividly narrated in rural domestic settings and educational institutions for purposes of entertainment. In parts of rural Africa, narrators in the past three decades have moved beyond casual telling and formed professional storytelling associations that entertain communities at wakes and other important events. Storytelling has also moved to the mass media in recent times, and may be heard or seen on radio and television, either independently or incorporated in popular culture. Within the realm of modern governance, the folktale has been helpful to musicians and raconteurs as a literary megaphone, enabling the voiceless to comment discreetly on contemporary politics, without fear of sanctions.

Bibliography

Abrahamsson, Hans. 1951. *The Origin of Death: Studies in African Mythology*. New York: Arno.

Agovi, J. K. 1973. "Preliminary Observations on the Modern Short Story and African Folktale Tradition." *Research Review* (Legon: Institute of African Studies, University of Ghana) 9: 123–29.

Arewa, Ojo E. 1966. "A Classification of Folktales of the Northern East Africa Cattle Area by Types." Diss. University of California, Berkeley.

Bascom, William. 1969. *Ifa Divination: Communication between Gods and Men in West Africa*. Bloomington: Indiana University Press.

1972. "African Dilemma Tales: An Introduction." In *African Folklore*. Ed. Richard Dorson. Bloomington: Indiana University Press: 143–55.

1975. *African Dilemma Tales*. The Hague: Mouton.

Beier, Ulli. 1966. *The Origin of Life and Death: African Creation Myths*. London: Heinemann Books.

Ben-Amos, Dan. 1972. "Two Benin Storytellers." In *African Folklore*. Ed. Richard Dorson. Bloomington: Indiana University Press: 104–14.

1975. *Sweet Words: Storytelling Events in Benin*. Philadelphia: Institute for the Study of Human Issues.
Bleek, W. H. I. 1864. *Reynard the Fox in South Africa; or Hottentot Fables and Tales*. London.
Burton, Richard. 1865. *Wit and Wisdom from West Africa*. London: Tinsley Bros.
Cancel, Robert. 1989. *Allegorical Speculation in an Oral Society: The Tabwa Narrative Tradition*. Berkeley: University of California Press.
Cardinall, A. W. 1931. *Tales Told in Togoland*. London: Oxford University Press.
Chatelain, H. 1894. *Folktales of Angola*. Memoirs of American Folklore Society 1. Boston / New York: Houghton Mifflin.
Clarke, Kenneth. 1957. "A Motif Index of the Folktales of Culture Area V, West Africa." Diss. Indiana University, Bloomington.
Dugaste, Idellete. 1975. *Contes, proverbes et devinettes des Banen*. Paris: SELAF.
Dundes, Alan. 1971. "The Making and Breaking of Friendship as a Structural Frame in African Folktales." In *Structural Analysis of Oral Tradition*. Ed. Pierre Maranda and Eli Kongas Maranda. Philadelphia: University of Pennsylvania Press: 175–81.
El-Shamy, Hasan. 1980. *Folktales of Egypt*. Chicago: University of Chicago Press.
1995. *Folk Traditions of the Arab World: A Guide to Motif Classification*. Bloomington: Indiana University Press.
Evans-Pritchard, E. E. 1967. *The Zande Trickster*. Oxford: Clarendon Press.
Finnegan, Ruth. 1967. *Limba Stories and Storytelling*. Oxford: Clarendon Press.
1970. *Oral Literature in Africa*. Oxford: Clarendon Press.
Galli, Silvano. 1983. "Storytelling among the Agni-Bona." In *Cross Rhythms*. Ed. Kofi Anyidoho *et al*. Bloomington: Trickster Press: 13–42.
Guillot, René. 1946. *Contes et légendes d'Afrique Noire*. Paris: Société d'Editions géographiques, maritimes et coloniales.
Haring, Lee. 1972. "A Characteristic African Folktale Pattern." In *African Folklore*. Ed. Richard Dorson. Bloomington: Indiana University Press: 165–79.
1982. *Malagasy Tale Index*. Helsinki: FF Communications 231. Suomalainen Tiedeakatemia.
Herskovits, M., and Frances Herskovits. 1958. *Dahomean Narrative: A Cross Cultural Analysis*. Evanston: Northwestern University Press.
Hesler, Albert. D. 1930. *African Stories*. New York.
Johnson, John. 1986. *The Epic of Son-Jara*. Bloomington: Indiana University Press.
Jones-Jackson, Patricia. 1987. *When Roots Die: Endangered Traditions on the Sea Islands*. Athens: University of Georgia Press.
Kilson, Marion. 1976. *Royal Antelope and Spider. West African Mende Tales*. Massachusetts: Language Associates.
Klipple, Mary. 1938. "African Folktales and their Foreign Analogues." Diss. Indiana University, Bloomington.
Knappert, Jan. 1971. *Myths and Legends of the Congo*. London: Heinemann Books.
Koelle, Sigismund. 1854. *African Native Literature or Proverbs, Tales, Fables, and Historical Fragments in the Kanuri or Bornu Language*. London: Church Missionary House.
Konrad, Zinta. 1994. *Ewe Comic Heroes: Trickster Tales in Togo*. New York: Garland.
Lambrecht, Winifred. 1967. "A Tale Type Index for Central Africa." Diss. University of California, Berkeley.
Mwangi, Rose. 1982. *Kikuyu Folktales*. Nairobi: Kenya Literature Bureau.

Nabasuta, Helen. 1983. "The Dynamics of the Storytelling Process: Kiganda Prose Narratives." In *Cross Rhythms*. Ed. Kofi Anyidoho *et al*. Bloomington: Trickster Press: 43–67.

Noss, Philips. 1972. "Description in Gbaya Literary Art." In *African Folklore*. Ed. Richard Dorson. Bloomington: Indiana University Press: 73–101.

1977. "The Performance of the Gbaya Tale." In *Forms of Folklore in Africa*. Ed. Bernth Lindfors. Austin: University of Texas Press: 135–43.

Okpewho, Isidore. 1983. *Myth in Africa: A Study of Its Esthetic and Cultural Relevance*. Cambridge: Cambridge University Press.

1992. *African Oral Literature: Background, Character, and Continuity*. Bloomington: Indiana University Press.

Parrinder, Geoffrey. 1986. *African Mythology*. New York: Peter Bedricks.

Pelton, Robert D. 1980. *The Trickster in West Africa: A Study of Mythical Irony and Sacred Delight*. Berkeley: University of California Press.

Radin, Paul. 1952. *The Trickster*. New York: Schocken.

Rattray, R. S. 1916. *Akan-Ashanti Proverbs*. Oxford: Clarendon Press.

1930. *Akan-Ashanti Folktales*. Oxford: Clarendon Press.

Scheub, Harold. 1972. "The Art of Nongenile Mazithathu Zenani. A Gcaleka Ntsomi Performer." In *African Folklore*. Ed. Richard Dorson. Bloomington: Indiana University Press: 115–42.

1975. *The Xhosa Ntsomi*. Oxford: Clarendon Press.

Seitel, Peter. 1980. *See So That We May See: Performances and Interpretations of Traditional Tales from Tanzania*. Bloomington: Indiana University Press.

Sekoni, Ropo. 1990. "The Narrator, Narrative-Pattern, and Audience Experience of Oral Narrative-Performance." In *The Oral Performance in Africa*. Ed. Isidore Okpewho. Ibadan: Spectrum: 139–59.

1994. *Folk Poetics: A Sociosemiotic Study of Yoruba Trickster Tales*. Westport, CT: Greenwood.

Stanley, Henry M. 1906. *My Dark Companions and Their Strange Stories*. New York: Charles Scribner's Sons.

Tremearne, A. J. N. 1913. *Hausa Superstitions and Customs: An Introduction to the Folklore and the Folk*. London: John Bales, Sons, and Danielsson.

Werner, Alice. 1925. *African Mythology. The Mythology of All Races*, vol. VII. Boston: Marshall Jones.

Woodson, Carter G. 1928. *African Myths*. Washington: Associate Publishers.

Yankah, Kwesi. 1983. *The Akan Trickster Cycle: Myth or Folktale?* Bloomington, IN: Indiana University African Studies Program.

1984. "The Folktale as a True Experience Narrative." *Folklore Forum* 17.2: 220–29.

1989. "From Africa to the New World: The Dynamics of the Anansi Cycle." In *Literature of Africa and the African Continuum*. Ed. Jonathan Peters, Mildred Mortimer, and Russell V. Linnemann. Washington, DC: Three Continents Press and African Literature Association: 115–28.

1995. *Speaking for the Chief: Okyeame and the Politics of Akan Royal Oratory*. Bloomington: Indiana University Press.

3

Festivals, ritual, and drama in Africa

TEJUMOLA OLANIYAN

African performance traditions entered the orbit of European discourse – which, by virtue of language, supplies the operative terms "festival," "ritual," and "drama" – primarily as negative examples. As a result, the origins of that entrance were marked in the main by condemnation, inferiorization, and general disregard. It was asserted or implied that blacks either had no traditions of drama indigenous to them, or had traditions that, in comparison with Europe and Asia, were merely "proto-dramatic" or "quasi-dramatic," cretinous forms in a state of developmental arrest in terms of style, esthetic canons, formalization of technique, and mode of historical transmission. Wherever "properly dramatic" traditions were found, they were marked off as but products of the African encounter with Europe – a way of claiming that the "properly dramatic" traditions are nothing less than derivatives of western forms and traditions (Jeyifo 1990: 242–43). There is a larger context, of course, to these deeply ethnocentric claims. They were part and parcel of the implacable inferiorization of African corporeality and cultural forms that matured in Europe in the eighteenth century and remains a major constituent of Eurocentrism. In the operations of the discourse, the inferiorization of a cultural practice becomes a shorthand to the inferiorization of the bearers of that culture and practice.

This is not the appropriate space exhaustively to engage the Eurocentric archive in all its details and dimensions. I will, instead, exemplify the discourse with the work of the distinguished contemporary scholar Ruth Finnegan. The chapter titled "Drama" in her influential work *Oral Literature in Africa*, published in 1970, still remains for many the canonical survey. Her opening lines alone reveal her restrictive methodology:

> How far one can speak of indigenous drama in Africa is not an easy question. In this it differs from previous topics [treated in the book] like, say, panegyric, political poetry, or prose narratives, for there it was easy to discover African analogies to the familiar European forms. (1970: 500)

When concepts describing cultural practices or forms cross cultural borders without some form of domestication before speaking the realities of their new abode, some excess, misrepresentation, or violence, is produced. For Finnegan, it is only if Africa could supply indigenous "analogies to the familiar European forms" that it would be established as a continent with drama. There is no other way. So she keeps looking for European drama on the African continent: "what . . . *we* normally regard as drama" (500); what "*we* are accustomed [to]" (516). The "definition" of drama she proposes, in all its pedantry and formal rigorism, is designed to achieve little else if not failure:

> It is clearly necessary to reach at least some rough agreement about what is to count as "drama". Rather than produce a verbal definition, it seems better to point to the various elements which tend to come together in what, in the wide sense, we normally regard as drama. Most important is the idea of enactment, of representation through actors who imitate persons and events. This is also usually associated with other elements, appearing to a greater or lesser degree at different times or places: linguistic content; plot; the represented interaction of several characters; specialized scenery, etc.; often music; and – of particular importance in most African performances – dance. Now it is very seldom in Africa that all these elements of drama come together in a single performance. (501)

Her – undeniably productive – failure prepares and authorizes her thesis, even against acknowledged contrary evidence: "Though some writers have very positively affirmed the existence of native African drama, it would perhaps be truer to say that in Africa, in contrast to western Europe and Asia, drama is not typically a wide-spread or a developed form" (500).

It is important to understand Finnegan's concept of difference, given her insistence that Africans in Africa produce European drama. To the extent that we are all the same, her work becomes unnecessary. If it is difference that enables her project, then her insistence on its erasure becomes paradoxical. But we must not assume that this illogicality lacks any logic, or that it thus self-destructs in the realm of power. Difference here is not erased but whipped into conformity and *hierarchized* (see also Graham-White 1974; Havemeyer 1966). It is interesting then to note that Ibadan, where Finnegan stayed for a time while working on her book, and where she signed the preface, is one of the main centers of the still vibrant Yoruba traveling theater movement, with a recorded tradition going back to the late 1590s. Apparently, this theater refused to provide Finnegan with "analogies to the familiar European forms."

If, today, such ethnocentric demands have ceased being made on Africa, it is because of the gargantuan effort of a host of African scholars such as Joel Adedeji, Wole Soyinka, Oyin Ogunba, Bakary Traore, Ebun Clark, Biodun Jeyifo, Penina Mlama, and others, who gave voice to the varieties of dramatic traditions in Africa while also redefining "drama" away from its received, Aristotle-centered conception, to the great profit of world theater history scholarship.

Africa is home to several traditions of theater, conceived as an ensemble of culturally marked and consciously staged practices in space and time and before an audience. Many of these traditions are of ancient origin, while others emerged with formal European colonization of the continent in the nineteenth century and the subsequent imposition of western education, religion, and culture. The older traditions are mostly nonscripted, improvisatory, and performed in indigenous African languages. Their conceptions of theater space is fluid, and stage–audience relations are not governed by inflexible rules: any space can be turned into a performance stage, while the audience, within acknowledged boundaries, is free to interact with the performers and performance in a variety of ways and even move in and out of the theater space during performance. The performance is often public and the audience non-fee-paying, though performers could be rewarded in cash or kind for their artistry. On the other hand, many of the newer theater traditions are text-based, written in European languages or indigenous African languages of European alphabet. The plays are designed to be performed in more or less formal theater buildings with fixed relations between performers and audience. The audience is usually fee-paying though the theater may not be expressly commercial. In all cases, as indeed in all societies, the functions of the theater traditions are broadly similar in their mixing of the pleasing and the pedagogical: their representations provide the audience with pleasurable entertainments while simultaneously channeling its passions and sentiments in certain directions.

Theater in Africa could be categorized into four distinct traditions: festival theater, popular theater, development theater, and art theater.

Festival theater and ritual

In many African communities, the foremost indigenous cultural and artistic institution is the festival. Organized around certain deities or spirits, or to mark generational transitions or the passage of the seasons whether of climate or agricultural production, festivals are sprawling multimedia occasions – that is, incorporating diverse forms such as singing, chanting, drama, drumming, masking, miming, costuming, puppetry, with episodes of theatrical enactments ranging from the sacred and secretive to the secular and public. Festivals could last for a few hours to several days, weeks or months. Each festival dramatizes a story or myth – or related sets of stories or myths – connecting the particular subject of the festival, be it a deity or the season of the harvest, to significant events in the life of the community and to its place in sustaining communal harmony, plenty, and stability. Artistically, the performances also serve to showcase the community's new artistic forms and talents as well as advancements and mutations in existing ones.

Festival theater is performed in an open space in the town square or a similarly appointed location. The audience sits or stands in rings of circles around the performers, and is able to drift in and out of the performance. The audience closes in or fans out depending on perceptions of the volume of space needed by the performers at particular moments of the action. There is a close relationship between the performers and the audience, with the latter even serving as chorus, but there are also distinctions, and it is treasured cultural knowledge to know when to and when not to interject in the performance. Esthetically, the performance is most often nonillusionistic, with acting or dancing occurring in the full range from realism to surrealism and spirit possession. This is partly why an empty space, with few prop or theatrical fripperies, is all that is needed for the communion between performer and audience on one hand, and the performance and society on the other.

There are two ways in which scholars have tried to understand African festivals. Some scholars label the festival as "pre-drama" or "traditional ritual" or "ritual drama," because of its expansive multimedia format, its firm integration of the dramatic amidst the other arts, and the presence of both religious and secular re-enactments (Echeruo 1981). The assumption of the scholars, whether acknowledged or not, is often that the twentieth-century western theater, with its packaged three hours, strict compartmentalization of the arts, and the virtual absence of the sacred, constitutes the norm of "theater." Other scholars have argued that the festival is full-fledged theater that is dynamic, spectacular, and inventive, and that the contemporary western theater could in fact be seen as nothing more than severely abbreviated festival. The argument of Wole Soyinka, Africa's leading dramatist and winner of the Nobel Prize in Literature, best exemplifies this view. He insists that festivals be seen as constituting "in themselves *pure theatre* at its most prodigal and resourceful . . . the most stirring expressions of man's instinct and need for drama at its most comprehensive and community-involving" (1988: 194).

In one sweeping move, he turns a colonialist interpretation of the festival on its head: "instead of considering festivals from one point of view only – that of providing, in a primitive form, the ingredients of drama – we may even begin examining the opposite point of view: that contemporary drama, as we experience it today, is a contraction of drama, necessitated by the productive order of society in other directions" (195).

Even the sacred core of many festivals – much maligned as "ritual" or "pre-drama" – do have consciously staged performances in space and time, though before a more restricted audience, and in language that may be more arcane, composed of incantations and elliptic proverbs. In many instances, such performances could be produced with very elaborate plots and costuming, indicating that even within the sacred, the more secular concerns of the artistic and pleasurable are never short-changed. A few useful studies of festival theater and ritual in Africa include works by scholars such as Oyin Ogunba (1978), Ossie Enekwe (1987), and Nnabuenyi Ugonna (1983).

Popular theater

"Popular" is a much-debated concept in African theater studies. It is important therefore to begin with a working definition. "Popular" as used here refers to those theater forms that have large followings at the point of reception. This mass – and indeed, massive – audience cuts across class or status boundaries. One reason for such wide appeal is that the theater is most often performed in the indigenous languages, or hybrids of them designed to be understood across linguistic borders. Increasingly, many subtraditions are being produced in simplified forms of the European languages that came with colonization, or in "pidgin" – a distinctive mixture of one such foreign language and an indigenous language. The last two – simplified European languages and pidgin – constitute much of the language of urban Africa today.

Early dramatic forms that have their roots in sacred ceremonies and involve elaborate masking, such as the Alarinjo and Apidan theaters of Nigeria, are composed mainly of male performers. With the famous exception of the Ghanaian Concert Party, it is generally the case that more recent forms – such as the Yoruba Popular Travelling Theatre, the Chikwakwa Theatre of Zambia, and the South African Township Theatre – are composed of both male and female performers.

The recurring themes in African popular drama are those with broad appeal, and are intimately linked with genre. Particularly common in comedies and melodramas are themes such as unrequited love, marital infidelity, unemployment, pretensions to wealth, status, or sophistication, the conundrums of modern city life, dreams of travel abroad, and so on. Satires predominate and have targeted egotistical chiefs, the rich but miserly, the strange manners of Europeans (explorers, missionaries, or colonial administrators and their spouses), corrupt politicians, overly westernized African men and women, prostitutes, the rural village teacher, and so on. Matters of fate and predestination, and the mythological lives of deities, legends, and powerful historical figures have been explored in tragedies and other serious dramas.

Most popular theater forms are not scripted but based on improvisations, giving the performers much leeway but also demanding an unusual dexterity in speech, movement, and gesture. Partly for economic reasons (size of troupe) and partly for artistic preferences (most popular plays are multimedia performances), performers are often skilled in many aspects of the enterprise such as acting, singing, costuming, playing a musical instrument or two, set designing, and business management. The performers are in most cases organized as traveling troupes, performing in a variety of available spaces: open squares, enclosed courtyards of kings and chiefs, school classrooms, concert or cinema halls, bars or nightclubs, and well-equipped theaters. Troupes are either kin- or lineage-based, or composed of close friends or understanding partners and acquaintances. The performers are generally professionals and the troupes run as commercial enterprises. It is not infrequent, though, that performers hold other jobs such as clerks, traders, crafts makers, and sedentary herbalists during lulls or off seasons.

The economic fortunes of the troupes ebb and flow with the sociopolitical and economic health of their societies. In Nigeria with the largest number of professional popular theater troupes, the boom decades were the 1970s and 1980s. Figures such as Hubert Ogunde, Moses Olaiya, Isola Ogunsola, Ade Love, Lere Paimo, and others became very successful entrepreneurs and even went into filmmaking as a result, making their most popular plays even more widely available on celluloid. Those who survived the harsh economic climate of the late 1980s and through the 1990s have branched into video production as a cheaper and low-tech alternative to crosscountry road shows (with no guarantee of sizeable audience) and capital-intensive filmmaking. In South Africa, Gibson Kente reigned supreme from 1966 until his detention by the apartheid government in 1976. Popular culture in Africa is generally understudied, but African popular theater has been the subject of valuable attention by scholars such as Robert Kavanagh (1977), Biodun Jeyifo (1984), Kwabena Bame (1985), David Kerr (1995), Karin Barber (2001), and Catherine Cole (2001), among others.

Development theater

In certain radical or leftist traditions of African theater scholarship, "development theater" is also known as popular theater, but the conception of the "popular" in this case is vastly different from that in the preceding section. While in popular theater the "popular" is measured at the point of consumption or reception, in development theater, the "popular" is marked at the point of production; the theater need not be popular at all in terms of reaching a wide audience. In other words, "popular" here means produced by an alliance of discriminating and ideologically astute intellectuals, workers, and peasants and expressly constructed to advance the interests of the underprivileged classes in society. Because the underprivileged classes constitute the majority of the people in the society, the theater is also known more polemically as "people's theater."

The conception of the "popular" operative in development theater is inspired by the radical Marxist German dramatist Bertolt Brecht, who writes:

> "Popular" means intelligible to the broad masses, taking over their own forms of expression and enriching them/adopting and consolidating their standpoint/representing the most progressive section of the people in such a way that it can take over the leadership: thus intelligible to other sections too/linking with tradition and carrying it further/handing on the achievements of the section now leading to the section of the people that is struggling to lead. (1964: 108)

This form of theater is geared toward raising the consciousness of the exploited classes so they can recognize their interests, band together against their common enemies, and struggle for liberation. To liberate themselves, in the Marxist understanding, is also to liberate the productive forces of the society from private appropriation and so ensure genuine development – a development in which there is no private appropriation of public wealth. It is in this sense that this tradition of theater is called "development theatre." In addition to Brecht, other significant conceptual supports for development theater come from Latin America: Augusto Boal, whose theater experiments are documented in his book *Theatre of the Oppressed* (1979), and Paulo Freire, adult educator and author of the famous *Pedagogy of the Oppressed* (1970).

A minor form of development theater practice is the "guerrilla theater," in which committed activist groups emerge unannounced at carefully chosen public locations and stage provocative performances, usually against particular government policies, and disappear before the agents of law and order appear. For a time in the early 1980s, the Obafemi Awolowo University Drama Department had a famous Guerrilla Theatre unit, under the direction of Wole Soyinka. However, not all forms of development theater are obviously ideologically charged. Many are designed as adult education programs to teach literacy, explain the political process to bridge the gap between the rulers and the ruled so people can better know their rights and responsibilities, communicate better agricultural techniques, teach new and improved ways of treating or preventing certain diseases, and encourage community mobilization for self-help projects and general rural development. In many instances where this is the case, the designation is the populist and less polemical "community theater." Workshops are held regularly by development theater practitioners to teach the people how to organize themselves to use the theater both as an expression of culture and as a tool for fostering social, political, and economic development.

Development theater practitioners are mostly professional intellectuals, often affiliated with a university, or educated individuals affiliated with a development agency or nongovernmental organization. They work with a variety of groups in mostly rural areas – areas that are in much of Africa the least recipients of the "benefits" of "modernity" and therefore the target of development schemes by states, nongovernmental organizations, as well as World Bank and United Nations agencies. Indeed, most – though not all – development theater practices in Africa receive funding from such institutions. The theater is noncommercial and most of those involved have regular occupations or are funded by grants. Given the direct, instrumentalist goal of the theater, the performances are often didactic and exhortatory, though the more skilled adult educators go to great lengths to emphasize esthetics and even incorporate popular forms from the people's indigenous performance traditions.

An important example of development theater practice is the Laedza Batanani of Botswana in the mid-1970s, which subsequently served as model and inspiration for similar experiments in Lesotho, Zambia, Malawi, Sierra Leone, and especially the well-known practice at Ahmadu Bello University in Nigeria. Perhaps the most oppositional of the experiments was the Kamiriithu Education and Cultural Center, led by Ngugi wa Thiong'o, the leading Kenyan writer. The center was so successful in mobilizing the community to explore critically their history and culture and contemporary situation through theater that Ngugi was imprisoned for a year without trial in 1977. By 1982, the Kenyan government had razed the center and banned all theater activities in the area. Scholars such as Robert Mshengu Kavanagh (1977), Michael Etherton (1982), Ingrid Bjorkman (1989), Penina Mlama (1991), David Kerr

(1995), Jane Plastow (1996) have produced illuminating work on development theater tradition in Africa.

Art theater

Art theater is the tradition of African theater most familiar to the outside world through the published works of the continent's notable playwrights such as Wole Soyinka, Athol Fugard, Femi Osofisan, Ama Ata Aidoo, Zulu Sofola, Efua Sutherland, Ola Rotimi, J. P. Clark-Bekederemo, Sony Labou Tansi, Guillaume Oyono-Mbia, Werewere Liking, and Tess Onwueme, among others. Art theater in Africa is of colonial origin; it emerged with the training of Africans in European languages and literatures and dramatic traditions, and it is most often written in the European colonial languages. The label "art theater" signifies the tradition's relationship to, and investment in, notions of "high art" or "great works" characteristic of western bourgeois cultural discourse since the nineteenth century.

The practitioners of art theater are usually professional intellectuals affiliated with universities or other institutions of higher education. Although the best dramas of this tradition borrow richly from indigenous performance forms, the overall "mold" of drama into which those borrowings are poured, as well as the languages in which they are written and performed, are European and greatly circumscribe their popularity with the majority of Africans who are not schooled in those esthetics or languages. After a successful career writing in English, Ngugi wa Thiong'o switched to his native Gikuyu language in the 1980s. The Nigerian dramatist J. P. Clark once considered the matter and observed that, in comparing the Yoruba Popular Travelling Theatre with the art theater, "Some would say that the latter has its head deep in the wings of American and European theatre! The works of Mr. Wole Soyinka, Dr. Ene Henshaw, and my own plays, I am told, clearly bear this badge, but whether of merit or infamy it is a matter still in some obscurity" (1970: 85). Clark hints here at a charge sometimes leveled against African art theater: whether it could really be original and authentically African as long as it borrows esthetic structures from and speaks the language of Europe. Such a charge and its subtending purist conceptions of transcultural relations and of its vehicle, cultural translation, has never represented much of a handicap for the truly creative minds of African art theater. They continue to confront the colonial inheritance and revise it from a variety of perspectives, without any surrender of initiative. For them, the centuries of African unequal contact with Europe are undeniable, and cultural purism, absolutism or insularity are not necessarily worthy coordinates of "originality." The Mexican writer Octavio Paz speaks for the writers of the ex-colonial world, from Africa to Asia and Latin America, when he argues that "The special position of our literatures, when compared to those of England, Spain, Portugal, and France, derives precisely from this fundamental fact: they are literatures written in transplanted tongues," but that they "did not passively accept the changing fortunes of their transplanted languages: they participated in the process and even accelerated it. Soon they ceased to be mere transatlantic reflections. At times they have been the negation of the literatures of Europe; more often, they have been a reply" (1990: 4–5).

The hub of art theater activity in Africa is mostly the urban areas, cities, and universities. This is also where most of the audience, those schooled in western languages, is located. Performance takes place in formal theater buildings, frequently with the proscenium stage that is hegemonic in Europe and America. Art theater is primarily state-subsidized and rarely self-sustaining as a commercial enterprise. Indeed, art theater is consumed more as dramatic literature – read widely in schools and colleges – than as theater.

Many practitioners of art theater have attempted to ameliorate the obvious elitism of the tradition by establishing community theaters or traveling theaters run by university resident professionals or drama students. These efforts, in less formal surroundings, make art theater performances – sometimes of plays in translations or in pidgin, or of text-based improvisations – available to audiences that would otherwise not have access to them. These projects designed to take the art theater to the masses of the people are often very expensive and have existed only intermittently. Some of the famous examples are the University of Ibadan Travelling Theatre (Nigeria, in the 1960s), the Makerere Free Travelling Theatre (Uganda, 1960s and 1970s), the University of Malawi Travelling Theatre (1970s), and the University of Zambia Chikwakwa Theatre (1970s and 1980s). There is the particularly unique case of the South African Athol Fugard, who broke for some time from his normal routine of formal playwriting in the 1970s to collaborate with the actors Winston Ntshona and John Kani. Their improvisations led to many well-received plays against the apartheid state and inaugurated a genre of popular theater labeled South African Protest theater. The most performed of such plays is *Sizwe Bansi Is Dead* (1973).

Although the four traditions of African dramatic performance described above exist simultaneously and often share, or overlap at the level of, deep formal structures, it is nevertheless the case that the social relations among them is hierarchical. Festival performances are still going on, though the scale has obviously been affected by the continent's economic downturn since the mid-1980s. More significantly, festivals no longer occupy a central position in civil society and are therefore no longer a preeminent instrument of sociopolitical and cultural socialization of the young. Since the last half century, that position has been taken over by cultural forms of westernization such as western-style schools and religious institutions and their myriad offshoots. The point is this: festival performance, the most widespread and truly mass African cultural form, no longer has the cultural capital it used to have, mainly because the cultural knowledge festivals impart no longer has much value in a person's quest for social mobility. Development theater is by no means widespread, and depends too much on institutional sponsorship, whether of a government or nongovernmental agency. In some instances, the charge that development theater is no more than elitist condescension to rural folks, a kind of "planning from above" to bring "modernity" to the "uncivilized," is not entirely unjustified. With the participation of a large number of western nongovernmental organizations in the last decade, including religious ones, it is also not out of place to query the level of agency rural Africans have in the development theater process. Because popular theater is basically commercial, it has to be close to urban centers where most of its clientele who can afford the price of tickets reside. Its thematic and esthetic choices are determined to a large extent by the preferences of its audience; and while many of its performances may have profound cultural significance for the collective, popular theater is not often catalyzed by any grand and well articulated idea of a cultural direction to which to steer the audience. Like all businesses, it does what it has to do to survive.

By far the most prestigious of the traditions is the art theater. Art theater tradition – scripted plays written in European languages or African languages of European alphabet, and made widely available by large and often multinational publishing houses – is the tradition by which Africa is known globally, and the primary bridge by which nationals of different African countries come into contact with one another's dramatic traditions. The practitioners of art theater are nearly exclusively the internationally well-known "African dramatists." Hubert Ogunde may be the father of modern Nigerian theater tradition, but it is Wole Soyinka who is known globally, the one whose works are easily available and weightily read as classic representations of Yoruba African culture to the world and in the world marketplace of cultural transactions. Because this tradition shares similar origins with the contemporary African state, and its bureaucracy and system of education – it is westernized and speaks a European language – it occupies a significant space in the ruling, dominant civil society.

Although many of the distinguished art theater practitioners are employees of one institution of higher learning or the other and few to none have lived solely on the proceeds of their writings, it is nevertheless the case that competence in this tradition is a sure means of social mobility in the larger society, and in the world. This, then, is the fundamental reason for the tradition's prestige.

We come to a profound irony, one that, after more than four decades, is only now being substantively addressed by the practitioners. Art theater may hold all the cultural capital according to the logic of what constitutes that resource in contemporary Africa, but it is the case that this would-be representative tradition speaks, by virtue of its predominant European language of expression, to only the small percentage of Africans who are literate in that language. The irony is made more poignant by the fact that art theater is the main tradition that most directly and persistently confronts the issue of colonial cultural deracination of African societies and the need for vigorous African cultural self-reclamation. It has performed that task by plumbing the depths of indigenous African performance traditions and both critically and creatively anchoring itself simultaneously in autochthonous forms as well as those borrowed from Europe. The tradition's deployment of the colonial languages goes beyond mimicry to contribute in very original ways to those languages. As early in Soyinka's career as 1965, a British reviewer of *The Road* wrote of the dramatist's use of English: "Every decade or so, it seems to fall to a non-English dramatist to belt new energy into the English tongue. The last time was when Brendan Behan's 'The Quare Fellow' opened at Theatre Workshop. Nine years later, in the reign of Stage Sixty at the same loved Victorian building at Stratford East, a Nigerian called Wole Soyinka has done for our napping language what brigand dramatists from Ireland have done for centuries: booted it awake, rifled it pockets and scattered the loot into the middle of next week" (Gilliatt 1965: 25).

But to return to the irony, the majority of Africans simply can not read or speak European languages. Art theater practitioners themselves have endlessly debated the issue (for a review of the question, see Ngugi 1986), suggesting solutions such as infusing the European languages with African imagery, writing in a mixture of African and European languages, translating between African and European languages, and writing in African languages. The more practical solution that is becoming widespread today is cross translation, as leading dramatists such as Soyinka and Osofisan have encouraged the translation of their classics from English to Yoruba. If this trend continues apace and becomes widespread, the art theater tradition will have done a lot to justify its throne of prestige among African theater traditions.

Bibliography

Adedeji, Joel A. 1969. "The Alarinjo Theatre: The Study of a Yoruba Theatrical Art Form from Its Earliest Beginnings to the Present Time." PhD diss. University of Ibadan.

Bame, Kwabena N. 1985. *Come to Laugh: African Traditional Theatre in Ghana*. New York: Lilian Barber.

Banham, Martin, Errol Hill, and George Woodyard, eds. 1994. *The Cambridge Guide to African and Caribbean Theatre*. Cambridge: Cambridge University Press.

Barber, Karin. 2001. *The Generation of Plays: Yoruba Popular Life in Theatre*. Bloomington: Indiana University Press.

Barber, Karin, John Collins, and Alain Ricard. 1997. *West African Popular Theatre*. Bloomington: Indiana University Press.

Barber, Karin, and Bayo Ogundijo, transcribed, trans., and ed. 1994. *West African Popular Theatre: Three Plays by the Oyin Adejobi Company*. USA: ASA Press.

Bjorkman, Ingrid. 1989. *Mother, Sing for Me: People's Theatre in Kenya*. London: Zed.

Brecht, Bertolt. 1964. *Brecht on Theatre: The Development of an Aesthetic*. Ed. and trans. John Willet. New York: Hill and Wang.

Clark, Ebun. 1980. *Hubert Ogunde: The Making of Nigerian Theatre*. Oxford: Oxford University Press.

Clark, J. P. 1970. *The Example of Shakespeare*. London: Longman.

Cole, Catherine. 2001. *Ghana's Concert Party Theatre*. Bloomington: Indiana University Press.

Conteh-Morgan, John. 1994. *Theatre and Drama in Francophone Africa: A Critical Introduction*. Cambridge: Cambridge University Press.

De Graft, J. C. 1976. "Roots in African Drama and Theatre." *African Literature Today* 8: 1–25.

Echeruo, Michael J. C. 1981. "The Dramatic Limits of Igbo Ritual." In *Drama and Theatre in Nigeria: A Critical Sourcebook*. Ed.Yemi Ogunbiyi. Lagos: Nigeria Magazine: 136–48.

Enekwe, Ossie. 1987. *Igbo Masks: The Oneness of Ritual and Theatre*. Lagos: Nigeria Magazine.

Etherton, Michael. 1982. *The Development of African Drama*. London: Hutchinson.

Finnegan, Ruth. 1970. *Oral Literature in Africa*. Nairobi: Oxford University Press.

Gilliatt, Penelope. 1965. "A Nigerian Original." *The Observer* 19 Sept.: 25. Cited in *Critical Perspectives on Wole Soyinka*. Ed. James Gibbs. Washington, DC: Three Continents Press: 106.

Gotrick, Kacke. 1984. *Apidan Theatre and Modern Drama*. Stockholm: Almqvist and Wiskell.

Graham-White, Anthony. 1974. *The Drama of Black Africa*. New York: Samuel French.

Havemeyer, Loomis. [1916] 1966. *The Drama of Savage Peoples*. New York: Haskell House.

Jeyifo, Biodun. 1984. *The Yoruba Popular Travelling Theatre of Nigeria*. Lagos: Nigeria Magazine.

1990. "The Reinvention of Theatrical Tradition: Critical Discourses on Interculturalism in the African Theatre." In *The Dramatic Touch of Difference: Theatre, Own and Foreign*. Ed. Erika Fischer-Lichte, J. Riley, and M. Gissenwehrer. Tübingen: Gunter Narr: 239–51.

Kavanagh, Robert Mshengu. 1977. *Making People's Theatre*. Johannesburg: Witwatersrand University Press.

1985. *Theatre and Cultural Struggle in South Africa*. London: Zed.

Kerr, David. 1995. *African Popular Theatre*. London: Heinemann.

Kidd, Ross. 1982. *The Popular Performing Arts, Non-Formal Education and Social Change in the Third World: A Bibliography and Review Essay*. The Hague: Centre for the Study of Education in Developing Countries.

Kirby, E. T. 1974. "Indigenous African Theatre." *Theatre Drama Review* 18. 4 (Dec.): 22–35.

Mlama, Penina M. 1991. *Culture and Development: The Popular Theatre Approach in Africa*. Uppsala: Scandinavian Institute of African Studies.

Ngugi wa Thiong'o. 1986. *Decolonising the Mind: The Politics of Language in African Literature*. Oxford: James Currey.

Obafemi, Olu. 1996. *Contemporary Nigerian Theatre: Cultural Heritage and Social Vision*. Bayreuth: Eckhard Breitinger.

Ogunba, Oyin. 1978. "Traditional African Festival Drama." In *Theatre in Africa*. Ed. O. Ogunba and A. Irele. Ibadan: Ibadan University Press: 3–26.

Ogunbiyi, Yemi, ed. 1981. *Drama and Theatre in Nigeria: A Critical Sourcebook*. Lagos: Nigeria Magazine.

Olaniyan, Tejumola. 1995. *Scars of Conquest/Masks of Resistance: The Invention of Cultural Identities in African, African-American, and Caribbean Drama*. New York: Oxford University Press.

1999. "African Theatre." In *Microsoft Encarta Africana*. Ed. Henry L. Gates and Kwame A. Appiah. CD-ROM.

Paz, Octavio. 1990. *In Search of the Present*. 1990 Nobel Lecture. New York: Harcourt Brace Jovanovich.

Plastow, Jane. 1996. *African Theatre and Politics: The Evolution of Theatre in Ethiopia, Tanzania and Zimbabwe: A Comparative Study*. Amsterdam: Rodopi.

Schipper, Mineke. 1982. *Theatre and Society in Africa*. Johannesburg: Ravan.

Soyinka, Wole. 1988. *Art, Dialogue and Outrage: Essays on Literature and Culture*. Ibadan: New Horn.

Traore, Bakary. 1972. *Black African Theatre and its Social Functions*. Ibadan: Ibadan University Press.

Ugonna, Nnabuenyi. 1983. *Mmonwu: A Dramatic Tradition of the Igbo*. Lagos: Lagos University Press.

Wertheim, Albert. 2000. *The Dramatic Art of Athol Fugard: From South Africa to the World*. Bloomington: Indiana University Press.

4

Arab and Berber oral traditions in North Africa

SABRA WEBBER

Background and research trends

North African oral traditions have left early and powerful traces despite their apparent ephemeral nature. The *Golden Ass* by the Roman writer Apuleius, born in Algeria in the middle of the first century of the Common Era drew, in text and texture, on the North African oral culture of his era. Apuleius, whose first language was probably Punic rather than Libyan (Berber), nonetheless claimed membership of two distinct Berber communities. To these African connections were attributed both his strengths (a facility for verbal artistry, a seeming naturalness and lack of artifice in his writing, an infusion of the techniques of African oral literature and magical and religious traditions in his work) and his weaknesses (the same). His work, like other literary works of the "African School," enlivened Greek and Roman metropolitan literature – displaying vivid color, a fondness for allegory, and a grotesque realism harvested from, by that time in western North Africa, a rich blending of Phoenician and various Berber cultures and in eastern North Africa, ancient Egyptian culture. Until recently, the influences of the Berber or Egyptian languages and culture(s) on Punic, Latin, or Greek have remained mostly unconsidered (but see Scobie 1983 for a discussion of the influence of Berber nannies and their storytelling on the children of Phoenician or Latin-speaking households and Black Athena and the controversy surrounding it). Recently, scholars have attended more to the cultural backgrounds of Latin writers from ancient North Africa noting that, for example, "much of [the native North African writer, Macrobius's] treatment of gods is colored by Egyptian and North African mythology . . ." (Chance 1994: 69); and, "Most likely [Fulgentius] lived in Africa: he intended to use the twenty-three letters of the Libyan alphabet for the twenty-three books of *De aetatibus mundi* and mentions the alphabet in the prologue; in one manuscript he is identified as 'carthaginiensis . . .'" (Chance 1994: 97). Further, his style, like that of the "African mythmakers" Martianus Capella and

Apuleius, was labeled "tumor Africanus" for its "pompous elegance" (97). The work of the Carthaginian Martianus, then, with its "humanization and feminization of Mythology" achieved by tempering Greek and Roman mythology and religion with that of North Africa and the Middle East was enthusiastically received within old French, German, and Irish schools after the early fifth and the twelfth centuries (Chance 1994: 298 and 245). Again, verbal art was and is achieved in the Mediterranean region not only by a lively intermingling of languages and cultures, but by the interplay of the oral and written.

With the seventh-century Arab invasion more than one thousand years after the Phoenician invasion, Berber gradually gave way in the southwestern Mediterranean periphery and in the cities of the Maghrib to Arabic and then a substantial Turkish element (especially in Egypt), during the Ottoman expansion. French (Morocco, Algeria, and Tunisia), Italian (Libya), and English (Egypt) during the 150 years or so of the European colonial presence became political languages of domination – again more dominant in the larger urban and southwestern Mediterranean periphery of North Africa, but these languages did not banish Arabic and Berber. Today verbal art continues to flourish in North Africa, still draws upon multiple linguistic sources of inspiration, now centrally Arabic and Berber, and still is a source of inspiration for written literatures that transcend national and regional borders. Tewfik al-Hakim draws upon children's rhymes to frame his play *Ya Tali al-Shajara* (Tree Climber), Tahar Ben Jelloun uses *Thousand and One Nights* themes in *L'enfant de sable* (*The Sand Child*), and Paul Bowles's work is infused with North African folktales, legends, and even personal-experience narratives. In general, as Mona Mikhail remarks of Yusuf Idris, they use the folktale form "to give shape to the content which is also inspired by the traditional lore" (1992: 86). Not only do the oral and written borrow across linguistic boundaries, interacting with and enhancing each other, but various verbal art genres (poems, proverbs, riddles, jokes) interweave – emerge from or are integrated into, combine with or are explicated – through folktales, epics or legends. And North African verbal artistry continues to contribute to the art scene north of the Mediterranean (and elsewhere) most notably today with the current powerful infusion of raï lyrics and music, a style that seems to have spread across the sea after its 1930s introduction to Oran by Berber and Arab Algerian rural women of the night who found it a useful performance tool to draw upon while trying to make a living. Lyrics, now performed more frequently by young men, mix Berber, varieties of North African Arabic, and French.

What follows reviews both the changing plurilingual language situation(s) in North Africa over the centuries and the shifting, especially European, theoretical approaches to the study of these oral traditions emerging out of changing and inextricably linked political and scholarly trends. How and why particular genres have been foregrounded or ignored over decades and centuries by scholars and aficionados will be touched upon – all the while acknowledging the slipperiness of generic categories in any case and the tendency of verbal artists to trouble, refuse, or erase those genre boundaries. This chapter goes on to consider briefly a few North African oral traditions – riddles, poems, jokes, narrative forms, market cries, "politesse," children's rhymes, lullabies, word play, and song lyrics.

There have been Berbers (*Tamazight* is thought to be the indigenous term) in the northern part of Africa from the western Nile region to the Atlantic for thousands of years. Ancient Egyptians mingled with and fought with Berber tribes since at least 3500 BCE. Gradually, as other groups moved into North Africa (Phoenicians from the Greater Syria region, Romans, Greeks, and especially Arabs), numbers of Berber speakers have proportionally declined although they are still an important presence in the region. Today, there are several Berber languages in North Africa as well as in Mali and Niger with Berber speakers ranging from less than one percent in Tunisia and Egypt to around forty percent in Morocco and perhaps twenty percent in Algeria. Berber is predominantly oral, but there are examples of Berber writing from at least the fifth century BCE and it continues to be written today. Arabic is a relatively recent arrival to North Africa, spreading rapidly beginning in the seventh and eighth centuries CE with the Arab conquest of North Africa, displacing Berber as well as Punic, Roman, and Greek.

Until recently, even most scholars of North African oral traditions have considered literary forms artistically superior to verbal art forms for one reason or another – because they were later to evolve, were considered more complex, more durable, or more compatible with "modernity." And regional (usually spoken) Arabic has commonly been subordinated to classical ("correct" and usually written) Arabic since the latter is considered closer to early poetic and Qur'anic language and essential to pan-Arabism. Still, challenging the colloquial–classical hierarchy is not new to the last century. The much-traveled historiographer of North Africa, Ibn Khaldun (1332–1406 CE) recorded lengthy examples of the oral epics about the Beni Hilal tribes in the three volumes of his *Muqaddimah* (Prolegomena). He observed that, "Most contemporary scholars . . . disapprove of these types [of poems] when they hear them, and refuse to consider them poetry . . . They believe that . . . they are [linguistically] incorrect and lack vowel endings . . ." He insists, however, "Vowel endings have nothing to do with eloquence" (III: 4, 12–80).

Felicitously, the devaluing of the oral over the written (for Arabic and Berber) and the colloquial (regional) over the classical (for Arabic) has had the effect over the centuries of keeping various forms of verbal art culturally vital because it was not considered worthy of appropriation or manipulation for symbolic purposes by a central authority. As René Maunier remarked more than sixty years ago in his work, *Introduction au folklore juridique*, folklore is local not national, and when it is appropriated by larger entities, it becomes something very different. One could add that with centralization, it tends to leave behind its counterhegemonic dimension, its critique of sociopolitical realities, along with many of its creative possibilities. With notable exceptions (*malouf* and perhaps shadow puppet plays in Tunisia, public storytelling or street theater in Morocco and Egypt), oral traditions in North Africa have been largely free of the systematic appropriation and "folklorization" or sanitation by colonizers or by governmental and other officialdoms that have sometimes been the fate of folk genres elsewhere. And for Arabic, the situation of diglossia and concomitant privileging of classical Arabic combines with the domination of the region by Arabic speakers (despite the colonial presence) so that regional Arabic speech is particularly free to innovate. Further, there is no movement to keep colloquial Arabic "pure" because it has never been considered pure. Today, depending somewhat on the esthetic or social and political requirements of the genre of artistic speech, speakers flavor their local Arabic with words adapted from Berber, French, Italian, Spanish, English, Turkish, or classical Arabic and code switch with (seemingly) whimsical abandon. In Cairo and other North African cities and towns, for example, one hears jokes and speech play that hinge on an understanding of some mix of French, English, classical and colloquial Arabic (Webber 1987). Furthermore, oral and written, colloquial and modern standard Arabic are interwoven by the unlettered as well as among the lettered population. Excerpts from colloquial Arabic poems or plays like the Tunisian colloquial *Kalam al-layl* both draw from and are received back into the world of verbal art (Booth 1992b).

The creative possibility of mixing colloquial with classical Arabic or with other languages was exploited early. Historically, poets from Andalusia, influenced by Hispano-Arabic folk poetry, when reciting *Zajal*, a playful poetry, did not use grammatical declension but rather used colloquial language, mixing it with a classical or semi-classical register at times. When it was recited to a bilingual audience of Romance and Arabic speakers, the author could also include Romance terms in the compositions and this melange could also contribute to the hilarity the poet wanted to evoke. The *muwashshahat*, another form of Andalusian strophic poetry, would be in classical Arabic but the ending, the *kharja*, could mix colloquial and classical Arabic with Romance languages. After those Jews now living in North Africa fled like the Arab Muslims from Andalusia in the fifteenth century, they continued to mix Hebrew and Spanish into their Arabic verbal (and sometimes written) art forms. Speech play interweaving French and Arabic is probably most common in the former French colonies. In the realm of 1940s Algerian politics, Malik Bennabi, among others, captured his despair at the state of party politics by using the term *la boulitique* for the French *la politique*. Playing on the pan-Arabic pronunciation of "p" as "b," the first syllable in French evokes the ubiquitous public bowling game for older men and, in Arabic, "piss." Thus, party leaders were playing a pissatic game of "defiling the public realm with private waste" (Christelow 1992: 72).

These often evocative and powerful linguistic concoctions as well as the interplay of Arabic and Berber esthetic speech need further attention. Finally, even though Arabic language purists do not consider that "good" literature can be in dialect or that dialect can be written, these "oral" literatures are not uncommonly written down, especially when the author wants to convey a sense of intimacy, informality or realism (Booth 1992a). Two obvious examples are local poetry and letters to family members and close friends. Today, e-mail is another medium that invites colloquial artistic communication.

Changing interests and theoretical foci of researchers over the centuries have influenced which oral traditions from various eras have been preserved. Researchers can expect that the more visible colonial period studies of the nineteenth and early twentieth centuries will be informed by European folklore theories of the time, or will find easily available collections, such as *Thousand and One Nights,* that appealed to European imaginings of a sensual, earthy, Orient. Interest in Berber verbal art, in particular folktales, often was focused on a search for remnants of ancient Roman, Greek, or Phoenician literature or religious beliefs. In the latter case these survivals in turn helped bolster justification for western colonization for, with few exceptions, scholars did not consider that the influence could have been mutual or might have moved from Africa north and west rather than from the Middle East and Europe to North Africa. As the self-proclaimed inheritors of Greek and Roman civilization, then, the French and Italians sometimes claimed that they were not occupying but returning to reclaim what once had been theirs. Berber studies were also encouraged by many western Europeans who considered Berbers more exotic, more "authentic" (native to the region, isolated, rural), more challenging linguistically, or less Muslim, than Arab populations.

Nineteenth-century scholars like Johann Gottfried von Herder and the linguist Jacob Grimm were convinced that the oldest (read "purest," "best") examples of any language could be found by seeking out the stories told by the oldest, least "contaminated" by other cultures and languages, speakers of language. These stories were found likely to contain even more archaic – purer, closer to origins – language than "everyday" speech. Thus, Arabic or Berber tales would be collected to provide insights into "authentic" Arabic or Berber grammatical or linguistic structures. An example of this motivation can be found in the careful work during the last years of the nineteenth century of Hans Stumme, where he included, along with careful linguistic analysis, tales in dialectical Arabic, plus transliterations and translations into German. Several of the many works of Ester Panetta, the Italian linguist and ethnographer/folklorist doing fieldwork in twentieth-century Libya, continue in this tradition, although her ethnographic interests in Libya ranged very broadly. At the same time, the European passion for establishing global classification systems sparked the collecting, sorting, and classifying of folktales by tale types and motifs. Panetta also classified folktales, loosely categorizing them using European genres such as fables, fairytales, and legends. In her work she also sorted out the recurrent themes found in the fairytales – for example, women dressing as men, a theme that continues in Arab literature of today. She matched Libyan examples to similar motifs in folktales from other regions, especially those of other regions of North Africa. She speculated about the social reasons informing the impulse to tell stories with these particular themes. Panetta, like many other European scholars, was particularly interested in Berber folklore, including folk narrative, and again this interest seems to stem in part from the link of the Berbers to pre-Arab (Phoenician, Greek, Roman) communities.

Scholars of the nineteenth century also sought to identify, through study of Arab or Berber culture's religious practices and folklore (assumed to be communally created among the rural and culturally less "evolved"), common evolutionary paths from savage to civilized among all culture groups. Joseph Desparmet (1932) observed that one reason to study the North Africans' orature was to catch the human spirit between savage and civilized, although he also speculated that Europeans had something of psychotherapy to learn from the Maghribians. The nineteenth-century searches for the "soul" of a people though their folklore, although no longer a major scholarly preoccupation (but see Paques 1964), continues to be used in popular writing as explanation for the importance of studying oral traditions in North Africa. Scholars were also preoccupied with origins of lore, especially of folktales and myths, and with clarifying the roles of three variables – shared common ancestors, diffusion, and polygenesis – in accounting for the widespread commonality of tales and motifs. Other collections of verbal arts were intended to illustrate a common humanity emphasizing, for example, the similarity of certain proverbs or religious or mythical stories shared by European and North African cultures. Others studied Berber to determine the origins of the people (Henri Basset 1887) or for unabashedly political motivations. Henri Basset writes, "Si l'on parle leur langue, ils perdent beaucoup de leurs moyens de résistance; ils sont comme désarmés." "If one speaks their language, they lose much of their means of resistance; they are as if disarmed" (Basset 1920: 37). Knowledge among researchers of Berber and Arabic languages varied widely as independence became a reality in the region during the second half of the twentieth century. Many have had to rely heavily on translators (see Aubin 1904 and his translators such as Si Kaddour ben Ghabrit).

During the second half of the twentieth century, attention to process and structure in the study of oral literature as well as its rhetorical power as a kind of counterhegemonic discourse has been foregrounded. Attending to creative process in oral literature necessarily requires consideration of the cultural and situational contexts of that verbal art leading to interesting, though fleeting to date, study of similarities between the production of oral literature and of other cultural forms – carpets, vernacular housing, and so on (see Harries 1977; Webber 1991; and for an earlier example, Maunier 1926). Scholarly preoccupations at any one time or place affected, of course, what got studied and preserved, but so did the fact that certain genres of verbal art tended to be more culturally effective as commentary on particular social conditions and thus to be more visible at any given historical moment. Today, the joke, quickly adaptable to comment on changing political and social realities, seems to be the favored form in hectic cities, notably Cairo, where time for more leisurely verbal artistry is in short supply. Personal experience narratives and proverbs are all pervasive today – among country people and city people, among men and women. Performances of epics (in poetry or rhymed prose) and folktales are shortened and become fewer, even in rural areas, as the eight-hour day takes the place of the cycle of the seasons for many men and women. But any of these latter genres and others – from patter heard in markets and from door-to-door merchants, to verbal dueling, to love poetry to children's rhymes – can undergo a florescence that may be limited to a small group, a community, a particular class or occupational group, or an entire region.

Genres, their performers, and their audiences

Due to the particular and changing interests of collectors and scholars as described above, one finds examples of Arabic and Berber oral traditions either more or less abundant by region and by language over time. The following is a sampling of verbal artistry that can be located from Egypt to Morocco, but the richness of particular examples can only be appreciated by the microstudies such as those listed in the bibliography and the many that yet need to be done.

Narratives

Contes or *Märchen*, whether in Arabic or Berber, can be identified as fiction by their introductory and usually concluding formulae. They tend toward vagueness as to time and setting, although "storied" settings such as Baghdad during the age of Haroun al-Raschid or a far away Persian city are popular options. It is not surprising to find cities as the final loci of stories about human characters – even if part of the action takes place in the countryside – but movement between city and country, Bedouin and settled settings is common. Boundaries between nature and culture, animal and human, and the natural and supernatural can become blurred so that humans may address the sea or talk to animals or ogres. Movement between the natural and supernatural, waking and sleeping, even life and death occurs without question. Women and girl characters are often educated, actively seek their own spouses, and travel to far and exotic lands. These stories can be presented orally by men or women and are also sometimes read aloud to entertain others who are doing sedentary chores – embroidering or applying henna, weaving mats, mending fishing nets, taking a store inventory – or who are simply less literate. Women storytellers (sometimes poor relations) in the past might live in the home of well-to-do patrons, providing a source of entertainment for the secluded women and the children.

The humorous trickster tales are very popular. The famous Juha (J'ha, Djoh'a, Goha) challenges all sorts of authority – religious, state, and class (although not commonly that of men over women) – shaking up, often rather more overtly than other folk genres, common cultural assumptions about the proper order of things. These tales are common throughout North Africa and among all faiths. Another subgenre, explanatory stories or folk etymological stories, can be about how a musical instrument or a place or a person was named. These narratives can be legends or tales depending on their presentation. Other kinds of fictional stories center on sea-lore, tales of generosity and hospitality, of the hazards of drink, and animal stories. Unlike *contes*, legends do not have introductory formulae. They can be presented as local history legends or personal experience narratives (two genres lacking study as artistic communication until recently) and overlap with the category "epic." Legends, at least at their core, are believed to varying degrees, and often contain some reference to the supernatural. The protagonist figures are larger-than-life examples of the brave, the holy, the foolish, the verbally or physically adept. Stories of *awliya'*, or for Jews, *tsaddiqim* (both words having the implication of "friends" [of God]), and for Coptic Christians, *quddisin* (holy ones), and their deeds, during their lives and especially after their deaths, continue to be powerful resources for community and smaller group self-representation.

The stories themselves center on help given by the godly person during a personal or communal crisis, often when the person or community is relatively powerless vis-à-vis a seemingly more powerful figure – usually, but not always, an outsider. Legends include such subcategories as stories about the lives, miracles, or visions of holy people or the heads of Sufi brother- or sisterhoods, of famous ancestors, including famous musicians and the spectacular power of their music, or famous executioners. According to André Levy, Jewish Moroccans use stories of *tsaddiqim* to address and resolve their continued love for Morocco – despite their fall from privileged to minority status since decolonization. Oral stories about the perfidy of one confessional group vis-à-vis the others are common, though each group within its popular and local religious practices also makes room to honor particular holy members of other confessional groups in poetry and prose narratives. Stories of a glorious ancient heritage are especially common in Coptic verbal art repertoires as are the glorification of martyrdom and death for the sake of the religion. Local stories of hidden wealth also abound, since any number of people who have been forced to flee the area for one reason or another leave wealth behind. Certain monuments become rumored to be fake (Roman or other ruins or *zawiyyas*, shrines built for *walis*), built to conceal arms or wealth. There are also stories of neighbors who claim to be married to genies (*jinn*, feminine: *jinniya*).

Market cries and other public patter

In the weekly markets of North Africa as well as among the street vendors or buyers, a well-turned phrase or a lengthy verbal concoction can grease the wheels of commerce or simply brighten an encounter between strangers. Sometimes what are sold are artful words, as in the case of the itinerant female fortune tellers that city and village women sometimes invite into their homes. Still today, one finds women fortune tellers who in the warm months travel together or with their husbands and children, sleeping out, and being ushered up to patios, porches, or verandas as a source not only of artistically, poetically presented information about the future, but of stories, poems, jokes, or songs. Other times door-to-door sellers of herbs or spices, beauty aids for women, or fresh water also are known and loved for their artistic speech. The street sellers are artistically invested in the shouting of their wares and also might offer along with their customers a gift of an appropriate riddle or joke. Until recently, some men acted as town criers, shouting out the news near gathering places, cafés, or marketplaces.

Riddles and proverbs

Riddles can stand alone, be told in sets, or be incorporated into legends or stories. Both Berber and Arabic riddles have a poetic form and appeal that has been likened to haiku – short, powerful images usually of everyday objects or phenomena. For example the Tunisian riddle *"It's about silver ground and a golden plow, the seeds speak, what a miracle"* evokes an appealing image that doesn't depend on its answer (paper, pen, and the letter itself) for its charm. Riddles often rhyme and possess assonance, have a deceptively simple vocabulary, and offer the created words and the syntactic layering more common in poetry than in prose. Riddles fall between definition and description as they attend to the sensory or the affective. Riddles can be quite difficult to master. Neither in Arab nor Berber culture is the riddle strictly a game or pastime for children, although children have guessing routines in both languages and rewards for guessing correctly and punishments for not guessing or for taking too long. The ancient neck riddle continues to be told (Webber 1999).

Proverbs are probably the most consistently practiced verbal art among adults today in North Africa. Men and women from all walks of life have a repertoire of proverbs in active use. Unfortunately, there are no studies that actually address this art in situational context, although there are dozens of publications simply listing proverbs from particular regions or ethnicities.

Jokes

Jokes are a particularly powerful form of counterhegemonic discourse. They seem especially favored in cities, among students and intellectuals, and frequently comment harshly but extremely wittily on corruption among the moneyed classes and on government ineptitude and more gently on country bumpkins. They also are a means of defusing tensions among the conflicting groups – religious, national, ethnic, rural/urban – that encounter each other in large cities. As one Cairene remarked to me, "When the joking stops [between these groups] it is time to worry." The joke *"A Saidi girl is walking with her boyfriend when they see her father coming toward them. 'Oh no, Papa,' says the girl. 'Don't worry,' comforts the boy, 'just tell him I'm your brother,'"* quickly sums up a host of contemporary communal concerns – changing male–female courtship practices, city–country tensions as country people move to Cairo and other big cities, and generational issues, to list only three.

Poems

Poetry tends to be foregrounded as a cultural source of pride for Berbers and Arabs, considered superior to other forms of verbal art. Topics range from falconry or war to love, or longing for a lost home (e.g., Andalusia). Professional folk poets, "merchants of art" (Slyomovics 1987), are scarcer today. They need a means to travel and reach people if they are to be heard. Traveling poets or poet-musicians of a certain reputation could, in the past, travel from place to place being taken in by the rich (perhaps to settle in as a resident entertainer) or performing in marketplaces or at weddings and festivals. Historically, these bearers of songs and poetry as well as of stories and heroic epics often accompanied their performances by a flute or tambourine carried in the hoods of their burnooses. Verbal artists could also be pious travelers, men or women, whose graves eventually become the sites of pilgrimages or small teaching centers, especially during the colonial period, for children of the urban poor or those located in the most rural areas. Until the mid-1800s criers, *l'ait*, are still reported, the famed poets of the battlefield celebrated since the Jahiliyya (pre-Islamic) period. "Voices like copper," Auguste Margueritte reports (1869), putting fear into the enemy and urging his or her tribe on to victory.

Other bearers of folk poetry (antigovernment, anticolonial, humorous, predictive, or bawdy) are water carriers – known in small towns or the neighborhoods of big cities during the colonial period as purveyors of enigmatic anticolonial poems; dervishes ("wise fools"); women – often bearers of prurient or comic poems – brought into the home to build clay ovens or to assist in the preparation of foodstuffs for storage; travelers; or salespeople. To find active bearers of oral traditions, one needs to look for those whose occupation/lifestyle results in contact with various households and both men and women. Over and over again the singers or tellers of the epic legendary biographies (*sira/siyar*) of the ancient Arab heroes like those of the Banu Hilal tribe are referred to as "gypsies." While they may in fact have homes (some towns or villages all over North Africa are known as the homes of fortune tellers, poets or musicians – Tella, al-Bakatush, Jahjouka, for example), it is true that to have an appreciable audience most verbal artists have to move around.

Politesse

Polite phrases are a central, but not much studied, genre of North African verbal art. Children and newcomers are quickly initiated into the intricacies and creative possibilities of polite speech – a conversational genre that depends on an appealing phrase, well placed, well timed, and effectively and appropriately delivered. Even poor speakers of colloquial Arabic who have a grasp of the basic politeness formulae will be complimented on how well they speak Arabic. Artful and less perfunctory politesse is truly foregrounded – noticed and remembered. Speakers choose from a panoply of vocabulary even for the simplest of greetings, "good morning" and "good night," so that those required greetings, esthetically pleasing, cleverly personalized to listener and context, can become long-remembered and repeated compliments. Aside from the "obligatory" phrases to (or by) beggars such as "may God provide" (uttered by the petitioner when refusing a petition), to parents regarding the health and success of their children (in school, in marriage), to workers encountered in the street, particular phrases relevant only to the person addressed and the situation addressed are especially valued. Reminiscences about a particularly well-turned compliment or conversely a pithy critique of a mannerless clod also are traditional artistic speech – celebrating the speaker, no matter how otherwise socially marginal, as well as the speech, and creating a sense of connection or community. Some very nice insults for those with no table manners can be found in Daumas 1864. For example, to be said to the greedy, "*From the rate at which you are making that goat disappear, one would think that while living it gored you,*" or (to the sloppy eater) "*In light of your familiarity with [the cooked goat meat] you would think his mother nursed you.*" Daumas also mentions over fifty ways to wish a person well in Algerian Arabic as well as numerous creative phrases to offer when someone is sick or wounded, when a loved one dies, when someone loses money, marries, has a child, or brings good news. Besides "*Good morning,*" one can wish another "a day of *dates and milk,*" or "*sugar and honey,*" for example, or, for the fishermen on the island of Kerkennah, Tunisia, a good early morning greeting is "*[May you have] fish up to your armpits.*" It remains for future studies to determine how flexible these polite phrases and reproaches can be and how much they vary from region to region.

Song

Sung narratives or poetry are common in Arabic or Berber. Similar poems or rhymed prose pieces are put to a spectrum of tunes depending on region and personal preference. Lullaby lyrics are set to various tunes depending on region and family practices. Touareg poetry in Ahaggar (Berber) might be recited, but can be sung (accompanied by a violin or sometimes a small drum) to any of several tunes that correspond to the particular rhythm of the "text." And any one of a number of rhythms can be chosen. Among other groups a flute might be used (the Jurqra of the Kabyles). Women's nonprofessional singing tends to be in private (Abu-Lughod 1986), except at traditional weddings. They sing while at work – spinning, weaving, grinding wheat – and when their words waft into the nearby community they subvert in interesting ways the public–private dichotomy, by making "public" emotions and opinions commonly considered suitable only for private utterance. A lullaby recorded in western Tunisia is simultaneously a song and warning to a nearby lover. Women and children also have songs and rituals to bring rain. In parts of North Africa, these rituals and songs are thought by some to be playful adaptations of Punic human sacrifices to the goddess Tanit. Religious ballads about the life of the Prophet or other important Islamic figures both construct and reveal a local, authoritative, "lived" religion, a very lively counterpoint to the textual tradition. Coptic Christians in Egypt have rediscovered the art of hymns – songs about Jesus, the church, or saints – sung in homes and at informal family gatherings. These two examples underscore most emphatically the importance of studying any of the North African religious traditions as lived traditions, often orally constructed and transmitted.

Although there are master poet-singers, long remembered and quoted, informal poetic compositions are set to music and are very widespread across classes and among men and women, young and old. As is the case with much folk speech by definition, only the author or close associates can understand allusions, omissions, additions to or rearrangements of verses. Often singers draw upon a specialized poetic vocabulary. As is the case with Arabic poetry, sung poetic duels can occur, including those by young mothers debating the merits of girl and boy babies. There is popular and some scholarly belief that this kind of dueling harks back to conflicts during which each side fought with the words of champion poets as well as with warriors.

Malouf (perhaps from *alifa*, "familiar" or "customary"), like the *sira* genre of legend, is an art form that has been tampered with by institutions. This song and musical style is said to have been brought from Andalusia by Muslims and Jews who were expelled during the fifteenth century, but it is far from clear that this is the case (see Guettat 1980; Abu-Haidar 1993). In any event, it became a form shared by both religious brother- and sisterhoods (where it is often considered chanting, not music) and by secular performers, whether dedicated amateurs, usually with some status in the community, or by professionals, both Muslims and Jews (of a lower class until the second quarter of the century). Some of the religious groups would also perform during weddings or circumcisions, even in street processions and in cafés. The texts, a combination of literary Arabic art forms – *qasida*, *muwashshahah*, and *zajal* – with (often very) local dialects are transmitted orally, as is the accompanying music. Leaders of local groups could alter the words or music, and borrowing occurred among religions and from sacred to secular and vice-versa. Until the last sixty years or so, secular *malouf* seems to have been performed either by Jewish performers or lower-class urban or middle- to upper-class rural Muslims. In *zawiyyas* all members chanted with the leaders changing words or melodies as necessary. Melodies could be traded between popular and sacred texts so that Jews on the island of Djerba, in Tunisia, borrowed from popular music texts in Arabic to sing *piyyutim*, or Hebrew poetic texts performed on religious occasions. Innovations, including the addition of western instruments continue to occur. Institutional, governmental or academic, interference has resulted in the following: a rupture between younger and older players, an attempt to codify and "correct" words, a downplaying of the religious *malouf* of Sufi brotherhoods, and a freezing in place of words (and music) choices by poets or musicians who tend not to be well-versed in *malouf*.

Lullabies

As in other parts of the world, lullabies can be any songs that appeal to the singer – often love songs. North African lullabies specifically for girls have focused on imagining the tender and supportive relationship the young girl will have with her mother, her future stunning beauty as a young woman, her success in the "womanly" skills of embroidery, fancy needlework, and weaving, and her successful marriage. For boys, the lullabies attend again to a close relationship with the mother, but imagine him coming to her from school, how desirable he will be to young women – *"One said, 'I'll marry him,' one said, 'I yearn for him,' one said, 'I swear I dreamed of him while he was still in his mother's womb,'"* – how successful and generous he will be as a man. Both lullabies and nursery rhymes refer back to the time that young men were conscripted into the Ottoman army (*"and Haneena is crying, her son is in Istanbul"*). The child and mother and father are likened to precious metals or the moon or stars – families of related symbols. The mother moves from one lullaby to another, often connecting them by drawing on the same tune. Lullabies are much less likely to involve linguistic code-switching, perhaps because they represent such a private moment between parent and small child.

Coded speech / speech play

"Small" artistic strategies such as multilayered, extended metaphors, naming practices, use of diminutives, and "secret" languages are important to the underpinnings of orature, but also embellish everyday speech and conversational genres like riddles, proverbs, and jokes. Henri Basset (1920), among others, mentions the artistic speech of women and children, remarking that among the Kabyles there are women who can speak so that men don't understand and that children's language is also specialized. Children's games, lullabies and rhymes are especially full of diminutives, although Arabic employs diminutives to great effect in various sorts of verbal art – stories, legends, proverbs, and so on – and they may also be nuggets of artistic speech embedded in everyday talk. Jeanne Jouin (1950) uses the Moroccan example of a double diminutive: *bint* (girl) to *bnita* (little girl) to *banutta* (little, little girl) or, alternatively, *binti* (my girl), *binati*, *binuti*, in Tunisia (Webber, personal observation). The pattern differs from place to place, but the concept is widespread.

Children's rhymes and games

Little rhymes and games for children (clapping rhymes, naming, or counting rhymes using fingers or toes, rhymes for learning to walk, rhymes in the ceremony for loss of the first tooth) also employ the diminutive and fantastic talk. The fingers become little people or the castle of a sultan; the armpit becomes the cave for a little mouse creeping up the child's arm in a game similar to "this little piggy went to market." But a rhyming or clapping game chanted in sing-song voices or sung can also simply be the story of something close to home. "*Daddy brought a little fish, we'll fry it in a little oil . . . What did daddy bring us? He brought us henna, I'm going to put some on, and I'll share it with Shoshena*" (probably a young, brown-skinned, servant girl). Creative pet names are common for children and often cannot be understood without reference to family or even Arab or Berber world history and relationships. Rhymes by children are extremely creative, often mixing multiple languages.

Today research into North African oral traditions represents a lively field of investigation – both for Berber and for Arabic. Researchers are once again requiring of themselves knowledge of local speech and seem willing to celebrate life at the margins, the interstices of verbal art and material culture, verbal art and written art, Berber, Arabic, and French at a minimum and so on. There is also in a postmodern era a willingness (not previously entirely unknown, of course) to explode western genre categories and an openness to attending to and (re-)appreciating cultural difference.

Finally, recognition by scholars of North Africa of the political dimension of artistic speech, standing alone, or in conversation with written texts, or with visual art or material culture, has resulted in powerful critical analyses that speak not only to local or regional concerns, but offer important insights into crosscultural relations writ large. Scholars of North Africa, like scholars of Africa in general, have often led in their understanding of the need to take into account the power of oral expressive culture in the contexts of both local and regional studies – political, literary, cultural, and religious. Now, however, what was once an artistic medium relegated to the simplest of building blocks for more important genres and media is broadly recognized as a highly complex and absolutely central resource in the critical need for understanding across cultures the powerful affective dimension of communities anywhere and everywhere.

Bibliography

Abnoudy, Abderrahman. 1988. *Al-Sira al-hilaliyya*. 3 vols. Cairo: Matabi' al-akhbar.

Abu-Haidar, Jareer A. 1993. "The Case for the Arabic Origins of the Muashshahat: Court Poetry and Burlesque in Al-Andalus." *The Maghreb Review. Majallat al-Maghrib* 18.1: 88–96.

Abu-Lughod, Lila. 1986. *Veiled Sentiments: Honor and Poetry in a Bedouin Society*. Berkeley: University of California Press.

1993. *Writing Women's Worlds: Bedouin Stories*. Berkeley: University of California Press.

Al-Hakim, Tawf iq. 1978. *Ya Tali' al-shajarah*. Beirut: al-Kitab al-Lubnani.

Al-Marzouki, Mohammad. 1967. *al-Adab al-sha'bi fi Tunis*. Tunis: Maison Tunisienne d'Editions.

1968. *Abd al-Smad qal kilmat*. Tunis: Maison Tunisienne d'Editions.

1971. *Al-Jaziya al-Hilaliyya*. Tunis: Maison Tunisienne d'Editions.

Amrouche, Jean, ed. and trans. 1947. *Chants berbères de Kabylie*. New edn. Paris: Charlot.

Ardant, Gabriel, and Jean Paul Charnay. 1965. *De l'impérialisme à la décolonisation*. Paris: Editions de Minuit.

Aubin, Eugène. [1904] 1922. *Le Maroc d'aujourd'hui*. 9th edn. Paris: A. Colin.

Ayoub, Abderrahman. 1982. *Approches de la poésie bédouine hilalienne chez Ibn Khaldoun*. Algiers: Société Nationale d'Edition et Diffusion: 321–45.

Bamia, Aida Adib. 2001. *The Greying of the Raven: Cultural and Sociopolitical Significance of Algerian Folk Poetry*. Cairo: American University in Cairo Press.

Basset, André, ed. 1925. *Poésies touarègues, dialecte de l'Ahaggar, recueillies par le P. de Foucauld*, vol. 1. Paris: E. Leroux.

1930. *Poésies touarègues, dialecte de l'Ahaggar, recueillies par le P. de Foucauld*, vol. II. Paris: E. Leroux.

Basset, Henri. 1883. *Contes arabes: histoire des dix vizirs (Bakhtiar-Nameh)*. Paris: E. Leroux.

1901. *Moorish Literature: Comprising Romantic Ballads, Tales of the Berbers, Stories of the Kabyles, Folk-lore and National Traditions*. Rev. edn. New York: Collier.

1920. *Essai sur la littérature des Berbères*. Algiers: Jules Carbonel.

1921. "Les influences puniques chez les Berbères." *Revue Africaine* 62: 340–75.

Basset, René Marie Joseph. 1887. *Contes populaires berbères recueillis, traduits et annotés par . . .* Paris: E. Leroux.

1924. *Mille et un contes, récits et légendes arabes*. 3 vols. Paris: Maisonneuve Frères.

Beguinot, F. 1922–23. "La letteratura berbera, secondo un'opera di H. Basset." *Oriente moderno* 2: 437–48; 505–10; 561–70.

Bel, Alfred. 1906. *Quelques rites pour obtenir la pluie en temps de sécheresse chez les musulmanes maghrébins*. Algiers: Fontana.

Ben Ali, A. 1941. "A travers les berceuses tunisiennes." *Institut des belle lettres arabes* 4: 131–44.

Ben Jelloun, Tahar. 1985. *L'enfant de sable: roman*. Paris: Seuil.

Benachehon, A. 1960. *Contes et récits du Maroc*. Rabat, Morocco: OMNIA.

Bentolila, Fernand. 1986. *Devinettes berbères*. 3 vols. Paris: Conseil International de la langue française (CILF).

Bernal, Martin. 1987. *Black Athena: The Afroasiatic Roots of Classical Civilization*. New Brunswick, NJ: Rutgers University Press.

Berque, Jacques. 1940. "La criée publique à Fès: Etude concrète d'un marché." *Revue Ec. Polit*. May: 320–45.

Biarney, S. 1917. *Etude sur les dialectes berbères du Rif*. Paris: E. Leroux.

1924. *Notes d'ethnographie et de linguistique nord-africaine*. Ed. L. Brunot and E. Laoust, vol. XII. Inst. des hautes-études marocaines. Paris: E. Leroux.

Bilu, Y. 1987. "Dreams and Wishes of the Saint." In *Judaism Viewed from Within and Without: Anthropological Studies*. Ed. Harvey E. Goldberg. SUNY series in anthropology and Judaic studies. Albany, NY: State University of New York Press: 285–313.

Bloch, Isaac. 1888. *Inscriptions tumulaires des anciens cimetières israëlites d'Alger: recueillies, traduites, commentées et accompagnées de notices biographiques. Grand Rabbin d'Alger*. Paris: Armand Dulacher.

Booth, Marilyn. 1992a. "Colloquial Arabic Poetry, Politics, and the Press in Modern Egypt." *International Journal of Middle Eastern Studies* 24: 419–40.

1992b. "Poetry in the Vernacular." In *Modern Arabic Literature*. Ed. M. M. Badawi. Cambridge: Cambridge University Press: 463–82.

Bougchiche, Lamara, and Lionel Galand. 1997. *Langues et littératures berbères des origines à nos jours: bibliographie internationale et systématique*. Paris: Ibis.

Boulifa, A. [1904] 1990. *Recueil de poésies kabyles*. Paris/Algiers: Awal.

Bowles, Paul. 1963. *Their Heads Are Green and Their Hands Are Blue*. New York: Random House.

Brown, Kenneth L., and A Lakhassi. 1981. "Everyman's Disaster: The Earthquake of Agadir: A Berber (Tashelhit) Poem." *Maghreb Review* 6.

Brunot, Louis. 1921. *La mer dans les traditions et les industries indigènes à Rabat et Salé*. Paris: Publications de l'Ecole Supérieure de Langue Arabe et de Dialectes Berbères de Rabat.

1931a. *Les joyeuses histoires du Maroc*. Rabat: Direction générale de l'instruction publique des beaux-arts et des antiquités.

1931b. *Textes arabes de Rabat*. Ed. Inst. des hautes-études marocaines. 2 vols. Paris: P. Geuthner.

Brunot, Louis, and Elie Malka. 1939. *Textes judéo-arabes de Fès*. Rabat: Typo-litho Ecole du livre.

Cachia, Pierre. 1989. *Popular Narrative Ballads of Modern Egypt*. Oxford and New York: Oxford University Press and Clarendon Press.

Chance, Jane. 1994. *Medieval Mythography: From Roman North Africa to the School of Chartres, AD 433–1177*. Gainesville: University Press of Florida.

Charhadi, Driss ben Hamed, and Paul Bowles. 1964. *A Life Full of Holes*. London: Weidenfeld and Nicolson.

Christelow, Allen. 1992. "An Islamic Humanist in the 20th Century: Malek Bennabi." *The Maghreb Review* 17.1–2: 69–83.

Colin, Georges Séraphin. 1939a. *Textes Ethnographiques*. Paris: A. Maisonneuve.

1939b. *Chrestomathie marocaine: textes citadins en transcription latine*. Paris: Adrien-Maisonneuve.

1942. *Recueil de textes en arabe marocain*. Paris: A. Maisonneuve.

Connelly, Bridget. 1986. *Arab Folk Epic and Identity*. Berkeley: University of California Press.

Daumas, Eugène, 1864. *Moeurs et coutumes de l'Algérie: Tell, Kabylie, Sahara, par le général E. Daumas*. 4th edn. rev. and enlarged. Paris: L. Hachette and Co.

Davis, Ruth. 1986a. "Modern Trends in the 'Arab-Andalusian' Music of Tunisia." *The Maghreb Review* 11.2–4: 58–63.

1986b. "Some Relations Between Three Piyyutim from Djerba and Three Arabic Songs." *The Maghreb Review. Majallat al-Maghrib* 11.5–6: 134–44.

Dermenghem, Emile. 1945. "Le mythe de Psyche dans le folklore nord-africain." *Revue Africaine* 89: 41–81.

Desparmet, Joseph. 1932. *Ethnographie traditionnelle de la Metidja. Le mal magique*. Université d'Alger. Publications de la Faculté des lettres d'Alger. Ancien bulletin de correspondance africaine. 1st series, vol. 63. Université d'Alger. Faculté des lettres et sciences humaines. Algiers: J. Carbonel; Paris: P. Geuthner.

Destaing, Edmond. 1907–11. *Étude sur le dialecte berbère des Beni-Snous*, vols. 34–35. Eds. De l'Université d'Alger et de la Faculté des lettres et sciences humaines. Paris: E. Leroux.

1937. *Textes arabes en parler des Chleuhs du Sous Maroc*. Paris: P. Geuthner.

1940. *Textes berbères en parler des Chleuhs du Sous (Maroc)*. Paris: P. Geuthner.

Dubouloz-Laffin, Marie Louise. 1946. *Le bou-mergoud, folklore tunisien, croyances et coutumes populaires de Sfax et de sa région*. Paris: G. P. Maisonneuve.

Eickelman, Dale F. 1977. "Form and Composition in Islamic Myths: Four Texts from Western Morocco." *Anthropos* 72: 447–64.

El-Fasi, M. 1967. *Chants anciens des femmes de Fès*. Paris: Seghers.

El-Fasi, M., and Emile Dermenghem. 1926. *Contes fasis, recueillis d'après la tradition orale*. Paris: F. Reider.

El-Shamy, Hasan M. 1980. *Folktales of Egypt*. Chicago: University of Chicago Press.

Falls, J. C. Ewald. 1908. *Beduinen-Lieder der libyschen Wüste*. Cairo: F. Diemer Finck and Baylænder succ.

Fanjul, Serafin. 1977a. "The Erotic Mawwal in Egypt." *Journal of Arabic Literature* 8: 104–22.

1977b. *Literatura popular árabe*. Madrid: Editora Nacional.

Foucauld, Le Père Ch. de. *Poésies touarègues: dialecte de l'Ahaggar*. 2 vols. Paris: Ernest Leroux.

Galand, Lionel. 1979. *Langue et littérature berbères: vingt cinq ans d'études: chroniques de l'Annuaire de l'Afrique du Nord*. Paris: Editions du Centre national de la recherche scientifique.

Galand-Pernet, Paulette. 1965. "Poésie berbère du sud du Maroc et 'motifs économiques.'" In *De l'impérialisme à décolonisation*. Ed. Jean-Paul Charnay. Paris: Les Editions de Minuit. 263–79.

1972. *Recueil de poèmes chleuhs*. Paris: Klincksieck.

1987. "Littérature orale et représentation du texte: les poèmes berbères traditionnels." *Etudes de littérature ancienne*, vol. III. Paris: Presses de l'Ecole Normale Superieure (PENS): 107–18.

1998. *Littératures berbères: des voix, des lettres*. Islamiques. 1st edn. Paris: Presses Universitaires de Paris.

Galley, Micheline, and Abderrahman Ayoub. 1983. *Histoire des Beni Hilal et de ce qui leur advint dans leur marche vers l'ouest: versions tunisiennes de la Geste hilalienne*. Paris: A. Colin.

Galley, Micheline, and Aouda Galley. 1971. *Badr az-zîn et six contes algériens*. Paris: A. Colin.

Gaudefroy-Demombynes, Maurice. 1894. *Contes en arabe vulgaire de Tlemcen*. Extrait du Journal Asiatique. Paris: Imprimerie nationale.

Germain, Gabriel. 1935. "Ulysse, le Cyclope et les Berbères." *Revue de Littérature Comparée* 15: 573–623.

Graf de la Salle, Madeleine. 1950. "Contributions à l'étude du folklore tunisienne." *Mélanges W. Marcais*. Paris: Maisonneuve: 161–84.

Guettat, Mahmoud. 1980. *La musique classique du Maghreb*. Paris: Sindbad.

Guiga, Tahar. 1968. *La geste hilalienne*. Tunis: Maison Tunisienne d'Editions.

Hanoteau, Adolphe. 1867. *Poésies populaires de la Kabylie du Jurjura*. Paris: Impr. Impériale, 1867.

1906. *Essai de grammaire kabyle renfermant les principes du langage parlé par les populations du versant nord du Jurjura et spécialement par les Igauaouen ou Zouaoua, suivi de notes et d'une notice sur quelques inscriptions en caractères dits tifinar' et en langue tamacher't*. 2nd edn. Algiers: Typographie A. Jourdan.

Hardy, Georges, ed. 1928. *Mémorial Henri Basset: nouvelles études nord- africaines et orientales*. 2 vols. Paris: Librairie orientaliste Paul Geuthner.

Harries, Jeanette. 1977. "Pattern and Choice in Berber Weaving and Poetry." In *Forms of Folklore in Africa: Narrative, Poetic, Gnomic, Dramatic*. Ed. Bernth Lindfors. Austin: University of Texas Press: viii, 281.

Hodgson, W. B. [1829] 1934. *Grammatical Sketch and Specimens of Berber Language*. Transactions of the American Philosophical Society. 4.1 (new ser.). Philadelphia: American Philosophical Society.

Hoffman, Valerie J. 1995. *Sufism, Mystics and Saints in Modern Egypt*. University of South Carolina.

Houdas, Octave. 1886. *Ethnographie de l'Algérie*. Paris: Maisonneuve Frères & C. Leclerc.

Hurreiz, Sayed Hamid A. 1977. *Ja'aliyyīn Folktales: An Interplay of African, Arabian and Islamic Elements*. African series, vol. VIII. Bloomington: Indiana University.

Hurreiz, Sayed Hamid A., and Herman Bell. 1975. *Directions in Sudanese Linguistics and Folklore*. Ed. Institute of African and Asian Studies. Khartoum: Khartoum University Press.

Ibn Khaldun. 1967. *The Muqaddimah*. Trans. Franz Rosenthal. 3 vols. London: Routledge and Kegan Paul.

Jouad, H., and B. Lortat-Jacob. 1978. *La saison des fêtes dans une vallée du Haut-Atlas*. Paris: Seuil.

Jouin, Jeanne 1950. *Chants et jeux maternels à Rabat*. Extrait de Hesperis: archives berbères et bulletin de l'Institut des hautes-études marocaines 37. Paris: Larose.

1954. "Chansons de l'escarplette à Fès et Rabat-Salé." *Hesperis* 41: 341–63.

Justinard, Louis. 1928. "Poésie en dialecte du sous-marocain, d'après un manuscrit arabico-berbère." *Nouveau journal asiatique* Oct.–Dec.: 217–521.

Kapchan, Deborah A. 1996. *Gender on the Market: Moroccan Women and the Revoicing of Tradition*. Philadelphia: University of Pennsylvania Press.

Lacoste-Dujardin, Camille. 1972. *Le conte Kabyle*. Paris: Maspero.

1974. "Le conte en berbère: l'exemple du conte kabyle." *AAN* 12 (1974): 249–57.

1999. *Contes merveilleux de Kabylie: narré par Amor ben Moh'ammed ou 'Ali de Taoudouchth et notes en kabyle par Auguste Moulieras*. Collection "Bilingues." Aix en Provence: Edisud.

Laoust, E. 1921. "La littérature des Berbères d'après l'ouvrage de M. Henri Basset." *Hesperis. Archives berbères et Bulletin de l'Institut des Hautes-Etudes marocaines* 1: 194–207.

1929. "Chants berbères contre l'occupation française." *Mémorial Henri Basset*. Paris: Inst. des hautes-études marocaines.

1949. *Contes berbères du Maroc*. Publications de l'Institut des hautes-études marocaines, vol. L. Paris: Larose.

Legey, Doctoresse. *Contes et légendes populaires du Maroc, recueillis à Marrakech et traduits par. . . .* Paris: Inst. des hautes-études marocaines.

Levi-Provençal, Evariste. 1922. *Textes arabes de l'Ouarghah, dialecte des Jbala du Maroc septentrional*. Paris: Leroux.

Levy, André. 1994. "The Structured Ambiguity of Minorities toward Decolonization: The Case of Moroccan Jews Today." *The Maghreb Review* 19.1–2: 133–46.

Lortat-Jacob, Bernard, and Hassan Jouad. 1979. *Berbères du Maroc: Ahwash*. Chant du monde.

Lortat-Jacob, Bernard, Gilbert Rouget, and Hassan Jouad. 1971. *Musique berbère du Haut Atlas*. Disques Vogue.

Loubignac, V. 1952. *Textes arabes des Zaër: transcription, traduction, notes et lexique*. Ed. Inst. des hautes-études marocaines, vol. VII. Paris: Librairie orientale et américaine M. Besson.

Louis, André. 1977. *Bibliographie ethno-sociologique de la Tunisie*. Tunis: Imprimerie N. Bascone.

Mammari, Mouloud. 1980. *Poèmes kabyles anciens*. Paris: La Découverte.

1982. *Littérature orale: actes de la table ronde, juin 1979*. Ed. Markaz al-Buhuth. Algiers: Office des publications universitaires.

Marçais, Philippe. 1954. *Textes arabes de Djidjelli; introd., textes et transcription, traduction, glossaire*. Publications XVI. Ed. de l'Université d'Alger Université and Faculté des lettres et sciences humaines. Paris: Presses Universitaires de France.

Margueritte, Auguste. 1869. *Chasses de l'Algérie, et notes sur les arabes du sud*. 2nd edn. Paris: Furne Jouvet.

Massignon, Genevieve. 1963. "Supplément à la 'Bibliographie des recueils de contes traditionnels du Maghreb.'" *Fabula: Zeitschrift für Erzählforschung; Journal of Folktale Studies; revue d'études sur le conte populaire* 6: 162–76.

1961. "Bibliographie de recueils de contes traditionnels du Maghreb (Maroc, Algérie, Tunisie)." *Fabula* 4: 111–29.

Maunier, René. 1926. *La construction collective de la maison en Kabylie; étude sur la coopération économique chez les Berbères du Djurjura*. Paris: Institut d'ethnologie.

Mikhail, Mona. 1992. *Studies in the Short Fiction of Mahfouz and Idris*. New York: New York University Press.

Mouliéras, Auguste, and René Basset. 1892. *Les fourberies de Si Djeha: contes kabyles*. Paris: E. Leroux.

Mouliéras, Auguste, and Camille Lacoste. 1965. *Traduction des légendes et contes merveilleux de la Grande Kabylie*. 2 vols. Paris: P. Geuthner.

Murtad, Abd al-Malik. 1982. *al-Alghaz al-shabiyah al-Jazairiyah: dirasah fi alghaz al-gharb al-Jazairi*. al-Jazair: Diwan al-Matbuat al-Jamiiyah.

Norris, H. T. 1968. *Shinqiti Folk Literature and Song*. Oxford: Clarendon Press.

1972. *Saharan Myth and Saga*. Oxford: Clarendon Press.

Noy, Dov. 1965. *Soixante et onze contes populaires: racontés par des Juifs du Maroc*. Jerusalem: Organisation sioniste mondiale, Département d'organisation, Section des recherches.

Panetta, Ester. 1940. *Pratiche e credenze popolari libiche: testi in arabo bengasino tradotti e annotati*. Rome: Istituto per l'Oriente.

1943. *Forme e soggetti della letteratura popolare libica*. Milan: Istituto per gli studi di politica internazionale.

1956. *Poesie e canti popolari arabi*. Modena: Guanda.

1963. *L'Italia in Africa: Studi italiani di etnografia e di folklore della Libia. Testo di Ester Panetta*. Rome: Istituto poligrafico dello Stato.

1973. *Studi italiani di etnologia e folklore dell'Africa Orientale: Eritrea, Etiopia, Somalia*. L'Italia in Africa: Serie scientifico-culturale. Rome: Istituto poligrafico dello Stato.

Paques, Viviana. 1964. *L'arbre cosmique dans la pensée populaire et dans la vie quotidienne du nord-ouest africain*. Travaux et mémoires de l'Institut d'ethnologie 70. Paris: Institut d'ethnologie.

Paul-Margueritte, Lucie. 1935. *Chants berbères du Maroc*. Paris: Editions Berger-Levrault.

Pellat, Charles. 1955. *Textes berbères dans le parler des Ait Seghrouchen de la Moulouya*. Paris: Larose.

Quéméneur, Jean. 1944. *Enigmes tunisiennes; textes recueillis*. Publications de l'Institut des belles lettres arabes 2. Tunis: S. a. P. I.

Rabia, Boualem. 1993. *Recueil de poésies Kabyles des Aï Ziki: Le viatique du barde: bilingue français–berbère*. Paris: L'Harmattan / Awal.

Reynolds, Dwight Fletcher. 1995. *Heroic Poets, Poetic Heroes: The Ethnography of Performance in an Arabic Oral Epic Tradition*. Ithaca, NY: Cornell University Press.

Sandy, Gerald N. 1997. *The Greek World of Apuleius*. Mnemosyne, bibliotheca classica Batava. Supplementum 174. Leiden: Brill.

Scobie, Alexander. 1983. *Apuleius and Folklore: Toward a History of ML 3045, AaTh567, 449A*. London: Folklore Society.

Sinaceur, Zakia Iraqui, and Micheline Galley, trans. 1994. *Dyab, Jha, La'âba – le triomphe de la ruse: contes marocains du Fonds Ed. Colin*. Issy les Moulineaux: Classiques africains.

Slyomovics, Susan. 1987. *The Merchant of Art: An Egyptian Hilali Oral Epic Poet in Performance*. Berkeley: University of California Press.

Socin, Albert, and Hans Stumme. 1895. *Der arabische Dialekt der Houwara des Wad Sus in Marokko*. Leipzig: S. Hirzel.

Sonneck, C. 1902. *Chants arabes du Maghreb, étude sur le dialecte et la poésie populaire de l'Afrique du nord*. 2 vols. Paris: Guilmoto.

Stern, S. M., and L. P. Harvey. 1974. *Hispano-Arabic Strophic Poetry: Studies*. Oxford: Clarendon Press.

Stumme, Hans. 1893. *Tunisische Märchen und Gedichte. Eine Sammlung prosaischer und poetischer Stücke im arabischen Dialecte der Stadt Tunis nebst Einleitung und Übersetzung*. Leipzig: J. C. Hinrichs.

1894. *Tripolitanisch-tunisische Beduinenlieder*. Leipzig: J. C. Hinrichs.

1895. *Märchen der Schluh von Tázerwalt*. Leipzig: J. C. Hinrichs.

1898. *Märchen und Gedichte aus der Stadt Tripolis in Nordafrika*. Leipzig: J. C. Hinrichs'sche Buchhandlung.

Tahar, Ahmed. 1975. *La poésie populaire algérienne (melhûn): rythme, mètres et formes*. Littérature populaire. Ed. Algiers, vol. 1. Algiers: Société nationale d'édition et de diffusion (al Maktabah al Wataniyah).

Vassel, Eusèbe. 1905–1907. *La littérature populaire des Israélites Tunisiens*. Ed. Inst. de Carthage (Tunisia). vol. 1. Paris: E. Leroux.

Webber, Sabra. 1969. *Lis-sigharina (For Our Children)*. Tunis: National Publishing House.

1977. "Four Tunisian Lullabies." In *Middle Eastern Muslim Women Speak*. Ed. E. Fernea and B. Bezirgan. Austin: University of Texas Press: 87–93.

1985. "Women's Folk Narratives and Social Change." In *Women and the Family in the Middle East*. Ed. Elizabeth Fernea. Austin: University of Texas Press: 310–16.

1987. "The Social Significance of the Cairene Nukta: Preliminary Observations." *ARCE (American Research Center in Egypt) Newsletter* 138 (Summer): 1–10.

1990. "Les fonctions communicatives des devinettes de Kelibia (Tunisie). (A Sociostructural Analysis of Tunisian Riddles.)." *La Revue IBLA (l'Institut des belles lettres arabes)* 53. 166: 1–21.

1991. *Romancing the Real: Folklore and Ethnographic Representation in North Africa*. Philadelphia: University of Pennsylvania Press.

1999. "Tunisian Storytelling Today." In *Traditional Storytelling Today*. Ed. Margaret Read MacDonald. Chicago: Fitzroy Dearborn.

Westermarck, Edward. 1926. *Ritual and Belief in Morocco*. 2 vols. London: Macmillan.

Yacine, T. 1988. *L'izli ou l'amour chante en kabyle*. Paris: Maison des sciences de l'homme.

1995. *Cherif Kheddam ou l'amour de l'art*. Paris: La Découverte/Awal.

Yelles-Chaouche, M. 1990. *Le hawfi. Poésie féminine et tradition orale au Maghreb*. Algiers: Office des publications universitaires.

Zafrani, H. 1980. *Littératures dialectales et populaires juives en Occident musulman*. Paris: Geuthner.

Zenagui, Abd el Aziz, and Maurice Gaudefroy-Demombynes. 1904. *Récit en dialecte tlemcénien*. Paris: Impr. Nationale.

5

Heroic and praise poetry in South Africa

LUPENGA MPHANDE

Praise poetry is central to any delineation of southern African literature since praising is an important part of the peoples' political and literary expression. The genre of praise poetry called *izibongo* in Zulu (used in its plural form) is a political art form found in southern African societies like the Nguni- and Sotho-Tswana-speaking peoples. The term refers to the form of poetic expression that defines and names an individual, and is characterized by bold imagery expressed in carefully selected language. This type of poetry applies to the personal set of praise names of individuals, comprising cumulative series of praises and epithets bestowed on them by their associates, from childhood onwards, interspersed with narrative passages or comments. These praises, composed and recited by professional bards, often embody concise allusions to historical incidents and memorable achievements or characteristics connected with each family, and may amount to verses of considerable length and excellence. Among the Nguni linguistic groups, the characteristically colorful heroic praise poetry has a rich body of collected literature dating back four hundred years, and such poetry is treasured by people in this subregion as their highest form of literary expression. The major function of praise poetry is to conserve and transmit social consciousness, while simultaneously entertaining the audience. Because it deals with happenings in and around the individual being praised, informing the audience of his/her political and social views, praise poetry is documentary, and speakers of many (and similar) southern African languages have retained this cultural expression to aid them in remembering their past.

Research into heroic praise poetry is still relatively scanty. The first recording, in the southern African region, was published by Eugene Casalis in 1841: *Etudes sur la langue Sechuana*. This was in reality a grammar of southern Sotho, and not of Setwana as the title suggests. Casalis published another collection in 1859, *Les Bassoutos*, which was translated into English in 1961 as *The Basutos*. In 1882 the "Song of the Assega," the *izibongo* of Lobengula of the Zimbabwe

Ndebele, was published by H. Depelchin and Croonenberghs in *Trois ans dans l'Afrique Australe: le pays des Matabélés, débuts de la Mission du Zambèse*. These publications did not include texts in the source language. The first praise poem published in an African language was Thomas Arbousset's praise of King Dingana of the Zulu in *Relation d'un voyage d'exploration au nord-est de la Colonie du Cap de Bonne Espérance* published in 1842, and translated into English in 1852. Some of the early recordings of praise poetry were published in newspapers before being re-issued in the form of anthologies. In 1906, *Zemk'iinkomo Magwalandini* containing, among other things, praise poems gathered from Eastern Cape newspapers by well-known Xhosa authors such as S. E. K. Mqhayi and J. T. Jabavu, and edited by W. B. Rubusana, was published. Similarly, in 1915, A. M. Sekese published *Lilotho tsa Sesotho*, a collection of praises in Sesotho taken from *Leselinyana la Lesotho*, the journal of the Paris Evangelical Mission Society. Zulu praise poems were published *in Ilanga laseNatali*, a newspaper started by J. L. Dube in 1903. After the First World War there followed a remarkable outburst of heroic praise-poetry publication in African languages, including those in southern Sotho (Z. D. Mangoaela 1921), Zulu (James Stuart's five collections, 1923–26, C. L. S. Nyembezi 1958), Xhosa (H. M. Ndawo 1925, 1939) northern Sutho (D. M. Phala 1935), and Malawi Ngoni (M. Read 1937).

In the 1920s, D. C. T. Bereng published praise poems of the Sotho King Mshweshwe, depicting him as the founder of the Sotho nation, and interspersing his description of heroic battles with passages of personal reflection, thought, and experiences. The end of the Second World War saw the publications by E. M. Ramaila (1935) on northern Sutho praise poetry, and the momentous annotated volumes of the Oxford University Press series "The Oxford Library of African Literature" that includes I. Schapera's volume for Setswana (1965), Trevor Cope's volume for Zulu (1968), D. P. Kunene's (1971) and M. Damane and P. B. Sanders's (1974) volumes for Sesotho, and Margaret Read's volume on praise poetry of the Malawi Ngoni (1956). In 1932 Cambridge University Press also came up with *The Growth of Literature*, in three volumes, edited by Chadwick and Chadwick (1932–40).

Later publications on praise poetry have been of a more critical nature, and these have included C. L. S. Nyembezi's "The Historical Background to the Izibongo of the Zulu Military Age," in *African Studies* 8 (1948): 110–25, 157–74; Harold Scheub's *The Xhosa Ntsomi* (1975); Jeff Opland's *Xhosa Oral Poetry* (1983); David K. Rycroft's *The Praises of Dingana* (1988); the seminal work by Leroy Vail and Landeg White, *Power and the Praise Poem: Southern African Voices in History* (1991); and Elizabeth Gunner and Mafika Gwala's *Musho! Zulu Popular Praises* (1994). The *Power and the Praise Poem: Southern African Voices in History*

(1991) takes a subcontinental view of the occurrence of heroic praise poetry and analyzes examples of such poems from Malawi, Mozambique, Zimbabwe, Swaziland, and South Africa to describe and substantiate the esthetics of praise poetry. The authors also deliver a powerful indictment against the anthropological theories that dominated earlier research in oral expression because of their reinforcement of an evolutionist attitude toward Third World cultures as primitive, and criticize the subsequent emphasis on the internal form of oral expression which results in a neglect of pertinent questions about the content of oral expression in its social setting. Lupenga Mphande's "Ngoni Praise Poetry and the Nguni Diaspora" (1993) extends the study of praise poetry to those Nguni communities that left South Africa during the *mfecane* and settled in lands as far away as East and Central Africa. David Copland, in *In the Time of Cannibals: The Word Music of Basotho Migrants* (1994) examines aspects of hybridity in praise poetry in an urban setting and the artistic repertoire of migrant workers in southern Africa.

The word *izibongo* comes from the Nguni verb /-bonga/, "to praise, give thanks, express gratitude, worship, pray to, offer sacrifice, give and be appreciative by evoking the clan name of the one being praised," etc. Thus the word has social, political, and religious connotations, all of which are important in its interpretation. The Zulu word also refers to the "praise name(s)" that an individual is given or gives himself/herself, and means to "praise," "laud," "extol," "utter praises of." Naming means "identifying," and the "praise names" are meant to give a concise description or epitomization of an event or action in the person's life, his achievements or failures, or a peculiar physical characteristic.

A praise name is different from a clan name, which usually is the name of the founder of the clan, and, as such, represents social identity and is often used for tracing genealogy and kinship relationship. Because praise poetry expresses publicly, and therefore reaffirms, social identity whenever it is performed, *izibongo* never take place in isolation but are always embedded in social life. Although the types of praise poems vary widely from birth praises, wedding praises, dirges, beer party praises, workers' praises, war praises, love praises, political praises, topical praises, to heroic praises, they all unite in naming, identifying, and therefore giving significance to the named person or object. The language used in praise poetry is characterized by the use of formulaic poetic devices (e.g., repetition, linking, parallelism, etc.) and by an accentuation of rhythm that leads the performer to chant rather than recite the poem, which in turn helps the audience to participate and remember. What distinguishes praise poetry from everyday speech is its unlimited use of the common euphonic qualities of alliteration, assonance, and onomatopoeia, buttressed by extended simile. The most formalized language, and thus the one indicating the highest social significance, is reserved for heroic praise poems, which are like eulogies, odes, and epics in that they project their subjects in a favorable light and record historical events. Unlike epics, which are projected as complete historical records, heroic praise poems deal with current, and therefore partial, historical events. While odes are inclined to reflect on philosophy and philosophical theory, heroic praise poems are based on social theory and action, and this multifunctional, multifaceted aspect of the heroic poetry art form makes it difficult to define because it incorporates a spectrum of political, poetic, and literary qualities. The praises of the rulers have a special status because the political leader is traditionally conceived as the center and symbol of unity of the community, and must thus be portrayed in the most impressive way. The greater the social significance involved, the greater the skill of praising needed for an adequate representation. Consequently, the *izibongo* of rulers constitute esthetically the most highly appreciated subgenre.

In southern African societies, social power relations intertwine with inherent oral art forms, so that if the object of praise is a ruler, the art of praising inevitably becomes the art of criticizing. In this regard, *izibongo* are central to the local language of politics, not only because of the esteemed genre of verbal art, but also because they are recognized as an important medium of political discourse that reflects the current political atmosphere in the community. In heroic praise poetry, praising always incorporates some negative characteristics into their subject's praises, marking what is laudable and what should be condemned. The praise poet applauds, and if necessary criticizes, political leadership in accordance with established values of the community. Therefore, even praise poets of the most powerful rulers cannot be regarded as mere flatterers at court because although they compose heroic poems as eulogies to powerful people, their compositions also have other social significances. Besides legitimating and entrenching the rule of the powerful ruler, heroic praise poetry provides a rallying point for communal identity and solidarity. For this reason, the political aspect of *izibongo* is itself part of its esthetics.

The basic structure of heroic praise poetry is a succession of praise names, arranged in such a way that there is a statement, extension, development, and conclusion. When reciting praises, the pauses that the artist makes after a praise name create the basic units of verses and stanzas. The most distinctive characteristics of heroic praise poetry in Nguni languages are its various structures of repetitiveness, such as alliterations, assonances, and parallelisms. Assonances, the means by which praise names are extensively linked to various human actions and qualities, usually dominate the *izibongo* literary text because of the characteristically elaborate noun-class system in Bantu languages. The subtle interplay of such linguistic features that comes about by the act of "nominalizing" things or actions by changing the prefix of the word to the noun-class produces a fascinating and much appreciated harmony and acoustic impact on the audience. The lyricism thus created is then synchronized with the repetitions at the content level to produce audial-rhymes so characteristic of poetic speech. The created harmony is just as important for an appreciation of praise poetry as the semantic import since praise poetry, like oral poetry as a whole, is performative. The performative nature of this genre of oral art also means that the whole range of "body-language," evident during recitation, is part of its normative form that underlines the narrated meaning in tone, mime, gesture, as well as audience responses. This wide range of stylistic repertoire in lyrical presentation of the individual praised is what makes praise poetry the highest form of literary expression among the Nguni-speaking people.

Praise poems are composed not only about chiefs, famous warriors, and prominent members of the nobility, but about ordinary people also, including women and herdsmen. There are, in addition, praise poems of clans and subdivisions of clans, of domestic animals, of wild animals, of trees and crops, of rivers, hills, and other scenic features, and of such inanimate objects as divining-bones. In modern times praise poems have even been composed about schools, railway trains, and bicycles (Schapera 1965:1). One of the most popular songs at workers' rallies in southern Africa today, "Shosholoza," is based on a praise poem to a train that used to transport migrant workers from the far outposts of the southern African subcontinent to the South African gold mines. There are praise poems to ancestors, and when praise poetry evokes the names of ancestors it provides the medium of communication between the living and the departed, and between the natural and the supernatural. Thus, naming of the ancestors in the praises is not simply an act of commemoration, but also a moment of invocation, a way of making them present.

Generally, praise poetry tends to have gender-specific themes, men's praises preoccupied with themes of war, honor, devotion, courage and bravery, chivalry, daring, adventure, combat, confrontation with the wild, manhood, etc., and women usually narrating themes concerned with domestic matters, womanhood, filial relationships, jealousies, but also with peace, courtesy, agricultural chores, futility of war, and so on. Elizabeth Gunner (1979) recorded many praises among Zulu women dealing with themes of identity, social status, and achievements articulated in discourses structured in traditionalist, polygamous households in contentious social relationships. Such poetry is regarded as a socially acceptable way of giving public expression to personal emotion.

The formal occasions at which praise-poetry performance has ceremonial functions include harvest festivals, weddings, and times of initiation. Because its esthetics are intrinsically linked to history, which is dramatically re-enacted in performance, praise poetry cannot be viewed in isolation from its social meaning. At each performance, therefore, the poet's words turn the physical presence of the praise poet and the audience into a metaphorical re-creation of history. Although we have no way of knowing when or how heroic praise poetry originated, it is likely that the recitation of praise names and praises was part of the socialization process, and that it was used to construct individual and collective identities. Supervisors of rites of passage ceremonies, regiment commanders, chiefs, princes, and princesses must have been largely responsible for the creation and memorization of praise poems. In the modern-day context, chiefs, kings, and politicians play an important role in the composition and recitation of heroic praise poems. Some heroic praise poems, such as "Praises for Mandela" by Zolani Mkiva which were performed during Nelson Mandela's inauguration as South Africa's first black president in May 1994, were composed in the recent past, as shown in their content. In contrast, however, others are generations old – for example, "Praises for first Zulu kings," recorded by James Stuart in *uKulumetule* (1925), A. T. Bryant in *Olden Times in Zululand and Natal* (1929), "Praises to Lobengula," first recorded by H. Depelchin and C. Croonenberghs (1882), and "Praises to Zwangendaba," first recorded in the 1930s by Margaret Read and published in *The Ngoni of Nyasaland* (1956). New praise poems are being composed all the time, especially by political functionaries, and in many cases variant forms of a particular poem exist, sometimes changing with location or generation. The differences in versions of the same poem come from the fact that praise poems are not static compositions; they are always revised and reformulated to incorporate new material relevant to the community for which they are composed, or to suit the changing times.

Heroic praise poetry can belong to literate peoples as well as to those lacking a written form of expression; it can be factual or fictional, modern or traditional. It is not of concern whether such folk narratives are based on some historical event or whether they are credible, though a great many do have value for the student of history. What is important is that they represent a form of art, and that they arise directly from the cultural bases of the communities in which they are found. While admitting that oral literature is not different from other forms of literature, Ruth Finnegan states that oral literature is "characterized by particular features to do with performance, transmission, and social context" (1970: 25). Mazizi Kunene says that heroic poetry such as that found in the Zulu language, being communal, requires a special method of presentation: "The poet does not just recite his poetry but acts it, uses variations of pitch, and aims at communicating his poem through the simulation of all the senses. He produces at one level a symphonic chant, at another, a drama, and at still another, a dance" (1970: 12).

Praise poetry, as folk narrative, is hardly distinguishable from a dramatic presentation and its rendering in written form falls short of achieving its goal of representing oral traditions. The praise poem is usually an act dramatically presented to an audience that frequently is itself part of the act. In interpreting the praise poem, therefore, the whole social context of the performance must be understood because the actor is performing within the confines of space, time, and social context. The fact that he belongs to a particular sex, age, and social group influence his narration, his narrative, and its reception by his audience. Although praise poetry contains all the elements generally found in the folk narrative, it is a highly stylized poetic form rendered by the speaker in chant rather than an ordinary speaking voice and accompanied by rhythmic body movements or even wild jumps during which stabbing movements are made with a spear or wooden staff. On the whole, words and acts complement each other in the recitation of praise poems. While heroic praise poetry like that of the Nguni- and Sotho-speaking peoples is historically based and event interpretive, it is not strictly a historical account, but a eulogy.

Scholars have viewed heroic praise poetry from different perspectives: historical, personal, social, political, and religious. David Rycroft, for example, states that the Zulu praise poems "play an active and essential role within traditional religion as a medium of communication between the living and the dead" (1988: 25). He refers to the special ceremonies held in the cattle byre (*kraal*) and involving the whole family, when praises are recited by the family head, and says that the appeal or prayer to the ancestors is expressed by the offering of the sacrificial beast. Thus, according to Rycroft, the poet/performer "becomes the intermediary between the ancestors and the people present." The problem with this historical perspective is that it puts orality and performance off stage from the contemporary political discourse.

The second perspective from which praise poetry is viewed is that which projects praise poetry as something "personal" to the poet/performer. Herbert Dlomo offers an idealized version of this view when he states that "praise poems were used as an urge to courage and endurance" (1947: 48), and that no one wanted to fall short of his "praises," in the sense that praise poems were bestowed on the heroes, thus "people would rather die than lose them." The advantage of this perspective is that it avoids the overemphasis on the text to the exclusion of all other features of praise poetry as was the case with the first perspective, and it projects the poet at the center stage of the contemporary social engagement. The weakness, though, is that in highlighting the individual it ignores the collective social function of praise poetry.

The third perspective emphasizes the social/political function of praise poetry. Trevor Cope states that *izibongo* are "the expression of public opinion, and provide an effective means of social control, for they are shouted out for all to hear" (1968: 21) and E. Krige states that they "are an important instrument in the educational system. Not only do they act as an incentive to and reward for socially approved actions, but their recital is a reminder to all present what qualities and conduct are praiseworthy" (quoted in Cope 1968: 21). The advantage of this perspective is that it focuses on the function of praise poetry, and projects praise poetry as part of the dominant culture and its performance as part of the process of socialization. But this perspective ignores the poet as an active agent in this process, and the poet's ability and capacity to manipulate the process for specific ends. It also neglects to acknowledge the possibility within the socialization process of resisting domination and the capacity of the poet to mediate between the dominant and dominated.

When analyzing heroic praise poetry, it is important to remember that orality and performance have to be approached from a balanced perspective that avoids projecting orality as a fossilized artifact, or the performer and audience as passive, disengaged bystanders. The perspective adopted by Vail and White (1991) situates the heroic praise poetry analysis within the theory of power relations and the dynamics of political dominance. Such a perspective has several advantages for analyzing praise poems – for example, it explains the logic of their organization: why they are the way they are, socially, culturally, politically, and religiously. It helps answer the question: why is it that some praises are peculiarly male, and what are the material justifications for that situation? It also highlights and explains the social control function they perform, and offers an insightful approach by creating a convergence of three perspectives: that from poet as agent, that from audience as object, and that from the praised as subject. This perspective has to be structured around and respond to the total performance as context; it enables us not only to say that heroic praise poetry in societies where it occurs is performed for heroes and chiefs, but also to explain that its performance is organized hierarchically because those societies are organized hierarchically. Thus the most famous recorded Zulu and Ndebele praise poems are about Shaka and Lobengula, respectively, because these Nguni societies are patriarchal and praise poetry is employed to both maintain and challenge the existing social structures. Therefore, although many cultures have praise poetry, we must examine how and by whom these are performed.

Praise poetry, as an institution, has long been part of the rural community in southern Africa. Vail and White state that praise poetry is a special form of expression among southern African societies whose oral performance is used in political discourse, and they declare it:

> is the region's oral poetry, subject to the esthetic we have described as poetic license, that gives access to the past and present intellectual life of the communities we describe. The poetry is the arena where competing "histories" clash, subjected not only to political revaluation but to moral and spiritual reassessment. (1991: xiii)

Singing praises of rulers and ruled has been a way of consolidating power and regulating the community. Traditionally, heroic praise poetry was performed only at court, usually inside the kraal, by a man recreating the battlefield, with a staff and/or shield, and before chiefs, kings, and the nobility. It was recited to a varied audience, of men and women, that included elders, important dignitaries, judges, and children. Nowadays, praise names can be recited to one's age group, and heroic praise poetry is also performed at festivals. The staff that the poet carries and the costume he wears help create the praise poetry tradition as well as a mystic aura. The praise poet, who is usually given enough space at performance site to allow movement, usually walks up and down when reciting, staff in hand. He shouts out the praises at the top of his voice as fast as he can, as if trying to cast a spell on the audience with a shower of words. Today praise poetry can also be performed in any of the modern sites of political life, including school halls, stadiums, trade union meetings, and parliament.

Praise poets enjoy considerable privileges since chiefs and those praiseworthy usually have a lot of wealth at their disposal. As a result, praise poets are usually employed by the rulers they praise and from whom they earn their income and receive gifts and major assets such as cattle and land. This fact may raise a serious question about their credibility: if they are recorders of history, whose history do they record? Praise poetry is performed for social maintenance, and the chiefs and politicians use praise poets to make claims to power, and thus legitimize their power against other claimants. From this standpoint, the advantage of studying heroic praise poetry from a "political dominance" perspective is that it forces us to focus on the language used in the performance, and enables us to re-examine traditional cultures and interrogate how ideas become hegemonic.

In studying praise poetry, it is as important to pay attention to the moment of its production as to its reception. The former helps us to tie the past to historical interpretation, while the latter helps us to understand how the past is recovered in the context of present demands. In terms of its production, praise poets are trained, within their cultural environment, by more experienced poets who provide the model and supervise the rehearsals. A praise poet may be recognized as such from early childhood, and may then be entrusted as an apprentice to an experienced poet from whom he learns the traditional way of presenting the art form. The initiate and experienced poet train and rehearse in relative seclusion, and many poets learn the art of reciting praises within their families before they can perform in public. Praise poetry involves public rendition because although there are domestic praises performed, the most memorable ones are done at large events before a substantial audience. The trainee recites the praises, including the accompanying nonverbal behavior, and trainers discuss the performances and make comments. It is here that the initiate learns the appropriate voice qualities for effective performance, learns how to hold the traditional poet's staff, how to jab with it, how to stomp and pace the ground with his feet, how to position his body, and what costume to wear at what occasion. The young poet also learns the language of praise poetry: what form to use, what epithets, what imagery, what mnemonic devices to employ, and how to improvise. In the case of southern African societies, during the process of training and learning, full advantage is taken of the strong rhythmical patterning of Bantu languages, which is characteristic of the diction of praise-poetry presentation.

A praise poet, known as an *imbongi* in Zulu, can be a man or woman, ranging from twenty years to middle age. The poet has to be a person of repute because one of his tasks is to create solidarity within society by presenting himself as a "negotiator" in the power discourse between the ruler and ruled. This show of solidarity is intended to entrench political power, and is achieved through the imposition of the official transcript of history. However, there is always resistance to such imposition by the subordinate class, and the praise poet is deployed to negotiate such tensions in society. The structure and function of the praise poetry institution is not fixed but is highly flexible and adaptable, and the poet's qualities as performer include an ability to adapt to the immediate sociopolitical environment. Therefore, the poet is able to criticize the ruler when it is most appropriate to do so, and praise him on other occasions. In other words, the poet has to adapt, reconfigure, or compose afresh whenever he is in a new space.

Any discussion of praise poetry would be incomplete without further examination of the institution of the praise poet, who is, after all, the composer of praise poetry. For effective performance, the praise poet, appreciating the immense value of the visual image in bringing home a scene to the general audience, makes a note of any authentic details in the people's experiences that he can discover which are likely to assist in creating a visual image – names of rivers and mountains, position of the sun, weather condition, appearance of characters, etc. – things probably of little consequence in themselves. These are observations of the visual detail of history that the praise poet musters and puts to imaginative use. The details about the people's migration and adventure, about geography, community, history, mothers and herdsboys are all selected, organized, and related to the story of the hero being praised in such a way as to illuminate, in an elevated style, the essentials of his life, personality, and achievements. These poems, then, collectively constitute an epic celebration of the hero, and illustrate the relationship between literary or esthetic sensibility and history. In the vast knowledge about the hero that the praise poet has accumulated over the years, he or she selects a few striking details that light up praises about the personal appearance and characteristics of the hero, projected against a great event of history. The praise poet is thus interested not in history but in the reformulation of culture based on historical knowledge; the poet makes the imaginative leap that all literature must perform to strike through the surface facts to some deeper, less expressible truth about life and death, and the reality of imagination.

In his or her function as a historian, the praise poet attempts to mediate, within the historical field, among the unprocessed historical record, other historical accounts, and an audience. The structure of praise poetry, therefore, can be defined as belonging more to that of a chronicle than a story. "Chronicle" differs from a "story" in that, according to White (1973: 6), the latter traces the sequence of events that lead from inaugurations to termination of social and cultural processes, whereas the former is open-ended: it has no inauguration; it simply begins when the praise poet starts recording events. In other words, a chronicle has no culmination or resolution, and can go on indefinitely, and the task of the praise poet is to explain the past by "finding," "identifying," or "uncovering" the stories that lie buried in chronicles. The basic difference between "history" and "fiction," therefore, resides in the fact that the historian has to "find" his stories, whereas the praise poet "invents" his.

It is the characteristic of the praise poet as a "negotiator and catalyst" that renders the praise poetry genre easily adaptable to other uses, and a popular feature of modern-day political performance. The ambiguous political role of the praise poet facilitates this process, because not only is he or she privy to strategies of encoding and decoding of both the powerful and the powerless, but both groups acknowledge to a greater or lesser extent his/her role as a performer of the negotiation. The praise poet, as an intermediary between the ruler and the ruled, redraws the boundaries of experience according to the spaces in which he or she works, and according to the power dynamics at work in those spaces. The poet's position in the community relies on his or her ability to gauge the political currents in the community, to extemporize and compose, and to use the esthetics of persuasion to sway audiences with his or her performance. It is precisely these qualities that make the praise poet (and praise poetry) susceptible to appropriation by powerful forces in society, such as chiefs, politicians, and organizations. In the southern African case, with the vast migrant labor system that came with industrialization and urbanization, many of the cultural activities of the rural communities followed the migrant worker into the city. Because they were performing now to a more diverse audience, the praise poets were also being asked to create and recite in English as a lingua franca.

The recitation of heroic praise poetry among the Nguni-speaking people opens and closes with an antiphonal call-and-response formula: for example, *Wena we ndlovu,* "You of the elephant," at the beginning, and *Bayeede! Ndabe zitha,* "Hail to the king!" at the end. These are not just opening and closing devices, they are also meant to enlist audience participation in the performance. The style employed in performing heroic praise poetry depends on many factors. The sex and age of the performer, for example, determine the vigor of the performance and the costume used: younger performers tend to be more vigorous than older ones; and male performers wear skins, carry long sticks, spears, and shields, while their female counterparts wear colorful beaded cloths, carry shorter sticks, leaves, or fly whisks. In the more traditional setting, there are no restrictions on the performer's movement, but in an urban setting, because of the use of microphones and public address systems, praise poetry performers tend to be rooted in one spot on the stage during performance, usually near the microphone. The restrictions in movement of the urban performer may seriously limit his ability to deploy some nonverbal features, such as gesture and pacing, as effective tools in the execution of his performance.

As regards its reception, the performance of heroic praise poetry is a display of the people's linguistic and literary culture, and exposes the younger generation to their cultural heritage. One of the functions of praise-poetry performance is entertainment: the sheer delight and beauty of praise poetry is regarded by Nguni-speaking people as their highest form of literary expression. Praise poetry also teaches the young, and reminds the old, of their past: their history, heroes, culture, and identity. Furthermore, praise poetry instructs about nature, human destiny, human relationships, and the relationship between man and nature. It expands the audience's worldview and ensures that children have access to their rightful heritage.

Use of appropriate and effective language is of paramount importance to the praise poets in executing their trade because they have to create an emotional atmosphere and touch the imagination of their audience. Praise poetry uses cadences and tonal fluctuations characteristic of the southern Bantu languages, and the linguistic features of alliteration, rhyme, symmetry, parallelism, harmony, repetition, simile and comparison, and idiomatic and symbolic language. If the execution is successful, there is always the sheer delight of the rhythm of the praise poem for the attentive audience. The following is an example of a praise poem, "Praises of Nzibe, son of Senzangakhona," recorded by James Stuart (1925: 238–39):

"Praises of Nzibe, son of Senzangakhona"

Unombambamajozi, kaQengwa!
Ubhukudi's abantu esizibaneni,
Ize bashone nezinjotshana zabo;
Umsuka wezul' eliphezulu.
Usompomp' odlel' endlebeni yendlovu
Unyakawumbe uzodlela kwengonyana.
Usokhethabahle naseMnyameni.
Zidla la bekudla khon' amadube nezindlovu.
ZinjengezikaNgudu emaMbatheni.
UNingizimu-vimbel'-nyakatho;
Ugcwayis' iziziba.
Inkom'-ekhal'-ehlungwini, kwaMlambo;
INgweny'-edl'-umuntu, inxe imlinde;
USihlangu sibukelwa undiyaza;
UGogod' -oyihluzayo.
UNkhon' -unamagabel'-amanxeba;
UMzimb'-unabenge lazitha.
INkayishan' encinyane, kaMenzi;
Uchachaz'-amathaf'-akulingene.
(WuNzibe-ke lowo)

Grabber-of-broad-stabbing-spear, son of Qengwa!
He plunges people into a river pool,
Until even their little loin-cloths disappear;
Msuka of the high heavens.
Bold-speaker who eats in the ear of an elephant,
Another year and he will eat in a lion's.
Chooser-of-handsome-ones even at Mnyameni.
The-one-whose-cattle-eat-on-the-Lubombo-mountains-without-falling,
They eat where zebra and elephants were eating;
Resembling Ngudu's cattle, of the emaMbatheni.
South-wind-opposing-the-North-wind;
He causes the river-pools to fill up.
Cow-lowing-in-the-burnt-veld, at Mlambo
Crocodile-that-mauls-a-person, and stands guard over him.
Shield watched only by the Ndiyaza trees;
Clean-licker-of-the-pot who reduces himself.
Forearm-with-wounds like the hide-strips on a shield;
Body-like-a-heap-of-meat-strips of the enemies.
Tiny fearless bird of Menzi;
Trampler-of-dry-river-beds.
Fast-runner-over-plains-that-are-your-equal.

(That is Nzibe)

In this poem we can see how praise poetry displays a wide range of stylistic devices and encompasses a variety of layers of meaning. Nzibe, who died young, was King Mpande's younger brother, and was brother also to Shaka and Dingana. The poet contrasts the images of gruesome destruction and the bloodbath wrought by the young Nzibe with those of a more settled existence that would perhaps have been more fitting for the young prince. Nzibe is described as a ruthless, merciless warrior: a courageous fighter, a bold speaker, a "crocodile-that-mauls-a-person, and stands guard over him," and a "fearless bird," and these qualities are declaimed with boastful relish: "He plunges people into a river pool / Until even their little loin-cloths disappear." This bold imagery of the ruthless killing of rivals is contrasted with a description of a serene landscape of another more peaceful period in history when these same battlefields were grazing grounds for "zebra and elephants." The poet does this by use of vivid imagery drawn from sharp epithets, simile and comparison.

In southern African languages, praise poetry also enables the display of fascinating language features, such as clicks and laterals, peculiar to Southern Bantu languages that add melody and luster to praise poetry performance.

The poet's task in reciting praise poetry, therefore, is to use tone and pitch in a way that maximizes the advantages of these linguistic features in creating an emotional atmosphere and touching the imagination of his audience. It also enables the younger members of the audience to expand their vocabulary and master the figurative use of the language.

In discussing heroic praise poetry context is indispensable; without it certain critical aspects of praise poetry's interpretation would be missed, and context provides the distinctive controlling motifs that determine its structure. In early Nguni praises, like the praise to Nzibe above, it is easy to see how praise poetry, as a mode of performance and a form of cultural production, is profoundly embedded in the historical context of its production. For an accurate interpretation of heroic praise poetry of that period, an awareness of the impact of the *mfecane,* or the scattering of the various Nguni and Sotho ethnic groups over the broad range of southern, central, and eastern Africa, is absolutely crucial. It is generally agreed that this "scattering" of people resulted largely from the rise of Shaka Zulu in Natal, and his attempts to forge a Zulu nation out of the fragmented social landscape of the time. From oral tradition, Shaka was a junior son of Senzangakhona, ruler of a small Nguni chiefdom known as Zulu, who wrested the throne from his father's nominated heir by brilliant military innovation and ceaseless conquest. Between 1818 and 1828, Shaka Zulu welded several Nguni clans into one powerful Zulu nation, while dispersing his enemies across the subcontinent as far afield as Zimbabwe, Mozambique, Zambia, Malawi, and Tanzania. In 1828, Shaka was assassinated by his half-brother, Dingana, who then took over as the ruler of the Zulu nation until he too was ousted by his other half-brother, Mpande.

Some of the most colorful Nguni heroic praise poems are about Shaka and those of his contemporaries who participated in, or were affected by, the *mfecane*, depicting their military campaigns and string of victories in their efforts to subdue their rivals and legitimize their claim to power. Both the adulation of Shaka as an early African (and Zulu) nationalist, and the resultant migrations and movements of the Nguni and Sotho peoples have been richly recorded in a fascinating corpus of heroic oral poetry. The following, for example, is a praise poem to Shaka recorded in Mzimba district, northern Malawi in 1996, and performed by J. C. Dlamini, one of the three official praise poets of the current Zulu ruler, King Zwelethini Zulu. The praise poet had accompanied the king's sister, Princess Thembi, on her official delegation to the Northern Ngoni of Malawi, descendants of Zwangendaba, one of the war heroes of the *mfecane* who had broken away from Shaka in 1820 and migrated northward with his followers. The poem was first recorded by James Stuart and published in 1925:

"Izibongo kaShaka (Inkondlo yenkosi Ushaka)"

Wena wendlovu!
Wena wendlovu!
Bayeede!

Udlungwane luka Ndaba
Oludlunge emanxulumeni
Kwaze kwasa amanxuluma esebikelana

Ilembe eleqa amanye amalembe ngoku khalipha
Unodum'ehlezi kaMenzi
Usishaya kashayeki
UShaka ngiyesaba nokuthi uShaka
Ngoba uShaka kwakuy'inkosi yaseMashobeni

Uteku lwababafazi bakwa noMgabi
Obelutekula behlezi emlovini
Bethi uShaka kayikubusa
Bethi kayikuba yinkosi

Kanti kulapho ezakunethezeka khona
Umlilo obuthethe kaMjokwana
Umlilo obuthethe osh'ubuhanguhangu
Oshise izikhotha ezisedlebe
Kwaze kwaye kwasha neziseMabedlana

Inkomo ekhale emthonjaneni
Izizwe zonke ziyizwile ukulila
Izwiwe udunga wase yengweni
Yazwiwa umancengetha wakwaKhali
Okhangele ezansi kwama Dungelo

Izinkomo zawosihayo zamlandela
Uye walandelwa ezakwa Mfongosi
Ezazisengwa lindiki okwakungela kwaMavela

UNgamende odle amabele engakadliwa
UNdabezitha wamaShongololo
Bampheke ngembiza ebipheke amakhosi akwaNtombazi
Bazi ukuthi uShaka akancengwa
Wazilanda izinkomo zazilandwe nguMakhedama ekhaBonina
Izulu elidume enhlakomuzi nasekuqabekeni
Lidume lazithatha izihlangu nezaMaphela kwaduma amahlanjwana
Ezalwa uZwide eMapheleni

Wadla unqabomi ezalwa uZwide eMapheleni
Wadl' unkondo kwela kwaZwide eMapheleni
Wadl' uMdadlathi kwabakaGagca
Wadl' unoziGcabo kwabakaNtatho
Wadl' uNkayitshana kwabaseCocweni
Wadl' uNkayitshana kwabaseCocweni

Odade ngankhalo obunye ngankhalo
Odabule emathanjeni
Abantwana bakwaTeya
Ababegodola kwabakaMacingwane lapho engonyameni

Inkonyane ekhwele phezu kwendlu kaNtombazi
Bathi iyahlola kanti sekuyibona abahlolayo
Indlovu ethe ibuka babehlokovukela abakwaLanga
Indlovu ebuyise inhloko yadl'amadoda
Usishaya ndlondlo kaMjokwane
Ubusika nehlobo kwehluleke abakwaNtombazi

AbakwaLanga bathi behlezi phezulu
Banquma ukuba abakwaNyuswa
Kwaku ngalutho nabaNyuswa
Kwakuzinqakuva nje!
ZiseManxiweni
Zizinteke-nteke zizidlel'amajuba

Inyathi ejame ngomkhonto lapho phezu komzimvubu
AmamPondo ayisabile njengenyoka yehlela
nani boGambushe
nani boFaku
Nize ningamthinthi nomntakaNdaba
Kuyothi kubanimthintile nobe nithinthe ithuna nathinth'uMageba
Usiba gojela ngale Nkandla
Lugojela njalo ludla amadoda namadojeyana
UGasane olwakithi kwaBulawayo
Kade kwasa lugasela imizi yamadoda
Lugasele uPhungashe ezalwa kwa Buthelezi
Lugasele uMacingwane engowa seNgonyameni
Lwagasela uGambushe engowa seMampondweni
Lwagasela uFaku engowa seMampondweni
Yayingasakhali inkomo yakwaNtombazi
Inkomo yayisikhala inthi
Nani bakwaBulawayo uhlanya lusemehlweni lwamadoda

Inyoni kaNdaba ethe isadl'ezinye yaphinde yadl'ezinye
Yath' isadl'ezinye yabuye yadl'ezinye

Yath' isadl'ezinye yabuye yadl'ezinye
Yath' isadl'ezinye yabuye yadl'ezinye

Hlanga lomhlabathi

Wena wendlovu!

(Translation by Phiwase Dlamini)
You, (born) of the elephant!
You, (born) of the elephant!
Hail to the king!

Dlunga, descendants of Ndaba
Who rises from poor heritage
Like waves that rise above all others
Who overtakes all others because of his intelligence
You are popular posing as you do, son of Menzi
They are trying to defeat you
But nobody calls Shaka's name in vain
Because Shaka you are a king of Shobani

The women ridiculers of Mgabi
Women ridiculers of Emlovini
Who said Shaka will never rule, will never be king
Yet now they are the ones proven wrong

Fire that caught quickly of Mjokwana
Flames that leapt suddenly
That burnt the overgrowth of Dlebe
And reached Mabedlana

The bull that bellows at Mthonjaneni
All the nations heard that bellow
Dunga heard it from Yengweni
Mancengetha from Khali heard it
Who gazed down at the Dungelo

Then Sihayo's cattle followed the bellow
Mfongosi's cattle did the same
Milked by initiate from Mavera

The Ngamende who ate the sorghum before it was ripe
The prince of the Shongololo
Who cooked him in a pot where by the kings of Ntombazi are cooked
Knowing that you Shaka is not coaxed
He collected his cattle of Makhedama of Ekhabonina
The thunder that roared from outside the village at Qabekeni
It roared and smashed the shields of Maphela

There roared/ scattered little leaves
Born from Zwide at Mapheleni
Seized Nqaboni born of Zwide of Mapheleni
Seized Nkondo in Zwide's land at Mapheleni
Seized Mdadlathi from the Gagca
Seized Lady Zigcabo from the Ntatho
Seized Nkayitshana from Concweni
Seized Nkayitshana from Concweni

Odade ngankhalo obunye ngankhalo
Odabule emathanjeni
Abantwana bakwaTeya

Who were feeling cold of Macingwane there at Engonyameni
The calf that climbed on top of the house of Ntombazi
They said it was an omen and yet they were part of its revelation
The elephant that when it looks, people of langa flee for their lives
The elephant that brought sense to men
The one that defeated the python of Mjokwane
In both winter and summer it felled people of Ntombazi
People of Langa as they sat on top (proudly)
They resolved to call themselves the Nyuswa
It meant nothing to be a Nyuswa
It is people deserving no respect at all
They are like waste left at the ruins
These weaklings who cannot even catch a pigeon

The hippo, poised to fight with a spear there on top of an alligator
They feared the snake slithering down the descent
You too the Gambushe
You too the Faku
Do not provoke the son of Ndaba
Otherwise you lead yourself into the grave

You provoke Mageba
The feather that destroys beyond Nkhandla
It destroys everything, it captures men, useless men
Gasane is one of us in Bulawayo
He has forever been attacking villages of men
He attacked Phungase born of the Buthelezi clan
He attacked Macingwane who is from Engonyameni
He attacked Gambushe who is from Emampondweni (Pondoland)
He attacked Faku who is from Emampondweni
He was bellowing so loud, the bull of Ntombazi
Then the bull bellowed thus:
To you people of Bulawayo the madman is before the men

The insatiable bird of Ndaba that eats others, and again eats others
While eating others it comes back to eat more
While eating others it comes back to eat more
While eating others it comes back to eat more

The reed of the soil
You of the elephant!

As can be seen, the historical context of *mfecane* in interpreting this poem is indispensable, otherwise references to the brutal clubbing of Shaka's enemies would be rendered incomprehensible, as would the catalogue of rival players and clans, and phrases like "To you people of Bulawayo the madman is before the men." The multiple repetition in reference to "The insatiable bird of Ndaba that eats others, and again eats others" is shorter than the one found in Cope (1968) and contains an ambiguity central to the discussion of the political/social mediative function of the praise poet. The reference to his insatiability could not have been said with such bluntness before Shaka himself, but since this poem is recited before a present-day Malawi Ngoni audience, themselves victims of Shaka's ruthlessness, the audience is likely to interpret the poet's words as vindicating them: that their ancestors were right to leave South Africa almost two hundred years ago because Shaka had gone crazy and become "insatiable" for human blood. Shaka's bravery, strength, power, and ruthlessness can, in this depiction, be said to be lauded as well as indirectly criticized. Since the Ngoni audience's own identity is partly based on Shaka's depiction as an insatiable killer as a plausible justification for their leaving South Africa that long ago, the past becomes a re-usable capital by both the performer and the audience, an important function of praise poetry, a strategic gesture of the bond between the Nguni in the diaspora and those who were left behind.

Similarly, praises of the Sotho King Mshweshwe display the same characteristic preoccupation with the *mfecane*. D. C. T. Bereng's praise poems, for example, derive their strength not only from the description of Mshweshwe as the founder of the Sotho nation, but also from a memorialization of the numerous battles fought, and victories won, by gallant Sotho soldiers fleeing Shaka's invaders. As an instrument of history, heroic poetry reveals an interesting correlation between the imaginative function of literature and the use of narrative in the construction of a collective identity. A study of the *mfecane*-related heroic praise poems reveals how the literary tradition substantiates history, and clarifies the nature of the interplay between the history of migration and the literary expression. It also reveals the social-historical forces that led to the construction of myths from historical realities, and enables us to examine the basic functions of praise poetry in society (i.e., as a source of collective identity), the changes in these functions that may have occurred over time, and the extent to which praise poetry performance is a forum for the articulation of power politics.

Going farther afield from the immediacy of the South African praise poetry landscape, the case of the Ngoni of Malawi, Mozambique, Tanzania, and Zambia offers the best example of how this genre of literary expression can be adequately organized around the theme of migration, partly because these groups traveled the longest distance from their original "base" in KwaZulu-Natal in South Africa to Lake Victoria in East Africa. Because praise poetry is set within a clearly identifiable time scale and deals with acknowledged historical events, it is quite feasible to organize it within specific controlling motifs. The first such organizing motif is the theme of the "diaspora," which can be defined by differentiating it from the word "migration," a word that researchers have used to describe the migrating Nguni and their heritage. The movement of a population from one geographical area to another, in this sense, the movement of the Nguni people out of their original area in KwaZulu-Natal to their various new locations throughout the subcontinent, can be described as migration. But migration presumes no continued relationship, physical or abstract, with the original base. Diaspora, on the other hand, not only refers to the dispersal of a population from its original base, but also the population's continued connection, physical or spiritual, with its "homeland." This relationship can also manifest itself in the imaginative expression – art, music, dance, song, poetry, and other cultural forms – some of which might revolve around the very theme of the diaspora. Therefore, the use of the term diaspora helps us to describe and explain the complex series of events and processes of migrations, but also assists in bringing about a cognitive grasp of what caused the departure from the original base, and the impact the rupture has had on the people who participated in it or those with whom the migrating groups came into contact.

The second organizing motif in Nguni and Sotho heroic praise poetry is found in the underlying theme of departure, so that there is constant reference to forced departure, as we find in the Zimbabwe Ndebele and Malawi Ngoni praise poetry. This theme of departure shows two aspects of migration: the actual, physical departure from South Africa, and the symbolic departure from the "homeland." The actual departure of the Ndebele and Ngoni from South Africa is depicted in their praise poetry as having been a very traumatic experience, one that tore them not only from their native soil, but from their kith and kin. In "Praises of Lobengula" and "Praises of Zwangendaba," there is a description of pillage and destruction of wars, and the language used is lofty, symbolic of its patriotic appeal. The poet chooses the language designed to engage the audience in the people's heroic struggle to defend themselves against formidable odds posed by Shaka's armies. Thus the language reflects not only the Ndebele and Ngoni splendor and ceremony as ruling classes in the respective communities where they eventually settled, but also the history of hardships they endured as a consequence of the upheaval caused by the *mfecane*.

There is another aspect of the departure motif, particularly relevant to Ngoni praise poetry, which comes from their symbolic break with their "homeland" symbolized by the crossing of the Zambezi River. This event, more than any other, seems to have had the deepest impact on the Ngoni creative imagination. The crossing of the Zambezi has also a religious value in the sense that it becomes a landmark and a point of transition in Ngoni history and subsequent social organization. The Ngoni had lived in Zimbabwe for about eight years, and had no doubt kept abreast of what was happening in their "homeland" across the Limpopo, particularly in matters relating to their kith and kin. With the crossing of the "mighty" river, that umbilical cord was being finally severed, with clear psychological consequences to the individuals. In many of the praise poems composed by the Ngoni on the crossing of the Zambezi River, the praise poet, as chronicler of events, picks out the threads that link this event to other different historical factors, identifying and tracing the threads outward into the natural and social space within which the event occurred, and both backward in time to the *mfecane* in order to determine the "origins" of the crossing, and forward in time, in order to determine its "impact" and "influence" on subsequent events. The following poem, describing how the Malawi Ngoni crossed the Zambezi, reveals how traumatic this event must have been for them as a final break from their "homeland":

Siwel' IZembezi sawela ngenthambo
    Samwela ngenthambo
    Samwela ngenthambo
Mnawo yayoya
    Sekwahlw' emini
Mnawo yayoya
    Se kwash' ubhani

When crossing the Zambezi we crossed with a rope
    We crossed it with a rope
    We crossed it with a rope

The sky darkened at day time
The lightning flashed.

The repetition of "We crossed it with a rope" highlights the means by which such a break was accomplished, and emphasizes the significance of rope in Ngoni society. Rope is the means by which things are bound together, it is the means by which people construct bridges that link areas on either side of a river. But the term "rope," is ambiguous, for it stands for the means by which desperate people commit suicide – a means by which a final break is made! Rope in the poem above is, therefore, symbolic of the new umbilical connecting all the Ngoni in a new community, and their final break with the past.

Because the Zambezi River is such an important landmark in the people's collective experience, there are many stories among the Ngoni about how they crossed the mighty river, and this multiplicity is a reflection of the ambiguity of poetic language – a single word can mean different things to different people in different situations. Where several versions of the same incident exist, what the ordinary person says about such an incident becomes crucial to its interpretation. Sometimes separate poems on the same event are composed which may eventually merge into one, but often one composition may crystallize into different versions, depending on the performer and situation. Although it remains an analysis of a specific Ngoni event situated in time and place, the incident involving the crossing of the Zambezi is a good example of multiple narration in praise poetry. Ngoni chronicles, as alluded to in the poem above, claim that soon after crossing the Zambezi sudden darkness descended on them and that the sun disappeared at midday: "The sky darkened at day time / The lightning flashed." This reference to the darkening sun has been attested by the recording of the total eclipse of the sun in November 1835, and this has helped historiographers date the time of Zwangendaba's crossing of the Zambezi – thus raising this incident out of its oral timelessness. Therefore, the praise poem's image of the crossing of the Zambezi has been explained by astronomy, and, in a measure, the historicity of praise poetry has been vindicated.

Wandering and adventure form the third major motif of the heroic praise poetry of the Ngoni. The Zwangendaba Ngoni could be said to originate from their crossing of the Zambezi, and that, from then onward, Ngoni history (and therefore Ngoni memory) becomes divided into how they refer to the people they left behind and the people they met, and how these two facts impacted their culture and way of life. Ngoni language, through heroic praise poetry, is called upon to mediate these two dialectically opposed references. To the Ngoni, the separation from their kind was not just a reminder of the dangers of their wandering and bitterness of their suffering, but was also a mark of the resilience of their culture, the survival of their traditions etched in the folds of the fondness of their imagination. This self-confidence gave the Ngoni the ability to integrate into, and absorb, other cultures – a point of loss and gain. Praise poetry thus fulfills an ideological function in the Ngoni society: it rationalizes Ngoni conquest and legitimizes Ngoni chieftaincy and the political system of dominance.

The religious beliefs of Africans and the lofty and persuasive nature of their language and poetry made it more tempting for the Christian missionaries to appropriate and adapt the praise poetry for their proselytization. Margaret Read recounts a typical example of the process of appropriation of African cultural expressions such as praise poetry by European colonizers. She says when "the party of Europeans . . . watched the rhythm and dignity of the dances they were so favorably impressed that they asked the Paramount Chief to send senior men to teach the songs and dances to the boys in the mission schools." After that, she continues, "the songs were used in the churches of the Scottish mission with different words written for them" (1956: 45). The points of appropriation of these indigenous cultural expressions were the sacred places, such as the kraal at the chief's court, which is the usual site of Ngoni praise poetry performance. It is important to note here that, in this appropriation process, the chief's "senior men" do not have to be converted to Christianity before their culture can be taken over – the initial aim is not to convert, but to take over the cultural production and through it establish domination.

It is not just Europeans and the Christian missions who have learned how to dominate and control indigenous African people through their cultural expressions; African leaders themselves also practice a degree of appropriation for their own political capital. With rapid social and political change in Africa, it was soon recognized that here was an art form not typical of Eurocentric culture, one deeply ingrained in black cultural power. Politicians realize that the praise poets are a vital feature in the rejuvenation of African traditions, and systematically use them to re-valorize the precolonial "authentic" cultural values, and also utilize selected phenomena taken from their traditional cultures to legitimate their power through the orally transmitted recitations of their various accomplishments. Therefore, in southern Africa praise poetry continues to function in that contentious space between politics and power. Many scholars have lamented the "decline" or disappearance of praise poetry due to the invasion of modernity in the political sphere, but such a lament is premature and ignores the capacity of the praise poetry institution to adapt to new situations. This capacity is based, among other things, on praise-poetry flexibility in content and form.

The adaptation is also evident in modern literary expression. To give but a few examples, in Xhosa praise poetry tradition, poets David Yali-Manisi and S. M. Z. Burns-Ncamashe, following the example of S. E. K. Mqhayi in the 1920s, use praise poetry to foreground issues of desegregated educational opportunities. In the Zulu tradition, praise poets such as J. C. Dlamini have found themselves entrapped in sectarian politics that have pitted the African National Congress (ANC), whose government pays their king and chiefs, against the forces of Inkatha who want to use the praise-poetry tradition to rekindle passions of past Zulu glory and claim more regional autonomy. Alfred Temba Qabula devotes his praise poems not to the eulogy of Xhosa chieftaincy, but to the trades union movement that is now depicted as the true "protector" of the workers as the traditional Nguni chiefs were the protectors of their subjects.

Praise poetry can be studied because of the insights it offers into the topic of oral heritage that continues to flourish in written literature today as regards the thematic and stylistic foundations. It would be nearly impossible to study and comprehend Mazisi Kunene's *Emperor Shaka the Great*, for example, without a full understanding of the structure, functions and meaning of Zulu praise poetry. In fact, Kunene's work demonstrates that, in southern Africa at least, praise poetry is not something of the past, but has a vibrant coexistence with modern African written literature.

Bibliography

Arbousset, T. 1842. *Relation d'un voyage d'exploration au nord-est de la Colonie du Cap de Bonne Espérance*. Paris: Arthus Bertrand.

Bryant, A. T. 1929. *Olden Times in Zululand and Natal*. London: Longmans. Republished in 1965 by Stuik in Cape Town.

Casalis, E. 1841. *Etudes sur la langue Sechuana*. Paris: L'Imprimerie Royale.

Chadwick, H. M., and N. K. Chadwick. 1932–40. *The Growth of Literature*. 3 vols. Cambridge: Cambridge University Press.

Cope, Trevor. 1968. *Izibongo: Zulu Praise-Poems*. Oxford: Clarendon Press.

Copland, David B. 1985. *In Township Tonight: South Africa's Black City Music and Theatre*. London: Longman.

1994. *In the Time of Cannibals: The Word Music of Basotho Migrants*. Chicago: University of Chicago Press.

Damane, M., and Sanders, P. B. 1974. *Lithoko: Sotho Praise-Poems*. Oxford: Clarendon Press.

Depelchin, H., and C. Croonenberghs. 1882. *Trois ans dans l'Afrique australe: le pays des Matabélés, débuts de la Mission du Zambèse*. Brussels: Polleunis, Ceuterick et Lefébure.

Dhlomo, H. I. E. 1947. "Zulu Folk Poetry." *Native Teachers' Journal* [Natal] 27: 4, 5–7, 46–50, 84–87.

Finnegan, Ruth. 1970. *Oral Literature in Africa*. Oxford: Clarendon Press.

Gunner, Elizabeth. 1979. "Songs of Innocence and Experience: Women as Composers and Performers of *Izibongo* Zulu Praise Poetry." *Research in African Literatures* 10.2: 239–67.

Gunner, Elizabeth, and M. Gwala. 1994. *Musho! Zulu Popular Praises*. Johannesburg: Wits University Press.

Kunene, D. P. 1971. *Heroic Poetry of the Basotho*. Oxford: Clarendon Press.

Kunene, Mazisi. 1970. *Zulu Poems*. London: Heinemann.

1976. "South African Oral Tradition." In *Aspects of South African Literature*. Ed. C. Heywood. London: Heinemann: 24–41.

1979. *Emperor Shaka the Great*. Trans. from the Zulu by the author. London: Heinemann.

Mangoalea, Z. D. 1921. *Lethoko tsa Marena a basotho*. Morija Press.

Mphande, Lupenga. 1993. "Ngoni Praise Poetry and the Nguni Diaspora." *Research in African Literatures* 24.4: 99–122.

Ndawo, H. M. 1925. *Izibongo zenkosi zaHlubi nezomaBaca*. Natal: Marianhill Mission Press.

1939. *Isiduko*. London: Longman.

Ntuli, D. B., and Swanepoel, C. F. 1993. *Southern African Literature in African Languages*. Pretoria: Acacia.

Nyembezi, C. L. S. 1948. "The Historical Background to the Izibongo of the Zulu Military Age." *African Studies* 8: 110–25, 157–74.

1958. *Izibongo Zamakhosi*. Pietermaritzburg: Shuter and Shooter.

1961. *A Review of Zulu Literature*. Pietermaritzburg: University of Natal Press.

Omer-Cooper, J. D. 1966. *The Zulu Aftermath: a Nineteenth-Century Revolution in Bantu Africa*. London: Longman.

1991. "The Mfecane Defended." *Southern African Review of Books* 4/5 (July/October): 12–16.

Opland, Jeff. 1983. *Xhosa Oral Poetry*. Cambridge: Cambridge University Press.

Phala, D. M. 1935. *Kxoma thowa*. N.p.

Phiri, D. D. 1982. *From Nguni to Ngoni*. Limbe (Malawi): Popular Publications.

Ramaila, E. M. 1935. *Tsa bophelo bya moruti Abraham Serote*. Transvaal: Berlin Missionaries Literature Commission.

Read, Margaret. 1937. "Songs of the Ngoni People." *Bantu Studies* 11: 1–35.

1956. *The Ngoni of Nyasaland*. Oxford: Oxford University Press. Republished in 1970 in London by Frank Cass.

Rycroft, D. 1988. *The Praises of Dingana*. Durban-Pietermaritzburg: University of Natal Press.

Schapera, I. 1965. *Praise Poems of the Tswana Chiefs*. Oxford: Clarendon Press.

Scheub, Harold. 1975. *The Xhosa Ntsomi*. London: Oxford University Press.

Sekese, A. M. 1915. *Lilotho tsa Sesotho*.

Stuart, James. 1923. *uTulasizwe*. London: Longman.

1924. *uHlangakula*. London: Longman.

1925a. *uKulumetule*. London: Longman.

1925b. *uBaxoxele*. London: Longman.
1926. *uVusezakiti*. London: Longman.
Vail, Leroy, and Landeg White. 1991. *Power and the Praise Poem: Southern African Voices in History*. Charlottesville: University Press of Virginia.
White, Hayden. 1973. *Metahistory: The Historical Imagination in Nineteenth Century Europe*. Baltimore: Johns Hopkins University Press.

6

African oral epics

ISIDORE OKPEWHO

The study of the African epic was born in denial. In the third volume (1940) of their classic *Growth of Literature*, H. Munro and N. Kershaw Chadwick, discussing the "distribution of literary types" across the world, conclude there is no "narrative poetry . . . at all in Biblical Hebrew or anywhere in Africa." Assuming a difference between such poetry and "saga," by which they mean a narrative form with an admixture of prose and verse, they conclude the latter is found in "several African languages" (1940: 706).

In his equally epochal book, *Heroic Poetry* (1952), C. M. Bowra also has difficulty in recognizing the existence of epic or "heroic" poetry in Africa. Adopting an evolutionist approach in his discussion of "the development of primitive narrative poetry" across nations, he concludes, on the one hand, that, in cultures like Africa, heroic poetry had not quite graduated from a tradition of predominantly panegyric forms to one of sustained heroic narratives, and, on the other, that such narratives of heroic pretensions as might be found on the continent were centered around figures who achieved their feats more by magic than by force of sheer physical might. Bowra's language is particularly alarming: in discussing pieces of historical panegyric and lament songs from Uganda and "Abyssinia," he observes that in spirit they are "close . . . to a heroic outlook" but that "the intellectual effort required" to advance such texts to the level of heroic poetry "seems to have been beyond their powers" (1952: 10–11)!

A third notable disclaimer came from Ruth Finnegan. In her groundbreaking book *Oral Literature in Africa* (1970), she presents the most extensive challenge to claims made by various ethnographers and researchers before her of the existence of epic traditions in Africa. To begin with, she follows the Chadwicks in dismissing these claims on the basis of the form in which the available texts were presented by editors: they do not really qualify to be called "epics," because they have been transcribed mostly in ordinary prose, with occasional snatches of song. For this reason, according to her, they do not have the sustained formal characteristic of the established European traditions.

Secondly, the African texts seem to exist in independent episodes, though efforts have been made by scholars to put these together into coherent wholes of considerable length; there is little to show that they were ever "conceived of and narrated as a unity prior to . . . recording (and perhaps elaboration) in written form." Finnegan recognizes the presence of certain texts like the (then) "less celebrated *mvet* literature" in areas like Gabon and southern Cameroon, a tradition of musical performances that "seem to include some historical poetry not unlike epic." She is also aware of "the many Arabic-influenced historical narratives in the northerly areas of the continent and the East Coast." But she remains convinced that the evidence is not conclusive enough, and more work needs to be done, to establish the claims for "epic"; until then, she says, "epic seems to be of remarkably little significance in African oral literature" (108–10).

The fact is, by 1970 when Finnegan published these views, there already existed enough texts of "epic" qualities to excite the curiosity, not dampen the interest, of a discerning mind like hers. For instance, by 1949 P. Boelaert had published the "Nsong'a Lianja: l'épopée nationale des Nkundo," and before he published *The Mwindo Epic from the Banyanga* in 1969, Daniel P. Biebuyck had drawn attention, in journal articles, to epic traditions of various Congolese peoples. In 1963, the Nigerian poet-dramatist J. P. Clark[-Bekederemo] gave notice in an article entitled "The Azudu Saga" of the text of an Ijo tradition he had collected from a stupendous performance lasting seven days; he was later to publish the text in a massive volume of face-to-face Ijo and English translation under the title *The Ozidi Saga: Collected and Translated from the Oral Ijo Version of Okabou Ojobolo* (1991 [1977]). There was also the extensive text of Fang epic published by Stanislaus Awona as "La Guerre d'Akoma Mba contre Abo Mama" (1965–66). Admittedly, some of these texts were presented in prose-verse form, entirely the choice of the editors; but closer examination of them could have made their generic claims easier to concede.

Further into western Africa, Amadou Hampaté Bâ and Lilyan Kesteloot had published texts of Bambara (1966b) and Fulani (1968) heroic narratives, giving due notice of long-established traditions of the epic in the vast Sahelian region. Although the verse forms of these texts seem to have been subject to some ordering by the editors, they nevertheless reflect the prosodic influence of the musical format in which these Sahelian traditions have traditionally been performed. No doubt also, they give an early indication of the form in which versions of the Sunjata story – first brought to our attention by Ibn Khaldun in the fourteenth century and in the early twentieth by Léo Frobénius, but raised to the status of a classic in Djibril Niane's *Soundjata, ou l'épopée mandingue* (1960) – was traditionally performed by bards in the region. Shortly after Finnegan's disclaimer, from the 1970s, there appeared a spate of epics from West Africa confirming the vibrancy of the tradition. Besides other versions of the Sunjata story, the best of which was recorded from the Gambia by Gordon Innes (1974), there were others like the hunters' epic from Mali, *Kambili* (1974), recorded by Charles Bird and colleagues, and more Bambara texts recorded by Bâ and Kesteloot (1966b). Texts of epic traditions from other regions of Africa, north and south of the Sahara, have also been published.[1]

With so much that had come to light, the claim by European scholars that the epic did not exist in Africa was obviously due for a re-examination. A survey of known traditions had, in fact, been published by Jan Knappert in an article titled "The Epic in Africa" (1967); although she was aware of it, Finnegan chose to subsume it in her general view that existing claims were not conclusive evidence of the existence of the genre. However, the first real challenge to Finnegan's position came in my article titled "Does the Epic Exist in Africa?: Some Formal Considerations" (1977), which, while directing attention to issues of the physical form in which texts of African epic were presented, suggests larger formal and cultural questions about the tradition as a whole. These issues, addressed from the perspective of a literary scholar, are more fully addressed in my full-length study, *The Epic in Africa: Toward a Poetics of the Oral Performance* (1979). In 1978 anthropologist Daniel Biebuyck published a more extensive survey of published epic traditions (1978b). In 1980 John W. Johnson, a folklorist, published another response to Finnegan, "Yes, Virginia, There is an Epic in Africa." By the 1980s, the subject of the African epic had earned a solid niche in investigations and teaching of African literature.[2]

What is the nature of this African epic? In *The Epic in Africa*, I offer the following definition of the genre: "An oral epic is fundamentally a tale about the fantastic deeds of a person or persons endowed with something more than human might and operating in something more than the normal human context and it is of significance in portraying some stage of the cultural or political development of a people. It is usually narrated or performed to the background of music by an unlettered singer working alone or with some assistance from a group of accompanists" (1979: 34). The crucial ingredients of what has come to be known as "epic" are clearly outlined in this definition: the extraordinariness of the events; of the characters engaged in them; of the scale or circumstances in which the events are waged; and the historical, cultural, and political import of the events to the people who tell or own the tales about these events. The second sentence of the definition gives some recognition to the very act of *performance* of the epic. This recognition is quite significant, because in the final analysis it suggests that, whatever the known facts of a tale might be, the results of any presentation of them will depend to a greater or lesser degree on the competence of the storyteller and the situation enabling the presentation. Let us see how the available texts of the African epic support the definition of the genre presented above.

We begin with the characters who perform the actions described in the tales, who are, in significant ways, hardly the kinds of people we meet in our daily lives. First, many of them come from privileged (royal) families and simply continue the line of rulership from which they come; others may not exactly be born into so much privilege, but in the end they rise to the position of leadership that rewards their achievements. Whatever the case may be, there is often something out of the ordinary in their birth, development, and overall career. A few examples will do.

In the tradition of tales relating to Sunjata,[3] he is said to be the son of a Mande king, Nare Makhang Konate, and a woman of Do who has the mystical powers of a buffalo; thus, from his mother, Sunjata will be blessed with some mystical powers that put him above the human rank and file. Unlike normal children born after nine months, Sunjata stays in his mother's womb for many years. He is finally born at about the same time as the king's first wife delivers her own son; news of the latter is announced to the king first, thus robbing Sunjata, who according to the king's fortune tellers will inherit the kingship after his father, of the right of succession. According to one version, the child is so angry that he decides to crawl on all fours for many more years. He is finally forced to rise when his mother, who has appealed to the king's first wife to lend her baobab seasoning for her stew, is insulted with the condition of her crippled son. Crushing huge rods of iron fashioned by smiths to help him to his feet, Sunjata simply leans on a stick brought to him by his mother, walks over to the massive baobab tree, uproots it, and replants it in his mother's backyard so she may have all the seasoning she will ever want. By this time, Sunjata's father has died and been succeeded by the rival son. Sunjata's mother, seeing there will only be trouble between the two branches of the family should she and her children (including Sunjata's sisters) remain, decides to take them with her into exile.

The Mande kingdom is soon annexed by Sumanguru, powerful king of the Susu kingdom who has been overrunning several kingdoms in the region; so finding a place of exile is not easy for Sunjata and his family. But they finally settle in the kingdom of Mema, where Sunjata is able to put his mystical as well as physical powers to the proof, earning himself honors from the host king for his extraordinary feats in hunting and war. His mother finally dies in Mema and, after initial difficulties with his host in procuring a burial plot, Sunjata at last lays her to rest and prepares to answer the call of his people to come over and recover the Mande kingdom from the hands of Sumanguru. The war between the two men turns out not to be easy, because they are both armed with mystical powers, involving disappearing acts at certain stages of the conflict.[4] Sunjata is finally able to overcome Sumanguru because one of his sisters, finding her way into Sumanguru's camp and feigning a love affair with him, is able to gather from him the secret of his magical powers: the spur of a white cock, mixed with gold and silver dust and attached to a weapon. With this, Sunjata is able to destroy Sumanguru and return as king of the Mande. From here, he and his generals move on to other conquests that unite the surrounding regions into what ultimately amounts to a far-reaching empire.

The extraordinariness of the events narrated above may seem tame, but that may be due to the constraints imposed on the narrative imagination partly by the sparse Sahelian ecology and partly by the restraining influence of Islam. The epics from the luxuriant and largely "pagan" communities in the tropical rain forests are, on the contrary, far more stupendous in scale. In *The Ozidi Saga* from the Ijo of the Niger Delta (Nigeria), the hero (Ozidi Junior) is born after his father (Ozidi Senior) has been killed by rival war generals in his community, and is reared by his grandmother, the powerful sorceress Oreame, with extraordinary magical powers. Thus, even as a little child, he is already beating children much bigger than himself, scaring off a leopard in the jungle, cutting down and lifting a massive tree to his mother's doorstep when she complains she has no wood to cook with, and performing other extraordinary feats. It is also Oreame who procures for him, through the services of a forest wizard and a smith conjured from the earth, the tools with which he is to fight the battles of his career: a potion compounded from forest fauna and herbs and hurled into his stomach, and a seven-pointed sword that hurtles out of his stomach and into his grip as the combined screams of the ingested fauna summon the killing rage within him.

Oreame has fortified Ozidi with these overpowering resources because she can see the boy faces equally daunting dangers from a community that is determined to wipe out whoever in his family is likely to inherit the paramountcy earlier held by his father. True enough, as soon as word of the young hero gets around, he is challenged by a whole string of opponents: not only the men who killed his father but even nonhuman figures of monstrous physical features – one has seven heads, another has twenty limbs, another walks on his head, another is a half-man head to foot, another has an egregious scrotum, and so on – who are determined to nip the young pretender in the bud.

In these interminable contests, waged both inside and outside environments known to man,[5] we can clearly see that it is Oreame who engineers the hero's triumphs, a token perhaps of the mystical role of the female in the traditionally matrilineal Ijo society. But it is equally clear that here magic and the supernatural serve basically to ritualize the extraordinary potential and estimation of the heroic personality. Ozidi destroys every one of his opponents, including the "Smallpox King" who in the tradition symbolizes the cleansing rite that terminates a career of blood, and lays down his conquering sword presumably in readiness to assume his hard-earned paramountcy over his people.

Among the Fang of Gabon, southern Cameroon, and Equatorial Guinea there is a cluster of *mvet* epic traditions. Of these, the best known and in some ways central figure is the hero Akoma Mba, who is conceived of incestuous relations between a brother and sister and born after staying in his mother's womb for one hundred fifty years.[6] A rather interesting tale in this cluster concerns a long drawn-out war in which the human community of Oku, under its leader Zong Midzi, is determined to steal from the community of Engong, led by Abo Mama, the resource of immortality possessed by them. Zong Midzi launches the war under the pretext that a certain Angone Endong of Engong does not let him breathe freely. The conflict between Zong Midzi and Angone Endong soon becomes complicated with the entry of a woman into their relations: the beautiful and much sought after Nkudang commands the attention of Angone, yet is obsessed with love for Zong whom she has not even met. Along the way a young man, Nsure Afane, wins the favor of Nkudang and comes between her and Zong; in an ensuing encounter, Zong kills Nkudang and later engages Nsure in a fierce battle. Nsure wins the support of Engong warriors, who are equipped to fly on iron wings and have almost captured Zong, when the latter suddenly disappears under the earth where his ancestors equip him with magic weapons. Though he is captured by the Engong, he is still able to make his escape back to his ancestors, who this time try to make him immortal like the Engong.

Akoma Mba uses magic to see these events from a distance, and is able to prevail on the ancestors to halt their transformation of Zong. As a compromise, the ancestors equip Zong with a magic gun whose bullets trail their target wherever it goes. But the Engong warriors neutralize this by latching a magnetic shield to Zong's back and firing a shot that propels him all the way to the privy council of their land, where he is stripped of his charms by Akoma Mba and killed.[7]

Our final example is the Congolese *Mwindo Epic*, recorded by Daniel Biebuyck and his assistant Kahombo Mateene. Briefly, Shemwindo, king of

Tubondo, is anxious that none of his wives bear a male child to succeed him. But one, named Mwindo, is finally born to the king's favorite wife. A mysterious child who chooses (after various escapades in his mother's womb) to come out not through the womb but the middle finger, he is born equipped with a magic *conga*-scepter and shoulder bag, has the gift of premonition, and can already walk and talk. His father tries to kill him by (among other devices) having him locked up in a drum. When Mwindo will not die, his father flees into the underworld, with Mwindo in pursuit. Aided by the lightning god Nkuba, husband of his aunt Iyangura, and his magic scepter, Mwindo executes many Herculean tasks set him by supernatural beings, finally capturing his father and returning him to Tubondo. The quarrel between them is settled by having the kingdom divided into two between them.

But Mwindo's problems are hardly over. While they are out hunting, his subject Pygmies are swallowed up by a forest dragon, Kirimu. Armed with his *conga*-scepter, Mwindo kills the dragon and frees his pygmies. Unfortunately, that rouses the anger of his erstwhile ally Nkuba, god of lightning who is patron also of the dragon. Mwindo is consequently translated to heaven, where he is severely chastised during a one-year sojourn, but finally restored as king of Tubondo.

The above is a very small sampling of the vast number of heroic narrative traditions that have been brought to light since serious collection and study of them began in the first half of the twentieth century. Although Europeans were the first to show interest in this enterprise, the zeal with which indigenous African scholars have lately gone into the field does say something about the significance of the texts as an index of national identity. There has, of course, been a great deal of controversy as to how seriously tales with such fantastical content should be taken in the reconstruction of a people's past history or their social and cultural traditions. But there has been no lack of painstaking effort by social scientists wading through the dense imagery of the texts for such purposes. Nationalist ideology has, at any rate, embraced the tales either as evidence of past glory or as charter of present conduct, or both. For instance, the story of Sunjata has been shown to be an account not only of the greatness of a Mandinka warrior-king of the thirteenth century but of his role in the dispersal of branches of the ethnic family especially west of their original homeland. Today, oral artists who narrate the story of Sunjata trace the roots of several Mandinka legacies to the days of Sunjata, and the Mali nation has enshrined the spirit of the hero in its consciousness in many ways, not least by adopting praises of the hero for its national anthem.[8] The Ozidi story among the Ijo does not lend itself to anything like dependable dating. But an examination of its mythic images and nomenclature does indicate marks of the stresses between some elements of the Ijo ethnic stock and the powerful kingdom of Benin, in the days when the kingdom was building itself up as an imperial force in the region. The epics from other tropical forest cultures, like the Fang and the Nyanga, are no more helpful as evidence of datable history. But the wars and conflicts they narrate evidently suggest the dynamics of fragmentation of politically uncentralized groups across the region.

Whatever difficulties these epic texts may pose, however, they contain large amounts of cultural data that link the past to the present and bear witness to the significance of the traditions to societies that have continued to keep them alive. Something of this significance may be seen in the very practice of performance of the epics. There may be no special terms for these epics in many African societies; despite claims that have been made about the terms *jali* and *griot* – used for the performers of these epic tales among the Mandinka of West Africa – there are often no special titles for the narrators either. But they appear to occupy a special place in the estimation both of themselves and of their fellow citizens. Each one of them is blessed with an innate skill in the oral arts, which is then augmented by training, formal or informal, in many cases lasting many years. The uniqueness of their position may be underlined either by the circumstances and processes of their preparation, by the objects they wield to identify them with the personalities they celebrate in their texts, or by the roles assigned them in the society. For instance, as part of his preparation the bard may be attached to a cult devoted to the worship of the spirit connected with the epic, as bards of the *Mwindo Epic* are to the cult of the god Karisi.[9] The *mvet* performer among the Fang is given certain magic objects designed to stimulate his imagination and to guide his performance successfully. In the course of the performance the bard may also hold certain objects peculiar to the hero he celebrates: thus the narrator of the *Ozidi* story often holds a sword (the hero's main weapon) in one hand and in the other a fan (wielded by the sorceress Oreame); the *Mwindo* bard holds in one hand a scepter representing the hero's *conga*-scepter. In terms of social position, the *griots* of the Sunjata tradition come from a caste recognized solely for their proprietorship of the oral arts, which in the past gave them the special privilege, as guardians of the wisdom of the past, of advising the rulers of their people. But even in the noncasted societies there was always some reverence shown for those who had the skill for weaving the traditional lore into words of uncommon impact and appeal.

The circumstances in which these narrators tell their tales are not exactly uniform. Some may be so accomplished in the craft that they both tell the tales and play the musical instruments that accompany them. More often, the main performer is accompanied by at least one apprentice who does any number of services: playing the accompanying instrument (for example, a stringed harp or wooden percussion), singing choral refrains, aiding the master's memory by whispering the odd forgotten detail, or generally encouraging the expansion or curtailment of episodes depending on the interests of the audience. There is, indeed, no doubt about the centrality of an audience to the processes and success of a performance. For instance, in a performance of one of the Sunjata versions recorded by Gordon Innes in the Gambia, considerable space is devoted to celebrating certain families that trace their descent from one of Sunjata's major generals, Tira Makhang, who was responsible for spreading the Mandinka empire to this region; the effort was suggested by the narrator's accompanist, who must have seen that a large proportion of the audience would be cheered to hear the names of their families mentioned in this roll call of honor. In other instances, the performance may be so rousing that members of the audience are inspired to ask occasional questions of the bard, provide random comments and reactions to details of his performance, even assume roles to lend dramatic effectiveness to certain episodes: such was the atmosphere in the performance of *The Ozidi Saga* that has made it an outstanding classic of the African heroic epic. Performed in a town far away from its Ijo homeland, it brought so much patriotic pride to the Ijo members in the audience that they aided the narrator and his accompanists in realizing the full theatrical impact of the story.

To give a good account of himself as a performer, the narrator depends not only on his music but, in some cases, on movements made with appropriate parts of his body to dramatize certain situations, to indicate the nature of an object or event, or to mimic the peculiarities of objects or characters in the tale. If the audience is drawn to laugh at these things, he has made his point! The epic being a tale of considerable scope, and the audience right before him, the narrator is also invariably forced into a performative mold that enables him to sustain material of such a scope. For instance, he utilizes a structure of repetitions for narrating details and episodes that have such a close resemblance to one another that he does not need to think up new words to describe them whenever they occur. From their researches into traditions of epic storytelling by Homer and Slavic *guslari* in former Yugoslavia, Milman Parry and Albert Lord have, in their publications, used the terms *formula* (for a limited unit of description, for example, a phrase) and *theme* (for a larger unit, for example, a scene or event) for these functional repetitions. These devices are also present in quite a few epic traditions in Africa.

Take the theme. In the Fang story of the conflict between Akoma Mba and Awo Mama recorded by Stanislas Awona (1965–66), each time a character has to make a quick dash on an errand or in flight, we are told he

> dashed like the branch of a broken tree,
> Like a young antelope in furious flight,
> Like a bird that takes off without bidding the branch goodbye
> (lines 59–61 = 190–92 = 364–66 = 526–28, etc.)

In the hunters epic *Kambili* recorded by Charles Bird and colleagues in Mali, various characters executed by Samory Toure are said to have had their heads "cut off by the neck," while their "shoulders became inseparable friends" (lines 397–99 = 435–57 = 505–07, etc.). Although the Chadwicks and Finnegan do not think that stories transcribed in "prose" qualify to be called epics, repetitive units of description abound in *Mwindo* and *Ozidi*. In the former, when a magical weapon (scepter or belt) is sent to punish the embattled Mwindo, he is brutalized in very much the same way each time: his mouth is crushed to the ground (or tree); he is breathless; and his urine and excrement are forced out of him, with no one around to help him clean up (for example, pp. 99, 100, 102). But it is in *Ozidi* that we find that tales of epic combat are constructed basically on a repeated sequence of moves. The confrontation between the hero Ozidi and an opponent usually begins with the opponent threatening to put an end to the career of the upstart hero, who is soon drawn into the opponent's presence; although Ozidi's powers initially destabilize the opponent, the early stages of the fighting go in favor of the latter, forcing the witch Oreame to scour the environment for herbal and other kinds of antidote to the opponent's powers. The fighting eventually turns in Ozidi's favor, and when the moment for disposing of the enemy comes, all those animals used in concocting Ozidi's charms erupt in a tumultuous howl; the conquering sword hurtles out of Ozidi's mouth, the "slaughter song" resounds, and off goes the opponent's head, which is right away dumped into the hero's shrine. His strength now augmented by the enemy's appropriated powers, Ozidi is driven by so much killing urge that he levels the vegetation in his homestead; his idiot uncle Temugedege, who has been cowering in the nearby bush, is so frightened that he pleads that the community put an end to the mad youth so the old man can live in peace.

Whatever the pragmatic value of this repetitive design in epic narratives, it nonetheless bears witness to the rhythmic basis of their composition: in other words, there is a certain lyrical impetus driving the sequence of narrative episodes. The tale is in essence a narrative song – Lord has called such a storyteller a "singer of tales" – and discerning members of the audience are often touched emotionally upon recognizing how skillfully a familiar move has been adjusted to fit a new episode in the development of the tale's plot. Narrators of epic tales are generally subject to such formal organization of their material, but the skill of each will depend essentially on how well he balances the imperative of form with the appeal of the various textual (affective diction) and paratextual (music and body movement) devices that constitute his performance.

Considering that physical form has been a major factor in the generic assessment of these African traditions, let us now examine to what extent some of the editions have done justice to the epic as an artistic vehicle of a people's cultural record. The documentation of African epics has been carried on by essentially three schools of endeavor – history, anthropology (including linguistics and folklore), and literature – and so far the record has been a little uneven. Niane's edition of the Sunjata story may be seen as representative of the historical interest and especially rooted in the preoccupations of the time. As a scholar, Niane was influenced by the ideology of Negritude that was embraced by the creative writers of his generation, in effect using his work on Sunjata as an opportunity to justify the historical achievement of an African people. The text he collected from his Guinean narrator, Djeli Mamoudou Kouyate, was not only hand-copied but reconciled with other sources. Although it bears many of the characteristic marks of the heroic narrative tradition and is no less valuable to us in assessing the heroism of Sunjata, we rather suspect that the bard's frequent emphasis on his role as "historian" is largely a product of Niane's editorial control. And although Niane has succeeded in recovering some of the atmosphere of the recording event, the resultant text reveals itself more as a historical novel than as a transcript of an oral performance, thanks to the anxiety of the historian Niane to present a *coherent* narrative.

A parallel weakness may be seen in the anthropologist Biebuyck's edition of the *Mwindo* story. Like Niane, he and his assistants hand-copied all the versions of the epic so far presented. Again, while these versions have provided valuable material for understanding the nature of the African epic, the "prose" form in which they have been transcribed hardly does justice to what was evidently a rousing musical event. There is evidence enough of the context of the narrative event – especially in the bard's comments on the dancing and other exertions of himself and his accompanists – and the occasional songs no doubt represent authentic musical interludes in the performance. But more energy seems to have been invested by the editors in achieving a coherent narrative that highlighted the functional relation of text to culture than in providing a text truly representative of the physical results of the performance. The least of Biebuyck's achievement, however, is in the English translation of his texts which, as I have demonstrated in my essay "The Anthropologist Looks at the Epic" (1980), have often sacrificed the esthetic merits of the artist to the functionalist project of the anthropologist.

Like Niane and Biebuyck before him, the Nigerian poet-playwright John Pepper Clark-Bekederemo has presented his edition of the Ijo epic of *Ozidi* in the "straight prose" (as he tells us in his introduction) in which he believes the story was told. But his results are rather different. It must be granted that, here and there in his translation, he has taken undue poetic liberties with the indigenous Ijo text in order to render the frequent Ijo ideophones into what he considers to be English of corresponding appeal. He has not – as I argue in my introduction to the 1991 edition of the work and as the (Ijo) linguist Teilanyo has more exhaustively demonstrated (2001) – been quite so successful in that effort. But *The Ozidi Saga* has emerged as the most convincing record of an African epic narrative performance so far published. Despite the prose form of the work, we do not miss the sheer musical infrastructure as well as accompaniment to the event. And it is to the credit of Clark-Bekederemo the dramatist that the full effect of the dialogue of emotions between the performing team on the one hand and a fully responsive audience on the other is conveyed. In his introduction Clark-Bekederemo recognizes the performance he recorded as more a multifaceted theater, an "opera – especially the Wagnerian type," than literature as conventionally understood. The result is a text in which we hardly miss anything that happened at the scene of the performance: from the narrator's self-conscious comments on his daunting task (the performance lasted seven days, as demanded by tradition) and the menace of the tape-recorder; to the call by the hostess Madam Yabuku for more songs from the performers; to the often motivating but sometimes disorienting interventions of Ijo members of the audience, especially challenging the narrator's preference of English loan words over indigenous Ijo forms for various items.

In a seminal paper he published in 1977 on the business of transcribing the texts of oral performance, Dennis Tedlock has argued that "prose (as we now understand it) has no existence outside the printed page" and that "spoken narratives are better understood as 'dramatic poetry' than as the analogue of our written prose fiction" (1977: 513; see also Tedlock 1983). It is true that verse has more frequently been used in transcribing the texts of heroic narratives collected in recent times, thanks perhaps to the growing recognition of the musical texture and contexture of the performances. But there are still rather few transcriptions that bear signs of the "dialogic" interaction (to invoke Tedlock 1977 once again) between the various persons present at the scene. Although the concept *epic* as denoting "large scope" has become fairly accepted in our understanding of the genre, somehow transcriptions of epic narrative performances remain constrained by the old etymology of *epos* as "word"; hence editors are narrowly concerned with the bare text of the story told by the narrator (often only the *main* narrator), leaving contributions made by other persons present – members of the audience making contributory comments, even the narrator's accompanist(s) offering helpful asides – totally out of the picture. Admittedly, in performances recorded especially by non-native investigators the atmosphere might be rather subdued, largely out of deference to the presumed seriousness of the recording process. But we really should do more to put the performers at their accustomed ease, and recognize that within the collectivist ethos in which epics are traditionally narrated, the *epos* is as much the total verbal input of everyone gathered to recreate the cherished cultural legacy of the community as the specialized reflections of the spotlighted performer.

It is no doubt fitting that the continuity of Africa's traditions is guaranteed not only by oral performance and improved methods of transcription and translation but especially by their incorporation into modern-day artistic creativity. Although Niane's edition of the Sunjata epic was an effort to inscribe the oral traditions into the historiography of the Mande, he has in fact rendered the story in the form of a historical novel, under the inspiration of the ideology of Negritude. A more conscious literary reconstruction of the story may be seen, however, in Camara Laye's *Le maître de la parole* (1978, trans. as *Guardian of the Word*, 1980). Other literary exploitations of this tradition have been reported by various scholars (e.g., Diawara 1992 and McGuire 1999). J. P. Clark [-Bekederemo] indeed made a play (1996) out of the Ozidi story before he finally published the Ijo and English versions of the performance he had collected on tape in 1963. The traditions relating to the Zulu leader Shaka have long been the source of creative reconstructions by various nationalist writers on the continent. Of special interest are Senghor's poetic drama on the subject (1964) and Oswald Mtshali's tautly drawn heroic portrait of the leader in the poem "The Birth of Shaka" (*Sounds of a Cowhide Drum*, 1971). In his long poetic statement, *Ogun Abibiman* (1976), celebrating Samora Machel's declaration of a state of war against Ian Smith's Rhodesia, Wole Soyinka presents the Shaka of history and the (Yoruba god) Ogun of myth as poised to lead a united African challenge to white supremacist rule in the continent. Finally, in the area of music technology, Robert Newton has reported (1997, 1999) the growth of a vast industry of audiocassette and compact-disc recordings of epic and other oral traditions in the Mande.

*

As scholars, we need to free ourselves from narrow-minded attitudes that have marked much of the scholarship on this subject. One of these involves the investigative or discursive strategy to be adopted in our study. Ever since my publications – especially *The Epic in Africa* – contesting claims by earlier scholars that the epic did not exist in Africa, a few protests have been raised against my comparative approach whereby I sought to demonstrate that, despite obvious cultural differences, there were epics in Africa existing on *essentially* the same principles as the well-known Indo-European classics, and that indeed certain *performance* qualities discernible in the African epics would help us better understand tendencies in some texts like Homer's that have been subject to some misapprehension. It seems to have been forgotten that the word *epic* is not even an African word; if we *all* use it in describing these magnificent heroic tales we find on the continent, we already adopt a comparatist mindset whatever the level of our discussion. In other words, *the study of the African epic is of necessity a comparatist enterprise*. Those who resist this imperative either do not really understand the Indo-European traditions they so eagerly separate from the African, or are not willing to do the demanding work entailed by this field of study. To insist that the African epic should be studied only on its own terms is to promote a narrow-minded ethnocentrism of dubious merit and intent.

More seriously, however, the study of the epic in Africa seems today to be going round in circles, and has not begun to address issues of contemporary African life in which such a study is inevitably imbricated. Very few of us involved in celebrating the great epic traditions of Africa have reflected deeply enough on the political ramifications of the texts, especially their status as charters for certain power configurations both within and beyond the geographic zones within which they are traditionally set. Nor have we examined seriously enough the processes by which the heroes we admire acquire their authority or the mechanics of empowerment their careers may seem to legitimize: who gets to be favored, and who rejected; how just are the considerations on which these decisions are based; and what legacies of social engineering have such political acts bequeathed to the communities that uphold these iconic figures as their culture heroes?

Let us examine a few details from the Sunjata story, no doubt the most celebrated of the traditions of the African epic. Most of the known versions state that Sunjata's mother Sogolon, the Buffalo Woman from the royal house of Du, is given to two itinerant hunter brothers of the Taraware clan as a reward for subduing her and terminating her ravages in a kingdom that has denied her her rights. But then the story makes them surrender the woman to Nare (Fa-)Maghan Konate (or Keita), for whom the woman has been destined to bear a son who will rule over the Manding nation after his father. In his rather insightful discussion of "The Buffalo Woman Tale" (1990), Stephen Bulman tells us the woman becomes Nare Konate's wife so that Sunjata will be shown to have descended from royalty on both his father's and his mother's side. But what does this say of the Tarawares? Bulman suggests that "the epic" presents them as mere itinerant hunters "with no overt royal connections." But this is not the picture we get from Bamba Suso, one of the bards in the Innes edition of Sunjata versions (1974), nor from Fa-Digi Sisoko in the Johnson edition (1986), both of whom present the Taraware clan as nobility. So what, beyond the myth of manifest destiny, justifies the surrender of that prize to a king about whose personal merits the tradition is largely silent?

Political alliance, perhaps? This may well be so, for later on in the Sunjata story we find the embattled hero putting the highest premium on Tira Makhang, a prince of the Taraware clan, as his most dependable ally in the war against Sumanguru. So where does that leave Faa Koli, an outstanding warrior of the smith caste whose defection from Sumanguru's side is no mean factor in the weakening of the Susu resistance? Faa Koli, of course, protests the prejudice, as do the other allies. Having defeated Sumanguru, Sunjata plans other wars, the best known being his attack of the Jolof king for ridiculing Sunjata's request for horses. In Johnson's edition, both Faa Koli and Tira Makhang vie for the honor of leading the campaign against the Jolof; again Tira Makhang is favored over Faa Koli, and for the rest of the Sunjata legend little is heard about Faa Koli. One is left to wonder whether Faa Koli's status as a "smith" cost him the estimation of his upper-caste leader. The logic of political decisions in these traditions leaves one wondering about the fate of the social structure.

Sometimes these decisions are so arbitrary, so capricious, as to be entirely indefensible. For instance, in Niane's edition of the story, Fran Kamara, king of Mema, first makes the exiled prince Sunjata his viceroy, then names him successor to the throne if Sunjata would decide to remain in Mema rather than press plans to return to Manding. Kamara's advisers endorse the offer, clearly because it has been announced as a royal fiat that may not be gainsaid, and we of course wonder on what moral or constitutional ground a king would award succession to his throne not to a qualified native (his son, perhaps) but to a total outsider, however well endowed. Then there are those panegyric epithets, recited by Banna Kanute in Innes's edition of the story, to the effect that as a result of Sunjata's frequent war-mongering, his people revolted against him, whereupon

> He waged war against Manding nineteen times,
> He rebuilt Manding nineteen times.
> (Innes 1974: 237, lines 2062–63)

The great hero and king, making war on his own people just to safeguard his paramountcy?

These are not idle questions. Even if we allow that there is no more than a mythic or symbolic import to many details in these traditions, we are at any rate justified in questioning the logic of the powers claimed by our epic heroes and the fate of communities that find themselves at the receiving end of their whims. We are justified because, in the post-independence record of indigenous African governance of nearly every African nation, we find the same capriciousness in our real-life leaders that we find in the legendary ones, and wonder by what unkind fate the lines between myth and reality so easily blur in Africa. The problems we all face, whether we are scholars reflecting on epic texts in the comfort of our study or peasants on whom the cost of our leaders' whims rests far less easily, are too real for us to pretend the epics we celebrate have no bearing on our present condition. This does not mean we should stop collecting epics. It only means that, in studying them whether as literary or cultural legacies, we also ask questions that might help our people address problems of today created by the fault-lines of history. The fault may lie with outsiders who imposed certain systems and outlooks on us. But it may also lie with ourselves.[10]

Notes

1. Sunjata seems to account for the largest amount of documentation so far: see Bulman 1997. Of North African epics, examples may be found in Reynolds 1995 and Slyomovics 1988.
2. There have been various regional and continent-wide discussions and surveys of African epic traditions by various scholars, such as Amadou Hampaté Bâ and Lilyan Kesteloot (1966a, 1966b, 1968), Robert Cornevin (1966), Christiane Seydou (1982), and Stephen Belcher (1999). Anthologies also exist in translation, such as those edited by Kesteloot and Dieng in French (1997) and by John W. Johnson, Thomas Hale, and Stephen Belcher in English (1997).
3. Several versions of this name exist in various regions where his story is told: Soundjata, Son-Jara, Mari Jata, etc. We shall restrict ourselves to "Sunjata" in this essay.
4. In Djibril Niane's version, Sunjata and Sumanguru are said to be taunting each other, before the start of hostilities between them, through their personal owls!

5. One of Ozidi's opponents, Ofe, disappears in the earth for a good while before reappearing to continue the fight with Ozidi.
6. *Mvet* is the name for both heroic tale and the accompanying stringed instrument. The story of the birth, heroic development, and career of Akoma Mba appears in Awona 1965.
7. This account, in Fang and French translation, is contained in Pepper 1972.
8. The continuity of the tradition is also guaranteed by a ceremony, held once every seven years in the town of Kangaba, Mali, in which a House of Speech (*kama blon*) is re-roofed and the story of Sunjata narrated by bards from the Diabate family of Kela, who are said to possess the story's official version. An account of this ceremony is contained in a lengthy article by Germaine Dieterlen, "Mythe et organisation sociale" (1955, 1959).
9. Divine inspiration has also been claimed by narrators of both the Mwindo and Ozidi traditions of the epic: see Biebuyck and Mateene, eds. (1969), *The Mwindo Epic*: 12, 14 and Clark (1963): 9.
10. See Okpewho 1998b for a discussion of these ethical issues.

Bibliography

Awona, Stanislas. 1965–66. "La guerre d'Akoma Mba contre Abo Mama (épopée du mvet)." *Abbia* 9–10 (1965): 180–213; 12–13 (1966): 109–209.

Bâ, Amadou Hampaté and Lilyan Kesteloot. 1966a. "Les épopées de l'Ouest Africain." *Abbia* 14–15: 165–69.

1966b. "Da Monzon et Karta Thiema." *Abbia* 14–15: 179–205. A Bambara epic.

1968. "Une épopée peule: 'Silamaka.'" *L'Homme* 8: 5–36. A Fulani epic. Rpt. 1993 in *Da Monzon de Segou: épopée bambara*. Ed. Lilyan Kesteloot. Paris: Harmattan.

Belcher, Stephen. 1999. *Epic Traditions of Africa*. Bloomington: Indiana University Press.

Biebuyck, Daniel P. 1978a. "The African Heroic Epic." In *Heroic Epic and Saga*. Ed.Felix J. Oinas. Bloomington: Indiana University Press.

Biebuyck, Daniel P., ed. 1978b. *Hero and Chief: Epic Literature from the Banyanga (Zaire Republic)*. Berkeley: University of California Press.

Biebuyck, Daniel P., and Kahombo C. Mateene, eds. 1969. *The Mwindo Epic from the Banyanga*. Berkeley: University of California Press.

Bird, Charles, Mamadou Koita, and Bourama Soumaouro, eds. 1974. *The Songs of Seydou Camara*, vol. I. *Kambili*. Bloomington: African Studies Center, Indiana University.

Boelaert, P. 1949. "Nsong'a Lianja: l'épopée nationale des Nkundo." *Aequatoria* 12: 1–75. Rpt. 1949. Antwerp: De Sikkel.

Bowra, Cecil Maurice. 1952. *Heroic Poetry*. London: Macmillan.

Bulman, Stephen. 1990. "The Buffalo Woman Tale: Political Imperatives and Narrative Constraints in the Sunjata Epic." In *Discourse and Its Disguises: The Interpretation of African Oral Texts*. Ed. Karin Barber and Paolo de. F. Moraes Farias. Birmingham: Centre of West African Studies: 171–88.

1997. "A Checklist of Published Versions of the Sunjata Epic." *History in Africa* 24: 71–94.

Chadwick, H. Munro, and N. Kershaw Chadwick. 1940. *The Growth of Literature*, vol. III. Cambridge: Cambridge University Press.

Clark, J. P. 1963. "The Azudu Saga." *African Notes* 1: 8–9.

Clark[-Bekederemo], J. P. 1966. *Ozidi: A Play*. London: Oxford University Press.

Clark-Bekederemo, J.P., ed. 1991. *The Ozidi Saga: Collected and Translated from the Ijo of Okabou Ojobolo.* Washington, DC: Howard University Press. With a Critical Introduction by Isidore Okpewho. First published 1977, Ibadan: Ibadan University Press and Oxford University Press (without Okpewho's Critical Introduction).

Cornevin, Robert. 1966. "Les poèmes épiques africains et la notion d'épopée vivante." *Présence Africaine* 60: 140–45.

Diawara, Manthia. 1992. "Canonizing Soundiata in Mande Literature: Toward a Sociology of Narrative Elements." *Social Text* 31–32: 154–68.

Dieterlen, Germaine. 1955, 1959. "Mythe et organisation sociale au Soudan Français." *Journal de la Société des Africanistes* 25 (1955): 39–76; 29 (1959): 119–38.

Finnegan, Ruth. 1970. *Oral Literature in Africa.* Oxford: Clarendon Press.

Innes, Gordon, ed. 1974. *Sunjata: Three Mandinka Versions.* London: School of Oriental and African Studies, London U.

Johnson, John William. 1980. "Yes, Virginia, there is an Epic in Africa." *Research in African Literatures* 11: 308–26.

Johnson, John William, ed. 1986. *The Epic of Son-Jara: A West African Tradition.* Text by Fa-Digi Sisoko. Bloomington: Indiana University Press.

Johnson, John William, Thomas A. Hale, and Stephen Belcher, eds. 1997. *Oral Epics from Africa: Vibrant Voices from a Vast Continent.* Bloomington: Indiana University Press.

Kesteloot, Lilyan, and Bassirou Dieng, eds. 1997. *Les épopées d'Afrique noire.* Paris: Karthala and UNESCO.

Knappert, Jan. 1967. "The Epic in Africa." *Journal of the Folklore Institute* 4: 171–90.

Laye, Camara. 1978. *Le maître de la parole: Kouma lafolo kouma.* Paris: Plon.

1980. *The Guardian of the Word.* Trans. James Kirkup. London: Collins.

Lord, Albert B. 1960. *The Singer of Tales.* Cambridge, MA: Harvard University Press.

McGuire, James R. 1999. "Butchering Heroism?: Sunjata and the Negotiation of Postcolonial Mande Identity in Diabate's *Le boucher de Kouta.*" In *In Search of Sunjata: The Mande Oral Epic as History, Literature, and Performance.* Ed. Ralph A. Austen. Bloomington: Indiana University Press: 253–73.

Mtshali, Oswald. 1971. *Sounds of a Cowhide Drum.* London: Oxford University Press.

Newton, Robert C. 1997. "The Epic Cassette: Technology, Tradition, and Imagination in Contemporary Bamana Segou." PhD diss. University of Wisconsin, Madison.

1999. "Out of Print: The Epic Cassette as Intervention, Reinvention, and Commodity." In *In Search of Sunjata: The Mande Oral Epic as History, Literature, and Performance.* Ed. Ralph A. Austen. Bloomington: Indiana University Press: 313–27.

Niane, Djibril Tamsir. 1960. *Soundjata, ou l'épopée mandingue.* Paris: Présence Africaine.

1965. *Sundiata: An Epic of Old Mali.* Trans. G. D. Pickett. London: Longman.

Okpewho, Isidore. 1977. "Does the Epic Exist in Africa?: Some Formal Considerations." *Research in African Literatures* 8: 171–200.

1979. *The Epic in Africa: Toward a Poetics of the Oral Performance.* New York: Columbia University Press.

1980. "The Anthropologist Looks at the Epic." *Research in African Literatures* 11: 429–48.

1998a. "African Mythology and Africa's Political Impasse." *Research in African Literatures* 29: 115.

1998b. *Once Upon a Kingdom: Myth, Hegemony, and Identity.* Bloomington: Indiana University Press.

Parry, Milman. 1971. *The Making of Homeric Verse: The Collected Papers of Milman Parry.* Ed. Adam Parry. Oxford: Oxford University Press.

Pepper, Herbert, ed. 1972. *Le mvet de Zwe Nguema: chant épique fang.* Paris: Armand Colin.

Reynolds, Dwight Fletcher. 1995. *Heroic Poets, Poetic Heroes: The Ethnography of Performance in an Arabic Oral Epic Tradition.* Ithaca: Cornell University Press.

Senghor, Léopold Sédar. 1964. "Shaka." In *Selected Poems.* Ed. John Reed and Clive Wake. London: Oxford University Press.

Seydou, Christiane. 1982. "Comment définir le genre épique? Un exemple: l'épopée africaine." *Journal of the Anthropological Society of Oxford* 13: 84–98. Special issue on *Genres, Forms, Meanings: Essays in African Oral Literature.* Ed. Veronika Görög-Karady. Trans. into English in 1983 as "The African Epic: A Means for Defining the Genre." *Folklore Forum* 16: 47–68.

Slyomovics, Susan. 1988. *The Merchant of Art: An Egyptian Hilali Oral Epic Poet in Performance.* Berkeley: University of California Press.

Soyinka, Wole. 1976. *Ogun Abibiman.* London: Rex Collings.

Tedlock, Dennis. 1971. "On the Translation of Style in Oral Literature." *Journal of American Folklore* 84 (1971): 114–33. Rpt. 1983 in *The Spoken Word and the Work of Interpretation.* Philadelphia: University of Pennsylvania Press: 31–61.

1977. "Toward an Oral Poetics." *New Literary History* 8: 507–19.

1983. "The Analogical Tradition and the Emergence of a Dialogical Anthropology." *The Spoken Word and the Work of Interpretation.* Philadelphia: University of Pennsylvania Press: 321–38.

Teilanyo, Diri I. 2001. "Translating African Ideophones." In *Perspectives: Studies in Translatology* 9.3. Ed. M. G. Rose, H. Gottlieb, and V. H. Pedersen. Clevedon, UK: Multilingual Matters: 215–31.

7

The oral tradition in the African diaspora

MAUREEN WARNER-LEWIS

Orality is the exercise of human verbal communication. Orality transmutes into orature, oracy, or oral literature when either unconsciously or deliberately couched in esthetic forms rather than when deployed in perfunctory manner or primarily for content transmission. Chirograph-centered analysts such as Walter Ong (1982: 11–14) consider the term "oral literature" an oxymoron. However, if the concept of "literature" is not indivisibly tied to language inscription, and its esthetic function foregrounded, then it equates with "verbal art." Esthetic structures are culture-specific to the extent that they are grounded in the sound, syntax, semantic and idiomatic configurations of a particular language system, but such structures occur universally and attract hearer attention within each language community. Among these structures are syntactic and semantic parallelisms which produce rhythmic phrasing; stock attributions and idioms, and their converse – syntactic inversions and unexpected semantic manipulation; imagery, metaphor, and simile; rhyme and alliteration; irony in plot or word-choice; dialogue which advances plot and consolidates character and setting; witty verbal exchange producing humor or surprise; conflictual situations; opposed character traits; the evocation of contrasting moods. These are also the very structures employed in scribal literature.

Given the traditionally limited use of literacy in most African societies (see Gregsen 1977: 174–93; Gérard 1981), orature genres, themes, styles, and performance techniques have historically been primary vehicles of communication, enculturation, entertainment, and societal acclamation. As cognitive and performative skills, these verbal traditions were among the few but highly significant possessions brought to the Americas by the enslaved survivors of transatlantic crossings.

Conversation and song

One of the distinctions of African and diasporan conversation is its contrapuntal patterning (see Reisman 1974). These conversations, like Suriname Maroon discussions, "are punctuated by . . . listeners, who offer supportive comments such as "That's right," "Yes indeed," or "Not at all" (see Price and Price 1980: 167). "Okay," and the vocables "Uh-huh," "Eh-heh," intoned on contrasting pitches and glides are among African American and Caribbean equivalents, indicating that the listener is emotionally responsive. This antiphonal pattern of verbal interaction leads to the observation of "frequent role-switching between soloist and other participants." In storytelling sessions, similarly in song, dance, and drum performances, this structure balances "the complementary values of communal participation and individual virtuosity" (Price and Price 1980: 168).

The link between speaking/narrating conventions and music is *a propos.* One of the distinctive structures of African song is its call-and-response patterning. Correspondingly, when Akan speech-makers declaim, "heralds" echo their words, and in Mandinka epic performances, back-up vocalists/instrumentalists hum at the beginning of the lead singer's lines and then intone the line-endings, the humming allowing them time to anticipate the lead artist's completion of the breath-group (see also Akpabot 1986: 104–05). Indeed, the responsorial structure often overlaps with unison singing when the solo melodic attack precedes the conclusion of the choric line. One manifestation of this performance concept in African-influenced modern pop music is the presence of a back-up chorus whose role is not confined to a stanza-end refrain, but more to intercalating rhythmic or melodic phrases with the lead singer's lyrics.

Another call-and-response mechanism is the alteration of pitch ranges within the same song. Because responses may traditionally have been sung in a higher octave than the solo in certain types of African music, African American female singers have startled audiences by their wide pitch variations in differing segments of a rendition. Similarly, African American male vocalists often change their normative vocal range to a falsetto. In the Caribbean, solo performers of African songs may move between three octaves from stanza to stanza. This is their way of replicating the tonal shifts that differentiate soloist from respondents.[1] Yet another musical characteristic is extempore composition within performance. Improvisation produces heterophony since singers may follow the lead melody for the most part but depart from it when tones are too high or too low, or when any singer wishes to create special emphasis, or wishes to introduce harmonic variation (see Southern 1983: 197). Improvisation continues to be positively valued in African and diasporan musical culture, being contemporaneously demonstrated in both jazz and gospel singing and instrumentation. Another musical characteristic is the downward glide or "flattening/bending" of notes, and the treatment of sustained notes by melisma – the extension of a syllable over a widely ranging series of notes. An associated device is tremolo, a wavering note produced by glottal constriction. It is typical of Arabic music, is used in the Senegambian region, as well as in Yoruba *apala* songs, divination and *eso* chants, these being of a philosophical or sacred nature, and thus conveying emotional and mental intensity. The microtonality of the tremolo, "the use of passing notes of unequal weighting, with elongated, trailing notes at the end of the piece" gives these songs "a haunting, meandering effect" (Warner-Lewis 1991: 147). The tremolo in the Suriname Djuka singing style was also used in Trinidad stickfight songs (Whylie and Warner-Lewis 1994: 142).

In the case of the calypso, the textual fixity induced during the twentieth century by composer literacy and less spontaneous performance events has made extempore performance rare, though still highly regarded. This improvisation is enabled by resort to predictability of theme, phraseology, and melodic patterns. A similar methodology was used in creating new African American spirituals since several prior song texts could be combined to produce a new one (in much the same way as is done with folktales), or known melodies were modified to accommodate new verbal texts (see Southern 1983: 172). Similar tendencies are at work in Jamaican dance-hall and African American hip-hop music: as an innovative rhythm gains ascendancy, new lyrics are composed to "ride" that rhythm, while melodic phrases, along with vocal and enunciatory techniques are intertextually appropriated.

Thematically, African and diaspora songs have inclined in the direction of work accompaniment, social commentary and derision, historical markers and reminders (see Price 1983: 25; Warner-Lewis 1994), dirges, incitement to dance and reproductive activity (see Edwards 1982: 181–92), invitations to make merry and deflect sorrow and anxiety, praise of the art form itself and self-praise of the singer, celebration and supplication of human antecedents and spiritual forces (see Price 1983: 8; de Carvalho 1993; Warner-Lewis 1994; Hart and Jabbour 1998). On the other hand, the cultivation of love and nature lyrics seems, in Africa, to have resulted from Arab contact, perhaps the same source which led via the Crusades to the growth of medieval Europe's courtly love tradition and the consolidation of the love theme in European, American, and Latin popular music into the present. As for nature poetry, Africans have tended to lyricize those plants and animals that hold for them supernatural power and/or economic value. However, Caribbean musical genres such as calypso, reggae, and their antecedent folk musics have tended to shun nature paeans as well as the theme of sentimental love, acknowledging rather love for mother, and treating heterosexual relations with disillusionment, as pragmatic alliances, or as sexual delight. In the case of the last, discourse has traditionally been metaphoric, but more recently – in the case of Jamaican dance-hall lyrics and American hip-hop – unabashedly direct. No doubt reflective of the overcrowding, educational marginalization, social malaise and economic unemployment produced by intense urbanization, these two musical genres have largely devoted their attention to social and interpersonal violence, leading to an antiromanticization of life and sex. Calypso on the other hand has so far retained the tradition of indirection with regard to sex, employing ambiguous pronunciation, or metaphors of agriculture, sports, doctor–patient relations, and automobile care to camouflage and/or humorously encode sexual allure and intercourse. Meanwhile, love songs of sentimental joy and heartbreak characterize rhythm-and-blues music of the United States and the anglophone Caribbean, as well as the Martinique/Guadeloupe beguine and zouk, Dominican Republic merengue, Cuban rhumba, mambo, and so on. Social and political critique has been carried in the old harvest songs of the United States, the later jailhouse blues, the folk and popular songs of the Caribbean (see d'Costa and Lalla 1989; Parrish 1992; Elder 1994), among them Eastern Caribbean calypso (see Rohlehr 1990), Jamaican reggae, and Haitian rara (see Yonker 1988).

Songs have had overlapping functions, as work songs could also be songs of ridicule, against employers, the other gender, and the deviant within the in-group. But there was also solo singing of lament and self-pity. Such songs tended to use the minor key and carried plaintive cadences, much like dirges; melodies and themes of this genre are no doubt the models upon which the African American spirituals and blues emerged. *Moans* are either precursors to and were certainly concurrent with the rise of spirituals; they still surge, unaccompanied by instrumentation or words, as groans and tremulous melodic snatches of spirituals from the scattered independent voices of older folk in southern black churches before the service begins; these overlapping doleful wails, outside of church use, are intoned to signal some inner grief.

The blues were a secular outgrowth of the spirituals, conveying similar feelings of "rootlessness and misery." They were first noted at the end of the nineteenth century being sung by wandering, often blind, performers whose themes bemoaned "the fickleness or departure of a loved one" (Southern 1983: 331), perhaps an extension of the kinless "motherless child" trauma of slavery. The spirituals themselves had first attracted attention early in the nineteenth century, having developed out of the often covert Christianization of the American slave population. Like the "ring shouts" which slaves sang in their "praise houses" till they were possessed by the Holy Spirit, some of the themes of these religious songs were hymn-based, some bewailed a luckless destiny and longed for release in death, others compared their slavery with the "experiences of frustration and divine deliverance, as set forth in the stories of the Hebrews in bondage" (Thurman 1990: 14). The Old Testament prophets and warriors along with the New Testament Messiah therefore became the inspiration for their delivery from an oppressive slavery (see Roberts 1989: 134–66):

> Ride on, King Jesus
> No man can he hinder thee

Indeed, in a Christian context, singing about the biblical heroes represented "a way of invoking a sense of the slaves' own collective past" in their self-identification as "the oppressed children of God" (Roberts 1989: 159); but this remark also held for the power icons represented by African divine forces. In Haitian *vodun*, Brazilian *candomble*, Trinidad's *orisha* or *shango*, and Cuban *regla de ocha* and *palo monte* (see Simpson 1970; Cabrera 1986), deities and ancestors were and still are invoked for help and guidance. The conviction that the body may be hurt but the spirit strengthened by trials and eventually freed by death led to the bewildering bravado and defiance on the part of rebels about to be hanged or tortured:

> O-o freedom . . .
> An' before I'd be a slave
> I'll be buried in my grave
> An' go home to my Lord
> An' be free

In the United States the influence of orthodox Christian hymnody on African diasporic music was extended by the practice of non- or semi-literate congregations having to wait for hymn lines to be called out. One consequence was prolongation of line-end words. The result was the nineteenth-century birth of gospel music, since the "combination of the very slow tempo and surging melismatic melody gave the impression of a music without rhythmic patterns" (Southern 1983: 447). This type of singing was also known as *sankey*, after Ira Sankey, an American evangelist who with others published a hymnal in 1875 (see Southern 1983: 445). This singing mode spread to the anglophone Caribbean through nineteenth-century African American proselytizers and the mode is still used in Caribbean Afro-Christian churches (see Seaga 1969; Henney 1973; tracks 23, 33 in Hill 1998; Glazier 1999). By the early decades of the twentieth century instrumental accompaniment was allowed in some of the United States churches, and the employment of piano, jazz-linked wind instruments, and tambourines introduced a new "rhythmic intensity formerly associated with dance music" (Southern 1983: 448). These *jubilees* or *holy rollers* were the origin of the ecstatic, highly melismatic gospel music that, now a specialty of the US music industry, has spread beyond color, denomination, and geographic boundaries.

Formal speech

Witty speech is "an important way in which one distinguishes oneself in public" (Abrahams 1974: 241). Oral performance in conversation becomes then a means of self-dramatization, display, and garnering "reputation" (Abrahams 1974: 243). The significance attached to words in both primary oral and orally oriented societies[2] underlies the admiration extended to individuals who display talent and artistry in their deployment of words and their perlocutionary force.[3] In African societies a connection exists between oratorical skill, public respect, and access to political, judicial, and religious power (see Albert 1964; Finnegan 1970: 448–52; Boadi 1972).

Various texts remark on eloquent, even grandiloquent speech among Caribbean-based Africans and their descendants during plantation times (see Abrahams 1983; Abrahams and Szwed 1983). Such grandiloquence must have sprung from an African sensitivity to the role of words in giving definition to moments in the time continuum by formalizing these occasions – the use of Austinian "performative language" (see Finnegan 1969); it also represented the exhilaration at acquiring new language/s. As such, these newly learnt phrases and vocabulary were often inappropriately applied in relation to social context and semantic intent. Malapropisms made for comedy to those who discerned the disjuncture between language style and speech event, but to the audience of formally unlearned and semiliterate gatherings at weddings, festivals, debates, and other public occasions, the speakers won admiration for their bombastic use of strange polysyllabic words and glibly delivered idioms: "Ek-kee homo, behold the man; Ek-kee homo, here I stand: I will now rise from my esteemed seat and I will say Bon Swar or Good Evening to the ladies and gentlemen of this nocturnal congregation" (in Lynch 1959; see also Abrahams 1977).

Other favorite techniques of public speaking have been rhyme, rhythmic parallelisms, and punning. These characterize the structure of the informal "dozens" as well. Such verbal strategies were honed at barbershops, verandahs, and drinking sessions in the United States and the Caribbean, and in a more technological age have come to be displayed by radio and dance-hall disc jockeys. But the formal addresses of some of the best exponents of African American public speaking demonstrate these arts as well. Gullah public prayers were "expected to be elevated and elaborate," incorporating "hymns, scriptural passages, and traditional expressions" heard and memorized by church deacons with little formal training (Jones-Jackson 1982: 26).

Characteristically, preacher/politician Jesse Jackson established enthusiastic rapport with a Jamaican audience,[4] not only by his speech's content, but also by the wit of his formulations:

> We're on a journey, an incomplete voyage, somewhere between slave ship and Championship . . .
>
> My mind is a pearl;
> I can learn anything in the world . . .

He then galvanized the audience to say after him:

> I am – somebody
> Respect me
> Protect me
> Never neglect me . . .
> If my mind can conceive it
> And my heart can believe it
> I can achieve it.

In a more meditative delivery at a graduation ceremony in Jamaica,[5] Martin Luther King, Jr., addressed the theme of sociohistorical transition, using the Revelations text "The former things are passed away . . . Behold I make all things new." He juxtaposed "the dying old [order] and the emerging new," urging therefore that "We must all learn to live together in this world or we must all perish together as fools" since

> We all are caught in an inescapable network of mutuality tied in a single garment of destiny, and whatever affects one directly, it affects me indirectly . . . I can never be what I ought to be until you are what you ought to be, and you can never be what you ought to be until I am what I ought to be. This is the interrelated structure of reality. Canon John Donne caught it years ago and placed it in graphic terms: "No man is an island . . . "

But, he warned with the quasi-proverbial truth of observation: "It's just a practical fact that he who gets behind in a race must forever remain behind or run faster than the man in front," and counseled that "The time is always right to do right." Again playing on semantic polyvalency, he critiqued with an aphorism: "The old insight of an eye for an eye ends up leaving everybody blind," and in a longer commentary: "We have spent far too much of our national budget establishing military bases around the world rather than bases of genuine concern and understanding." Then, in one of his signature concluding crescendos he urged excellence:

> If it falls to your lot to be a street sweeper,
> sweep streets like Raphael painted pictures,
> sweep streets like Michelangelo carved marble,
> sweep streets like Shakespeare wrote poetry,
> and like Beethoven composed music . . .

His delivery had been slow, with pauses after "and . . . " and "because . . . "; nouns, verbs, and adjectives had been stressed; the wealth of images and literary quotations had been dazzling; and the cultivation of a repeated pattern of falling cadences marking the end of breath-groups, together with sustained phrase-endings like held notes in a voice resonant and quivering, constituted the structural and paralinguistic magic of his oration. This shading of speech into song at which King's style had hinted is in fact one of the stylistic elements of African American sermonizing. Indeed, the slippage from one medium to another remains in the vocal mimicry of musical instruments in African and diasporan song, and in the scattering of nonce syllables. The performance of the epic of the thirteenth-century Mande king, Sunjata, is itself characterized by three delivery modes: speech for narrative segments; high-pitched recitative for philosophic comment as well as declamation of ancestral and clan relationships; while song is the channel for summary and commemorative eulogy. All these modes carry stringed and percussive xylophone accompaniment (see Innes 1974: 17–20). The form of present-day Jamaican dance-hall music and African American hip-hop, characterized by rhythmic speech over ostinato instrumentation and occasional melodic interludes, represents an unconscious return to this aspect of orature tradition.

Proverbs

In African speech culture appropriate use of proverbs and riddling idioms is a hallmark of high rhetoric. The centrality of European languages in the transatlantic diaspora has deprived proverbs of pride of place in formal address, nor do they operate as mechanisms of argument and precedent in European legal systems as they do in African indigenous courts (see Christensen 1958;

Messenger 1959). But proverbs still function in the diaspora as discursive summaries, evidence of precedent, warnings, child-rearing strategies, and arsenals in verbal attack. Competitive games of rapid proverb exchange at social events in some African societies seem a pastime that has faded out in the West Atlantic, though practiced into this century at funeral wakes in Guyana. But in many Caribbean territories where proverb use is patently alive, proverb retorts add pungency to verbal sparring. While proverbs in the Americas derive from multiple cultural heritages, cognates exist throughout the Americas. This suggests intraregional diffusion, on account of the extensive movement of Africans during the slavery era, as runaways, sailors, or in the company of their masters' migratory, business, or vacation travels. But there is also evidence that many of these proverbs calque those in several African cultures, carrying both semantic resemblance and image correlation. In Africa, shared cultural traditions and ethnic mingling have produced cognate proverbs among contiguous peoples, and it is therefore likely that many West Atlantic proverbs have multiple African sources. Among parallels between Caribbean and Nigerian proverbs are (see Ojoade 1987): "Doh cuss alligator long mout' till yuh cross de river" – Tiv and Jukun; "Dog sweat, but long hair cover it" – Igbo and Yoruba; "God fan fly fi 'tumpa tail (stump-tailed) cow" – Kuteb, Igbo, and Yoruba. Yoruba and Caribbean people advise against substituting a serviceable item for a less utilitarian one despite surface similarity: "Don't swop black dog for monkey"; and Yoruba reference to the hawk or crow that seeks to hide intentions under the excuse of fortuitous circumstance is rendered in Jamaica: "When jonkro (vulture) wan' (want) go a gully/grasspiece/ windward, he say is cool breeze blow him there" (in Ajibola 1969); similarly "While the master of a house is alive, the front garden will not lack attention" (in Ajibola 1969:52) becomes in Jamaica "When man dead, grass grow at 'im door." The Efik observation is Caribbean-wide: "The higher monkey climb, the more his ass/tail is exposed"; and the Edo, Jamaicans, and Guyanese warn of the inevitable combination of maturity and disillusionment: "Pig ask 'im mooma 'Wha' mek yuh mout' so long?' Pig mooma answer 'Yuh a grow, yuh will learn.'" Several Igbo proverbs reproduced in Achebe's novels are paralleled in Jamaica: "He who will swallow udala seeds must consider the size of his anus" is reproduced as "Cow must know 'ow 'im bottom stay before 'im swallow abbe (Twi for oil palm) seed,"or "Jonkro must know what 'im a do (is doing) before 'im swallow abbe seed"; "The fly who has no one to advise it follows the corpse into the ground" becomes "Sweet-mout' fly follow coffin go a (to) hole"; "The sleep that lasts for one market day to another has become death" contains the same metonym, "Take sleep mark death (Sleep is a foreshadowing of death)" (see Achebe 1975: 226).

The query "Where are the young suckers that will grow when the old banana tree dies?" is a rhetorical rendering of "When plantain wan' dead, it shoot (sends out new suckers)"; "A man who makes trouble for others is also making one for himself" (Achebe 1969: 59–60, 88) echoes "When you dig a hole/ditch for one, dig two." The Akan "The offspring of an antelope cannot possibly resemble a deer's offspring" (in Danquah 1944: 197) is one of several African cognates for "Goat don't make sheep." The Caribbean awareness of unequal power relations, "Cockroach nuh business inna fowl fight," replicates the Congo "In a court of fowls the cockroach never wins his case" (in Weeks 1911: 33) just as: "Teach a child before it goes to the dance not after it has come back" (in Claridge 1969: 251) is echoed in Jamaica's "Learn to dance a yard (at home) before you go a foreign (abroad)"; and advocacy of patient judgment: "It is best to let an offence repeat itself at least three times; the first offence may be an accident, the second a mistake, but the third is likely to be intentional" (in Claridge 1969: 252) has its Jamaican reflex: "One time a mistake, second time a purpose, third time a habit."

Banter and abuse

The best known of a bewildering array of African American terms for double-talk is *signifying*, speech whose essential element is indirection (see Mitchell-Kernan 1972: 315, 316, 326), a significant communicative strategy in sub-Saharan Africa (see Piot 1993). But this is not the only African American term for this form of interaction. Terms not only change over time, but vary from one locale to another, and there is tremendous semantic slippage and overlap among them (see Abrahams 1974). A similar situation obtains for Jamaica, a much smaller space, since there are generational and regional differences in referents. In Trinidad, with half of Jamaica's population, there is less an issue of regionalism than a slippage of semantic range between *fatigue, heckle, tone, mamaguy,* and *picong.* In the Trinidad instance semantic indeterminacy also stems from a layering of terms from indigenous languages such as Spanish, French, and English. *Fatigue, heckle* and *give tone* mean "to tease," "to harrass by poking fun at"; *mamaguy* means the same, except that it embodies flattery with the intent to mildly embarrass the addressee and even deflect an anticipated taunt; while *picong* may function as a synonym for *mamaguy*, but often touches on an annoying (possible) truth or rumor that leaves the addressee peeved at the possibility that what had been said in jest was a concealed deprecation. *Mepwi* (from French *mépris*) was a once common term for taunt and insult, either directly or through metaphor and name-substitution.

In general, however, within African American signifying modes, one may distinguish the "clean" and "dirty" *dozens*. These may take the structure of rhymed couplets, but must necessarily contain an extravagant simile (see Labov 1972: 274). In a *clean dozens* exchange at a Southern rural workcamp, one man claimed, "Ah seen a man so ugly till they had to spread a sheet over his head at night so sleep could slip up on him," which another *capped* with the comparison: "Those men y'all been talkin' 'bout wasn't ugly at all . . . Ah knowed one so ugly till you could throw him in the Mississippi river and skim ugly for six months." Yet another rejoined: "He didn't die – he jus' uglied away" (in Hurston 1970: 94). By their obscenity and surface misogyny, *dirty dozens* resemble the male contests in derogatory songs and utterances during certain Ghanaian festivals (see Abrahams 1970: 40–41; Labov 1972: 274; Agovi 1987).

African American *loud talking* (Mitchell-Kernan 1972: 329–30) is commonly known in the Caribbean as *droppin'/throwin' word(s)'*. *Drop word* takes place when an unfavorable comment is made by X to Y within earshot of Z for whom the remark is actually intended. Another type of indirect speech, its aim is to offend, and if Z responds, a full-blown *quarrel* or *cuss out* may ensue, with X and Y defending themselves with proverbs such as "If me throw stone inna pig sty, the one that bawl out is the one that get lick [hit]," or "Who the cap fit, make them wear it," and "Me throw me corn, me na call no fowl."[6] Rather than reply to offending remarks, Z could begin loudly singing hymns that function as indirect critiques of and threats to the aggressor, or the aim may be to drown out further belittling remarks: "At the Cross, at the Cross / Where I first saw the light," or "When God get ready / You got to move."

Caardin', *ribbin'* or *mout'in'* in Jamaica is comparable with *tantalize* in Guyana (see Edwards 1978) and witty clean signifying or *rappin'* in the United States (see Mitchell-Kernan 1972: 322–26). As either flattery or a back-handed compliment, this activity shades into Jamaica's *lyrics/lyricisin'*, or Trinidad's *sweet mouth/talk*. This category of comments is an important interactive medium of playfulness among an in-group, particularly young people at street corners, in classrooms, or at the workplace. But these types of comment, repartee, and dialogue can transmute into ritual insults very similar to the *dozens*, or to antagonistic *'busin' out* or *war* in Guyana (see Edwards 1978: 195, 196, 204, 206), *cussin'* and *meli* (from French *mêlée*) in Antigua (see Reisman 1974: 119–22), *tracin'* in Jamaica. Such boundary crossing may be signaled by the onset of obscene language. Verbal aggression involves each side in hurting the other by exaggerated accusations of ugliness (see Samarin 1969); promiscuous, unorthodox, or ineffective sexual performance; unhygienic habits; poverty; and possibly derogatory comments about the opponent's antecedents and relatives.

Middle-class verbal assaults take on a more logical and explanatory tenor called in the anglophone Caribbean *quarrellin'* and *tellin' off*. Whereas these are heated exchanges, Jamaican *runnin' up one's mouth*, or *makin' up fuss*, similar to Euro-American "blowing hot air," implies that a speaker is continuing a monologue of complaint or even issuing threats, but these are treated dismissively by the object of the complaint and other hearers.

Boasts, the epic, and narratives

In Trinidad *makin' gran' charge* – originally a French-inspired military image – infers a promise or boast that is hardly likely to be effected. When its tenor is defiance or challenge, it becomes *robber talk*, named for a carnival masquerade called "the robber." The robber reels off grandiose boasts of his terror and invincibility: "when I clash my feet together the earth crumble, famine follow. Wherever I stand, grass never grows, sun never shine, far more for mankind to go . . . I bite off bits of the moon to lengthen the days and shorten the season . . . There's no gun, dagger made of steel, can make me feel or heal . . . " (in Crowley 1956: 264 fn. 125). This language style closely resembles that of a masquerade in Achebe's *Arrow of God*:

> There is a place, Beyond Knowing, where no man or spirit ventures unless he hòlds in his right hand his kith and in his left hand his kin. But I, Ogalanya, Evil Dog that Warms His Body through the Head, I took neither kith nor kin and yet went to this place . . . the first friend I made turned out to be a wizard. I made another friend and found he was a leper. I, Ogalanya . . . made friends with a leper from whom even a poisoner flees. (Achebe 1975: 48)

Apart from its masquerade connections, the discourse of awe-inspiring self-projection is known as *ese* in Ibibio and *ase* in Efik. This is a spoken poetic "(auto)-biography or commemorative toast of an heroic nature . . . narrated at funerals but also occurring during male drinking sessions" (Ikiddeh 1966: 21), a genre continued in the African American toasts and boasts which project a central character such as Stagolee or Toledo in physical, mental, sexual, or verbal situations during which he outshines others (see Abrahams 1970: 43–49, 88–96).

Folk narratives

These form yet another orature category that are in large measure inherited from Africa. Yet because of the cultural disruptions characterizing the transatlantic migration, no epics have evolved. While slave entertainment defied the plantation regime, confining itself to after-work night spaces and holidays, slave life was insufficiently leisurely to accommodate the sustained, sometimes daily, performance needed for epic re-enactments; at the same time, epics contain culture-specific genealogical, migration and military histories unsuitable for multi-ethnic audience appeal and translinguistic participation (see Okpewho 1979). Insofar as there exist in the West Atlantic germs of epic narrative material, these are to be found in the charter legends of various Maroon or runaway slave communities. These however tend to be short accounts, but do recall community founders, migration treks, and mythically stated rationalizations regarding their relationships with other groups (see Price 1983: 8). As in Africa, these myths of association are couched in kinship metaphors (see Bilby 1984; Vansina 1990). On the religious plane, sacred narratives about Yoruba divinities have been retained in the lore of African-derived religions such as Cuba's santería or *regal de oct* (rules/order of the *orisha* or deities), and *candomble* of Bahia, Brazil (see Cabrera 1961; Verger 1980; Martínez Furé 1986; de Carvalho 1993). These are accounts of creation, and the attributes, adventures and interrelationships of the divinities.

While originary African epics have not survived the disintegration of earlier regional and national aggregations, the epic as an inclusive genre embraces self-contained narratives, paeans, philosophic commentary, proverbs, and songs. There is thus some evidence that narratives that may have formed part of epics have survived the Middle Passage, but this may result from the fact that similar tale motifs occur within oral genres other than the epic. However, Raymond Relouzat postulates the likely origin of several Caribbean tales about the Seven-headed Beast as the Segu epic of the Bambara hero, Bakary Dian. Bakary destroys the monster Bilissi (Arabic "the Devil"), but before he can claim his reward, an impersonator claims it (see Relouzat 1988: 81–83; Parsons 1933: 268–71, 1936: 95–97; Tanna 1984: 113–15). Again, the Mandinka epic of Sunjata contains the story of a hunter rescued by his three dogs from the machinations of an attractive witch who attempts to discover the secret location of the hero's protective talisman. Similar tales are the Dahomean "Flight Up the Tree: Why the Abiku Are Worshipped in the Bush" (Herskovits and Herskovits 1958: 275–84) and Jamaica's "Old Witch Woman an Hunta" and "Blam Blam Sinday, Dido" (Tanna 1984: 125–28). As such, these tales and motifs are less likely derived from particular epics than from the commonly shared sources on which both epics and segmentary tales drew.

Other widespread tales in Africa and the Americas concern amphibious animals like tortoise or frog who borrow bird feathers but, after offending the birds, fall from heaven when vengefully deprived of the borrowed trappings; tortoise or rabbit/hare deceptively winning a race by placing his children in relays along the race route; and the Tar Baby debacle (see Harris 1880: 7–11; Weeks 1911:3 67, 388–90; Barker and Sinclair 1917: 69–72; Bascom 1992). Another group recalls the "Complete Gentleman" (see Tutuola 1952: 17–25). A girl attracted by the physical appeal of a dashing male and entering precipitately into marriage with the cannibal/devil is taken to his deathly domain. Her rescue is sometimes effected by a magic formula in song. The role of songs in plot progression and action segmentation is common in African folktales (see Scheub 1975: 50–54). This tradition has been partially retained in the transatlantic diaspora, though it is likely that many tales have lost their earlier song component. Another narrative inheritance is the use of ideophones, words which by their sound symbolism and iteration convey not only onomatopoeia, but also size, gait, speech, or affect (see Noss 1970: 45–46).

Either the same characters people the tales on both sides of the Atlantic, or diasporan substitutes are either translation contingencies or reflect different ecological environments. Among the constants are the tricksters: spider – commonly known in the Caribbean by the Akan name Anansi – tortoise, and a creature variously referred to in the Americas as "cunny [coney] rabbit," or "hare."[7] Their dupes are Tiger/Leopard, Elephant, Monkey, and Hyena, who becomes Dog or Bouki.[8] Intellectual acuity and agility are the assets that enable tricksters to overcome difficulties and compete with others. But in some tales the trickster is condemned to defeat because his conduct leads to social disintegration by fracturing relationships of trust.

In both African and diasporan tales, animals carry the titular address of *tío/cha,* or "uncle," *compère,* or "god-father," "brer/bra/brother." Another structural analogue lies in tale formulaic preludes and epilogues. Folktale sessions may be preceded by riddle contests. The Jamaican storyteller then cries, "Story time!" the Bahamian shouts, "Bunday," the audience echoing these words or responding, "Yeah," "Alright" (Crowley 1954: 219). In the francophone Caribbean, the *conteur* rallies his listeners with "People, crick!" to which the audience replies "Crack!" This formulation intimates the Yoruba concretization of artistic inspiration as a load falling *gbalagada* from the sky, breaking a tree bough. Or the narrator cries, "Tim, Tim!" to which listeners shout, "Bwa shess! [Dry wood]." The narrator may then add, "Everything God put on earth! / What God put on earth?" with the predictable reply, "Everything" (see Shillingford 1970; Charlemagne 1997). The "Crick" / "Crack" device is interspersed throughout the narration as a means of ensuring audience alertness and to heighten suspense by slightly delaying the recount of events. The tale itself may commence with the European fairytale formula "Once upon a time," or "There was once . . ." But it may parallel the Igbo "When lizards were in ones and twos" (Achebe 1975: 14, 70), with the Jamaican nonspecific time reference "When Wapi kill Fillup," or "When mih eye de a me knee (When my eyes were at my knees, i.e. when I was very small)," which translates Yoruba *nigba ti oju si wa lorunkun* (see Olayemi 1971: 33), and "When saltfish was a shingle house-top (When salted fish was used as roof shingles)," like the Bahamian "In old people time when they used to take fish scale to make shingle, and fish bone to make needle" (see Crowley 1954: 220). Closing formulae in the Eastern Caribbean include "You lie well!," a compliment from the audience to the narrator, or the storyteller's own rhyming couplets, "Crick Crack, / Monkey break he [his] back," or "The wire ben', / The story en'." Lying as a synonym for "fiction" replicates the Eastern Caribbean extension of the term "nansi 'tori" to mean "lie," but in the storytelling context reference to lying recalls the Akan narrator's closing "I have not said," signifying disengagement from the awful powers of the Word (see Izutsu 1956; Tambiah 1968; Peek 1981). His Jamaican counterpart asserts, "Jack Mandora,[9] me no choose none (I have no opinion)," thereby dissociating him/herself from the imaginary characters and situations conjured up through word and gesture.

Conclusion

Despite the "pressures of the text"[10] in literate and complex chirographic societies, the oral traditions have largely survived, even transforming themselves into new genres and usages as evident in the magic, quest, and conflict motifs of print and video cartoons, electronic games, product promotions, films, and *Harry Potter*-type novels. Furthermore, scribal artists and musical composers have resorted to oral traditions, whether out of cultural nationalism – the need to ground their conceptions and representations in the "thought, word, and deed" of a particular people – or to project and mine the resources of inherited poetics. The intention, techniques, and cultural matrices of aspects of the writings of Paul Lawrence Dunbar, James Baldwin, Ralph Ellison, Derek and Roderick Walcott, Kamau Brathwaite, Toni Morrison, Simone Schwarz-Bart, Erna Brodber, Olive Senior, Merle Hodge, Merle Collins, Earl Lovelace, Edwidge Danticat, and Nalo Hopkinson, to name a miserly few, are but partially understood and appreciated without reference to traditional verbal esthetic strategies.

Notes

1. See Lewin 1974: 127; evidenced also in Yoruba songs by Margaret Buckley in Hill 1998.
2. Ong (1982: 11) uses this term to refer to nonliterate societies. By "orally oriented societies" I mean the cultures and subcultures, even in a high-technology ambience, which preserve much of the mindset of primary orality and also cultures with "restricted literacy" as elaborated in Goody and Watt 1968: 11–20.
3. "Perlocution" defines the speech act, either its conscious or unwitting "consequential effects upon the feelings, thoughts, or actions of the audience, or of the speaker, or of other persons" (Austin 1962: 10).
4. At the People's National Party's Founder's Day commemoration, Assembly Hall, University of the West Indies, Jamaica, September 1985.
5. At the Graduation Ceremony, University of the West Indies, Jamaica, 20 June 1965.
6. The last two occur in Marley 1976. Another variant, "If the shoe fits, wear it," concludes the verbal exchange in Mitchell-Kernan 1972: 318.
7. Among the Mende of the Senegambia region, Hagbe is a rabbit-sized antelope. See Kilson 1976: 42, fn2. The Mende trickster is Spider, and proverbs aver that both Spider and the folktale represent human behavior (Kilson 1976: 32).
8. Wolof for "hyena." See Crowley 1954; Gaudet 1992.
9. As cryptic as "Wapi and Fillup."
10. Phrase borrowed from the title to Brown 1995.

Bibliography

Abrahams, Roger. 1970. *Positively Black*. New Jersey: Prentice Hall.

1974. "Black Talking on the Streets." In *Explorations in the Ethnography of Speaking*. Ed. Richard Bauman and Joel Sherzer. London: Cambridge University Press: 240–62.

1977. "Tea Meeting: An Essay in Civilization." In *Old Roots in New Lands: Historical and Anthropological Perspectives on Black Experiences in the Americas*. Ed. Ann Pescatello. Westport: Greenwood: 173–208.

1983. "Traditions of Eloquence in Afro-American Communities." In *The Man-of-Words in the West Indies. Performance and the emergence of creole culture*. Baltimore: Johns Hopkins University Press: 21–39.

Abrahams, Roger, and John F. Szwed. 1983. "Ways of Speaking: Speech, Letters, Names, Proverbs." In *After Africa: Extracts from British Travel Accounts and Journals of the Seventeenth, Eighteenth, and Nineteenth Centuries concerning the Slaves, their Manners, and Customs in the British West Indies*. Ed. Roger Abrahams and John Szwed. New Haven: Yale University Press: 77–107.

Achebe, Chinua. [1958] 1969. *Things Fall Apart*. London: Heinemann.

[1964] 1975. *Arrow of God*. London: Heinemann.

Agovi, Kofi. 1987. "Black American 'Dirty Dozens' and the Tradition of Verbal Insult in Ghana." In *Black Culture and Black Consciousness in Literature*. Ed. Chidi Ikonne, Abele Eko, Julia Oku. Ibadan: Heinemann Educational Books: 243–54.

Ajibola, J. O. [1947] 1969. *Owe Yoruba*. Ibadan: Oxford University Press.

Akpabot, Samuel. 1986. *Foundations of Nigerian Traditional Music.* Ibadan: Spectrum.

Albert, Ethel. 1964. "'Rhetoric', 'Logic,' and 'Poetics' in Burundi: Culture Patterning of Speech Behavior." *American Anthropologist* 66.6, pt. 2: 35–54.

Austin, J. L. 1962. *How to Do Things with Words*. Cambridge, MA: Harvard University Press.

Barker, W. H., and Cecelia Sinclair, eds. 1917. *West African Folk Tales*. London: George Harrap.

Bascom, William. 1992. *African Folktales in the New World*. Bloomington: Indiana University Press.

Bilby, Kenneth. 1984. "'Two Sister Pikni': A Historical Tradition of Dual Ethnogenesis in Eastern Jamaica." *Caribbean Quarterly* 30.3–4: 10–25.

Boadi, Lawrence. 1972. "The Language of the Proverb in Akan." In *African Folklore*. Ed. Richard Dorson. New York: Anchor: 183–91.

Brown, Stewart, ed. 1995. *The Pressures of the Text: Orality, Texts and the Telling of Tales.* University of Birmingham: Centre of West African Studies.

Cabrera, Lydia. 1961. *Cuentos negros de Cuba*. Havana: Ediciones Nuevo Mundo.

1986. *Reglas de Congo: Mayombe, Palo Monte*. Miami: Ediciones Universal.

Charlemagne, Lydia. 1997. "Content, Structure and Characterisation in St. Lucian Folktales." Caribbean Studies Project, University of the West Indies, Jamaica.

Christensen, James. 1958. "The Role of Proverbs in Fante Culture." *Africa* 28. 3: 232–43.

Claridge, G. Cyril. [1922] 1969. *Wild Bush Tribes of Tropical Africa*. New York: Negro Universities Press.

Crowley, Daniel. 1954. "Form and Style in a Bahamian Folktale." *Caribbean Quarterly* 3.4: 218–34.

1956. "The Midnight Robbers." *Caribbean Quarterly* 4.3–4: 263–74.

Danquah, J. B. 1944. *The Akan Doctrine of God: A Fragment of Gold Coast Ethics and Religion.* London: Lutterworth.

D'Costa, Jean, and Barbara Lalla, eds. 1989. *Voices in Exile: Jamaican Texts of the 18th and 19th Centuries*. Tuscaloosa: University of Alabama Press.

De Carvalho, Jose Jorge. 1993. *Cantos sagrados do Xango do Recife.* Brasilia: Fundacao Cultural Palmares.

Edwards, Walter. 1978. "Tantalisin and Busin in Guyana." *Anthropological Linguistics* 20.5: 194–213.

1982. "A Description and Interpretation of the Kwe-kwe Tradition in Guyana." *Folklore* 93.2: 181–92.

Elder, J. D. 1994. *Folksongs from Tobago: Culture and Song in Tobago*. London: Karnak House.

Finnegan, Ruth. 1969. "How to Do Things with Words: Performative Utterances among the Limba of Sierra Leone." *Man* 4.4: 537–52.

1970. *Oral Literature in Africa.* Oxford: Clarendon Press.

Furé, Rogelio Martínez. 1986. "Patakin: Sacred Literature of Cuba." *African Cultures*. Paris: UNESCO: 41–83.

Gaudet, Marcia. 1992. "Bouki, the Hyena, in Louisiana and African Tales." *Journal of American Folklore* 105.415: 66–72.

Gérard, Albert. 1981. *African Language Literatures: An Introduction to the Literary History of Sub-Saharan Africa.* Washington, DC: Three Continents Press.

Glazier, Stephen. 1999. "The Noise of Astonishment: Spiritual Baptist Music in Context." In *Religion, Diaspora, and Cultural Identity: A Reader in the Anglophone Caribbean.* Ed. J. W. Pulis. New York: Gordon and Breach: 277–94.

Goody, Jack, and Ian Watt. 1968. "The Consequences of Literacy." In *Literacy in Traditional Societies*. Ed. Jack Goody. Cambridge: Cambridge University Press: 27–68.

Gregsen, Edgar. 1977. *Language in Africa: An Introductory Survey*. New York: Gordon and Breach.

Harris, Joel Chandler. 1880. *Uncle Remus: His Songs and His Sayings*. New York: Appleton-Century-Crofts.

Hart, Mickey and Alan Jabbour, producers. 1998. *The Yoruba/Dahomean Collection: Orishas across the Ocean*. RCD 10405. Washington, DC: Library of Congress Endangered Music Project.

Herskovits, Melville and Frances Herskovits. 1958. *Dahomean Narrative*. Evanston: Northwestern University Press.

Hill, Donald, producer. 1998. *Peter Was a Fisherman: The 1939 Trinidad Field Recordings of Melville and Frances Herskovits*. Cambridge, MA: Rounder Records, CD 1114.

Henney, Jeannette Hillman. 1973. "The Shakers of St. Vincent: A Stable Religion." In *Religion, Altered States of Consciousness, and Social Change*. Ed. Erika Bourguignon. Columbus: The Ohio State University Press: 219–63.

Hurston, Zora Neale. [1935] 1970. *Mules and Men: Negro Folktales and Voodoo Practices in the South*. New York: Harper and Row.

Ikiddeh, Ime. 1966. "Ibibio Folktale Night: An Introduction to Ibibio Oral Literature." MA thesis, University of Leeds.

Innes, Gordon. 1974. *Sunjata: Three Mandinka Versions*. London: School of Oriental and African Studies.

Izutsu, Toshihiko. 1956. *Language and Magic: Studies in the Magical Function of Speech*. Tokyo: Keino Institute of Philological Studies.

Jones-Jackson, Patricia. 1982. "Oral Tradition of Prayer in Gullah." *The Journal of Religious Thought* 39.1: 21–33.

Kilson, Marion. 1976. *Royal Antelope and Spider: West African Mende Tales*. Cambridge, MA: Langdon Associates.

Labov, William. 1972. "Rules for Ritual Insults." In *Rappin' and Stylin' Out: Communication in Urban Black America*. Ed. Thomas Kochman. Urbana: University of Illinois Press: 265–314.

Lewin, Olive. 1974. "Folk Music Research in Jamaica." In *Black Communication: Dimensions of Research and Instruction*. Ed. J. Daniels. New York: Speech Communication Association.

Lynch, Louis. 1959. "Tea Meeting." In *West Indian Eden: The Book of Barbados*. Glasgow: Robert Maclehose: 231–36.

Marley, Bob. 1976. "Who the Cap Fit." *Rastaman Vibration*. Bob Marley and the Wailers, Island Records. ILPS 9383.

Messenger, John. 1959. "The Role of Proverbs in a Nigerian Judicial System." *Southwestern Journal of Anthropology* 15: 64–73.

Mitchell-Kernan, Claudia. 1972. "Signifying, Loud-Talking and Marking." In *Rappin' and Stylin' Out: Communication in Urban Black America*. Ed. Thomas Kochman. Urbana: University of Illinois Press: 315–35.

Noss, Philip. 1970. "The Performance of the Gbaya Tale." *Research in African Literatures* 1.1: 41–49.

Ojoade, J. O. 1987. "Nigerian Folklore in the African Diaspora." In *Black Culture and Black Consciousness in Literature*. Ed. Chidi Ikonne, Ebele Eko, and Julia Oku. Ibadan: Heinemann Educational Books: 243–54.

Okpewho, Isidore. 1979. *The Epic in Africa: Toward a Poetics of the Oral Performance*. New York: Columbia University Press.

Olayemi, Kayode. 1971. "Salient Features of the Yoruba Oral Tale." MA diss. University of Leeds.

Ong, Walter. 1982. *Orality and Literacy: The Technologizing of the Word*. London: Methuen.

Parrish, Lydia. [1942] 1992. *Slave Songs of the Georgia Sea Islands*. Athens: University of Georgia Press.

Parsons, Elsie Clews. 1933. *Folk-Lore of the Antilles, French and English*. New York: American Folk-Lore Society, vol. I.

1936. *Folk-Lore of the Antilles, French and English*. New York: American Folk-Lore Society, vol. II.

Peek, Philip. 1981. "The Power of Words in African Verbal Arts." *Journal of American Folklore* 94. 371: 19–43.

Piot, Charles. 1993. "Secrecy, Ambiguity, and the Everyday in Kabre Culture." *American Anthropologist* 95. 2: 353–70.

Price, Richard. 1983. *First-Time: The Historical Vision of an Afro-American People*. Baltimore: Johns Hopkins University Press.

Price, Sally, and Richard Price. 1980. *Afro-American Arts of the Surinam Rain Forest*. Berkeley: University of California Press.

Reisman, Karl. 1974. "Contrapuntal Conversations in an Antiguan Village." In *Explorations in the Ethnography of Speaking*. Ed. Richard Bauman and Joel Sherzer. London: Cambridge University Press.

Relouzat, Raymond. 1988. "Le conte créole des Amériques et deux légendes ouest-africaines d'avant la Traite." *Tradition orale et imaginaire créole*. Martinique: Ibis Rouge: 81–88.

Roberts, John. 1989. *From Trickster to Badman: The Black Folk Hero in Slavery and Freedom*. Philadelphia: University of Pennsylvania Press.

Rohlehr, Gordon. 1990. *Calypso and Society in Pre-Independence Trinidad*. Port-of-Spain: Gordon Rohlehr.

Scheub, Harold. 1975. *The Xhosa Ntsomi*. Oxford: Clarendon Press.

Seaga, Edward. 1969. "Revival Cults in Jamaica: Notes Toward a Sociology of Religion." *Jamaica Journal* 3.2: 3–13.

Shillingford, Toni. 1970. "French Creole Folktales from Dominica: An Analysis of Their Content and Form." MA diss. University of the West Indies, Jamaica.

Simpson, George. 1970. *Religious Cults of the Caribbean: Trinidad, Jamaica, and Haiti*. Puerto Rico: Institute of Caribbean Studies.

Southern, Eileen. 1983. *The Music of Black Musicians: A History*. New York: Norton.

Tambiah, Stanley J. 1968. "The Magical Power of Words." *Man* 3: 175–208.

Tanna, Laura. 1984. *Jamaican Folk Tales and Oral Histories*. Kingston: Institute of Jamaica.

Thurman, Howard. 1990. *Deep River and the Negro Spiritual Speaks of Life and Death*. Richmond, IN: Howard Thurman.

Tutuola, Amos. 1952. *The Palm Wine Drinkard*. London: Faber and Faber.

Vansina, Jan. 1990. *Paths in the Rainforests: Toward a History of Political Tradition in Equatorial Africa*. Oxford: James Currey.

Verger, Pierre. 1980. "Yoruba Tales from Brazil." *Kiabàrà* 3.2: 139–58.

Warner-Lewis, Maureen. 1991. *Guinea's Other Suns: The African Dynamic in Trinidad Culture*. Dover, MA: The Majority Press.

1994. *Yoruba Songs of Trinidad*. London: Karnak House.

Weeks, John. 1911. *Congo Life and Folklore*. London: Religious Tract Society.

Whylie, Marjorie, and Maureen Warner-Lewis. 1994. "Characteristics of Maroon Music from Jamaica and Suriname." In *Maroon Heritage: Archaeological, Ethnographic and Historical Perspectives*. Ed. Kofi Agorsah. Kingston: Canoe: 139–48.

Yonker, Delores. 1988. "Rara in Haiti." In *Caribbean Festival of Arts*. Ed. John Nunley and Judith Bettelheim. Seattle: Saint Louis Art Museum and University of Washington Press.

8

Carnival and the folk origins of West Indian drama

KEITH Q. WARNER

In the amalgam of languages and cultures that is the Caribbean, it is almost impossible to reach complete agreement on the origin of any of the art forms that have emerged as distinctly Caribbean. In colonial times, the European masters naturally replicated their cultures in this new-found milieu, although they did make a few concessions to the presence and input of other communities – the indigenous ones they found on arrival, and those from Africa and from India in particular. In the postcolonial societies of the Caribbean, the newly independent states have found themselves faced with an intriguing cultural choice. On one hand, they can discard what was brought by the Europeans and stick to what they have produced themselves – often labeled "folk" or "local" to set it apart from the more established extra-Caribbean equivalents. On the other, they can retain Eurocentric values, traditions, and art forms, and in so doing risk giving the impression that they are renouncing their cultural independence. Naturally, it would be highly impractical for societies in the West Indies – still the familiar name for the anglophone territories referred to in our title – to attempt to choose one of the foregoing over the other. In reality, several values and traditions have come together to produce authentic, unique art forms that are both similar to those of Europe, and sufficiently dissimilar from them to be distinctly Caribbean or West Indian. Carnival fits this pattern, as does drama.

West Indians have been stereotypically portrayed as carefree and fun-loving, and as not taking seriously matters of the gravest import. At one end of the chain of island territories, Jamaicans have been seen as reacting to any difficult situation with the popular response: "No problem." At the other end, Trinidadians have been known to take a characteristically light-hearted view of any crisis. This was evident in 1990 when the country, under curfew following an attempted coup, saw many of its citizens having curfew parties wherever they ended up, as restrictions went into effect. Throughout the West Indies, success in cricket at the international level is almost always followed by a carnival-type celebration, and lack of success is attributed to the cavalier attitude of the players: their carnival or calypso style of play. This propensity has led observers outside the region to conclude that West Indians, and Trinidadians in particular, have a carnival mentality. It is a description that causes those so branded to bristle at its negative connotation, but it is also one that, upon further reflection, is not without its positive attributes. Carnival, as it has evolved in Trinidad, and as it has expanded to the other English-speaking territories of the Caribbean, pervades the popular culture of the islands. It is only natural that it would be a key contributor to the folk origins of the drama produced by the people of the region.

Early researchers maintained that carnival in Trinidad evolved from celebrations by French settlers. This claim is bolstered by the fact that in the anglophone territories, it is only in Trinidad that this spectacle took on the grandeur that we now see, and this from approximately the time slavery was abolished. Carnival as eventually celebrated by the masses was seen as originating from the minority French settlers who had flocked to the island with the promise of land holdings and inexpensive labor to work them. This French influence may in part explain why this festival did not develop in the same manner in the other anglophone territories that were without a similar influx. The fact remains that the Trinidad carnival prospered where the other territories had none, or at least no exact equivalent. This situation is not unlike that which obtained with the development of the calypso, with Trinidad being given credit for its origin despite the existence of similar-type songs throughout the Caribbean. There is little dispute that carnival and calypso are Trinidad's contribution to West Indian popular culture.

With the added importance finally given to the African presence in the islands, there have been those who claim that carnival came to the West Indies from Africa. To support such a claim, they cite similarities in some of the carnival characters – the stilt walker or moko jumbie, and the overall style of masking, for example – as proof of this origin. There is also the view that the French, like other Europeans, merely copied what originated in Africa, since the African continent had been seen as a vast no man's land where all who so desired could go plundering.

Both camps may be correct, in that elements from both Europe and Africa are certainly in the carnival, but so are elements found in neither of these cultures. Indeed, until other West-Indian territories belatedly began to promote a recognizably Trinidad-style carnival, Trinidad's version was hailed as "the" carnival of the region, and has even chauvinistically been billed as "the greatest show on earth." Worldwide acclaim and replication further justify looking principally at Trinidad's carnival when examining the relationship between this spectacle and the origins of what one could arguably call West-Indian drama.

In this regard, and with respect to the staging of plays in some internationally recognized format, there is a great deal of similarity between the islands. In other words, theater per se can be found all the way from Jamaica, where its presence is quite strong, to Trinidad, where it is less so. Still, differences are significant enough to raise questions about the emergence of a national drama in the West Indies. The islands each have peculiar, distinguishing events that are the popular artistic expressions of the national psyche, the folklore, so to speak. In the Bahamas, it may be the John Canoe; in Jamaica, it may be the annual pantomime. In Trinidad, it is the carnival.

The theater created by West Indians does not always satisfy the definition of "theater" as determined by those who purportedly brought this art form to the region. But if the theater developed in the West Indies is valid, though often encumbered with the ever-present "folk" epithet, and given that a truly West Indian drama might be more mirage than reality, then carnival and its folk aspects are not merely influences on the conventional theater. It is not enough simply to insert a carnival character, a costume, or a song into the conventional theater. The entire carnival is, in fact, the national theater of Trinidad, it being understood that the concept of theater would have evolved significantly along with everything else in the society. Carnival is obviously not the only theater, but it is sufficiently developed to warrant examination as a truly West Indian creation.

Of the carnivals celebrated in the West Indies today, Trinidad's is the most engaging, infectious, and widely experienced by both artist and audience. Apart from those characteristics it is the one carnival that encompasses to a significant degree all the aspects that comprise theater. That it may not, to the purists, satisfy all the attributes of the conventional theater cannot serve to disqualify it as theater or classify it solely as another form of presentation. For in reality what carnival and the people of Trinidad and Tobago – the official name of the twin-island republic, though there is the tendency to speak more so of Trinidad carnival – have done is to redefine the notion of theater. Combined with the purists' studious avoidance of seeing carnival as theater is the fact that fine art has mainly been associated with the elite, while folk art is associated with the masses. Connoisseurs have therefore tended to see the two as opposites. The notion that carnival is theater has been opposed precisely among those – the middle and upper classes, who had almost succeeded in having carnival banned – whose pro-active support for it would be of invaluable help in the advancement of the art form. This support would be more substantial if carnival were seen to be closer to the fine art end of the spectrum than to the folklore and popular culture end. It is an irony born of the colonial situation that the very ones who withheld their support for this aspect of the island's culture were among those who derived the most financial benefit when they belatedly cashed in on the commercialization of the annual festival. They had seen the lower classes, in particular the segment of the population largely comprised of former slaves, gradually snatch carnival from their grasp, and the ensuing popular nature of this celebration had made them uneasy. Calypsos were vilified. Steelband music was deemed mere noise. And carnival was called an excuse for licentious behavior. The people persevered in their observations of the annual ritual, to the extent that it became part and parcel of their culture. All things considered, the attitude of the masses has prevailed, and the middle and upper class have been swayed, almost to the point of retaking control at times. In the end, however, Trinidad carnival as a significant element of West Indian popular culture is now well established, with different sections of the population enjoying all or some of its varied elements.

Carnival as practiced in Trinidad is multifaceted. It is the season that usually begins immediately after Christmas and extends until the Monday and Tuesday immediately preceding Ash Wednesday. It is the Dimanche Gras show that starts the carnival, which then carries on until the final two-day revelry. It is *jouvay* (the creole version of the French words *jour ouvert*), the pre-dawn start to Carnival Monday, a time of visual satire, puns, and inversion, a symbolic triumph of the masses over the establishment and the "respectable." It is Carnival Tuesday, the climactic day of street parading and costumes, the final opportunity to participate in the masquerade, to "play mas'." It is increasingly a blend of traditional characters – clown, jab jab or devil, pierrot, bat, dragon, midnight robber, moko jumbie, Dame Lorraine, fancy sailor – with the newer portrayals and disguises that comprise the popular bands. There are those who are committed to certain characters, and return to them year after year, usually portrayed as individuals; there are those who base their decision to be part of a particular band on the popularity of the band leader, or on the fact that they simply want to be part of a group of friends seeking to have fun together. But in addition to all those who don disguises, there are those who are dedicated spectators, who prefer to admire costumes and characters from a distance, but who nonetheless see themselves as participating fully in carnival. In other words, it is not farfetched to see both spectators and revelers as playing well-defined roles.

Carnival is, all told, a massive presentation comprising several major productions typical of those associated with the theater anywhere else. It is calypso tents, where the new calypsos are sung, and where eager audiences gather to hear not only the latest dance songs, but also the latest update on political and other intrigue in the society. It is the community yards where steelbands rehearse in preparation for their shot at the Panorama championship, symbol of their superiority in pan, as this music is known. It is mas' camps where revelers, tourists, students, and designers view costume designs and production. It is the attendant competitions that reward all aspects of this national festival, the spirit of rivalry ensuring that almost every sector of the population has its interest piqued. It is the seemingly ceaseless rounds of parties – called fetes – that, incredibly, keep some carnival lovers sleepless for nights on end. It is the flourishing of many forms of art and craft: music (arrangement, playing, and composition), design, costuming, drama, and fine art. It is widespread audience participation and subscription. It is increasing commercial sponsorship, underwriting, financial management, profiteering, and spin-off industries. It is production and human resource management. Finally, it is mass appeal and support.

The climax of the massive presentation is the parade of the bands on Carnival Monday and Tuesday, the single largest event of the entire season, and often compared to one long theatrical performance in several acts. The success of this show depends heavily on design, performance, and music, and these elements are also interdependent on each other. The design of a band and its costumes influences the performance, which in turn is propelled, or even dictated, by the music, another integral part of the entire presentation.

The theme and design of the band, and preparation of the profusion of costumes of varying styles, textures, sizes, colors, and prices, for tens of thousands of participants, or mas' players as they are commonly called, are extremely important, and demand nothing less than consummate professionalism from beginning to end. The delivery of the costumes to the mas' player often involves an intricate, factory-like organization in which many professionals are engaged, although many of these workers would modestly see themselves as working simply for the sheer love of carnival. It is in their blood, many claim when asked why they spend so much time and energy preparing for the two days of revelry, only to start all over again as early as the Ash Wednesday following each carnival season.

While in years gone by bandleaders would be responsible for designing the costumes, in recent times they often use dedicated designers under contract. In some instances, designers may also be bandleaders, as is the case with

Peter Minshall and Wayne Berkeley. Of the designers who work on carnival costumes, a significant number have been educated formally, or by apprenticeship in mas' camps. Some of the designers spend approximately six months in Trinidad, and the rest of the time designing for Trinidad-style carnivals abroad. Outside of carnival many of these designers are engaged in other aspects of theater, entertainment, and fashion, with the result that there is some blurring of the lines separating their carnival work from their work in other areas.

Bands are usually under the direction of a single leader, a committee, or a combination of the two. The design and production of costumes begin with the selection of the theme of the band followed by a mandate to the designer to submit sketches for approval. Once the imprimatur has been issued, the bandleader and the designer arrange for the selecting of materials. The acquisition, normally wholesale, of materials may include trips abroad, or the employment of buyers already living outside of Trinidad; it may also involve private arrangements with wholesalers in Trinidad, ensuring an ample supply of fabric and other materials needed to make costumes. Designers are fiercely competitive, and seek to be innovative in the selection of these materials, which can be as varied as dried leaves, clay, glass, scrap iron, wax, aluminum, sacking, or burlap.

The production of costumes engages the talents of numerous artists and artisans: seamstresses, tailors, shoemakers, painters, wire benders, welders, screen printers, sculptors, and even engineers. These talents ordinarily work in the mas' camp where the band is produced and where there is a centralized system of production, though in other cases they work out of their own homes, enabling them to hire themselves out to more than one band. In the mas' camp there are cells of activity supervised by one or more persons. In each cell something different but pertinent is done, and incrementally, costumes are embellished as they move from one place to another along the quasi-assembly line. There are some workers who are contracted months in advance and who suspend their alternative, personal, bread-earning activities to honor these contracts. Of the persons working on costumes some may be highly skilled, and some semiskilled; some are apprentices and others just helping a friend. The same range can be found in the method of remuneration for the tasks. Some are highly paid on contract, and some are paid according to the piece or task; some are given a costume in exchange for their time, and some work for food and drink; some work for the feeling of community that exists in the camp, while others work for love and excitement.

The delivery of the costumes is another aspect of the production and which has now become an orchestrated event. In the majority of cases the costumes are delivered according to a plan. Some bands publish in the print media the dates and times that costumes are to be collected. The delivery is staggered, and the costumes distributed to the players in some sort of container: a bag or a box, or both, depending on the costume. The player is also instructed on how the costume is to be worn, since ultimately the optimal effect in the presentation of the band is being sought. There are also instances where the player is told when to wear the costume – Tuesday and not Monday, for example – to maximize the effect on the audience and judges in the annual competition.

The design aspect, though, is not confined to the sketches, but extends to the preparation and building of the costumes to get the desired replication of the drawing. The more elaborate ones require a high degree of engineering and other technical skill in order that the costume blend smoothly in with its wearer, for an ungainly outfit detracts not only from the enjoyment of the masquerader, but also is not viewed too kindly by the judges. Consequently, It is from this *mise-en-scène* that the drama will emanate.

Band and costume design have now become a source of instruction for students and professionals. For instance, American students of art from the University of Madison, Wisconsin, spent two weeks in Trinidad in 1997 studying art and craft, costume making, and production; and in 1993, Irish puppeteers visited Trinidad during carnival to study costume making. But, the costume in isolation, on a stationary form is still a work in progress. It is in the performance of the mas' that the design becomes complete.

Carnival is theater in the street, with characters, individually or in groups, performing on this vast stage. Performance at carnival dates back to the 1800s with the introduction of the now traditional characters, and the first of the military and naval masquerades. These bands originally imitated the military exercises carried out by the militia of Queen Victoria's government that had come to the West Indies to flex their muscles in the face of threatened slave rebellions. During the ensuing years, these bands appeared with improved drills and mock engagements, and evolved into the popular military bands, mainly played by members of the steelbands. They have continued to perfect their performances to include the state-of-the-art military maneuvers and simulated hardware found in the military of their choice (usually that of the United States).

Performances were not confined to bands. Individual traditional masquerades were characterized by costume and performance. The pierrot, for example, was a character whose costume came to be associated with a certain type of performance. This character usually wore a resplendent costume, and had two assistants carrying his train and his weapon. According to Errol Hill, this character "recited grandiose speeches dwelling on his own prowess, invincibility and impressive lineal descent, and the dire things in store for all his enemies" (1972: 29). Of course, wherever two pierrots met, bystanders would gather to view and judge, as was the case with another stock character, the midnight robber, who also exploited the grandiose, the frightening, the quasi-horrific to coax a few pennies from his listeners into his miniature coffin-cum-piggy bank. His was a performance of dance and mesmerizing oratory, and his influence permeates even everyday life in the language of the people, who deem any overly boastful, and thus empty, stance as "robber talk." This is a most striking example of how carnival and popular culture are intertwined, for no further explanation is necessary whenever the robber talk accusation is made. The entire society is aware that the allusion stems from the familiarity of the people with this character and with what he stands for in the context of carnival.

The long line of characters now recognized as part of traditional carnival comes with specific rituals and performances, so that one does not don the costume simply to dance in the streets to the music. One plays the part of the character. It is an opportunity for even the lowliest of individuals to fantasize, to equalize, in short to be dramatic and theatrical. From the Dame Lorraine with its mockery of the French creole upper class to imps and devils with names of evil-doers inscribed on their oversized books of reckoning; from dragons and scaled beasts breathing fire and venom to Wild Indians, red, blue, or black, and their elaborate headpieces; from Yankee minstrels, a case of blacks imitating whites imitating blacks, to Tennessee cowboys; from bats and clowns to fancy sailors with their dance steps simulating drunkenness or the rocking of a boat, all go beyond the outer disguise to play for an ever-appreciative mass audience that is in tune with the requirements of the various roles or costumes. Increasingly, the contemporary carnival is evolving away from some of the stock characters in favor of presentations that are the visual embodiment of the fantasy of the designer, though there is still the tendency to have a king and queen in many of the larger bands, on whose extravagant costumes a significant amount of time would have been spent. These kings and queens participate in a separate competition prior to the two days of street parading, and usually have the enthusiastic support of the rest of the players in their bands. However, in times of economic stringency, simpler costumes are becoming the norm for the various sections comprising a band. These are worn mainly for the sheer joy of "playing mas'" and their wearers normally have little to do that is considered "in character."

There are many competitions associated with carnival, and their influence can be seen in the concerted attempts made by bandleaders to outdo each other to gain the nod of the various judges, and the attendant prestige that goes with winning particular prizes or titles. With the growing popularity of the spectacle and its attraction for tourists, the Trinidad and Tobago government has sought, through its National Carnival Commission, to formalize the structure of the presentations by fixing the principal competition venues. The most prestigious is at the Queen's Park Savannah, and the sprawling stage erected every year provides an ideal locale to blend theaters – street and conventional – as the costumed masquerader of the street becomes the costumed character on the stage. It is here that the main judging takes place for the Band of the Year, and that innovation and originality are rewarded. It is, according to Peter Minshall, one of the main proponents of carnival as theater, the only place available for the proper presentation of just not his, but all mas'.

Now, while it is Minshall who is mostly associated with the concept of carnival as theater, at least in the 1980s and 1990s, his bands were by no means the first to dramatize portrayals on stage in the Savannah. Harold Saldenah's *Imperial Rome*, and *Glory that was Greece*, George Bailey's *Ye Saga of Merrie England*, and *Byzantine Glory*, dating back to the 1950s, all had players knowingly choreograph their movements to enhance the authenticity of their portrayals. This development is not without its share of controversy. First, from the point of view of the revelers in the band, there is the complaint that many of the spectators who follow popular bands, but are not in costume, do not vacate the stage so the masqueraders can put on the best possible performance for the judges. Second, from the point of view of the rival bands, there is the complaint that some bandleaders are given more than their fair share of time on stage, to the dismay of those who are left waiting, sometimes almost at standstill, for their turn to show their array of costumes and characters.

Peter Minshall, with performances different from what the public had seen prior to his entrance into the world of carnival-as-theater, took center stage in the 1980s and 1990s. His performances were abstract and symbolic, but no less intriguing. Minshall has produced bands in trilogies, with presentations and performances spanning three years. He has also presented bands in what he has termed two acts, striving for theatrical effect, and thereby emphasizing that mas' is theater. In the 1983 presentation of *The River*, for example, on Carnival Monday, act one, the Washerwoman, his queen of the band, wore an all-white costume. She symbolically washed the clothes of her folk, and their clean clothes hung on a line – erected over her head as part of her headpiece – to blow innocently in the breeze. Each section of the band symbolized a tributary of the main stream, represented by a twenty-five foot wide, half-mile long, stretched nylon canopy held over the entire band on poles by selected revelers. The pure waters represented by each section, converged in the river above the heads of the participants. Act two on Tuesday began with Mancrab and his bloodstained shroud, and the dead queen with her clothes soaked in red. The half-mile river canopy had become a polychrome river indicating pollution. It was not until 5:30 p.m. that the band, numbering well over 2,000 – thus large by current standards – reached the Savannah stage, and proceeded to complete the symbolic struggle of good versus evil, a favorite Minshall theme that his masqueraders were being called upon to stage (see Nunley and Bettelheim 1988: 108). The timing of the band's arrival coincided with the start of the evening sunset, with its special rays reflected on the costumes of the revelers.

Minshall had stage-managed his presentation for maximum visual impact. He has been persistent in emphasizing that carnival is theater, and has incurred the wrath of his bandleader colleagues for spending too much time acting for the judges, a reasonable complaint when one considers the logistics of moving large numbers of masqueraders on and off the vast open stage erected for the occasion. His answer to his critics is that the logistics problem is not of his making, and that he should not be stymied in his attempt to present carnival's surviving traditions in a particular way. "I do absolutely believe in the power of the mas'," he has said, "so I will play it in the fashion that best allows for that power to be appreciated by all who look upon it" (quoted in Joseph 1997).

Carnival is inconceivable without music. The hypnotic state to which many masqueraders are driven is the result not only of their total involvement with the new self beneath the disguise, but also from the infectious music that accompanies all carnival activity. In this regard, therefore, one must pay attention to another aspect of the drama that is carnival, namely that of the voice of the people, for it is the so-called people's performer, the calypsonian, who provides the music, even the societal context for the mas'.

Throughout the carnival and calypso season that starts immediately after Christmas, as the various preparations are being made for the street parade that is the climax of the carnival, the society partakes of a massive serving of oral literature and popular culture, the new calypsos. These eagerly awaited songs are presented, sometimes in dramatized fashion, at various venues – calypso tents – by calypsonians, the contemporary version of the lead singers, the chantwells, that were part of early carnival bands. The calypsonians have evolved away from direct association with masked bands as such. But it is their music that bandleaders use to accompany their presentations, though calypso is often much more than the music it supplies.

If carnival is the national theater, then calypso is the national literature. In a society that prides itself on its literacy, on its love of book learning, the oral tradition is still vibrant, and very much alive in the calypso. Calypsos constantly interpret events in Trinidad and Tobago society, and monitor activities within and without it. They are the mirror of the national ethos, moving far beyond mere information as supplied by the media (see Warner 1982). Their earlier role of people's newspaper has nowadays more correctly evolved into that of people's magazine. Even in the remotest of country villages, people no longer depend on the itinerant calypsonian to bring them news of what is taking place in the society. Since improved technology provides instant worldwide coverage of any newsworthy occurrence, new calypsos appear with some distance in time from events they depict. Nevertheless, while the "news" factor is no longer uppermost in the minds of the calypsonians, calypsos do analyze social and political events, and do reflect prevailing moods and attitudes. They are an integral part of the popular culture, and come closest to explaining what makes this society distinctly Trinidadian, even distinctly West Indian or Caribbean. Such calypsos hold the interest of the public mainly through their lyrics, thus through what they "say."

Many of the new calypsos are presented at venues – any such place being dubbed tents – in the six- to eight-week period between the start of the new calendar year and the two days of street parading. Aware of the appeal of dramatic presentations, calypsonians have often resorted to staging the story line of many of their calypsos. These presentations are characteristically done in slapstick fashion, with little or no attempt to disguise the calypsonians playing the various characters. This is not usually a problem, and is even expected of the presentation, since the audience is more interested in the slant the performance gives to whatever is the latest imbroglio being dramatized. For instance, calypsonians are seen by the people as being constantly in touch with the shenanigans of those in power, or the covert activities of all politicians in general. This is so much so that in one of his early renditions, popular calypsonian The Mighty Sparrow, boasted that "if Sparrow say so, is so," thus granting unto himself moral and poetic license not easily claimed by others in the society. Yet this is not seen as extraordinary, for it is what the public has come to expect over the years, and those who step over the line of decency are immediately greeted with sharp disapproval.

All in the calypso is not protest and social commentary, however, and the public has come to expect other things from its bards, most of whom have traditionally sung under an interesting array of sobriquets, from the early fear-inspiring Roaring Lion, Growling Tiger, or Attila, to the newer, less awesome

Mighty Sparrow, Cro Cro, or Sugar Aloes. Calypsonians provide a healthy portion of literary fulfillment for a society more attuned to its oral tradition than it would like to admit. As such, they sing of love, of life, of episodes, humorous or otherwise, that illustrate the human condition, and the public listens and appreciates. Indeed, it gets involved with these singers, as happens whenever a controversial topic is raised, and a national debate ensues.

Throughout the carnival/calypso season, then, calypsos provide the background to the preparation for the festivities. But while one type of calypso sets the mood for reflection, or pricks the conscience of the people, leading a bandleader like Peter Minshall to use a specific calypso to present an overall theme for his band, it is another type that sets the masqueraders dancing. Even when it narrates a story, what this other type of calypso "says" matters relatively little. It exists as a vehicle for the music, tune and melody being more important than lyric. It is this type of calypso, like Arrow's "Hot, hot, hot," that easily captures international audiences, and accounts for the impression that the calypso is mainly a danceable folksong from "the islands." With the rapid ascendancy of reggae from Jamaica, due in large part to the worldwide popularity of the late Bob Marley, calypso has found itself competing, even in Trinidad and Tobago, with this Jamaican import at the level of popular appeal. Calypso's response in terms of access to world audiences is soca – coined from soul of calypso – but its marketing has not been as aggressive as that of reggae. Nevertheless, there is great interpenetration of one territory's music into another, with reggae influencing calypso in Trinidad, and calypso influencing reggae in Jamaica. The resulting mixture is appreciated by the public as a whole, for it is aware that this blend is something authentically Caribbean, and something born of the masses and their culture. Jamaica has now begun to host an annual carnival, as do most of the other Caribbean territories, but Trinidad's carnival remains undoubtedly the premier celebration of the region.

As the climax of carnival approaches, it becomes clear which of the dance type of calypso will dominate the street parades – the most popular being designated the Road March. In recent times, a new sort of call and response has developed, as the calypsonians have urged their listeners to participate by doing certain dance steps or movements. "Get something and wave" and "Put your hands in the air" were two of the more popular exhortations made in the 1990s. The result is a communal dance – a new one every year – a communal participation in an experience that is renowned for its ability to coax the inhibited, the reserved, or the conservative out of their noninvolvement. It is noticeable, for instance, that carnival bands are increasingly dominated by women, and that many appear on the streets in scanty costumes that lead some spectators to complain annually that there is too much lewdness in carnival. In their defense, such revelers maintain that carnival is a time for total freedom, and that the suggestive dancing in public is nothing more than an open and harmless celebration of the vibrancy that lies at the depth of the society's soul. They see the complaints as yet another attempt by the establishment to stifle any show of enjoyment and creativity by the masses. This inability to deal with what has evolved in the popular culture is seen as another of the legacies of colonialism.

It is the same situation that existed with regard to the acceptance of the music produced by the novel instrument called the steelpan, fashioned, almost incredibly, from discarded oil drums. The social stigma that was attached to association with the steelbands and their members was similar to that attached to association with calypsonians. Popular culture in both these instances was not given any credibility by the establishment, which grudgingly paid occasional lip service when it was convenient for its own self-interest. Fortunately, both calypsonian and steelband player stuck together in the face of social pressure to abandon their art form and their music, and in the lead-up to carnival, they work harmoniously together. Almost all the music played by steelbands for the carnival season is calypso.

Carnival and calypso are thus intimately interwoven. Both have redefined the concept of audience participation, and both have evolved into barometers of the mood of the society. Community involvement is key to them both, for in the oral arena in which calypso is performed, there is constant interchange between performer and listener, just as the carnival spectator is invariably swept into the action, onto the stage, so to speak (the symbolic sprinkling of baby powder on spectators by one carnival character, the fancy sailor, being evidence of this interaction).

It would seem perfectly natural for the blend of carnival and calypso to end up on the conventional stage, there to be an example of what postcolonial societies can produce when they marry the inherited with the newly minted, when popular culture is allowed to be fully expressed. Indeed, there have been many attempts to develop a specifically carnival theater by taking carnival characters and rituals and integrating them into proscenium-style plays. These efforts have produced plays such as Errol Hill's *Man Better Man* (1957), Derek Walcott's *The Charlatan* (1954), Godfrey Sealy's *To Hell Wid Dat* (1990), and Felix Edinborough's *Mas in Yus Mas* (1980) and *J'Ouvert* (1982). These productions were first and foremost examples of conventional theater with carnival characters, carnival songs, and carnival dances incorporated, as opposed to the open, and admittedly difficult to define and delimit, street theater. The short-lived experiment of the Trinidad Tent Theatre of the early 1980s, which also showcased the incorporation of carnival characters into a conventional type of drama, showed that it was not sufficient merely to write plays that incorporated traditional characters and scenes, however noble such a venture might seem. This type of carnival theater still had as its premise the idea that something "local" – an unfortunate term even in this postcolonial phase – was being made to fit a pre-conceived model, one that was accommodating a bit of local color and folk input, and one that was reserved, all things being equal, for "real" theater. There was once more the misguided notion that popular culture was only a complement to true culture.

One noteworthy development in the continuing marriage of carnival and folk theater is the Jouvay Process as conceived by Tony Hall's Lordstreet Theatre, which turns the microscope on carnival and extracts traditional characters. The process involves familiarizing members of the theater group with the history of carnival, with the early calypso/carnival music of kalinda, and with the movements of stick fighters, all of which centers on an appreciation for the use of the street. Members eventually blend a traditional carnival character with a contemporary one, and portray it, going to various outdoor or community locales, where they draw in bystanders, and so try to discover how animators prod others to respond, such as at carnival time in the street.

It must be emphasized that the folk origin under discussion is not a mere stepping stone to the more conventional theater, which has existed, and no doubt will continue to exist, in the West Indies. Carnival as theater stands on its own; in fact, it cannot work totally on the proscenium, where it seems somewhat out of place and out of character, despite the theatricality inherent in the various portrayals. It needs the street, or a street-like atmosphere, which it is not likely to find with an audience seated quietly indoors. Carnival has its own life, and has even given birth to other similar attempts, as Trinidad and Tobago nationals and other aficionados have taken this phenomenon to the rest of the Caribbean nations, and to the metropolitan areas of Europe and North America where there are large concentrations of Caribbean immigrants.

There is heavy emphasis on participation by the people, even when, to all appearances, spectators are mere bystanders. The passive observation of floats passing by is not what the Trinidad carnival is about, and it is for that reason that there are problems when a band presents itself before the judges at the designated venues. Revelers, whether or not in costume, deem it their right to enjoy the music, to "jump up" as they say, for, to use another popular expression of Trinidad revelers: "Carnival is we t'ing." In other words, it belongs exclusively to them and they are going to enjoy it come what may. The matter of interfering with the competitive chances of the very band in which they are "jumping" seems to be of minimal importance. Such participants would no doubt be quite surprised to hear they were part of a theatrical performance as such, and in fact they do not use the term "theater" to describe the event of which they are a vital part. However, they would be acutely aware of being an integral part of the popular culture of a nation that now proudly advertises this event as one of the cultural wonders of the world.

From the beginning, carnival has been about drama: the Dame Lorraine, the pierrot, the midnight robber, wild Indians, all costumed characters with set roles on the street stage. The drama has been about the formerly illicit calypso tents, the police raids they suffered, and the clever use of the *double entendre* to prevent detection by colonial authorities. The drama has also been about the outlawed *cannes brûlées* processions ("canboulay" of popular parlance) that evolved out of the burning of the sugar cane, and ended in riots with the police. It has been about the seasonal kalinda dance, and about the stickfights, where Trinidad males externalized and ritualized their quest for dominance. The drama has been about jouvay with the revelers emerging in the pre-dawn daubing themselves with mud and presenting the grotesque and the obscene. It has, finally, been in the struggle of the urban blacks to have upper-class society accept their steelbands as making music, thus as contributing to the corpus of fine arts that the establishment thought its preserve.

It is clear then that, as of old, the drama in carnival is not in the single story being told, and hence confounds all who look for a single plot. The drama is in the performance of the costume and band, the delivery and topic of calypsos, the arrangement and playing of the accompanying music. The drama is in the fierce competitions of steelband and masked band, the feverish preparation for these contests, even in the stage-management of the grand theatrical event.

Further, there is little doubt that carnival, born of the folk and intrinsically tied to the folk, is the national theater of Trinidad. Whereas in former times dancing in the street, masked characters, and music created by the lower classes or folk were frowned upon by the colonial upper class, the mulatto and black middle classes, today people of all social and financial levels participate in and support this annual presentation. Hence from the lowly beginnings, from the bowels of the folk, there is now a flourishing, widely appreciated national theater in Trinidad, and it is carnival. It is a significant contribution to drama in the West Indies, for it shows that postcolonial societies can indeed develop their own art forms with an original blend of the imposed culture and the indigenous.

Bibliography

Anthony, Michael. 1989. *Parade of the Carnivals of Trinidad 1839–1989*. Port of Spain: Circle Press.

Caribbean Quarterly. 1956. 4: 3–4.

Gill, Mary. 1994. "Presence, Identity, and Meaning in the Trinidad Carnival: An Ethnography of Schooling and Festival." PhD diss. University of Wisconsin.

Hill, Errol. 1972. *The Trinidad Carnival: Mandate for a National Theater*. Austin: University of Texas Press.

Joseph, Terry. 1997. Comments. *Sunday Express* (Trinidad). 20 April 1997. Section 2: 7.

Nunley, John, and Judith Bettelheim. 1988. *Caribbean Festival Arts*. Seattle: University of Washington Press.

Van Koningsbruggen, Peter. 1997. *Trinidad Carnival: A Quest for National Identity*. Basingstoke: Macmillan.

Warner, Keith Q. 1982. *Kaiso! The Trinidad Calypso: A Study of the Calypso as Oral Literature*. Washington, DC: Three Continents Press.

9

Africa and writing

ALAIN RICARD

Africa is everywhere inscribed. From rocks to masks, sculptures, pyramids, and manuscripts one needs but a stubborn and narrow-minded commitment to alphabetic writing to deny that the continent has left graphic marks of its history everywhere. Graphic representation is indeed present, but is it writing? One of the best books on the topic, written from an Asian angle, *Visible Speech*, subtitled "The Diverse Oneness of Writing Systems," by John De Francis, will be my guide on what can be called the "African chapter in the history of writing" (see Figure 9.1). Speech communities always generate material means to keep and retrieve information – this is not always writing. I will then reflect on graphic representation of sounds and the competition generated between several systems of graphic representation, before considering the contribution of a new kind of artist, the alphabet inventor, who belongs to the history of art, and not to the history of literature.

De Francis makes two useful distinctions that have a practical bearing on the analysis of writing in Africa. He divides students of graphic systems into two camps, the inclusivists and exclusivists, using as a discriminating criterion their definition of writing:

> Partial writing is a system of graphic symbols that can be used to convey only some thought.
>
> Full writing is a system of graphic symbols that can be used to convey any and all thought.
>
> Inclusivists believe that both partial and full writing should be called writing; exclusivists believe that only full writing deserve this label. (De Francis 1989: 5)

Africa is the continent with the largest number of recorded rock art paintings: from the Drakensberg and the Matopos in Southern Africa to the Air in the Sahara, the continent seems to have been populated by crowds of painters eager to record, to pray, or to celebrate. A recent book, *L'art rupestre dans le monde*, by Emmanuel Anati, director of Unesco World Archive of Rock Art

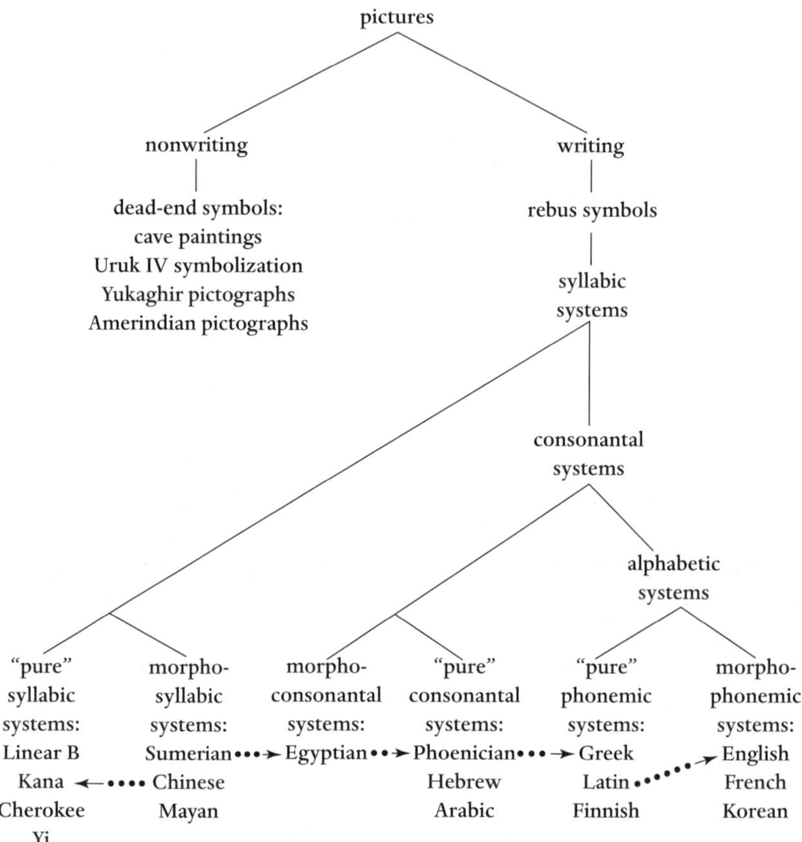

Figure 9.1 De Francis's Writing Classification Scheme. (From De Francis 1989.)

(WARA), based on an extensive survey of several millions of pictures and engravings, attempts to demonstrate that cave paintings are indeed a kind of writing, and that we have here a universal code. Studies by Henri Lhote on the Sahara and by Henri Breuil and Victor Ellenberger in southern Africa are of course part of this model that organizes graphic production according to two axes: a diachronic series taking into account the mode of subsistence of the artists and a synchronic dealing with the syntax of the pictograms. For Anati, some pictograms are ideograms and point to a universal code of graphic expression. In his view, Central Tanzania offers what is probably the longest sequence in the world of such images and is probably the "cradle" of this art (Anati 1997: 191–92). They are an exceptional testimony of the development process of thinking, of intellectual achievement, and of the cultural changes that have marked East Africa within the last 40,000 years. Especially impressive are the pictures of the Kundusi gatherers, with their heads masked, arranged in a triad, as if captivated by a special myth:

> Painted walls stand for a cathedral. In it are kept myths and legends, i.e., the capacity to keep a living relationship with the past or the future, which is usually done in palaces or sanctuaries.
>
> What is called the White Bantu style offers us a true historical archive, full of pictograms and ideograms, which remains to be interpreted. It provides extraordinary information on the concepts and beliefs of Bantu people. (Anati 1997: 221; 223)

Anati's attempts to relate recent findings to Nyau ritual and dance are especially interesting: they allow us to read the paintings as pictograms of masks and dance and provide a bridge to present-day Chewa society (Anati 1997: 235; Probst 1997).

Africa is full of inscriptions of what the Angolan writer Luandino Vieira calls "illiterate writing." Paintings and engravings that encode stories and rituals belong to writing, if we adopt an inclusivist position. So does graphic symbolism in a different way. In her book, *Symboles graphiques en Afrique noire* (1992), C. Faik Nzuji undertakes a semiological analysis of the code of representation in different groups. This is an avenue that was explored long ago by Marcel Griaule and Germaine Dieterlen (1951). Dogon graphic symbolism has been the topic of several studies. It is indeed of the utmost importance because these symbols are in close relation to speech: they are produced within speech communities and demand interpretation by these communities. They fulfill one of the essential functions of writing: recording information and enabling its retrieval. They do this in a specialized way not available for any kind of messages. But many writing systems suffer from the same constraints. The "African Chapter in the History of Writing" (Raum 1943) is the study of ways to keep and retrieve information by graphic means:

> When Livingstone entered the country of the Lunda he observed that all trees along his route bore incisions, which are said to have resembled faces reminiscent of Egyptian pictures. (Raum 1943: 181)

These signs – incisions etched on trees and marked by colored dots on sticks – even if they are not pictographs (why not?) – fulfill some functions of writing, by reminding us of the words, spells, and prayers of those who inscribed them:

> Symbols are cultural creations that derive their meaning from rituals and cults, intense moments that punctuate the life of their users. In most cases, the body is marked, objects are carved, modeled to this end. Scarifications are thus messages sent to the ages. (Faik-Nzuji 1992: 122)

Marking of property, what Raum calls "crystallizing and registering thought processes" (1943: 9), as well as graphic and colored symbols are used by African peoples; they serve

> three main purposes: the perpetuation of expressions of emotional states and volitional tendencies in inscriptions which bear a magical, and sometimes religious, significance; the regulations of social relations by supplying distinguishing marks for private and clan property and by affording a medium of communication between individuals; finally graphic symbols serve to record the shape, name and number of objects as well as subjects of conversations and negotiations and thus act as instruments of intellectual processes. (1943: 187)

As is well known, graphic symbolism fulfills different functions: magical and numerical. Certain systems have been particularly well perfected, such as the Nsibidi script (Dalby 1986). Some objects elicit a verbal response and thus encapsulate a text. The systematic use of such objects can function like writing. It is especially important to recall these propositions to prevent a confusion of perspectives. These pictograms have been used for centuries. As David Dalby explains, the graphic symbolism of the Egyptian ideograms probably belongs to symbolic repertories long used in Africa, whether on rock, on wood, or on skin. The Egyptian system of writing is of course full writing, capable of recording any thought: it recorded a literature used in an actual society. These pictographs have been enriched by what De Francis calls the rebus principle:

> Pictographs used as pictographs lead nowhere. Pictographs used as phonetic symbols lead to full writing . . . The rebus principle formed the basis of three systems of writing, generally thought to have been independently developed, which were created at intervals of about fifteen hundred years: first by the Sumerians about 3000 BC, then by the Chinese about 1500 BC, and last by the Mayas about the beginning of our era. (1989: 50)

As De Francis demonstrates convincingly – and paradoxically for those with a superficial and often ideological knowledge of Chinese writing – Chinese ideograms note essentially the sounds of syllables, while Egyptian hieroglyphs note the sounds of consonants. Of course not all the system is phonetically based but it has a central phonetic component, and it is precisely this that makes it capable of recording any kind of thought, of being full writing. The operation of the "rebus principle," substituting images of things to represent the sounds of their names, is the key to the development of a writing system. Pictograms serve to complete the picture, to enrich, to make the texts precise. The oldest written African language is thus Egyptian, to which we can add Nubian. The Meroe pyramids and the Sudan desert have yielded stones with inscriptions, allowing us to decipher Meroitic script but not to understand the language:

> In addition to its use in religious contexts, Meroitic was without doubt also the written language of both the administration and of daily life.
>
> The variety of preserved inscribed monuments is so great that we can assume both knowledge and use of writing for a significant portion of the population . . . a comprehensive body of source material is now at hand for the Meroitic Period of the kingdom. Its value, however, is certainly weakened by the fact that the texts can be read, but not translated. A few basic rules of the linguistic structure are recognizable, showing that Meroitic might belong to a group of northern Sudanese languages to which Nubian is also ascribed. But the chronological and genetic distance from these languages is so great that not much help can be expected by making comparisons. The meaning of divine and personal names, place-names, and individual titles can be grasped, especially in those cases that stem from Egyptian. Among these are words like . . . *ato* ("water"), *at* ("bread"). (Priese 1996: 253)

The Kingdom of Kush and its capital Kerma were in dynastic times (25–15 centuries BCE) at the center of an ancient Nubian empire and of the relations between Egypt and Black Africa. The inscriptions found are written in Egyptian, but Meroe, the successor kingdom, had its own written language. Written with a selection of Egyptian demotic hieroglyphs, it is indeed an African language, related to languages still spoken in the area. But it is also fascinating by reason of the mystery it presents: we know the consonants and the vowels but we cannot organize the discourse, as if the written image of the language were too far removed from an actual language. Many African languages have been written with rather inadequate systems: perhaps Meroe was the first one of the series and this is the cause of its present opacity.

The highly tonal, largely monosyllabic West African coastal languages would probably need something like the Chinese system to be efficiently written, whereas the class and tone languages of the Bantu would certainly be reduced to bare consonantal skeletons in the Egyptian writing system. In other words, these languages need another approach of representation where phonemic analysis would go along with symbolic representation. It is already difficult to write vowels, with aperture and length: how can we represent pitch as well in a phonemic (or alphabetic) system? The Vietnamese have succeeded in a context of an exceptionally strong feeling of national consciousness, ready to bear many sacrifices. The balance between phonemic and other kinds of representation (symbolic, pictographic) in a system is achieved over centuries: a writing system does not live divorced from a society. It is very important to realize, for instance, that a system which looks cumbersome and inefficient, like the hieroglyphs, had special advantages for the world within which it was required to function:

> The central complaint is that the Egyptians evidently lacking in imagination, failed to take what is deemed to be the obvious step: simply to use their uniconsonantal signs in the manner of an alphabet, abandoning the other types of signs. Such criticism, which is based essentially on the assumed superiority of alphabetic script over all others, is quite misplaced. It not only overrates the efficiency of alphabetic systems, it also undervalues the merits of others. The Egyptian system has the disadvantage of containing a relatively large number of signs. In compensation however, its mixed orthography creates visually distinctive word patterns that actually enhance legibility. (Davies 1987: 35)

In Africa only Egyptian, Nubian, Ge'ez, and Tamazight have, over the centuries, developed their own systems of full writing. A literature, a community of writers and readers were thus created. The Ethiopian syllabary (whether in Ge'ez or in Amharic) is the only syllabary still in practical use in Africa today. Other African languages have borrowed scripts, whether Arabic or Roman. In the last two centuries, inventions of specific syllabaries, in the Mande area for instance (Vai syllabary), have occurred in a context of intensive culture contact with Islam, but remained local and did not produce a literature (Dalby 1970). All these inventors should be remembered as graphic artists more than as writers or inventors. Only the Bamun sultan Njoya, at the beginning of the twentieth century, devised a syllabary in which original works of history were written; unfortunately the development of this original creation was stopped by the destruction of his printing shop at the time of French colonization. Arabic itself was probably the most commonly used written language in Africa up to the nineteenth century. It was written in Timbuktu in the fifteenth century and there still exists an Arabic literature in West Africa.

To borrow a script is not to borrow a language, and some adaptations are necessary. Arabic, for instance, has only three vowels, while many African languages have more (for instance, Kiswahili has five vowels) and some even have tones. Fula and Hausa were written in the Arabic script, using the *ajami* script created in the eighteenth century; as was Kiswahili on the Indian Ocean. But of course these adaptations are not without problems. As Amadou Hampaté Bâ, a well-known Islamic scholar as well as francophone writer put it:

> We do not even know for how long Fula was written in Arabic script . . . No linguistic study of the western system had been made to fix for each phoneme a specific sign . . . So writing varied with each different area. The result was that a writer who did not know his text by heart had difficulties rereading his text six months later . . . The only known exception is the Futa Jallon where, thanks to a long practice of writing, people could reread themselves, not without difficulties. (Bâ 1972: 28–29, my translation)

Arabic does not have certain phonemes, for instance *-ng,* so often present in Bantu languages. Tippu Tip, the famous slave dealer from Zanzibar wrote his autobiography in Kiswahili in 1899 using the Arabic script and the text was transliterated by the German Consul and published in romanized Kiswahili (Whiteley 1958) as well as in European languages; it is probably one of the first Swahili narratives in which Islam is not the dominant theme. Many Swahili Arabic-script manuscripts have been transliterated to become romanized books – *Al Inkishafi*, for instance, which is probably the greatest Swahili poem, written at the beginning of the nineteenth century – and spread in book form in 1939 thanks to W. Hitchens's work.

There has been a large movement towards romanization, along with the spread of colonial education and missionary Christian activity, not so much to convert Muslims to Christianity as to prevent the conversion of non-Muslim Africans to Islam by providing alternative ways of writing their languages, detached from any association with Arabic. This was the rationale for writing down in Roman script many African languages, in Nigeria especially. At the same time a romanized version of the Hausa script – *boko* – was printed and widely disseminated. It may have been a colonial plot in the 1930s, but its continuing success is due to other factors, especially its standardization. Let us also remember that the Turkish language was romanized at the same time. The same is true for Kiswahili, which was used as a medium by Catholic missionaries at the end of the nineteenth century, while Protestants were more reluctant to engage in the theological dialogue with Islam that this kind of linguistic appropriation required, since a large part of Swahili conceptual vocabulary came from Arabic. Finally, Somali was romanized in the 1970s and became the official language of the defunct Socialist Republic of Somalia.

The switch from Arabic to Roman script inspired a massive effort to write down previously unwritten languages. Some posed rather complex problems, as can be seen from the chart showing the different ways of writing down Khoi sounds such as clicks (see Figure 9.2). The creation of an International Phonetic Alphabet, in 1854, provided a useful comparative tool to compare different languages, previously recorded in rather haphazard ways, according to the different linguistic backgrounds of their students. French missionaries would write *-ch* while English would write *-sh*: Thomas Mofolo behaved as a proper student of the Paris Mission when he wrote the name of the Zulu hero *Chaka* (*ch-* French spelling of the Zulu fricative) and not *Shaka*.

The spread of writing and especially of printing has been the task of missions in Africa (see Coldham 1966) but without some measure of agreement on transcription, the dissemination of the written version of each African language is heavily handicapped. The Yoruba reached an agreement between themselves in 1875 (see Ade Ajayi 1960), thanks to the pioneering work of Bishop Samuel Ajaiyi Crowther, linguist, explorer, translator, and a Yoruba by birth: a fact that helped considerably the development of their written literature. Religious differences made for different writing systems, based on conventions of the European tongues. Sometimes nationalistic concerns were in force, and lasted long, as demonstrated by the differences between South African and Lesotho spellings (*Shaka* or *Chaka*) of the same language, Sesotho. Today the size of the South African Sotho market is a powerful magnet that has helped to convert the orthography of Lesotho publishers, without any linguistic conference.

The issues in graphization leave us with a legacy of competition between churches and between states. The Gu people of Porto Novo (Benin Republic) never wrote their language like their Yoruba neighbors (Nigeria): to divide was a prerequisite of imperial rule and the invention of different graphic forms of mutually understandable languages was a great tool of division between competing powers (see Ricard 1995: 145–49).

In a typically romantic worldview, writing the language of an African group – of any group – meant, in the nineteenth century, bringing this group to light, making it emerge from the Dark Ages. The world was classified according to the "Great Divide": with Gutenberg the "Night has passed away and the Day has come," sings the choir in Mendelssohn's Second Symphony performed in 1840 to commemorate the four-hundredth anniversary of the invention of the movable type (Vail and White 1991: 1). A general theory of graphic expression cannot consider alphabetic writing to be the apex of human culture. It should reject well-known theories that have a rather ethnocentric bias: other paths have been followed by other cultures, in Asia or in Africa, for instance, but

Hottentot Language.

PUBLICATIONS AND MANUSCRIPTS.				CLICKS.			
Nos.	TITLES.	Date.	Catal.	Dent.	Lat.	Gutt.	Pal.
1	Sir Thomas Herbert, Bart.,...	1638	28.	i s t			
2	G. Fr. Wrede, Compendium....	1664	*30.				
3	God. Guil. Leibnitii, Collect...	1717	35.	t? k?			
4	M. P. Kolbe's Travels	1719	33.	∩ (or) ~			
5	Andrew Sparrmann, M.D.,......	1782	23.	t'			
6	C. P. Thunberg, M.D.,...........	1789	24.	a	A	á	
7	F. Le Vaillant, Travels.........	1790	25.	∧	∨		△
8	John Barrow, F.R.S.,............	1801	26.	—		⊍	
9	Dr. van der Kemp, Catech.....	1805	*21.	By 6 differ. Numer.			
10	H. Lichtenstein, M.D.,..........	1808	18. ·19.	t'[1]	t'[2]		t'[3]
11	Kafir and Zulu Books, since...	1824	43.216.	c	x	q	(qc)
12	Will. J. Burchell, Travels......	1824	20.	ɔ	c cc		
13	Joh. Leon. Ebner, Travels	1829	*	—			
14	J. H. Schmelen, Manu., before	1830	10.	—	⊃	|	∩
15	H. C. Knudsen, Spell.-book.....	1842	5. 6.	·	⊃	⊃⊃	:
16	H. C. Knudsen, Luke's Gospel	1846	15.7.4.	·	⊃	⊂	:
17	C. F. Wuras, Catech., before...	1848	21.	·	⊃	⊂	
18	C. F. Wuras, Grammar.........	1850	16.	f	y	q	v
19	H. P. S. Schreuder, Zulu Gr...	1850	178.	ϟ	≷	·≷·	·
20	R. Lepsius, Manuscript.........	1853		ıc	ıx	ıq	ıc
21	Rich. Lepsius, Stand. Alphab...	1854		/	//	!	¦
22	F. H. Vollmer, Spelling-book..	1854	8. 12.	v	q	f	x
23	Rhenish Mission Conference...	1856		/	//	⊬	≠
24	Henry Tindall, Grammar, &c.	1856	2. 3.	c	x	q	v
25	Wm. H. I. Bleek, Rese., &c....	1857	215.36.	c	x	q	o
26	C. F. Wuras, Manuscript.......	1857	16.21.*d*	∧	π	∩	
27	Manuscript Notes..................		6.	ts	kl	gkt	kt
28	J. W. Gibbs, Remarks, &c......	1852	174.	□	[]	⊆	

Figure 9.2 Different ways of writing sounds. (From Bleek 1958.)

this is often forgotten. Misconceptions regarding non-alphabetic systems have long been the rule, such as believing in the totally non-phonetic nature of Chinese writing (Goody and Watt 1972: 349–52) and assigning, by contrast, to the alphabet the property of developing logical methods. As De Francis rightly comments: "There is in this approach [Goody and Watt's] no concrete analysis of why . . . the consonant-plus-vowel system should be singled out as the primary factor in the intellectual ascendancy of Greece over its Near Eastern neighbors, who had achieved their inferior literacy half a millennium earlier" (De Francis 1989: 245). These Manichean oppositions marked by remnants of an Orientalist posture have been even stronger in the African case and have prevented research from looking at the Egyptian data in an African context.

Going back to our inclusivist position we can safely say that the African chapter in the history of writing is probably one of the longest in human history and that the obsession with orality – what Leroy Vail and Landeg White (1991) call "the invention of oral man" – is more an ideological and political posture than a well-informed theoretical stand.

Bibliography

Ade Ajayi, J. F. 1960. "How Yoruba Was Reduced to Writing." *Odu* 8: 49–58.

Anati, Emmanuel. 1997. *L'art rupestre dans le monde. Imaginaire de la préhistoire*. Paris: Larousse.

Bâ, Amadou Hampaté. 1972. *Aspects de la civilisation africaine*. Paris: Présence Africaine.

Battestini, Simon. 1997. *Ecriture et texte*. Québec: Presses de l'Université Laval/Paris: Présence Africaine.

Bleek, Wm. H., comp. 1858. *The Library of His Excellency Sir George Grey, K. C. B., Vol. 1, Part I: Africa, Philology*. London, Leipzig.

Breuil, Henri. Preface to Ellenberger, Victor. 1952. *La fin tragique des Bushmen*. Paris: Amiot-Dumont.

Celenko, Theodore, ed. 1996. *Egypt in Africa*. Bloomington: Indiana University Press.

Coldham, Geraldine. 1966. *A Bibliography of Scriptures in African Languages*. 2 vols. London: British and Foreign Bible Society.

Dalby, David. 1984. *Le clavier international de Niamey*. Paris: ACCT.

1986. *L'Afrique et la lettre*. Lagos: Centre culturel français, Fête de la lettre / Paris: Karthala.

Dalby, David, ed. 1970. *Language and History in Africa*. London: Frank Cass.

Davies, W. V. 1987. *Reading the Past: Egyptian Hieroglyphs*. London: British Museum.

Deacon, Jeanette, and Thomas Dowson, eds. 1996. *Xam Bushmen and the Bleek and Lloyd Collection*. Johannesburg: Witwatersrand University Press.

De Francis, John. 1989. *Visible Speech: The Diverse Oneness of Writing Systems*. Honolulu: University of Hawaii Press.

Ellenberger, Victor. 1952. *La fin tragique des Bushmen*. Paris: Amiot-Dumont.

Faik-Nzuji, Clémentine Madiya. 1992. *Symboles graphiques en Afrique noire*. Paris: Karthala / Louvain: Ciltade.

Fishman, J., Charles Ferguson, and J. Das Gupta, eds. 1968. *Language Problems of Developing Nations*. New York: John Wiley.

Geary, Christraud. 1994. *King Njoya's Gift, a Beaded Sculpture from the Bamum Kingdom Cameroon in the National Museum of African Art*. Washington, DC: National Museum of African Art, Smithsonian Institution.

Gérard, Albert. 1981. *African Languages Literatures*. Harlow: Longman.

Goody, Jack, and Ian Watt. 1972. "The Consequences of Literacy." In *Language and Social Context: Selected Readings*. Ed. Pier Paolo Gilioli. Harmondsworth: Penguin: 311–57. Rpt. from *Comparative Studies in Society and History* 5 (1962–63): 304–26, 332–45.

Griaule, Marcel, and Germaine Dieterlen. 1951. *Signes graphiques soudanais*. Paris: Hermann.

Kendall, Timothy. 1997. *Kerma and the Kingdom of Kush 2500–1500 BC: The Archeological Discovery of An ancient Nubian Empire*. Washington, DC: National Museum of African Art, Smithsonian Institution.

Kihore, Yaredi M. 1984. "Kiswahili katika hati za Kiarabu." *Mulika* 16: 38–45.

Lhote, Henri. 1972. *Les gravures du Nord Ouest de l'Aïr*. Paris: Arts et métiers graphiques.

Lacroix, P. F. 1965. *Poésie peule de l'Adamawa*. Classiques africains. Paris: Julliard.

Nasir, Sayyid Abdallah A. 1972. *Al Inkishafi, The Soul's Awakening*. Ed. W. Hitchens. Nairobi: Oxford University Press.

Niangoran-Bouah, G. 1984. *L'univers akan des poids à peser l'or*. Abidjan: Nouvelles éditions africaines.

Priese, Karl-Heinz. 1996. "Meroitic Writing and Language." In *Sudan: Ancient Kingdoms of the Nile*. Ed. Dietrich Wildung. Paris: Flammarion: 253–62.

Probst, Peter. 1997. "Danser le sida. Spectacle du nyau et culture populaire chewa dans le centre du Malawi." In *Les arts de la rue. Autrepart*, vol. 1. Ed. Michel Agier and Alain Ricard. *Cahiers des sciences humaines* (IRD): 91–112.

Raum, O. F. 1943. "The African Chapter in the History of Writing." *African Studies* 2: 178–92.

Ricard, Alain. 1995. *Littératures d'Afrique noire*. Paris: CNRS / Karthala.

Vail, Leroy, and Landeg White. 1991. *Power and the Praise Poem: Southern African Voices in History*. Charlottesville: University Press of Virginia; Oxford: James Currey.

Whiteley, Wilfred, trans. and ed. 1958. *Maisha ya Hamed bin Muhammed El Murjebi, yaani Tippu Pip*. Kampala, Nairobi, Dar es Salaam.

Wildung, Dietrich, ed. 1996. *Soudan, royaume sur le Nil*. Paris: Institut du monde arabe, Flammarion.

Yoruba Orthography Committee. 1969. *Kaaaro . . . oojiire, a Report on Yoruba Orthography*. Ibadan.

Zima, Petr. 1969. "Language, Script and Vernacular Literature in Africa." *African Language Review* 8: 212–24.

10

Ethiopian literature

TEODROS KIROS

Ethiopian literature falls into three broad categories: classical literature, including historical narratives, heroic poetry, and works of philosophical reflection cast in an imaginative mode; romantic and political literature in Amharic, and, since the Second World War, the new literature in English. The classical literature is expressed in Ge'ez, a Semitic language that is also the oldest written language in Africa, with its unique orthography going back nearly two thousand years. The Holy Bible and all other Christian texts have been translated into Ge'ez, which survives today as the language of the Ethiopian clergy; in this respect, it has a status similar to Latin in the western world. Ordinary Ethiopians neither spoke nor wrote in Ge'ez. Therefore, the texts written in that language did not seep into the soul of the people, and did not produce a national literary culture. The classical literary texts, hymns, and songs circulate today only among the priestly class and highly specialized students and teachers of Ge'ez. This is part of the reason that the modern Ethiopian state which emerged in the late nineteenth century had to forge a new language aimed at producing a popular national culture through the medium of Amharic.

Classical literature

This category comprises a substantial number of devotional books, many of them works translated from foreign sources. They include biblical scriptures, exegesis, service books of the Coptic church, texts detailing the lives of saints of the Universal Church who flourished before the schism at the Council of Chalcedon in 451 CE and of saints of the Coptic church, especially the Desert Fathers,[1] and homilies by the early Church Fathers, such as John Chrysostom, Athanasius of Alexandria, Severus of Antioch, and Cyril of Alexandria (Haile 1995: 40). It is widely believed that the translation of the Bible into Ge'ez began in the fifth century, one hundred years after the conversion of the Aksumite kingdom to Christianity, and that it was completed by the seventh century (Knibb 1999: 2). This translation, based on a Greek text, was revised in light of Arabic and Hebrew texts during the literary revival that marked the reign of Amda Tseyon (1314–44) in the fourteenth century. Literary activity, which had stopped with the decline of the Aksumite kingdom in the seventh century, was revived with the establishment of the Solomonic dynasty (1268–1975). Ge'ez versions of many sacred books have disappeared (Haile 1995: 43), but some have survived. The main religious books of this period are the *Book of Enoch*; the *Book of Jubilee* (on the Sabbath), and the *Book of Joseph and Asenath*. These books were unknown to the authors of the Old Testament but were apparently well known by the authors of the New Testament. They have now become fully incorporated into the body of Ethiopian sacred books; thus, they form the Bible, which for Ethiopians consists not of sixty-six but of eighty-one books. In the Ethiopian Christian community, all the texts grapple with distinctly Ethiopian problems, out of which develops a distinct Christian literature by Ethiopians and for Ethiopians. This was the first exercise in the indigenization and localization of Christianity in the African experience. A broader view of this interpretive literature must include these texts as contributions to global Christian literature.

Classical Ethiopian literature also includes a large body of philosophical writings in literary language, in genres such as fables and poetry, deriving from different external and internal sources. Classical Ethiopian philosophy itself results from a confluence of Greek, Egyptian, Aramaic, and Arab sources. The *Fisalgos* (second century CE) is a transcription from the Greek *Physiologos*. It is primarily symbolic of moral values. In these texts, various animals, plants, and natural objects function as symbols of moral instructions, and thus compose a distinctly Ethiopian interpretation of the Bible. They revolve around a discourse that emphasizes the duties of children toward their parents, as in this passage from the *Fisalgos*:

> The young one of the hipwopas,[2] when their father grows old, pluck off his molting feathers, peck his eyes, keep him in a hot place, welcome him under their wings, feed him, and guard him, as if they were saying to their father: "As a reward for having kept us, we shall do likewise to you." And they do so until (these aged birds) are imparted with renewed vitality; they are rejuvenated and are young once more. (Sumner 1994: 25–26)

The Book of the Philosophers also uses images in the same way as the *Fisalgos*. In contrast to the *Fisalgos*, *The Book of the Philosophers* is a collection of sayings that illuminate tradition as a source of philosophy, in other words, that consecrate philosophy as a product of orality. Most of the sayings are Ethiopianized interpretations of classical Greek philosophers – Pythagoras, Plato, and Aristotle – but the texts retain their Ethiopian roots and cadence. They are not merely appropriations, but rather transformed interpretations. As Claude Sumner has argued, Ethiopians never translate literally: they adapt and modify, add and subtract; thus, a translation always bears a typical Ethiopian stamp. The results are always texts that distinguish themselves from the original sources.

One of the outstanding texts of the fourteenth century concerns the story of Skendes (Greek, Sekondos), a story that has fired the imaginations of Greek, Syrian, Arabic, and Ethiopian scholars over the centuries. The Ethiopian text is based on the Arabic, although some scholars contend that its style is modeled on the Greek. The Ethiopian version recalls the story of Skendes, the son of sagacious parents, who decided to send him to Berytus (modern Beirut) and Athens for a classical education. Skendes was thirteen years old at the time of his departure to the foreign lands. While he was abroad, he encountered a statement of the wise philosophers that declared, "All women are prostitutes." He was greatly perturbed by the statement and determined to verify it. After staying abroad for twenty-four years he returned to his homeland. He recalled that disturbing statement about the nature of women, and decided to test his own mother. Through the services of a maidservant whom he met at a public well, he managed to trick the maid into letting him into his mother's house, to spend the night with her mistress in exchange for one hundred dinars. So he spent the night with his own mother. In the morning he revealed himself to his mother as her very own son. Shocked by the discovery, she hanged herself.[3]

Skendes regretted his words that had caused the death of his mother, and vowed never to speak again; from that moment on, he became permanently silent. The emperor at the time was Andryanos, and when he heard the extraordinary and tragic story of Skendes, he invited him to his court. When Skendes was ordered to speak, he refused; instead he wrote down his thoughts, and the king also communicated with him through writing. His responses were organized into two books, with fifty-five questions in the first and 108 questions in the second. After the emperor had carefully read his responses, he was deeply impressed, and did not order the philosopher to speak. Instead, it was officially decided that the work of Skendes be treated as a national treasure and be preserved in the priests' archives.

The philosopher developed in his discourses systematic theories about the essence of God, the angels, the universe, and the elements, and about the soul, human nature, and the spirit. Many of his other discourses speculate about the emotions and states of being. According to Sumner, the obstinate silence of Skendes produced an implacable dialectic of speech and silence in classical Ethiopian philosophy. The importance of silence and wisdom, the need to control the tongue, became powerful ethical and sapiential themes in classical Ethiopian philosophy.

The *Book of the Philosophers*, *Fisalgos*, and *Skendes*'s sayings are both literary and philosophical. At issue is not the status of the texts. They are broadly speaking philosophical in their own right. It is the case, however, that they are derivative transformations of non-Ethiopian texts to which Skendes and many others contributed. Some of the sayings are natively Ethiopian, based on observation, reports, readings of the Bible, and other sources. Given Ethiopia's location and history, it is not an accident that the sapiential themes are at once Arabic, Syrian, biblical, and Greek. Ethiopia is clearly at the confluence of world cultures, and its philosophical tradition precisely reflects that confluence.

These philosophical reflections are interesting in several senses. To begin with, the ethical counsels become transformed by Ethiopian thinkers into much more than their original form. The various traditions, customs, and belief systems impose themselves on the original forms and radically alter them. Furthermore, they provide us with a novel opportunity to inspect closely the meaning of tradition in the Ethiopian context. The inner architectonics of the Ethiopian texts can be understood and appreciated only if we take account of the multicultural tapestry out of which they are woven and which they radically transform into their very own African literary forms. Sumner offers a striking example of this process of integration:

> One example taken from *The Book of the Philosophers* will suffice to drive this point home. The well-known conversation between Diogenes and Alexander of Corinth, which is recorded by Diogenes Laertius, is found in our Ethiopian work. But it is transformed beyond recognition. "Move away from my shadow" of Diogenes is ascribed to Socrates in Ethiopic, as it already was in the Arabic. The whole passage has been given such a specifically Christian form and development that one seems to be listening to an Oriental monk speaking through the mouth of Socrates. Alexander the Great is simply called "The King" – and the Arabic does as well. As in most other passages in our manuscript, he is placed in an inferior position in relation to the wise man. The whole dialogue hinges around one point: life. For Socrates the real life is the spiritual one. But the king misses the point, and thinks that Socrates is speaking of the temporal life. (Sumner 1994: 51–52)

Royal chronicles

The *Kebra Nagast* (Glory of the Kings), dating to the early fourteenth century, is a characteristically original text that traces the origin of the Solomonic dynasty in Ethiopia as part of the elaboration of the Judeo-Christian tradition. The text can be read as a legitimation of the dynasty, a justification of its right to rule based on the divine rights of kings. In marvelous poetic-analytic language, it describes the amorous relationship between Sheba, the beautiful and shrewd Ethiopian queen, and the wise Solomon (Bezold 1909). Another section of the work describes the military genius of Alexander the Great. *Kebra Nagast* is simultaneously mythical, allegorical, and more fundamentally apocalyptic. This story gives Ethiopia the first legendary king, Menelik, who became the first self-conscious founder of the Ethiopian dynasty. He is purportedly the son of Solomon and Sheba. A long line of kings traces their genealogy to this legendary story. Different books of this period also describe the deeds of heroes, such as during the wars of the Ethiopian emperor Amda Tseyon (1314–44), celebrated in *The Glorious Victories of 'Amda Tseyon, king of Ethiopia* (Huntingford 1965).

These texts are one source from which Ethiopian historians chronicle Ethiopian history; they represent one of the two fountains from which Ethiopian history flows. The other source is *Gedlat* (Acts of Saints). Getatchew Haile finds the *Gedlat* exceptionally useful, the simplicity of the Ge'ez in which they are written being one its attractions; while the rich tapestry of the Ethiopian setting that grounds the texts is another (Haile 1995: 50). This period also gave Ethiopia one of its finest emperors, Zara Yacob, who was also an accomplished literary figure.

Hymns and poetry

The emperor Zara Yacob (1434–68) is remembered for his vivid hymns and his devotion to the cult of Mary. He pleaded that the "goddess" should be revered by the faithful; painters heeded to his demands and personified her in breathtaking paintings. According to Haile, "The king ordered thirty-three feasts to be observed in Mary's honor, some monthly and some annually" (1995: 50). Zara Yacob's literary texts are filled with hymns to Mary. A foundational hymnody called *Igziabher Negse*, is considered his main literary output. The following passage from Zara Yacob's *Book of Hours* is representative of its style and atmosphere of devotional piety:

> What should we call you, O full of grace;
> You are the gate of Salvation;

You are the portal of light;
You are the daughter of the palace
Should we call you a golden basket?
Your son is the bread of life;
His apostles are your stewards,
The sacrifices of the body of your First-born.
(Haile 1995: 52)

One of the genres of Ge'ez poetry is that associated with *Qine*. These poems are employed as panegyrics and eulogies of political and religious personalities, to honor the saints and as hymns to celebrate particular religious ceremonies. The poems are rhymed and rhythmical, and are performed by trained singers. The composers must follow strict rules of composition as regards the length of the lines, rhythm, and grammatical structure. The singers are expected to display exceptional powers of expression. Students are carefully instructed in the mastery of the genre, before they can aspire to compose these intricately woven *Qine* poems. One such book of rhymes is *Diggua*, a book of hymns attributed to a sixth-century Aksumite priest (Haile 1995: 51). *Aksum Tsion*, a famous church, uses *Qine* to celebrate "the conception of Mary" as a special religious event; this church prohibits the use of *Qine* for any other purpose. The most famous poem in this genre is *Mezmure Dawit*, which closely follows *"Psalms of Dawit,"* written by an anonymous poet who lived probably in the sixteenth century.

The fifteenth century witnessed ferocious conflicts between Orthodox Christians and other denominations. Islam was also seeking to penetrate Ethiopia by force, and Ethiopian Christianity was asserting its autonomy and repelling foreign intrusion. The great religious books of the century are literary documentations of these conflicts. Among them can be mentioned *Egiazhar Ngse* (The God King); *Kisaitan Herdet* (Satan's Dance); and finally the *Gedlat,* a book that narrates the "deeds and miracles" of the saints. The fifteenth century was also a century of king worship. Divinized Ethiopian kings are praised in literary homilies. The most powerful literary figure of the time was Enbakom, a Muslim merchant who converted to Christianity and became prior of the monastery of Debre Libanos. He is the author of *Anqas'a amin* (Gate of Faith); *Fetha Nagast* (Justice of the Kings); and *Hawi Mesthafe*, a theological encyclopedia translated by Salik of Debre Libanos.

Unfortunately, the fifteenth century also witnessed the destruction of books consequent upon the Muslim incursion (1527–43). As Islamization spread, the destruction of Christian books increased, crippling Ethiopian literary life. All this resulted in mitigating the verve and imagination of those who wrote in Ge'ez, which lost its expressive vigor and presence. It became reduced to a "liturgical" language of the Church. Except among Ethiopian Falashas, Ethiopian Jews who continued to use Ge'ez, the language has been replaced in all the secular sectors of Ethiopian national life by Amharic.

Romantic and political literature in Amharic

It took several centuries before Amharic replaced Ge'ez as the language of writing. Amharic had emerged by the fourteenth century as an independent language, replacing classical Ge'ez as the spoken language of the royal court under the Solomonic dynasty (Molvaer 1997: xiii). The oldest writings in Amharic are poems and songs in praise of Emperors Amda Tseyon and Emperor Ghelawdewos; these writings appeared in the fourteenth century. Amharic achieved official status as the literary language of Ethiopia during the reign of Emperor Menilik (1881–1913); Menilik's own extensive chronicle was written in Amharic (Demoz 1995: 17). Emperor Tewodros (1855–68) introduced the idea that the unification of Ethiopia required the use of a national language. Amharic thus gained prominence in the late nineteenth century, opening the way to the flowering of a new national literary culture. Amharic became the official language of Ethiopia in 1955, as promulgated in the country's revised constitution.

The establishment of the first government press in 1906, and the setting up of more presses later on, facilitated the publication of the books that were beginning to be written (Molvaer 1997: xiv). Scholars have described the years between 1900 and 1935 as "the renaissance of Ethiopian writing." A new crop of Ethiopian writers emerged during this period, writers who were experimenting with new forms of fiction. Afework Gebra Yesus published his first novella in 1908. Hiruy, "the father of Amharic literature," is reputed to have written about twenty-eight books. Among these books, *Wedaje Libbe* (I Am My Own Best Friend, 1925) is the most popular. Tekle Hawariyat produced the first Ethiopian play in 1930 (Molvaer 1997: 48). After the restoration of Ethiopian independence, following the Italian invasion (1936–41), and spurred by the support of Emperor Haile Selassie, Ethiopian writers began to produce poetry and novels of considerable literary merit. Reidulf Molvaer has featured some of these Ethiopian writers in his collection of interviews (Molvaer 1997).

T'obbiya Lebb Wallad Tarik (literally, "history born of the heart"), by Afework Gebre (1868–1947), is perhaps the most famous work of this period. It announces the arrival of the novel written in Amharic. Gebre recalls in this novel the perennial conflict between Christianity and Islam. As Yonas Admassu has observed,

> this foundational novel confronts us, at first sight, with the simplicity of a tale. Yet, it would be difficult, even erroneous, to classify it as a simple tale. If anything, the work defies classification. It reads at once as myth, legend, adventure, romance, fantasy, all put together rather hastily, but with a clearly defined moral and political intent that only invites (indeed, demands at every turn it negotiates), the reader's serious interpretive participation. (Admassu 1995: 95)

Afework is followed by a string of great novelists such as Haddis Alemayehu (b. 1902), the author of the modern classic, *Fikir Eske Mekabir* (Love until Death), first published in 1958. This powerful novel contains a scathing criticism of the static institutions of feudal Ethiopia. The story of a forbidden love between the peasant Bezzabeh and the aristocrat Seble, the novel is at once romantic and realistic. The tension between the demands of love and the dead weight of backward institutions is resolved in favor of the rights of the peasant to love, and Seble, the slave of honor, sings the language of freedom.

Other novelists have taken the path opened up by Afework. Mangestu Lemma's *Yegitim gubae* (Synod of Poetry) was published in 1955. Kebede Mikael, also known as "the grand old man of Amharic" reportedly wrote more than a hundred books, but only twenty-two have been published. He adapted and translated *Romeo and Juliet*, as well as *Faust* (Molvaer 1997: 74). Belau Girma's first novel, *Ke Admas Bashager* (Beyond the Horizon) is another novel of disillusionment, widely admired for its narrative of the misery and deprivation of the Ethiopian poor. Germachew Tekle Hawariyat's *Araya* is an educational novel that recounts in a captivating style the adventure of a gifted boy, Araya, who is presented to a French visitor, Mme. Dubonne Foi. He is taken to France by her, is educated there, and returns home as a young man. Araya has developed a profound respect for western technology and efficiency, but he prefers and admires the values of discipline and self-control, which are heralded as Ethiopia's own cardinal virtues.

The novels cited above are now classics of modern Ethiopian literature in Amharic. The succeeding generation of writers was to focus on Ethiopian life under Emperor Haile Selassie. Abe Gubenya (1933/34–1980) is the author of the longest novel (602 pages) in Amharic, *And lennatu* (His Mother's Only Son), about the famous Ethiopian Emperor Tewodros. Another novel, *Alwelledim*

(I Refuse / Do Not Want to Be Born), is a social novel that confronts the feudal regime of Haile Selassie's Ethiopia, by exposing the vacuity of religion insofar as religion is used to mystify and justify the oppression of the peasants by absentee landlords. The novel is notable for its prophetic anticipation of the socialist autocracy of the Ethiopian Derg (or "Committee"), the repressive regime that ruled the country from 1974 to 1991 under Colonel Mengistu. In its depiction of a repressive state, the novel can be considered an Ethiopian equivalent to Orwell's acclaimed *1984*. The Israelis in *Alwelledim* are represented as a people living under a garrison state, as this was to be perfected later by the Derg. The novel was banned during Haile Selassie's reign, and the Derg briefly embraced it, during its short-lived democratic phase. But once the Derg consecrated repression as a way of life, its leaders quickly realized that the novel was after all a perfect representation of the State they had created. So the novel was banned again. Abe Gubenya's death coincided with the rise of State terrorism under the Derg.

The implicit indictment of the Derg in Abe Gubenya's work is extended by the direct attack of the regime in Belau Girma's novel *Derasiw* (1980, The Writer), which examines the life of a writer who confronts oppressive regimes and cannot speak truth to power. Following the footsteps of Gubenya, Girma examines the inner workings of repression by focusing on the vulnerability of the writer who dares to speak the truth. His characters are modeled after the inept and incompetent officials he knew, and his novel documents their lust for power, their unscrupulous methods, and indeed some of their crimes. The failed campaigns in Eritrea and the derogation of the idea of state socialism itself form part of his indictment. Girma's second novel, *Oromai* (Enough), even goes further. *Oromai* is the work of a witness who has seen all and decided he had had enough of the perversities of political life in contemporary Africa, in which the writer speaks truth to power at the risk of his life. Indeed, *Oromai* is said to have sealed Girma's fate. The writer, who was director-general of the Ministry of Information after having been an editor of the government's newspaper, *Addis Zemen*, was summarily dismissed by the Mengistu regime and barred from holding any further employment. Predicting his own death in *Derasiw*, Grima wrote,

> I do not have any plans on how to live life except simply existing. The purpose of life is merely living. I live this precious piece of life, like Abraham without dwelling in a house, and like Moses, nobody knowing the site of my grave. I survive and write with the hope of living in the future and looking back at the past. (Girma 1980: 209)

Ethiopian writing in English

There is a dearth of fiction writing in English across the Horn of Africa. In light of this well-known fact, the emergence of writing in English in Ethiopia is an impressive new development. Although French was for a long time the lingua franca of the Ethiopian intelligentsia, it was superseded by English after 1941 (Zewde 1991: 108–09), a position that was consolidated after the return of the emperor, Haile Selassie, who had taken refuge from the Italian invasion, during the war, in England. After the war, English was introduced to the court and became the language of instruction in the schools and at the University of Addis Ababa.

Some limited writing in English began in the early 1960s, inspired by a new sense of curiosity about other cultures and ways of being that the postwar period initiated. Some Ethiopian writers who have lived abroad and become diasporic writers have adopted English as a second language. Others have managed to write both in English and their native tongues. These writers have internalized the contours of European literature, and can only write in its conventional forms. The reasons for the choice of English by Ethiopian writers are as varied as the writers themselves. For some, it is simply a matter of taste, a preferred medium of esthetic form; for others, it is a matter of convenience, of gaining access to a wider public through a language of wide international diffusion. However, all these authors write about aspects of Ethiopian life, thereby staying true to their Ethiopian / African origins even though they write in English.

B. M. Sahle-Sellassie has dominated Ethiopian writing in English. His fourth novel in English, *Firebrands*, is considered his best work; because of its uncompromising stand against politicians, Tadesse Adera has compared the work to Ayi Kwei Armah's *The Beautyful Ones Are Not Yet Born* (Adera and Ahmed 1995b: 164). Other lesser known but very able writers have written novels and plays in English. Abe Gubenya wrote two books in English, in addition to twenty books in Amharic (Molvaer 1997: 183); Mengistu Lemma translated two of his pre-revolutionary plays into English, *Telfo bekise* (Marriage by Abduction) and *Yalaccha gabiccha* (The Marriage of Unequals) (Molvaer 1997: 278); Daniachew Worku, who studied creative writing at Iowa University in the US, wrote a novel, *The Thirteenth Sun*, published in 1973; Tsegaye Gebre-Medhin wrote plays and poems in English and Amharic (Molvaer 1997: 272). The contribution of this major poet and dramatist have been been well summed up by Biodun Jefiyo in these terms: "All told within the social context of pre-Revolutionary Ethiopia of the Emperor, his ecclesiastical potentates, and their aristocratic, anti-people pretensions, Gebre-Medhin's plays constitute an intense, passionate ideological contestation of the religion which underpins and sustains the misrule of the oligarchy and the denigration of the governed" (Jefiyo 1995: 186).

In *Collision of Altars*, the poet sings:

I am a Kush, and of this land of Ra
On whose roots the first sun rose,
My body living
As my head is true.
Mine is unlike your hybrid
Devious, little Sabean mind
Where the quibbles of your Ge'ez tongue
Outlive the living body by far.
With us, the body has language
The mind cannot speak.
Both live. Without the one
The other is dead: and
The one cannot live
The other's complete life.

His other work, *Oda Oak Oracle*, calls for a new humanism built on the foundations of compassion and reciprocity (Jefiyo 1995: 187). The principal character Shanka represents this new consciousness, as indicated by this passage from the play:

We cry
Only to join your hands
Come
Abortive cry against darkness
Come
The truer the love
The thornier the fate
And the more reason to die
Come darkness, come.

The development of Ethiopian literature in English has been brought to a new and exciting high point with the publication of Nega Mezlekia's novel, *Notes From the Hyena's Belly* (2000). In a powerful blend of autobiography and social history, the novelist explodes the contemporary stereotypes of Ethiopia and incites our imagination to revisit the grandeur and stubborn sovereignty of this ancient empire. In intricately woven stories told with verve and imagination, Mezlekia treats Ethiopia as the site of a classic conflict between modernity and tradition. Along with a gripping story of his childhood, he introduces us to a living Ethiopian culture: its customs, religious traditions, and the nuanced ways of seeing and knowing. The book's beginning with his birth "in the year of the paradox," in the labyrinthine city of Jijiga, displays the author's textual mastery, in a narrative texture that frames local myths, beliefs, and practices in powerful evocative language. As the young Mezlekia navigates the complexity of family and culture, he leads us through the local scene – its ethnic tensions and its religious universe – all the while focused on a vision that incorporates the classical Ethiopian metaphors of the human world as an animal world, with its central characters: the vicious hyena, the brave lion, the shrewd fox, and hardworking donkey. This work is without question a monumental contribution to the modern Ethiopian literary culture.

Ethiopian literature in English is a recent development, but it already includes some of the most significant works in African literature today, most notably the plays of Tsegaye Gebre-Mehdin. Moreover, as Mezlekia's remarkable work demonstrates, it is a literature that remains in close touch with its roots in the literary and poetic tradition of the national community, as this community has evolved over millennia of a dramatic history.

Notes

1. This is a collection of sayings known in the Coptic Church as "bustan al-rohban" "the monk's garden," also known in English as "the paradise of the Desert Fathers." It consists of accounts of the lives of Desert Fathers of Egypt.
2. A species of bird.
3. The parallel with the Greek tragedy of Oedipus is of course obvious.

Bibliography

Primary works

Alamayehu, Haddis. 1972. *Fikr Isqe Mekabir*. Addis Ababa: Birhanena Selam Printing Press.

Beylot, R., and M. Robinson. 1995. *Répertoire des bibliothèques et des catalogues de manuscrits éthiopiens*. Paris and Turnhout: Institut de Recherche et d'Histoire des Textes.

Bezold, C., ed. and trans. 1909. *Kebra Nagast: Die Herrlichkeit der Könige*, vol. 23. Munich: Abhandlungen der philosophisch Klasse der königlich bayerischen Akademie der Wissenschaften.

Budge, E. A. Wallis. 1896. *The Life and Exploits of Alexander the Great, Being a Series of Ethiopic Texts Edited from Manuscripts in the British Library and the Bibliothèque nationale, Paris, with an English Translation and Notes. The English Translation*, vol. II. London: Cambridge University Press.

1922. *The Queen of Sheba and Her Only Son Menelik: Being the History of the Departure of God and His Ark of the covenant from Jerusalem to Ethiopia, and the Establishment of the Religion of the Hebrews and the Solomonic Line of Kings in the Country*. London: M. Hopkinson.

ed. and trans. [1923] 1976. *Barlaam and Joseph, being the Ethiopic Version of a Christianized Recension of the Buddhist legend of the Buddha and the Bodhisattva*. Amsterdam: APA-Philo Press.

trans. [1928] 1976. *The Book of the Saints of the Ethiopic Church*. Hildesheim: Georg Olms Verlag.

trans. 1933. *One Hundred and Ten Miracles of Our Lady Mary, translated from Ethiopic manuscripts for the most part in the British Museum*. London: Oxford University Press.

Conti Rossini, Carlo, ed. and trans. 1964–65. *Il libro della luce, Mashafa Berhan*. Louvain: Corpus Scriptorum Christianorum Orientalium.

Fusella, Luigi, Salvatore Tedeschi, and Joseph Tubiana. 1984. *Trois essais sur la littérature éthiopienne*. Antibes: Aresae.

Gebre, Afework. 1964. *T'obbiya*. Addis Ababa: Commercial Printing Press.

Gebre-Medhin, Tsegaye. 1965. *Oda Oak Oracle*. London: Oxford University Press.

1977. *Collision of Altars*. London: Rex Collings.

Girma, Bealu. 1980. *Derasiw*. Addis Ababa: Ethiopian Book Center.

1983. *Oromai*. Addis Ababa: Kuraz.

Haile, Getatchew. 1983. *The Different Collections of Nägs Hymns in Ethiopic Literature and Their Contributions*. Erlangen: s.n.

trans. 1991. *The Epistle of Humanity of Emperor Zär'a Ya'eqob*. 2 vols. Louvain: E. Peeters.

1992. *The Mariology of Emperor Zär'a Ya'eqob of Ethiopia: Texts and Translations*. Rome: Pontificium Institutum Studiorum Orientalium.

Huntingford, G. W. B., ed. and trans. 1965. *The Glorious Victories of 'Amda Tseyon, King of Ethiopia*. Oxford: Clarendon Press.

Knibb, Michael A. 1978. *The Ethiopic Book of Enoch. A New Edition in the Light of the Aramaic Dead Sea Fragments*. 2 vols. Oxford: Clarendon Press.

Macomber, William F., and Gatatchew Haile. 1975–93. *A Catalogue of Ethiopian Manuscripts Microfilmed for the Ethiopian Manuscript Microfilm Library, Addis Ababa, and for the Monastic Manuscript Microfilm Library, Collegeville*. 10 vols. Collegeville, MN: Monastic Microfilm Library, St. John's Abbey and University.

Mezlekia, Nega. 2000. *Notes From the Hyena's Belly*. Toronto, New York: Penguin.

Molvaer, Reidulf K. 1997. *Black Lions. The Creative Lives of Modern Ethiopia's Literary Giants and Pioneers*. Lawrenceville, NJ: Red Sea.

Sahle-Sellassie, B. M. 1979. *Firebrands*. Washington, DC: Three Continents Press.

Sumner, Claude. 1974. *Ethiopian Philosophy. The Book of the Wise Philosophers*, vol. IV. Addis Ababa: Central Printing Press.

1978. *Ethiopian Philosophy. The Treatise of Zara Yacob and of Walda Heywat. Text and Authorship*, vol. II. Addis Ababa: Commercial Printing Press.

Tadesse Tamarat. 1964. "Tobbya." *Ethiopia Observer* 7. 3: 242–67.

Uhlig, S. 1988. *Äthiopische Paläographie*. Stuttgart: F. Steiner.

Wendt, Kurt, ed. and trans. 1962. *Des Mashafa Milad (Liber Nativitatis) und Mashafa Sellase (Liber Trinitatis) des Kaisers Zara Yaqob*, vols. 221–22. Louvain: Corpus Scriptorum Christianorum Orientalium.

Worku, Daniachew. 1973. *The Thirteenth Sun*. London: Heinemann.
1998. *Zabat elfitu*. Addis Ababa: Tewanney Studio plc.

Secondary works

Adera, Tadesse, and Ali Jimale Ahmed. 1995a. *Silence Is Not Golden. A Critical Anthology of Ethiopian Literature*. Lawrenceville, NJ: Red Sea.

1995b. "From Apologist to Critic: The Dilemma of Bealu Girma." In Adera and Ahmed 1995a: 155–66.

Admassu, Yonas. 1995. "The First-Born Amharic Fiction: A Revaluation of Afework's T'obbiya." In Adera and Ahmed 1995a: 93–112.

Cerulli, Enrico. 1968. *La letteratura etiopica*. Milan: Sansoni-Accademia.

Guidi, I. 1932. *Storia della letterature etiopica*. Rome: Istituto per l'Orient.

Haile, Getachew. 1995. "Highlighting Ethiopian Traditional Literature." In Adera and Ahmed 1995a: 39–60.

Jeyifo, Biodun. 1995. "Art and Ideology in the Plays of Tsegaye Gebre-Medhin." In Adera and Ahmed 1995a: 183–90.

Knibb, Michael B. 1999. *Translating the Bible: The Ethiopic Version of the Old Testament*. Oxford: Oxford University Press.

Levin, Donald. 1972. *Wax and Gold: Tradition and Innovation in Amhara Culture*. Chicago: University of Chicago Press.

Littman, E. von. 1909. "Geschichte der Aethiopische Litteratur." In *Geschichte der christlichen Litteraturen des Orients*. Ed. Carl von Brockelman *et al*. Leipzig: C. F. Amelang.

Molvaer, Reidulf. 1980. *Tradition and Change in Ethiopia: Social and Cultural Life as Reflected in Amharic Fictional Literature 1930–1974*. Leiden: E. J Brill.

Sumner, Claude. 1994. *Classical Ethiopian Philosophy*. Los Angeles: Adey.

Tolassa, Fikre. 1983. "Realism and Amharic Literature." PhD diss. University of Bremen.

Ullendorff, E. 1968. *Ethiopia and the Bible*. London: British Academy.

Zewde, Bahru. 1991. *A History of Modern Ethiopia 1855–1974*. London and Addis Ababa: Ohio University Press and Addis Ababa University Press.

11

African literature in Arabic

FARIDA ABU-HAIDAR

The Arabic language is a rich and flexible tool that, over the centuries, has been shaped and molded by the many different peoples that came to express themselves in it. In Africa, Arabic spread with the advent of Islam. It became the official language throughout northern Africa, from the Sudan to the western Sahara, and as far south as Mauritania. The first Arabic works in Africa date from about the tenth century and are mostly religious treatises written by Muslim jurists. Creative writing in Arabic initially consisted of poetry, a genre much esteemed and perfected by Arabs since pre-Islamic times. Prose works continued to be scholarly and religious, right up to the end of the nineteenth century when genres new to Arabic literature, like the novel, the short story, and drama emerged.

The region now has a thriving national literature in Arabic. Egypt, in particular, has a rich tradition of Arabic creative writing, predating the emergence of modern Arabic literature elsewhere in Africa. The Maghreb countries, once under French rule, have a globally renowned francophone literature. It was only after independence that the Arabic creative writing of the Maghreb began to reach a wide readership in other parts of the Arabic-speaking world. In sub-Saharan Africa, and particularly in West Africa, where Islam is the main religion, Arabic is a religious language, introduced by Muslim scholars. It spread with the establishment of centers of Arabic learning in several African cities. Some parts of sub-Saharan Africa have been prolific in the production of Arabic works. In Nigeria, Muslim scholars were producing works in Arabic as early as the thirteenth century. But throughout the sub-Saharan region, any literary production in Arabic, whether in prose or verse, has been concerned primarily with religious themes. It is generally folk poetry and legends, orally transmitted from one generation to the next, that focus on secular topics, notably the history of famous tribes and the heroic deeds of warriors.

Oral poetry and storytelling have always been part of the African cultural heritage. It is not surprising, therefore, that some Arabian romances and epic poems, introduced into Africa through various channels, but largely via Egypt, became part of African folklore. Foremost among these is the romance of the Banu Hilal, an Arabian tribe who, in the tenth century, moved first to Egypt and later to Tunisia. Their exploits in battle, particularly those of their heroes, among them Abu Zayd al-Hilali, fired the imagination of later generations of folk-poets and storytellers. The wanderings of the Banu Hilal in the Arabian Desert, their seeking new territory, and their settlement in northern Africa constitute the main themes of a voluminous epic known in Arabic as *Sirat Bani Hilal*. Stories interspersed with poems from this romance are to this day related in coffee houses and other public places throughout northern Africa and in some parts of sub-Saharan Africa, by storytellers often referred to as poets, who, in a way, performed and continue in many places to perform the roles of medieval *jongleurs*.

Another well-known popular epic, *Sirat 'Antar* (The Adventures of 'Antar), whose hero is 'Antara ibn Shaddad, the sixth-century Arabian warrior-poet, was just as popular in Egypt, the Sudan, and the northern African countries as it was in the rest of the Arab world. Its central character 'Antara is, after all, half-African. 'Antara, the poet, is moreover the author of one of the seven *Mu'allaqat*, the well-known select *qasidas* (odes) of pre-Islamic Arabia. A *qasida* is a long poem – often of more than sixty or seventy verses, all having the same meter and rhyme scheme – that became formalized in the eighth century.

As pre-Islamic Arabic poetry held the fascination of the numinous for Arabs everywhere, Arabic poetry, imitative of the style of the classical Arabian *qasida*, became popular in territories conquered by the Arabs, like northern Africa and Spain. From about the tenth century, cities in the region now known as the Maghreb, among them Fez, Tlemcen, and Tunis, became important centers of Arabic learning, and produced a number of scholars and poets who looked to the Arab east for guidance and inspiration. The eleventh-century poet and scholar Ibn Rashiq (1000 – *c.*1070), who was born not far from the present city of Constantine in Algeria, urged fellow poets to give up imitating the classical *qasida* with its descriptions of imaginary desert journeys, and to concentrate on depicting the environment they lived in and knew best. Ibn Rashiq's major contribution to Arabic literature is his encyclopedia of poetry, *Al-'Umda fi Sighat al-Shi'r* (The Sourcebook on the Art of Poetry), describing the function, structure and forms of Arabic poetry. It is a work that has been praised by a number of later scholars, among them Ibn Khaldun (1332–1406), one of the best-known medieval historians and thinkers, who described Ibn Rashiq's *Al-'Umda* "as an epoch-making work" (Nicholson 1956: 288).

Ibn Khaldun was born in Tunis to a family of Arabian descent who had lived in Islamic Spain. He is considered to be "the greatest historical thinker of Islam" (Nicholson 1956: 417). His renown rests on his *Muqaddimah* (*Prolegomena*), the introduction to his monumental work, *Kitab al-'Ibar* (The Book of Examples), on the history of Arabs, Berbers, and neighboring races, as well as all the Muslim dynasties of northern Africa. In the *Muqaddimah*, Ibn Khaldun presents his readers with a philosophical theory of history, tracing the religious, economic, scientific, and artistic developments of the civilizations he knew. He states at the outset that the true purpose of history is to make people aware of different societies and civilizations. He firmly believes that history is subject to universal laws. And it is in these laws that truth can be found. He divides the human race into nomads and citizens, claiming that all races are originally nomadic before they inevitably become settled. Once they are fully urbanized, they form states and conquer new territory. When they have achieved all that they set out to do they become effete and corrupt and begin to lose the very qualities that had helped them to develop and prosper. It is then that they turn weak and defenseless and become a prey to other less developed civilizations who in time conquer them. R. A. Nicholson states that no one before Ibn Khaldun took such a comprehensive and analytical view of history or "attempted to trace the deeply hidden causes of events, to expose the moral and spiritual forces at work beneath the surface, or to divine the immutable laws of national progress and decay." Nicholson goes on to say that Ibn Khaldun's "intellectual descendants are the great mediaeval and modern historians of Europe – Machiavelli and Vico and Gibbon" (1956: 438–39).

Pilgrimage to Mecca, the *hajj*, being one of the five pillars of Islam,[1] most Muslim scholars attempted to make the journey to the holy city of Islam at least once in their lifetime. For those in the western extremities of Muslim lands, the journey entailed traveling through unfamiliar landscapes and terrains, often fraught with danger. Some scholars chose to describe their journeys and adventures in writing. This trend during the Middle Ages gave rise to a wealth of geographical and travel literature in Arabic. Among the best-known geographical works that display a good deal of originality are those by al-Bakri (d. 1094) of Cordova, al-Idrisi (1100 – *c.*1162) who was born in Ceuta and studied in Cordova, and Ibn Jubayr (1145–1217) who was born in Valencia and died in Alexandria. Al-Bakri was a prolific writer whose works, many of which have not survived, cover different subjects, among them theology, botany, and philology. He is said to have written also a number of wine poems. Among al-Bakri's surviving works are a dictionary of the place names that occur in pre-Islamic Arabic poetry, and extracts of a work titled *Al-Masalik wa al-Mamalik* (The Book of Roads and Dominions), which contains valuable descriptions of West Africa. It is because of these two works that al-Bakri has gained a prominent place among medieval Arab geographers. Al-Bakri influenced younger geographers, among them al-Idrisi who settled in Palermo where he worked under the patronage of Roger II, King of Sicily. In compiling his geographical works, al-Idrisi used European maps and relied on the verbal reports of European travelers. He was also influenced by the works of Ptolemy. Al-Idrisi's younger contemporary, Ibn Jubayr, was a prolific traveler who wrote at length of his journeys (*The Travels of Ibn Jubayr*), leaving for posterity valuable documents of medieval life in Spain and North Africa. Like many another geographer and travel writer, Ibn Jubayr's first venture eastwards occurred during a pilgrimage to Mecca.

The works of geographers who came after al-Idrisi and Ibn Jubayr showed little originality. From about the thirteenth century, travel literature became a popular genre. Perhaps the best-known medieval Arab traveler is Ibn Battuta (d. 1368–69 or 1377) who was born in Tangier. In 1325 Ibn Battuta traveled across North Africa to Egypt and Syria. His journeys east took him to Iran and the heartlands of Asia, as far as China. Arriving in the Indus Valley in 1333, Ibn Battuta spent some time in the Indian subcontinent. He visited Constantinople and southeastern Europe. He first made the pilgrimage in 1326, and was to return to Mecca several times after that. He traveled into the interior of Africa, reaching East Africa. The account of his numerous journeys was dictated by him to Ibn Juzayy, a secretary of the sultan of Fez. Much of what he related to Ibn Juzayy was reconstructed from memory. Ibn Battuta also drew on the works of earlier geographers and travel writers. In spite of the fact that he may have been given to exaggeration, his descriptions of the people and places he came across constitute a highly important landmark in Arabic travel writing and provide valuable information on the social geography of Muslim territories in the fourteenth century (*Ibn Battuta: Travels in Africa and Asia 1325–1354*). Another writer who left important records of his time and milieu is al-Maqqari (*c.* 1577–1632). Born in Tlemcen, he spent most of his life in Morocco. Al-Maqqari wrote a number of works, some of which are considered to be valuable documents, describing the people and places he knew. His *Rawdat al-As* (Meadows of Myrtle) consists of biographies of Moroccan scholars and also describes his own life and education. Al-Maqqari's masterpiece, *Nafh al-Tib* (The Rich Fragrance), provides a wealth of information on the political and literary history of Muslim Spain.

In sub-Saharan Africa where there is a long-standing tradition of Arabic religious and didactic writing, Sufism (Islamic mysticism) played a significant role in the development of Arabic scholarship and literature. The majority of scholars who wrote in Arabic were followers of Sufi orders known as *tariqas* (paths, ways). Their works cover a wide range of Islamic disciplines, comprising *fiqh* (jurisprudence), *tafsir* (Qur'anic exegesis), *hadith* (Prophetic traditions), and *'ilm al-tawhid* (theology). Their poetry, also with a religious bias and moralistic overtones, is of several types, including *madih* (eulogy), often in praise of the Prophet Muhammad, *ritha'* (elegy), and *hija'* (satire). Among the Sufi orders that flourished in West Africa and had many followers are the Qadiriyya and the Tijaniyya. In Senegal, Shaykh Ahmadou Bamba (1853–1927), originally a member of the Qadiriyya brotherhood, established the Muridiyya order. The Muridis distinguished themselves in Islamic scholarship. In 1866, under the leadership of Shaykh Bamba, they founded the city of Touba, which became a center of Islamic pilgrimage and Arabic scholarship. A good number of Shaykh Bamba's writings were motivated by his nationalist feelings against the French colonial powers. One of his best-known works, *Masalik al-Jinan* (The Roads to Paradise), explains the various Sufi stages. Shaykh Bamba chose to write in Arabic because he felt that the Arabic language "reflected a spiritual obligation due to his own initiation into Sufism, and to an ardent desire to commune with God and with the prophet Muhammad" (Camara 1997: 170). A prolific writer and educationalist, Shaykh Bamba's works, and especially his religious poems, written in classical Arabic, have inspired younger generations of Senegalese Wolof-language poets, while he himself is mentioned in some Wolof poems.[2] The Tijaniyya *tariqa*, founded by Ahmad al-Tijani (d. 1815), also played an important role in the development of Arabic literature in Senegal. One of the leading followers of this *tariqa* was the twentieth-century scholar Ibrahim Niasse (d. 1975) who published several books and also wrote poetry. Niasse had followers in other parts of West Africa, and especially in northern Nigeria, where in Kano a local literature emerged, inspired primarily by his teachings.

Arabic scholarship in what is now Nigeria dates from the thirteenth century. One of the first known writers is thought to have been Abu Ishaq Ibrahim of Kanem (d. *c.*1212) who was a grammarian and poet. Until the end of the eighteenth century, Nigerian Arabic writing consisted only of religious works. It was shortly before the beginning of the nineteenth century that Arabic writing received a new impetus following an Islamic revivalist movement, led by Fulani scholars. Shaykh 'Uthman ibn Muhammad Fudi (d. 1817), his brother 'Abdullah (d. 1829), and his son Muhammad Bello (d. 1837) together produced a large number of prose works and poems. 'Abdullah ibn Fudi wrote a commentary on the Qur'an under the title, *Diya' al-Ta'wil* (Lucid Interpretation). Muhammad

Bello wrote several biographies of Sufi saints. These three scholars tried to free Islam of the non-Islamic elements that they felt had crept into it over the years. 'Uthman ibn Fudi fought neighboring rulers who did not prohibit pagan practices infiltrating Islam. Other notable Nigerian scholars include al-Mukhtar al-Kunti (d. 1811) and his son Muhammad (d. 1826), followers of the Qadiriyya order, who wrote extensive prose works. Their teachings helped to spread Arabic learning in the region. In Yorubaland, in southwestern Nigeria, Ilorin became a prosperous center of Islamic learning, attracting scholars from other parts of Africa, including Arab settlers. The prose works they produced deal with all the disciplines of Islamic scholarship. A number of scholars wrote religious poetry also. Secular oral poetry, particularly praise poetry, has always been popular in Yoruba culture. In the nineteenth century, written praise poems in Yoruba, modeled on classical Arabic poetry, were introduced by Muslim scholars. These, together with animal fables and other texts in Yoruba, were translated into Arabic, introducing a new trend in Nigerian Arabic scholarship.

In Mauritania, which became a French protectorate in 1903 and a French colony in 1920, gaining independence in 1960, Arabic scholarship has always been highly esteemed. Sufism in Mauritania also played a significant role in the development of Arabic writing, just as it did in Senegal and Nigeria. As far as creative writing is concerned, poetry, both written and oral, has always been a highly popular art form in Mauritania, as it has been in most of the western Sahara. Mauritanian written poetry in classical Arabic follows the meters and rhyme schemes of the Arabic *qasida*. Poetry is also composed in Hassaniya, a colloquial variety of Arabic whose use is widespread in Mauritania. Hassaniya verse is syllabic and draws on local folksong rhythms. It is either recited or sung, and is known in its latter form as *leghna* (from Arabic *al-ghina'*, or "song"). Although poetry in the region was composed as far back as the fifteenth century, some of the best-known poets lived during the eighteenth and nineteenth centuries, foremost among them being the Sufi poet and scholar Shaykh Muhammad al-Mami (d. 1865). A comprehensive account of Mauritanian poetry can be found in *Al-Wasit* by al-Shinqiti (d. 1913). Apart from being a compendium of poems in classical Arabic and Hassaniya, the work consists also of important data on the history, geography, and folklore of the region.

A younger contemporary of Shaykh Bamba, who was also a Sufi and a committed nationalist, was the Algerian Emir Abdelkader (1808–83), who led an unsuccessful rebellion against the French. Abdelkader was a notable scholar and poet. The author of a number of prose works on military and religious issues, his writings paved the way for the next generation of Algerian scholars and reformists. The Arabic works that were published in Algeria during the first decades of the twentieth century are nearly all didactic. Apart from his prose works, Abdelkader left a number of patriotic poems, most of which were collected and published posthumously. His nationalist sentiments, expressed in the poems, inspired Arabic-language poets throughout the Maghreb in the early decades of the twentieth century when feelings of national awakening began to be openly expressed in writing.

It was in Arabic newspapers and periodicals that the beginnings of modern Arabic literature in Egypt and the Maghreb emerged. A number of Arabic newspapers appeared in Egypt at the start of the nineteenth century. One of the best-known Arabic newspapers, which is still printed today, is the Egyptian *Al-Ahram*, founded in 1876 as a weekly. It became a daily in 1881. *Al-Ahram*'s service to modern Arabic literature has been immeasurable and unprecedented. The newspaper has always carried articles dealing with literary topics, as well as book reviews, poems, and short stories. It was in its pages that a number of outstanding literary works were first serialized, including some of Naguib Mahfouz's award-winning novels. The earliest newspaper in the Maghreb is thought to have been the Tunisian *al-Ra'id al-Tunisi* (1860, The Tunisian Pioneer), which was an official publication. It was not until the beginning of the twentieth century, however, that independent newspapers in Arabic began to appear in the Maghreb. In Algeria, which was a French colony (1830–1962), and not a protectorate like Morocco (1912–56) and Tunisia (1881–1956), the first decades of the twentieth century are marked by the publication of three Arabic periodicals, *Al-Muntaqid* (1925) (The Critic), *Al-Shihab* (1925) (The Meteor), and *Al-Basa'ir* (1936) (Insights), founded by the Association of Ulema ("learned men"). The Ulema were a reformist group who, under their leader Abdelhamid Ben Badis (1889–1940), adopted the slogan "Islam is my religion, Arabic is my language and Algeria is my homeland." The articles they published in their newspapers were mostly religious or didactic, calling for social and political reforms. The Ulema advocated spreading the true message of Islam, freeing it of any superstitious beliefs, and encouraging Arabic scholarship throughout French-occupied territories. Among Ben Badis's many works was a commentary on the Qur'an that appeared in *Al-Shihab*. The Ulema included two poets among their founding members, Tayyib al-'Uqbi (1888–1960) and Muhammad al-'Id Khalifa (1904–79). They frequently published selections of classical poetry in their newspapers and also welcomed original new verse. Much of the poetry written during the first decades of the twentieth century, however, is imitative of the style of classical poetry and hence lacking in originality.

Twentieth-century Arabic poetry is usually divided into three main stages: neoclassical, which began in the nineteenth century and continued until the early years of the twentieth; romantic, which was fashionable during the first half of the twentieth century; and modernist, which became widespread from about the 1950s. In Egypt neoclassical poetry enjoyed considerable popularity. The leading exponent of the neoclassical movement was Ahmad Shawqi (1868–1932), whose poems include eulogies and panegyrics, imitative of the style of Arab poets of the classical era. Known in the Arab world as the "Prince of Poets," Shawqi also wrote a number of plays in verse, mainly with classical themes, including *Masra'Kilyobatra* (1929) (The Death of Cleopatra) and *'Antar* (1931) based on the hero of the *Adventures of 'Antar*. Neoclassical poetry was also popular in the Maghreb countries. In Algeria al-'Uqbi and Khalifa wrote in the neoclassical style. As the new trends that were being introduced into Arabic poetry were of western provenance, Algerian poets were reluctant to allow what they considered to be non-Arab influences into their compositions. In Morocco also, the *salafiyya* ("return to the past") movement, which had a number of followers from among scholars and poets, was opposed to any literary innovation. Some distinguished Moroccans, among them 'Allal al-Fasi (1910–74), a highly respected Moroccan academic and writer who was also a poet, encouraged the development of patriotic poetry known as *al-Shi'r al-Nidhali* ("protest poetry"). Written in the classical mode, patriotic poetry became widespread in other African countries. In Algeria the best-known patriotic poems are by the nationalist poet Mufdi Zakaria (1913–77), who wrote the famous exhortative song *Min Jibalina* (1932, From Our Mountains). Apprehended by the colonial authorities for his anti-French writings, he was imprisoned. It was from his prison cell, in 1955, that he composed the poem *Qasaman* (An Oath), which has become the Algerian national anthem. *Qasaman* has been published in a collection entitled *Al-Lahab al-Muqaddas* (The Holy Spark) that comprises Zakaria's best-known poems. Tunisians also wrote protest poetry in the first decades of the last century, when poets joined forces with essayists and religious leaders to protest against the French occupation of their country.

The "first major literary figure from the Maghreb to make an impact on Arabic literature is undoubtedly the Tunisian poet Abu'l-Qasim al-Shabbi (1909–34)" (Martínez Montávez 1974: 99), who was hailed as a nationalist. The poems he wrote during his short life have been published in a collection, *Aghani al-Hayat* (1955) (Songs of Life). Written in a spontaneously simple, yet lyrical style, they convey the poet's feelings of love, his veneration of nature, and his longing for freedom. Al-Shabbi was influenced by western literature, which he read in Arabic translation. His poetry, in which mystical elements can be detected, is representative of the romantic movement in Arabic poetry that was then emerging. The initiators of the romantic movement in Egypt founded a monthly periodical in 1932 that they called *Apollo*. They also established the Apollo Society, whose first president was Shawqi. The society welcomed members from all over the Arabic-speaking world whose contributions they published in their periodical. Although *Apollo* was founded just two years before al-Shabbi died, some of his later poems were published in it. Another important poet who emerged during this period is the Sudanese Yusuf Bashir al-Tijani (1912–37). Like al-Shabbi, he too venerated nature and "enriched Arabic romantic poetry by his moving accounts of his mystical experiences" (Badawi 1993: 50). Al-Tijani's poems reflect influences of an Arabic literary tradition, western romantic poetry, and Sudanese sung poetry with its African rhythms. Although not as dominant a figure in Arabic literature as al-Shabbi, al-Tijani made a worthy contribution to Sudanese literature, which, three decades later, gained international acclaim with the fictional works of Tayeb Salih.

Al-Shabbi paved the way for future generations of poets from the Maghreb who gradually turned away from the traditional meters and rhyme schemes of classical Arabic poetry. His successors began to introduce new forms and meters, drawing inspiration from western models, as well as from the free verse movement which gained momentum in the Middle East in the early years of the 1940s, and which was highly influenced by western norms. From about the 1950s a number of outstanding Moroccan poets emerged. They include Muhammad al-Habib al-Furqani (b. 1922), Muhammad al-Sabbagh (b. 1930), 'Abd al-Karim Tabbal (b. 1931), and Muhammad Bannis (b. 1950), who all write innovative verse that is free of the rigid rules of classical Arabic poetry. Tunisia also boasts a number of outstanding contemporary poets, among them Salah Garmadi (1933–82), Abdelaziz Kacem (b. 1933), and Tahar Bekri (b. 1951), who have all written poetry in both Arabic and French. In Algeria, apart from Zakaria, a number of poets emerged during the war of independence and in the first years of independence, although none among them has to date made much of an impact on modern Arabic poetry. Much of contemporary Algerian poetry is imitative of Middle Eastern poetry, dwelling on patriotic themes and particularly the Algerian war of independence.

Algeria, Morocco, and Tunisia have a wealth of oral poetry in both Arabic and Berber. Many of these poems are now in print. Arabic oral poetry, composed spontaneously and transmitted orally, is usually in the vernacular, although some oral verse is composed in literary Arabic. The themes of oral poetry are varied. Apart from relating legends and histories of local populations, and celebrating the lives of local heroes, there are also exhortative war poems and amatory verse, the latter describing the poet's yearning for the beloved. Some poems, particularly those in a more literary language, are in praise of the prophet. In the twentieth century, oral poetry came to contain political and nationalist themes, evoking each country's history and the way of life of its people. A type of traditional oral verse in colloquial Arabic that has always been popular with audiences, and is sometimes set to music, is the *malhun* ("vernacular"), an important aspect of the cultural heritage of the Maghreb.

Twentieth-century Egyptian literature is one of the earliest, and to date the most prolific, in the Arabic-speaking world. Most studies of Arabic literature tend to focus on Egyptian writers, to the exclusion of authors from some other Arab countries. In the *Encyclopedia of Arabic Literature* (Meisami and Starkey 1988), for example, there is no mention of Libyan or Mauritanian writers. In this chapter, however, I propose to include very few Egyptian writers and to concentrate on a more general survey of Arabic writing in Africa, focusing on literatures that are often overlooked. Before the twentieth century, Egypt, which was occupied by the British (1822–1914) and subsequently made a British Protectorate (1914–22), led the way in modern Arabic literature and thought. Napoleon's invasion in 1798 and the British occupation of the country turned the Egyptian outlook towards Europe. Literary works in English and French were translated into Arabic, giving Egyptian intellectuals an insight into western letters and culture. Western influence on Arabic literature was further enhanced by the arrival of Syrian Christian intellectuals who, fleeing religious persecution in their country, settled in Egypt, which they found to be a safe haven. They established publishing houses and founded newspapers and magazines. They were also instrumental in introducing genres hitherto unknown to Arabic literature, like the short story and drama.

Among the earliest writers to make an impact on modern Arabic literature are the Egyptian writers Muhammad Husayn Haykal (1888–1956), Tawfiq al-Hakim (1898–1987), and Taha Husayn (1889–1973), whose literary careers span the beginnings and development of twentieth-century Arabic literature. All three, who were sent to France to complete their studies, succeeded in introducing western ideas into Arabic literature. Haykal was a novelist, critic, and politician. Early in his career he wrote what could be described as a pastoral novel, *Zaynab* (1913), credited with being the first truly Egyptian novel, and an important landmark in the development of Arabic fictional writing. Haykal was a strong believer in an Egyptian national literature. Both *Zaynab* and his second novel, *Hakadha Khuliqat* (1955) (She Was Born Thus), are set in rural Egypt and give a romantically nostalgic depiction of the Egyptian countryside and the way of life of the people. Al-Hakim, who was a playwright, a novelist, and short-story writer, also believed in the importance of national literature. He composed patriotic songs during the nationalist revolt of 1919. Al-Hakim, however, is best remembered for being one of the most prolific playwrights in the Arab world. Having begun by publishing novels and collections of short stories, he took up drama, with which his name has become synonymous in the Arab world. Taha Husayn was one of the advocates of the purity of the Arabic literary language. He was totally opposed to any colloquialism in creative writing and shunned folk literature. Husayn's works of literary criticism are highly influenced by western norms. Husayn, who had a long and distinguished literary career, wrote several novels in which he introduced characters drawn on people from the poorer walks of life, a theme that characterizes the prolific output of Naguib Mahfouz.

Naguib Mahfouz (b. 1911), who was awarded the Nobel Prize for literature in 1988, is considered to be the writer who almost single-handedly made modern Arabic literature globally known. Mahfouz far outstrips most Arab writers in the quality and quantity of his output, produced over a period of fifty years. In spite of the fact that he wrote short stories and plays, his name is associated with the development of the Arabic novel. Mahfouz began by writing historical novels set in the Pharaonic era, before turning to sociorealistic themes. He wrote a number of works that portray the Cairo lower middle classes among which he was born and raised. His highly acclaimed family-saga trilogy – *Bayn al-Qasrayn* (1990) (*Palace Walk*), *Qasr al-Shawq* (1991) (*Palace of Desire*), and *al-Sukkariyya* (1992) (*Sugar Street*), whose titles are Cairo street names – concentrates on three generations of a traditional Egyptian family between the years 1917 and 1944. Published between 1956 and 1957, all three volumes were written before the 1952 revolution that overthrew the Egyptian monarchy. In all his works Mahfouz excels in depicting convincing scenes and dialogue. In his inimitable way he succeeds in turning literary Arabic into a language that approximates spoken Arabic, making his works easily accessible to a wide readership. Mahfouz has not been without his critics. His allegorical novel *Awlad Haratina* (1959) (Children of Our Quarter, trans. *Children of Gebelawi*, 1981) was the subject of a great deal of controversy when it was initially serialized in the Egyptian press. Set in an imaginary quarter of old Cairo, inhabited by characters whose names evoke Adam, Moses, Jesus, and Muhammad, among others, the novel was condemned by religious authorities and Mahfouz accused of blasphemy. The work was later published in book form in Lebanon in 1967, and has since been reprinted and translated into other languages, including English.

Another Egyptian writer who has become internationally known is Nawal El Saadawi (b. 1931). Born in a small village north of Cairo, El Saadawi trained as a doctor. She was subsequently posted to a village in a rural area in 1955. It was there that she began her literary career, publishing her first collection of short stories in 1957. A year later her first novel, *Mudhakkirat Tabiba* (1958) (The Memoirs of a Woman Doctor, 1988), appeared. The novel is an autobiographical work, based on her life and experiences as a doctor in rural Egypt. It is also a controversial work that criticizes, in uncompromising language, the malaise affecting Egyptian society, particularly in the countryside. This theme was to recur in her other works, most of which have been translated into the major world languages. Her nonfictional work *Al-Mar'a wa al-Jins* (1972) (Woman and Sex) appeared while she was working as Director of Health Education in the Egyptian Ministry of Health. Soon after its publication, the book was censored and El Saadawi dismissed from her post at the ministry. She continued to write controversial novels, among them *Imra'a 'inda Nuqtat al-Sifr* (1975) (*Woman at Point Zero*, 1983) and *Mawt al-Rajul al-Wahid 'ala 'l-'Ard* (1976) (The Death of the Only Man on Earth, trans. *God Dies by the Nile*, 1985a). In all her works, whether fictional or factual, El Saadawi speaks openly of the plight of women in patriarchal societies. What emerges in nearly all her writings is her "authorial domination" that "encloses her protagonists within a monologous discourse in which there is little sign of interior development" (Manisty 1993: 268).

El Saadawi's may be the only Egyptian woman's voice to date that has made an impact globally on feminist literature and women's studies. Yet in Egypt she is not the only woman writer expressing utter dissatisfaction with the status of women. Several other Egyptian women writers have challenged gender roles and patriarchal values within their society, among them Sakina Fu'ad (b. 1942), Radwa 'Ashur (b. 1946), and Salwa Bakr (b. 1949). Bakr, some of whose works have already been translated into other languages, including English, is set on challenging the power of patriarchy and presenting female characters in a new light. In her novel *Al-'Araba al-Dhahabiyya la Tas'ad ila al-Sama'* (1991) (The Golden Chariot Does Not Go Up to Heaven, trans. *The Golden Chariot*, 1995), she depicts several women from different walks of life, presenting her readers with the many faces and viewpoints of Egyptian women.

Despite the fact that Sudan has a fairly rich literary tradition, it was not until the latter half of the twentieth century that the country gained a place on the literary map of the Arab world, thanks to the efforts of one writer: Tayeb Salih (b. 1929). Salih became one of the best-known writers from Africa, following the publication in English of his award-winning novel, *Mawsim al-Hijra ila al-Shimal* (1966) (*Season of Migration to the North*) in 1969. The setting of Salih's novels and short stories is Wad Hamid, an imaginary Sudanese village by the Nile. The Nile is depicted as both generous and cruel. As a navigable river, it provides a link with the outside world, and waters the doum-palms that are an essential part of the landscape. Yet it also claims lives. In *Mawsim*, Mustafa Sa'eed, the stranger who settles in Wad Hamid, drowns in the Nile, and his body is never recovered. In *Daw al-Bayt* (1971), the eponymous character, a white stranger, washed up on the riverbank in Wad Hamid, disappears in the Nile when he is engulfed by its waters. Salih's storytelling, in all his works, is reminiscent of the oral narratives of African *griots*. When he first began writing in the 1950s he developed the technique of the oral storyteller, talking directly to his readers and relating the events in a tone of intimacy and confidentiality. In this way the reader becomes not only an observer, but is directly involved in the narrative and the events described. The journey or migration motif in Salih's works is another aspect that is evocative of African folklore. In spite of the fact that Salih presents other settings, as in *Mawsim*, when the plot moves to England in flashbacks, Wad Hamid and the Nile remain the pivots around which the characters and the events revolve. For Salih, as for the majority of African writers, "life begins in the village" and wherever the characters go, "they carry the village with them" (Obiechina 1972: 201).

In the Maghreb, the short story was the first Arabic fictional genre to emerge during the early decades of the twentieth century. Short stories developed from the didactic prose pieces that appeared in newspapers during the first half of the twentieth century. The novel, a much later genre than the short story, developed in Tunisia and Morocco in the 1940s, while in Algeria it did not make its appearance until the 1970s. The person who is considered to be instrumental in preparing the ground for the Algerian Arabic novel is Réda Houhou (1911–56), a member of the Association of Ulema who was educated in Saudi Arabia. On his return to Algeria, Houhou joined the association and began to publish in their periodicals. The earliest pieces he wrote were essays, similar in vein to those written by Ben Badis and other Ulema, urging Algerians to rid Islam of the superstitions that had crept into it. Houhou also called for the emancipation of women and for secular education in Arabic for all Algerians. He gradually turned his essays into short narrative pieces to make them more appealing to readers. It was not until the war of independence (1954–62), that the Arabic short story became a full-fledged genre in Algeria when some Algerians, moved by events in their country, felt the need to express themselves in writing. Several writers who emerged during the war of independence abandoned writing after independence. The few who continued to produce short stories were instrumental in the emergence of the Algerian Arabic novel.

The two best-known authors who have had a lasting influence on the development of Arabic fictional literature in Algeria are Abdelhamid Benhedouga (1925–96) and Tahar Ouettar (b. 1936). *Rih al-Janub* (1971) (South Wind) by Benhedouga is considered to be the first important example of Arabic novel writing in Algeria. Set in the countryside in the first years of independence, it introduces a variety of characters, including a young educated woman who is torn between the traditional world of her environment and the more liberated one that she discovers as a student. Benhedouga in this and later novels succeeds in tackling the question of women's rights and other important social issues. His novels are nearly all written in a linear style with the events set out in chronological order. Tahar Ouettar, on the other hand, adopted at the outset an experimental technique that has continued to characterize his fictional production. The war of independence, social malaise, and injustice are the themes that recur in his works. A committed Socialist, he documents important developments in post-independence Algeria, notably the Agrarian Revolution of the 1970s. Benhedouga and Ouettar dominated Arabic fictional writing in Algeria before they were joined by Rachid Boudjedra (b. 1941), a well-known francophone author who began to write in Arabic from 1981. Boudjedra's Arabic novels echo the iconoclastic, anti-patriarchal diatribes voiced in his francophone works. Boudjedra tends to experiment with the Arabic language, often coining his own expressions. For both Ouettar and Boudjedra, introducing innovation into language symbolizes a complete break from the established norms of classical Arabic. It is their way of forging a new Algerian identity in literature paralleling the country's emergence as an independent nation after years of colonial rule.

Arabic fictional writing in Algeria flourished during the 1980s when there was a certain freedom of expression in the country. A number of bilingual Algerians chose to write in Arabic, thus giving Algerian writing of Arabic expression a new verve. Nearly all these writers are men, the only two women to date being Zhor Ounissi (b. 1936) whose writings have been greatly influenced by Houhou's works, and Ahlem Mostaghanmi (b. 1952). Both Ounissi and Mostaghanmi are concerned mainly with political issues. They devote little space in their novels and short stories to feminist themes. With the rise of Islamic fundamentalism in the country many Algerian writers were threatened with death for daring to broach the taboo subject of sex and to question religious beliefs and practices. Several of those threatened fled the country. Some, like Waciny Larej (b. 1954) and Amin Zaoui (b. 1956), both well-established writers of Arabic fiction, now live in France where they have begun to write in French.

In Morocco, where Arabic continued to be written while the country was a French Protectorate, novels began to appear from about the 1940s. Abdelmajid Benjelloun's (1915–81) two-part autobiographical work, *Fi al-Tufula* (1957, 1968) (On Childhood), is considered to be one of the earliest examples of the Arabic novel in Morocco. There are a number of outstanding Moroccan novelists, foremost among them being 'Abd al-Karim Ghallab (b. 1919), whose works portray Moroccan social reality. In one of his best-known novels, *Dafanna al-Madi* (1966) (We Have Buried the Past), he describes how Moroccans became politically conscious in the twentieth century. In an earlier novel, *Sab'at Abwab* (1965) (Seven Doors), Ghallab depicts the world of political prisoners, imprisoned merely for daring to criticize the status quo. Ghallab tackles a number of important topics, like the exploitation of poor rural workers who flock to the city in search of their livelihood. He stresses the importance of secular education on the eve of the twenty-first century. Issues of paramount importance in the Arab world, like the Palestinian question, are also themes that occupy Moroccan writers. Mubarak Rabi' (b. 1935), in his novel *Rifqat al-Silah wa al-Qamar* (1976) (The Companions of Arms and the Moon), focuses on the 1973 Arab–Israeli war. The novel won the prize of the Arab League Academy in 1975.

Both Ghallab and Rabi' have distinguished themselves as short-story writers, a genre that continues to flourish in the hands of able writers, among them Mohamed Berrada (b. 1938). Berrada began to write novels in the 1980s. His first novel, *Lu'bat al-Nisyan* (1987, reprinted 1992) (*The Game of Forgetting*, 1996) has been translated into English, French, and Spanish. Set during the last years of the protectorate, the work explores the ways in which childhood memories affect adult life. Narrated by several voices, it vividly depicts Morocco's modern history. Berrada is one of the co-founders of the Union of Moroccan Writers, some of whose members have gained international recognition.

A writer who distinguished himself both in the field of the short story and the novel was Mohamed Zafzaf (1944–2001). One of the most prolific of present-day Moroccan authors, Zafzaf began writing in the 1970s and published more than twenty volumes of fiction. His work portrays both positive and negative aspects of Moroccan society. Early in his career Zafzaf came in for a lot of criticism because he dared to speak openly about sexual matters, especially in his novel *Al-Mar'a wa al-Warda* (1972) (The Woman and the Rose) where he presents a central character who is obsessed with sex, drink, and drugs. In most of his works Zafzaf succeeded in presenting his readers with tormented individuals desperate to express themselves freely in a taboo-laden society.

As in Algeria, Moroccan women authors of Arabic expression are still too few and relatively unknown. The two women who are known outside Morocco are Khannata Bannuna (b. 1940) and Leila Abouzeid (b. 1950). Bannuna's works are concerned mostly with political issues. She too has dealt with injustices committed against Palestinians. Abouzeid often introduces assertive women characters who are determined to establish themselves as individuals in a society that still sees women as dependent on men.

Tunisia is, without doubt, the largest producer of Arabic works in the Maghreb, despite its having been a French protectorate for three-quarters of a century. Perhaps the first Tunisian to become well known as a short-story writer is 'Ali al-Du'aji (1909–49) who also wrote radio plays and song lyrics. One of the most important novelists is al-Bashir Khurayyif (1917–83), who also wrote short stories. His highly acclaimed novel *Al-Digla fi 'Arajiniha* (1969) (Dates in Their Clusters) is set in the oasis of Nefta where the author himself was born. The novel describes the harshness of life in rural areas in southern Tunisia, and the animosity that develops between people because of deprivation and poverty. Khurayyif takes up a number of social issues. He is particularly concerned with the way women are treated, and this is vividly brought out in his works. A great believer in racial equality, he condemns racism in his novel, *Barq al-Layl* (1961), which tells the story of the eponymous character, a sixteenth-century black slave. Khurayyif was the first Tunisian novelist to introduce extracts of Tunisian colloquial Arabic into his narratives, a technique adopted by younger writers, among them Alia Tabaï (b. 1961) in her first novel, *Zahrat al-Subbar* (1991) (Cactus Flower). Tabaï is one of a number of Tunisian women writers, which includes Arusiyya al-Naluti (b. 1950), who explore contemporary issues affecting Tunisian society in their novels, collections of short stories, poems, and plays.

In Libya, scholarly prose and poetry in Arabic continued to be written during the Italian colonial period (1912–47). Fictional writing began in the mid-1930s. It did not become fully established, however, until well after Libya was declared independent in 1951. Yet Libyan literature remains purely for the home market. Libyan authors are rarely known beyond the country's borders, with the exception of Ibrahim al-Kawni (b. 1948) and Ibrahim al-Faqih (b. 1942). Al-Kawni, who began writing in the 1970s, has established himself as the best representative of contemporary Libyan literature. His many novels and collections of short stories have been translated into several languages. Al-Faqih also began writing in the seventies. He published fictional and nonfictional pieces in various Arabic periodicals. It was not until the 1990s when his trilogy, *Hada'iq al-Layl* (1990) (*Gardens of the Night*, 1991), was published that he became well known in the Arab world.

Al-Kawni's works are steeped in African mythology and history. The majority are set in the vast desert that stretches westwards to the Fezzan, eastwards to the Hoggar Mountains, and southwards to Lake Chad, Kano, and Timbuktu. Al-Kawni, who is a Tuareg, was born in the desert but moved to Tripoli where he received Arabic formal education. His novels and short stories are written in Arabic, yet they resonate with the rhythm of Tamasheq speech, his Berber mother tongue. He often introduces Tamasheq words and expressions, which add color and authenticity to his works. Just as the Nile in Tayeb Salih's works is both bounteous and treacherous, the desert in al-Kawni's fiction can be welcoming and at the same time menacing. Travelers find refuge in it. Yet it is also the place where many of them die of thirst or are buried in the sand when the ferocious East Wind blows without mercy. The desert in al-Kawni's short stories and novels, notably his two-volume novel *Al-Majus* (1991) (The Pagans), is inhabited by both humans and *jinn*. Mixing reality with mythology is characteristic of al-Kawni's works. The humans are either white, nomadic, and Muslim, or black, sedentary, and animist. There is a lot of violence in most of his stories, and he dwells on descriptions of violent death. Living with nature, sometimes awake, and at other times hallucinating or having nightmares, al-Kawni's characters seem to be in search of an ephemeral paradise, the illusory oasis of Waw, which they yearn to reach.

The desert also plays a significant role in Ibrahim al-Faqih's trilogy. The first volume is set in Scotland, where the central character, Khalil, a Libyan, is studying at Edinburgh University. The six main characters include an Indian as well as a Frenchwoman, and two Arab men, one of them the central character. There are constant references to the desert where Khalil was born. The desert predominates as a setting in the second and third volumes in which the characters are all Libyan, with the main difference being that some of them are real, while others appear only in Khalil's dreams and hallucinations. Khalil is presented as a tormented, restless man, constantly in need of love, which he is denied. In his search for happiness and peace of mind, he goes to the desert to visit the tombs of his ancestors and to seek the advice of Sufis. By describing Khalil's dreams, the author is able to mix the real with the imaginary, and by choosing the desert as a setting, he is able to delve into the mythical past of Libya with its world of magic and holy men.

The Arabic novel in Mauritania dates from the early 1980s. Ahmad Wuld 'Abd al-Qadir, in his two novels, *Al-Asma' al-Mutaghayyira* (1981) (Changing Names), and *Al-Qabr al-Majhul* (1984) (The Unknown Grave), evokes rural Mauritania in the nineteenth century, before the onset of modernity transformed the country and changed the way of life of its people. The first novel tackles the theme of identity. It describes how the central character, a young boy sold into slavery, changes his name several times during his life, in order to be accepted by the various people among whom he has to live. The second novel is a nostalgic evocation of pre-twentieth-century life in the Mauritanian countryside. *Ahmad al-Wadi* (1987) by Shaykh Ma' al-'Aynayn, set in the present, depicts the struggle between urban and rural values. The central character, who is seduced by a western way of life, is gradually convinced by Ahmad al-Wadi, a recluse, to settle in the country and to lead a life totally removed from western influence.

Twentieth-century Arabic drama, drawing on both the western and African oral genres, is a flourishing art form throughout most of Africa. In Egypt there is a long tradition of modern drama in both classical and colloquial Egyptian Arabic that is known and liked throughout the Arabic-speaking world. In the Maghreb, theater has been an important medium, thanks to the efforts of people of the caliber of Abdelkader Alloula (1939–94) in Algeria, Tayeb Saddiki (b. 1938) in Morocco, and 'Izz al-Din al-Madani (b. 1938) in Tunisia, among others. Alloula built a varied repertoire of plays in his native city of Oran. He translated masterpieces of western theater and wrote his own plays, all in colloquial Arabic. His theater and the ensemble he formed became well known throughout the Maghreb. Tayeb Saddiki's repertoire is as prolific as Alloula's. His plays are greatly influenced by the oral folk literature of Morocco. He frequently introduces into his plays the character of the storyteller, a popular sight in market places throughout Morocco. Saddiki writes and produces plays in French, classical and colloquial Arabic. Al-Madani, who is known for his avant-garde writings, is a leading playwright in Tunisia. He cleverly camouflages contemporary social issues in his plays by setting them in an historic era. In Nigeria the increase in Arabic-educated intellectuals and the spread of institutes for the teaching of Arabic have given rise to the translation of modern English plays into Arabic, notably Wole Soyinka's *The Trials of Brother Jero*. The year 1994 saw the publication of the first original Arabic language play, *Al-'Amid al-Mubajjal* (The Honorable Dean). Written by an academic, Zakariyau I. Oseni (b. 1950), it describes corruption in Nigerian universities.

At the close of the twentieth century Egypt still dominates as the most prolific producer of Arabic literature, whereas Arabic creative writing is still in its infancy in Mauritania. In Libya, only al-Kawni and al-Faqih have to date made their mark internationally. In Sudan, Tayeb Salih is still the predominant voice, despite the emergence of several other Sudanese writers. In the Maghreb, Arabic writing is on the increase, and published material is becoming widely available, with the exception of Algeria where works are rarely distributed outside the country. In Nigeria, Arabic writing "seems to be well on its way to broader forms of expression" (Abubakre and Reichmuth 1997: 205). Despite the many stages of development Arabic creative writing in Africa has gone through in the course of the twentieth century, it is difficult to predict at the present time how it will develop and what the future holds for it in the twenty-first century.

Notes

1. The other four pillars are: *salat* (prayer), *sawn* (fasting), *shahada* (the [Muslim] creed), and *zakat* (almsgiving).
2. See for example Camara 1997, where he quotes and translates verses from Seri ñ Musa Ka's poetry in Wolof in which Shaykh Bamba's name occurs.

Bibliography

A selective bibliography of primary sources in English translation.

Classical literature

'Antar. 1980. *The Adventures of 'Antar*. Trans. and ed. H. T. Norris. Warminster: Aris and Phillips.

Ibn Battuta. 1957. *Ibn Battuta: Travels in Asia and Africa 1325–1354*. Trans. and ed. H. A. R. Gibb. London: Routledge and Kegan Paul.

Ibn Jubayr. 1952. *The Travels of Ibn Jubayr.* Trans. R. J. C. Broadhurst. London: Goodwood.

Ibn Khaldun. 1958. *The Muqaddimah: An Introduction to History*. 3 vols. Trans. Franz Rosenthal. London: Routledge and Kegan Paul.

Modern literature

Bakr, Salwa. 1995. *The Golden Chariot*. Trans. Dinah Manisty. Reading: Garnet.

Benhedouga, Abdelhamid. 1971. *Le vent du Sud*. Algiers: SNED.

1977. *La fin d'hier*. Algiers: SNED.

Berrada, Mohamed. 1996. *The Game of Forgetting*. Trans. Issa Boullata. Austin: University of Texas at Austin Press.

Boudjedra, Rachid. 1982. *Le démantèlement*. Paris: Denoël.

1985. *La Macération*. Paris: Denoël.

1987. *La Pluie*. Paris: Denoël.

1991. *Le désordre des choses*. Denoël.

Al-Faqih, Ibrahim. 1991. *Gardens of the Night, A Trilogy*. Trans. R. Harris. London: Quartet.

Mahfouz, Naguib. 1981. *Children of Gebelawi*. Trans. Philip Stewart. Pueblo, CO: Passeggiata. Rpt. 1997.

1985. *Autumn Quail*. Trans. Roger Allen. London: Doubleday. Rpt. 1990.

1990. *Palace Walk*. Trans. W. M. Hutchins and O. E. Kenny. London: Doubleday.

1991. *Palace of Desire*. Trans. W. M. Hutchins and L. M. Kenny. London: Doubleday.

1992. *Sugar Street*. Trans. W. M. Hutchins and A. B. Samaan. London: Doubleday.

1995. *Al-Harafish*. Trans. Catherine Cobham. London: Doubleday.

1997. *Echoes of an Autobiography*. Trans. Denys Johnson-Davies. London: Anchor/Doubleday.

Ouettar, Tahar. 1977. *Le séisme*. Algiers: SNED.

1980. *Les martyrs reviennent cette semaine*. Algiers: ENAP.

El Saadawi, Nawal. 1983. *Woman at Point Zero*. Trans. Sherif Hetata. London: Zed.

1985a. *God Dies by the Nile*. Trans. Sherif Hetata. London: Zed.

1985b. *Two Women in One*. Trans. Ousman Nusairi and Jana Gough. London: Al Saqi.

1986. *Memoirs from the Women's Prison*. Trans. Marilyn Booth. London: Women's Press.

1988. *Memoirs of a Woman Doctor*. Trans. Catherine Cobham. London: Al Saqi.

1988. *Fall of the Imam*. Trans. Sherif Hetata. London: Methuen.

1989. *Circling Song*. Trans. Shirley Eber. London: Zed.

1991. *Searching*. Trans. Marilyn Booth. London: Zed.

1997. *The Nawal El Saadawi Reader*. London: Zed.

Salih, Tayeb. 1968. *The Wedding of Zein and Other Stories*. Trans. Denys Johnson-Davies. London: Heinemann.

1969. *Season of Migration to the North*. Trans. Denys Johnson-Davies. London: Heinemann. Rpt. 1980.

1996. *Bandarshah*. Trans. Denys Johnson-Davies. London: Routledge and Kegan Paul.

Secondary works

Abouzeid, Leila, and Heather Logan Taylor. *Return to Childhood: The Memoir of a Modern Moroccan Woman*. Austin: University of Texas Press.

Abubakre, Razaq D., and Stefan Reichmuth. 1997. "Arabic Writing between Local and Global Culture: Scholars and Poets in Yorubaland." *Research in African Literatures* 28.3: 183–209.

Allen, Roger, ed. 1982. *The Arabic Novel: A Historical and Critical Introduction*. Syracuse: Syracuse University Press.

Badawi, Mustafa M. 1993. *A Short History of Modern Arabic Literature*. Oxford: Clarendon Press.

Bois, Marcel. 1992. "Arabic Language Algerian Literature." *Research in African Literatures* 23. 2: 103–11.

Brett, Michael. 1998. *Ibn Khaldun and the Medieval Maghreb*. Aldershot: Ashgate.

Cachia, Pierre. 1990. *An Overview of Modern Arabic Literature*. Edinburgh: Edinburgh University Press.

Camara, Sana. 1997. "*A'jami* Literature in Senegal: The Example of Sëriñ Mousaa Ka." *Research in African Literatures* 28. 3: 163–82.

Déjeux, Jean. 1975. *La littérature algérienne contemporaine*. Paris: Presses contemporaines de France.

El-Enany, Rasheed. 1993. *Maguib Mahfouz: The Pursuit of Meaning*. London: Routledge.

Fontaine, Jean. 1991. "Le centième roman tunisien: *Zahrat al-Subbar* (Fleur de cactus) de Alia Tabaï." *Institut des belles lettres arabes* (IBLA) 54: 223–34.

1992. "Arabic Language Tunisian Literature (1956–1990)." *Research in African Literatures* 23.2: 183–93.

1998. *Recherches sur la littérature arabe*. Tunis: IBLA.

Gibb, Sir Hamilton. 1963. *Arabic Literature*. Oxford: Clarendon Press.

Hunwick, John. 1995. *Arabic Literature of Africa*, vol. II. *The Writings of Central Sudanic Africa*. Leiden: Brill.

1997. "The Arabic Literary Tradition of Nigeria." *Research in African Literatures* 28.3: 210–23.

1998. *Arabic Literature of Africa*, vol. III. *The Writings of the Muslim Peoples of Eastern Africa*. Leiden: Brill.

Irele, Abiola. 1981. *The African Experience in Literature and Ideology*. London: Heinemann. Rpt. 1990. Bloomington: Indiana University Press.

1993. "Narrative, History and the African Imagination." *Narrative* 1. 2: 156–72.

Kharmash, Muhammad. 1998. *Al-Naqd al-Adabi al-Hadith fi al-Maghrib* (Modern Literary Criticism in the Maghreb). Ifriqiya al-Sharq: Casablanca. In Arabic.

Manisty, Dinah. 1993. "Changing Limitations: A Study of the Woman's Novel in Egypt (1960–1991)." Unpublished PhD thesis. University of London.

Martínez Montávez, Pedro. 1974. *Introducción a la literatura árabe moderna*. Madrid: Revista "Almenara."

Meisami, Julie Scott, and Paul Starkey, eds. 1998. *Encyclopedia of Arabic Literature*, vols. I and II. Routledge: London.

Mortimer, Mildred. 1990. *Journeys through the French African Novel*. Oxford: James Currey.

Nicholson, R. A. 1956. *A Literary History of the Arabs*. Cambridge: Cambridge University Press.

Norris, H. T. 1968. *Shinqiti Folk Literature and Song*. Oxford: Oxford Library of African Literature.

Obiechina, Emmanuel. 1972. *Culture, Tradition and Society in the West African Novel*. Cambridge: Cambridge University Press.

Soyinka, Wole. 1978. *Myth, Literature and the African World*. Cambridge: Cambridge University Press.

Takieddine-Amyuni, Mona, ed. 1969. *Season of Migration to the North by Tayeb Salih: A Casebook*. Beirut: American University of Beirut.

Wuld Muhammad, Mustafa. 1996. *Al-Riwaya al-'Arabiyya al-Muritaniyya* (The Mauritanian Arabic Novel). Cairo: Al-Hay'a al-Masriyya al-'Amma lil-Kitaba. In Arabic.

12

The Swahili literary tradition: an intercultural heritage

ALAMIN M. MAZRUI

Swahili literature, broadly defined as that body of verbal art originally composed in the Swahili language, is a product of what Ali Mazrui (1986) has termed Africa's triple heritage. It emerged out of a confluence of three forces: the indigenous tradition, the Islamic legacy, and the western impact. The indigenous contribution has, of course, featured primarily in the realm of orature; but, over the years, it has continued to affect the destiny of Swahili *written* literature that is the focus of this chapter. One must also bear in mind that the boundary between what is written and what is oral in the various genres of Swahili literature is not always easy to determine.

With regard to the interaction between the Arab-Islamic and indigenous factors, in particular, the general tendency, until relatively recently, was to privilege the former (usually seen as the "donor") over the latter (regarded as the "recipient") to a point where it has supposedly lost its local identity. But as Rajmund Ohly observes, "The overlapping of these two cultures – the local, Bantu and the Oriental – took place on the basis of mutual adjustment and not, as has been thought until now, on the basis of assimilation, so that a two tiered development of literature can be observed which embraces both the pure elements of Bantu folk culture and the inflowing Muslim-Oriental elements" (1985: 461). In fact, the so-called layers became integrated into a new organic synthesis and, in time, fused with other influences reflecting, among others things, the tensions between town and country, and between "gentry" and "commoner."

Particularly indicative of this cultural bias in the interpretation of Swahili literature is the controversy surrounding the earliest Swahili poet on record, the poet-king Fumo Liyongo wa Bauri. To the Swahili people, Fumo Liyongo has become almost an iconic representation of the depth, the achievement, and the ambience of their culture as a whole: "That Fumo Liyongo was at once a major poet and a 'hero' in the social world makes him, for the collective imagination, the embodiment of that combination of the poetic utterance and social practice which epitomizes the Swahili ideal of a fully developed human potential" (Shariff 1991b: 154). Placed between the tenth and thirteenth centuries by oral sources, Fumo Liyongo has often raised questions about his religious affiliation on the evidence of his own poetry: Was he a "pagan" as suggested by Ohly (1985: 462), a Muslim (Shariff 1991b: 162), or a Christian (Knappert 1979: 68)? The record of Swahili literature over the centuries is replete with such examples of cultural intermarriages that continue to confound literary critics in search of easy answers.

The rise to prominence of a Muslim clergy, however, led to a systematic bias in the preservation of the Swahili literary heritage. Poems that were more "purely" Islamic now stood a much greater chance of preservation for posterity than those that were deemed to be less so in orientation. In the words of Assibi A. Amidu, "while the poems of Liyongo are much older than the Swahili version of the Hamziya [the thirteenth-century praise-poem on the prophet of Islam originally composed in Arabic] and were probably written down long before the 17th century, only the Islamic ones such as the Hamziya were approved of and preserved while the secular poems of Fumo Liyongo and his contemporaries were either suppressed or allowed to perish" (1990: 4).

With their modal partiality towards the written over the oral word, European colonizers later gave further credence and legitimacy to this Oriental-Islamic bias within Swahili literature. What existed in a written form – predominantly religious – was quickly and mistakenly taken to define virtually the entire scope of the Swahili literary experience. The fact that the Swahili themselves accorded greater value to their oral tradition and that at no point in their history did they produce a greater proportion of homiletic than secular literature now became submerged under new layers of Eurocentric prejudices.

The beginnings of writing in Swahili literature can be traced to the Afro-Arab contact in the East African seaboard that goes back to antiquity. According to the accounts of *The Periplus of the Erythrean Sea* (by an unknown Greek author), Arab and Persian traders must have frequented the East African coast as early as the first century CE, if not earlier. There were also recurrent waves of Arabian migrants who were displaced by internecine wars in their own countries and found refuge, and eventually settled, in the East-African city-states. Over time, many of these settlers intermarried with the local population and Islam, once it established itself in the area soon after it was founded in Arabia, became an additional force in the consolidation of this Afro-Arab heritage. It is out of this cultural intercourse that the Swahili written tradition was born.

This first wave of writing used Swahilized versions of the Arabic alphabet akin to what is referred to as *ajami* in West Africa. Exactly when this mode of writing came into being in the Swahili literary tradition is difficult to determine. The Hamziya poem celebrating the life of Prophet Muhammad, for example, is said to have been composed no later than 1652 CE (Knappert 1979: 103). The earliest surviving manuscript, however, dated about 1728 CE, is Mwengo wa Athumani's *Utenzi wa Herekali* (The Epic of Herakleios) – also known as *Chuo cha Tambuka* (The Book of Tabuk) – on the seventh-century military encounter between the troops of the Byzantine Emperor, Herakleios, and those of the Prophet Muhammad (Gérard 1981: 96).

This pre-twentieth-century literature was replete with homiletic *tenzi* or *tendi* (singular: *utenzi* and *utendi,* respectively) verses with a didactic or hagiographic thrust. The term *utenzi* generally refers to an extended narrative poem of defined meter and rhyme even though it often assumes an epic form and function. Structurally, the *utenzi* verse is made up of four lines – or, in the opinion of some, two with a caesura – with eight syllables to a line and an *aaab* rhyming pattern. Its language is often simple, making little use of such features as extended metaphors, allegories, and symbolism. And because of its structural and stylistic simplicity it has lent itself well to lengthy versification of historical events and fictional narratives. There are *tenzi* on legendary characters like Fumo Liyongo, on the lives of various prophets of Islam, on wars and battles within Swahililand and elsewhere, and on many other subjects requiring extensive articulation. In length, the *utenzi* can run into thousands of verses. Shaaban Robert's *Utenzi wa Vita vya Uhuru* (1967a), an account of the Second World War from a Tanzanian perspective, for example, is comprised of some three thousand verses.

Prosodic developments in the Swahili verse tradition, however, were by no means limited to the *utenzi*. Indeed, by the turn of the nineteenth century, again under the impetus of the Afro-Arab contact, the entire Swahili poetic tradition had come under an elaborate prosodic system governing the use of meter and rhyme. The golden period of Swahili literature, with poetry as its pivotal force, had now been properly ushered in.

Much of the earliest written Swahili literature was predominantly Islamic both because of the subject it treated and because of the influence of the wider Muslim culture on canons of composition in East Africa. What Thomas Hodgkin said of Ghana's Islamic literary tradition, then, was also true of the earlier stages of much of written classical Swahili literature: "It is a literature which can be properly called 'Islamic' in the sense that its authors were Muslims, trained in the Islamic sciences, conscious of their relationship with the Islamic past, and regarding literature as a vehicle for the expression of Islamic values" (1966: 442).

Some of the verse forms that emerged during this period have, in fact, continued to be used for themes that are almost entirely religious. These have included: the *wajiwaji* and the *ukawafi* – compositions of five-line and four-line verses, respectively, with fifteen syllables to a line and caesuras between the sixth and seventh and, again, between the tenth and eleventh syllables; and the *inkishafi* (with four lines to a verse, ten syllables to a line, with a caesura between the sixth and seventh syllables). These types continue to defy any separation between form and substance.

Significant also is the fact that much of the poetry was composed by the *ulamaa,* scholars versed in Islamic theology and jurisprudence, all with a high sensitivity to the metaphysical relationship. These early poets "lived and worked on the northern coast of Kenya . . . writing religious and didactic verse in the Arabic script and using one of the northern dialects of Swahili" (Whiteley 1969: 18). It is reasonable to assume, then, that the *ajami* tradition in Swahili literature may itself have arisen out of a need to reach the common Mswahili (Swahili person) spiritually through the effective medium of poetry. In the course of Qur'anic instruction many Swahili acquired the capacity to read in the Arabic alphabet without the capacity to understand the Arabic language. *Ajami* became the bridge between the legacy of a foreign medium and literacy in an indigenous language.

One of the most renowned of these *ulamaa*-poets was Sayyid Abdalla bin Ali bin Nasir (1720–1820 CE), a descendant of a long line of Swahili scholars. His best-known composition is the *Al-Inkishafi* (Self-Examination). In the poem, Nasir draws inspiration from the historical ruins of Pate and draws the analogy of death from them. By reflecting on the once accomplished and splendid achievements of the Swahili people of Pate, the poet castigates his own heart and urges it to take its cue from the fallen ruins and ephemeral nature of life. Describing the depths beneath and beyond the grave with terrifying clarity reminiscent of Dante's *Divine Comedy*, he urges his heart not to take this world seriously:

Ewe moyo wangu nini huitabiri!
  Twambe u mwelevu wa kukhitari
Huyui dunia ina ghururi
  Ndia za tatasi huzandamaye?

Suu ulimwengu uutakao
  Emale ni lipi upendeyao?
Hauna dawamu hudumu nao
  Umilikishwapo wautendaje?

Why, O my soul, heed'st not thy Future Fate!
Soothly, if thou wert wise, discriminate
Would'st not perceive this world of rain frustrate?
Why to its turmoiled path dost ever turn? . . .

This mortal life, this vale of thy desire,
Where doth its virtue lie, that thou admire?
Nor Earth, nor man, for ever shall endure
E'en had'st thou mortal power, what could'st attain?
(Trans. by Hichens 1969: 58–65)

He then almost begs his heart to repent its past sins and pray for eternal peace and happiness that can only be found in the life after death. Other celebrated *tenzi* of this period include Sayyid Abdalla bin Ali bin Nasir's *Takhmisa ya Liyongo* (on the events surrounding the life and tragic end of the Swahili poet-hero Fumo Liyongo); Abdalla Mas'ud Mazrui's *Utenzi wa Al-Akida* (an historical chronicle in verse of the intrigues in the power struggles between the *akida* [commander], Muhammad bin Mbarak Mazrui, and the Omani governor of Mombasa); and Abubakar Mwengo's *Utenzi wa Katirifu* (on the supposed romance between a wealthy Muslim man and Hasina, the daughter of a slain "pagan" king, that leads to conspiracies and, subsequently, to a series of battles between Muslim forces and those of non-believers in Islam).

It is also from this period that we have records of the celebrated woman poet, Mwana Kupona binti Mshamu (1810–60), and her poem, *Utendi wa Mwana Kupona*. Composed in 1858 shortly before her death, the poem was intended to be an instructional guide for her seventeen-year-old daughter, Mwana Hashima binti Mataka, on the place, roles, duties, and responsibilities of a woman in respect of her husband. Today, the work stands as one of the most famous among the *tenzi*. Its accomplishments can be attributed as much to its tone and humor as to the flow of its language and the style intrinsic to the work: "The poem is a masterpiece of allusions that play up the male ego in a society where men see themselves as masters over their womenfolk, while at the same time instructing the intelligent woman to treat the opposite sex as she would an infant" (Shariff 1991a: 46). More recently, in fact, the poem has begun to generate some controversy as to its ideological orientation. Some argue that it affirms and reinforces the patriarchal order in Swahili society, while others see in it a subversive, if disguised, anti-hegemonic discourse. Amidst this controversy, however, Mwana Kupona continues to enjoy a place of note among Swahili poets: shops, restaurants, sewing businesses, and cultural forums are some of the projects that bear her name.

While Mwana Kupona has rightly attracted the greatest attention among women poets, women have generally had a profound influence on Swahili verse. Even when they do not receive the acclaim that they deserve, some of the best verse in the Swahili literary tradition continues to be the product of female genius. Furthermore, women have been central in the conservation of works of poetry of the classical type, both in their oral and written forms, and it is to them that people usually turn for the most eloquent recitations. Ali A. Jahadhmy has noted, in connection with the Swahili of the island of Lamu, that its women "in the past as well as in the present have been the custodians of Swahili poetry; in fact, some of the best verse literature has come from the pen of women . . . Zena Mahmud has just completed a most authoritative work on Swahili poetry . . . She is, with a few others, carrying on the tradition of the women of Lamu as keepers of the Swahili verse tradition" (1975: 28).

The nineteenth century, however, also saw the rise of a written poetic tradition posturing towards the secular. Everyday issues of social and political importance were captured in verse and preserved for posterity in the Swahili-Arabic alphabet. The leading spirit behind the popularization of this more secular poetic tradition was the inimitable Muyaka wa Mwinyi Haji (1776–1840), who lived and composed in Mombasa on the coast of Kenya. Muyaka marks the beginning of a gradual shift of the Swahili poetic genius from the northern coast of Kenya (Lamu and its archipelago) to Mombasa, a shift precipitated in part by a conjucture of new historical and political circumstances in the region.

In the hands of Muyaka, the quatrain (or *shairi* in the Swahili language) attained its rightful place as an important genre in the Swahili poetic diction. The *shairi*, comprised of four-line verses, a sixteen-syllable meter with a middle caesura and a final rhyming pattern, is often used for the more grave subject matter. Muyaka produced *shairi* poems with an unmatched mastery on the topical issues of his period. He wrote of love and infidelity, prosperity and drought, the sex-exploits of key figures of his time, and the calamities of the Mombasans. Above all, Muyaka became the celebrated poet of the Mazrui reign of Mombasa in the first half of the nineteenth century. And his war poetry, during the rivalry between Mombasa and other city-states, continues to excite the imagination of the Swahili to the present. In one of his war-inspired poems, for example, he boasts:

Ndimi taza nembetele, majini ndimi mbuaji
Nishikapo nishikile, nyama ndimi mshikaji
Ndipo nami wasinile, nimewashinda walaji
Kiwiji samba wa maji, msonijua juani!

Maji yakijaa tele, huandama maleleji
Pepo za nyuma na mbele, nawinda wangu windaji
Huzamia maji male, male yasofika mbiji
Kiwiji simba wa maji, msonijua juani!

I roam the seas, a hunter bold, in waters deep I slay!
And in my fearsome grip I hold, relentlessly, my prey.
My foes would rend my flesh! Behold! Tis them I hold at bay!
For I am fierce and valiant, aye! The lion of the seas.

When high the surging rollers leap and squall, toss white the spray,
When back and forth the wild winds sweep, I hunt my hunter's way!
I sink in the depths of the water's deep, whose surge no ship may stay!
For I am fierce and valiant, aye! The lion of the seas.

(Trans. by Gérard 1981: 103)

So central was Muyaka's poetry in the power struggles between Swahili city-states during his time, that scholars of his works liken him to the court-poets of Europe.

Muyaka's genius lay partly in his linking the social relationship with the relationship of the ego. The poetry of the private self is more limited in Afro-Islamic literature than in Afro-European literature. But poets like Muyaka helped to build bridges between individual privacy and public concern.

The secularization of Swahili written poetry within the traditional prosodic framework continued into the colonial period. In the words of Albert Gérard, "while Muslim subject-matter remained paramount in Swahili literature, colonial enterprise fostered the growth of a [new] trend . . . the use of the epic forms for handling secular topics and contemporary events" (1981: 119). Of particular significance is poetry seeking to document colonial conditions and anticolonial struggles in what had become German East Africa. Hemed al-Buhry's *Utenzi wa Wadachi Kutamalaki Mrima* (The Epic of German Invasion of Mrima, 1955), and Abdulkarim bin Jamaliddin's "Utenzi wa Vita vya Maji Maji" (The Epic of the Maji-Maji War, 1957) are some prominent examples of this new poetic development.

The classical Swahili tradition, however, continued to exert an impact on the postcolonial period. The themes, style, and tone of Muyaka's poetry, in particular, have continued to influence modern poets like Abdilatif Abdalla, Kaluta Amri Abedi, Zena Mahmud, Mwalimu Hassan Mbega, Ahmad Sheikh Nabhany, and Ahmad Nassir. Their poetry is replete with archaisms drawn from the work of poets who preceded Muyaka. To fully assimilate, appreciate, and evaluate their work often requires grounding in classical poetry. Swahili culture is so vital a component of their poetry that it is often difficult to understand the nuances without some familiarity with the various registers of the Swahili language. Furthermore, the very fact that they have continued to compose on a variety of themes that are of direct relevance to the realities of modern Africa has vindicated the assumption that modern themes and issues are capable of being versified within the traditional poetic diction. Their poetry is both classical and inventive without being stilted.

The public concerns of some of these poets are not only secular, they are also sometimes political. Abdilatif Abdalla is particularly renowned for his politically oriented poetry. Radical in his politics, he was imprisoned essentially for supporting an opposition party in Kenya at a time when the political system was becoming increasingly autocratic. After a five-year term in jail on charges of sedition and libel, he compiled an anthology of his prison poems that span his entire experience in Kenyan prisons. His poems are militant and unrepentant in tone. The sense of isolation and the effects of solitary confinement are vividly recaptured in the imagery he uses. The anthology is reminiscent of the poems of Muyaka in which he castigated the treasonable conduct of some of his compatriots. Equally striking is Abdalla's nationalism. In one poem, reflecting on whether to embark on a self-imposed political exile by a finer flight of imagination, he puts himself in a position not unlike that of a crab: "Where else can a crab run to save into its own shell?" (Abdalla 1973: 77).

Unlike many of the African poets writing in European languages, the poets writing in Swahili within the traditional prosodic framework are seldom groping for identity. There is a conspicuous absence of poems obsessed with cultural alienation or with cultural conflict with Europe, or even poetry of the surrealist type. The only genre that comes close to the theme of "alienation" is the so-called poetry of political combat. This includes those poems, which appear regularly in Swahili newspapers, composed to condemn the evils of neocolonialism in its political sense and poems that recount the virtues of *Ujamaa* in Tanzania. The poets themselves were trained in the classical Islamic education system and, in most cases, suffered a minimum of cultural alienation. While the traditional Islamic system of education accommodated aspects of African traditional culture, the western system of education alienated and sometimes suppressed traditional value systems. The recipients of traditional Islamic education came out equipped with both the Arabic alphabet and the Roman alphabet and tended to use the two interchangeably. They became conscious of the existence of the legacy of Swahili literature before being initiated into the heritage of literature in European languages. They accepted the legacy of the *ulamaa*, the priestly poets of old, and at the same time searched for a new idiom commensurate with their time and place.

In their contributions to poetry columns in Swahili newspapers, these poets also seek to influence standards of language use in the society at large. The poets constitute an *ipso facto* Swahili academy, serving as the custodians of the "very best" of the Swahili linguistic tradition that they seek to conserve and promote. As Ali A. Mazrui once observed, "There is a school of thought in English poetry . . . to the effect that poetry should approximate the ordinary language of conversation. But in Swahili culture there is a school of thought which would argue that ordinary conversation should try to approximate the elegant language of poetry" (1986: 245).

Closely related to the destiny of Swahili literature, however, was the development of the Swahili language itself. Even before the inception of European colonial rule, Swahili had managed to spread well beyond the frontiers of Swahili ethnicity and had acquired an important role as a medium of interethnic communication. But precisely because the language was still primarily circumscribed to trade functions, Swahili literature continued to be the exclusive preserve of people who were themselves ethnically Swahili. This status quo, however, was to be drastically transformed by the German invasion of Tanganyika in 1885, and British colonization of Kenya, Uganda, and Zanzibar around 1895, as a new Swahili literature began to evolve from outside the traditional boundaries.

The earlier phase of this colonial linguistic history was virtually dominated by Christian missionaries who, inspired by their evangelical concerns, struggled to learn Swahili and in time rendered various sections of the Bible into the language using the Latin script. The missionaries were also initially responsible for exposing the west to Swahili literature by making its folktales available both in writing and in translation in European languages, as well as for introducing the west to Swahililand by having some English texts translated into Swahili. The Swahili versions of some of Charles Lamb's *Tales from Shakespeare*, Bunyan's *Pilgrim's Progress*, and *Aesop's Fables*, for example, were all produced during this early phase of the colonial dispensation (Rollins 1983: 113–14).

Later, the Germans widened the use of Swahili and raised its status by making it the official language at the lower levels of their colonial administration. The British after them continued with this policy in Tanganyika and extended it, to a lesser extent, to parts of Kenya. But the British also went a step further by introducing the language into schools and by encouraging its teaching as a subject in much of the Swahili-speaking area. They also promoted its use as a medium of instruction in lower elementary education throughout Tanganyika and Zanzibar – the two constituting what is today called Tanzania – and the native Swahili-speaking area of Kenya.

This new role of Swahili as an academic language naturally placed the question of instructional materials for schools on the colonial educational agenda. An (East African) Inter-Territorial Language Committee was thus set up in 1930, partly to standardize the language and its new Latin-based orthography, and to encourage local Africans to write creative works in the language. What came to be known as "Standard" Swahili was now in the making based, supposedly, on the Zanzibar dialect of the language. Though initially opposed by the Swahili themselves, especially in Kenya, due to its seeming artificiality, the new imposed norm rapidly established roots in East Africa, especially among non-native speakers. The orthographic Latinization of Swahili was now also in full swing and would gradually marginalize Swahili-Arabic writing altogether.

In their continued efforts to address the urgent need for school readers in Swahili, the British translated even more of their own literary classics into the language. Between the late 1920s and early 1940s, therefore, there was a proliferation of translated creative works, which included R. L. Stevenson's *Treasure Island*, Rudyard Kipling's *Mowgli Stories*, Jonathan Swift's *Gulliver's Travels*, Rider Haggard's *Allan Quatermain* and *King Solomon's Mines*, Lewis Carroll's *Alice in Wonderland*, and others. By 1940, these British models in Swahili had sufficiently inspired the local population to stimulate new writing by East Africans themselves. These efforts were given further encouragement through the establishment of the East African Literature Bureau in 1948 with its primary focus on publishing Swahili language texts.

European involvement in setting a new written norm for the Swahili language and its literature within the first half-century of colonial rule, therefore, was immense. According to Jack Rollins, "In terms of literary influence, one set of figures alone will explain more than several paragraphs. Between the years 1900 and 1950, there were approximately 359 works of prose published in Swahili; 346 of these were written by Europeans and published mainly in England and Germany. Many of these were translations: Swift, Bunyan, Moliere, Shakespeare, but none more pervasive, in more abundance, and having more effect than the Bible" (1985: 51). These biblical narratives in Swahili included not only the books of the Bible itself, but also hymn books, catechisms, prayer books, and booklets on the lives of individual saints.

There were also Swahili journalistic ventures of one type or another, going back to the time of German rule in Tanganyika and which, sometimes, carried short stories. *Msimulizi* (The Narrator) came into being in 1888, and

Habari za Mwezi (Monthly News) in 1894. The two were soon followed by *Pwani na Bara* (The Coast and the Inland) and *Rafiki* (Friend) by the competing German Protestant Mission and the German Catholic Mission, respectively. These experiments continued during the period of British colonial rule, initially under the impetus of British colonial administrators like A. B. Hellier.

In his statistics, Rollins is unlikely to have included the works published by Muslim scholars like Sheikh Al-Amin bin Ali Mazrui and Sheikh Abdalla Saleh Farsy. Nonetheless, the overwhelming proportion of the widely circulating Euro-Christian-produced materials, using what was conceived to be Standard Swahili, came to set the linguistic standard to which East Africans, including the Swahili people themselves, were now expected to adhere. The dis-Islamization of Swahili, its ecumenicalization, was now rapidly under way and was to affect the destiny of Swahili literature in some major ways in the decades to come.

But unlike the classical period of Swahili writing which emanated from the Kenya coast, the more modern phase of Swahili literature that was partly set in motion by the African–European encounter, developed its strongest roots in Tanzania, where Standard Swahili was supposedly born. And while colonialism helped in consolidating the secular tradition in Swahili literature, it also impelled the emergence of new genres and subgenres, including prose fiction and written drama.

Prior to the colonial period the only Swahili prose writing of significance was in the form of historical chronicles. Preserved ones among these include court chronicles such as *Tarekhe ya Pate* (The Pate Chronicle) covering the years 1204 to 1885 and the *Khabari za Lamu* (The Lamu Chronicle) covering the eighteenth and nineteenth centuries. There are also other chronicles dealing with the history of Kilwa, Shungwaya, Mombasa, and other city-states. This genre continued to be encouraged by both the Germans and the British and set the background against which modern prose fiction was to emerge.

Following in the tradition of the chronicles was James Mbotela's *Uhuru wa Watumwa* (The Freeing of the Slaves, 1934) a semi-historical narrative that is widely regarded as the precursor of the Swahili novel. Though composed by an African, *Uhuru wa Watumwa* is essentially colonial in its style, content, and ideology to the extent of exonerating the west in African enslavement. But it is nonetheless important "for the history of Swahili literature because it exemplifies how a new trend was arising in modern-educated circles that were alien and even hostile to the predominantly Muslim and/or Arabic elements in traditional Swahili culture" (Gérard 1981: 136).

The artist who is considered to have been most decisive in the development of modern Swahili writing, however, is Shaaban Robert (1909–62) from Tanga,

Tanzania. Though a poet of note, his most important contribution to Swahili literature was in prose fiction, and his early writings are a clear demonstration of the multicultural heritage at work. His first novellas, *Kufikirika* (The Imaginable, written in 1946 but published posthumously in 1967), *Kusadikika* (1951) (The Believable), and *Adili na Nduguze* (1952) (Adili and His Siblings) are all a fusion of a medium of composition of western influence and a stylistic tendency towards fantasy with a didactic orientation that express the legacies of both the African tradition and the *Alfu-lela-ulela* stories from the *Arabian Nights*. In his later works, *Utubora Mkulima* (1968a) (Utubora the Farmer) and *Siku ya Watenzi Wote* (1968b) (The Day of Reckoning), however, Shaaban Robert moves closer to the novel in the western sense, making little appeal to the fantastic, having a multiplicity of plots and a large number of concrete characters clearly described in some depth and located more precisely in time and place.

Inspired by a strong sense of nationalism with a literary mission to raising the status of the Swahili language, Shaaban Robert is widely acclaimed for the colorful and rich quality of his language. And his renowned poem on Swahili continues to galvanize Tanzanians in their attempts to enrich the language in various ways. Robert urges his compatriots to cherish the language, for Swahili is to the Tanzanian what a mother's breast is to a child:

Titi la mama litamu
  hata likawa la mbwa
Kiswahili naazimu
  sifayo iliyofumbwa
Kwa wasiokufahamu
  niimbe ilivyo kubwa
Toka kama mlizamu
  funika palipozibwa
Titile mama litamu
  jingine halishi hamu

Mother's breast is the sweetest
  Canine it may be
And thou, Swahili, my mother-tongue
  Art still the dearest to me.
My song springs forth from a welling
  heart, I offer this my plea
That those who have not known thee
  may join in homage to thee.
Mother's breast is the sweetest,
  no other satisfies.
    (Trans. by Jahadhmy 1975: 3)

A Mswahili of Yao origin (from Malawi), Shaaban Robert served as a symbolic bridge between the Swahili and non-Swahili cultural universes at a time when Swahili literature was rapidly ceasing to be an exclusively Swahili ethnic phenomenon. Its boundaries were expanding beyond the East-African coast, beyond the home of the Swahili where it was born. The trend towards the de-ethnicization of Swahili literature in Tanzania was further consolidated by the country's leftist move to *Ujamaa,* a policy that fostered the rise of Swahili as the national and official language of the new East-African state.

But if the Swahili language and its literature had become de-ethnicized in a demographic sense, Tanzanian society itself was becoming increasingly Swahilized in a cultural sense. The cultural label "Swahili" and the national label "Tanzanian" were gradually becoming synonymous. In the words of Kiango and Sengo, "Here at home [in Tanzania] Swahili is our guardian; it has reared us from the colonial era and united us to the period of our independence. It is the language that expresses our social reality . . . A Swahili means a Tanzanian" (Kiango and Sengo 1972: 10).

With his mastery of the language and his creative genius Shaaban Robert became a pioneer in the Swahilization of Tanzanian culture. His prose contributed to setting in motion a new trend in the Tanzanian imagination towards a trans-ethnic Swahili literature. He clearly anticipated Tanzania's nationalist spirit, if not its revolutionary ideals. His was work that "expressed the views of a generation which saw the necessity for social changes but turned away from the road of violent revolutionary transformation" (Ohly 1985: 474).

But if Shaaban was the greatest inspirational figure in the emergence of Swahili prose fiction, it fell to his national compatriot Euphrase Kezilahabi to raise it to greater heights of artistic achievement. After the publication of his first novel, *Rosa Mistika* (1971), Kezilahabi quickly distinguished himself as a writer of extraordinary talent with the courage to test the boundaries of cultural censorship in addressing topical issues of social and political concern in Tanzania. More significantly it was Kezilahabi who placed the "psychological novel" firmly on the Swahili literary map, addressing, perhaps for the first time in Swahili prose writing, psychological themes like alienation, with vivid imagination. A product of a university education both in Africa and the USA, Kezilahabi is described as "the greatest novelist of the Tanzanian mainland, who more than any other Swahili writer has been influenced by western literary trends" (Bertoncini 1989: 107). His national compatriots have likened him to Thomas Mann and Albert Camus because of the existentialist orientation of some of his writings (Mlacha and Madmulla 1991: 31).

Representing almost the opposite trajectory is another, equally accomplished writer of the modern period, Said Ahmed Mohamed of Zanzibar. With a university education from both Tanzania and Germany, Mohamed is a prose-fiction writer, playwright, and poet, even though he is best known for his novels. Like his celebrated compatriot Mohamed Suleiman Mohamed – the author of *Kiu* (1972) and *Nyota ya Rehema* (1976) (Rehema's Fortune), winner of the 1973 Kenyatta Prize for Literature, and one of the most skilled Swahili novelists of the twentieth century – Said Ahmed Mohamed has demonstrated remarkable dexterity in language use and great ingenuity in crafting the structures and plots of his stories. But perhaps more than any other Swahili novelist, he is the writer most strongly identified with "socialist realism." His works have a persistent focus on class exploitation and the class struggle. As a result, he has sometimes been regarded as the Ngugi wa Thiong'o of Swahili literature.

The works of Shaaban Robert, Kezilahabi, and Mohamed fall under the larger taxonomic scheme discussed by Mlacha and Madmulla who distinguish various types of Swahili prose fiction: the psychological and the social, the historical and the political, the autobiographical and the ethnographic, the utopian as well as the dystopian (Mlacha and Madmulla 1991: 29–43). There is also a rapid mushrooming of popular fiction, encouraged especially by the expansion of individually and locally owned publishing houses. The earliest seminal figure in this new Swahili fiction is the Zanzibar-born Mohamed Said Abdalla, the writer of, among other novels, *Mzimu wa Watu wa Kale* (1960) (The Ancestors' Graveyard), *Kisima cha Giningi* (1968) (The Well of Giningi), and *Siri ya Sifuri* (1974) (The Secret of Zero). This subgenre was soon to grow in leaps and bounds as Faraji Katalambulla and others began to make their contributions, with detective stories becoming particularly attractive. And underlying all this growth and diversification of Swahili prose fiction was an increasing tendency towards greater realism even as the oral heritage continued to exercise its influence, especially in matters of linguistic style.

A prose genre that has received far less attention than the novel has been the short story. East-African Swahili newspapers like *Mambo Leo*, *Taifa Leo*, *Baraza*, and *Mzalendo* seem to have served as the initial outlets for short-story compositions, going back to the early years of colonial rule. Later, beginning in the 1960s, *Kiswahili*, the official journal of the Institute of Swahili Research in Dar es Salaam, also began publishing Swahili short stories on an irregular basis. Anthologies of short stories, however, do not seem to have appeared until the early 1970s. An important stimulus in this direction was the BBC radio Swahili short-stories competitions that were launched in 1967. Some of the submissions were later selected for publication under a series entitled *Hekaya za Kuburudisha* (Entertaining Tales), produced by Longman Kenya between 1970 and 1977.

A writer who has come to be recognized as one of the most gifted in this genre is the distinguished novelist from Zanzibar, Mohamed Suleiman Mohamed. His stories invariably won the first prize in every BBC competition. With a general tone that swings between irony and humor, his stories are lyrical, full of suspense and surprise, with characters that are rich and dynamic. Mohamed's creative genius in short-story writing was later capped by his single-authored collection of six stories, *Kicheko cha Ushindi* (1978) (Laughter of Triumph).

Equally accomplished in this genre is another Zanzibar-born writer, Saad A. Yahya, best known for his collection *Pepeta* (1973) (Rice Flakes). Assuming the voice of a detached insider, Yahya explores, with penetrating insight, the various spaces in the complex lives of residents of Zanzibar (his original home) and Nairobi (his adopted home) in the postcolonial period. Weaving tragedy and irony, Yahya proves to be an acute observer of the East-African condition, and his collection is a demonstration not only of his creative genius but also his profound humanity.

At the heels of Mohamed and Yahya has been their compatriot, the internationally acclaimed Said Ahmed Mohamed. Like Mohamed Suleiman Mohamed, Said Ahmed Mohamed also made his initial appearance in the short-story scene through the radio competitions of the BBC. Winning several literary awards, his stories were among those that later appeared in the Longman series *Hekaya za Kuburudisha*. Said Ahmed Mohamed also took part in the short-stories competition organized by the Swahili service of Radio Deutsche Welle, coming at the very top in every instance. A selection of the latter eventually went into making his anthology *Si Shetani si Wazimu* (1985) (It's Neither Spirit nor Insanity).

At this same period, Gabriel Ruhumbika produced his collection of four short stories, *Uwike Usiwike Kutakucha* (1978) (Crow or Not, Dawn Will Break). Varying widely in style, from quasi-realistic to re-crafted fables, Ruhumbika's stories are strongly didactic in their general orientation. But it is his compatriot Alex Banzi who seems to show even greater fidelity to didacticism and to the traditional *ngano* (story) in his choice of form as demonstrated, especially, in his *Nipe Nikupe na Hadithi Nyingine* (1982) (Give Me and I Shall Give You, and Other Stories).

Other distinguished writers of the short story have included the poet Mugyabuso M. Mulokozi (concentrating, in particular, on political satire and quasi-revolutionary themes) and the outstanding and most influential Swahili novelist, Euphrase Kezilahabi (with his continued emphasis on the existential). Their stories have appeared in several places, including newspapers, magazines, journals, and edited volumes, but neither of them has produced single-authored collections in this genre.

Of all these writers, however, it is Mbunda Msokile who has emerged as the single most important beacon of the Swahili short story. He too began by contributing his short stories to local newspapers. After experimenting with a couple of novelettes, he came to acquire special prominence as a short-story writer with the release of his anthology entitled *Nitakuja Kwa Siri* (1981) (I Will Come Secretly). But it is his pioneering study of the short story, *Misingi ya Hadithi Fupi* (1992) (Foundations of the Short Story) that finally distinguished him as the most dedicated advocate of the genre. The first part of this lengthy text deals with theoretical and historical questions in the development of the Swahili short story. The second part is a vibrant collection of short stories by himself, Euphrase Kezilahabi, Mugyabuso Mulokozi, John Rutayisingwa, and Mohamed Suleiman Mohamed.

In spite of the many attributes that distinguish the stories of these various writers, however, most of them bear the unmistakable imprint of the *ngano* (oral tales), demonstrating the affinity and synthesis between the "old" and the "new." In the majority of cases, it is even impossible to tell where orality ends and the written begins in the continuing evolution of the modern Swahili short story.

The contribution of indigenous verbal arts to the development of Swahili literature is equally noticeable in written drama, even though the latter is more decidedly a product of the western educational system than prose writing. Inspired by English dramatic works studied in schools during the colonial period, Swahili written plays first made their appearance in the late 1950s, beginning with *Mgeni Karibu* (1957) (Welcome Guest) by a British expatriate teacher, Graham Hyslop, and *Nakupenda Lakini . . .* (1957) (I Love You, But), by Henry Kuria. Though this literary experimentation began in Kenya, however, it was in Tanzania that its greatest genius was to emerge, in the person of Ebrahim Hussein.

Hussein's career as a playwright covers virtually the entire spectrum of Swahili dramaturgical experience in the twentieth century. His first two plays, *Alikiona* (1970) (She Learnt Her Lesson) and *Wakati Ukuta* (1970) (Time Is a Wall), produced while he was still a student at the University of Dar es Salaam, were modeled on Aristotelian design. The frame of reference for these plays, as of many Swahili plays by other playwrights, is "a theatre that created and sustained Aristotelian illusion, that used a curtain or at least blackouts by electric light to mark or, more precisely, to conceal changes of scenes (scenery), and that, first of all, constructed a series of actions all leading to a single climax" (Fiebach 1997: 22).

This early postcolonial period was also one of growing cultural nationalism as African intellectuals sought to affirm an independent African esthetic. In Tanzania this spirit of reculturation was further galvanized by the politics of *Ujamaa*. And it is against the background of this political mood that Hussein produced his best-known drama, *Kinjeketile* (1969). Not only did the play center on a nationalist theme of historical importance, the Maji-Maji war against German colonial rule in Tanganyika, it adopted Brechtian dramaturgy, which was widely regarded as having a closer affinity with African performance arts than Aristotelian dramaturgy.

As an independent playwright, however, Hussein soon moved away from strict adherence to Aristotelian or Brechtian theater. Instead, he tried to synthesize the legacy of the western theater and the tradition of indigenous arts. This is the dramaturgic trend that unfolds in his other plays, *Mashetani* (1971) (Devils), *Arusi* (1980) (Wedding), and *Kwenye Ukingo wa Thim* (1988) (At the Edge of Thim). In particular, "Hussein discarded the illusionist components of received European artistic models" and in the process created a uniquely African drama out of Aristotelian foundations (Fiebach 1997: 28–29).

In the mid-1970s, Hussein also published two dramatic monologues, *Ngao ya Jadi* (1976, Shield of the Ancestors) and *Jogoo Kijijini* (1976, Rooster in the Village), which draw almost exclusively from the *ngano* (storytelling) and *kitendawili* (riddle) traditions of the Swahili. But it is Hussein's compatriot Penina Mlama (alias Penina Muhando) – the producer of *Hatia* (1972, Guilt), *Pambo* (1975, Decoration), and *Lina Ubani* (1982b, There Is a Remedy), among other plays – who has more consistently been associated with the African performance experience in her dramaturgy. Her plays have often been refreshingly sensitive to the different registers of the Swahili language and have been quite successful in integrating song, dance, and ritual, adding to the Africanness of their theatrical form. Commenting on one of her productions, Micere Mugo has noted that Penina "succeeds in this play, as few artists can, in engaging the emotions of the audience, so that they become completely and involuntarily absorbed in the fate of the characters. *Hatia* has an easy-flowing style, is arresting and commanding in effect, mainly because the playwright has such a tremendous capacity for creating suspense" (Mugo 1976: 139).

In the meantime, the appearance of Said Ahmed Mohamed's *Amezidi* (1996) (Gone Beyond the Limits), with its inclination toward an African theater of the absurd, demonstrates the continuing potential of a multicultural synthesis in Swahili dramaturgy. Ahmed himself acknowledges the influence of Samuel Beckett's *Waiting for Godot* and Eugene Ionesco's *Rhinoceros*, *The Chairs*, and *The Lesson* on his composition of *Amezidi* (Njogu 1997: iv). But there is little doubt, in the final analysis, that *Amezidi* is a synthesis of traditions that is peculiarly Swahili in literary experience.

In addition to prose writing and drama, East Africa's contact with the west also stimulated creative experimentation in written poetry, as a new generation of poets sought to break away from the hitherto more strict confines of meter and rhyme. The first collection of Swahili free and blank verse was published by a British settler in Tanzania. The poet, Cory, was convinced that Swahili poetry as hitherto composed by some of its leading poets was inaccessible except to the highly learned scholar of Swahili language, reducing it to a sophisticated dialog between an elitist few. He attributed this problem to the impact of Arabic poetics on Swahili poetry. As a way of "remedying" the situation, therefore, Cory suggested that Swahili poetry seek a break from the Arabo-Islamic legacy, as an aspect of its modernization, and allow itself to come under the European influence (1958: vii). And it is on the inspiration of this mission that he proceeded to produce what is perhaps the first anthology of Swahili free verse. Similar sentiments were later to be expressed by African writers, like Kezilahabi, who contended that "For a long time Swahili poetry had turned into a dialog among a few people who understand it . . . There is need to bring it down to the level of the common person and get it to spread" (1974b: xiv; my translation). Contrary to the classical legacy, therefore, Swahili poets were now being called upon to adopt a poetic idiom that was close to the everyday language of conversation of "common folk."

But it was Mwalimu Julius Nyerere's Swahili translation of Shakespeare's *The Merchant of Venice* and *Julius Caesar* that sparked an entire debate on the boundaries of Swahili poetics. Nyerere followed the English originals by rendering his Swahili translation of the plays in blank verse. Was this artistically admissible in the Swahili poetic universe? This debate was to grow, both in intensity and acrimony, with the appearance of more Swahili poems in blank and/or free verse by such leading writers as Ebrahim Hussein and Euphrase Kezilahabi. Some of its practitioners, like K. K. Kahigi and M. M. Mulokozi in *Malenga wa Bara* (1976, Poets of the Uplands), Alamin Mazrui in *Chembe cha Moyo* (1988) (Arrow in my Heart), and Said Ahmed Mohamed in *'Sikate Tamaa* (1980c) (Do Not Despair), have sought to maintain a delicate balance between received prosody and free versification. The result has been the continued use of meter and rhyme but in a manner that is non-traditional and more flexible.

Though still lacking in popular appeal, this new poetic style now seems to have succeeded in establishing a certain degree of legitimacy within Swahili literature. As a result, "free verse and metrical poetry are currently coexisting in a more tolerant manner than was hitherto the case. What is likely to result eventually is a dynamic coexistence of verse genres, and this will be enriching to both forms of poetic composition" (Njogu 1995: 149).

Whatever the genre or the style, however, much of the modern literature – especially in prose and drama – has tended to revolve around certain common themes of conflict of values. The most prominent of these is the conflict between tradition and modernity, which, in most cases, is intertwined with the conflict between the rural and the urban. While some works idealize the traditional, others are critical of it or aspects of it, the difference sometimes being determined by the class background of the writer. Saad A. Yahya's collection of short stories *Pepeta* (1973), Ebrahim Hussein's play *Wakati Ukuta* (1971b) (Time Is a Wall) and Mbunda Msolike's *Nitakuja Kwa Siri* (1981) (I will Come Secretly) all exemplify this thematic trajectory in Swahili literature. Relations between men and women, especially in matters of love, sex and marriage, have been especially productive as a topic for the exploration of this particular clash of values.

This same conflict, however, is sometimes presented in narrower terms as one between Africa and the west, between the indigenous and the foreign. This was particularly true of earlier writings that pitted Christianity against indigenous African religions, as in Samuel Sehoza's *Mwaka Katika Minyororo* (1921) (A Year in Chains). But other themes of conflict, like the indigenous versus western systems of education – for example, I. C. Mbenna's *Kuchagua* (1972) (A Matter of Choice) – and indigenous versus western traditions of healing have also been explored. In the realm of politics, examples of this thematic clash include Farouk Topan's *Aliyeonja Pepo* (1973) (The Taste of Paradise), J. R. Nguluma's *Chuki ya Kutawaliwa* (1980) (Hatred of the Colonized), O. B. N. Msewa's *Kifo cha Ugenini* (1977) (Death in a Foreign Land), and Mugyabuso Mulokozi's *Mukwawa wa Uhehe* (1979). And in some rare cases, as in William B. Seme's *Njozi za Usiku* (1973) (Night Visions), the indigenous is presented nostalgically as a past that has been obliterated by western and modern encroachments.

The emergence of the educated class, influenced by western liberal ethos and political ideologies, has also made the conflict between the individual and society a theme of growing attention in Swahili literature. Of particular concern has been the location of the individual in modern African nation-states where national unity is often promoted at the expense of sub-national identities, or in more "traditional" societies that value collective welfare over individual rights and freedoms. The question of individualism features in many of Ebrahim Hussein's works. Euphrase Kezilahabi, on the other hand, has explored not only the problem of individual alienation (in his *Kichwamaji*, 1974a), for example, but also the conflict between private property and the more socialist land tenure system wrought by *Ujamaa*, as captured in his *Dunia Uwanja wa Fujo* (1975) (The World is a Stage of Confusion).

The clash between individual rights and collective concerns brings us directly to the theme of conflict between socialism and capitalism. Unlike most of the other themes in Swahili literature that have been approached from a more "universalistic" angle, the concern with alternative politico-economic systems betrays greater regional variation. The socialist-oriented Swahili literature from Kenya, for example, is essentially a reaction to the country's more overt neocolonial reality. It tends to locate the possibility of radical change within the context of specific class tensions emanating from center-periphery relations tied to global capitalism. Mass class uprising (of the proletariat, peasantry, petite bourgeoisie or some alliance / s of these classes) is often depicted as the preferred strategy of revolutionary change. Katama Mkangi's satiric novels *Mafuta* (1984) (Grease) and *Walenisi* (1996), Rocha Chimerah's *Nyongo Mkalia Ini* (1995) (Pancreas, the Liver's Oppressor), and Alamin Mazrui's play *Kilio cha Haki* (1981) (Cry of Justice) all fall within this domain of socialist literature to one degree or another. The socialist trajectory in this literature is generally utopian, in the loose sense of the word as an ideal to be aspired to, without the socialist system itself being explicitly articulated.

More experientially rooted is the socialist-oriented literature of Tanzania. But we do need to draw a distinction between the socialist literature of *mainland* Tanzania (or what was known as Tanganyika before its union with Zanzibar in 1964) and *island* Tanzania (encompassing the islands of what was once the independent nation of Zanzibar). The socialist literature of mainland Tanzania is more explicitly inspired by the living experiences of *Ujamaa* villages. Though there are some texts that are critical of the excesses of their leaders or that highlight some practical problems in the process of formation and management of *Ujamaa* villages, much of it seeks to demonstrate the socioeconomic and/or moral superiority of *Ujamaa*.

Within this socialist tradition we have, for example, K. K. Kahigi's and A. A. Ngerema's *Mwanzo wa Tufani* (1976, The Beginning of a Storm), in which the domestic worker, Kazimoto, who is exploited and abused by his employers, gains the sympathy and love of their daughter, Tereza; the two finally run away and find refuge and support in a socialist village. In John Ngomoi's *Ndoto ya*

Ndaria (1976, Ndaria's Dream), the leading character, Ndaria, is a rich farmer who uses every means at his disposal to prevent the introduction of *Ujamaa* to his village of Ranzi. But once he notices how flourishing a neighboring *Ujamaa* village had become in a few years' time, he becomes guilt-ridden, and subsequently does his utmost to turn Ranzi into an *Ujamaa* village.

Along the same lines, in the socialist literature of mainland Tanzania, we find writings that again support the ideals of *Ujamaa,* but are critical of the excesses of some of the leaders involved in the formation and management of the *Ujamaa* villages. These excesses include forced villagization, administrative mismanagement, and corruption. Some of this literature also highlights more practical problems of socialism, and of the socialist construction of *Ujamaa* villages without, however, interrogating the validity of *Ujamaa* ideals and claims. Examples of texts belonging to this category of critical *Ujamaa* literature include *Kijiji Chetu* (1975) (Our Village) by Ngalimecha Ngahyoma, *Nyota ya Huzuni* (1974) (The Star of Grief) by George Liwenga, and *Dunia Uwanja wa Fujo* (1975) (The World is a Stadium of Confusion) and *Gamba la Nyoka* (1979) (The Snake's Skin) by Euphrase Kezilahabi.

The socialist literature of island Tanzania, on the other hand, derived its inspiration not from the living experiences of *Ujamaa,* but from the bloody agonies of the Zanzibar revolution of 1964. When *Ujamaa* was promulgated as the politico-economic policy of the federated nation of Tanzania, Zanzibar was already on its revolutionary march towards socialism. As Kimani Njogu (1997) demonstrates, it is this revolution, and its class background and precipitating conditions, which have continued to inform the socialist-oriented literature of Zanzibar and Pemba writers like Said Ahmed Mohamed and Shafi Adam Shafi.

The important point to bear in mind here is that the road to *Ujamaa* in mainland Tanzania, though pursued bureaucratically rather than democratically, was ultimately peaceful, enjoying much popular goodwill and meeting no militant opposition from antisocialist interest groups. The road to socialism in island Tanzania, on the other hand, was marked by a tremendous amount of violence. For historical reasons connected with "race" relations on the island, and due to fears of counter-revolutionary attempts, Zanzibar experienced an undue amount of bloodshed in its quest for a socialist order.

Against this backdrop, therefore, the socialist imagination in island Tanzania became virtually entrapped in a discourse of rationalization. Socialist-inspired writers of island Tanzania seemed to be under moral pressure to explain the very basis and justification for the Zanzibar revolution. They have sought to highlight the feudal-cum-capitalist relations of exploitation and the inhuman conditions of the life of the underprivileged classes in pre-revolutionary

Zanzibar. The impression is thus created that the magnitude of exploitation and oppression in pre-revolutionary Zanzibar was bound to trigger a violent revolutionary upsurge with socialist aims. Mohamed S. Mohamed's *Nyota ya Rehema* (1976) (Rehema's Luck), Shafi Adam Shafi's *Kasri ya Mwinyi Fuad* (1978) (Lord Fuad's Palace), and Said Ahmed Mohamed's *Dunia Mti Mkavu* (1980a) (The World Is a Dry Tree), all betray this rationalizing tendency in Zanzibar's socialist-inspired literature.

In spite of its internal differences, however, much of the socialist literature of Tanzania has tended to omit reference to neocolonial capitalism and dependency. This is a trajectory that clearly distinguishes it from the socialist-inspired literature of neighboring Kenya. The focus on the home-grown system of *Ujamaa* in mainland Tanzania, and on the locally induced revolution at the dawn of independence in Zanzibar, have relegated the problem of neocolonialism to the periphery of Tanzania's literary imagination in Swahili. But now that *Ujamaa* has virtually been abandoned and the Zanzibar revolution discredited, we can expect new trends in socialist-oriented writing in Tanzania. This possibility is clearly demonstrated by Said Ahmed Mohamed's play *Amezidi* (1996), which explores, among other issues, the broader theme of Africa's dependence on the west.

The contrast between Kenya and Tanzania brings us to a fundamental anomaly of the East-African esthetic situation. It is Kenya, and not Tanzania, that is the home of Swahili esthetic genius at its richest. Most of the classical masterpieces of Swahili poetry came from the Kenya coast. Tanzania's contribution to Swahili literature has much more recent origins, attaining new heights of achievement only in the second half of the twentieth century. But the home of the older poetic traditions of the Swahili language, and the source of most of the great epics, was the Kenya coast.

Yet, in terms of general dissemination, Swahili culture is more widespread in Tanzania than in the Kenya nation as a whole. Tanzania, among African countries, has the smallest number of creative writers writing in English. The largest output in drama, prose, and poetry is in Swahili. The literature in general is a reflection of the nationalist character of Tanzanian society. Once the most radical nation in East Africa, it managed to decolonize the various aspects of life there, ranging from the emphasis on Kiswahili for legislative deliberations to the politicization of the so-called masses. Finding themselves in a radically tempestuous climate, the poets and novelists also preoccupied themselves with the problem of "development." An entire state-sanctioned movement of dialogic and dramatic *ngonjera* political poetry has evolved to extol the virtues of Tanzanian nationhood and the pitfalls of too excessive a dependence on external cultural models. Day after day the predominant Swahili newspapers are inundated with poems urging greater reliance on the land as the backbone of the Tanzanian economy and lauding the beauty of the Swahili language, customs, and political and literary culture.

Kenya, on the other hand, continues to have a more limited geographical area of concentrated aesthetic achievement in Swahili. Most of the country's noted writers continue to come from the narrow coastal province. Outside this region, it is the Swahili language as a neutral medium of communication rather than Swahili culture as a rich vessel of heritage that has spread (Mazrui and Mazrui 1995: 119).

This situation may, of course, be only transient. As the language is becoming more consolidated in the country, Kenyans have begun to realize the value of "nationalizing" the cumulative esthetic accomplishments of the Kenya coast. In addition, the whole region continues to be in the throes of a cultural reappraisal that has received added impetus from the end of the Cold War, the entrenchment of global capitalism, the collapse of *Ujamaa,* and the increasing pressure for pluralism. And as these dynamics and counter-dynamics continue to unfold, only the future can confirm their full implications for the destiny of Swahili literature and its multicultural heritage.

Bibliography

Primary works

Abdalla, Abdilatif. 1971. *Utenzi wa Adamu na Hawaa*. Nairobi: Oxford University Press.
1973. *Sauti ya Dhiki*. Nairobi: Oxford University Press.
Abdalla, Abdilatif, ed. 1973. *Utenzi wa Fumo Liyongo* by Mohamed Kijumwa. Dar es Salaam: Institute of Kiswahili Research.
Abdalla, Mohamed Said. 1960. *Mzimu wa Watu wa Kale*. Dar es Salaam: East African Literature Bureau.
1968. *Kisima cha Giningi*. London: Evans Brothers.
1973. *Duniani Kuna Watu*. Dar es Salaam: East African Publishing House.
1974. *Siri ya Sifuri*. Dar es Salaam: East African Publishing House.
Abdulaziz, Mohamed H. 1979. *Muyaka: Nineteenth-Century Popular Poetry*. Nairobi: Kenya Literature Bureau.
Abedi, K. Amri. 1954. *Sheria za Kutunga Mashairi na Diwani ya Amri*. Dar es Salaam: Eagle.
Abedi, Suleiman H. 1980. *Sikusikia la Mkuu*. Ndanda-Peramiho: Benedectine Publishers.
Akilimali Snow-White, K. H. A. 1962. *Diwani ya Akilimali*. Nairobi: Kenya Literature Bureau.
Al-Buhry, Sheikh Hemed. 1955. *Utenzi wa Wadachi Kutamalaki Mrima*. Ed. J. W. T. Allen. Kampala (Uganda).
Amana, B. 1982. *Malenga wa Vumba*. Oxford: Oxford University Press.
Balisidya, N. 1975. *Shida*. Nairobi: Foundation Publishers.

Banzi, Alex. 1972. *Titi la Mkwe*. Dar es Salaam: Tanzania Publishing House.
1977. *Zika Mwenyewe*. Dar es Salaam: Tanzania Publishing House.
1980. *Tamaa Mbele na Hadithi Nyingine*. Ndanda-Peramiho: Benedectine Publishers.
1982. *Nipe Nikupe na Hadithi Nyingine*. Ndanda-Peramiho: Benedectine Publishers.
Burhani, Z. 1981. *Mali ya Maskini*. Nairobi: Longman.
Chacha, Nyaigotti Chacha. 1982. *Mke Mwenza*. Nairobi: Heinemann.
1986. *Marejeo*. Nairobi: Kenya Literature Bureau.
Chimerah, Rocha. 1995. *Nyongo Mkalia Ini*. Nairobi: Jomo Kenyatta Foundation.
Chiraghdin, Shihabuddin. 1987. *Malenga wa Karne Moja*. Nairobi: Longman.
Chiume, M. W. K. 1969. *Dunia Ngumu*. Dar es Salaam: Tanzania Publishing House.
Chogo, Angelina. 1974. *Wala Mbivu*. Nairobi: East African Publishing House.
1975. *Kortini Mtu Huyu*. Nairobi: Foundation Books.
Farsy, A. S. 1960. *Kurwa na Doto*. Nairobi: East African Literature Bureau.
Hussein, Ebrahim. 1969. *Kinjeketile*. Dar es Salaam: Oxford University Press.
1971a. *Mashetani*. Dar es Salaam: Oxford University Press.
1971b. *Wakati Ukuta*. Nairobi: East African Publishing House.
1976. *Ngao ya Jadi/Jogoo Kijijini*. Dar es Salaam: Oxford University Press.
1980. *Arusi*. Nairobi: Oxford University Press.
1988. *Kwenye Ukingo wa Thim*. Nairobi: Oxford University Press.
Hyslop, Graham. 1957a. *Afadhali Mchawi*. Nairobi: East African Literature Bureau.
1957b. *Mgeni Karibu*. Nairobi: East African Literature Bureau.
1974. *Mchimba Kisima*. Nairobi: Nelson.
1975. *Kulipa ni Matanga*. Nairobi: Nelson.
Jamaliddin, Abdulkarim. 1957. "Utenzi wa Vita vya Maji Maji." Supplement to the *Journal of the East African Swahili Committee* 27: 57–93.
Kahigi, K. K., and A. A. Ngerema. 1976. *Mwanzo wa Tufani*. Dar es Salaam: Tanzania Publishing House.
Kahigi, K. K., and M. M. Mulokozi. 1976. *Malenga wa Bara*. Dar es Salaam: East African Literature Bureau.
Kandoro, Saadan. 1978. *Liwazo la Ujamaa*. Dar es Salaam: Tanzania Publishing House.
Kareithi, Peter Munuhe. 1969. *Kaburi Bila Msalaba*. Nairobi: East African Publishing House.
1975. *Majuto Mjukuu*. Nairobi: Gazelle.
Katalambulla, F. 1965. *Simu ya Kifo*. Nairobi: East African Literature Bureau.
1975. *Buriani*. Nairobi: East African Literature Bureau.
1976. *Lawalawa na Hadithi Nyingine*. Nairobi: East African Literature Bureau.
Kezilahabi, Euphrase. 1971. *Rosa Mistika*. Dar es Salaam: East African Literature Bureau.
1974a. *Kichwamaji*. Dar es Salaam: East African Publishing House.
1974b. *Kichomi*. Nairobi: Heinemann.
1975. *Dunia Uwanja wa Fujo*. Dar es Salaam: East African Literature Bureau.
1979. *Gamba la Nyoka*. Arusha: Eastern Africa Publishers.
1987. *Nagona*. Dar es Salaam: Educational Publication Centre.
Khatib, M. S. 1975. *Utenzi wa Ukombozi wa Zanzibar*. Nairobi: Oxford University Press.
Kibao, Salim. 1975. *Matatu ya Thamani*. Nairobi: Heinemann.
Kiimbila, J. K. 1966. *Lila na Fila*. Dar es Salaam: Longman.
1971. *Ubeberu Utashindwa*. Dar es Salaam: Taasisi ya Uchunguzi wa Kiswahili.
1972. *Visa vya Walimwengu*. Dar es Salaam: Longman.

King'ala, Yusuf. 1984. *Majuto*. Nairobi: Oxford University Press.
Kitsao, Jay. 1981. *Tazama Mbele*. Nairobi: Heinemann.
1983a. *Bibi Arusi*. Nairobi: Oxford University Press.
1983b. *Malimwengu Ulimwenguni*. Nairobi: Oxford University Press.
Kitsao, Jay, and Zachariah Zani. 1975. *Mafarakano na Michezo Mingine*. Nairobi: Heinemann.
Komba, Serapius M. 1978. *Pete*. Dar es Salaam: Institute of Kiswahili Research.
Kuria, Henry. 1957. *Nakupenda Lakini*. Nairobi: East African Literature Bureau.
Lihamba, Amandina. 1980. *Hawala ya Fedha*. Dar es Salaam: Tanzania Publishing House.
Liwenga, George. 1974. *Nyota ya Huzuni*. Dar es Salaam: Tanzania Publishing House.
Mazrui, Alamin, M. 1981. *Kilio cha Haki*. Nairobi: Longman.
1988. *Chembe cha Moyo*. Nairobi: Heinemann.
Mbenna, I. C. 1972. *Kuchagua*. Dar es Salaam: Maarifa.
1976. *Siuwezi Ujamaa*. Dar es Salaam: East African Publishing House.
Mbonde, J. P. 1974. *Bwana Mkubwa*. Nairobi: Transafrica.
Mbotela, James. 1934. *Uhuru wa Watumwa*. London: Sheldon.
Mhina, G. 1971. *Mtu ni Utu*. Dar es Salaam: Tanzania Publishing House.
Mkangi, Katama. 1975. *Ukiwa*. Nairobi: Oxford University Press.
1984. *Mafuta*. Nairobi: Heinemann.
1996. *Walenisi*. Nairobi: East African Educational Publishers.
Mnyampala, Mathias. 1965. *Diwani ya Mnyampala*. Nairobi: Kenya Literature Bureau.
Mohamed, Mohamed Suleiman. 1972. *Kiu*. Dar es Salaam: East African Publishing House.
1976. *Nyota ya Rehema*. Nairobi: Oxford University Press.
1978. *Kicheko cha Ushindi*. Nairobi: Shungwaya.
Mohamed, Mwinyihatibu. 1980. *Malenga wa Mrima*. Dar es Salaam: Oxford University Press.
Mohamed, Said Ahmed. 1978. *Asali Chungu*. Nairobi: Shungwaya.
1980a. *Dunia Mti Mkavu*. Nairobi: Longman.
1980b. *Utengano*. Nairobi: Longman.
1980c. *'Sikate Tamaa*. Nairobi: Longman.
1984. *Kina cha Maisha*. Nairobi: Longman.
1985. *Si Shetani si Wazimu*. Zanzibar: Zanzibar Publishers.
1988. *Kiza Katika Nuru*. Nairobi: Oxford University Press.
1996. *Amezidi*. Nairobi: East African Educational Publishers.
2001. *Babu Alipofufuka*. Nairobi: Jomo Kenyatta Foundation.
Msewa, O. B. N. 1977. *Kifo cha Ugenini*. Dar es Salaam: Tanzania Publishing House.
Mshamu, Mwana Kupona binti. 1972. *Utenzi wa Mwana Kupona*. Ed. Amina A. Sheikh and Ahmed S. Nabhany. Nairobi: Heinemann.
Msokile, Mbunda. 1981. *Nitakuja Kwa Siri*. Dar es Salaam: Dar es Salaam University Press.
1992. *Misingi ya Hadithi Fupi*. Dar es Salaam: Dar es Salaam University Press.
Mtendamema, G. 1978. *Utotole*. Dar es Salaam: Longman.
Muhando, Penina. 1972. *Hatia*. Nairobi: East African Publishing House.
1974. *Heshima Yangu*. Nairobi: East African Publishing House.
1975. *Pambo*. Nairobi: Foundation Books.
1982a. *Nguzo Mama*. Dar es Salaam: Dar es Salaam University Press.
1982b. *Lina Ubani*. Dar es Salaam: East African Literature Bureau.

Mulokozi, M. M. 1979. *Mukwawa wa Uhehe*. Nairobi: East African Publishing House.
Mushi, J. S. 1969. *Baada ya Dhiki Faraja*. Dar es Salaam: Tanzania Publishing House.
Muyaka, wa Mwinyi Haji. 1940. *Diwani ya Muyaka bin Haji Al-Ghassany*. Ed. William Hichens. Johannesburg: Witwatersrand University Press.
Mwaduma, S. 1974. *Simbayavene*. London: University of London Press.
Mwanga, Zainab M. 1983. *Kiu ya Haki*. Morogoro: Spark International Consultants.
Mwangudza, J. A. 1986. *Thamani Yangu*. Nairobi: Oxford University Press.
Nabhany, Ahmed Sheikh. 1985. *Umbuji wa Kiwandeo*. Nairobi: East African Publishing House.
Nasir, Sayyid Abdalla bin Ali. 1977. *Al-Inkishafi*. Nairobi: East African Literature Bureau.
Nassir, Ahmed. 1971. *Malenga wa Mvita*. Nairobi: Oxford University Press.
Ndibalema, Charles. 1974. *Fimbo ya Ulimwengu*. Nairobi: Heinemann.
Nduguru, E.A. 1973. *Walowezi Hawana Siri*. Dar es Salaam: Tanzania Publishing House.
Ngahyoma, Ngalimecha. 1975. *Kijiji Chetu*. Dar es Salaam: Tanzania Publishing House.
Ngare, Peter. 1975. *Kikulacho ki Nguoni Mwako*. Nairobi: East African Publishing House.
Ng'ombo, Amina Hussein. 1982. *Heka Heka za Ulanguzi*. Ndanda-Peramiho: Benedictine Publishers.
Ngomoi, John. 1976. *Ndoto ya Ndaria*. Dar es Salaam: Tanzania Publishing House.
Nguluma, J. R. 1980. *Chuki ya Kutawaliwa*. Dar es Salaam: Swala.
Omari, C. K. 1971. *Mwenda Kwao*. Dar es Salaam: Institute of Kiswahili Research.
1973. *Barabara ya Tano*. Dar es Salaam: Tanzania Publishing House.
1976. *Kuanguliwa kwa Kifaranga*. Nairobi: Heinemann.
Omolo, L. O. 1971. *Uhalifu Haulipi*. Nairobi: Longman.
Osodo, Felix. 1979. *Hatari kwa Usalama*. Nairobi: Heinemann.
1982. *Mama Mtakatifu*. Nairobi: Heinemann.
Rajab, Hammie. 1982. *Miujiza ya Mlima Kolelo*. Dar es Salaam: Busara.
1984. *Roho Mkononi*. Dar es Salaam: Busara.
Robert, Shaaban. 1945. *Koja la Lugha*. Nairobi: Oxford University Press.
1947. *Pambo la Lugha*. Johannesburg: Witwatersrand University Press.
1951. *Kusadikika*. London: Nelson.
1952. *Adili na Nduguze*. London: Macmillan, 1952.
1953. *Kielelezo cha Insha*. Johannesburg: Witwatersrand University Press.
1967a. *Utenzi wa Vita vya Uhuru*. London: Oxford University Press.
1967b. *Kufikirika*. Nairobi: Oxford University Press.
1968a. *Utubora Mkulima*. Nairobi: Nelson.
1968b. *Siku ya Watenzi Wote*. Nairobi: Nelson.
Ruhumbika, Gabriel. 1974. *Parapanda*. Dar es Salaam: East African Literature Bureau.
1978. *Uwike Usiwike Kutakucha*. Dar es Salaam: Eastern Africa Publications.
Sehoza, Samuel. 1921. *Mwaka Katika Minyonyoro*. Dar es Salaam.
Seme, William B. 1973. *Njozi za Usiku*. Dar es Salaam: Longman.
Senkoro, Fikeni E. M. 1978. *Mzalendo*. Nairobi: Shungwaya.
Shafi, Shafi Adam. 1978. *Kasri ya Mwinyi Fuad*. Dar es Salaam: Tanzania Publishing House.
1979. *Kuli*. Dar es Salaam: Tanzania Publishing House.
Simbamwene, J. 1972. *Kwa Sababu ya Pesa*. Dar es Salaam: Longman.
1978. *Kivumbi Uwanjani*. Dar es Salaam: Transafrica.

Somba, John Ndetei. 1968. *Kuishi Kwingi ni Kuona Mengi*. Nairobi: East African Publishing House.

1969. *Alipanda Upepo na Kuvuna Tufani*. Nairobi: Heinemann.

Topan, Farouk. 1973. *Aliyeonja Pepo*. Dar es Salaam: Tanzania Publishing House.

Ugula, P. 1969. *Ufunguo Wenye Hazina*. Nairobi: Evans Brothers.

Yahya, A. S., and David Mulwa. 1983. *Buriani*. Nairobi: Oxford University Press.

Yahya, Saad A. 1973. *Pepeta*. London: University of London Press.

Secondary works

Amidou, Assibi A. 1990. *Kimwondo: A Kiswahili Electoral Contest*. Vienna: Beiträge zur Afrikanistik.

Bertoncini, Elena Zubkova. 1989. *Outline of Swahili Literature: Prose Fiction and Drama*. Leiden: E. J. Brill.

Cory, H. 1958. *Sikilizeni Mashairi*. Mwanza: Lake Printing Works.

Fiebach, Joachim. 1997. "Ebrahim Hussein's Dramaturgy: A Swahili Multiculturalist's Journey in Drama and Theatre." *Research in African Literatures* 28.4: 19–37.

Gérard, Albert S. 1981. *African Language Literatures: An Introduction to the Literary History of Sub-Saharan Africa*. Washington, DC: Three Continents Press.

Hichens, William. 1969. *Al-Inkishafi: The Soul's Awakening*. Nairobi: Oxford University Press.

Hodgkin, Thomas. 1966. "The Islamic Literary Tradition in Ghana." In *Tropical Africa*. Ed. I. M. Lewis. London: Oxford University Press: 442–60.

Jahadhmy, Ali A. 1975. *Anthology of Swahili Poetry*. London: Heinemann.

Kiango, S. D., and T. S. Y. Sengo. 1972. "Fasihi." *Mulika* 4: 11–17.

Knappert, Jan. 1979. *Four Centuries of Swahili Verse*. London: Heinemann.

Mazrui, Ali A. 1986. *The Africans: A Triple Heritage*. London: BBC Publications.

Mazrui, Ali A., and Mazrui, Alamin M. 1995. *Swahili, State and Society: Political Economy of an African Language*. Nairobi: East African Educational Publishers; Oxford: James Currey.

Mlacha, S. A. K., and Madmulla, J. S. 1991. *Riwaya ya Kiswahili*. Dar es Salaam: Dar es Salaam University Press.

Mugo, Micere G. 1976. "Gerishon Ngugi, Peninah Muhando and Ebrahim Hussein: Plays in Swahili." *African Literature Today* 8: 137–41.

Njogu, Kimani. 1997. *Uhakiki wa Riwaya za Visiwani Zanzibar*. Nairobi: Nairobi University Press.

1995. "Poetic Serialization: Kiswahili Metapoetry on Prosodic Knots." *Research in African Literatures* 26.4: 138–50.

Ohly, Rajmund. 1985. "Literature in Swahili." In *Literatures in African Languages: Theoretical Issues and Sample Survey*. Ed. B. W. Andrzejewski, S. Pilaszewicz and W. Tyloch. Cambridge: Cambridge University Press: 460–92.

Rollins, Jack D. 1983. *A History of Swahili Prose*. Leiden: E. J. Brill.

1985. "Early Twentieth-Century Prose Narrative Structure and Some Aspects of Swahili Ethnicity." In *Toward African Authenticity, Language and Literary Form*. Ed. Eckhard Breitinger and Reinhard Sander. Bayreuth: Bayreuth University Press: 49–68.

Shariff, Ibrahim N. 1991a. "Islam and Secularity in Swahili Literature." In *Faces of Islam in African Literature*. Ed. Kenneth W. Harrow. Portsmouth, NH: Heinemann: 37–57.

1991b. "The Liyongo Conundrum: Reexamining the Historicity of Swahilis' National Poet." *Research in African Literatures* 22.2: 153–67.

Whiteley, Wilfred. 1969. *Swahili: The Rise of a National Language*. London: Methuen.

13

Africa and the European Renaissance

SYLVIE KANDÉ

If for the period extending from the end of the nineteenth century to the present, Africa's contribution to art, ideas, and especially world literature has been duly recognized, its contribution has yet to be acknowledged for preceding centuries, and in particular for the period from the decline of the Roman Empire up until the first European explorations along the continent's great river highways.

It has not gone unnoticed that in effect this category of African literature was "invented" in circumstances that make it more accessible to Europe, since its written beginnings are substantially in European languages and it takes over from, and sometimes counterbalances, ethnographic studies. Just as African art was "discovered" at the turn of the twentieth century and studied for the answers it might bring to the questions of form posed by Cubism, so African literature – that which emerged at the end of the nineteenth and beginning of the twentieth centuries – seems to raise questions that concern Europe itself, which was engaged forcefully and improvisationally in the process of colonization that inevitably radically modified the relationships of colonizers as well as colonized to history, language, and identity.

On the other hand, literary criticism seems to have contented itself with the absence of African (europhonic) letters from the time, roughly speaking, of St. Augustine (354–430) to Olaudah Equiano (1747 – *c.*1801) – an absence supposedly offset through a recourse to orality that is often abusive because exclusive. Thus, the Renaissance and the beginning of modern times, of crucial importance in the transformation of the visions of the world and in the constitution of national literary histories, seem, *a priori*, to owe nothing to Africa, its writers, and its texts.

As a means of periodizing western history, the Renaissance affords a break with the Middle Ages and an acknowledgment of the west's dynamism that opened it up beyond its previous geographic, intellectual, cultural, and religious boundaries. Placed under the sign of conquest, secularization, and officialization of common languages enriched by a broader knowledge of ancient languages, the Renaissance interlaces tales of triumph, built upon the binary opposition of Us/the Others, "a holy saga of mythic proportions" (Mudimbe 1994: xii), placing under erasure another story of triumph that has heretofore been overshadowed in the west – that of the conquest of Islam over western Europe (seventh to fifteenth centuries), redirected, at the completion of the Reconquista, toward Constantinople, which was taken in 1453. Thereafter seeing themselves as the center of a system that admitted change, westerners ventured to the periphery where they "discovered" and subjugated the Other, sowing children and planting the Christian cross on the lands they had confiscated. At this stage, *métissage* was not envisioned as having a destiny beyond the places of colonial encounter, and especially not in the metropole. According to that logic, it can be understood that the presence in Europe of individuals of African origin was not discussed, except when the fame they had accrued protected them from oblivion, as was the case for Juan Latino and Anton Wilhelm Amo. The very paucity of information on one such as Juan Latino, for example, has led certain critics to consider his existence as purely legendary (Gates and Wolff 1998: 16).

In a useful inversion of perspective, one can nevertheless consider that it was the circumnavigation of Africa, that "third continent," by the Portuguese, who came to Kongo in 1482 and to the Cape of Good Hope in 1487, that gave the Renaissance its first impetus. Their installation in São Tomé and Principe in 1480 inaugurated the cycle of tropical production of sugar destined for Europe, thanks to manual slave labor. Again it is two African reference points that mark geographically the success of the Reconquista: the victory over Ceuta in 1415 by the Portuguese, and over Oran by the Spanish in 1509. All in all, the epoch was favorable to the circulation of people and ideas between America and the "old" continents, and also, despite the tendency to forget it, between Europe and Africa. It has been estimated that two-thirds of the gold that circulated in Europe and North Africa during the fourteenth century, an assurance of economic stimulation, came from commerce with West Africa, the reason for which a famous Spanish map drawn in 1375 shows the King of Mali holding in his hand a gold nugget. The accounts of the Arab travelers of the fifteenth century, such as Al-Bakri, Ibn Battuta, and Ibn Khaldoun, who informed the world of the existence of powerful African kingdoms, come to mind, as well as the undeniable similarity between the European university towns and African towns such as Timbuktu, between Columbus's enterprise and that of Abubakar, the predecessor of Emperor Kankan Moussa of Mali, who in the fourteenth century launched his flotillas towards America. There is a wealth of syncretisms, of which Leo Africanus is a magnificent incarnation; and there is an abundance of mutual influences, illustrated for example by the introduction of the Sudano-Sahelian style in West Africa by the Grenadine poet-architect El-Saheli whom Kankan Moussa brought back with him at the completion of his pilgrimage to Mecca.

Although sporadic and insufficiently documented, the presence of Africans in Europe from the Renaissance to the Age of Enlightenment is a reality. We know that beginning in 1444 the first Africans to be deported as slaves were sent to farms in the south of Spain and in Portugal. European literature and painting of the period attest to the social roles that devolved in society to Africans, who were subalterns for the most part – minor pages or musicians – but sometimes endowed with power and dignity: we think of the portrait of Juan de Pareja by the Spanish painter Diego Velásquez (1650).

As a result, most often, of planters' absenteeism, this African presence, numerically important around ports such as Lisbon, Seville, London, Nantes, Bordeaux, and Amsterdam, elicited three kinds of reactions. The first was psychosis and rejection, which were legally translated in decrees of expulsion – from England in 1596 and 1601 (File and Power 1981: 6), and from France in 1777 (Deveau 1994: 242). As shown by the James Somerset case in Great Britain (1772), the reaction consisted in reinforcing the prohibition of slavery in the metropolis, which gradually led to a reconsideration of the legitimacy of the slave trade, then of slavery in the colonies. The third effect was integration, since a large percentage of these Africans mixed through *métissage* into the rest of the European population.

We must be wary of envisioning this presence as a simple reservoir of manual labor or as an exotic "Court of Wonders." We know that numerous Africans transported to the Americas – because they were Muslims – were literate in Arabic: the writings of Job ben Salomon (captured in 1713), Omar Ibn ben Said (1831), and Abu Bakr ad Siddiq (1834), among others, have been catalogued (Diouf 1998: ch. 4). In America or in Europe, those and others wished to maintain and extend their mastery of writing, or to become literate in European languages. From this point of view, Francis Williams (*c.*1700 – *c.*1770) and Phillis Wheatley (1754–84) are not exceptional figures, but alongside Juan Latino, Jacobus Elisa Joannes Capitein (1718–47), Anton Wilhelm Amo, Olaudah Equiano, Ignatius Sancho (1729–80), and others took part in an intense effort to affirm their humanity by claiming their entitlement to writing, which has proved to be one of the most powerful – although least often evoked – manifestations of resistance to slavery.

Let us turn especially to Juan Latino and Anton Wilhelm Amo who, individually renowned in their respective places of exile, chose, however, to engage their identity and their history in their writings.

*

Juan Latino (Juan de Sesa) (*c.*1518 – *c.*1597) was in all likelihood born in sub-Saharan Africa, less probably in Spain. This man of letters owes his surname – conferred upon him by one of his co-disciples and adopted by Latino himself, and meaning "Latin teacher" – to the permanence and quality of his intellectual activities. He probably arrived in Seville, Spain, with his mother and was sold in Baen, then worked in the household of the Count of Cabra, Don Luiz Fernandez de Cordoba, as a footslave of the young Don Gonzalo, the third Duke of Sesa. Latino profited from the classes to which he accompanied the young duke to assure his own education at the Cathedral and the University of Granada – a city in full cultural bloom since its reconquest in 1492 at the end of the long crusade against the Muslims. Latino obtained several diplomas in succession: the Bachillerato in 1546; the Licenciado in 1556; and the Master of Arts in the following year. In 1566, after several years of study, he began to teach the humanities, probably at the Cathedral of Granada, with whose history his name remains associated. At that same time, he had developed a private practice, based on his literary and musical talents. Moreover, he married one of his pupils, Ana, the daughter of the Licenciado of Corlobal, which indicates that he gained manumission, either before or simultaneously. They had four children: Juana (1549), Bernardino (1552), Ana (1556), and Juan (1559).

The first African to publish poetry in a European language, Latino was also a teacher, grammarian, and translator. A member of literary circles, according to the critic Menéndez y Pelayo (Gates and Wolff 1998: 21), a companion of Don Diego Hurtado de Mendoza, Hernando de Acuna, and Gregorio Silvestre, he appears as a major figure in the humanist movement in Grenada: a specialist of *studia humanitatis* (rhetoric, grammar, and poetry, especially), he was known for his ability to write elegantly, synthesizing classical culture and Christianity. Juan Latino is known through the numerous references that other intellectuals, critics, and writers, have made to his life and his work, which, for lack of translation, remains relatively unknown outside hispanophone and Latinist circles.

The extant works of Juan Latino are in Latin: in all probability they represent the essential element of his work, since Latino was considered one of the masters of the new Latinity, a literary tendency that developed in reaction to the officialization of Spanish (for which the first grammar book was published in 1492) and to the preponderance of Arabic (banished in 1556). The *Austriad* (1573) is a famous set of 1,837 hexameters divided into two volumes of 763 and 1,074 verses. The preface contains biographical details and epigrams dedicated to Philip II on the occasion of his son's birth. A celebration of the military victories of Don Juan of Austria, the son of Charles V and the half-brother of Philip II, whom Latino had moreover met, the *Austriad* recounts the events of the Battle of Lepanto in the Gulf of Corinth between Christians and Muslims. In neoclassical style, the *Austriad* presents *exempla,* and is inspired by the metrics and vocabulary of Virgil, Martial, and Horace, yet with numerous Christian references.

A commemoration of the transfer of the royal remains to the monastery of El Escorial has also been preserved, in 600 lines in the same style (1576). There also remains a short, twelve-page pamphlet published in 1585, a tribute of the House of Sesa in which Latino grew up and a homage to his close friend, the third Duke of Sesa. Also attributed to him is an elegy bearing the compliments of Pope Pius V to Philip II for his military victories. His texts in Spanish include, notably, his address at the opening ceremony for the academic year 1565. Sanchez Martin mentions as an example of his translations from Latin into Spanish an epigram dedicated to Seville (Gates and Wolff 1998: 25).

Juan Latino's spectacular social ascent was attributed to the social and cultural climate in Europe which, from the sixteenth century, was more liberal than that in the New World and thus would have allowed certain Africans to be recognized for their talents (Fikes 1980: 212). Nevertheless, one senses that Juan Latino's itinerary was marked by a "sentiment of race" that was relatively active among his entourage and in his own consciousness (Erickson 1993: 503). Sometimes the object of pleasantries of a racial nature, Latino attracted interest in large part because of his marriage with a noble Spanish woman. Furthermore, despite his abilities, Latino only attained the rank of Professor at the Cathedral of Granada, in 1556, after strong polemics. Even then he was threatened with removal from his classrooms. Without minimizing the political nature of the conflicts in a society strongly marked by the Inquisition, which was as hostile to Jews as it was to *Mudejars* and those called Moors, and without minimizing the tension between Latino's humanism and the university's metamorphosis into a conservative center for the transmission of utilitarian knowledge (Martinière and Varela 1992: 288), it is likely that the specificity of his identity worked against him. On the other hand, it would be anachronistic to wish to see Latino as a writer preoccupied with affirming his Negritude. Nevertheless, we should note that Latino did not renounce Africa, and he even on occasion claimed all of it, for example, in the preface of the

Austriad where he writes, "The writer was not engendered in this region, he comes, Latino, from the land of the Ethiopians." We can thus imagine Latino as a man of letters who is at peace with his African origins, but working, in the humanist vein, toward the promotion of the Europe of the future.

The reception of his work attests to his importance in the world of letters in the Renaissance. The oldest sources are Bermudez de Pedraza, *Antiguidad y Excelencias de Granada* (1608, Antiquity and Marvels of Granada) and Ambrosio Salazar, *Espejo de Gramatica* (1615, Example of Grammar). Cervantes alludes to Latino's erudition in the preface of *Don Quijote* (1605). Diego Jimenez de Enciso dedicated a theatrical work to him, *La comedia famosa de Juan Latino* (1620, The Famous Comedy of Juan Latino), often interpreted as his biography (Ivory 1979: 613–17). Poets such as Gabriel Rodriguez de Aridilla have paid him homage. In the twentieth century, the works of the scholars A. Marín Ocete, Calixto C. Maso, and Valurez B. Spratlin should be mentioned, as well as the analytical and synthesizing article by Henry Louis Gates, Jr., and Maria Wolff (1998).

The Age of Enlightenment has strong ties to the Renaissance. The two periods should be understood as systemic bursts of energy directed at greater clarity in the understanding of the order of things, creative autonomy, and domination of the world of nature. Both are built upon opposition to the order that preceded them, supposedly obscurantist and strictly hierarchized. Between them there is a genealogical link: the *philosophes* of the Enlightenment pursued and perfected the movement of modernization begun in the fifteenth century. Numerous other parallels can be established between the Renaissance and the Age of Enlightenment, notably, for our purposes here, the desire to discover worlds as yet unexplored and human beings uncorrupted by civilization – a desire soon formalized in a new science, anthropology, and in a renewed literary genre, the travelogue. Another similarity: whatever its ties with power, politics, and religion, the university remained the crucible where an emerging European culture was elaborated and cemented by the still preponderant use of Latin.

In the Age of Enlightenment, Europe's relation to Africa enters a period of transition: the question of slave trade, in full force, becomes the touchstone for new debates in all of Europe concerning the freedom and equality of the individual. Sometimes dissertation topics concerning slavery are even proposed for intellectuals in training (Anton Wilhelm Amo, Thomas Clarkson, Montesquieu and Jean-Jacques Brissot among others). Nevertheless, the prevailing market relationship excludes the possibility of Europe turning toward Africa with concern for observable truths and tolerance of differences that are characteristic of the Enlightenment. The slave trade, on the contrary, relaunches the capital of myths and received ideas already enveloping Africa and Africans. The myth of the Noble Savage embraced by a certain elite is no less injurious. The establishment in 1788 of the African Association that sent Mungo Park to Timbuktu, inaugurated the first explorations into the interior of sub-Saharan Africa, which were gradually to ensure the succession of the slave trade by colonialism.

It is therefore remarkable that despite the historical circumstances, marked by slavery and the subsequent invention of racism, two Africans distinguished themselves in the domains that best represent the respective spirits of these epochs: humanism for the Renaissance, and philosophy for the Enlightenment. It should be emphasized that Latino and Amo both took part, within the framework of their academic and literary functions, in two crucial stages in the elaboration of European culture, stages whose effects are still discernible.

*

Anton Wilhelm Amo (*c.*1700 – *c.*1754) was born near Axim in the Gold Coast (today's Ghana). He was sent to Europe, in all probability to be educated as a priest of the Reformed Dutch Church. While still a child, he was taken into the household of Duke Anton Wilhelm Brunswick-Wolfenbüttel of Saxony, who gave him to his son after having him baptized according to Lutheran rites. As a young man, he was, moreover, confirmed in the same chapel in 1721 under the name Anton Wilhelm Rudolph Mohre. Amo was educated in that household, either by reason of the promise he represented in a country and age filled with Enlightenment thinkers preoccupied with pedagogy and equality, or by reason of the positive impression produced by Pushkin's ancestor, Ibrahim Hannibal. Hannibal was a lieutenant general of African descent of the artillery in the service of Peter the Great in Russia who, upon returning to France, stopped at the court of the Brunswicks, relatives of the czar (Sephocle 1992: 183; Bess 1989: 390).

Educated in classical languages, French, German, and Dutch, Amo enrolled in 1727 in the college of philosophy at the University of Halle, considered one of the capitals of the new spirit and endowed with a cosmopolitan student population. There he wrote a legal paper (now lost) entitled "De Jure Maurorum in Europa" (1729, The Rights of Blacks in Europe), then left Halle for the University of Wittenberg where his successes earned him the rector's written congratulations in 1733, as well as an active participation in the public life of the institution. Amo taught classes as a lecturer in several universities. He also taught private classes and developed a good reputation. As the first African to obtain a diploma at the completion of higher studies in Europe, in 1734 he received a doctorate in philosophy, with a thesis entitled "De humanae mentis apatheia" (On the Impassivity of the Human Mind). In the same year, he prepared a study entitled "Disputatio philosophica continens ideam distinctam eorum quae competunt vel menti vel corpori nostro vivo et organico" (A Philosophical Discussion Distinguishing between what Belongs to the Mind and to the Living and Organic Body). Giving courses on systems of classical modern thought, he taught in the universities of Wittenberg, Halle, and Jena. In 1738 he began his major work, "Tractatus de Arte Sobrie et Accurate Philosophandi" (On the Art of Philosophizing with Sobriety and Accuracy), a series of readings clarifying his philosophical positions. According to Blumenbach (who cites "Von den Negern," *Magazin für das Neueste aus der Physik* and *Naturgeschihte*, Gotha, 1787; see Hountondji 1983: 130) and Abbé Grégoire (who cites the *Monthly Magazine* of 1800; see Grégoire 1996: 134, n. 8), Amo is said to have received the title of Chancellor of the State at the court of Berlin.

Living in what was to become Germany, until at least 1747 – the year of the production of a theatrical play satirizing his person, as mentioned in the periodical entitled *Hallische Frage-und-Anzeigen Nachrichten* – Amo, who was approaching fifty years of age, decided to return to Ghana. That departure may be due to the loosening of his ties with his protector; to the increasing hostility in society; and to his relative isolation in a place where, unlike Ibrahim Hannibal and Olaudah Equiano, for example, he had not succeeded in marrying. The last written testimony on Amo comes from David Henry Gallenger, a scientist who traveled to Ghana in 1753. Amo was said to have set up his household not far from his parents and in a section close to the Dutch fort of Saint Sebastien. The date of his death remains uncertain.

Amo enjoyed uncontested recognition as a philosopher and teacher in Germany in the first part of the eighteenth century. His extraordinary itinerary was even further enhanced by the rumored existence of a brother – a slave in Surinam.[1]

A contemporary of Leibnitz, Christian Thomasius, and Christian von Wolff, Amo was strongly influenced by the western intellectual tradition of his time. As a man of the Enlightenment, he was more concerned with classification and verification than with totalization and thus did not produce a specific theoretical system; but he did not hesitate to categorize the philosophical theories of other great thinkers for his students. He often commented on them in critical fashion, in a language appreciated for its clarity. Involved in the philosophical debates of his time, he was engaged in the question of the relationship between the body and the mind, the subject of slavery, among other debates. Distancing himself from Aristotle, Descartes, and Stahl, Amo strove notably to demonstrate that the human mind is impassive, and is not the seat of sensations, which themselves depend upon the circulation of the blood. But it is this proximity of the body and the mind that allows the latter to understand and act by means of ideas. Some scholars even advance the idea that with his thesis on apathy, he anticipated Kant's question on the conditions of possibility of *a priori* judgments (Bess 1989: 388). Positioning himself in the quarrel between the vitalists and the mechanists, he pronounced himself in favor of Enlightenment thinkers, and on the sidelines with respect to Pietism. In his inaugural thesis, he took a position against the slave trade, contrary to his contemporary, the Ghanaian Capitein, who for his admission to the University of Leiden unwaveringly upheld the thesis of compatibility between Christian principles and the slave commerce.

Abolitionists such as Abbé Grégoire, in his *De la littérature des Nègres,* or Lydia M. Child in her chapter "Intellect of Negroes" from the essay *An Appeal in Favor of Americans Called Africans* (1836), found in Amo the material to demonstrate the existence of intellectual faculties among those whose servile status had abolished all their rights, including the right to respect. In the twentieth century, Kwame Nkrumah, engaged with his *Consciencism* (1964) in a project of synthesis and evaluation of European philosophy as a preliminary to the development of his own theory, also alluded to his compatriot and predecessor, Amo. More recently, in the framework of the debate on African philosophy / ethnophilosophy, Amo has been a subject of interest for his ambivalence (see Hountondji 1983:128–30 and Nwodo 1985: 36–39).

Is it possible to evaluate the part Africa has played in the life and work of Amo? We observe that Amo kept and even specified his Ghanaian name by signing *Amo-Guinea-Afer* or *Amo-Guinea-Africanus*, "as though he was afraid that his long European adventure might make him or his circle forget his African origins and ties" (Hountondji 1983: 111). Furthermore, as has been seen, Amo's first writings convey the mark of his interest in the African cause. He was determined to demonstrate that slave trading is unjustified: that the past grandeur of Africa, all the skills of Africans are opposed to it, as are Christian principles. His "return" to Ghana – where he had not spent much time – allows us to measure his attachment to the idea of a land of origin, given that the risks he incurred were enormous, since the slave trade was quite active on that section of the coast. Critics nevertheless judged that Africa occupies a minimal place in Amo's research and mode of thought – because of his early acculturation and the absence of intellectual partners of African origin around him. One could nuance this view by indicating that his participation in activities in the public sphere can be understood as a personal strategy meant to change the representations of Africa and Africans. Moreover, if we admit that there is often a metaphorical relationship between the nature of research and a personal existential problematic, it is important that Amo, who cannot by any means be considered Senghorian, redirected attention to the body as the seat of sensations, at a time when the African body was sold, bought, bartered, tortured, and disdained on a daily basis by virtue of its sudden visibility.

Note

1. For a list of archival material relating to the course of his life, see the article about him written by Hountondji (1983: 113).

Bibliography

Primary works

Child, Lydia. 1836. *An Appeal in Favor of Americans Called Africans.*

Clarkson, Thomas. 1785. *An Essay on the Slavery and Commerce of the Human Species*. London.

Grégoire, Henri. 1808. *De la littérature des Nègres, ou recherches sur leurs facultés intellectuelles, leurs qualités morales et leur littérature; suivies de Notices sur la vie et les ouvrages des Nègres qui se sont distingués dans les Sciences, les Lettres et les Arts*. Paris: Maradan.

1996. *On the Cultural Achievements of Negroes*. Amherst: University of Massachusetts Press. Trans. of *De la littérature des Nègres.*

Latino, Juan. 1971. *Ad catholicum pariter et invictissimum Philippum dei gratia hispaniarum regem, de foelicissima . . . / per magristrum Ioannem Latinum. Tractatus de arte sobrie accurate philosophandi / Antonius Guilielmus Amo. Dissertatio politico-theologica, de servitute, liberati christianae non contraria / Jacobus Elisa Joannes Capitein*. Nendeln: Kraus, Rpt. Includes reprints of Juan Latino's *Ad catholicum pariter et invictissimum Philippum* . . . Granada, 1573; A. W. Amo Afer's *Tractatus de arte sobrie accurate philosophandi* . . . Hall, 1738; J. E. J. Capitein's *Dissertatio politico-theologica* . . . Leiden, 1742.

Secondary works

Bess, Reginald. 1989. "A. W. Amo: First Great Black Man of Letters." *Journal of Black Studies* 19. 4: 387–93.

Bodunrin, P. O. 1985. *Philosophy in Africa: Trends and Perspectives*. Ile-Ife: University of Ife Press.

Dathorne, O. R. 2001. *Worlds Apart: Race in the Modern Period.* Westport, CT: Bergin and Garvey.

Deveau, Jean-Michel. 1994. *La France au temps des négriers*. Paris: France Empire.

Diouf, Sylviane A. 1998. *Servants of Allah: African Muslims Enslaved in the Americas*. New York: New York University Press.

Erickson, Peter. 1993. "Representations of Blacks and Blackness in the Renaissance." *Criticism* 35. 4: 499–527.

Fikes, Robert, Jr. 1980. "Black Scholars in Europe during the Renaissance and the Enlightenment." *The Crisis* 87. 6: 212–16.

File, Nigel, and Chris Power. 1981. *Black Settlers in Britain 1555–1958*. London: Heinemann.

Gates, Henry Louis, Jr., and Maria Wolff. 1998. "An Overview of Sources on the Life and Work of Juan Latino, the 'Ethiopian Humanist.'" *Research in African Literatures* 29. 4: 14–51.

Hountondji, Paulin. 1983. "An African Philosopher in Germany in the Eighteenth Century: Anton Wilhelm Amo." In *African Philosophy. Myth and Reality*. Bloomington: Indiana University Press: 111–30.

Ivory, Annette. 1979. "Juan Latino: The Struggle of Blacks, Jews, and Moors in Golden Age Spain." *Hispania* 62: 613–18.

Marín Ocete, A. 1925. "El Negro Juan Latino." *Revista de Estudios Históricos de Granada y su Reino*. Granada.

Martinière, Guy, and Consuelo Varela. 1992. *L'état du monde en 1492*. Paris and Madrid: La Découverte.

Maso, Calixto C. 1973. *Juan Latino: Gloria de España y de su raza*. Chicago: Northeastern Illinois University Press.

Mudimbe, V. Y. 1988. *The Invention of Africa: Gnosis, Philosophy, and the Order of Knowledge*. Bloomington: Indiana University Press.

1994. *The Idea of Africa*. Bloomington: Indiana University Press.

Nkrumah, Kwame. 1964. *Consciencism: Philosophy and Ideology for Decolonization and Development with Particular Reference to the African Revolution*. London: Heinemann.

Nwala, T. Uzodinma. 1978. "Anthony William Amo of Ghana on the Mind-Body Problem." *Présence Africaine* 108: 158–65.

Nwodo, Christopher S. 1985. "The Explicit and the Implicit in Amo's Philosophy." *Philosophy in Africa: Trends and Perspectives*. Ed. P. O. Bodunrin. Ile-Ife: University of Ife Press: 27–39.

Sephocle, Marilyn. 1992. "Anton Wilhelm Amo." *Journal of Black Studies* 23. 2: 182–87.

Shyllon, Folarin. 1977–78. "Olaudah Equiano: Nigerian Abolitionist and First National Leader of Africans in Britain." *Journal of African Studies* 4. 4: 433–51.

Spratlin, Valaurez Burwell. 1939. *Juan Latino, Slave and Humanist*. New York: Spinner Press.

14

The literature of slavery and abolition

MOIRA FERGUSON

One infamous 300-year battle over slavery was waged in Britain and the Americas, a period that is culturally rich with texts written by first-, second-, and sometimes third-generation Africans (in Britain and the Americas), including the United States and the Caribbean. Geography as an organizing principle helps to illuminate the similarities and differences within that literature of slavery and abolition.

African writers in Britain

From the sixteenth to the nineteenth centuries, slaves and ex-slaves in the African diaspora, kidnapped in West Africa, shipped across the notorious Middle Passage, and sold into slavery, wrote unflinchingly about their brutal life experiences. In petitions, poems, fictions, and autobiographies, also known as slave narratives, they recreated their environment and their mature selves as human beings enduring grievous lives, in Britain, the Americas and the Caribbean. They wrote in conscious opposition to proslavery stereotypes.

The earliest recorded English slave trader was John Hawkins, who, in 1562, on behalf of the English government, traded Africans to the Portuguese African and Spanish planters. By 1618, the English government held monopolies to slave trading-companies. The Royal African Company was founded in 1672 and was granted exclusive rights of trade between the west coast of Africa and the British colonies in the Americas. In the next five years, the company had shipped 100,000 African slaves to the West Indies and 5,000 to the North American colonies. After the Treaty of Utrecht in 1713, England assumed imperial dominance in the slave trade by acquiring the right – the *Asiento* – to deliver 144,000 slaves to the Spanish colonies.

Slaves also worked as domestic servants in Britain itself, often for absentee plantation owners, and slave-ship and military personnel (Fryer 1984: 14–19). By the 1660s, the Royal Adventurers had received a charter permitting slaves to be a supply source (Fryer 1984: 20). It was not uncommon in Britain to see slaves wearing metal collars around their necks, inscribed with the names of their owners. In those early centuries, people turned a blind eye to palpable evidence of slavery in aristocratic and slave-owners' homes.

The strength of the "West India" lobby in parliament made the cause of abolition an uphill battle. With few exceptions before 1750, most of the writing about black communities in Britain appeared in such official documents as ships' records, and often in advertizements for runaway people. That situation, however, dramatically changed after Lord Mansfield's decision in the celebrated James Somerset case in 1772, when James Somerset who had petitioned for freedom in Britain was granted such, provided he did not try to return. The judge, that is, ruled that slaves, even if they were slaves in the country from which they came could not be transported out of Britain involuntarily, and this was widely interpreted to mean that slavery was illegal. This decision indirectly extended a positive effect to the black communities, who numbered about 15,000 people.

By 1772, several African slaves and former slaves were beginning to write about their situation, sometimes with the assistance of amanuenses. White abolitionists encouraged this "literature of repudiation," in O. R. Dathorne's phrase (1981), and public affirmation of African literacy. Ukawsaw Gronniosaw (James Albert) was one of the first Africans to have his life story published. He dictated his experiences to a woman who lived in Leominster, entitling the text *A Narrative of the Remarkable Particulars in the Life of James Albert Ukawsaw Gronniosaw, an African Prince, Related by Himself.* Born between 1710 and 1714, he begins by chronicling his life as a child living in Bornu in the northeast of today's Nigeria, and his kidnapping and enslavement as a teenager. He records living in America with a Dutch pastor who freed him after eighteen years when Gronniosaw converted to Christianity. Debt-ridden, he worked as a cook and a privateer to support himself, and having traveled to England, he married. In dire financial straits, he and his family subsequently moved to Kidderminster, where he related his narrative to earn money to support his family. The original publication of his narrative probably appeared around 1774. Nothing is known of the later life of Gronniosaw or his family (Fryer 1984: 90–91).

In contrast to Gronniosaw, who was born in Africa and sold in the American colonies before reaching England, Ignatius Sancho was born aboard a slave ship in 1729 and reached England at the age of two, his parents having died while he was an infant. After the second Duke of Montagu, who had become something of a mentor to Sancho, died in 1749, Sancho assumed a position in the Duchess's household. Later he married and had six children. Many of his *Letters* (1782) deal with family and business life, and are filled with striking contemporary insights. For example, Sancho speaks vividly about the Gordon Riots and eloquently to Laurence Sterne about the plight of slaves. Nonetheless, he always remembers his African heritage and ethnicity: he uses "Africanus" as his pen name in letters to the press, and consistently acknowledges his "brother Negro" and "my poor black brethren." He referred to himself as "poor blacky grocer." Multitalented, Sancho also composed music, wrote poetry, two stage plays, and a theoretical tract on music (since lost). After a "long illness aggravated by gout and corpulence," he died in 1780.

In 1787, the year that the Anti-Slavery Society was founded, Quobna Ottobah Cugoano's *Thoughts and Sentiments on the Evil and Wicked Traffic of the Slavery* was published in London. Cugoano was born in 1757 on the coast of present-day Ghana and in 1770 was kidnapped, taken to Grenada as a slave, then freed by his owner in England. A community leader, Cugoano worked closely with Granville Sharpe, a white abolitionist involved in the James Somerset case, and Olaudah Equiano, who was one of the most celebrated African writers in eighteenth-century England. A truncated version of Cugoano's *Thoughts and Sentiments* was published in 1791, after which scant information about him exists. Purposefully polemical, Cugoano contributed powerfully to the antislavery debate and the pseudoscientific question about the so-called superiority of white people. Such claims were also brought out by the outspoken brilliance of his friend, Olaudah Equiano.

A member of the Ibo nation, Equiano was born in the interior of Nigeria. When he was eleven, he and his sister were captured by slave traders and sold to British slavers bound for North America. A ship's steward, he served under several Mediterranean commanders and Caribbean traders. Having been brought to Virginia where he was sold to Michael Henry Pascal, an officer in the Royal Navy, he was renamed Gustavas Vassa, after a sixteenth-century Swedish monarch.

After many maritime adventures and a harsh human betrayal, the determined, highly literate Equiano purchased his freedom in 1766 and continued traveling throughout the Caribbean and the American colonies. Fearing harassment and recapture, he relocated to England where he worked for Dr. Charles Irving, a scientist experimenting with salt-water purification. Equiano then traveled to Italy, Turkey, Portugal, and the Arctic, and studied opera and architecture. First published in two volumes, his autobiography, entitled *The Interesting Narrative of the Life of Olaudah Equiano, or Gustavas Vassa, the African, Written by Himself* (1789), is hailed as one of the finest slave narratives. He begins with his experiences aboard the slave ship, chronicles his mastery of navigation, his naval service in Canada during General Wolfe's campaign, and his labor in the Mediterranean as a gunpowder carrier, then his learning to be a barber while continuing as a sailor to many countries. With his diverse and unsurpassed talents, he emerged as one of the first community leaders and intellectuals of the age. Equiano's two-volume autobiography has remained a classic of the slave narrative genre, as well as in the global genre of autobiography.

African and African diasporic writers in the Americas / United States

Slavery increased in the Americas during the 1600s when thousands of African slaves were forced to that continent and sold. By the 1780s, many northern states had enacted legislation to abolish slavery, and the ordinance of 1787 prohibited slavery in the Northwest Territory. Not only did the Declaration of Independence question the validity of slavery, but for many northerners, the practice was unprofitable. Discontent was rife. In 1800, for instance, in the Gabriel Plot, Gabriel Prosser led over a thousand slaves and marched on Richmond, Virginia. Thirty-five people were executed for participating in the plot. In 1822, a free black man named Denmark Vesey organized an insurrection of slave artisans in urban areas, but someone betrayed the plotters: nearly 150 slaves were arrested and forty executed. During the 1830s, northern antislavery societies worked for the emancipation of slaves. Understandably, the antislavery movement included many freed slaves. In the south, by contrast, slavery increased as the population grew from 650,000 in 1790 to 3.2 million in 1850 (Roberts 1993: 184–85). Just as much to the point, slavery increasingly divided the North and South, and by February 1861, Alabama, Florida, Georgia, Louisiana, Mississippi, Texas, and South Carolina had withdrawn from the Union and formed the Confederate States of America.

Briton Hammon probably wrote the first published work by a black author in North America. Entitled (in its shortened version) *A Narrative of the Uncommon Sufferings, and Surprizing Deliverance of Briton Hammon, a Negro Man – Servant to General Winslow, of Marshfield, in New-England: who Returned to Boston, after having been absent almost Thirteen Years* (1760), it tells of his many unusual adventures. At the end, Hammon expresses his delight in finding his old master and "the Truth was joyfully verify'd by a happy Sight of his Person which so overcome me, that I could not speak to him for some Time" (Starling 1988: 52–53). He preferred a long incarceration in a dungeon in Havana rather than board a pirate ship. By 1760, in Marion Starling's words, "life had sobered him up a trifle" (1988: 53).

In 1773, *Poems on Various Subjects, Religious and Moral* by Phillis Wheatley was published to favorable reviews. Born around 1753 in West Africa, possibly in the country now known as Senegal, the young woman was captured, brought to the Boston market as a slave, and sold in 1761 to John Wheatley. An early poem suggests a shrewd awareness of her situation: "On Being Brought from Africa to America." The 1770s brought significant changes to Wheatley's life: in 1774, she was freed three months before Susanna Wheatley's death on 3 March, and on 1 April 1778, she married a free black man named John Peters. On 5 December 1784, she died in Boston while working as a cleaning maid at a boarding-house, a sure sign, presumably, of contemporary attitudes.

Perhaps the first explicit antislavery poet, George Moses Horton was a slave who exemplified the basic contradictions endured by a black poet in the Americas at that time. Born in North Carolina, he published his first volume of African American poetry, *The Hope of Liberty, Poems: George Moses Horton, Myself* in 1829. Three of the poems addressing slavery included: "On Hearing of the Intentions of a Gentleman to Purchase the Poet's Freedom,"

> Some philanthropic souls from afar,
> With pity strove to break the slavish bar.
> (Gates and McKay 1996: 193)

As more slaves escaped from the South, advertizements and posters calling for their return were common sights. Fugitive slaves, known or unknown, became a regular northern presence. Attempts to rescue fugitive slaves accelerated in the 1840s and 1850s. In this volatile atmosphere, Harriet A. Jacobs, Jarena Lee, Harriet Wilson, Nancy Prince, and Mary Ann Shadd Cary penned their bold, controversial narratives. Most often they used the first person to proclaim their experiences – though sometimes in the third – but they never surrendered their need to mask the distance, rearrange chronologies, and alter characters – all in the service of individual and collective representation and preservation. They apprehended only too well their dangerous political milieu.

Harriet A. Jacobs's *Incidents in the Life of a Slave Girl, Written By Herself* (1861) marks in an unprecedented fashion a departure for slave narratives, frequently told from a female perspective. As never before, her narrative paved the way for gendered reconstructions of a slave's experience. She speaks about the persistence of sexual harassment and the vulnerability of female slaves and white-male manipulation of motherhood in an unprecedentedly open fashion. For many years, Jacobs had concealed herself in her grandmother's attic. Her owner, Dr. Flint, continued to stalk her for many years, even after she traveled north to join her children (Edwards and Dabydeen 1991: 176). The complex life of Harriet Jacobs – "the black fugitive slave author and creator of Linda Brent," in Jean Fagan Yellin's compact phrase – necessitated a pseudonym, her persona integral to her survival (Yellin 1987: xxxi). Under a *nom de plume*, she could attack with some impunity perpetrators of racist violence and sexual abuse.

No less heroic in a different context was William Wells Brown, born into the household of Dr. John Young, a farmer and physician in 1814 in Lexington, Kentucky, the son of a slave mother and a slaveholder. In 1827, after Young bought a farm in St. Louis and moved there, Brown worked at a variety of jobs, until escaping to Ohio in 1834, where some Quakers assisted him. The exchange between William Wells Brown and the Quakers displays Brown's devotion to his master who named him William, as well as his self-determination: "I am unwilling to lose my name of William. As it was taken from me once against my will . . . " Then "said [the Quaker, a Mr. Wells Brown], 'I shall name thee William Wells Brown'" (Starling 142).

Two years later, in Buffalo, his home doubled as an important station on the Underground Railroad. In 1843, after Frederick Douglass came to Buffalo to hold antislavery meetings, Brown lectured for the Western New York Anti-Slavery Society.

Brown's memoirs, *The Narrative of William Wells Brown, a Fugitive Slave, Written by Himself*, were published in Boston in 1847, followed the next year by his song-poems, *The Anti-Slavery Harp.* He then went on to lecture for the Massachusetts and the American Anti-Slavery Societies. In 1849, Victor Hugo invited him to the Paris Peace Congress. Brown was obliged to stay in England for five years after the passing of the Fugitive Slave Law in 1850. There he published the earliest version of his novel, *Clotel; or, The President's Daughter: A Narrative of Slave Life in the United States* (1853). *Clotel* is generally considered the first novel written by an African American author, although Harriet Wilson's *Our Nig*, printed in 1859, is the first such work originally published in the United States. In line with other antislavery writers, Brown foregrounds the hypocrisy of Christianity and the complicity of all levels of society in that religion. During the Civil War, Brown recruited members of the Massachusetts 54th and 55th regiments, legendary black troops led by white officers. Intent on his quest for social justice, Brown fought to gain equal pay and improved medical services for the black troops.

Also in 1855, a fugitive slave wrote a novel that would change the definition of the genre of slave narrative and permanently alter an individual's perception of slavery. Written by Hannah Crafts and recently discovered by Professor

Henry Louis Gates, Jr., *A Bondwoman's Narrative* suggests a need to reassess US culture on the subject of slavery and abolition. Theories of racial difference collapse in the presence of the narrator's unmediated, private voice. Crafts draws from the sentimental and gothic conventions, as well as antislavery polemic; she destabilizes the definition of the slave narrative as presently constituted. Traditionally, slave narratives provide a reader with basic biographical details (such as birth and death), while establishing a claim to an artistic identity as the writer philosophizes about the human condition. That *A Bondwoman's Narrative* remained unpublished is telling. What were the financial difficulties? What was the level of white support? How was Crafts prepared to deal with inevitably mixed consequences?

Along with Jacobs, Brown, and Douglass, David Walker pressed even further. Born to a slave father – whose birthplace is currently unknown – and a free mother on 28 September 1785, in Wilmington, North Carolina, he taught himself to read and write and traveled through the South to observe the hideous condition of slaves. After the founding of the abolition movement, he wrote for *Freedom's Journal*, an antislavery weekly. He concealed his radical pamphlet, *Appeal . . . to the Coloured Citizens of the World . . . (1829)*, in the pockets of clothes that sailors bought in his used-clothing store before re-embarking. In this way Walker hoped his philosophically pioneering pamphlet would reach southern ports and win distribution. Walker's exceptional call for armed resistance threatened white security so intensely that many people urged him to flee to Canada. He refused. His murdered body was found near his shop, inducing numerous reprintings of the *Appeal*.

The most celebrated African American of the nineteenth century was Frederick Douglass who marched, philosophically speaking, alongside Jacobs, Brown, Walker, and many others, known and unknown. Douglass's initial act of resistance against slaveowner Edward Covey enacted Walker's call for armed resistance. As Douglass himself puts it: The "turning-point in my career as a slave" came when a "Negro-breaker" tried to assault him. Douglass energetically retaliated and was not beaten again. "I now resolved," he wrote later, "that, however long I might remain a slave in form, the day had passed forever when I could be a slave in fact. I did not hesitate to let it be known of me, that the white man who expected to succeed in whipping me, must also succeed in killing me." Returning to Baltimore, he learned the trade of a caulker and hired himself out, thereby coming into contact with the free-black community in the city. He disguised himself as a sailor to escape slavery.

In 1841, Douglass gave his first antislavery lecture for William Lloyd Garrison's Massachusetts Anti-Slavery Society and published his *Narrative of the Life of Frederick Douglass* four years later to rebut current ideas about slaves' literacy. An overnight success, the narrative chronicled his personal life while it concurrently delivered a mordant critique of a slave-owning society. Ubiquitous racial bigotry, he asserted, meant even free people were only "half-free."

When his whereabouts as a fugitive slave were revealed, he undertook a two-year lecture tour of Great Britain, arranged by British antislavery friends. In 1846, these friends negotiated the legal purchase of his freedom from his master, Thomas Auld, in Maryland. Returning as a free man to the United States in 1847, Douglass founded his own newspaper, the *North Star*, in Rochester, New York. From 1847 to 1863, Douglass edited the most successful black-abolitionist journal, alternately under the logos, *Frederick Douglass' Paper* and the *Douglass Monthly*. In 1855, *My Bondage and My Freedom* appeared.

Like his friend, William Wells Brown, Douglass harbored fugitive slaves and supported the conspiracy that led to John Brown's heroic raid in 1859 at Harper's Ferry. Later Douglass came to agree with Walker and Brown that armed struggle was necessary to win abolition. He served in various political positions, and during Reconstruction, Douglass argued that freedmen should have access to land and private property. From 1889 to 1891 he served as minister to Haiti. He died in Washington on 20 February 1895.

Born in 1825 to free parents, Frances Ellen Watkins Harper published *Poems on Miscellaneous Subjects* in 1854, the same year she joined the Underground Railroad. During that summer, she spoke on "The Elevation and Education of Our People," after which she conducted a lecture campaign for the Anti-Slavery Society of Maine.

During Reconstruction, Harper lectured in southern states, urging people to work together, regardless of race. Although Harper fought for black women's suffrage, she believed that black men's need for suffrage was a more important goal. In addition to lecturing, in 1892 she published *Iola Leroy*, one of the earliest novels by a black woman. She died in 1911 of heart failure.

African and African-diasporic writers in the Caribbean region

Fewer books on slavery by slaves or ex-slaves were published in the Caribbean region than in Britain and in the Americas/United States. Those that have surfaced to date are the narratives of Mary Prince, Ashton Warner, Asa-Asa, Juan Francisco Manzano, and Esteban Montego. Manzano's account is, in general, an exceptional one, regardless of geography, having been the only one written by a slave during slavery in this region.

Several factors account for this scarcity of slave narratives, most of all a society rigidly divided into workers and landowners that discouraged even white writers from discussing slavery (Honychurch 1995: 102). Fear of punishment also played its part. Almost two million Africans lived in the Caribbean Islands out of a total population of nearly three million in 1825; about 400,000 "mulattos and mixed" were counted within the "non-negro" population. Altogether, the population count was 2,361,000 African Caribbeans and "mulattos" and a white population of 482,000 (Coulthard 1962: 9). Although Britain abolished the slave trade in 1807/08 and declared emancipation in 1834, emancipation in the British Caribbean did not effectively begin until 1839, when so-called apprenticeship ended (Claypole and Robottom 1989: 1).

According to Michael Craton 1982: 335–39, the chronology of resistance from 1638 to 1857 in the British West Indies was intense and continuous, ranging from a revolt in Providence in 1638; in Bermuda in the seventeenth and eighteenth centuries; in St. Lucia, Grenada and St. Vincent in the eighteenth century; in Barbados, Jamaica, Antigua, and St. Kitt's, slave revolts were frequent through the seventeenth, eighteenth, and nineteenth centuries. They occurred also in Tortola, Guyana, Bahamas, Belize, Tobago, and Dominica in the eighteenth and nineteenth centuries and in Trinidad in the nineteenth century. In 1737 in Antigua, a captured slave describes an Alcan priest named Quancou after Tacky's rebellions:

> I saw this Obey Man at Secundi's House after I waked at Midnight, I found him and Hunts Cuffy there. Secundi gave him a Chequeen, a bottle of Rum and a Dominique Cock and Quawcoo put Obey made of Sheeps Skin upon the ground, upon and about the bottle of Rum, and the Chequeen upon the bottle. Then he took the Cock, cut open his Mouth, and one of his Toes, and so poured the Cocks blood Over all the Obey, and then Rub'd Secundi's forehead with the Cocks bloody Toe, then took the Bottle and poured Some Rum upon the Obey, Drank a Dram, and gave it to Secundi and made Secundi Sware not to Discover his name to any body. Secundi then Asked him when he must begin to Rise. Quawcoo took a String Ty'd knots in it, and told him not to be in a hurry, for that he would give him Notice when to Rise and all Should go well, and that as he ty'd those knots so the Bacararas [whites] should become Arrant fools and have their Mouths Stoped, and their hands tyed that they should not Discover the Negro's Designs. (Craton 1982: 123, 190)

Victor Hugues's proclamation was in St. Vincent in 1786:

> Behold your chains forged and imposed by the hands of the tyrannical English! Blush, and break those ensigns of disgrace, spurn them with becoming indignation, rise in a moment, and while we assist you from the motives of the

> philanthropy and zeal for the happiness of all nations, fall on these despots, extirpate them from your country, and restore yourselves, your wives and children to the inheritance of your fathers, whose spirits from the grave will lead on your ranks, inspire you with fury, and help you to be avenged.
>
> (Craton 1982: 190)

Over fifteen islands fought for freedom from slavery for well over 300 years. The slaves in Jamaica, often called Maroons, held a celebrated, though contended, reputation as very fierce fighters (Campbell 1990: 11ff.).

One of the earlier Caribbean writers was Francis Williams, born to free parents about 1700 and "adopted" by the Duke of Montagu as a protégé. Williams studied the classics at an English grammar school and mathematics at Cambridge (Dance 1986: 493ff.). Between 1738 and 1748, he returned to Jamaica, and opened a school in Spanish town where he taught classics and mathematics to local white children. Williams welcomed each new governor with a dedicatory Latin ode, one of which is repeated in *History of Jamaica* by the commentator Edward Long. The poem for which Williams is most celebrated is a Latin ode to George Haldane, governor of Jamaica in 1759. In the words of critic Arthur Drayton, Williams transformed the formulaic prose of odes and subtly exposed the atrocities of slave experience. In Williams's own words:

> Under your leadership all that had been perpetrated ill-advisedly is now vain, never to recur in your presence. So all the people, not to mention the lesser throng, may see that you have relieved them of the yoke that would have clung to their necks and the evils which this innocent isle had formerly suffered with grievous torment. (Dance 1986: 495)

Thus Williams argues for human dignity and freedom, signaling a consciousness well-attuned to contemporary realities, despite the traditional form.

Francis Williams's circumlocuitous references to the horror of slavery could not readily be used by Ladies' Anti-Slavery Societies who pamphleteered door-to-door. Not so with Mary Prince's polemic, entitled *The History of Mary Prince: A West Indian Slave, Related by Herself*, published in London in 1831, sponsored by the Anti-Slavery Society. It went into three editions that year, and was probably the first published slave narrative by a woman in English.

Born around 1788 in Bermuda (the date of her death is unknown), Mary Prince was the daughter of slaves and had at least ten siblings. At an ultimate degree of vulnerability, she stood up for herself after running away from her owner, then returning to her father, her heroic actions comparable to Frederick Douglass's in the same general period. She goes on to record vile experiences on Turks Island where she stood all day long in salt marshes, infested with boils and in great pain. When she went to Antigua with new owners, she witnessed the murder of a pregnant, exhausted co-worker. In London, she "walked" from these very owners and made her way to the Anti-Slavery headquarters. Like Gronniosaw, Mary Prince dictated her experiences to an amanuensis, who probably edited out anything too "steamy" for the Christian readership. Her tale is one of suffering endured, but ultimately of the human spirit triumphant (Ferguson 1997: 48–53).

While Mary Prince dictated her experiences in London, Ashton Warner was penning his own experiences as a slave in St. Vincent. Unfortunately, he died while the volume was in progress, the proceeds going to his aged mother, as he requested. Warner describes the condition of slaves graphically, including the fact that his pregnant wife "was flogged for not coming out early enough to work, and afterward, when far advanced in pregnancy, she was put into the stocks by the manager because she said she was unable to go to the field" (Warner 1831: 45). He ends by echoing Mary Prince's contention: that they write to help the plight of others, not just themselves. In a sense, they speak with a community voice.

In Cuba, *Autobiografia* by Juan Francisco Manzano struck some slightly different notes, due to his unusual circumstances. Born in 1797 and living with his parents who were servants to aristocrats, he escaped to Havana. While serving as a page, he taught himself to read and write and was freed by a patron, Domingo del Monte, who admired Manzano's famous sonnet, *Mis treinta anos* (My Thirty Years) and collected the money to emancipate the slave. Del Monte also encouraged Manzano to write his *Autobiografia*, which was first published in 1840 in an English translation by Richard Madden.

Proffering an invaluable sociohistorical document, Manzano writes about his life as a slave, narrating his experiences as a child and young man who fears a cruel mistress. He stresses insecurity, dependence on arbitrary matters, and the futility of obtaining justice. One graphic detail concerns the accusation that he stole a chicken and then was tormented and punished into confessing to a crime he did not commit. Even when he proves his innocence, he cannot appeal.

In 1841, Manzano wrote a five-act tragedy titled *Zafira* and many articles for literary magazines. Four years later, colonial authorities imprisoned him for participating in a conspiracy, but he was released in 1845 when he was found innocent. From then until his death, Manzano published very little. The reasons for his long silence remain unknown. In 1868, Manzano's autobiography appeared in a book entitled *Coloured Poets*, which included biographies of four poets of color, all born slaves. The book's profits were used to manumit Jose de Carmen Diaz, a slave poet, again under the auspices of del Monte.

Esteban Montejo's *Biografia de un Cimarron*, edited by Miguel Barnet, and entitled in English *Autobiography of a Runaway Slave* (1968), belongs in the category of the dictated slave narratives to which Mary Prince's and Gronniosaw's texts belong. Barnet is the amanuensis to Esteban Montejo, a centenarian-plus, who assumed many roles in his lifetime: first a slave, then a maroon, after that a resistance fighter, and finally a waged worker. Montejo speaks of his early moments of awareness:

> I felt within me the overwhelming spirit of the maroon from which I could not escape . . . I saw many horrors of punishment under slavery. That's why I didn't like that life. In the boiler house there were the stocks, which were the most cruel. There were stocks for lying down and for standing. They had wide slabs with holes through which they made the slave place his feet, hands, and head. They had them [the slaves] immobilized thus two or three months for some insignificant mistake. (Montejo 1968: 9)

Montejo reflects on his bold and resourceful life, focusing on his escape from slavery and years of solitary hill-dwelling as a maroon. As with Equiano, Mary Prince, Frederick Douglass, Harriet Jacobs, and countless others, rebellion is the keystone of Montejo's life.

Conclusion

The literature of slavery is vast and varied, its heterogeneity springing from a host of factors, among the most important of which were people coming from and being transported to different countries and continents; constantly changing landscapes; rich, diverse ancient cultures, where often kinship- and community-based concepts are in conflict with newly emerging cultures; and philosophically speaking people with freedom on their minds doing battle with their adversaries, owners, entrepreneurs, personnel of every description bent on human enslavement. Changing times, changing historical circumstances, changing attitudes, also played a large role.

So the literature of slavery, as a genre, is multifaceted and never stationary. Sometimes highly charged emotions explode on the page; at other times, people talk mutedly about the need for slaves to arm themselves. As Anthony Appiah puts it, "[t]he slave narrative is a polemical genre; it makes no bones about it" (1990: x). The literature of slavery is also, of course, housed in other genres: among them, the sentimental novel and other "fictions," a Latinate ode, a gothic tale, a sentimental or historical poem, especially autobiography, biography, travelers' tales, and as-told-to memoirs. Among its common characteristics would be the refusal of silence, creative reconstruction, illiteracy, white protectionism, tactical omissions or expansions, docility and seeming docility, and some related stereotypes. Class and gender also play their roles because slavery cuts across these boundaries. Claiming counts too, especially the claiming of personhood, authorship, authenticity, intuition, inspiration, awareness, stoicism, witnessing, a sense of dignity and delicacy as well as bereavement, horror, incredulity, and anger.

Olaudah Equiano and Quobna Ottobah Cugoano said it well when they withdrew support from the Sierra Leone Company's scheme to repatriate Africans (who had been captured originally from many different African countries) to Sierra Leone. They heard the double-voiced narrative of that repatriation plan: "Let's help the 'black poor,' and let's send them on their way as well."

In the end, the literature of slavery and abolition displays the nature and construction of colonialism, how its exploitative ontology shaped texts and people, countries and continents. It remains relevant to this day because of its close connection to the literature of Civil Rights, to prison writings, to discourse about alleged contemporary slavery and to anti-apartheid writings. The condition of human freedom and of those who wage the struggle for that freedom on behalf of others is, as former President Nelson Mandela reminds us, a birthright that cannot be sold (1994: 523).

Selected bibliography

Primary works

Andrews, William L., ed. 1992. *The African-American Novel in the Age of Reaction: Three Classics.* New York: Mentor.

Appiah, Anthony, ed. 1990. *Early African-American Classics*. New York: Bantam.

Asa-Asa, Louis. 1997. "Narrative of Louis Asa-Asa, a Captured African." In *The History of Mary Prince: A West Indian Slave, Related by Herself.* Ed. Moira Ferguson. Ann Arbor: University of Michigan Press: 132–35.

Brown, William Wells. 1847. *Narrative of William Wells Brown, a Fugitive Slave, Written by Himself.* Boston: Anti-Slavery Office.

[1853] 1969. *Clotel; or, The President's Daughter: A Narrative of Slave Life in the United States.* New York: Citadel.

Craft, William, and Ellen Craft. 1860. *Running a Thousand Miles for Freedom; or, The Escape Of William and Ellen Craft from Slavery*. London: W. Tweedie.

Crafts, Hannah. [1855] 2002. *A Bondwoman's Narrative*. Ed. Henry Louis Gates, Jr. New York: Warner.

Cugoano, Quobna Ottobah. [1787] 1999. *Thoughts and Sentiments on the Evil and Wicked Traffic of Slavery*. Ed. Vincent Carretta. London: Penguin.

Davis, Arthur P., J. Saunders Redding, and Ann Joyce, eds. 1971. *Selected African American Writing from 1760 to 1910*. New York: Bantam.

Douglass, Frederick. [1845] 1987. "Narrative of the Life of Frederick Douglass, an American Slave, Written by Himself." In *The Classic Slave Narratives*. Ed.Henry Louis Gates, Jr. New York: Mentor: 243–331.

1855. *My Bondage and My Freedom*. New York, Auburn: Miller, Orton, and Mulligan.

Equiano, Olaudah. [1789] 1967. *Equiano's Travels*. Ed. Paul Edwards. London: Heinemann.

[1789] [1814] 1987. "The Interesting Narrative of the Life of Olaudah Equiano, or Gustavus Vassa, the African, Written by Himself." Also in *The Classic Slave Narratives*. Ed. Henry Louis Gates, Jr. 1814. New York: Mentor.

Garrison, W. P. and F. J. 1885. *William Lloyd Garrison, 1805–1879. The Story of His Life*. 4 vols. New York: Houghton Mifflin.

Gronniosaw, James Albert Ukawsaw. n.d. *A Narrative of the Most Remarkable particulars in The Life of James Albert Ukawsaw Gronniosaw, An African Prince, as Related by Himself.* 2nd edn. n.p.

Hammon, Briton. 1760. *A Narrative of the Uncommon Sufferings, and Surprizing [sic] Deliverance of Briton Hammon, a Negro Man*. Boston: Printed and sold by Green and Russell, in Queen-Street.

Hammon, Jupiter. 1787. *An Address to the Negroes in the State of New York. By Jupiter Hammon, Servant of John Lloyd, jun. Esq. of the Manor of Queen's Village, Long Island*. New York: Printed by Carroll and Patterson.

Harper, Frances Ellen Watkins. [1854] 1988. *Complete Poems of Frances E. W. Harper*. New York: Oxford University Press.

[1893] 1988. *Iola Leroy; or Shadows Uplifted*. New York: Oxford University Press.

Horton, George Moses. 1829. *The Hope of Liberty, Poems: George Moses Horton, Myself.* Raleigh, NC: J. Gales and Son.

Hugues, Victor. [1798] 1977. *Rapport Fait aux Citoyens Victor Hugues et Lebas, Agens Particuliers du Directoire Exécutif aux Isles du Vent*. Basse-Terre: Société d'histoire de la Guadeloupe.

Jacobs, Harriet A. [1861] 1987. *Incidents in the Life of a Slave Girl, Written by Herself.* Ed. L. Maria Child. Boston, 1861; ed. and with introduction by Jean Fagan Yellin. Cambridge, MA: Harvard University Press.

Mandela, Nelson. 1994. *The Autobiography of Nelson Mandela*. Boston: Little.

Manzano, Juan Francisco. [1840] 1996. *The Autobiography of a Slave*. Detroit: Wayne State University Press.

1981. *The Life and Poems of a Cuban Slave: Juan Francisco Manzano, 1797–1854*. Ed. Edward J. Mullen. Trans. Richard Robert Madden. Hamden, CT: Archon.

Montejo, Esteban. 1968. *The Autobiography of a Runaway Slave*. Ed. Miguel Barnet. Trans. Jocasta Innes. New York: Pantheon.

Prince, Mary. [1831] 1987. *The History of Mary Prince: A West Indian Slave, Related by Herself.* Ed. Moira Ferguson. Ann Arbor: University of Michigan Press.

Proper, David R., and Lucy Terry Prince. 1995. "Bars Fight." In *Lucy Terry Prince, Poet of Deerfield*. n.p.

Roper, Moses. 1837. *A Narrative of Moses Roper's Adventures and Escape from American Slavery*; with a preface by Reverend T. Price. London: Darton, Harvey, and Darton.

Sancho, Ignatius. [1782] 1998. *Letters of the Late Ignatius Sancho, an African*. Ed. Vincent Carretta. London: Penguin.

Sancho, Ignatius and Joseph Jekyll, Esq., M. P. [1803] 1968. *Letters of the Late Ignatius Sancho: An African to Which are Prefixed Memoirs of his Life*. 5th edn. London: Dawsons.

Smith, Venture. 1798. *A Narrative of the Life and Adventures of Venture, a Native of Africa; but Resident about Sixty Years in the United States of America. Related by Himself.* New London: Printed by C. Holt.

Stewart, Maria W. 1987. *Maria W. Stewart, America's First Black Woman Political Writer*. Ed. Marilyn Richardson. Bloomington: Indiana University Press.

Truth, Sojourner. [1850] 1973. *Narrative of Sojourner Truth, a Northern Slave, Emancipated from Bodily Servitude by the State of New York in 1828*. Boston: Printed for the Author.

Walker, David. [1829] 1993. *Walker's Appeal, in Four Articles. Together with a Preamble to the Coloured Citizens of the World, but in particular, and very expressly, to those of the United States of America, Third and Last Edition Revised and Published by David Walker.* Introduction by James Turner. Baltimore: Black Classic Press.

Warner, Ashton. 1831. *Negro Slavery Described by a Negro Being the Narrative of Ashton Warner, a Native of St. Vincent's: With an Appendix Containing the Testimony of Four Christian Ministers Recently Returned From the Colonies on the System of Slavery as it Now Exists.* London, S. Maunder.

Wheatley, Phillis. [1786] 1976. *Poems on Various Subjects, Religious and Moral*. New York AMS Press.

Wilson, Harriet E. [1859] 1983. *Our Nig: or, Sketches From the Life of a Free Black, in a Two-Story White House, North: Showing That Slavery's Shadows Fall Even There*. Ed. Henry Louis Gates, Jr. New York: Vintage.

Secondary works

Aptheker, Herbert. 1943. *American Negro Slave Revolts*. New York: Columbia University Press.

Baker, Houston A., and Patricia Redmond, eds. 1989. *Afro-American Literary Study in the 1990s*. Chicago: University of Chicago Press.

Ball, Charles. [1837] 1969. *Slavery in the United States: A Narrative of the Life and Adventures of Charles Ball*. New York: Negro Universities Press.

Bayliss, John F., ed. 1970. *Black Slave Narratives*. New York: Macmillan.

Boehmer, Ellen. 1995. *Colonial and Postcolonial Literature: Migrant Metaphors*. Oxford: Oxford University Press.

Bontemps, Arna Wendell, ed. 1969. "The Slave Narrative: An American Genre." In *Great Slave Narratives*. Boston: Beacon.

Campbell, Mavis C. 1990. *Maroons of Jamaica 1655–1796: A History of Resistance, Collaboration and Betrayal*. Trenton, NJ: Africa World Press.

Chapman, Abraham, ed. 1971. *Steal Away: Stories of the Runaway Slaves*. New York: Praeger.

Claypole, William and John Robottom. 1989. *Caribbean Story*. 2nd edn. Vol. II. Essex: Longman. 2 vols.

Coulthard, George Robert. 1962. *Race and Colour in Caribbean Literature*. London: Oxford University Press.

Coulthard, George Robert, ed. 1966. *Caribbean Literature: An Anthology*. London: University of London Press.

Craton, Michael. 1974. *Sinews of Empire: A Short History of British Slavery*. Garden City: Anchor.

1982. *Testing the Chains: Resistance to Slavery in the British West Indies.* Ithaca: Cornell University Press.

Craton, Michael and James Walvin. 1970. *A Jamaican Plantation: The History of Worthy Park 1670–1970*. Toronto: University of Toronto.

Craton, Michael, James Walvin, and David Wright. 1976. *Slavery Abolition and Emancipation: Black Slaves and the British Empire*. London: Longman.

Dabydeen, David, ed. 1988. *A Handbook for Teaching Caribbean Literature*. London: Heinemann.

Dance, Daryl Cumber, ed. 1986. *Fifty Caribbean Writers: A Bio-Bibliographical Critical Sourcebook*. New York: Greenwood.

Dathorne, O. R. 1981. *Dark Ancestor: The Literature of the Black Man in the Caribbean*. Baton Rouge: Louisiana State University Press.

Davis, Charles T., and Henry Louis Gates, Jr., eds. 1985. *The Slave's Narrative*. London: Oxford University Press.

Donnell, Alison, and Sarah Lawson Welsh, eds. 1996. *The Routledge Reader of Caribbean Literature.* London: Routledge.

Edwards, Paul, and David Dabydeen, eds.1991. *Black Writers in Britain 1760–1890*. Edinburgh: Edinburgh University Press.

The Encyclopedia Americana-International. 1997. Vol. 9. Danbury, CT: Grolier.

Ferguson, Moira, ed. 1987. *The History of Mary Prince: A West Indian Slave, Related by Herself.* Ann Arbor: University of Michigan Press.

1989. *Nine Black Women: An Anthology of Nineteenth-Century Writers From the United States, Canada, Bermuda, and the Caribbean*. New York: Routledge.

Fisher, Dexter, and Roberto S. Stepto, eds. 1979. *Afro-American Literature: The Reconstruction Of Instruction*. New York: MLA.

Foster, Frances Smith. 1979. *Witnessing Slavery: The Development of the Ante-Bellum Slave Narratives.* Westport, CT: Greenwood.

Fraser, Henry, Sean Carrington, Addington Forde, and John Gilmore, eds. 1990. *A–Z of Barbadian Heritage*. Kingston, Jamaica: Heinemann.

Fryer, Peter. 1984. *Staying Power: The History of Black People in Britain.* London: Pluto.

1993. *Black People in the British Empire: An Introduction*. London: Pluto.

Fyfe, Christopher. 1962. *A History of Sierra Leone*. London: Oxford University Press.

1991. *Our Children Free and Happy: Letters from Black Settlers in Africa in the 1790s*. Edinburgh: Edinburgh University Press.

Gates, Henry Louis, and Nellie Y. McKay, eds. 1996. *The Norton Anthology of African American Literature*. New York: Norton.

Gilroy, Paul. 1993. *The Black Atlantic: Modernity and Double Consciousness*. Cambridge, MA: Harvard University Press.

Honychurch, Lennox. 1995. *The Caribbean People: Book Two*. Walton-on-Thames: Thomas Nelson.

Jackson, Richard L. 1979. "Slave Poetry and Slave Narrative: Juan Francisco Manzano and his Black Autobiography." In *Black Writers in Latin America*. Albuquerque: University of New Mexico Press.

James, C. L. R. 1963. *The Black Jacobins: Toussaint L'Ouverture and the San Domingo Revolution.* New York: Vintage.

Jefferson, Paul, ed. 1991. *The Travels of William Wells Brown*. New York: Markus Wiener.

Katz, William Loren. 1968. "Southern Views on the 'Peculiar Institution.'" In *Five Slave Narratives: A Compendium*. New York: Arno.

Loggins, Vernon. 1931. *The Negro Author*. New York: Columbia University Press.

Lowenberg, Bert James, and Ruth Bogin, eds. 1996. *Black Women in Nineteenth-Century American Life: Their Words, Their Thoughts, Their Feelings*. University Park: Pennsylvania State University Press.

McKay, John P., Bennett D. Hill, and John Buckler. 1991. *A History of Western Society*. 4th edn. Boston: Houghton Mifflin.

Peterson, Carla L. 1995. *"Doers of the Word": African-American Women Speakers and Writers in the North (1830–1880)*. New York: Oxford University Press.

Potkay, Adam, and Sandra Burr, eds. 1995. *Black Atlantic Writers of the Eighteenth Century: Living the New Exodus in England and the Americas*. New York: St. Martin's Press.

Roberts, Paul M. 1993. *Review Text in United States History*. 2nd edn. New York: Amsco.

Smorkaloff, Pamela Maria, ed. 1994. *If I Could Write This in Fire: An Anthology of Literature From the Caribbean*. New York: New Press.

Starling, Marion Wilson. 1988. *The Slave Narrative: Its Place in American History*. 2nd edn. Washington, DC: Howard University Press.

Stewart, Maria W. 1987. *America's First Black Women Political Writers*. Ed. Marilyn Richardson. Bloomington: Indiana University Press.

Williams, Eric. 1944. *Capitalism and Slavery*. New York: Capricorn.

Williams, Lorna Valerie. 1994. *The Representations of Slavery in Cuban Fiction*. Columbia: University of Missouri Press.

Willis, Susan. 1985. "Crushed Geraniums: Juan Francisco Manzano and the Language of Slavery." In *The Slave's Narrative*. Ed. Charles T. Davis and Henry Louis Gates, Jr. London: Oxford University Press: 199–224.

Woodson, Carter G. 1915. *Education of the Negro Prior to 1861*. New York: Putnam.

Yarborough, Richard. 1989. "The First-Person in Afro-American Fiction." In *Afro-American Literary Studies in the 1990s*. Ed. Houston A. Baker and Patricia Redmond. Chicago: University of Chicago Press: 105–34.

Yellin, Jean Fagan, ed. 1987. Harriet A. Jacobs. [1861]. *Incidents in the Life of a Slave Girl, Written by Herself*. Ed. L. Maria Child. Cambridge, MA: Harvard University Press.

15

Discourses of empire

ROBERT ERIC LIVINGSTON

"The conquest of the earth," declares Charlie Marlow, principal narrator of Joseph Conrad's 1899 novella *Heart of Darkness*, "which mostly means the taking it away from those who have a different complexion or slightly flatter noses than ourselves, is not a pretty thing when you look into it too much." "What redeems it," he continues, "is the idea only." Thus does Marlow look back on his voyage up the great African river, at the moment when the King of the Belgians was tightening his grip over what he called the "Congo Free State," at the cost of close to six million African lives. The remark comes at the opening of Marlow's extended "yarn," both a bitter memory and the canny opening gambit of a master storyteller. Marlow's first words represent the closing remarks of a history whose moral climax turns on the evasion of last words. Though he has witnessed the horror that resounds in the life of that "remarkable man," Mr. Kurtz, Marlow's "inconclusive experiences" in Africa are – so we are given to understand – not amenable to final judgments.

Heart of Darkness is, for better and worse, both a chillingly clear-sighted account of imperial violence and a self-implicating instance of the moral blindness it denounces. Conrad's story raises the discourse of empire to an excruciating pitch of self-consciousness. Deliberately provocative and self-loathing, the text combines a frank acknowledgment of colonial brutality with an exquisite aversion to moral judgments; and it opts, ultimately, to align itself with what it sees as the corrupting lie of "civilized" morality. Both inviting and discounting its readers' desire to "look into it too much," *Heart of Darkness* continues to fascinate and scandalize: it forms an inescapable point of entry into the discourse of empire.

For however we may want to complicate the analysis of particulars, the brute fact remains that the "western" relation to Africa has been marked by structures of domination, an imbalance of power that comes to distort even the most benevolent of intentions. This disparity has produced a discourse (defined, roughly, as knowledge built on power) largely self-validating and, until quite recently, inconsiderate of indigenous views or claims; just as Marlow's address to "ourselves" establishes the racial contours of his audience of insiders, so a history of conquest hardens the third-person position ("them") into objecthood. For "Africanist" discourse, as Christopher Miller terms it, the land and its inhabitants are at best a backdrop for imperial schemes, at most an obstacle to ambitious projects, be they economic, political, or moral (Miller 1985). Elaborated with little regard for indigenous claims or knowledges, the archive of western discourse on Africa has sheltered no end of self-willed blindness and fantasy, often of the most bizarre and noxious sort; its stock of stereotypes, having percolated into the public imagination, tends to recirculate at critical moments. To sketch the historical dimensions of imperial discourse is not, therefore, to presume on its disappearance. Indeed, analysis of such knowledge needs to be archeological, in Michel Foucault's sense, insofar as the discourse consists of layers laid down at different historical moments, so that an utterance in the present may partake of several disparate "discursive formations" (Foucault 1972). To reconstruct this discourse is thus to trace the convolutions of an understanding at once made possible and disfigured by a history of domination.

One further comment on the relation between "discourse" and literature may be in order here. It would be needlessly reductive to suggest that literary texts merely reiterate the terms of domination. Neither, however, would it be plausible to claim that such texts simply transcend ideology, or that they invariably enact a critical distance from the instances of racial prejudice or colonialist arrogance they portray. Writers are no less susceptible than readers to the lures of simplification and crude caricature. Due to their inclusion in esthetic canons and their widespread dissemination, however, literary texts often have a staying power that results in a certain privilege for their treatment of ideological motifs. Literature regularly both perpetuates the pernicious and makes it available to colder and more critical scrutiny.

In short, literature and imperialism are complexly intertwined, and any particular case requires careful and specific analysis. Nevertheless, the concept of "imperial discourse," as a formation that includes literary texts alongside travel, natural history, anthropology, and philosophy, seems crucial for moving our understanding beyond the first-line defense of esthetic autonomy. What *Heart of Darkness* records by enacting is the powerful tendency to retreat behind the redemptive "idea," to evade judgment by not looking too closely; as Conrad shows, such a tendency has deep roots in the gendering of moral judgment and historical action, and in what psychoanalysis calls the process of idealization. The obverse of this tendency – the desire to have every text bear the cumulative weight of historical guilt – may be more excusable, but can hardly be more satisfactory. Critical judgment must keep both ethical and esthetic considerations in scrupulous play, especially where the demand for absolutes is strong. If a certain flattening of literary nuance is unavoidable, it seems a fair price for the gain in historical and cultural perspective.

What anthropologists politely term "culture contact" is rarely an egalitarian affair. Whatever the mundane occasions that draw people into proximity and exchange, such contacts are inevitably surrounded by a penumbra of differences – of language, behavior, belief, custom, and expectation. Where irregular contacts congeal into ongoing social relationships, differences are readily arranged into oppositions – between us and them, familiar and strange – that acquire explanatory force as marks of belonging. Such binary arrangements serve to stabilize patterns of contact, and, by making them intelligible, to perpetuate them. Where the relationship is asymmetrical, the simplicity of the binary scheme can legitimize hierarchy by giving it the unquestionable status of nature. Efforts to challenge or transform such naturalized oppositions must then fly in the face of "logic," reverse the terms of the opposition, or else displace one binary with another.

In the relation between Europe (a designation that, for our purposes, can provisionally be extended to the United States) and Africa, the pivotal contrast is, of course, between black and white. Nowhere is the simplifying effect of the binary more evident than in this reading of the vast range of skin pigmentation: there is, as biologists have regularly observed, as much variation within each side of this culturally charged contrast as between them. Yet this opposition retains a powerful foothold in ordinary language and the popular imagination, and consequently serves both to shape identities and to delineate terms of political struggle. Particularly given the predominance of visual media, what Frantz Fanon terms the "epidermal scheme" continues to be the master trope of the Euro-African relationship (Fanon 1967).

Historically, this basic structure has come to be encrusted with a host of futher binaries, each serving to reinforce the fundamental inequality. Thus, the black/white contrast has been given a moral valence, producing what Fanon again calls the "Manichean" view: the relationship is taken to embody a primordial struggle between good and evil, civilized and savage, or (now reversing the terms) between oppressor and oppressed, "the West and the Rest" (Fanon 1961). A similar set of oppositions finds its way into the cooler terms of Enlightenment rationality and its disciplinary offspring, the human sciences. Subject/object; modern/traditional; literate/oral: these pairs, while less overtly biased, still serve to essentialize differences, and thus to confirm historic asymmetries, often against the express intentions of those who deploy them. Because the binary inhabits a social relationship that cannot fully be dissolved into discourse, even critical and self-conscious treatments can rarely extricate themselves from the positioning force of the opposition.

Recast in narrative terms, the structure of binary oppositions results in what is perhaps the prevalent mode of the European experience in Africa, namely, the quest-romance. In this mode, the self stakes its identity or integrity on an encounter with a threatening or seductive Other, whose power must be overcome and incorporated for the self's destiny to be realized. Such a narrative puts otherwise static oppositions into play, generating suspense from categorical contrast. In its quasi-Hegelian casting as the dialectic of master and slave, the quest-romance has often been taken as the key to understanding the European-African relationship (if not the structure of history itself); the conflict between colonizer and colonized can readily be allegorized – by Fanon, among others – in these terms. Even where the characters are less clearly word-historical spirits, however, the quest-romance lends narrative drive and purpose to what might otherwise seem ambiguous or prosaic encounters.

To say that the quest-romance is a prevalent mode in Africanist discourse is to suggest that it is not limited to explicitly literary texts, but underlies nonfictional accounts as well. Indeed, the trope of "exploration" that endows much travel writing with an aura of glamour and heroism is a clear example of quest-romance at work. Nor does the mode exclude overtly "realistic" treatments: the negative or dialectical quest-romance forms a familiar subgenre, in which the quest-hero learns to recognize the spell cast by his own imagination and thus to master a disenchanted world through self-discipline. Separated from its cosmological or mythological roots, that is, the quest-romance finds both epistemic and ethical inflections. Thus, for one significant strand of imperial discourse, Africa represents the great unknown, a terrain to be systematically secured for reliable knowledge; its very existence poses a challenge to western conceptions of rationality, even a provocative limit to the power of Enlightenment. The rigors of climate, disease, or cultural resistance that historically frustrated European knowledge-claims, when not moralized as inveterate hostility, gave rise to the figure of Africa as "blank darkness," as Miller puts it, the very trope of a threatening ignorance, productive of bafflement or hysteria (Miller 1985).

In another variant, Africa appears as the quintessential land of adventure, a place for European manhood to display its prowess. This version acquires particular salience with the consolidation of modernity in Euro-America itself; Africa is seen to offer an outlet for actions and ambitions no longer credible in the "civilized" part of the world. Here the binary opposition transposes a spatial difference into a temporal one, producing what the anthropologist Johannes Fabian calls a "denial of coevalness" (Fabian 1983). As Marlow puts it, "Going up that river was like traveling back to the earliest beginnings of the world, when vegetation rioted on the earth and the big trees were kings" (Conrad 1899: 35). According to Fabian, this chronological trope underpins vast stretches of the anthropological enterprise, as observer and observed are taken to inhabit different cultural or evolutionary times, with the "primitive" assigned the task of revealing the prehistory of the more developed individual. Like other binaries, however, this opposition provides ample room for reversal and reinscription: thus, for instance, European modernism embraced "primitivism" as an alternative to the stifling conformity of bourgeois civilization, while mass-cultural fantasies (*Tarzan, King Kong*) exploited similar inversions for titillating ends.

Turning now to a more chronological overview, we may discern three major phases of the European engagement with Africa. These phases can be distinguished by the predominant forms of interaction between Europeans and Africans, the social relationship that gives imperial discourse its characteristic problematic. At the end of the fifteenth century, following a long period of intermittent contact, the first phase crystallized around the slave trade; discourse about Africans, their history, and their customs, was dominated by commercial imperatives or, later, the polemics between pro- and antislavery forces. During the middle years of the nineteenth century, with the abolition of the Atlantic slave trade, attention shifted to the possibility of appropriating the vast resources of the continent itself: this second phase brought the moment of colonialism proper, culminating in the "scramble for Africa" of the 1880s and accompanied by the growth of a "scientific" racism that justified domination in the name of a civilizational superiority. A third phase opens with the discrediting of imperialism in the wake of the First World War: faced, on the one side, by Wilsonian advocacy of national rights to self-determination and, on the other, by the example of revolutionary socialism, the imperial powers spent the 1920s and 30s fending off awareness of their own illegitimacy. After the Second World War, decolonization was officially on the world agenda. Protracted and uneven, the process of African liberation hardly spelled the end of imperial discourse; indeed, from one perspective, it may be preferable to speak of neocolonialism rather than postcoloniality. Nevertheless, the idea that discursive monopoly should give way to self-determination and cultural dialogue is widely recognized, in principle if more rarely in practice.

Awareness of a great land to the south, beyond the Mediterranean littoral, goes back to antiquity; the classical ethnographers, Herodotus and Pliny, include information about the area, some specific, some vague and legendary, in their surveys of the world known to Greco-Roman civilization. The crucial aspect of the Greek paradigm, as V. Y. Mudimbe (1994) terms it, is its classing of Africans as *barbaroi*, those living beyond the limits of the *politai*. The precise meaning of this contrast is a matter of debate, though it undoubtedly varied with the fortunes of the *imperium* itself. Pliny's famous tag "Ex Africa semper aliquid novi" (Out of Africa always something new) – indicates the region's status as a source of marvels – fascinating but not entirely trustworthy.

Knowledge of the continent and its inhabitants remained largely second-hand throughout the European Middle Ages, based on tradition, rumor, and speculation. A lingering classical influence meant that the landmass as a whole was variously referred to as Ethiopia, Abyssinia, or Libya. Not until the sixteenth century did the name Africa emerge as the most common designation, thanks to the popularity of the *Description of Africa* (1550) produced by El-Hasan ben Mohammed el-Wazzan ez-Zayyati, known to the west by his humanist sobriquet, Leo Africanus. When Africa entered the medieval imagination, it was in the context of a preoccupation with the spread of Islam; hence the widespread interest in the legend of Prester John, a Christian priest-king reputed to dwell somewhere in "middle Asia," cut off from his natural allies in the Mediterranean by the advancing Arab armies. Although loosely based on memories of the Coptic Kingdom of Abyssinia, stories of Prester John exhibited such fabulous accretions as gold-digging ants and magical mirrors; various (forged) "Letters from Prester John," urging his co-religionists on to greater feats of crusading spirit, circulated throughout Europe for several centuries (Reader 1998: 349–54).

A fusion of the classical interest in "marvels" with the martial religion of the Crusades can plausibly be regarded as the matrix of quest-romance. The idea of a sacred mission – to defeat the Moors, to find Prester John – certainly prompted Portuguese efforts to establish an imperial presence in North Africa (an effort that, conveniently, kept the restive Portuguese nobility occupied for much of the fifteenth century). When an expeditionary force seized Ceuta (across the Strait of Gibraltar) in 1415, a chronicler records that the Moorish mansions they ransacked made Portuguese dwellings look like pigsties by comparison (Boxer 1969: 13). Yet Ceuta also formed a terminal port for the trans-Saharan gold trade, and within a few decades, the Portuguese had managed to divert a substantial part of the Saharan trade to their own maritime shipping. The prospect of lucrative dealings, in gold, ivory, slaves, and spices, helped to inspire the Portuguese Prince Henry to style himself "The Navigator." While the nobility fought the Moors in North Africa, merchants and minor officials sponsored by Dom Henrique made their way around Cape Bojador, opened commercial relations in the Senegambia, proceeded to establish *feitorias* (fortified trading posts) down the West African Coast, eventually rounding the Cape of Good Hope (in 1488) and continuing up the East Coast to secure a share of the Indian Ocean trade as well. In 1490, the Portuguese dispatched a large mission to the kingdom of the Kongo and converted a segment of the ruling elite to Christianity, including Nzinga Mbemba, who took the title of King Afonso I in 1506, ruled as a Catholic monarch until 1543, and sent a number of young Kongolese nobles, including the future Bishop of Utica, to Portugal for their education.

As the Portuguese Empire spread, and especially following the development of the plantation system in the New World, the demand for labor created a booming market for human bodies. In the early years of the Portuguese expansion, slaves were generally captured by coastal raiding parties. "Often directed against unarmed family groups or undefended villages," C. R. Boxer writes, these raids "were written up by the Court chronicler, Gomes Eanes de Zurara, as if they were knightly deeds of derring-do equal to any feats on the battlefields of Europe" (1969: 24–25). The Portuguese court, that is, preferred to regard its African expeditions in chivalric rather than directly commercial terms: the flow of Guinean gold that enabled the royal treasury in 1457 to issue its new gold coin, significantly named the *cruzado*, sustained such vanities. Within a few years, however, the slave trade had been institutionalized, with upwards of 150,000 Africans, including relatives of the Christian King Afonso of Kongo, passing into Portuguese hands between 1450 and 1500.[1] The boom in coastal trading, meanwhile, aggravated economic and political pressures in the interior. Traditional forms of servitude and dependence began to collapse into chattel slavery, as human bodies became, first, a convenient form of currency and then a valuable, if troublesome, commodity. Periodic efforts, in Benin or Kongo, to stem the flow simply undermined their reputation as trading partners, and forced slave traders farther afield. Africa's reputation for cruelty, corruption, and political instability began to take shape, a helpful by-product, for the European conscience, of the process Marx termed "primitive accumulation" (Reader 1998: 377–433).

The chief literary monument of the Portuguese expansion is Luis Vaz de Camões's epic *Os Lusiades* (1572), conceived and published just as Portugal's imperial moment was drawing to a sudden close. Set *in medias res* in the Mozambique channel, the *Lusiads* celebrate the achievement of "the stalwart commander," Vasco da Gama (canto 1, line 12). Camões, whose involvement in various Indian Ocean ventures included two years in Mozambique, embroiders a mythopoetic account of Portuguese historical destiny with sharply drawn and vivid details of his own; his description of a water-spout ("As a purple leech may be seen swelling / On the lips of some beast . . . The more it sucks, the bigger it grows," canto 5, verse 21) is justly famous. From the first, the epic makes the civilizational stakes of da Gama's voyage explicit. "We are Portuguese from the Occident," announce the "powerful Lusitanians" forthrightly. "We seek the passage to the Orient" (canto 1, line 50), as the treacherous Sheikh of Mozambique plots their ruin: "Nothing showed in his face or gestures / As, behind a cheerful mask, he continued / Treating them with gentle condescension / Until he could act out his true intention" (canto 1, line 69).

Having escaped from the Sheikh, da Gama's crew finds refuge with the Sultan of Malindi. Cantos 3–5 are then taken up with a prolonged narrative (modeled on *The Odyssey* and *The Aeneid*) of Portuguese history, including an account of da Gama's voyage down the African coast and around the Cape. Among the episodes are two contrasting descriptions of landfalls on either side of the Cape (at St. Helen's Bay and Mosselbaai, respectively). In the first, the sailors bring back "a stranger with a black skin / They had captured, making his sweet harvest / Of honey from the wild bees in the forest" (canto 5, verse 27). The stranger is uninterested in gold, silver, or spices, but taken with "Tiny beads of transparent crystal, / Some little, jingling bells and rattles, / A red bonnet of a pleasing colour" (canto 5, verse 29); later an effort by Fernão Veloso to record the natives' customs ends in a brief skirmish ("It was not just those bonnets that they wear / Were crimson at the end of this affair!" canto 5, verse 33).

In the second episode, by contrast, the voyagers encounter a "cordial and humane" people: "Their wives, black as polished ebony, / Were perched on gently lumbering oxen, / Beasts which, of all their cattle / Are the ones they prize the most. / They sang pastoral songs in their own / Tongue, sweetly and in harmony, / Whether rhymed, or in prose, we could not gauge / But like the pipes of Virgil's golden age" (canto 5, verse 63). The contrast between the two episodes – one anthropological, the other pastoral – is pointed and significant: what separates them is the rounding of the Cape, which inspires one of Camões's most remarkable inventions, the Titan Adamastor, who curses the travelers for their transgression of the world's natural limits:

> O reckless people,
> Bolder than any the world has known,
> As stubborn in your countless,
> Cruel wars as in vainglorious quests;
> Because you have breached what is forbidden
> Daring to cross such remote seas,
> Where I alone for so long have prevailed
> And no ship, large or small, has ever sailed,
>
> Because you have desecrated nature's
> Secrets and the mysteries of the deep,
> Where no human, however noble
> Or immortal his worth, should trespass,
> Hear from me now what retribution
> Fate prescribes for your insolence.
>
> (verses 41–42)

Adamastor's curse inscribes future disaster at the very origin of the Portuguese imperial venture, overshadowing da Gama's heroic narrative with Camões's own late-imperial pessimism. The pastoral trope that follows is thus self-consciously idealizing, a nostalgic glimpse of a paradise forever barred ("For all our desire to converse with them, / Neither with words nor signs could we prevail, / So we once again raised anchor and set sail" canto 5, verse 64).

Epic aggrandizement undercut by guilt and a sense of futility: it is a recurrent pattern in reckonings of European experience in Africa – the mark, perhaps, of a literary distance from the furious ambitions of the empire builders. Literary rather than critical, for the melancholy of epic evokes fidelity to an ideal ("what redeems it is the idea only") and may demand rededication instead of ethical reflection. Unfulfilled ambitions are an open invitation to self-sacrifice, as Conrad's Marlow testifies. *Os Lusiades* breaks off with a condemnation of the present ("my throat is hoarse," writes Camões, "not from singing but from wasting song / On a deaf and coarsened people" – canto 10, verse 145) and an address to King Sebastião to resume the epic:

> In your service, an arm inured to battle;
> In your praise, a mind given to the Muses;
> All I lack is due approval where
> Merit should meet with esteem.
> If heaven grants me this, and your heart

> Embarks on an enterprise worthy of song . . .
> My triumphant, happy Muse will extol
> Your exploits throughout the world.
> (canto 10, verses 155–56)

Six years after *Os Lusiades* appeared, King Sebastião embarked on a disastrous invasion of Morocco, effectively putting an end to Portuguese designs in Africa for several centuries thereafter.

If Camões's despair brings the epic moment to a close, the pastoral interlude in southern Africa sets the stage for a quite different discursive formation. In 1652, the Dutch East India Company established a permanent settlement at the Cape of Good Hope, in order to supply fresh produce to ships plying the routes between Europe and Asia. At first, the colony sought to limit its conflicts with the local Khoikhoi ("Hottentot") and San ("Bushman") peoples, but within a few years, a category of "free burghers" claimed the right to establish their own farms on the indigenes' land. With the arrival, in 1689, of 150 members of the Dutch Reformed Church, the groundwork for "Boer" or "Afrikaaner" identity had been laid. Weakened by smallpox and increasingly repressive legislation, native groups were forced into subordinate status: "By 1778 the new governor Van Plattenburg reported finding no autonomous Khoikhoi communities in the Cape Colony" (Pratt 1992: 40).

In European discourse about Africa overall, the Cape Colony remained an anomaly until the nineteenth century, steady expansion of the Boer population notwithstanding. Its significance lay in being a way-station in the greater African coastal trade, rather than as an enterprise in its own right. Yet the routinization of the trade that produced the colony also inaugurated a shift in the forms of discourse about Africa, from what Mary Louise Pratt calls the "navigational paradigm" to one organized around Enlightenment science and "natural history." The project of natural history, as Pratt puts it,

> asserted an urban, lettered, male authority over the whole of the planet; it elaborated a rationalizing, extractive, dissociative understanding which overlaid functional, experiential relations among people, plants, and animals. In these respects, it figures a certain kind of global hegemony, notably one based on possession of land and resources rather than control over routes . . . Claiming no transformative potential whatsoever, it differed sharply from overtly imperial articulations of conquest, conversion, territorial appropriations, and enslavement. (1992: 38–39)

Natural history seeks to inventory the world; disavowing its relation to power, it claims to pursue disinterested knowledge. Where the navigational paradigm constituted itself around heroic figures like Vasco da Gama, the protagonist of natural-history writing is the self-effacing observer, mere servant of a progressive science of the world. Aiming, ideally, at a God's-eye survey of all that exists, natural history imagined the world arranged into a systematic grid of categories (Coetzee 1988: 12–19). Inspired in particular by Linnaeus's *Systema Naturae* (1735), which established the practices of classification as the leading edge of scientific understanding, monumentalized in Buffon's *Histoire naturelle* (1749), this descriptive imperative favored a static picture of the world, eschewed whatever refused to fit neatly into its categorical grid, and thus devalued change and its cognitive organon, narrative. The definitive monument of natural history is doubtless the *Description de l'Egypte* (1821–29) in twenty-one volumes, a by-product of the Napoleonic invasion.

The emergence of natural history is, of course, one aspect of the project of Enlightenment, the displacement of a divinely authored cosmos by the methodical investigation of a disenchanted but rationally intelligible natural order. In Africa, this ambition exacerbated the perceived difference between Europeans and natives; the former became the subjects of Enlightenment, the latter objects of its gaze. Narrative and its attributes – change, history, moral choice – gravitated towards the producers of knowledge, while the apparatus of natural history inscribed others, human and nonhuman alike, in the ledgers of a world known objectively.

The disparity in power thus precipitated a difference in discursive genres, a difference subsequently taken, all too often, as equivalent to a distinction in kind. It is in the context of this misprision that the well-documented propensity for uninformed and dismissive remarks about Africa, by eighteenth-century European philosophers otherwise champions of Enlightenment, needs to be grasped (see Eze 1997).

Here it is worth noting the significance of the Protestant Reformation, long linked to such phenomena as the rise of capitalism and the disenchantment of the world. Within the Catholic Church, the Spanish conquest of the New World had left a legacy of doctrinal debate about the status of other peoples: "whatever else might be said of non-Westerners," Philip Curtin remarks, "they were officially human beings and potentially Christians with full spiritual equality. Because of the religious difference, this position did not necessarily extend to Protestant Europe" (1964: 33). Indeed, Protestants were more inclined to search out biblical precedents for their treatment of Africans, especially where slavery was concerned. Thus the rise of natural history was accompanied by the resurgence of quasi-theological explanations for the inequality between Europeans and Africans, for instance, that the latter were descendants of Noah's son Ham, cursed by God to be "a servant of servants" (Genesis 9. 25). At the same time, even in Catholic territories, the gap between official Church doctrine and the actual treatment of native peoples remained, to put it mildly, considerable: "In reality what regulated the degree of exploitation was not the owner's nationality or religion but the extent to which there was a lucrative market for the products of slave labour" (Kiernan 1969: 196–97).

The discourse of Enlightenment had contradictory and ambivalent effects on the European understanding of Africa. On the one hand, according to Curtin, "18C Europeans knew more and cared more about Africa than they did at any later period up to the 1950's" (1964: 10). Product of an established and lucrative trade, such knowledge was far from being a mere tissue of generalizations and stereotypes. Works like the *Universal History* (1736–65), for instance, devoted as much space to Africa as to East, Southeast, and South Asia altogether: "The treatment of individual African countries included a short sketch of European activities; but the body of the work was concerned with the history, manners, and customs of the Africans themselves, and a quarter of the African section was given over to West Africa" (Curtin 1964: 13). On the other hand, the reliability of the information was due, in large measure, to its commercial value: those who were engaged in the slave trade needed to have a firm grasp on the customs of their business partners, not to mention the habits of their human merchandise. The profit motive sharpened the eye for precise distinctions, while pragmatic necessity rendered empirical observations as indisputable facts of nature. But the sheer volume of the traffic in human beings – recent scholarship puts the figure of slaves exported at over 61,000 per annum for the period 1701–1800 – and the associated rise in visible misery and brutality began to constitute a problem for the nascent Enlightenment conception of universal human freedom.

How to explain the sudden growth and influence of antislavery discourse from the mid-eighteenth century onward, after three centuries of near-universal acceptance, continues to be a matter of historiographical controversy.[2] Since Eric Williams's *Capitalism and Slavery* (1944), it has been common to connect the fortunes of abolition to the spread of capitalism; although Williams's own reduction of antislavery to an expression of economic interest has been largely discredited, it remains an unavoidable point of reference for subsequent studies. Much of the debate turns on what, exactly, is taken as needing explanation: the development of "humanitarian" sensibilities, the support for antislavery measures garnered among political and economic elites, or the ultimate outcome and long-term consequences of the move to suppress the slave trade. If there can be little question that early abolitionists – whether outsiders like the Quakers or more established figures like William Wilberforce or Henry Thornton – were largely inspired by religious ideals and principles, the politics surrounding the eventual success of the antislavery cause were less consistently high-minded. The French Revolution's abortive experiment with emancipation traversed the same trajectory more rapidly, though it did result in the Haitian Revolution (see James 1938).

For our purposes, however, the significant question is how the escalating debate about slavery affected European discourse on African and Africans. The campaign for abolition was one of the first attempts systematically to mobilize a newly emergent public opinion behind a moral cause; the rhetorical strategies it devised to call attention to social evil have an uncanny familiarity. As Patrick Brantlinger observes, antislavery literature organized itself around the revelation of atrocities, the exposure of unspeakable savagery (1988: 175–76). The organized practice of the slave trade is epitomized by vividly etched scenes of cruelty; shown as disrupting the rule of natural sentiment and pastoral tranquility, such scenes acquire the force of revelation through repeated shock. The strategy uncovers certain presuppositions about human dignity and ethical standards, soon to be codified into conceptions of the rights of man; its product is a culture of sentimentality dependent on recurrent waves of revulsion and disposed to condescending benevolence and moral self-congratulation. Imperial discourse, that is, inflected humanitarian rhetoric with an attitude of moral paternalism towards Africa, in which a sense of obligation carried undertones of disapproval, a moralistic rhetoric that proved an irresistible target for later satirists like Dickens and Carlyle.

A moral rather than merely a political cause, the campaign against slavery intervened in the public sphere with arguments and exposés; but it was poetry that rose to the task of sentimental reform. Indeed, abolitionist rhetoric and the humanitarian sensibility it cultivated is one of the seedbeds of European Romanticism, a forcing ground for the extension of sympathies. A comparison between William Cowper's verse-sermon "Charity" (1783) and Robert Southey's "To Horror" (1791) neatly encapsulates the development. Cowper's text, moving through the measured antitheses prescribed by his heroic couplets, elaborates opposition to slavery within the framework of traditional Christian morality: "Canst thou, and honoured with a Christian name, / Buy what is woman-born, and feel no shame? / Trade in the blood of innocence, and plead / Expedience as a warrant for the deed?" (quoted in Bender 1992: 89). A decade later, Southey draws on more Gothic conventions for the climactic stanza of his "To Horror": "Horror! I call thee yet once more! / Bear me to that accursed shore, / Where on the stake the Negro writhes" (in Brantlinger 1988: 175). What is remarkable here is not only the change in esthetic conventions, to the point that, for Southey, the emotion precedes and virtually overrides its ostensible cause, but also the ideological shift that displaces the argument from questions of justification to the unquestionable reality of physical pain. In place of the communal rhetoric of shame and justice through which Cowper addresses the slave trader, that is, the Romantic text mediates its appeal through an individualized moral sensibility ("I call . . . Bear me"). As the image of Africa came increasingly to be associated with the graphic depiction of cruelty and suffering, such ethical immediacy would have grave effects on the European understanding of African cultures and politics.

At the same time, however, the Romantic emphasis on suffering and sympathy was not driven simply by esthetic motives, but responded to broader shifts in the debate surrounding the slave trade. For as the abolitionist cause gained public influence, pro-slavery arguments grew coarser and more vehement. With their moral standing impugned and their economic interests threatened, those who profited from slavery, particularly the plantation owners of the West Indies, defended their practices by deepening the divide between themselves and those they held as property. Where earlier traders accumulated detailed knowledges about the peoples with whom they dealt, polemical defenses of slavery were increasingly based on generalizations about Africans, often extrapolated wildly from the behavior of populations that had undergone the Middle Passage. Edward Long's *History of Jamaica* (1774), in particular, presumed on the basis of his experience with slaves in the West Indies to offer testimony about the "nature" of the Negro. Casting vicious prejudice in the form of natural history, Long insisted that blacks and whites belonged to different species. According to Curtin,

> Long divided *genus homo* into three species: Europeans and similar people, Negroes, and "orang-outangs" . . . He arranged Africans on an ascending scale from the half-legendary Jagas of Angola upwards through Hottentots, Fulbe and Mandinka peoples of West Africa, to the Wolof and Ethiopians, the highest type of African man . . . Long's greatest importance was in giving an "empirical" and "scientific" base that would lead on to pseudo-scientific racism. The part of the *History of Jamaica* dealing with race was reprinted in America in the *Columbia Magazine* of 1788, where it became a support for later American racism. It was used again and again for three-quarters of a century by British and Continental polygenists . . . and it provided a set of ready made arguments for any publicist who wanted to prove the "fact" of African inferiority.
>
> (1964: 44–45)

In Long and others, the stylistic habits of the Enlightenment – systematic classification, naturalistic rationalism, moral skepticism – bring a fateful veneer of authority to the defense of slavery. Otherwise nonsensical claims about Africans' lack of capacity to feel pain, exercise self-restraint, or behave rationally were passed off as scientific gospel. Most ominously, the disparity between Europeans and Africans was grounded, not in social, economic, or technological differences – not, in short, in human practices and institutions – but in "nature." Ethical considerations were subordinated to a discourse of realism.

Needless to say, the debate over slavery followed larger trends in European intellectual history. The opposition between "science" and "poetry," taken as competing sources of authority and styles of ethical conviction, runs like a fault-line through nineteenth-century discourse. Broadly speaking, the pro-slavery position gravitated towards conceptions of natural inequality, framing its arguments in naturalistic and aggregative terms and elaborating a discourse of racial types and civilizational stages. Opponents of slavery remained within the orbit of Christian universalism, even as traditional religion modulated, over the course of the century, into missionary evangelism, on the one hand, and appeals to subjective or idealistic motives, on the other. The abolitionist cause invested heavily in figures of heroic or sentimental individualism: in addition to the slave narratives that often testified equally to the horrors of bondage and the power of Christian conversion, the Romantics saw the exiled and deracinated slave as a potent metaphor for poetic aspiration, as in William Wordsworth's tribute to Toussaint L'Ouverture (1803): "Toussaint, the most unhappy man of men! . . . There's not a breathing of the common wind / That will forget thee; thou hast great allies; / Thy friends are exultations, agonies, / And love, and man's unconquerable mind" (lines 1, 10–13). In the 1820s, the Brontë children set their imaginary Glass Town Confederacy in West Africa, in transparent homage to the founding of Liberia (1816); subsequently recast as "Angria," this post-Romantic colony sketched out ideas of passionate rebellion and imprisonment that would find their way into the sisters' mature fiction. Baudelaire's "Le cygne," linking an enslaved Andromache to a nameless "negress" dreaming of "superb Africa," gave the figure a powerful incarnation in French poetry as well.

By the middle of the nineteenth century, the cause of abolition had largely won the day, with England leading the way in barring the slave trade in 1833, France, guided by Victor Schoelcher, embracing emancipation in 1848, and the Civil War settling the issue in the United States during the 1860s. But legal and political victories did not entail triumph in moral or intellectual terms;

indeed the nineteenth century witnessed the eruption of race-thinking and racism on a grand scale. In Scotland, Robert Knox drew on his service as an army surgeon in South Africa (1817–20) to forge his system of "transcendental anatomy," most fully articulated in his monumental *The Races of Man* (1846): "Race is everything: literature, science, art – in a word, civilization depends on it" (quoted in Curtin 1964: 378). Benjamin Disraeli, and Edward Bulwer Lytton who served as Secretary of State for the Colonies, were only two of the many who drew inspiration from Knox. In France, the Comte de Gobineau based his own four-volume *Essai sur l'inégalité des races humaines* (1853–55) on Knox's work. Racial discourse also acquired a powerful new scientific vocabulary with the rise of Darwinism, especially as evolutionary biology tended to undermine the authority of Christian revelation. Although Darwin himself wrestled with the ethical implications of his evolutionary theory, "racists could use the theory of natural selection to 'prove' that human varieties must be vastly different from one another" (Curtin 1964: 364), while popular slogans about "the survival of the fittest" were given a racial or national gloss in "social Darwinism" and sanctioned a new ruthlessness in the pursuit of great-power interests.

As such ideas came to inform European thinking about cultural difference, antislavery discourse itself left a troubling legacy for Africa. Having washed their own hands of the trade, the British felt entitled to interdict the activities of others, a useful pretext for intervening more directly in African affairs. In *The African Slave Trade and Its Remedy* (1840), Thomas Fowell Buxton, who inherited the mantle of abolitionism from William Wilberforce, proposed to organize the Niger Expedition in order to bring Christianity and "legitimate commerce" to West Africa. Buxton's tract illustrates the close kinship between antislavery rhetoric and missionary fervor: "Bound in the chains of the grossest ignorance," he declared, Africa "is a prey to the most savage superstition. Christianity has made but feeble inroads on this kingdom of darkness" (quoted in Brantlinger 1988: 177). Advocates of a more aggressive "forward policy" in Africa likewise found the tradition of focusing on shocking atrocities helpful in mustering public support. In a turn that recurs regularly up to the present day, European humanitarianism could imagine itself as an exemplary corrective to the conduct of Africans.

The very prevalence of abolitionist discourse, in other words, meant that images of the slave trade became, for public opinion in Europe, indelible emblems for Africa itself. Historical reform, in fact, quickly came to reinforce the contrast between rational progress in the west and the "immemorial customs" of Africans. In the words of Victor Kiernan, "Formerly, the argument in defense of the trade, that removal from Africa was the Negro's only chance of redemption, had been repeated by men as prominent as [Lord] Nelson: now that he was no longer to be carried off to civilization, it might be right that civilization should be carried to him" (1969: 204). This shift laid the ideological groundwork for colonialism proper, as a passion for reform fed the conviction of a civilizing mission.

The counterpart to this enhanced self-righteousness was an intensified denigration of Africans themselves. As Brantlinger has demonstrated, it was during this period that the European myth of the "Dark Continent" ultimately crystallized (1988: 173–97). A rhetoric of "barbarism," distantly related to the Greek terminology of *polites* and *barbaroi*, was ratcheted up into the image of the "savage." Practices of human sacrifice and cannibalism, previously minor curiosities in western accounts of the continent's customs, became an obsessive motif: the encounter between cannibal and missionary is still a popular graphic residue (however humorously treated) of the stereotypes forged at this moment. Combined with ideas about racial typologies, this moral contrast congealed into a powerful representational schema, the "Manichean allegory" theorized by Fanon. The "Dark Continent" projected moral, racial, and geographical features onto the single axis of color (light/dark; white/black), etching the terms of cultural awareness deeply into the face of nature. Missionary discourse could speak fervently about saving souls, but the dominant idiom subordinated the fate of individuals to greater civilizational entities and the destinies of nations.

Contributing to the mythology of the "Dark Continent" was the reinvention of natural history in the more dynamic narrative form of geographical exploration. Mungo Park's 1799 account of his *Travels in the Interior Districts of Africa* had already yoked an ostensibly scientific purpose to an investigation of the Niger River.[3] Malarial fever limited European incursions during the first decades of the nineteenth century – Buxton's Niger Expedition came to grief upon losing forty-one of its western members to fever – but the development of quinine raised the survival rate, and set off a new fashion for African exploration. David Livingstone's sixteen-year stint in southern Africa, recorded in his *Missionary Travels and Researches* (1857), established his reputation as a Victorian saint.[4] Darwin's cousin, Francis Galton, later renowned for his theories of eugenics, published *The Art of Travel, or, Shifts and Contrivances available in wild countries* in 1855, described as "a thesaurus of African lore [containing] advice on everything from how to deal with scorpion stings to how to treat porters" (McLynn 1992: 56). The rivalry between Richard Francis Burton and John Speke to trace the course of the Nile River produced two bestsellers,

Burton's *Lake Regions of Central Africa* (1860) and Speke's *Discovery of the Sources of the Nile* (1864).

That the authors of these texts became legendary, stamping the character of the pith-helmeted African explorer onto the popular imagination, is testimony to the transformation of a tabular natural history into a narrative of discovery and adventure, in which obstacles to knowledge are morally weighted. "The great explorers' writings," Brantlinger observes, "are nonfictional quest romances in which the hero-authors struggle through enchanted, bedeviled lands toward an ostensible goal: the discovery of the Nile's source, the conversion of the cannibals. But that goal is also sheer survival and return home to the regions of light" (1988: 180–81). Record of a successful struggle against "darkness," that is, the text itself illuminates the lives of its readers, building their store of knowledge and securing their imaginative identification with the heroic advance of enlightenment.

The power of this narrative formula ensured that it would be replicated and exploited, as it was most notably by Henry Morton Stanley. Born John Rowlands in Wales in 1841, Stanley took the name of a New Orleans plantation owner who befriended him after he jumped ship; he served on both Confederate and Union sides during the US Civil War, and later covered Hancock's "pacification" of the Cheyenne Indians for the *Missouri Democrat*. The military experience shaped Stanley's conception of exploration, which he undertook with all the ruthless dedication of an organized campaign, acquiring the epithet Bula Matari – Breaker of Stones – for his use of dynamite. But his venture into Africa was in large part a journalistic stunt, cooked up by the publisher of the *New York Herald*, James Gordon Bennett. Alert to the potential of newly global communications – a transatlantic telegraph line had been laid in 1869 – Bennett dispatched Stanley to Africa with the assignment to find David Livingstone, whose precise whereabouts had been uncertain for several years. Much of the excitement generated by Stanley's expedition was due to the speed of his progress through the continent, and the relatively immediate coverage it received in the *Herald*.[5] When he reached Ujiji (on the shores of Lake Tanganyika) in October 1871, the journalist greeted the missionary with a phrase quickly viewed as a classic in understated punchlines ("Dr. Livingstone, I presume?"). Stanley's account of *How I Found Livingstone in Central Africa* appeared in 1872, to widespread acclaim.

The encounter between Stanley and Livingstone heralded more than just a passing of the baton between generations of "explorers." It represented a major shift in the locus of Africanist discourse and thus in the legitimation of Euro-American involvement in the continent. Livingstone had gone to Africa as a missionary, and although his exploring expeditions were often only tenuously connected to spreading the gospel, his reputation for sainthood was in part based on his opposition to the African slave trade. Stanley had no such moral justification: his motive was celebrity. "You are now as famous as Livingstone," Bennett cabled him in Aden, "having discovered the discoverer" (quoted in McLynn 1992: 91). The formulation is significant: henceforth, it would be news-value, and public interest as shaped and interpreted by journalism, that would steer western attention towards Africa. In keeping with the Social Darwinism so prevalent among the capitalist powers from the 1870s onward, self-interest and competition became the watchwords governing European behavior.

Among the quickest to realize the opportunities for aggrandizement made possible by the new discursive situation was King Leopold of Belgium, a monarch in search of a mission. In 1876, he convened a conference in Brussels with the purpose of opening "to civilization the only part of our globe where Christianity has not penetrated and to pierce the darkness which envelops the entire population" (quoted in Henessy 1961: 80). Out of the conference came an "International African Association" and then the "International Association of the Congo," both fronts for Leopold's designs on Central Africa. In 1879, Leopold hired Stanley to lead an expedition to the Congo region, setting up trading stations that would form the infrastructure for the "Congo Free State." Armed with modern artillery, Stanley waged a campaign of conquest, extorting "treaties" acknowledging the supremacy of the Belgian king from the native populations he encountered. In the Upper Congo, where Stanley's passage brought Arab slave traders in its wake, he became known as "Ipanga Ngundi" – Destroyer of the Country (Johnston 1910: 82). For his part, Stanley continued to boost his own intrepid reputation, publishing *Through the Dark Continent* (1878), *The Congo and the Founding of Its Free State: A Story of Work and Exploration* (1885), *In Darkest Africa* (1890), and *Slavery and the Slave Trade in Africa* (1893), not to mention *My Dark Companions and Their Strange Stories* (1893).

King Leopold's initiatives in Central Africa were viewed with alarm by the other European powers. To establish a legal framework for what threatened to become a frantic scramble for African territories, the powers arranged the Berlin Conference of 1884–85, in which the continent was decisively carved up and distributed among its European claimants. Leopold received exclusive rights to the region Stanley had staked out as the Congo Free State, owning it, as one observer put it, as completely as Rockefeller owned Standard Oil (McLynn 1992: 102). The Berlin Conference marked the onset of colonialism proper in

Africa: to secure their claims, states had to demonstrate their commitment to ruling the territories they owned.[6] For the inhabitants of Africa, the Berlin Conference left a legacy of arbitrary borders, drawn with little regard for language, culture, or kinship, and tailored to the demands of European national interests. The resultant map was a wrenching imposition of modern cartographic conceptions onto longstanding patterns of flexible identity and plural affiliation. Laying the groundwork for what Basil Davidson (1992) calls "the curse of the nation-state" in Africa, the Berlin Conference simultaneously allowed the continent to be imagined as a unity and inscribed it with ineradicable divisions.[7]

It is worth observing here that the plans for a colonized Africa largely preceded the actual practices of colonization. Cartography proved itself a technology of the imagination, capable of inciting a sustained project of social and political engineering. The map registers, not the reality of existing features, but the aspiration to systematic appropriation. Conrad's Marlow acknowledges the stimulus such charts offered to boyhood fantasy: "when I was a little chap, I had a passion for maps. I would look for hours at South America, or Africa, or Australia and lose myself in all the glories of exploration. At that time there were many blank spaces on the earth and when I saw one that looked particularly inviting on a map . . . I would put my finger on it and say: When I grow up I will go there" (Conrad 1899). Fed by the exploits of celebrities like Livingstone and Stanley, pumped up by the forces of the new mass culture, cartography nourished a sense of global reach.

The assumption of world-ordering responsibility displayed at Berlin finds its echoes in popular culture of the time, as the ever-less-distant corners of the world become available for imaginative occupation. No longer a static prop but a stage for the adventure of European expansion, the global map comes to support the literary projections of European boyhood. The most resonant title is no doubt Jules Verne's *Around the World in Eighty Days* (1873), but the appeal of cartography crosses national borders. Karl May populated the world's frontiers with heroic Germans, in the process teaching German boys more about geography than they ever learned in school. In England, the novels of G. A. Henty *By Sheer Pluck: A Tale of the Ashanti War* (1884) and *The Dash for Khartoum* (1891) ranged far afield, following the formation of the imperial spirit across borders of both space and time. In France, Pierre Loti (*nom de plume* for Julien Viaud) won election to the Académie Française in 1891, at the age of forty-one, for his contribution to the literature of French exoticism, including the virtual invention of the *roman colonial* (Quilla-Villéger 1998: 193–97). Heir to a tradition of post-Romantic travel reaching back to Chateaubriand, Loti led the peripatetic life of a "planetary pilgrim," discovering romance and disillusion in far-flung landscapes from Iceland to Arabia.

Like Conrad, Loti began his career as a naval officer; in 1873–74, he served aboard a ship monitoring the African coast from Dakar to Guinea. The experience became the basis for *Le roman d'un spahi* (1880), which detailed the travails of a French soldier stationed in Senegal.[8] Born in the Cévennes, the mountainous heart of provincial France, Jean Peyral – "a dreamer, like all mountaineers" (p. 25) – rapidly succumbs to the cynicism and lethargy of the colonial atmosphere:

> Environment, climate, nature, had gradually exercised all their enervating influence upon his youthful personality. Slowly he had felt himself gliding down unknown slopes – and today he was the lover of Fatou-gaye, a young Negro girl of Khassonké race, who had cast upon him I know not what sensual and impure seduction, what talismanic enchantment. (p. 20)

A decadent counterplot to traditional stories of social climbing, Loti's novel is fragmented and impressionistic, enlivening textual stasis with exotic descriptions and erotic reverie. A pseudo-scientific naturalism ("environment, climate, nature") here fuses clichés about military dissipation with beliefs about African primitivism and sexuality ("*Anamalis fobil!* . . . words whose translation would blister these pages . . . the first words, the motive and refrain of a diabolical song, delirious with licentious passion, the song of the spring *bamboulas*," p. 70). Peyral's degradation is effectively complete when Fatou-gaye steals and sells the soldier's watch, a paternal inheritance and "precious fetish" (p. 152); the loss confirms his irrevocable exile from civilized temporality. His hometown fiancée marries another; his African mistress bears him a son. In the novel's rather lugubrious conclusion, Peyral is killed in military engagement deep in the African interior, while Fatou-gaye commits infanticide.

If Loti's fictions typified *fin-de-siècle* decadence, Rider Haggard's novels resonated with the more vigorous strains of anglophone imperialism. Attached, at the age of nineteen, to the office of the Lieutenant-Governor of Natal, South Africa, Haggard hoisted the British flag over the Transvaal following its annexation in 1877, and witnessed the initial phases of the Anglo-Zulu war, recorded in his first book, *Cetewayo and His White Neighbours* (1880). On trek, he encountered the son of a former King of Swaziland, M'Hlopekazi (Umslopogaas), whose stories of warrior life impressed the young Englishman inordinately. As a native sidekick to the hero Allan Quartermain, Umslopogaas became a fixture of Haggard's run of African novels. Starting with *King Solomon's Mines* (1885) and *She* (1887), Haggard virtually invented the mass-market blockbuster in England,

and parlayed his colonial experience into a lifetime's literary capital; he felt particularly free when writing about Africa, he declared, "the land whereof none know the history, [and] the savages, whom I love, although some of them are almost as merciless as Political Economy" (quoted in Pocock 1993: 63). He specialized in romantic tales about the Zulu, including *Nada the Lily* (1892) and a pseudo-historical trilogy about the rise and fall of the Zulu kingdom (*Marie*, 1912; *Child of Storm*, 1913; and *Finished*, 1917).

When the first of Haggard's African novels appeared, just as the Berlin Conference was drawing to a close, his publisher plastered London with posters announcing "*King Solomon's Mines* – The Most Amazing Story Ever Written" (Pocock 1993: 62). The episode is significant, for it testifies to the intimate relation between mass culture and journalism, whose construction of the news exerted increasing pressure on the politics of empire. Public interest in southern Africa had been kindled by the opening of the Kimberly diamond mines in 1871, and ignited by the discovery of gold on the Witwatersrand in 1885; together, these two finds attracted an influx of new migrants, both European and African, and prompted the creation of pass laws that laid the foundations of South African apartheid. As in the American myth of the Wild West, the combination of an unregulated frontier and a newly powerful popular press spawned legends, pseudo-epic figures for a new age of conquest. Few men embodied such myths more fully than Cecil Rhodes, whose De Beers Consolidated had, by 1891, gained a monopoly on diamond production in Kimberly and an enormous stake in the gold mines as well. Shrewd and ruthless in his dealings, both financial and political, Rhodes drew up a Trust Deed for De Beers that "permitted the company to engage in any business enterprise, to annex land in any part of Africa, to govern foreign territories and maintain standing armies on those territories, if necessary" (Reader 1998: 513). Moreover, Rhodes knew how to identify his own interests with those of the British Empire as a whole. Plans for an "Africa British from the Cape to Cairo" bore his imprint, as a famous cartoon of Rhodes as the continent-bestriding colossus records.[9]

From the mid-1880s, then, through the first decades of the twentieth century, European visions of Africa were driven by a speculative frenzy, fed by exorbitant ambitions and dreams of personal enrichment comparable, in their way, to the Spanish Conquest of the New World. A capitalist economy in full swing, however, demanded measurable returns on its investments, and justified the exploitation of African resources, both natural and human. Such an atmosphere made the ventures of King Leopold in the Congo more representative of the European presence in Africa than even Conrad could acknowledge.

The gloom that suffuses *Heart of Darkness*, while at one level an attribute of *fin-de-siècle* malaise, can likewise be regarded as a symptomatic expression of this realization.

The devastation wrought by the First World War spelled the end of the imperial enterprise. Ideologically no less than esthetically, it opened a generational rift in Europe, between pre- and postwar sensibilities, between those who believed in the mission of western civilization and those who could only regard such talk with irony, contempt, or melancholy nostalgia. Following the Bolshevik Revolution in Russia, Lenin's view of imperialism as the last (or latest) stage of capitalism achieved widespread currency; the First World War was taken as the logical outcome of imperial rivalry and competition. Even those who rejected the Leninist thesis were unwilling to defend imperialism, looking instead to Woodrow Wilson's notion of self-determination, institutionalized in the League of Nations, as the guarantor of future peace. Only in Germany and Italy, defeated in the war itself, did the imperial cause retain its appeal. Indeed, Nazism and Fascism, as Hannah Arendt argued, turned the practices developed in the colonies onto the populations of Europe (Arendt 1951).[10]

The postwar moment marked the end of the imperial enterprise, but not, of course, the end of colonialism. The jingoist fever that fueled European expansion since the 1870s broke, and left behind vast territories viewed, more soberly, as problems for administration. With the judgment of generals largely discredited, rhetorical custody of the empire passed from the military to the civil service.[11] Restored communications and improved transportation also increased the number of intellectuals inspecting the colonial possessions. André Gide's *Voyage au Congo* (1927) and *Retour du Tchad* (1928), products of a mission sponsored by the French Colonial Ministry, echoed Conrad in bringing the treatment of the colonized into disrepute. Four years later, Michel Leiris signed on as "secretary-archivist" to the Dakar-Djibouti expedition organized by the ethnographer Marcel Griaule, recording his experiences and impressions at length in *Afrique fantôme* (1934). In *Remote People* (1931) and *Black Mischief* (1932), the English satirist Evelyn Waugh cast a similarly misanthropic eye on East and Central Africa, and later covered Mussolini's invasion of Abyssinia (*Waugh in Abyssinia*, 1936). Graham Greene, more originally, visited Liberia (*Journey without Maps*, 1934).

A comparison between Leiris and Waugh will prove instructive for grasping differences between the French and English patterns of disaffection from empire. Influenced by Surrealism, associated with the avant-garde intellectual Georges Bataille, Leiris was drawn to Africa in the spirit of modernist primitivism. African customs and beliefs seemed to offer a vital alternative to the stifling conformity of European civilization, and promised more intense experiences of the torments and ecstasies in life. Nourished by avant-garde interest in occultism, esoteric religion, and extreme psychic states, Leiris was fascinated by ritual practices and ideas of spirit possession; in Abyssinia, he attended a sacrificial ceremony, drinking and having himself anointed with blood. For the Parisian, in short, Africa looked to strip off the mask of civilization to reveal a more authentic being.[12]

Where Leiris's anthropological fantasies prompted a quest for primal spiritual power, *Black Mischief* takes the charade of civilization itself as its subject. Making the most of one winter spent visiting the region, Waugh invented an imaginary independent kingdom, ruled by "Seth, Emperor of Azania, Chief of the chiefs of Sakuyu, Lord of Wanda and Tyrant of the seas, Bachelor of the Arts of Oxford University" (Waugh 1932: 11). The notion of African self-rule is itself a comic conceit in Waugh's hands, harbinger of a world turned upside-down. In the novel's opening chapter, a rebellion against the emperor sets off an escalating series of pay-offs, betrayals, and murders before resulting in an unexpected victory for the status quo. Waugh's cheerful nihilism seeks, in a sense, to go Conradian disenchantment one better, by taking the claims of morality as the most ludicrous of pretexts. His satire is thus mercilessly even-handed. Despairing at one moment, the Emperor Seth is exuberantly modern-minded the next: "We are Progress and the New Age," he proclaims. "The world is already ours; it is our world now, because we are the Present . . . We are Light and Speed and Strength, Steel and Steam, Youth, Today and Tomorrow" (1932: 43). Meanwhile, remaining whites are shown "hanging around the bars and bemoaning over their cups the futility of expecting justice in a land run by a pack of niggers" (1932: 19). The device of free indirect discourse here allows the text to have its racist cake and diet, too; in the great tradition of conservative satire, Waugh delights in the spectacle of cultural degeneration, savaging moral laxity, miscegenation, stupidity, and corruption. From this perspective, the pretensions of colonialism are sheer folly; but so, too, are anticolonial aspirations and, indeed, all political schemes. For Leiris, Africa offered access to primitive powers; for Waugh, by contrast, primitivism is the febrile symptom of a diseased civilization.[13]

Waugh's text is, so to speak, deliberately superficial, using the colonial setting as a topical occasion for satirical wit. The novels of Joyce Cary present a more serious effort to portray the cultural effects of European rule, from a writer who served seven years (1913–20) as a colonial administrator in Nigeria. Cary's four African novels – *Aissa Saved* (1932), *An American Visitor* (1933), *The*

African Witch (1936), and *Mister Johnson* (1938) – are unusual in attempting to resist the structure of quest-romance and to employ instead the techniques of domestic realism in the colonial context. The premise is that imperialism itself can be de-romanticized, and African fiction writing brought within the mainstream of English fiction. In the background of Cary's texts stand the everyday routines of colonial administration – map-making, census-taking, road-building; in the foreground, the "cultural contacts" possible within this framework, particularly the various forms of conflict between "tradition and modernity." His setting is studiously contemporary, responsive to such cultural trends as the effects of tourism in *An American Visitor*, incipient nationalism in *The African Witch*. As a liberal, Cary takes ample note of colonialist prejudices; hidebound conservatives often supply a dash of comic relief in the novels, expressing shock at Africans dressed in European styles, for instance. But Cary's renderings of the Nigerian scene are regularly marred by the proprietary air of the old colonial hand. His sympathy has more than a touch of paternalistic indgulence, and he is given to authoritative pronouncements ("The faith in juju stands badly, a few dry years, a very little contamination from a government instruction destroy faith in the lingam," 1932: 8). Cary's novels arguably identify themselves with the rationalizing work of administration, the forces of progress, and the conventions of "mechanism," as he calls it. Within this apparatus, African beliefs and practices can be treated with compassion, curiosity, or exasperation, but they cannot, at bottom, be taken seriously. Natives fallen under the sway of European civilization, meanwhile, like the nationalist Aladi in *The African Witch* or the eponymous Mister Johnson, are ultimately regarded as victims, pathetic rather than tragic, of a historical process that exceeds them. In 1941, in the shadow of the Second World War, Cary produced a pamphlet, prefaced by George Orwell, on *The Case for African Freedom* (expanded in 1944), looking ahead to the issues of postwar reconstruction and advocating a commitment to African development. A brief historical survey, *Britain and West Africa* (1946) reiterated Cary's core belief that "The partition of Africa . . . was a blessing to the African masses. Its worse evils, even of the Congo under Leopold's concession, were not so bad as the perverse and ruinous cruelty of slave raiders and despots like the Ashanti kings" (Cary 1962: 176). Cary's dismissive picture of precolonial Africa provoked a rebuttal from the young Chinua Achebe.

If Evelyn Waugh viewed colonial society as yet one more instance of stupidity in the great parade of decadence, the Danish-born writer Karen Blixen, better known as Isak Dinesen, depicted life in Africa as an orderly counterweight to a Europe *entre-deux-guerres*. Set in Kikuyu country just north of

Nairobi, *Out of Africa* (1937) follows in the wake of Ernest Hemingway's *Green Hills of Africa* (1935) in picturing an Edenic world of eternal truths, pastoral labor, and big-game-hunting. The writing is deliberately simplified, sensuous, and keenly attuned to the natural landscape. In Dinesen's text, humans and their awkward histories dwindle before the spectacle of the Kenyan mountains; the "natives," as she typically calls them, are folded into the scenery, even when what is at issue is the politics of settlement. "I had six thousand acres of land," Dinesen writes,

> and had thus got much spare land besides the coffee plantation. Part of the farm was native forest, and about one thousand acres were squatters' land, what they called their *shambas*. The squatters are Natives, who with their families hold a few acres on a white man's farm, and in return have to work for him a certain number of days in the year. My squatters, I think, saw the relationship in a different light, for many of them were born on the farm, and their fathers before them, and they very likely regarded me as a sort of superior squatter on their estates. (1937: 9)

The term "squatters" here conveniently equates colonizer and colonized, both of them equally transitory in face of the permanence of nature. Dinesen's casual tone ("My squatters, I think . . .") bespeaks an aristocratic insouciance, an indifference to mere questions of rightful ownership or possession, as if moral questions were trivial compared to the realities of natural life.

In its naturalizing of the settler relationship, *Out of Africa* harks back to Defoe's *Robinson Crusoe*. Like Robinson, Dinesen presents herself as a splendid individual bringing productive order to an uncultivated part of the world: "In the wildness and irregularity of the country, a piece of land laid out and planted according to rule, looked very well. Later on, when I flew in Africa, and became familiar with the appearance of my farm from the air, I was filled with admiration for my coffee-plantation . . . and I realized how keenly the human mind yearns for geometrical figures" (1937: 7). Like the administrative projects that inform Joyce Cary's texts, this aerial perspective yields the satisfaction of long-term plans brought to fruition, the fulfillment of the cartographic ambitions adumbrated at the Berlin Conference. The counterpart of such magnificent self-regard ("the human mind yearns") is the virtually botanical tendency to regard the locals as a collection of essential specimens or types. As Dinesen herself confirms, this sense of mastery is deeply indebted to a military esthetic, a gaze enthralled by the spectacle of disciplined masses. "My father was an officer in the Danish and French army," she writes, "and as a very young lieutenant he wrote home . . . 'The love of war is a passion like another, you love soldiers as you love young womenfolk . . . But the love of women can include only one at a time, and the love for your soldiers comprehends the whole regiment, which you would like enlarged if it were possible.' It was the same thing with the Natives and me" (1937: 18). Like the officer's love for his soldiers, the plantation-owner's love for her natives gives an erotic overlay to a fundamentally authoritarian relationship. The clarity of Dinesen's portrait, that is, rests on the presumption of an inviolable distance. The closest analogue to this vision can perhaps be found in the work of Leni Riefenstahl ("Africa means more to me than any other country . . . I shall be homesick for Africa, its people, its animals, its deserts and savannahs as long as I live," Riefenstahl 1982: 7), whose photographs summon a comparable spectacle of pagan virility and primitive racial splendor.

Doris Lessing evokes a similar atmosphere in *The Grass is Singing* (1950), on a considerably diminished scale and without the aristocratic *hauteur*. Set on a small farm in Rhodesia (Zimbabwe), the novel rubs the assumption of unbridgeable racial distance up against the fact of physical proximity, raising psychic inhibition to the pitch of modernist hysteria (the title alludes to T. S. Eliot's *The Waste Land*). Appearing at a moment when the British Empire was dying but before colonial independence had been secured, Lessing's text addressed the leading edge of metropolitan opinion, and was received as a timely protest against the "color bar" recently enshrined in South African law, thanks to the 1948 victory of the Afrikaaner National Party, under the name *apartheid*. In Dinesen and Lessing, as earlier in Olive Schreiner's *The Story of an African Farm* (1888), the fact that author and central character alike are unmarried – "free women," as Lessing's *The Golden Notebook* (1962) called them, ironically – tends to domesticate the structure of quest-romance so prevalent in masculine fictions, and to open room for a protofeminist take on the social conventions of colonialism. Born in Rhodesia, Lessing herself was, during the Second World War, close to the Communist Party and shared its opposition to imperial rule, though, as *The Golden Notebook* testifies, generally without managing to cross the racial divide itself.

Decolonization first challenged and then stripped imperial discourse of its legitimacy; much of postcolonial theory, from Fanon onward, can be regarded as an extension of the struggle for self-determination into the western institutions of knowledge. In the process, artifacts of imperial culture, such as the colonial novel, have become a source of esthetic and ideological embarrassment, sites of a prolonged contest over the meaning of imperialism to western culture as a whole. At the same time, however, the stalled projects of national liberation, and the troubled formation of the African postcolonies, have left room for the re-examination, and even the redeployment, of imperial discourses. Rarely, to be sure, are such efforts as forthright as the call for a new colonialism issued by Norman Stone in the wake of political breakdown in Somalia and Rwanda/Burundi (Stone 1996). More sophisticated versions at least acknowledge the untenable legacies of imperial rule, legible in the continued fragility of the postcolonial states, and seek to devise more or less subtle strategies for negotiating the ensuing crisis of representation. Our survey can thus draw to a close by juxtaposing two significant efforts to reinscribe the traditions of imperial discourse. A comparison can be particularly illuminating in this case, since both V. S. Naipaul's *A Bend in the River* (1979) and Barbara Kingsolver's *The Poisonwood Bible* (1998) base themselves on the history of independence in the Congo. In doing so, both writers pay explicit homage to Conrad's *Heart of Darkness*, confirming Central Africa's standing as imaginative epitome of the continent itself.

Born in Trinidad of East Indian parentage, Naipaul early adopted as his own a stance of modernist deracination, following, as his author's note recurrently declares, "no other profession" but that of author. During the 1960s and 70s, as the decolonization movement gathered force, Naipaul constituted himself as a neo-Conradian witness to the wake of empire; in both travelogues and novels, his own ex-colonial identity lent authority to his increasingly disenchanted impartiality. Deliberately, even provocatively, refusing to take sides in the rhetorical conflict over the colonial legacy, Naipaul adopted a position of superiority perilously close to contempt: his writings compile an almost exhaustive catalogue of postcolonial failure, rage, and self-loathing, delivered with the icy precision of the truth-teller. No naïve spokesman for the glories of empire – indeed, his ear for the echoes of humiliation and envy is unsparing – Naipaul nevertheless urges an implacable stoicism, a nihilistic detachment laid out in the first paragraph of *A Bend in the River*: "The world is what it is; men who are nothing, who allow themselves to become nothing, have no place in it" (1979: 4).

Like Conrad, Naipaul leaves the Central African setting of his novel unnamed, allowing it to evoke more than a single national history. But he signals his revisionary ambitions by having his central character/narrator, Salim, approach Central Africa overland, from the East rather than the West Coast. In place of the river-pilot Marlow, whose status as a company man is at once a source of complicity and a saving grace, Salim comes from an East-African-Indian trading family; in the wake of independence, he sets off for Central Africa to become a shopkeeper, not so much to make something of himself as to stave off the threat of becoming nothing.

Methodically antinarrative, almost eerily affectless, *A Bend in the River* abjures traditional novelistic satisfactions in favor of an anatomy of resentments. The novel echoes the trajectory of independence in the Congo, from what Naipaul calls "the second rebellion" to the rise of the "Big Man" and the radicalization of nationalism associated with the campaign for *authenticité*. But events as such are relentlessly held at a distance: the characters in "the town" experience history at several removes, as a puzzling and ultimately lethal spectacle. "If there was a plan," Salim remarks toward the end of the novel, "these events had meaning . . . But there was no plan; there was no law; this was only make-believe; play; a waste of men's time in the world" (1979: 267). In place of significant plot, the novel proceeds through a series of fitful hopes and recurrent disillusions; in place of dialogue, which might reveal, through a clash of perspectives, an incipient social relation, Naipaul assembles a string of monologues. Like Waugh without the jokes, the novel takes grim delight in repeatedly exposing the pettiness of the characters, the vanity of their aspirations and the bitterness of their inevitable limitations. The premise of this bleak parade is the utter irrelevance of moral codes to the panorama of futility that is African history. "It's not that there's no right or wrong here," one character declares in an epigram worthy of Conrad's Marlow, "there's no right."

Naipaul's modernist nihilism has been understandably controversial. Appearing in 1979, in the wake of the phase of radicalism it records, *A Bend in the River* was freighted with enough ideological baggage to provoke the scorn of critics sympathetic to the liberation movements and the admiration of liberals tired of Third-Worldist rhetoric. The historical recession of Cold War antagonisms, however, may have deprived the novel's disenchantment of its contrarian novelty; its bleakness seems more wearying than warranted. In return, however, the text's affinities with the novel of postcolonial disillusionment, a genre to which African writers from Achebe and Armah to Ngugi have contributed, have become more visible and poignant. Moreover, as Michael Gorra has argued, Naipaul's fully Conradian skill as an ironist precludes any simple identification of author and character / narrator, pre-empting and problematizing casually dismissive judgments upon the text (Gorra 1997).

Naipaul, in other words, extricates the novel from imperial discourse by pursuing the modernist strategy laid out by *Heart of Darkness,* turning skepticism against all forms of political commitment. Adopting the paradigmatic perspective of petty commerce, *A Bend in the River* does not so much regret imperial power as mourn the loss of its saving illusions; for Naipaul's text, the retreat of the civilizing mission exposes sadly misplaced hopes for civilization itself. By contrast, Barbara Kingsolver's *The Poisonwood Bible* (1998) aims rather to expose the history of neo-imperial – particularly US – involvement in Africa. Its central characters are a family of Baptist missionaries, Nathan Price, his wife Orleanna, and their four daughters, who set off for the Congo in 1959, only to be caught up in the turmoil surrounding decolonization. The novel proceeds serially, with each of the women recounting the gradual breakdown of Reverend Price's redemptive mission.

Where Naipaul depicts a world of impotent rage and anomie, Kingsolver imagines a richly textured quotidian life in the Congo, the children's perspective often supplying a welcome streak of humor. Here the tradition of domestic realism, with its attention to the concerns of women, gathers into a feminist reproach to imperial arrogance. Moving from the sudden coming of independence and the US-backed murder of Patrice Lumumba through the career and eventual fall of Mobutu, the novel attempts to embed the serial disenchantments of postcolonial history within a sharply drawn political chronicle, on the one hand, and the doggedly renewed hopes of daily existence, on the other.

The Poisonwood Bible is particularly noteworthy for its efforts to engage with African writing. The novel draws equally on *Heart of Darkness* and Achebe's *Things Fall Apart*, constructing an intricate counterpoint between the disorientation of its American characters and their partial regrounding in African realities. Most interestingly, perhaps, Kingsolver explicitly thematizes issues of translation and (mis)interpretation. The novel's title alludes to Reverend Price's mispronunciation of a Kikongo word "meaning 'most precious' and 'most insufferable' and also 'poisonwood.' That one word brought down Father's sermons every time, as he ended them all with the shout 'Tata Jesus is *bängala*'" (1998: 504–05). Meanwhile, one of the daughters, Adah, suffers from a mysterious ailment that leaves her virtually speechless but gifted with preternatural verbal facility. Adah thus punctuates the text with a near-Joycean stream of puns, palindromes, and ironically subversive symbolism, disrupting the tranquil realist surface of the novel.

By making the Price women reluctant witnesses to the Reverend's self-righteous mission, Kingsolver gains a certain critical leverage over the forms of imperial discourse. The resistance to teleological closure provided by domestic realism – the story of daily life goes on, after all – manages to defuse the moral structure of the quest-romance, to expose its rigidities and idealizing blindness. At the same time, however, the text adumbrates an anti-imperialist allegory that threatens, particularly towards the drawn-out end of the novel, to lapse into its own schematic closures. As Kingsolver follows out the daughters' lives,

The Poisonwood Bible itself modulates into a utopian vision of Africa, hopes briefly vested in a revolutionary Angola, but then reverting to the dream of a pristine kingdom of Kongo, a private myth shared by the novel's only married couple, Leah Price and Anatole Ngemba. As Nathan Price's most dutiful daughter, Leah's marriage to a Lumumbist teacher and activist – they have children named Pascal, Patrice, and Martin-Lothaire – itself resembles the sacrificial fulfillment of a missionary endeavor. The novel thus suggests, without being able to explore, the kinship between Christian and secular political commitments.

In their different ways, *A Bend in the River* and *The Poisonwood Bible* seek to sum up the literary legacy of empire. For Naipaul, the demise of Conrad's redemptive "idea" leaves little more than morally bankrupt politics and shabby attempts at ideological self-deception. The aftermath of empire means an interminable disillusionment. "In time it would all go," Salim muses. "That certainty of the end . . . was my security" (1899: 202). For Kingsolver, by contrast, imperial history continues to provide a source of narrative coherence, as Euro-American interference stands in the way of the ultimate redemption of domestic life. The novel's anticlerical satire, along with its residual vision of interracial union as political progress, attach *The Poisonwood Bible* to a tradition of Enlightenment humanism that can perhaps be regarded as the silver lining of imperial discourse. Whether such a tradition can ever be fully disentangled from the history of domination is a question still awaiting an answer.

Notes

1. When Afonso wrote to the King of Portugal to protest the seizure of his subjects, the king "dismissed Afonso's complaint, and far from offering even the slightest support for his wish that the Portuguese trade in slaves from the Kongo cease, replied to the effect that the Kongo had nothing else to sell" (Reader 1998: 375).
2. See the illuminating exchange between David Brion Davis, Thomas L. Haskell, and John Ashworth assembled in Bender 1992.
3. In an application to the African Association (later fused with the Royal Geographical Society), Park described his motives: "I had a passionate desire to *examine into the productions* of a country so little known, and to become *experimentally* acquainted with the modes of life and character of the natives" (emphasis added); Quixote-like, he set off on his travels accompanied by "a slave named Johnson and a Mandingo interpreter called Demba . . . he packed no more scientific equipment than a sextant, a magnetic compass and a thermometer . . . his entire arsenal consisted of a couple of fowling pieces and a brace of pistols" (McLynn 1992: 13–14). Park's status as a legend was secured when he died by drowning on a subsequent expedition to the Niger.

4. The full title of Livingstone's work is revealing: *Missionary Travels and Researches in South Africa: Including a Sketch of Sixteen Years' Residence in the Interior of Africa, and a Journey from the Cape of Good Hope to Loanda on the West Coast; Thence across the Continent, down the River Zambezi, to the Eastern Ocean.*
5. Stanley's biographer, Frank McLynn, accounts for Stanley's dramatic progress as follows: "He left for the interior with some 200 porters and soldiers . . . He took on two white assistants and hounded them to death by refusing to stop when they contracted fever. Six months into the expedition both men were dead; but not before in desperation they had attempted to assassinate Stanley. By refusing to stop for adequate rest Stanley also killed off large numbers of his porters, who were debilitated by smallpox and other illnesses, and induced many more to desert" (1992: 89).
6. It was this provision that both inspired Leopold to institute the notorious system of forced labor that cost so many African lives, and authorized the inspection tours by outside witnesses that eventually drummed up outrage against Leopold's policies. See especially the reports on the Congo and the "Open Letter" to Leopold issued by the African-American journalist George Washington Williams, excerpted in Kimbrough's edition of Conrad 1899: 82–125.
7. Today, writes John Reader in 1998, "the continent is divided into forty-six states (plus five offshore island states), more than three times the number in Asia (whose land-surface is almost 50 percent larger); nearly four times the number in South America. The boundaries dividing Africa's forty-six nations add up to more than 46,000 kilometres (compared with under 42,000 in all Asia). . . . Fifteen states are entirely landlocked, more than in the rest of the world put together" (1998: 573–74).
8. Translated as *The Sahara*, by Marjorie Laurie. All references are to this edition.
9. Rhodes's ideological significance for the imperial cause can perhaps be gauged by a biographical entry prepared for the 1928 *Encyclopaedia Britannica*, apparently by Lord Lugard, the colonial governor of Nigeria: "A will exists, written in Rhodes' own handwriting, when he was still only twenty-two, in which he states his reasons for accepting the aggrandizement of the British empire as the highest ideal of practical achievement. It ends with a single bequest of everything of which he might be possessed for the furtherance of this great purpose . . . Five and twenty years later, his final will carried out . . . the same intention" (vol. 19: 258).
10. The thesis of the colonial roots of national cultures has recently been reiterated by Marc Fumaroli (*L'état culturel: une religion moderne*, 1991) and Gauri Viswanathan (*Masks of Conquest: Literary Study and British Rule in India*, 1989).
11. The essays of George Orwell, including "Shooting an Elephant" and "Marrakech," provide a compelling picture of the new generation of civil servants, forced into poses of authority ill-suited to their sensibilities. A good indication of changing standards for the evaluation of empire can be gleaned from the works of E. M. Forster. *A Passage to India* (1924) did much to define interwar attitudes, but its concerns are already delineated in *Howards End*

(1912), where the Wilcoxes' African rubber holdings are seen as promoting racial arrogance and bad manners.

12. Such feelings were closely connected to the heady experience of colonial power. Under the cloak of "scientific research," the expedition "requisitioned" vast quantities of ritual objects, going so far as to threaten villagers with police reprisals if they refused to surrender certain sacred figures. Michel Leiris registers the terror and panic induced by these threats, and the intoxicating sensation of sacrilege that resulted (see Wynchank 1992).
13. Waugh's counterpart in the French tradition is probably the doctor, novelist, and antisemite Céline (Louis-Ferdinand Destouches), who conjured up the imaginary French colony of Bambola-Bragamance in *Voyage au bout de la nuit* (1932, *Journey to the End of Night*), a title with deliberately Conradian echoes.

Bibliography

Arendt, Hannah. 1951. *The Origins of Totalitarianism*. New York: Harcourt, Brace.

Bender, Thomas, ed. 1992. *The Antislavery Debate: Capitalism and Abolitionism as a Problem in Historical Interpretation*. Berkeley: University of California Press.

Brantlinger, Patrick. 1988. *Rule of Darkness: British Literature and Imperialism 1830–1914*. Ithaca: Cornell University Press.

Boxer, C. R. 1969. *The Portuguese Seaborne Empire 1415–1825*. New York: Knopf.

Buxton, Thomas F. 1840. *The African Slave Trade and Its Remedy*. London: J. Murray.

Camões, Luis Vaz de. [1572] 1997. *The Lusiads*. Trans. Landeg White. Oxford: Oxford University Press.

Cary, Joyce. [1932] 1949. *Assia Saved*. London: Michael Joseph.

1946. *Britain and West Africa*. London: Longmans, Green & Co.

Clifford, James. 1988. *The Predicament of Culture: Twentieth-Century Ethnography, Literature, and Art*. Cambridge, MA: Harvard University Press.

Coetzee, J. M. 1988. *White Writing: On the Culture of Letters in South Africa*. New Haven: Yale University Press.

Conrad, Joseph. [1899] 1988. *Heart of Darkness*. Ed. Robert Kimbrough. 3rd edn. New York: Norton.

Curtin, Phillip. 1964. *The Image of Africa: British Ideas and Action 1780–1850*. Madison: University of Wisconsin Press.

Davidson, Basil. 1992. *The Black Man's Burden: Africa and the Curse of the Nation-State*. New York: Times Books.

Description de l'Egypte: ou, Recueil des observations et des recherches qui ont été faites en Egypte pendant l'expédition de l'Armée française. 1821–29. 21 vols. Paris: C. L. F. Panckoucke.

Dinesen, Isak. 1937. *Out of Africa*. New York: Modern Library.

Eze, Emmanuel Chukwudi, ed. 1997. *Race and the Enlightenment: A Reader*. Cambridge, MA: Basil Blackwell.

Fabian, Johannes. 1983. *Time and the Other: How Anthropology Makes Its Object*. New York: Columbia University Press.

Fanon, Frantz. 1961. *The Wretched of the Earth*. Trans. Constance Farrington. New York: Grove Weidenfeld.

1967. *Black Skin, White Masks*. Trans. C. L. Markmann. New York: Grove Weidenfeld.
Foucault, Michel. 1972. *The Archeology of Knowledge*. New York: Pantheon.
Fumaroli, Marc. 1991. *L'état culturel: une religion moderne*. Paris: Editions de Fallois.
Gobineau, Arthur, comte de. [1884]. *Essai sur l'inégalité des races humains*. Paris: Firmin-Didot.
Gorra, Michael. 1997 *After Empire: Scott, Naipaul, Rushdie*. Chicago: University of Chicago Press.
Henessy, Maurice. 1961. "The Congo Free State: A Brief History, 1876–1908." In *Heart of Darkness*. 1988. Ed. Robert Kimbrough. New York: Norton.
James, C. L. R. 1938. *The Black Jacobins: Toussaint Louverture and the San Domingo Revolution*. New York: Dial.
Johnston, Harry. 1910. "George Grenfell: A Missionary in the Congo." In *Heart of Darkness*. 1988. Ed. Robert Kimbrough. New York: Norton.
Kiernan, Victor. 1969. *The Lords of Humankind: Black Man, Yellow Man and White Man in an Age of Empire*. Boston: Little, Brown.
Kimbrough, Robert, ed. 1988. *Heart of Darkness*. New York: Norton.
Kingsolver, Barbara. 1998. *The Poisonwood Bible*. New York: HarperCollins.
Long, Edward. 1774. *The History of Jamaica*. London: T. Lowndes.
Loti, Pierre. *Le roman d'un spahi*. Trans. Marjorie Laurie as *The Sahara*. New York: Brentano, n.d.
McLynn, Frank. 1992. *Hearts of Darkness: The European Exploration of Africa*. London: Pimlico.
Miller, Christopher. 1985. *Blank Darkness: Africanist Discourse in French*. Chicago: University of Chicago Press.
Mudimbe, V. Y. 1994. *The Idea of Africa*. Bloomington: Indiana University Press.
Naipaul, V. S. 1979. *A Bend in the River*. New York: Knopf.
Pocock, Tom. 1993. *Rider Haggard and the Lost Empire*. London: Weidenfeld and Nicolson.
Pratt, Mary Louise. 1992. *Imperial Eyes: Travel Writing and Transculturation*. London: Routledge.
Quilla-Villéger, Alain. 1998. *Pierre Loti: le pèlerin de la planète*. Bordeaux: Auberon.
Reader, John. 1998. *Africa: A Biography of the Continent*. New York: Knopf.
Riefenstahl, Leni. 1982. *Leni Riefenstahl's Africa*. Trans. Kathrine Talbot. London: Collins / Harvill.
Stone, Norman. 1996. "Why the Empire Must Strike Back." *The Observer* 18 August 1996: 22.
Viswanathan, Gauri. 1989. *Masks of Conquest: Literary Study and British Rule in India*. New York: Columbia University Press.
Waugh, Evelyn. 1932. *Black Mischief*. London: Chapman and Hall.
Williams, Eric. 1944. *Capitalism and Slavery*. Chapel Hill: University North Carolina Press.
Wynchank, Anny. 1995. "Fictions d'Afriques: les intellectuels français et leurs visions." In *Afriques imaginaires: regards reciproques et discours littéraires*. Ed. Wynchank and Salazar. Paris: L'Harmattan.
Wynchank, Anny, and Ph.-J. Salazar. eds. 1995. *Afriques imaginairies: regards réciproques et discours littéraires*. Paris: L'Harmattan.

16

African-language literatures of southern Africa

DANIEL P. KUNENE

The beginnings of written literatures among the indigenous peoples of southern Africa are rooted in the nineteenth century, a period of intensive and extensive missionary activity in that region. As the word made visible, writing was ushered in by translations of Bible tracts, followed at a slower but steady pace, by the Bible and John Bunyan's *Pilgrim's Progress*. The writer most likely to be published was one who advocated the abandonment of indigenous customs and cultures and the acceptance of their rivals from the west. A typical and much quoted example is that of Thomas Mofolo's *Moeti oa Bochabela* (Sesotho, 1907) (*Traveller of the East*), which described the premissionary Lesotho as a place steeped in darkness in which "people ate each other like the animals of the veld," and was accepted with great enthusiasm by the Paris Evangelical Mission Society, while *Chaka* (Sesotho, 1925), a much superior work artistically, was kept from publication for a long time by the same missionary group because they did not like its message. Typically, in *Moeti oa Bochabela,* Mofolo created a protagonist, Fekisi, who rejects his people and their customs, and undertakes a journey similar to that of Christian in Bunyan's *Pilgrim's Progress*. Fekisi's "escape" from his culture is replayed over and over as African-language writers simulate Bunyan's hero, especially in the early missionary period. Henry Masila Ndawo's *Uhambo lukaGqobhoka* (Xhosa, 1909) (Gqobhoka's Journey) is another outstanding example of this motif. In his preface, Ndawo says that his first-person narrator, Gqobhoka ("Convert"),

> Tells us that every single person is born together with two companions, Light and Darkness. One of them [Light] does not stray from his original character till he comes face to face with the Final Judge. As for Darkness, he would one day be a roaring lion seeking someone to maul. Sometimes he would be a leopard, or a python. (1958: iii)

With their beginnings in the second half of the nineteenth century as literacy took root and spread, in the early part of the twentieth, African-language literatures assumed an identity, through thematic defining elements that were unabashedly political. The two basic themes were, first, the mostly overt, but sometimes implied, Manichean theme of good versus evil as constantly opposing forces represented by light or God or the soul (Good) on the one hand, and darkness or Satan or the body (Evil) on the other. Good and evil were, of course, often contending forces in African oral myths as well. But the integrity of the art form, namely the stories in which they were embodied, was always primary. The danger, to the emerging literatures, of this preoccupation with morality, was that it forced the writers to put the message before the art. Furthermore, the emerging literary tradition's definition of good and evil was politically motivated. The good comprised the new Christian dispensation, and the evil consisted of the traditional African life with all its cultural underpinnings. Or, if universal human traits were addressed, it was always in a simplistic manner in which characters represented absolutes, where the evil character was forever evil, and the good forever good, like animals in fables.

The second theme, strongly linked to the first, arose from the forced migration of the young men to the cities, especially Johannesburg, to find work either in the mines or secondary industries. After all, taxes were to be paid in cash. Furthermore land, under the native reserve scheme, was too small to raise cattle for sheer subsistence, let alone such ritualistic functions as the payment of *ilobolo* (Zulu), i.e., cattle given as part of the traditional marriage contract. Money was now the accepted substitute for cattle in these transactions.

All this meant that the traditional tight-knit social structure of earlier times was being seriously undermined. To reflect their concern about this state of affairs, the writers began to create characters who were "swallowed up" and corrupted by the city, and whose only salvation was a return to the innocence of the simple rural life. Thus was born the "prodigal son" theme that was to dominate African-language writing for decades. Matlosa's novel *Molahlehi* (Sesotho, 1946) (The Lost One), and Moloto's *Motimedi* (Setswana, 1953) (The Lost One), complete with their symbolic names, are good illustrations of this phenomenon. Good and evil found their concrete manifestation in stereotypical sets of characteristics. The good character was the obedient child, who went to church regularly, worked diligently at school and obtained good grades, and grew up to be a virtuous and exemplary adult. If one adds to these the adverse circumstances imposed on the character by human design, such as a cruel stepparent, then one has Nyembezi's novel *Ubudoda Abukhulelwa* (Zulu, 1953) (Manhood is not Reckoned by Age), or Guybon B. Sinxo's *Umzali Wolahleko* (Xhosa, 1933) (The Misguided Parent), as supreme examples. The evil character was the opposite of all this, and was doomed to a life of failure and misery.

The two types of character occurred in the same story as protagonist and foil, similar to oral tales in which siblings (usually girls) are launched on a journey into the unknown, face the same sets of trials, and the good one is rewarded, and the bad one punished. The literature was thus more than didactic; it was unabashedly moralistic.

But even before literacy had taken root, missionary influence on the traditional oral arts had begun to be felt. The story of Ntsikana, the nineteenth-century Xhosa chief who, somewhere between 1816 and 1820, declared his conversion with the words "This thing that has entered me enjoins that we pray, and that all must kneel" (quoted in Jordan 1973: 45), has been told many times as a legend of many versions. The core of it is that Ntsikana, variously described as "a great composer, singer and dancer, as well as a polygamist, adulterer, and diviner" (Jordan 1973: 44), became converted either directly by the Reverend Joseph Williams of the London Missionary Society, who arrived in the territory of the Ngqika people in 1816, or by the pervasive presence of the new religion. His "conversion" was marked by a renunciation of such traditional customs as polygamy and "tribal" dances that he considered incompatible with the new religion, and his creation of a worship group, or "church," that was a syncretism of Christian ritual and Xhosa musical idioms, and praise poetic images and rhythms. Of all his hymns, "UloThix' omkhulu" (You Are the Great God) became the best known because it was reduced to writing.

Ntsikana's hymn properly belongs to the genre of poetry variously labeled "praise," or "heroic." To Ntsikana, God was a hero as shown by the attributes the poem assigns to him. The praises are carried largely by epithets that reveal God as a benevolent Being: as a "Shield," a "Fortress," and a "Refuge," he protects *Truth*. And we know that truth is the highest value that human beings can aspire to, for it reveals their own godliness. God is also praised as the "Creator" who created life and the heavens and the galaxies; a "Hunter" who hunts for souls; and a "Peacemaker" who brings together those who reject each other; and also as the "Great Cloak" that is draped over us. All these are eulogies (see Kunene 1971: xxii–xxiii and 15n) more easily recognizable as such in their original Xhosa form, and thus Ntsikana the hymn-maker was also Ntsikana the praise poet eulogizing his warrior-hero, God.

A. C. Jordan states that Ntsikana's hymn was "the first literary composition ever to be assigned individual formulation – thus constituting a bridge between the traditional and the post-traditional period[s]" (1973: 51). The available evidence suggests that William Govan Bennie was the actual scribe who used Ntsikana's disciples, Zaze Soga and Makhaphela Noyi Balfour, and his son William Kobe Ntsikana as informants about their mentor's life (see Bennie 1936). Jordan is right about the ascription of this verbal art piece to an individual, rather than to the anonymity of a folk tradition. But there is something more, namely, that, as Bennie's informants, Ntsikana's disciples' accounts belong somewhere between legend, myth, and biography, and not "history" as documented evidence. Ntsikana died in 1820, two years after Joseph Williams, and many have interpreted this as symbolic of his devotion to his "mentor."

Xhosa, Ntsikana's language, belongs to one of two major linguistic groups in southern Africa, namely the Nguni and the Sotho groups. In addition to Xhosa, the Nguni group includes, Zulu, Ndebele, and SiSwati, while the Sotho group includes Sesotho (also popularly known as Sesotho sa Moshoeshoe, i.e., Moshoeshoe's Sesotho, and by linguists and anthropologists as either Sotho or Southern Sotho), Setswana (known to linguists and anthropologists as Tswana), and Sepedi (Pedi or Northern Sotho). The speakers of these languages were introduced at about the same time to western cultures and modes of thought through colonization and Christianization, which often worked hand in hand. Christianity challenged the Africans' notions of religious meaning and the rituals by which these were expressed in the people's daily lives. Among the many instruments and methods employed by the missionaries was the introduction of literacy. Christianity was, after all, a religion of the Book. Their proselytizing work required that the Bible be translated into the various African languages, and, more importantly, be read by their would-be converts. The establishment of schools was thus a natural consequence of these conspiring circumstances.

Some outstanding writers, educators, and spiritual leaders emerged from these early years of missionary activity among the Xhosa people. Tiyo Soga, born at Gwali in 1829, is known, *inter alia*, for his translation of Bunyan's *Pilgrim's Progress*. He also wrote numerous letters to the Xhosa newspaper *Indaba* (News) and published fragments of his large collection of African fables, proverbs, praises, customs, legends, histories, and genealogies of chiefs. Like many African converts, especially those who trained as ministers, Soga engaged in composing hymns, including the well-known "Lizalis' idinga lakho" (Fulfill Your Promise). These were in the Christian tradition, rather than Ntsikana's African idiom.

William Wellington Gqoba, born 1840, learned the trade of wagon building, but was also a translator of note in English and Xhosa. Between 1884 and 1888 he was editor of the newspaper *Isigidimi samaXhosa* (The Xhosa Messenger), the successor of *Indaba*, which was an important organ in the literary development of the Xhosa, and to which Gqoba himself contributed numerous articles. He composed two long dramatic poems. "Ingxoxo Enkulu YomGinwa NomKristu" (Great Discussion between the Non-Believer and the Christian) has two participants who bear the symbolic names "Present-World" and "World-To-Come" and espouse the positions symbolized by their names about the importance of the matters of this world versus those of the heavenly kingdom. It is divided into three parts and comprises a total of 896 lines. "Ingxoxo Enkulu Ngemfundo" (Great Discussion about Education), totaling 1,741 lines, brings together young people of both sexes, among them such characters as "Sharp-Eyed," "Crooked-Eyed," "One-Sided," "Miss Vagrant," "Miss Gossip," "Miss Truthful," and "Miss Upright." Their arguments are succinct encapsulations of the obstacles faced by the newly educated African in a white-controlled political environment. Jordan summarizes the opinions of the majority of debaters as follows:

> They are critical of the educational practice of the day. They are denied access to certain fields of knowledge; they are poorly paid. There is a conspiracy among the rulers, and it is this: "If they cry for Greek and Latin and Hebrew, given them a little. But make no mistake about the wages. Keep the wages low." (1973: 65–66)

One of them, "Tactless," complains about taxes and land dispossession: "a tax on firewood, a tax on water, a tax on grass even. We are deprived of our pastureland. – Today the land belongs to them." This position is countered by a small group of "moderates" who consider their opponents "ungrateful."

These "Discussions" deserve more than a passing mention. As realistic vignettes of serial problems resulting from a relentless imposition of the new order, they reveal many responses that would otherwise go unnoticed. The sense that missionary schools denied Africans "access to certain fields of knowledge" is one that was echoed in Lesotho as far back as 1886, when a teacher and later minister of the church, Cranmer 'Matsa Sebeta, who was also deeply involved in the debate concerning the Sesotho orthography, established an independent black-owned school at Matelile, with strong support from the chief of the area. Sebeta claimed that there were "certain subjects" he was not allowed to teach at the missionary school because they were not yet ready for the Basotho, which can be interpreted to mean the Basotho were not yet ready for them (Kunene 1989: 24–25).

Other political problems that emerge are: heavy taxation of blacks, even of basic necessities, a burden that was commented upon by Reuben T. Caluza, the Zulu composer, most of whose texts were directed at exposing and critiquing prevailing social problems. An example of such narrative lyrics is "Sixoshwa emisebenzini" (We Are Driven away from Our Jobs). In this piece, Caluza was reacting to the "civilized labor policy" sponsored by the Afrikaner Premier J. B. M. Hertzog in the mid-1920s, aimed at reducing white unemployment by laying off blacks and installing whites in erstwhile "menial" jobs reserved for blacks, which were now magically transformed into "civilized" jobs. This process was described by the newspaper *The Friend* as "a white man's front against the Africans, created for the purpose of raising white wages and ensuring jobs for 'poor whites,' the overwhelming majority of whom were Afrikaners" (Wilson and Thompson 1971: 379).

Space does not permit more than just a passing mention of other important Xhosa writers of the early twentieth century. They include John Henderson Soga, son of Tiyo Soga, John Knox Bokwe, a noted musician who, among other things, wrote a biography of Ntsikana; D. D. T. Jabavu, born in 1885, who wrote accounts, in Xhosa, of his travels to such places as Jerusalem, America, India; and also some substantial works in English, including a biography of his father, John Tengo Jabavu; Walter B. Rubusana, editor of the anthology *Zemk' Inkomo Magwalandini* (1906) (The Cattle Are Going, You Cowards), among his other writings. Enoch Sontonga, the schoolteacher and musician who, at the close of the nineteenth century, composed the text and music of "Nkosi Sikelel' iAfrika" (God Bless Africa), which has become the National Anthem of South Africa and other African countries, deserves special mention. Samuel Edward Krune Mqhayi is known for his dilemma drama *Ityala lamaWele* (The Case of the Twins) in which each twin claims seniority to the other, in order to take charge of the estate of their late father, and they bring their case to the king's court. But Mqhayi was perhaps best known as a poet and dramatic oral performer of his own poetry.

Lastly one should mention the best Xhosa novelist to date, namely, A. C. Jordan, author of *Ingqumbo Yeminyanya* (1940) (translated into English in 1980 by the author as *The Wrath of the Ancestors*), which created a great deal of excitement at its publication, as it departed radically from the usual schoolchildren type of book.

The above activities among the Xhosa had a close parallel in Lesotho where the first missionaries of the Paris Evangelical Mission Society (PEMS) arrived in 1833. The usual flurry of activity, especially printing excerpts from the Bible, took place. But the major event in terms of communicating through the printed word came about thirty years later when the Reverend Adolphe Mabille established the newspaper *Leselinyana la Lesotho* (Sesotho) (The Little Light of Lesotho), whose story parallels in many ways that of *Ikwezi* (The Morning Star) among the Xhosa.

In his *The Mabilles of Basutoland*, Edwin Smith writes that "Filimone Rapetloane wrote the introduction to the first number" of *Leselinyana la Lesotho* (1992: 127), quite obviously at Adolphe Mabille's invitation. Rapetloane, a teacher with very basic training, had been encouraged and given lessons by the Mabille family whom he helped in their translation work: "The importance of Rapetloane in the literary history of Lesotho cannot be over-emphasized, for here was a man, at the very first moments of the birth of literacy among his people, being involved at various levels in the launching of that literacy" (Kunene 1971: 49). Rapetloane's introduction is a little literary piece in its own right in which he creates two characters with the symbolic names of Sethoto (Fool) and Bohlale (Wisdom), who engage in an argument about the usefulness of the paper *Leselinyana la Lesotho*. It refers specifically to the communication, through letters, between Ramohato (Moshoeshoe) and "the queen of the white people" (Queen Victoria). Once again we see Bunyanesque features in the symbolic characters "Fool" and "Wisdom," whose argument harks back to the Xhosa "Great Discussions" by Gqoba.

Adolphe Mabille, by his own admission, had as his primary reason for the establishment of this paper, the challenging of the Basotho's customs, such as *bohadi*, that is, the symbolic payment of cattle to the bride's people in negotiating marriage, and in order to turn them away from such customs towards Christian ways. However, it did not take long before *Leselinyana* became the vehicle for an emerging literary tradition. In the years following its inception, it started publishing the traditional oral tales of the Basotho. Reverend François Coillard (often using the initials F. C.) set this in motion, and some Basotho began to follow his example. Typically, the missionaries, and later their Basotho imitators, sought to find analogies in these stories with some Christian messages. There was always a contrived appended explanation of a perceived parallel with some Christian tale, as for example, the story of Christ's offer to come to the Earth as The Savior, and the story of Senkatana, the precocious baby who grew into a fully armed young warrior in a matter of minutes, and offered to go and kill the Kgodumodumo, a monster that had swallowed all the people and their animals. He kills the monster, releases the people, who make him their king, but afterwards unaccountably turn against him and plot his death.

Azariele Sekese published his 226-page *Buka ea Pokello ea Mekhoa ea Basotho le Maele le Litsomo* (Sesotho) (Book that is a Collection of the Customs of the Basotho, and their Proverbs and their Folktales) in 1893. "H. D." (Hermann Dieterlen) gave the book an enthusiastic review as the first book "written by a Mosotho," and not one of the French missionaries. Sekese also wrote the fable *Pitso ea Linonyana le Tseko ea Sefofu le Seritsa* (Sesotho) (A Meeting of the Birds, as well as the Dispute between the Blind Man and the Cripple), which was published in 1928 – though there was a version of *Pitso ea Linonyana* that appeared in the *Leselinyana* in the latter half of the nineteenth century. A humorous but cutting satire on the miscarriage of justice against the powerless in Chief Jonathane's court, the first part takes the nature of a fable in which the smaller birds complain against the tyranny of the larger ones that cannibalize their own kind. The second part, namely the dispute between the blind man and the cripple, is in the nature of a dilemma tale involving not only justice, but also fairness. It is typically a story that ends up involving the audience in arriving at some just resolution. Needless to say, the debate is always lively precisely because there is no acceptable resolution.

One of the major writers to emerge from this new literary culture was Thomas Mofolo. His first novel, *Moeti oa Bochabela,* was serialized chapter by chapter in the *Leselinyana* before finally being published in 1907. The effect on the readers was electrical, and at least one reader suggested its publication even before the serialization was over. The Basotho readers quite clearly recognized the strong oral storytelling features in the narrative, which resonated so well with them.

The missionaries were excited for different reasons. Fekisi, the protagonist, was so much like Christian, Bunyan's "Pilgrim," and his journey so unequivocally inspired by his rejection of the old customs and ways of the Basotho, that he was doing the missionaries' job for them. Yet here too the author, in spite of himself, reveals some of the old religious beliefs of the Basotho, in the form of Ntswanatsatsi, the Basotho's "Eden," so to speak, which, for a considerable part of the story, runs parallel with the new Christian beliefs in influencing the direction of the story.

Mofolo's second published novel, *Pitseng* (1910), displayed a cautionary attitude that was totally lacking in *Moeti*. He took courtship and marriage, and openly endorsed it as an institution that was revered by the Basotho, and that was integrated into the culture of parental respect, respect for elders in general, and for the authority of socially appointed figures like teachers and ministers, that held society together. He lamented that this institution was being desecrated by the modern, educated, and westernized Basotho youth. He digressed many times to suggest that the new should not be accepted blindly on the assumption that it was all good, and by the same token the old should not be rejected out of hand on the assumption that it was all bad. It is evident from this that the renunciation of Basotho customs that was often so self-consciously flaunted, was more often than not skin deep, with a strong undercurrent of resistance often manifesting itself in some form of nostalgia, as illustrated by Sekese's research, but even more patently in the above novel by Thomas Mofolo.

Some Basotho writers who emerged from and carried forward this literary activity included Zakea D. Mangoaela, who compiled a collection of the praises of kings in his *Lithoko tsa Marena a Basotho* (Sesotho) (Praise Poems of Basotho Kings), Edward Lechesa Segoete, author of *Monono ke Moholi ke Mouane* (Sesotho, 1910) (Riches Are Mist, They Are Vapor), recounting the worldly actions of a man, Khitsane, who starts off "rich," experiences one misfortune after another and loses all his possessions, and ends up poor but spiritually rich after being converted to Christianity. The story is told in a series of flashbacks to the young man, Tim, who is in danger of following the same disastrous path.

Resistance to what might be called "negative change" sometimes manifested itself through an appropriation of the very religion the missionaries preached. It was often a deliberate and unabashed political statement. Among the Zulu, the person whose name is associated with this kind of mobilizing of the people's religious feeling into an intellectual political force was Isaiah Shembe, the founder and leader of *Isonto lamaNazaretha* (Church of the Nazarites). As a spiritual leader, Shembe composed hymns that reflected a syncretism of the Christian faith and strong belief in the validity of Zulu culture and religiosity. Absalom Vilakazi describes him as "a child of his culture, a Zulu," who "came on the scene when Zulu culture and many of its patterns like kinship grouping and family solidarity, the respect for seniors, and the ideal of Zulu womanhood . . . were breaking down due to the contact with western civilization and Christianity. Western ways which were not understood were being copied, and the result was social chaos" (1986: 28).

In some respects Shembe resembled Ntsikana. Many of his hymns were praise poems for God and Christ, as is illustrated by hymn 150, which gives warrior attributes to UMkhululi (The Savior, or The Emancipator). By contrast, hymn 21 recognizes the devastation of the people by the laws of the white colonizers, and asks desperately why "The Lord of the Sabbath," "The God of Adam," "The God of Abraham," has forsaken the people in their time of need: "Why have you forsaken us?" is the mournful refrain of this hymn which states, "We have become homeless vagabonds" in our own land. Part of hymn 216 "is concerned with self-identification and historical allusions" (Vilakazi 1986: 101–02) that link the Zulu people to their traditional kings, Senzangakhona, Shaka, Mhlangana, and Dingane.

This appeal to Zulu identity with historical links to past kings was a strong component of the texts of the previously mentioned Zulu composer, choirmaster and self-taught pianist Reuben T. Caluza. One particular composition of his was entitled "Elamakhosi" (Song of Kings), in which he refers to many Zulu kings by name, quite clearly to recall and revalidate a glorious past. But Caluza was also an outspoken social critic who engaged the political issues of the day in the texts of his songs. The enactment of the Natives Land Act of 1913, which uprooted blacks from the land and rendered them homeless, and was the subject of severe criticism by Sol T. Plaatje in his *Native Life in South Africa* (1916), also became the launching pad for Caluza's political commentaries in his songs. At that time he wrote the song "I-Land Act," whose constant motifs were, firstly, that "we have become homeless vagabonds in the land of our fathers," and secondly a call for the different African groups to unite to fight for their rights. This song was later sung routinely at political meetings.

Many of Caluza's songs addressed themselves to the evils of migrant labor, which broke up families, separated lovers, widowed women, and orphaned children while the men disappeared indefinitely in the gold mines and industrial centers such as Johannesburg and Durban. The texts were narratives that often included a first-person narrator who travels to these centers in search of his lost relative. There are implied participants in this saga in the nature of the people from whom he made inquiries. There are sometimes apostrophic calls to the brother to come back home, for his absence has created a lot of suffering. But Caluza also engaged in lighthearted satirical commentaries of human foibles and superstitions. His songs demonstrated the unity of the performative arts among the black people. Story, song, and dance became one dramatic presentation. No Caluza song was sung without some choreographed body movement.

Caluza studied, and then taught, at an educational institution established by one of the most innovative, versatile, and indefatigable products of missionary training, namely, John L. Dube, who was born in 1870, was taught in missionary schools, and got the opportunity to study in the United States where he came under the influence of James Booth, an English Baptist missionary who preached the doctrine of "Africa for the Africans." Having also seen and been impressed by Booker T. Washington's Tuskegee Institute, Dube returned to Natal and established a college first called the Zulu Christian Industrial School at Ohlange, but later renamed Ohlange Institute. In addition, Dube established a newspaper called *Ilanga laseNatali* (The Natal Sun, Zulu). Thus, Dube became not only a recipient of missionary efforts, but creatively took over the initiative in bringing about literacy among his own people. He wrote one historical novel entitled *Insila kaShaka* (1933), later translated by J. Boxwell as *Jeqe, the Bodyservant of King Tshaka* (1951).

Later more Zulu writers came on the scene. R. R. R. Dhlomo wrote mostly historical novels, which were more biographical than imaginative, namely *UDingane* (1936), *UShaka* (1937), *UMpande* (1938), *UCetshwayo* (1952), and *UDiniZulu* (1968). Thus Dhlomo maintained the preoccupation with Zulu identity through a study of the lives of their kings. B.W. Vilakazi, whose life was cut short by an untimely death at the age of forty-one while employed at the University of the Witwatersrand as a Language Assistant, was a brilliant poet whose poetry ranged in style from the traditional heroic/praise, to the lyrical inspired by English poets. He produced two volumes of poetry, namely *Inkondlo kaZulu* (1935, Zulu Songs) and *Amal' eZulu* (1945) (Zulu Horizons), which have since been translated into English by Frances Louie Friedman under the title *Zulu Horizons*. Vilakazi also wrote three novels, namely, *Noma nini* (Whenever It May Be), *UDingiswayo kaJobe* (Dingiswayo, Son of Jobe), and *Nje nempela* (Verily So), all of them having historical settings. There is clearly a fascination with Zuluness evinced by some of the Zulu writers we have seen so far, a characteristic not shared by other southern African groups.

Closer to our time is C. L. S. Nyembezi, who, like his mentor B. W. Vilakazi, taught at the University of the Witwatersrand as a Language Assistant, was later appointed Professor of Bantu Languages at the University of Fort Hare, and, resigning as a matter of conscience when university apartheid was introduced, joined the editorial staff of the publishing house of Shuter and Shooter in Pietermaritzburg, Natal, from which he retired in 1984. Nyembezi's major contribution to Zulu literature was in the form of three novels, namely, *Mntanami! Mntanami!* (1969) (My Child! My Child!), a conflict of parental control that goes out of hand, leading to one of the sons, Jabulani, absconding to Johannesburg where a powerful love story (the real story) begins; *Inkinsela YaseMgungundlovu* (1961) (The VIP from Mgungundlovu), in which a crook from the city tries to rob the country folk of Nyanyadu of their cattle, and minor family conflicts arise because the children see through the deception while their parents are lured by the promised riches; and *Ubudoda Abukhulelwa* (1953), in which an orphan cruelly treated by his foster mother, who is also his aunt, develops a resilience that leads him to success through dogged determination.

While Nyembezi's intention in *Ubudoda* is to chastise step- or foster parents whose favoritism leads to hardship for the stepchild, he indirectly holds up a mirror to the social, economic and political inequalities of South African society. Granted that his aunt throws Vusumuzi to the wolves through her inexplicable and undisguised hatred and ill-treatment of him, it is the "wolves" in the form of white racists, policemen who are not only permitted but indeed encouraged by the system to terrorize black people, the whites who control the economy and underpay the politically disenfranchised blacks, who are ultimately the "Valleys of Despond" that Vusumuzi has to wade through to reach his glorious destination.

Many black writers responded directly to the crisis of political disenfranchisement of Africans. Sol T. Plaatje, whose name was mentioned earlier in conjunction with that of Reuben Caluza, is a case in point. The two writers exposed the evils of the Natives' Land Act of 1913, Caluza through his songs, and Plaatje through his book *Native Life in South Africa*. The latter was a powerful indictment of the government of the then-recently formed Union of South Africa (1910). Born in 1876 and thus a contemporary of Thomas Mofolo, John L. Dube, and S. E. K. Mqhayi, among others, Plaatje has come to be known as the author of the novel *Mhudi* (written in English, published in 1930), and a translator of several of Shakespeare's plays into Setswana, his native language. *Diphosophoso* (*Comedy of Errors*), *Dintshontsho tsa boJuliase Kesara* (*Julius Caesar*) were published during his lifetime, but the manuscripts *Maswabiswabi* (*The Merchant of Venice*), *Matsapatsapa a lefela* (*Much Ado About Nothing*), and *Othello* (*Othello*) remained unpublished until after his death.

In 1901, Plaatje started a Tswana newspaper entitled *Koranta ea Becoana* (The Tswana Newspaper) of which he was editor till 1908 when it stopped publication for lack of funds. Then later, in 1912, he established another newspaper, named *Tsala ya Batho* (Friend of the People). Plaatje also took great interest in Tswana language and culture. His contributions in this regard include a 1916 publication entitled *Sechuana Proverbs and Their European Equivalents,* a collection of over 700 proverbs accompanied by approximate equivalents in English, French, Dutch and German, and *Sechuana Readers in International Phonetics,* supervised by the English phonetician Daniel Jones of the University of London, also in 1916.

In 1969, the anthropologist John Comaroff tumbled upon what turned out to be a diary that Plaatje kept during the Siege of Mafeking in the Anglo-Boer War (1899–1902).[1] In addition to the day-to-day events and experiences, the diary also reveals Plaatje's talent as a creative artist as he throws in pieces of brilliant and humorous character sketches that appear to be caricatures of some of the people he knew or met during the siege. These little sketches must have provided much needed relief from the tedium and uncertainty of life in captivity.

Other Tswana authors include D. P. Moloto, described by Josh R. Masiea as "the first author to write a Tswana novel" (1985: 639). Moloto's first novel, entitled *Mokwena,* and published in 1943, has a rural setting in which the protagonist, Mokwena, lives a traditional life. But the inevitable conflict between Tswana customs and Christian beliefs is not far behind. The protagonist of Moloto's second novel, *Motimedi,* published in 1953, has the appropriately symbolic name, Motimedi ("the lost one"); he is lost in more senses than one. First, he leaves his rural home, and "gets lost" in the city. Secondly, he is lost in a much deeper sense, in the cultural and moral desert of the city away from the security of family and community in the rural area.

Finally, M. O. M. Seboni's *Rammone wa Kgalagadi* (Rammone of the Kgalagadi Desert) continues the theme of the conflict between traditional customs and the new dispensation when his protagonist, Rammone, leaves the country for the city and experiences the cultural desert we described for Motimedi.

From the above, it is clear that literacy was never intended, in the first place, for the creation of literature for its own sake. Ownership of the printing presses gave the missionaries absolute control over what could or could not be published, which amounted to a virtual censorship. It is therefore appropriate to conclude this survey with an assessment of the influence of this control on the African-language writer. In the earliest part of writing, the predominant theme was that of the creation of what the missionaries considered a wholesome human being. The purpose of literature was to present moral lessons in which the characters depicted "good" and "evil." And since their purpose was to change the ways and customs of those among whom they preached, the missionaries too often defined evil as the continued belief in, and practice of, traditional customs. One of the consequences of this was the Prodigal Son theme, where a young man decides to leave his home in the country and go to the city to seek his fortune, and escape from parental and societal control. Happiness, if any, does not last long before the young man gets into trouble, is without a job, gets tangled up with the law, sometimes contracts disease, and then, like the biblical Prodigal Son, "arises and goes to his father." The theme of the total renunciation of the traditional way of life by defining it as evil, and undertaking a journey in search of goodness, is one that found a perfect model in Bunyan's *Pilgrim's Progress,* which explains why this book was such a constant companion of the Bible in the new missionary-inspired consciousness.

The South African government, in implementing the migrant labor system, and later the Bantu Homelands policy, was not far behind in taking advantage of the African-language writer through the education system, especially Bantu education, and Afrikaner-controlled publishing houses such as APB and

Die Nasionale Pers. They perpetuated the Prodigal Son theme, with a twist, namely, that the protagonist leaves the country now politically defined as his "homeland" according to his "tribe," but finds city life unappealing and with many disadvantages, and chooses to return to his "homeland" as the place where he can be best fulfilled.

In both these scenarios, the authority (whether missionary or government policy), dangled the carrot of the school market before the writer. The economic benefit for the publisher and the prestige for the writer came second only to the enormous benefit to these authorities through capturing the pliable minds of the young to perpetuate their policies.

But despite these deliberate hurdles, some writers did write novels that addressed adult themes, thus freeing themselves from the strictures of the Bible and government policy, and at the same time engaging in the complex storytelling techniques that writing makes possible. In other words, the art was demanding its freedom from being hostage to interests that retarded its growth.

Although this chapter concerns itself almost exclusively with literatures written in the African languages, I have broken this rule a little bit when that seemed unavoidable. To have left out Sol T. Plaatje simply because his novel *Mudhi* and his *Native Life in South Africa* were written in English would have been a travesty. It would have meant restricting myself to his *Sechuana Proverbs,* which would have given a very skewed idea of who and what he really was in the field of writing.

Finally, whichever way one looks at it, the dynamics of South African society in the early to mid-twentieth century formed a tangled web that we try in vain to separate into such constituent parts as literature, politics, religion, economics, and the like. Such a separate existence of these elements is an illusion. They belong together no less than the parts of a human body. Once we place the writing in this context, as part of an organic whole, it begins to make a great deal more sense, and we will not be in danger of vivisecting a society, but will see and appreciate it in its totality.

Note

1. While doing research in Botswana, and having made it known that he was interested in old papers that might be sitting in someone's house, Comaroff was handled a bundle that turned out to be Plaatje's diary in long hand. This was in 1969. In 1970, the University of California at Berkeley asked me to review Comaroff's first draft for them. It was published in 1973 by Ohio University Press under the title *The Boer War Diary of Sol T. Plaatje*. The current, revised,

edition, was published under Plaatje's name, by Meridor Books and James Currey Publishers in 1990.

Bibliography

Primary works

Caluza R. T. 1913. Composer of "I-Land Act," a four-part choral song with words highly critical of the (Natives) Land Act; he composed many other songs (words and music) in which he criticized the government's policies, and returned constantly to the themes of the African's homelessness in the land of his birth, and the need for unity across tribal lines to face the new threat.

Dhlomo, R. R. R. 1936. *UDingane.* Pietermaritzburg: Shuter and Shooter.

1937. *UShaka.* Pietermaritzburg: Shuter and Shooter.

1938. *UMpande.* Pietermaritzburg: Shuter and Shooter.

1952. *UCetshwayo.* Pietermaritzburg: Shuter and Shooter.

1958. *UDinizulu.* Pietermaritzburg: Shuter and Shooter.

Dube, John L. [1935] 1971. *Insila kaShaka.* Marianhill Misson Press.

1971. *Jeqe, the Bodyservant of King Shaka.* Trans. J. Boxwell. Lovedale: Lovedale Press.

Gqoba, W. W. 1911. "Ingxoxo Enkulu YomGinwa NomKristu"; and "Ingxoxo Enkulu Ngemfundo." For details and translations of titles see Rubusana 1906, below.

Jordan, A. C. 1940. *Ingqumbo Yeminyanya.* Lovedale: Lovedale Press.

1980. *The Wrath of the Ancestors.* Trans. A. C. Jordan. Lovedale: Lovedale Press.

Leselinyana la Lesotho, newspaper, publication started 1863, by Morija Printing Works; still in circulation.

Mangoaela, Z. D. 1921. *Lithoko tsa Marena a Basotho.* Morija.

Matlosa, S. [1946] 1971. *Molahlehi.* Morija.

Mofolo, Thomas M. 1907. *Moeti oa Bochabela.* Morija. (Reprinted many times.)

1910. *Pitseng.* Morija.

1925. *Chaka.* Morija; 1931, trans. into English under same title by F. H. Dutton in London: Oxford University Press for the International African Institute; 1981, a new English translation by Daniel P. Kunene was published by Heinemann in London.

1934. *The Traveller of the East.* Trans. H. Ashton. London: Society for Promoting Christian Knowledge.

Moloto, D. P. 1953. *Motimedi.* Johannesburg: Bona.

Mqhayi, S. E. K. 1914. *Ityala Lamawele.* Lovedale: Lovedale Press. [Ntuli and Swanepoel 1993: 31 give 1905; Scott 1976a: 5–8 discusses problems of dating Mqhayi's work.]

Ndawo, H. M. 1958. *Uhambo lukaGqobhoka.* Trans. Daniel P. Kunene. Lovedale: Lovedale Press.

Nyembezi, C. L. S. 1916. *Inkinsela YaseMgungundlovu.* Pietermaritzburg: Shuter and Shooter.

1953. *Ubudoda Abukhulelwa.* Pietermaritzburg: Shuter and Shooter.

1969. *Mntanami! Mntanami!* Johannesburg: Bona.

Plaatje, Sol T. 1916a. *Native Life in South Africa.* London: P. S. King and Son.

1916b. *Sechuana Proverbs with Literal Translations and their European Equivalents.* London: Kegan Paul, Trench, Trubner.

1916c. *Sechuana Reader in International Phonetics.* With Daniel Jones (Professor of Linguistics and Phonetics, University of London). London: University of London Press.
1930a. *Mhudi.* Lovedale: Lovedale Press.
1930b. *Dintshontsho tsa boJuliase Kesara.* Setswana trans. of Shakespeare's *Julius Caesar.* Johannesburg: Witwatersrand University Press.
1930c. *Diphoshophosho.* Setswana trans. of Shakespeare's *A Comedy of Errors.* Morija.
[Note: the following information about other reported translations of Shakespeare's works by Plaatje is quoted from Herdeck 1973: 347: "*Maswabiswabi* (Shakespeare's *The Merchant of Venice*); *Matsapatsapa a lefela* (Shakespeare's *Much Ado About Nothing*); *Otelo* (Shakespeare's *Othello*); the last three in manuscript." In addition to this source, these titles are also found listed on the reverse side of the title page of the 1957 edition of *Mhudi* as translations "by the same author."

The following further information will be found useful in resolving some of the nagging questions about Plaatje's translations of Shakespeare. It is quoted from Tim Couzens and Brian Willan's *Solomon T. Plaatje, 1876–1932: An Introduction*, in *English in Africa* 3.2 (September 1976): 1–99 (entire issue). Couzens and Willan quote from *The Star* of 26 July 1930 as follows: "News has been received from the French mission Press of Morija, Basutoland, of the issue of the first of four Sechuana translations of Shakespeare's works by Mr Sol Plaatje, author and journalist of Kimberley. Interviewed today, Mr Plaatje said the first translation was Shakespeare's *Comedy of Errors* . . . Mr Plaatje said he had translated *Julius Caesar* in 1917 . . . *Othello* was translated partly in 1923 . . . Other works still in the press are *Julius Caesar, The Merchant of Venice,* and *Much Ado About Nothing*" (p. 9).]
1973. *The Boer War Diary of Sol T. Plaatje.* Athens: Ohio University Press. [Revised edition published in 1990 as: *Mafeking Diary*, by Solomon T. Plaatje, John L. Comaroff, Brian Willan, and others. London and Oxford: Meridor and James Currey.]
Rubusana, W. B. 1906. *Zemk' Inkomo Magwalandini.* London: Butler and Tanner; 2nd enlarged edn. 1911. This is the source of, *inter alia,* W. W. Gqoba's "Ingxoxo Enkulu Phakathi KomGinwa NomKristu" (Great Discussion between the Non-Believer and the Christian), Part 1: 27–33, Part 2: 34–41, Part 3: 42–62; and "Ingxoxo Enkulu Ngemfundo" (Great Discussion about Education) 63–130, including a three-page introduction.
Seboni, M. O. M. n.d. *Rammone wa Kgalagadi.* Bloemfontein: Via Afrika. [Author's introduction is dated 1 January 1946; Gérard 1971: 217 gives 1947 as publication date.]
Segoete, Everitt L. 1910. *Monono ke Moholi ke Mouoane.* Morija.
Sekese, Azariele. 1893. *Buka ea Pokello ea Mekhoa ea Basotho le Maele le Litsomo.* Morija.
1928. *Pitso ea Linonyana, le Tseko ea Sefofu le Seritsa.* Morija.
Shembe, Isaiah. Founder of "iSonto lamaNazaretha" (Church of the Nazarites), preacher, poet, healer, and composer of all the hymns for his church, many of which were nationalistic and even downright political, and often included strong references to the need to revive the glory of Zulu culture and beliefs.
Shembe, J. G. 1940. *Izihlabelelo ZamaNazaretha.* Durban: W. H. Shepherd & Co.
Sinxo, Guybon B. 1933. *Umzali Wolahleko.* Lovedale: Lovedale Press.
Vilakazi, B. W. 1932. *Noma Nini.* Marianhill Mission Press.
1935. *Inkondlo kaZulu.* Bantu Treasury Series. Johannesburg: Witwatersrand University Press.

1943. *Nje Nempela*. Marianhill Mission Press.
1945. *Amal' eZulu*. Bantu Treasury Series. Johannesburg: Witwatersrand University Press.

Secondary works

Andrzejewski, B. W., S. Pilaszewicz, and W. Tyloch, eds. 1985. *Literatures in African Languages: Theoretical Issues and Sample Surveys*. Warsaw: Wiedza Powszechna and Cambridge University Press.
Bennie, William Govan. 1936. *Imibengo*. Lovedale: Lovedale Press.
Gérard, Albert. 1971. *Four African Literatures: Xhosa, Sotho, Zulu, Amharic*. Berkeley: University of California Press.
1981. *African-Language Literatures: An Introduction to the Literary History of Sub-Saharan Africa*. Washington, DC: Three Continents Press.
1986. *European-Language Writing in Sub-Saharan Africa*, vols. I and II. Budapest: Akademia Kiado.
Gray, Stephen. 1977. "Plaatje's Shakespeare." *English in Africa* 4. 1: 1–6.
Herdeck, Donald, comp. and ed. 1973. *African Authors. A Companion to Black African Writing: 1300–1973*. Washington, DC: Black Orpheus.
Jordan, A. C. 1973. *Towards an African Literature: The Emergence of Literary Form in Xhosa*. Berkeley: University of California Press.
Kunene, Daniel P. 1971. *Heroic Poetry of the Basotho*. Oxford: Clarendon Press.
1989. *Thomas Mofolo and the Emergence of Written Sesotho Prose*. Johannesburg: Ravan.
Kunene, Daniel P., and Randal A. Kirsch. 1967. *The Beginning of South African Vernacular Literature: A Historical Study, by Daniel P. Kunene, and A Series of Biographies, by Randal A. Kirsch*. Los Angeles: UCLA, African Studies Center.
Masiea, Josh R. 1985a. "Tswana Literature." In Andrzejewski, Pilaszewicz, and Tyloch. Powszechna and Cambridge University Press: 635–49.
1985b. "Southern Sotho Literature." In Andrzejewski, Pilaszewicz, and Tyloch: 610–34.
Ntuli, D. B., and C. F. Swanepoel. 1993. *Southern African Literature in African Languages: A Concise Historical Perspective*. Pretoria: Acacia.
Scott, Patricia E. 1976a. *Samuel Edward Krune Mqhayi 1875–1945: A Bibliographical Survey*. Grahamstown: Department of African Languages, Rhodes University.
ed. 1976b. *Mqhayi in Translation*. Grahamstown: Department of African Languages, Rhodes University.
Smith, Edwin. 1929. *The Mabilles of Basutoland*. London: Hodder and Stoughton.
Vilakazi, Absalom. 1986. *Shembe: The Revitalization of an African Society*. Johannesburg: Skotaville.
Wilson, Monica, and Leonard Thompson, eds. 1971. *The Oxford History of South Africa*, vol. II. New York: Oxford University Press.

17

Gikuyu literature: development from early Christian writings to Ngũgĩ's later novels

ANN BIERSTEKER

Written literature in Gikuyu is one of Africa's most dynamic and lively literatures. There are strong and active traditions of fictional and journalistic writing in the language. There have also been publications in a wide range of additional genres including studies of history and culture, autobiographical writing, and religious publications. Engagement with issues of human rights, economic and social equality, and political freedom has been central to many works written in Gikuyu and to nearly all contemporary writing in the language. Works written in Gikuyu were frequently banned by the British colonial government and more recent works have been suppressed by the two post-independence governments of Kenya.

The earliest publications in Gikuyu were Gikuyu / English (1903, 1904, 1905) and Gikuyu / Italian (1910, 1919 / 1921) vocabulary lists and grammatical sketches produced by Protestant and Catholic missionary presses primarily for the benefit of British and Italian missionaries in their work converting Gikuyu speakers to Christianity. These publications were produced as part of conversion and Bible translation projects, but were not made widely available. The Gikuyu / Italian materials were produced by Catholic missionaries from Italy. The New Testament of the Bible was first published in Gikuyu in 1926. The Old Testament was not published until 1951, but some books of the Old Testament were available earlier. Early missionary press publications directed at converts included religious publications such as J. M. Kelsall's *Ũhoro wa Ngoma ĩrĩa Njũru na Mũgate* (1931) (Information concerning the Njũru and Mũgate Dances). The major writers in Gikuyu have all been educated in Christian schools and have been familiar with biblical language, imagery, and narratives.

Nearly all writers in Gikuyu have also been and are trilingual in Gikuyu, Swahili, and English. Their writing has been informed by their reading of literatures in these three and other languages. In his political statements published in 1921 and 1922, Harry Thuku wrote in Swahili. Most of the memoirs of those who fought in the 1950s armed struggle, including those of J. M. Kariuki and Karari Njama, were written in English, as was Bildad Kaggia's autobiography *The Roots of Freedom*, and political history. For many writers the decision to write in Gikuyu has been a strategic political decision based upon consideration of the viability of alternative language choices. The earliest published works by speakers of Gikuyu were probably letters to the editor and articles written in English and Swahili by Harry Thuku and other members of the East African Association during the early 1920s.

The first newspaper published in Gikuyu was *Muigwithania* (The Unifier), a monthly publication founded and edited by Jomo Kenyatta (then Johnstone Kenyatta) on behalf of the Kikuyu Central Association (KCA). Kenyatta was at the time the General Secretary of the KCA and in this role he worked to expand the political base of support for the organization. *Muigwithania* was first published in 1928 as part of this effort. Its name is generally translated as "the reconciler," but a more literal translation would be "one who causes people to listen to each other." Bruce J. Berman and John M. Lonsdale suggest that the role of reconciler is the role that Kenyatta saw himself playing (1992: 17). The newspaper carried news items as well as advice features and reports on meetings of the KCA and on the activities of KCA officials. When Kenyatta traveled to London in 1929 as the representative of the KCA he continued to edit *Muigwithania* and sent editions by mail to Kenya. The issues edited in London included editorials as well as reports on events in London. In one issue Kenyatta reported on the opening of parliament and then stated what he saw as the lessons of this experience for his readers (Berman and Lonsdale 1992: 23). *Muigwithania* was later edited by Henry Mwangi Gichuiri, Crispin I. K. Keiru, and Josphat M. Kamau (Rosberg and Nottingham, 1966: 100). Carl G. Rosberg, Jr., and John Nottingham state that the "monthly appearance of [*Muigwithania*] was eagerly awaited throughout Kikuyu country" (p. 101). They also report that "Publication of the newspaper lapsed in the early thirties, but it was revived in June, 1935 and continued to appear intermittently up till the out-break of the Second World War" (p. 102). After the Second World War, the paper was banned by the colonial government (p. 212).

By the mid-1930s a wider range of publications was available to readers of Gikuyu, including Stanley Kiama Gathigira's 1934 ethnographic *Mĩikarĩre ya Agĩkũyũ* (The Customs of the Agikuyu) and Justin Itotia wa Kimacia's 1937 *Endwo nĩ Irĩ na Irĩĩri* (One Fortunate to Have Prosperity and Heirs). The most significant and widely read ethnography written by a Gikuyu speaker was Jomo

Kenyatta's *Facing Mount Kenya,* published in 1938. This work had a significant impact on pan-Africanist writing and it is considered to be a classic text in the field of anthropology. Kenyatta later became the first president of Kenya. *Facing Mount Kenya* was written in the mid-1930s while Kenyatta was studying anthropology with the eminent scholar Bronislaw Malinowski at the London School of Economics.

Stanley Kiama Gathigira's ethnography treated subjects such as clans, construction of homes, types of work, marriage, childbirth, religious practices, initiation, the role of elders, courts and the settlement of disputes, crops and foods, types of oral literature, ceremonial pollution, oaths, war, and death. Justin Itotia wa Kimacia's work included statements of moral and ethical positions, stories, and narratives of various types. *Facing Mount Kenya* addressed many of the same topics as the earlier works in Gikuyu, but Kenyatta addressed these topics in greater detail and placed more emphasis on issues of economic and political life.

Certainly a primary reason why ethnographies were written during this period was because cultural practices were major issues of contention among the missions, the colonial government, and the Kikuyu Central Association. Missions had been teaching against cultural practices such as "female circumcision," polygamy, certain dances, and not burying the bodies of all who died, but gradually mission ideologies and ways of imposing those ideologies began to be widely questioned. In 1929 many of the missions in central Kenya united in a policy to end the practice of "female circumcision." To implement this policy they barred from attending mission schools the children of those who refused to denounce the practice. The KCA opposed these policies and independent schools began to be established for children who had been barred from mission schools. Ethnographies were a means by which positions on these controversial issues were articulated and debated.

Gathigira first entered politics in the 1928 Nyeri Local Native Council elections as the successful candidate of the Progressive Kikuyu Party, a party sponsored by the Church of Scotland Mission. He stated in the preface to his ethnography:

> Ndiandĩkĩte maũndũ macio nĩ getha andũ marũmagĩrĩre marĩa moru, aca, nyandĩkĩte tondũ nĩnjũĩ atĩ gũtirĩ rũrĩrĩ rũngĩhota gũthiĩ mbere wega.
> (1934: iii)

> I have not written about these matters so that people should persist in those that are bad, no, I have written because I know that there are customs that might be able to continue in a positive sense.

Gathigira also expressed the hope that his work would be useful to European missionaries who "marutaga wĩra gũkũ Gĩkũyũ wa kũgarũra ngoro cia Agĩkũyũ cierekere Mwathani Jesu Kristo" ("work here in Gikuyu land to turn the hearts of Gikuyu people to the Lord Jesus Christ") (1934: iv). The longest section of Gathigira's book deals with the issues of initiation and circumcision. He argues against what he clearly saw to be "female genital mutilation" and he argues that it was not Europeans who raised this issue, but rather it was Agikuyu Christians who felt compassion for the suffering of women (1934: 55–56).

Facing Mount Kenya perhaps most specifically addressed the positions on Gikuyu cultural practices that were articulated by Kenyatta's fellow student in Malinowski's seminar, L. S. B. Leakey, who was also writing an ethnography of the Gikuyu that would be published forty years later (Leakey 1977). Yet it is likely that Kenyatta was also aware of Gathigira's work as well as of earlier ethnographies that had disparaged Gikuyu culture, such as those of Father C. Cagnolo and Katherine and William Scoresby Routledge. *Facing Mount Kenya* was a powerful answer to all of these works. Kenyatta did not deny that his work was political but he stated:

> My chief objective is not to enter into controversial discussion with those who have attempted, or are attempting, to describe the same things from outside observation, but to let the truth speak for itself . . . At the same time, I am well aware that I could not do justice to the subject without offending those "professional friends of the African" who are prepared to maintain their friendship for eternity as a sacred duty, provided only that the African will continue to play the part of ignorant savage so that they can monopolize the office of interpreting his mind and speaking for him. To such people, an African who writes a study of this kind is encroaching on their preserves. He is a rabbit turned poacher. (1938: xviii)

Facing Mount Kenya eloquently articulated KCA positions on the cultural issues of the 1920s and 1930s in central Kenya but, more importantly, it was a powerful critique of colonialism that had a long-term impact on struggles against colonialism and on writing within and about those struggles in a wide range of languages and contexts.

Facing Mount Kenya was first published by Martin Secker and Warburg Ltd. in London while Gathigira's *Mĩikarĩre ya Agĩkũyũ* was first published by the Sheldon Press. In contrast *Endwo nĩ Irĩ na Irĩĩri* was self-published by Justin Itotia, and was one of the first works published by an independent (i.e., non-missionary and non-government) press. Such presses have been central to the development of literature in Gikuyu because they have enabled writers to address issues and topics in works that would not have been published by the heavily censored missionary and government presses. To publish works in Gikuyu and works that addressed political and social issues of concern to Gikuyu speakers, it became necessary for writers to establish their own presses. These presses have played a critical role in the dissemination of literature in Gikuyu. Editions they have published have generally been inexpensive and have been sold by street vendors as well as in bookshops.

Disagreements between missionary publishers concerning orthography led to the establishment of the first Gikuyu orthography committee, the United Gikuyu Language Committee, in 1949. Such disagreements have remained a continuing problem for writers and publishers of materials in Gikuyu. In *Facing Mount Kenya*, Jomo Kenyatta used the orthography that had been developed by Catholic missionaries when he made reference to terms in Gikuyu. This orthography did not distinguish all of the vowel sounds of the language and did not require diacritics. The orthography adopted by the committee used the tilde (~), in contradiction to general linguistic practices, to distinguish vowel height. The Qur'an: *Kũrani Theru: Kikuyu Translation of the Holy Qur'an with Arabic Text*, was first published in Gikuyu in 1988, although a Muslim prayer was published in 1937 (believed to have been translated by Haji Mwalimu Hamis).

In 1980 an orthography committee composed of Gakaara wa Wanjaũ, Gerald G. Wanjohi, Rev. John G. Gatũ, Rev. John Mbũrũ, Karega Mũtahi, Kĩnũthia wa Mũgĩĩa, Magayũ K. Magayũ, Ngũgĩ wa Mĩriĩ, Ngũgĩ wa Thiong'o, and Peter Kĩarie Njoroge planned to begin work on revising the orthography. Subsequently, Ngũgĩ wa Thiong'o and Gakaara wa Wanjaũ have used double vowels to mark vowel length in their publications. Continuing work on orthography revision has been undertaken by the editors of *Mũtiiri* (The Supporter) and other scholars and by the recently established ŨŨGĨ language committee. ŨŨGĨ is an acronym of Ũrumwe wa Ũkuria wa Gĩgĩkũyũ. The word "ũũgĩ" also means "knowledge" or "wisdom."

Gakaara wa Wanjaũ was the most prolific of the second generation of Gikuyu writers. He was born in 1921 and began his writing career in 1946 when he published *Uhoro wa Ugurani* (And What about Marriage). This publication included the story *Ngwenda Unjurage* (I Want You to Kill Me). *Ngwenda Unjurage* concerns the suicide of a young woman whose father had kept greedily demanding additional bridewealth payments from her fiancé. When the young woman pleaded with her father to be reasonable, he beat her severely, locked her in the house and returned the bridewealth payments to the young man telling him never to return. The story's title comes from a final declaration that the daughter makes to her father:

> Baaba, nĩ ndooka rĩu na ngwenda ũnjũrage nĩ ũndũ ndũrĩ na bata na ni . . . Nĩ ngũthaithĩte mũno wĩtĩkĩre hikio nĩ mwanake ũrĩa ndũire nyendeete na nĩũregeete, ũkaanuma na ũkaahũũra nĩ ũndũ wa gũkũũria o gwiki. Nĩ ũnyonetie wega biũ atĩ nĩ wendeete indo makĩria, ũkariganĩrwo nĩ niĩ. (6)
>
> Father, I have come to you now, and I want you to kill me, because you have no use for me. . . . I have begged you to let me marry the man I've loved all this time and you have refused and cursed and beaten me just for asking you. You've really let me see that you prefer money and you've forgotten about me. (Gakaara 1946. Bennett translation, p. 4)

Ngwenda Unjurage was reprinted in 1951, 1961, 1966, 1967, and 1985.

Gakaara was one of an activist group of publishers and writers who during the late 1940s and early 1950s produced political newspapers, booklets, and pamphlets in Gikuyu. Writers in this group included Bildad Kaggia (who was then the General Secretary of the Kenya African Union (KAU)), John Kabogoro Cege, Isaac Gathanju, Kĩnũthia wa Mũgĩĩa, Stanley Mathenge (who later became a leader in the armed struggle), Victor Mũrage Wokabi, Mũthee Cheche, Morris Mwai Koigi, Mathenge Wacira, and Henry Mwaniki Muoria. Many of these writers were members of, and wrote in support of, the KCA and the KAU. The KCA had been banned in 1940 and a number of members had been detained, but groups of members continued to meet secretly even after the KAU was formed in 1944, and Jomo Kenyatta became its president in 1947. The works of this group of writers were nationalist, anti-colonial, and anti-racist. Most of the works produced by the group were published by Henry Mwaniki Muoria and Gakaara wa Wanjaũ.

Booklets and pamphlets published by Gakaara Book Service during this period included: Gakaara wa Wanjaũ's *Mageria Nomo Mahota* (an April 1952 translation of his 1951 Swahili publication *Roho ya Kiume na Bidii kwa Mwafrika*: The Spirit of Manhood and Perseverance for Africans), *Witikio wa Gikuyu na Mumbi* (1952) (The Creed of Gikuyu and Mumbi), Mwaniki Mugweru's *Kamuingi Koyaga Ndiri* ([1946]/1952a) (It Takes a Group to Lift a Mortar) and *Wiyathi wa Andu Airu* (1952b) (The Freedom of Black People), and *Kenya ni Yakwa* (1952) (Kenya is Mine) and *Miikarire ya Thikwota* (1952) (The Lives of Squatters). *Mageria Nomo Mahota* was later reprinted as an appendix to Gakaara's prison diary (see Gakaara wa Wanjaũ 1983a). The first chapter of

Mageria Nomo Mahota is "Tugutura Tutangikaga Nginya-ri?" (For How Long Will We Endure Oppression?). The chapter begins:

> Athungu ni moi wega ati twi na uhoti, ugi ona umenyo wa gwika maundu manene ta nduriri iria ingi ciothe cia thi, ni undu ona ithui turi na meciria ota o, no tundu Athungu ni mendaga gutura bururi-ini uyu witu magiikaraga magithahagia maundu maitu ona gutumenereria ni getha ati na ithui twimene. (1983a 222; orthography that of the original)

> It is the strategy of our white rulers, in order to ensure their dominant stay in this land, to cast aspersions on our abilities and even to sow seeds in us of self-hate and self-doubt; and this in spite of the fact that the white rulers are well aware that we are endowed, like all the other nationalities of the world, with the mental abilities and skills and wisdom to manage our own affairs for our own benefit and well being; they are quite well aware that we have a mind as good as theirs. (trans. by Ngigĩ wa Njoroge: 228)

In 1951 and 1952 four booklets containing political songs were compiled by Kĩnũthia wa Mũgĩĩa, Mũthee Cheche, Gakaara wa Wanjaũ, Stanley Mathenge, and Ndiba. The booklets were published by Henry Mwaniki Muoria and Gakaara wa Wanjaũ. Kĩnũthia wa Mũgĩĩa's *Nyimbo cia Kwarahura Agikuyu* (Songs to Awaken the Agikuyu) was the first of the books of songs to be published in October/November 1951 by Muoria's Mumenyereri Press. Kĩnũthia, the compiler, was a KCA and KAU activist. Muoria, the publisher, was an Assistant Secretary General of KAU and the editor of *Mumenyereri* (The Observant One), a weekly newspaper in Gĩkũyũ that had a circulation of 11,000 before it was proscribed. Mũthee Cheche (a pseudonym, probably that of an author by the name of Mũthemba from Kiambu) published the second song book. The third song book, *Nyimbo cia Gikuyu na Mumbi* (Songs of Gikuyu and Mumbi), was compiled and published on 15 August 1952 by Gakaara wa Wanjaũ, at the time also the editor of the newspaper *Waigua Atia* (What's New?). Gakaara composed some of the songs himself. Others were collected by Stanley Mathenge, who was then a young friend of Gakaara's. During the liberation struggle Mathenge became the legendary General Mathenge who was never captured and reportedly escaped to Ethiopia. Gakaara and Kĩnũthia were subsequently arrested in October 1952 along with the KAU leaders. Ndiba from Nyeri compiled the fourth song book, *Nyimbo cia Kwarahura* (Rousing Songs).

On 21 October 1952, leaders of the KAU were detained and publications found in their possession, including copies of the song books, were seized. Bildad Kaggia, Kungu Karumba, Jomo Kenyatta, Fred Kubai, Paul Ngei, and

Achieng Oneko were arrested and charged with "membership and management of Mau Mau" on 17 November 1952. The song books became primary and highly contested evidence in the trial as the prosecutors sought to prove that possession of the booklets and being named in the songs was proof of "membership and management of Mau Mau" even though it was acknowledged that none of the accused had compiled or published the song books. Since that time the songs in these books have been reissued in a variety of published and audiotape formats. They have been anthologized with earlier political songs as well as with songs that were composed during the armed struggle. Table 17.1 is an example of the first three verses of one of the songs and of three different translations.

In studying the history of political songs in Gikuyu it is useful to consider and distinguish contexts of composition, transmission, and performance and to bear in mind the conditions under which the texts were preserved and transmitted. The case of the books of political songs published by Kĩnũthia wa Mũgĩĩa, Mũthee Cheche, Gakaara wa Wanjaũ, Stanley Mathenge, and Ndiba provides relevant examples. In some instances the compilers or people known to the compilers composed and wrote the songs. In other instances, as illustrated above, lyrics seem to have been re-worked from those published in Christian hymnals. Some songs, in addition were heard at political meetings and written down and published by the compilers. There is considerable evidence that the songs were widely distributed in written form and that they were frequently sung at political meetings. This complex history of composition, transmission, and performance was subsequently reduced by L. S. B. Leakey in his discussion of the songs in *Defeating Mau Mau*. In his discussion, Leakey referred to the writers and publishers of the songs as "bards"/"singers" of "hymns" (1955: 55, 62), presumably to strengthen his argument that the songs were produced by "The leaders of the Mau Mau movement" (1955: 53) rather than by those who produced the song books. Leakey may have heard the songs sung, but as the translator for the prosecution in the Kapenguria trial he had access to the published versions that he translated in *Defeating Mau Mau*.

In 1963, at the time of independence in Kenya, a number of the songs from the 1952 song books were reclaimed and republished by one of the original compilers and publishers, Gakaara wa Wanjaũ. Gakaara's *Nyimbo cia Gukunguira Wiathi* (1963) (Songs to Celebrate Freedom) contained four groups of songs. The first group consisted of songs concerned with Olenguruone, a 1948–50 forced resettlement. The second group was made up of songs from the song books. The third group of songs were composed during the liberation struggle. The fourth group consisted of songs composed between 1961 and 1963.

Table 17.1 *Examples of original verses and translations.*

Karechu Mũruku's "Ngwĩka atĩa Thirwo Nĩ Thĩĩna" (*Nyimbo cia Mau Mau* 12)[a]	L. S. B. Leakey's translation of "Kigenyo" (hymn 27) for the Kapenguria prosecution	The Kapenguria defense team's translation of "Kigenyo" (hymn 27)	"Police Harassment" Maina wa Kinyatti's version (96)
	False Witness	*False Allegation / False Story*	
Ngũrora Nairobi ngakora Haraka	I go to Nairobi and I find Haste	When I go to Nairobi I find there that all is Haraka / When I go to Nairobi I come into contact with the police / When I go to London all I get is "Move on there"	In Nairobi I am harassed by the occupying forces And if I return to the countryside I am a Mau Mau "gangster".
Ndacooka Gĩkũyũ ndĩ wa Mau Mau	When I return to Kikuyu I am of Mau Mau	When I go back to Kikuyu I am alleged to be Of Mau Mau (Slater 1955: 92). Version 2 / verse 1: If I go into town I am harried by the police; if I go into the country somebody calls me Mau Mau (Slater 1955: 131).	

		Chorus
Ngwĩka atĩa, ngwĩka atĩa, Thirwo nĩ thĩĩna Ngwĩka atĩa, ngwĩka atĩa, Thirwo nĩ thĩĩna	What shall I do, what shall I do, to be freed of my sorrows? What shall I do, what shall I do to be freed of my sorrows?[b]	*What shall I do?* *What shall I do?* *To be free from this slavery?*
Nĩ ngũruta mbeca cia gũcaria ũtheri, Na rĩrĩa ũkoneka, ngaikara ta ndua.	I will give money to search for light And when it is found I shall be like a big beer gourd	I'll pay any price For the light of liberation, And when it comes I will live in dignity.
Nĩ twĩrutanĩrie twĩ Nyũmba ya Mũmbi, Tũnyitane ithuothe ta thiga rĩa koine.	Let us all work hard together, we of the house of Mumbi. And hold ourselves together like the corner stone (Slater 1955: 91).	We must struggle together as one people, Let us all unite And become like the foundation stone.

[a] Another version of this song is found in D.Kĩnũthia Mũgĩa's *Ũrathi wa Chege wa Kĩbiru*.

[b] Rev. Robert Philip volunteered in his testimony that, "the chorus itself is not an original composition, it is a chorus from one of our well-known hymns" (Slater 1955:91).

The songs from the 1952 song books received international recognition through their re-publication in Ruth Finnegan's much cited 1970 work, *Oral Literature in Africa*. Finnegan's edited versions of the songs were based entirely on the versions published in Leakey's *Defeating Mau Mau*. Finnegan reassessed and challenged Leakey's opinions of the songs and of the liberation struggle in her comparison of the struggle in Kenya to other African nationalist struggles. Yet like Leakey, Finnegan considered the songs part of African political "oral" literature, even though the lyrics for these songs for the most part had been written and had been published.

In the 1970s and early 1980s, the 1952 songs became part of the struggle in Kenyan academia over the meaning of Mau Mau in Kenyan history. In his 1976 paper delivered to the Historical Association of Kenya, "Politics, Culture and Music in Central Kenya: A Study of Mau Mau Hymns," Bethwell A. Ogot presented an "ethnic" view of the songs that was consistent with his arguments and those of his associates concerning the liberation struggle. It was their contention that Mau Mau was an internal struggle between groups within Gikuyu society and not a nationalist liberation struggle. Maina wa Kinyatti challenged Ogot's views of the songs and of the liberation struggle in Kenya in his 1980 *Thunder from the Mountains: Mau Mau Patriotic Songs.* This is the most complete collection of songs available.

Wanjikũ Mũkabi Kabira and Karega Mũtahi included a version of one of the 1952 song book songs as well as other 1950s resistance songs in their 1988 *Gĩkũyũ Oral Literature.* Wanjikũ and Karega's work provides evidence of the entry / re-entry of the songs into oral literature and of the transmission of the songs in oral literature after published versions had been proscribed. In 1989, at the beginning of "the second liberation" in Kenya, Gakaara wa Wanjaũ published *Nyimbo cia Mau Mau* and the musician Joseph Kamaru produced a cassette tape, *Nyimbo cia Mau Mau.* Cassettes of speeches of the late president Jomo Kenyatta were also produced. The cassettes were very popular and were frequently played in Nairobi and central Kenya *matatu* (privately owned public transport vehicles). Subsequently the government banned the playing of "vernacular" music and speeches in *matatu*. In 1994 music in Kenyan languages other than Kiswahili was banned from radio broadcasts and a new cassette of "Mau Mau songs," *Nyimbo cia Mau Mau*, which contained songs from the 1952 song books, was released by Irungu wa Kario.

While the independent presses in the late 1940s and 1950–52 were producing a wide range of lively political, creative, and cultural works, Eagle Press, the colonial government publisher, also became more active in publishing in

Gikuyu. One of its 1950 publications, presumably produced in response to the independent press coverage of the activities of nationalists such as Jomo Kenyatta and Mbiyu Koinage, presented George Washington Carver as an alternative role model (J. M. Rutuku's translation of Janet Schwab's *Mũndũ Mũịrũ Mũũgĩ Mũno–George Washington Carver* [A Very Wise Black Person – George Washington Carver]). A Highway Press publication during this era was a translation of John Bunyan's *Pilgrim's Progress* (*Rũgendo rũa Mũgendi*, 1949).

Gakaara wa Wanjaũ was arrested on 21 October 1952 and was detained until 20 July 1959. During his years in detention Gakaara secretly kept a prison diary that was published as *Mwandĩki wa Mau Mau Ithaamĩrio-inĩ* (1983a)/*Mau Mau Writer in Detention* (1986). The diary documents the experiences of Gakaara and other prisoners who were among the first arrested under a state-of-emergency decree on 21 October 1952. Many of these prisoners along with others were later transported to the Lamu prison and then to a prison camp on Manda Island. In 1956 Gakaara was transferred to the Athi River prison camp where he was forced to work on the building of a dam; it was here that he was later to write "anti-Mau Mau propaganda." Gakaara wrote a play, *Reke Aciirithio nĩ Mehia Maake* (Let the Guilt of His Crimes Weigh Heavy on His Conscience), which was performed a number of times in the camp during July 1956. Initially the play was well received but Gakaara was subsequently accused of writing a play "to foster hatred between detained people and loyalist home-guards" ([1983a]/1986: 191). He was interrogated and delayed from seeking parole.

Gakaara was transferred to a detention camp close to his home in February 1958 but was then "banished" to Hola, which "had become the dumping ground of the unreformable Mau Mau hardcore" ([1983a: 156]/1986: 199). The infamous Hola massacre took place here in March 1959. A heavily armed platoon of over a hundred soldiers set upon approximatedly eighty-five detainees and beat them: "Eleven detainees were battered to death; many others were maimed" ([1983a: 157]/1986: 201).

Gakaara was released from Hola in August 1959 and then lived as a restricted person in his home until May 1960. He had sent the pages of his diary home with fellow detainees when they were released and his wife had collected them upon her release from Kamĩtĩ Women's prison in 1957. After his release, Gakaara selected the songs that were eventually published in *Nyimbo cia Mau Mau* (1989) (Songs of Mau Mau). In 1961 he worked in Nairobi as a staff member of *Sauti ya* KANU (The Voice of KANU), the paper of the Kenya African National

Union. Later he returned to Karatina and again set up his own publishing company. Ngũgĩ wa Thiong'o urged Gakaara to publish his diary. The diary was awarded the NOMA prize in 1984. In 1986 Gakaara was detained and tortured on the basis of false charges that he had been associated with the Mwakenya movement.

Gakaara is probably most well-known to readers of Gikuyu because of his fictional works. He published a wide range of fictional works including forty installments in the wa-Nduuta series published in the magazine *Gikuyu na Mumbi*. In 1964 a short story by Gakaara won second place out of 300 entries submitted to Chemchemi Cultural Centre's short-story competition. The central character of the *Gikuyu na Mumbi Magazine* series, KĩWaĩ Wa-Nduuta, is a middle-aged former freedom fighter who struggles to survive and make sense of life in contemporary Kenya. The best-known installments in the series are three that were republished together as the short novel, *Wa-Nduuta: Hingo ya Paawa* (The Time of Power). In this 1983 novel Wa-Nduuta and his friend Conjo happen to arrive in Nairobi in the early morning of 1 August 1982, the day of the attempted coup. As they attempt to find out about the coup and then to escape the violent aftermath, they witness and become involved in the violence that took place in various parts of the city on that day and subsequently. In the final section of the story wa-Nduuta returns to Nairobi to recover Conjo's body. Others stories in the series deal with social issues such as alcohol abuse (*Wirirage Gutiri na Riene*, no. 2, and *Wa-Nduuta Gukinya Ikara kwa Bibikubwa* (Wa-Nduuta Comes to Stay at Bibi Kubwa's, no. 19), theft (*Wa-Nduuta Gukinya Ikara kwa Bibikubwa*, no. 19), violence (*Hingo ya Paawa)*, fraudulent land schemes (*Wa-Nduuta Kugaya Mugunda wa Thothaiti na Hinya* (Wa-Nduuta and the Dividing of the Society's Farm by Force, no. 31), family planning (*Wa-Nduuta Ugo-ini wa Kunyiihia Uciari* (Wa-Nduuta and the Matter of Decreasing the Number of Births, no. 24), and remembering the liberation struggle (*Wa-Nduuta Gukunguira Miaka 20 Ki-Mau Mau* (Wa-Nduuta Celebrating Twenty Years Since Mau Mau, no. 34). In *Wa-Nduuta Gukunguira Miaka 20 Ki-Mau Mau* Wa-Nduuta and Mũmbi, who were both guerillas in the liberation struggle, explain the history of the struggle to Mũmbi's children, who initially laugh when they hear their mother and Wa-Nduuta speak of Mau Mau. Mumbi's children become enthralled by the history they learn from their mother and her friend. When Wa-Nduuta returns home to his wives and tells them what happened they decide to invite their daughter and Mumbi and her children to their home for a celebration of the liberation struggle.

Gakaara wa Wanjaũ also published works in Swahili, and he frequently used English and Swahili in his fiction for stylistic effects. For example, in *Hingo ya*

Paawa the central character Wa-Nduuta hears the cries of a young Indian woman who is being sexually assaulted by a soldier:

> Bacha kuua! Mimi bana kataa kitu! Pilisi, pilisi, pilisi! kataa bana, ua bana! (1983c: 10)
>
> Don't kill me! I won't refuse anything! Please, please, please, I won't refuse! Don't kill me.

The young woman here speaks in broken Swahili. Wa-Nduuta speaks in Standard Swahili when he picks up the gun the soldier has left near the door, and orders, "Mikono juu! Tena juu!" ("Hands up! Up! Further!"). He then tells the young woman, "Toa nguo zake zote na uzilete hapa!" ("Take off his clothes and bring them here!") and he continues speaking Swahili to order the soldier to run outside in his underwear, "Kimbia! Toroka na uende mbio kabisa!" ("Run! Get out of here as fast as possible"). Wa-Nduuta adopts Swahili as the language of the military to threaten the soldier and then puts on the soldier's uniform to complete his disguise and to escape (1983c: 10).

Gakaara was also committed to the promotion of writing in African languages. He developed a series of instructional materials for use in teaching Gikuyu, the *Thooma Gĩĩgĩkũyũ Kĩega* (1988) (Read Gikuyu Well) series and he developed educational materials (the *Mwalimu wa Lugha Tatu* (Teacher of Three Languages) series for primary-school teachers who teach in trilingual instructional contexts where English, Swahili, and one of twenty Kenyan languages are the languages of instruction.

Historical studies written in Gikuyu have included Gakaara wa Wanjaũ's 1971 *Agikuyu, Mau Mau na Wiyathi* (The Agikuyu, Mau Mau and Freedom), his *Mwandĩki wa Mau Mau Ithaamĩrio-inĩ/Mau Mau Writer in Detention* (1983a, 1986), P. Kibaara Kabutu's 1963 *Mbaara ya Wiyathi wa Kenya Kuuma 1890–1963* (The War for the Freedom of Kenya from 1890–1963), D. Kĩnũthia Mũgĩa's 1979 *Ũrathi wa Cege wa Kĩbiru* (The Prophecy of Cege wa Kĩbiru) and Albert Wakang'ũ Mũnene's 1995 *Mũtaarani Mũgĩkũyũ* (The Gikuyu Advisor). A large number of ethnographic and cultural works have also been written in Gikuyu. In addition to works already mentioned, these have included: Gakaara wa Wanjaũ's *Kienyu wa Ngai Kirima-ini gia Tumutumu* (1952) (A Young Man at Tumutumu Hill), *Kiguni gia Twana* (1951) (The Benefit of Children), and *Mihiriga ya Agikuyu* (1967) (Clans of the Gikuyu), B. Mareka Gecaga's *Kariũki na Mũthoni* (1946) (Kariuki and Muthoni), Mathew Njoroge Kabetũ's *Kaguraru na Waithĩra* (1961) (Kaguraru and Waithĩra) and *Kĩrĩra kĩa Ũgĩkũyũ: Kuuma Mũndũ Amonyokio o Nginya Rĩrĩa Akahinga Riitho Aarĩkia Kwĩgaya* (1947) (The Wisdom of Gikuyuland: From the Time a Person is Born until S/he Shuts His/Her Eye

Having Made a Will) and Philip M. Ng'ang'a's *Mũũgĩ nĩ Mũtaare* (1996) (A Wise Person is an Advisor).

While most of these works have focused on standard ethnographic topics such as marriage and kinship, Gakaara wa Wanjaũ's undated *Ugwati wa Muthungu Muiru* (The Danger of the Black European) critiqued the linguistic and cultural practices of those he described as "Black Europeans." The book mocks the pretensions of Agikuyu who fashion themselves according to colonial models. In the first illustration in the book a father is welcomed home by his daughter who addresses him by saying, "Harũ ndandi" ("Hello Daddy"), to which he responds, "Harũ mbembi" ("Hello Baby") (p. 5). The second illustration depicts a man and a woman speaking English in an urban setting. They are being laughed at and are called "fools" by a European observer because of their claims of discomfort in using Gikuyu and of having forgotten how to speak Gikuyu (p. 9). In the dialogue that follows another illustration a woman applies to a clerk for a housework position in his home. She speaks to him in Gikuyu. He pretends that he doesn't understand the language and speaks rudely to her in English (p. 14). In a fourth illustration a stern teacher forbids unhappy students from speaking Gikuyu and tells them that they will be beaten if they speak the language (p. 17). The cover and final illustration in the book is of a man with a rooster in his head that speaks for him in English when he opens his mouth (p. 20).

Ngũgĩ wa Thiong'o is the most well known writer in Gikuyu. In 1976 while chair of the University of Nairobi Literature Department he worked, along with Ngũgĩ wa Mĩriĩ, with the Kamĩrĩĩthũ Cultural Center in the development and production of the play *Ngaahika Ndeenda (I Will Marry When I Want).* The play was developed cooperatively and incorporates historically significant resistance songs in Gikuyu. The initial productions of *Ngaahika Ndeenda* were perhaps the most enthusiastically received productions in the history of Kenyan theater. The play was regularly produced in the 1980s and 1990s, although some productions were closed down by government authorities. The play has had a continuing influence on the growth and expansion of resistance and of popular theatre in Kenya and elsewhere. The production and its reception were also the initial inspiration for Ngũgĩ's decision to continue writing in Gikuyu. In 1999, the play was translated into Tigrinya, a language of Eritrea. In January 2000, Ngũgĩ had his first opportunity in twenty-five years to see a performance of *Ngaahika Ndeenda* when it was produced in the Tigrinya translation for the "Against All Odds" conference in Asmara, Eritrea. Ngũgĩ, Nawal El-Saadawi, Ama ata Aidoo, and Mbulelo Mzamane were the chairs of this conference that celebrated African-language literatures.

Ngũgĩ wa Thiong'o was arrested on 31 December 1977. During the year of his detention he decided to write the novel *Caitaani Mũtharaba-inĩ*, his first novel in Gikuyu. *Caitaani Mũtharaba-inĩ*, later translated as *Devil on the Cross* (1980, 1982), concerns a group of people who have received invitations to attend a feast of thieves and robbers. The characters meet in a local taxi/bus on their way to the feast, a feast organized by the devil that becomes a competition between the planners to determine who has been and will continue to be the most exploitative. Ngũgĩ wrote this novel in prison on toilet paper. The novel was first published in 1980, as was the play *Ngaahika Ndeenda*, which he wrote with Ngũgĩ wa Mĩrĩ.

Upon his release from prison on 12 December 1978, Ngũgĩ wa Thiong'o composed the musical drama *Maitũ Njugĩra* (Mother, Sing for Me). This work incorporates eighty songs of resistance that were composed in eight Kenyan languages. According to Ngũgĩ, approximately 10,000 people attended the open rehearsals of the play, which were the only performances that took place before the production was closed down by government authorities. During this period Ngũgĩ published his prison diary *Detained* (1981) and also wrote a series of children's books in Gikuyu: *Bathitoora ya Njamba Nene/Njamba Nene's Pistol* (1984), *Njamba Nene na Mbaathi ĩ Mathagu/Njamba Nene and the Flying Bus* (1982), and *Njamba Nene na Cibũ Kĩng'ang'i/Njamba Nene and the Cruel Chief* (1986).

Ngũgĩ was forced into exile in 1982. There was a coup attempt in Kenya on 1 August of that year while Ngũgĩ was in Britain promoting the publication of the English translation of *Caitaani Mũtharaba-inĩ* (*Devil on the Cross*). Upon learning that he would be implicated as a conspirator in the coup and possibly executed, Ngũgĩ decided to remain in Britain. In 1986, Ngũgĩ published his first major work in exile – *Decolonising the Mind* – in which he made his famous declaration to write subsequently in Gikuyu and Kiswahili.

Ngũgĩ's *Matigari ma Njirũũngi* was published in 1986. This novel is a prose poem about neocolonialism and the ways in which it is comprehended by a survivor/survivors of the wars against imperialism. The characters in the novel struggle to understand and resist neocolonialism through the discourses of nationalism, Christianity, and liberalism. When these discourses prove unworkable in their struggles they turn to what Ngũgĩ in *Decolonising the Mind* termed "the language of struggle." The author notes in the preface to the translation of *Matigari ma Njirũũngi* (1986b) that the novel itself was forced into exile when the Kenya government searched for the main character and then confiscated the remaining copies of the novel from the publisher's warehouse. In addition to publishing fiction in Gikuyu, Ngũgĩ has also published articles of literary criticism. He published "English: A Language for the World?" in the *Yale Journal of Criticism* in 1990 and has published both criticism and poetry in the journal *Mũtiiri*.

Ngũgĩ wa Thiong'o and Ngũgĩ wa Mĩriĩ dedicated their translation of *Ngaahika Ndeenda* to writers in Gikuyu and in particular to Gakaara wa Wanjaũ. Ngũgĩ's early novels (*Weep Not Child, The River Between, A Grain of Wheat, Petals of Blood*), short stories, and plays (*The Black Hermit* and, with Micere Mugo, *The Trial of Dedan Kimathi*) were written and published in English. He also wrote and has continued to publish works of criticism (*Writers in Politics, The Barrel of the Pen, Decolonising the Mind, Moving the Center*) in English. Numerous scholars have found evidence in Ngũgĩ's fiction of his reading of novels in English. In his criticism, Ngũgĩ has frequently made reference to his reading of literature in Swahili and to his study of progressive, socialist, and anti-imperialist writers. Ngũgĩ's commitment to engagement and dialogue with the "languages of struggle" as he has explained in *Decolonising the Mind* has clearly been informed by his understanding of the history of writing in Gikuyu as well as by his readings of the works of Franz Fanon and Paolo Freire. Critics of Ngũgĩ's decision to write in Gikuyu have not indicated that they are aware of his study of Fanon and Freire nor have they acknowledged his understanding of the history of writing in Gikuyu. His critics often have dismissed Ngugi's decision to write in Gikuyu as an "ethnic" or "tribalistic" action that contradicts his socialist commitments. Yet those who have read Fanon and Freire or Ngugi's own descriptions of his struggles to write in Gikuyu and to establish dialogues with workers and peasants find his decisions on issues of language consistent with his progressive commitments.

There have been a number of recent intertextual studies of literature in Gikuyu. Simon Gikandi (1991, 2000), Gĩtahi Gĩtĩtĩ (1995), and Alamin Mazrui and Lupenda Mphande (1995) have provided ground-breaking studies in this area in their considerations of intertexuality in Ngũgĩ's works. Gikandi (1991) considers the ways in which Ngũgĩ uses Mau Mau legends and coded language in *Matigari*. In his 1995 study Gikandi reflects upon Ngũgĩ's use of Mau Mau songs and Gikuyu language versions of Christian iconography. One of the most important recent studies of Ngũgĩ's work is Gikandi's *Ngugi wa Thiong'o*. Gĩtahi discusses the figures of the gĩcaandi poet and of gĩcaandi poetry in *Caitaani Mũtharaba-inĩ*. Mphande and Mazrui clarify the ways in which Ngũgĩ wa Thiong'o has revised in his most recent novels the intertextual practices of engagement with forms of orature evident in his earlier works.

Eileen Julien asserts that Ngũgĩ's *Caitaani Mũtharaba-inĩ* as well as *Decolonising the Mind* challenge notions of the novel and of orality as "essences." She argues that in *Caitaani Mũtharaba-inĩ* "oral language" is presented as "a quality of Kenyan culture *now*" (1992: 143; emphasis in original). According to Julien, "The contemporaneity" of *Caitaani Mũtharaba-inĩ* "demonstrates that orality is neither of the past nor the elementary stage of an evolutionary process" (1992: 144). What she says of *Caitaani Mũtharaba-inĩ* seems equally valid to a discussion of *Matigari*:

> It does not use the "oral tradition" as a bulwark to inspire confidence or action by association with a people's past grandeur or wisdom and virtue. It is neither the "source of truth" nor an exemplary quality of African culture to be retreated into or represented textually; rather it offers verbal means and procedures for constructing and analyzing an issue. (1992: 146)

Through parody *Matigari* also challenges notions of biblical parables, legends, allegories, radio speeches, as well as Ngũgĩ's own earlier works as static authoritative texts. Julien's argument that spoken art forms are a means to analyze and discuss issues in *Caitaani Mũtharaba-inĩ* may also be applicable to Gakaara's fiction where Wa-Nduuta is neither hero nor anti-hero but a survivor who uses the range of verbal resources available to him to "get by" in the world.

Consideration of gĩcaandi and of the history of some political song books may extend and clarify the arguments concerning "orality" made by Julien in her discussion of *Caitaani Mũtharaba-inĩ*. In studying literature in Gikuyu it becomes apparent that what might seem obvious distinctions between orature and written literature may not be clearly evident. In *Caitaani Mũtharaba-inĩ* the character Gatuĩria asks, "Who can play the gĩcaandi for us today and read and interpret the verses written on the gourd?" (1992: 59). As this question makes clear and as has been explained in more detail in recent studies by Gĩtahi and Kimani, the performance of gĩcaandi involves extemporaneous sung poetic composition based upon readings and interpretations of ideographic symbols engraved on a calabash. The performance is dialogic as the poets comment upon each other's compositions. Simultaneously both poets read and interpret the ideographs. Kimani argues that "the text on the gĩcaandi gourd acts as an embodiment of the authority of the inscribed text" and that reading the gĩcaandi is "a recognition and re-activation of ideas previously expressed in preceding performances" (1993: 188). It is also possible that the gĩcaandi ideographs embody an even wider set of metaphors. Assessment of gĩcaandi ideographs is speculative without close comparison of a number of gĩcaandi gourds and without detailed explanations in Gikuyu of the symbols, yet even comparison of the two gourds diagrammed in Vittorio Merlo Pick's study (1973) suggests that the symbols are part of a shared system in which metaphors are pictured. For example, on both gourds, long narrow shapes that extend the length of the gourd and are filled with small dots embody rivers / running water seemingly as a metaphor for communication across boundaries. The cowrie shell that is explained as "the blacksmith's wife pregnant" seems mnemonic of key elements of the frequently told story in which the pregnant wife of a man who has gone to work at the forge is tormented by an ogre. Do the gĩcaandi ideographs embody metaphors? Are they the basis of a writing system that is used exclusively in the expression of verbal artistry? Reading gĩcaandi is clearly a topic that merits further study.

In 1994, Ngũgĩ wa Thiong'o founded the journal *Mũtiiri* (The Supporter), devoted to literary criticism, poetry, and memoirs. Writers who have contributed to *Mũtiiri* have included Cege Gĩthiora, Gĩcingiri wa Ndĩgĩrĩgĩ, Gĩtahi Gĩtĩtĩ, K. K. Gĩtĩĩri, Kĩmani Njogu, Maina wa Kĩnyattĩ, Ngĩna wa Kĩarĩĩ, Ngũgĩ wa Thiong'o, Ngũgĩ wa Mĩrĩĩ, and Waithĩra wa Mbuthia. The journal has also included translations into Gikuyu of poems by Abdilatif Abdalla, Alamin Mazrui, Ariel Dorfman, and Otto Rene Castillo. Gĩtahi Gĩtĩtĩ has recently published a volume of poetry, *Mboomu Ĩraatuthũkire Nairobi na Marebeta Mangĩ* (The Bomb Blast in Nairobi and Other Poems). The poem that provides the title of the volume concerns the 7 August 1998, US Embassy bombing in Nairobi.

Newspapers that are currently being published in Gikuyu include: *Mwĩhoko: Gũtirĩ Ũtuku Ũtakĩaga* (Trust: There is no Night without End), *Mũiguithania* (The Reconciler), and *Kihooto: Kĩhooto Kiunaga Ũta Mũgeete* (Justice: Justice Prevails over the Drawn Bow), published by the Mũrang'a Catholic Diocese. These newspapers publish news articles and commentaries on current events as well as poetry, fiction, and essays on history and language. Well-known Kenyan writers who contributed to 1997 issues of *Mwĩhoko* included essayist and novelist Wahome Mũtahi, editor Sam Mbure, and playwright Bantu Mwaũra. *Mwĩhoko* is a monthly publication with a circulation in 2001 of approximately 30,000 copies per issue. Earlier the Catholic Diocese of Mũrang'a published *Inooro*. *Inooro* was banned in 1992.

The survival and growth of Gikuyu literature despite the extensive colonial and post-independence efforts to ban and to suppress it ensure the future of literature in Gikuyu. Gikuyu literature's resistance and radical history and on-going engagement with political and social issues have made writing in Gikuyu relevant to contemporary readers and writers who continue to contribute to its growth. The growth of literature in Gikuyu has encouraged the development of literatures in other Kenyan languages and writers in Gikuyu such as Ngũgĩ wa Thiong'o and Gakaara wa Wanjaũ have been actively involved in the promotion of literature in Kiswahili and other Kenyan languages. Literature in Gikuyu has a secure position as a Kenyan national literature, as an East African and African literature, and as a literature of what Ngũgĩ wa Thiong'o has termed "the real language of humankind: the language of struggle" (1986a: 108).

Select bibliography

Primary works

Anon. 1952a. *Kenya ni Yakwa*. Nairobi: Gakaara Book Service.

1952b. *Miikarire ya Thikwota*. Nairobi: Gakaara Book Service.

Bunyan, John. [1949] 1960. *Rũgendo rũa Mũgendi*. Nairobi: Highway Press. 2nd edn. East African Literature Bureau.

Gakaara wa Wanjaũ. n.d. *Ugwati wa Muthungu Muiru*. Karatina, Kenya: Gakaara Press.

[1946] 1951. *Ngwenda Unjurage*. (Reprinted from *Uhoro wa Ugurani*, 1946.) Nairobi: Gakaara Book Service, 1951; Gakaara Publishing Service, 1961, 1966; Gakaara Book Service, *Atiriri Series*, no. 5, 1967; Karatina: Gakaara Press, 1985.

1983. *A Kenyan Market. Literature: Gakaara wa Njau and the Atiriri Series. Ba Shiru Literature Supplement*, 1. Trans. Patrick R. Bennett. Madison: *Ba Shiru:* vii-12.

1952. *Kienyu wa Ngai Kirima-ini gia Tumutumu*. Nairobi: Gakaara Book Service.

[1952] 1971. *Nyimbo cia Gikuyu na Mumbi*. Nairobi: Gakaara Book Service.

[1952] 1989. *Wĩtĩkio wa Gĩkĩkũyũ na Mumbi*. Nairobi: Gakaara Book Service. Rev. edn. Karatina: Gakaara Press. Reprinted in *Mwandĩki wa Mau Mau Ithaamĩrio-inĩ* (p. 187)/*Mau Mau Writer in Detention* (p. 250).

1963. *Nyimbo cia Gukunguira Wiathi*. Nairobi: Gakaara Publishing Service.

1967a. *Mihiriga ya Agikuyu*. Revised and enlarged edition of *Wikumie na Muhiriga Waku*. Karatina: Gakaara Press.

1967b. *Wirirage Gutiri na Riene. Gikuyu na Mumbi Magazine*, no. 2. Karatina: Gakaara Press.

1968. Rev. edn. 1988. *Turwimbo na Tumathako twa Twana*. Karatina: Gakaara Book Service.

n.d. [1971]. *Agikuyu, Mau Mau na Wiyathi*. Karatina: Gakaara Book Service.

1980. *Wa-Nduuta Gukinya Ikara kwa Bibikubwa. Gikuyu na Mumbi Magazine*, no. 19. Karatina: Gakaara Press.

1982. *Wa-Nduuta Ugo-ini wa Kunyiihia Uciari. Gikuyu na Mumbi Magazine*, no. 24. Karatina: Gakaara Press.

[1983a] 1986. *Mwandĩki wa Mau Mau Ithaamĩrio-inĩ/Mau Mau Writer in Detention*. Nairobi: Heinemann.

1983b. *Wa-Nduuta Gukunguira Miaka 20 Ki-Mau Mau. Gikuyu na Mumbi Magazine*, no. 34. Karatina: Gakaara Press.

1983c. *Wa-Nduuta: Hingo ya Paawa. Gikuyu na Mumbi Magazine*, nos. 28–31. Karatina: Gakaara Press. Republished in one volume, 1984.

1983d. *Wa-Nduuta Kugaya Mugunda wa Thothaiti na Hinya. Gikuyu na Mumbi Magazine*, no. 31. Karatina: Gakaara Press.

1988. *Thooma Gĩĩgĩkũyũ Kĩega*. Rev. edn. Karatina: Gakaara Press.

1989. *Nyimbo cia Mau Mau*. Karatina: Gakaara Press.

Gathigira, S. K. [1934] 1952. *Mĩikarĩre ya Agĩkĩkũyũ*. London: Sheldon. Rpt. 1973. Nairobi: Equatorial.

Gecaga, B. Mareka. [1946] 1971 and 1975. *Kariũki na Mũthoni*. Nairobi: Highway Press. Republished Nairobi: East African Literature Bureau.

Gĩtahi Gĩtĩtĩ. 1999a. *Mboomu Ĩraatuthũkire Nairobi na Marebeta Mangĩ*. Ngoro Njega Publications.

1999b. *Mũkũnga-Mbura*. Trenton: Africa World Press.

Haji Mwalimu Hamis. [1936] 1937. *The Muslim Prayer Translated in Gikuyu (Swahili – English – Urdu)*. Lahore: Feroze Din, Swahili Manzil. Translated in Bennett, n.d.: 230–31.

Justin Itotia wa Kimacia. [1937] 1961. *Endwo nĩ Irĩ na Irĩĩri*. Wangigi Market: Justin Itotia.

Kabetũ, Mathew Njoroge. 1947, 1966. *Kĩrĩra kĩa Ũgĩkũyũ: Kuuma Mũndũ Amonyokio o Nginya Rĩrĩa Akahinga Riitho Aarĩkia Kwĩgaya*. Nairobi: Eagle Press, East African Literature Bureau.

1961. *Kaguraru na Waithĩra*. London: Nelson.

Kabutu, P. Kibaara. 1963. *Mbaara ya Wiyathi wa Kenya Kuuma 1890–1963*. Nairobi: P. K. Kabutu.

Kelsall, J. M. 1931. *Ũhoro wa Ngoma ĩrĩa Njũru na Mũgate*. London: Sheldon.

Kĩnũthia wa Mũgĩĩa. 1951. *Nyimbo cia Kwarahura Agikuyu/Songs to Awaken the Agikuyu*. Nairobi: Mumenyereri Press.

Kũrani Theru: Kikuyu Translation of the Holy Qur'an with Arabic Text. 1988. Surrey: Islam International Publications.

Maina wa Kinyatti, ed. 1980. *Thunder From the Mountains: Mau Mau Patriotic Songs*. London: Zed.

Merlo Pick, Vittorio. 1973. *Ndaĩ na Gĩcandĩ: Kikuyu Enigmas, Enigmi Kikuyu*. Bologna: EMI.

Mũgĩa, D. Kĩnũthia. 1979. *Ũrathi wa Cege wa Kĩbiru*. Nairobi: Kenya Literature Bureau.

Mugweru, Mwaniki. [1946] 1952a. *Kamuingi Koyaga Ndiri*. Nairobi: Gakaara Book Service.

1952b. *Wiyathi wa Andu Airu*. Nairobi: Gakaara Book Service.

Mũnene, Albert Wakang'ũ. 1995. *Mũtaarani Mũgĩkũyũ*. Nairobi: East African Educational Publishers.

Ng'ang'a, Philip M. 1996. *Mũũgĩ nĩ Mũtaare*. Nairobi: East African Educational Publishers.

Ngũgĩ wa Thiong'o. 1964. *Weep Not Child*. London: Heinemann Educational Books.

1965. *The River Between*. London: Heinemann.

1967. *A Grain of Wheat*. London: Heinemann.

1968. *The Black Hermit*. London: Heinemann Educational Books.

1977. *Petals of Blood*. London: Heinemann.

1980. *Caitaani Mũtharaba-inĩ*. Nairobi: Heinemann.

[1980] 1982. *Caitaani Mũtharaba-inĩ/Devil on the Cross*. Nairobi: Heinemann.

1981. *Writers in Politics: Essays*. London: Heinemann Educational Books.

1982. *Njamba Nene na Mbaathi ĩ Mathagu*. Nairobi: Heinemann.

[1982] 1986. *Njamba Nene na Mbaathi ĩ Mathagu/Njamba Nene and the Flying Bus*. Trans. Wangũi wa Goro. Nairobi: Heinemann.

1983. *The Barrel of A Pen: Resistance to Repression in Neo-Colonial Kenya*. Trenton: Africa World Press.

1984. *Bathitoora ya Njamba Nene*. Nairobi: Heinemann.

[1984] 1986. *Bathitoora ya Njamba Nene/Njamba Nene's Pistol.* Trans. Wangũi wa Goro. Nairobi: Heinemann.

1986a. *Njamba Nene na Chibũ Kĩng'ang'i/Njamba Nene and the Cruel Chief.* Nairobi: Heinemann.

1986b. *Matigari ma Njirũũngi.* Nairobi: Heinemann.

1986c. *Njamba Nene na Cibũ Kĩng'ang'i.* Nairobi: Heinemann.

[1986d] 1989. *Matigari ma Njirũũngi/Matigari.* Trans. Wangũi wa Goro. Nairobi: Heinemann; London: Heinemann International.

1993. *Moving the Center: The Struggle for Cultural Freedoms.* Oxford: James Currey; Portsmouth, NH: Heinemann.

Ngũgĩ wa Thiong'o and Micere Githae Mugo. 1976. *The Trial of Dedan Kimathi.* London: Heinemann Educational Books.

Ngũgĩ wa Thiong'o and Ngũgĩ wa Mĩriĩ. [1980] 1982, *Ngaahika Ndeenda: Ithaako rĩa Ngerekano/I Will Marry When I Want.* Nairobi: Heinemann.

Schwab, Janet. 1950. *Mũndũ Mũirũ Mũũgĩ Mũno – George Washington Carver.* Trans. J. M. Ruthuku. Nairobi: Eagle Press/East African Literature Bureau.

Wanjikũ Mũkabi Kabira and Karega Mũtahi. 1988. *Gĩkũyũ Oral Literature.* Nairobi: East African Educational Publishers.

Secondary works

Bennett, Patrick Rowland. n.d. "The Development of Kikuyu Literature: A Survey of the Oral and Written, Traditional and Modern, Literatures of the Kikuyu of Kenya." Typescript.

Biersteker, Ann. 1994. "Mũtaratara wa Mabuku Marĩa Maandĩkĩĩtwo kana Gũtaũrwo na Rũthiomi rwa Gĩĩgĩkũyũ," *Mũtiiri*, 1. 3. (A comprehensive bibliography of works published in Gĩĩgĩkũyũ.)

Berman, Bruce J., and John M. Lonsdale. 1992. *Unhappy Valley: Conflict in Kenya and Africa.* Oxford: James Currey.

1998. "The Labors of *Muigwithania:* Jomo Kenyatta as Author, 1928–45." *Research in African Literatures* 29. 1: 16–42.

Cagnolo, Father C. 1933. *The Akikuyu: Their Customs, Traditions and Folklore.* Trans. V. M. Pick. Nyeri: The Mission Printing School.

Finnegan, Ruth. 1970. *Oral literature in Africa.* Oxford: Clarendon Press.

Gikandi, Simon. 1991. "The Epistemology of Translation: Ngũgĩ, Matigari, and the Politics of Language." *Research in African Literatures* 22. 4: 162–67.

1995. "Moments of Melancholy: Ngũgĩ and the Discourse of Emotions." In *The World of Ngũgĩ wa Thiong'o.* Ed. Charles Cantalupo. Trenton: Africa World Press: 59–72.

2000. *Ngugi wa Thiong'o.* Cambridge: Cambridge University Press.

Gĩtahi Gĩtĩtĩ. 1995. "Recuperating a 'Disappearing' Art Form: Resonances of Gĩcaandi in Ngũgĩ wa Thiong'o's *Devil on the Cross.*" In *The World of Ngũgĩ wa Thiong'o.* Ed. Charles Cantalupo. Trenton: Africa World Press: 109–27.

Julien, Eileen. 1992. *African Novels and the Question of Orality.* Bloomington: Indiana University Press.

Kaggia, Bildad. 1975. *The Roots of Freedom. 1921–1963.* Nairobi: East African Publishing House.

Kenyatta, Jomo. 1938. *Facing Mount Kenya: The Tribal Life of the Gikuyu*. London: Secker and Warburg.

Kimani Njogu, Simon. 1993. "Dialogic Poetry: Contestation and Social Challenge in East African Poetic Genres." Diss. Yale University.

1995. "Decolonizing the Child." In *The World of Ngũgĩ wa Thiong'o*. Ed. Charles Cantalupo. Trenton: Africa World Press: 119–40.

Leakey, L. S. B. 1955. *Defeating Mau Mau*. London: Methuen.

1977. *The Southern Kikuyu Before 1903*. London: Academic Press.

Mazrui, Alamin, and Lupenga Mphande. 1995. "Orality and the Literature of Combat: Ngũgĩ and the Legacy of Fanon." In *The World of Ngũgĩ wa Thiong'o*. Ed. Charles Cantalupo. Trenton: Africa World Press: 159–83.

Muoria, Henry. 1994. *I, the Gikuyu and The White Fury*. Nairobi: East African Educational Publishers.

Ngũgĩ wa Thiong'o. 1981. *Detained*. Nairobi: Heinemann.

1983. *Barrel of a Pen: Resistance to Repression in Neo-Colonial Kenya*. Trenton: Africa World Press.

1985. "On Writing in Gikuyu." *Research in African Literatures* 16.4: 151–56.

1986. *Decolonising the Mind*. Portsmouth: Heinemann.

1993. *Moving the Center: The Struggle for Cultural Freedoms*. Portsmouth: Heinemann.

Ogot, Bethwell A. 1976. "Politics, Culture and Music in Central Kenya: A Study of Mau Mau Hymns." *Kenya Historical Review* 5. 2: 275–86.

Pugliese, Cristiana. 1995. *Author, Publisher and Gikuyu Nationalist: The Life and Writings of Gakaara wa Wanjau*. Bayreuth: E. Breitinger, Bayreuth University.

Rosberg, Carl G., Jr., and John Nottingham. 1966. *The Myth of "Mau Mau": Nationalism in Kenya*. Stanford: Stanford University Press.

Routledge, William Scoresby, and Katherine Routledge. 1910. *With a Prehistoric People: The Akikuyu of British East Africa*. London: Edward Arnold.

Sicherman, Carol. 1989. *Ngũgĩ wa Thiong'o: A Bibliography of Primary and Secondary Sources, 1957–1987*. New York: Hans Zell.

1990. *Ngũgĩ wa Thiong'o: The Making of a Rebel: A Source Book in Kenyan Literature and Resistance*. New York: Hans Zell.

Slater, Montagu. 1955. *The Trial of Jomo Kenyatta*. London: Secker and Warburg.

18

The emergence of written Hausa literature

OUSSEINA ALIDOU

This chapter looks at the development of Hausa written literature from the formative stages to its modern status, beginning with a critical analysis of the dynamism and fluidity of the very identity of "Hausaness" it seeks to represent, as well as the sociohistorical and political conditions that have influenced its evolution over time, which demonstrate an important interplay between history, literature, language, and society. In mainstream Hausa scholarship, Hausaland has traditionally been seen to include northern Nigeria and, on rare occasions, Niger. This relatively narrow focus on the West African region populated by the Hausa people will be maintained in this chapter. But this demographic space will also be interrogated as a way of opening up new possibilities in the study of literary activities in the Hausa language in the Hausa diaspora, in places like the Sudan, Northern Ghana, and the Middle East, and of comparative literary experiences between the Hausa "motherland" and the Hausa diaspora.

Hausaness: language, culture, and identity

Hausaness as an identity does not encompass a monolithic unit. It is a convergence that reflects Ali Mazrui's notion of a triple heritage of indigenous African, Islamic, and European elements, and which extends, historically, from pre-Islamic, precolonial time to the present era. Demographically, it incorporates descendants of the original Hausa seven states, the descendants of other ethnic groups such as the Fulani, Arab, Tamajaq, and Nupe who have been linguistically and culturally assimilated as a result of sociohistorical contact, political affiliations, intermarriages, and other more recent "converts" in the region arising from both colonial and postcolonial dynamics. Each group in this constituency has become a supplier of valued cultural ingredients that today make up Hausa identity. But because a Fulani contribution to Hausaness has been prominent, the phenomenon may now be more appropriately described as the Hausa–Fulani formation.

In metaphorical terms, then, Hausaness is a space with many entrances that provide admission and accommodation to individuals of divergent ethnic and cultural origins. Each member occupies a portion of that space without being fully cognizant of the structural layout of the whole. Within the Hausa society, a certain intracultural relativity prevails, allowing for a multiplicity of interpretations of what Hausaness actually means – for it certainly means slightly different things to its different members depending on their location within that Hausa space.

Geographically Hausaness is a space that transcends present-day northern Nigeria, the supposed locus of Hausa "authenticity" as reflected in mainstream Hausa studies. It is thus a product of a dynamic interculturalism among people and ethnicities that share a collective consciousness about that identity in spite of the scattering of their entities across contemporary postcolonial boundaries. At the same time, however, Hausaness is constantly being reconfigured in its different locations, as its literary history has amply demonstrated, without losing its shared core values. In cultural terms, Hausaness must be understood "[not as] a given entity, but a resource that is being constantly re-worked both by jigsaw-makers and by jigsaw-doers. As tradition is invented so culture is also reconstructed" (Furniss 1996: 7).

Written Hausa literature: the formative years

While one can argue that in most Afro-Islamic cultures, the development of literacy, which led to the emergence of written literary traditions, coincided with the spread of Islam, these cultures differ in their choices of languages of written classical literatures. Although the Swahili, for example, developed a local written tradition based on the Arabic script over four centuries ago, Islamic Swahili culture hardly produced literary works in any genre in the Arabic language. This contrasts with the early development of a written literary tradition among the Somali. Until recently, traditional Somali written literature was composed primarily in Arabic, with literature in the Somali language being predominantly oral. Somali culture thus did not fully develop an *ajami* literary tradition in the Somali language. The genesis of Hausa literary tradition, on the other hand, combines both the Swahili and Somali experiences: Arabic literature and Fulfulde literature are the precursors of the written Hausa *ajami* literature which developed later in the eighteenth and nineteenth centuries, if not earlier.

In the early seventh and eighth centuries, the trans-Saharan trade fostered not only multicultural contacts among sub-Saharan ethnic groups such as the Hausa, Fulani, and Tamajaq, but also contacts between these groups and North African Arabs and Turkish populations. The contacts were very instrumental in the early spread of Islam in sub-Saharan Africa in general and more especially among the Hausa and later, the Hausa–Fulani.

During the fourteenth century, *jihadist* and Muslim scholars foresaw the limitation of an Islamic theological training which precluded new converts in the non-Arab world from acquiring a knowledge of Arabic language; to them Arabic was essential in gaining an adequate understanding of Islam. As a result the Islamic University Mosque of Sankore in the province of Timbuktu, situated in present-day Mali, was created and modeled upon older Islamic Universities of North Africa such as the University of Al-Azhar (founded 972 CE) and the Universities of Fez and Cordova to cater for students of Islamic studies from the western Sudanic belt. The graduates from the University of Sankore were in charge of spreading this formalized intellectual tradition of Islamic learning in newly converted regions. In the words of Hamidu Alkali:

> The period of instructional studies, which is parallel to a kind of Teacher-Training, depended on the ability of the individual. On completion of his training, the individual scholar would receive from his master, Murabi, Ustaz, a ja'izah (reward) which qualified him to explain to others in the way and manner his master had done. As the work of these scholars proved successful, more subjects were added to the curricula of the University. The study of Arabic grammar and literature was considered essential for the understanding of the Kur'an . . . The University of Sankore was said to contain copies of almost the whole of Arabic literature. (Alkali 1967: 10–11)

Thus, from both the early contacts with North African scholars in the fifteenth century and the scholastic training at the University Mosque of Sankore, an Arabic Islamic literary tradition began to emerge in Hausaland (Pilaszewicz 1985: 202).

Some studies also contend that since the early seventeenth century, the Bornu empire tradition of Arabic writing had strongly affected Hausa states, and had produced Hausa writers who contributed to the Arabic written literature in Bornu (see Gérard 1981b and Pilaszewicz 1985). These studies cite the earliest work of *nazm*, or versification, produced during that era by Abdullahi Sikka from Kano entitled "al-'Atiya li'l-mu'ti" (The Gift of River, or The Gift of the Donor), which reflects the author's advanced training in Sufi mysticism as developed in Hausaland. They also mention the work of a famous Hausa poet and religious commentator, Ibn al-Sabbagh, known in Hausa as Dan Marina, "the Son of the Dyers." He composed a poem of both political and historical significance in the form of a treatise – "Mazjarat al-fityan" (The Admonition to Young Men) – celebrating the victory of the Bornu King Ali B. Umar over the "pagan" tribes in the Benue Valley in present-day northern Cameroon.

The same studies also indicate the preeminence of Hausa scholars during the eighteenth century in Islamic jurisprudence. This is revealed in the works of the most eminent Islamic jurist of the time, Muhammad al-Barnawi of Katsina, also known as Dan Masani ("Son of the Scholar"). Al-Barnawi was a well-known disciple of Dan Marina, who was credited with writing more than ten Arabic treatises. In addition, we should not overlook the significant influence of Islamic intellectual centers such as Agadez, located in the northern part of present-day Niger, as well as those in Egypt and the Maghrib, on the late eighteenth-century and nineteenth-century scholars, among whom were the Sheikh Usman Dan Fodio.

Mention should also be made of the different levels of training that existed and continued to mark the distinction between the training of elementary school teachers known as the *mu'allim* (*malam*) and that of advanced Muslim scholars, the *'ulema* or *'ulemasi* who graduated from Sankore Mosque University. The *mu'allim*'s knowledge is limited to the study of the Qur'an, the *Hadith* (Sayings and traditions of the Prophet), and religious practice, with an Arabic language proficiency that extends beyond their recitation of basic religious texts. They use their native languages to interpret and convey their religious knowledge to other people who have no basic literacy skills in Islamic education. The *'ulema*, on the other hand, are also analysts and interpreters of Islamic doctrine within the scholastic tradition.

While there is no exact determination of when *ajami* literacy, the tradition of writing Fulfulde and Hausa in a modified version of the Arabic script, began, it is quite reasonable to surmise that it emerged as a byproduct of the dialogic interactions between the Arabized literate *'ulema*s and their subaltern *mu'allims*. *Ajami* literacy in Fulfulde and Hausa emerged as an indigenous tradition in the course of an evolving Hausa Islamic identity. Given also the highly mercantile tradition of Hausa society and its interaction with Middle Eastern traders, it is quite possible that the earlier writings in *ajami* were limited to trade transaction diaries, accounting notes, and other forms of literature related to business. These elementary forms of written texts might have predated both the bulk of manuscripts of homiletic Hausa poetry and the chronicles discovered in the early nineteenth century.

Relying entirely on the availability of written documents to trace the beginnings of a writing tradition in Hausa culture is quite problematic. First, there is the question of the value put on the written document, which differs from one culture to another. In Islamic Hausa culture, a product of Islamic knowledge is a collective property. An author (of written or orally produced literary pieces) sometimes parted with the single original version of a text in the spirit of sharing, advancing knowledge, and enriching the text through contributions from others. Thus, individual authorship becomes subsumed by collective appropriation of the work, which, in the absence of widespread literacy, gets reconfigured orally at the expense of its written original.

There is also the question of the nonexistence or rudimentary nature of print during that era that might have hindered the possibility of producing more than a limited number of copies of an original work. A fair amount of writing was and continues to be done on the wooden slate still in use in most Afro-Islam traditional schools. Such writing was read and memorized for future public recitation and, after fulfilling its functions, was washed off and the liquid absorbed for its medicinal or protective power. What is crucial here is the centrality of the power of memory in the oral transformation of a text that was originally written. Original authorship is not denied but becomes, in the process, virtually inconsequential.

It is also important to bear in mind the quality of the materials on which texts were written during that era. Commenting on the manner in which the works of Nana Asma'u (1793–1864), daughter of Sheikh Usman Dan Fodio, were preserved even as late as the early nineteenth century, for example, Beverly Mack and Jean Boyd observe:

> These *Ajami* [poetic] compositions [and treaties written by Nana Asma'u] were written with vegetable dye inks on unbound sheets of paper, and traditionally kept together in a leather bookbag called by the Hausa term *gafaka*. This is the way Nana Asma'u produced and stored her manuscripts, in the manner of her day. Her collected works have remained in storage in her home since her death in 1864. Owing to the vagaries of time and circumstance, it is possible that some of her works were lost by various means: perhaps some were loaned out and lost or destroyed; perhaps others disintegrated before they were copied, or were lost to weather and insect damage. (1997: xvii)

Given such rudimentary methods of preservation, then, it is not inconceivable that writing may have begun much earlier in Hausaland than the available evidence seems to suggest.

The birth of a Hausa *ajami* literary tradition

The wind of Islamic reformist movement in the early eighteenth century influenced to a great extent the shift of writing toward mainly creative literary texts of didactic and homiletic thrust. Sheikh Usman Dan Fodio (1754–1817), the Fulani Islamic reformer who launched a *jihad* between 1804 and 1810 against the Hausa leaders, did so strategically on two grounds: first, to gain the solidarity and trust of his Hausa followers serving in his battalion, most of whom belonged to the class of peasants and commoners who suffered from the oppressive authority of Hausa leaders; and secondly, to strengthen this alliance with the new converts through Islamic education. By 1808–09 Sheikh Usman Dan Fodio had replaced all the Hausa kings by members of his family who became the new emirs of the conquered Hausa states and consolidated the power of his empire under the Sokoto Caliphate with Sokoto as the administrative capital.

The *jihad* leader was aware that proper Islamic practice requires investment in Islamic education. However, most of his religious writings were not accessible to the majority of his followers who were not literate in Arabic or Fulfulde. Among these the Hausa speakers were predominant. In fact, by the time of the *jihad* most Fulanis and members of other ethnic groups had been culturally and linguistically assimilated to Hausa identity at a time when the Hausa language had already acquired a regional status as a lingua franca. But the Shehu himself produced little in Hausa, having been more fluent in Arabic and Fulfulde. It was not until

> the reign of Muhammad Bello (1817–1837) that the foundations of Hausa writing were laid by Usman's brother, Abdullah b. Muhammad (1766–1829), his daughter Asma'u (also known as Nana) bint Shehu (1794–1863) and such of his early disciples as Asim Degel and Muhammad Tukur. They handled in Hausa the favorite genres and the main themes of Islamic writing. (Gérard 1981b: 58)

As Mack and Boyd (2000) rightly point out, what these pioneers of writing in Hausa accomplished was not merely a translation of the Shehu's works, but their actual adaptation to the dictates of Hausa language and culture. They did to Shehu's works what Fitzgerald did to Omar Khayyam's *Rubaiyat*.

Sheikh Usman Dan Fodio's seminal works translated into Hausa focused on an Islamic orthodoxy against the Afro-Islamic syncretism prevalent in much Muslim Hausa practice and also on the unity of the Islamic *umma* (community), Islamic jurisprudence, and political leadership. These works cut across various literary genres although Dan Fodio's most favorite genre was Islamic versification, poetic compositions of a homiletic nature. His revival writings in Arabic include his first treatises, *Ihya al-sunna wa-Ikhmad al-bid'a* (1793) (Revivification of Orthodoxy and Extinguishing of Innovation), *Nûr al-albâb* (The Light of the Mind), *Masa'il Muhimma* (1802) (Important Matters), *Al-qasida al-Sudaniya* (1794) (The Sudanic Ode); *Kitab-al farq* (Book of the Difference between the Governance of the people of Islam and the Governance of the Unbelievers); *Bayan wujub al-hijra ala al-'ibad* (Explanation of the Necessity of Hijra to the Worshippers Divine Islamic Jurisprudence and Moral Ethic of Divine); and *Sirj al-Ikhwan* (The Lamp of the Brethren). "Tabbat Hakika," written in Fulfulde, is one of his most popular poetic compositions. The dedication of Sheikh Usman Dan Fodio's (close and extended) family members to the spread of the religious intellectual vision of their leader was an effort of tremendous collaboration:

> Verse written in one language by the Shehu was translated into another language by another member of the family. One member of the family would transform verse by another member of the family out of couplets into quintains by undertaking a *takhmis* [adding an explanatory or exemplification lines]. Sometimes translation would render additional commentary such that the new would constitute more an alternative version of the old translation.
> (Furniss 1996: 200)

Apart from the phenomenal input of the Fodio dynasty to the *jihad ajami* literature, it is important to take into account the original contributions of other *jihad* scholars of the time who used their literary creative abilities to express their affiliation to Islamic brotherhoods other than Sheikh Usman Dan Fodio's *Qadiriyya*. These include the famous religious poets of Katsina, Muhammadu na Birnin Gwari, known for his popular poem entitled "Gangar Wa'azu" (The Drum of Admonition), Malam Shitu Dan Abdurra'uhu, who contributed two lengthy poetic compositions – "Jimiyya" and "Wawiyya" – in both Arabic and Hausa in strong support of Sufism and the Tijaniyya brotherhood, and Sheikh Usman Dan Fodio's own dissident grandson who developed a new satirical genre within mainstream *jihad* verse to protest against his ostracization from the Sokoto Caliphate. To sum up, then, it is the mediated translation of Sheikh Usman Dan Fodio's works from Arabic or Fulfulde into Hausa undertaken by members of his family, and the remarkable contributions of his disciples and dissidents, which marked the beginning of a Hausa *ajami* literary tradition.

Because the Islamic revival movement was a religious war against the "pagan" and a call for orthodoxy for the already converted Muslims, the poetic content it inspired was both homiletic and didactic. Many Hausa studies contend that much of Hausa classical poetry of the nineteenth century was thematically a continuation of classical Arab-Islamic poetry. These classical subgenres include: *wak'ok'in wa'azi* (poems of warning and admonition), poetic compositions that describe the practical paths to hell and paradise on Judgment Day and inform the believers of the difference between the two; *wak'ok'in sira*, religious poems that focus on the life of the Prophet and other Muslim saints; *wak'ok'in madahu* (prophetic panegyric poems) whose content calls for the believer's devotion to God and his Prophet; *wak'ok'in farilla*, which describe Muslim legal obligations; *wak'ok'in hisabi*, devoted to numerological poems; *wakokin taurari*, poems related to astrology; and *wak'ok'in tauhidi*, poems devoted to theology and philosophy (see Hiskett 1975; Pilaszewicz 1985: 202; Gérard 1981a; and Furniss 1996).

There is some debate regarding the original structure of Hausa *ajami* poetry. Some scholars argue that nineteenth-century Hausa religious poetry was structurally inspired by classical Arabic poetic meters and can be described using the Arabic *xalilian* metric system. Others contend that rather than being an offshoot of Arabic, it is better accounted for by a more indigenous structure whereby the rhyme represents the unit of division into stanzas (Furniss 1996: 210). The debate then is framed in terms of a discourse of foreign hegemony versus that of nationalistic authenticity.

Of special note in the development of an *ajami* literature is the contribution of the *jihadist* women scholars, which has so far received little attention in mainstream Hausa scholarship. This marginalization has been a common trend even with regard to such prominent figures as Nana Asma'u, a leading intellectual authority in her own right. There has been a gender bias that has reinforced a false image of total absence of a women's intellectual and literary tradition in Afro-Islamic cultures in general and in Hausaland in particular. It is against this backdrop that the pioneering works of Jean Boyd in *The Caliph's Sister: Nana Asma'u 1793–1865, Teacher, Poet and Islamic Leader* (1989) and Jean Boyd and Beverly Mack, *The Collected Works of Nana Asma'u, Daughter of Usman Dan Fodiyo* (1997), and Beverly Mack and Jean Boyd in *One Woman's Jihad: Nana Asma'u, Scholar and Scribe* (2000) attain their monumental importance in filling the gap in the historical and critical study of the Hausa *ajami* literary tradition. By bringing to light the *ajami* literary work of the nineteenth-century Muslim women in Hausaland, Mack and Boyd have posed a fresh challenge even to western-trained feminist thinkers (of both western and African background) on the need to recenter modern Muslim women intellectuals working within a native (i.e., non-western) epistemological framework. These pioneering works, in other words, are a call for the adoption of more gendered approaches to the study of cultural (re)production.

European colonization and resistance *ajami* literature

The impressive Hausa classical literary movement that developed in the nineteenth century under the leadership of Fulani *jihad* lords was confronted in the early twentieth century with two destabilizing forces. First was the late nineteenth-century internal dissidence between the followers of Sheikh Usman Dan Fodio's *Qadiriyya* orthodoxy who continued to adhere to the original mission of the movement, on one hand, and the breakaway Mahdist scholars, on the other. The latter developed a new poetic genre that combines the traditional didactic and homiletic content with satirical commentaries about the corrupt state of the *Qadiriyya* leadership. As Stanislaw Pilaszewicz points out, for example, the political denunciation of exploitation and abuse of the poor by some of the *jihad* lords constitutes the theme of both Muhammadu na Birnin Gwari's Hausa poem with the Arabic title "Bi'llahi Arumi" (I Desire It through God) and Iman Daura's "Kogi" (The River), both written at the end of the nineteenth century (1985: 207). In spite of its religious concerns, this dissident trajectory opened up the space for the emergence of a secular tradition in Hausa written poetry.

The second force was of a menacing British invasion that threatened to erase Hausa precolonial history from the collective memory and triggered the desire of certain members of the Hausa *ajami* literati to produce historical texts and chronicles in order to document the reign of renowned emirs, important historical events that marked their reigns and also life in Hausaland during the pre-*jihad* era (Gérard 1981a; Pilaszewicz 1985). *The Chronicle of Kano*, also known as the *Song of Bagauda*, written in verse in the late nineteenth century, for example, covers the history of the town of Kano from the period of its legendary leader Bagauda to the reign of the Emir Muhammadu Bello. Other chronicles include the *Chronicle of Sokoto,* completed in the 1920s and authored by Abubakar Dan Atiku, the *Chronicle of Zaria*, which provides an historical account of the emirate of Zazzau, and the *Chronicle of Katsina*, which offers a list of the rulers of the town of Katsina up to 1807. The same period also produced *ajami* historiographies of other towns and important historical events that affected non-Hausa kingdoms as shown in the work of Hausa *malams* from the area.

The theme of Islamic resistance against British colonial occupation informed the poetic compositions of both Ibrahim Nagwamatse (1857–1922) and the Hausa trader Al-Hajj Umar Ibn Bakr (1858–1934) from the Gold Coast (present-day Ghana) who wrote in both Arabic and Hausa (see Hodgkin 1966: 442–43). Ibn Bakr is best known for his famous Hausa poem, *Labarin Nasara* or *Wak'ar Nasara* (The Story of the Christians), written in 1903, which is an attack on British colonization as it destabilized the Sokoto Sultanate's authority, leading to the fragmentation of its consolidated constituency and the exile of the sultan to the east. The following excerpt from his poem reflects Ibn Bakr's disdain of the new rulers:

> Idan ka ce akwai wahala ga tashi
> Lahan duka na ga masu biyan Nasara.
> Idan iko kakai kak ko k'I tashi
> Ina iko shi kai ikon Nasara.
> Idon sun ba ka kyauta kada ka amsa,
> Dafi na sunka ba ka guba Nasara.
> Suna foro gare mu mu bar zalama,
> Mazalunta da kansu d'iyan Nasara.
> Bak'ar fitina gare su da kau makida,
> Ta b'ata dinin musulmin Annasara
>
> You may say it is difficult to rise up
> All fault lies with those who follow the white man.
> If you have power, and so refuse to rise up,
> Where is your power since it comes from the white man?
> If they offer you a gift, do not accept it,
> It is poison that the white man offers you.
> They are warning us not to be oppressive,
> But they themselves are acting oppressively,
> They are evil and are trying, by trickery,
> To destroy the religion of Islam.
>
> (from Furnis 1996: 207)

European colonization and Hausa literary identity

In 1903, Sheikh Usman Dan Fodio's dynasty was invaded from the south – the regions situated in present-day Nigeria and northern Ghana – by the British and, from its northern borders (which includes part of the southeastern present-day Niger Republic and the northern part of present-day Cameroon) by French forces. After years of resistance, which for the Islamized indigenous population was regarded as a second *jihad* in Hausaland, a segment of the population associated with the Mahdist movement migrated eastwards to constitute a new Hausa-Fulani diaspora in Maiurno in present-day Sudan (Abu-Manga 1999; Al-Nagar 1972; and Yamba 1990). Thus began the division of Hausaland into demarcated French and British spheres of colonial authority.

French colonization was based on the so-called direct policy that implied French control of the colonial administration at all levels and cultural assimilation of the indigenous population through imposition of the French language. The British, on the other hand, adopted in their territories, in northern Nigeria more particularly, what is known as "indirect colonial policy," in which colonial rule was exercised through local authorities, and local languages, cultures, and traditions were to a large extent allowed to prevail.

These colonial developments and the ensuing colonial policies precipitated three forces that impacted on Hausaness and its literary tradition in colonially divided Hausaland. The new formation of diasporic Hausa in the Sudan embodied an Islamic Arabized identity, resulting in a reversal from Hausa *ajami* literacy / literary production to a Hausa–Fulani literature in Arabic. In French-controlled territories such as in the Niger Republic and Northern Cameroon, French assimilation policies officially quashed the Hausa *ajami* tradition by imposing a formal education exclusively in French. This policy also hindered the use of the Hausa language whether in *ajami* or Roman script in formal education in "francophone" Africa in general and Niger in particular where Hausa is the mother tongue of more than 50 percent of the country's thirteen million inhabitants and represents the most widely spoken lingua franca. The use of local languages in education and administration was banned during the colonial era and up to the 1970s when the failure of instruction in French became a serious national issue of debate. Inadvertently, then, French educational policy ended up reinforcing the oral literary tradition among the majority of Hausa-speaking peoples who did not have access to formal French education in the Niger Republic. The more organic *ajami* literacy became totally marginalized and remains marginalized, and its educational potential in the postcolonial period was deliberately disregarded by the western-trained elite. In effect, therefore, French colonization and its aftermath meant the near-death of Hausa *ajami* literature in Niger.

The British, on the other hand, encouraged the use of local languages and to some extent promoted literacy and formal education in those languages in northern Nigeria where more than forty million Hausa speakers reside. However, the British were not keen to retain the use of Arabic script and allow the continuation of Hausa *ajami* literary creativity. To the colonialists, *ajami* was a strong repository of Hausa-Islamic identity and an antithesis to the European colonial hegemonic agenda. Thus, by the 1860s European missionaries had begun to use the Roman script for writing the Hausa language and by 1903 this new system was established as a policy for recording Hausa texts by the department of colonial education. This marked the beginning of Hausa writing in the Roman alphabet in the former British colonies.

The introduction of the Roman script for writing Hausa met with resistance from some of the members of the traditional intelligentsia. And this reaction to the use of the Roman script for writing Afro-Islamic languages was not unique to Hausa. During the same period, for example, Islamic scholars on the East African coast opposed the conversion from Arabic to Roman script for writing Kiswahili on linguistic grounds.[1] Their rationale was that the new script would eventually obliterate the authenticity and sophistication of the Kiswahili sound system.

The first literary works to appear in the Hausa language during the early stages of the romanization of its script were primarily translations of gospel literature by European missionaries. The Gospel of St. Matthew was translated into Hausa in 1860 by Jacob Friedrich Schön. This was followed by a tradition of recording collections from the oral genres. Between 1911 and 1913, for example, Frank Edgar, then a British colonial administrative officer in Sokoto, published three impressive volumes, *Litafin Tatsuniyoyi na Hausa* (Book of Hausa Tales and Traditions). These were transliterations of oral folktales from Sokoto collected and transcribed in *ajami* by the *malammai*, the teachers trained within *ajami* tradition. Neil Skinner provided a critical restructuring of Edgar's collections by making a distinctive classification between Hausa *tatsuniyoyi* (trickster stories, caricatures, etiological stories) and *labaru* (short oral narratives relaying the heroic account of *jihad* leaders, legendary saints and leaders, stories of wars and other stories of miraculous events of the past). Both *tatsuniyoyi* and *labaru* are didactic genres with a moral thrust.

The western impact and the emergence of new literary genres

In order to consolidate the romanization of Hausa script in northern Nigeria, the British colonial government established, in the early 1930s, the Translation Bureau at Zaria under the supervision of Rupert East, who was also an instructor at the Katsina Teachers' Training College. East coordinated the development of educational materials in the Hausa language for use in schools, collaborated with some Hausa scholars to translate literary works from Europe and Asian cultures – *The Thousand and One Nights* and *The Assemblies*, for example. These translations were undertaken with the hope that they would inspire the literary imagination of potential Hausa writers to create modern prose fiction in all genres with a thematically secular orientation. This goal was pursued through creative-writing competitions organized by the Translation Bureau in the 1930s.

For several decades, the new script and the Hausa secular literature it sought to promote through the introduction of fiction writing remained unappealing to the majority of the members of the Hausa traditional literati who resisted the process. Both the attempt to introduce prose fiction and the foreignness of the genre were considered antithetical to the traditional literary paradigm, which associated the art of writing with either religious functions or recording of important and serious historical events. Storytelling, especially the *tatsuniya* or folktale associated with (older) women, was linked to "mere" entertainment and amusement. Thus, for the intellectual operating within the traditional *ajami* epistemology, the new literature that the Zaria Bureau of Translation was promoting was not concordant with the Hausa cultural realm of demarcation between what belongs to the world of facts worth recording in writing, and imaginative stories based on "falsehood" and not amenable to writing.

Interestingly, all laureates of the 1933–34 competitions were graduates of Katsina Teachers' Training College where East himself taught. The literary competition thus revealed a divergence between the traditional Hausa literati and those who had embraced the western literary influence. The writers from the former framework continued to suscribe to the *ajami* or Arabic writing while developing more and more secular prose, but still within the realm of non-falsehood. Those of the latter paradigm, on the other hand, produced a new literature that incorporated new genres such as the novel and play. The genres and subgenres that constitute modern Hausa literature in Roman script, however, are neither a replica ofliterary forms found in European literature nor romanized versions of the traditional Islamic Hausa literature. The features of this new literature are, in fact, a manifestation of the convergence of the various literary traditions that influenced its emergence.

Rupert East's prose-fiction competitions of the 1930s produced five novels that set in motion a new tradition in Hausa literature through its striking secular orientation as well its incorporation of themes that were absent in the more traditional written literature. These include crime and punishment, topics that draw on emotion (love, hatred, and revenge), social issues (crimes, prostitution, alcoholism) and their consequences (punishment, cultural alienation, social degeneration, and sorrowful end). The themes, plots and characterization of these European-instigated Hausa novels are developed within the imaginative world of realism and fantasy with a moral didacticism intimately rooted in Hausa Islamic education.

Jiki Magayi (The Body is the One to Tell) is a novel jointly written by Rupert East and Malam J. Tafida. It is a story of young Abubakar's revenge against a wealthy man, Shehu, who used a charm to seduce his bride Zainabu. The realization of what took place set Abubakar to get even with Shehu through the quest for an equally powerful if not more damaging charm. Abubakar eventually returns home and successfully injects Kyauta, Shehu's only offspring from that marriage, with a satanic potion acquired in the magic forest of Dawan Ruk'uki', which instills in the child severe criminal tendencies, eventually leading to his accidental murder of his biological father, Shehu. With the help of his mother, Kyauta escapes trial and learns from her the foundation of his own decadent behavior. Based on this knowledge, Kyauta decides to avenge himself by decapitating Abubakar. However, Kyauta miraculously escapes the danger of another criminal act, for he finds Abubakar already dead. Kyauta returns home to repent for his previous crime by giving back to the community whatever he had acquired from his days of degeneracy, and returns to an honest lifestyle.

Shaihu Umar is a historical novel written by Abubakar Tafawa Balewa (1912–66), former Prime Minister of the Federal Government of Nigeria. It presents a story about the destiny of two captives, a child named Umar who is also the main character of the novel and his mother, in the hands of an Arab slave-trader in Egypt. In spite of the harshness of slave conditions, Umar receives good treatment from his Arab master, who ensures that Umar gets adequate Islamic education, eventually becoming a shehu (religious leader). He becomes a learned Muslim scholar and is miraculously reunited with his mother in a foreign land, though she dies shortly after. Shaihu (Shehu) Umar manages to escape being captured by other Arab slave raiders in the Sahara. He returns to his native Hausaland, which he finds in a state of decay resulting from his people's lack of spiritual ideals. Shaihu Umar sets himself the task of educating the "pagans" in his Islamic ways and reinstating Islamic morals in the society.

This historical fiction reveals Tafawa Balewa's strong inclination toward Islamic didacticism and his ability to provide a detailed depiction of life in Hausa society before European colonization. Its moral decay is presented as the key factor that makes it vulnerable to European invasion. Shaihu Umar has a powerful determination to reinscribe Islamic social and moral values, which include submission to God, honesty, diligence, and virtue as a basis for sustaining a strong culture. Shaihu Umar reminds the reader of Okonkwo's struggle to maintain the valued traditions of Umuofian precolonial society in Chinua Achebe's *Things Fall Apart*. However, Shaihu Umar's peaceful, patient, and merciful nature, which defines his relationship with members of the community, is in sharp contrast with Okonkwo's strong and violent character. Tafawa Balewa's setting of the novel in Kantogora, a Hausa–Fulani town situated in present-day Niger, probably reveals his transnational Hausa consciousness, an understanding of Hausaness that goes beyond the boundaries drawn by European colonialism. This subtlety of setting as an ideological metaphor recurrent in Nigerian writers' work is often overlooked by literary critics.

Gandoki, written by Muhammadu Bello, was selected as the best among the five novels presented in the 1933 competition. It is a fictional autobiography of Gandoki, an Islamic mystic warrior shocked by the capitulation of his culture to British colonial authority and values, some of which he eventually begins to appreciate. Thus, Gandoki is a warrior with an orientation that is opposite to Okonkwo in *Things Fall Apart* whose quest for power and fame prevents him from compromising and adjusting to the reality of his people's adoption of new western ways, eventually leading him to his tragic suicide. The story in *Gandoki* is a follow-up to that of *Shaihu Umar,* for it offers the westernized elites a positive perspective of the impact of British colonization on Hausaland.

Ruwan Bagaji (The Water of the Cure) by Abubakar Imam was another major contribution to the emerging modern Hausa literature. The novel is a satire of greedy and corrupt *malams* in Hausa culture embodied in two main rival characters, Alhaji Imam and Malam Zurke. Drawing on Hausa wit and humor, the novel, structured around a series of episodic stories, depicts how Alhaji Imam tricks an ignorant, non-Islamized Hausa community to dismiss the authority of Malam Zurke, a learned Islamic scholar, and to take advantage of a series of other characters. All this trickery and mischief takes place in the course of a journey in search of the *Ruwan Bagaja* needed to heal the son of the leader of the town. This adventurous journey takes Alhaji Imam from the world of realism to that of spirits, *jinns* of all sorts. Befriending the king of *jinns* in a world of magic and fantasy earns him the secret to the main object of his quest, the curative water that he brings back to the real world.

Idon Matambayi (The Eye of the Questioner), written by Muhammadu Gwarzo in 1934, is another novel that focuses on the theme of crime and punishment pertaining to the handling of the undesirable members of society. The story is about four thieves skillfully competing to outsmart police vigilance and steal from a well-guarded house by cheating its wealthy owner. However, because of selfishness and greed they all end up losing the fruits of their robbery and eventually go their different ways.

Magana Jari Ce (The Art of Storytelling is an Asset) represents Abubakar Imam's second major contribution to the early writings of modern Hausa literature initiated by Rupert East's literary venture in Hausaland. It is also one of the writings that set the stylistic and literary standard for the evolving trend in modern Hausa literature. *Magana Jari Ce* is a novel that demonstrates Abubakar Imam's genius in inventing an authentic Hausa style built upon the convergence of various cultures. As Albert Gérard observes, "[The stories in *Magana Jari Ce*] draw from a wide variety of sources, African, European, Arabic, and Oriental" (1981a: 66). Inspired by *The Thousand and One Nights'* esthetic and stylistic structure adapted to Hausa idiom, *Magana Jari Ce* presents a series of interwoven stories focused on an intriguing and comic dependency-relationship between a king and his pet parrot. This parrot manages to render himself indispensable to his owner through his cleverness in relaying crucial information and providing advice useful for the preservation of his master's power and authority. As a result, the parrot usurps the human vizier of his privileged position in the palace and becomes the king's main confidant and adviser to his heirs.

The period between the Second World War and the late 1960s produced a few novellas, most of them fewer than forty pages. The majority are published by the Gaskiya Corporation or the Northern Nigerian Publishing Company (NNPC). These include Amadu Ingawa's *Iliya Dan Maikarfi* (Iliya, Son of a Strong Man), a story centered around the theme of the heroism of a sickly and paralyzed child, Waldima, born to parents who suffered years of childlessness and the pain resulting from this condition in a society where reproduction is highly valued. Using the miraculous powers conferred on him by the angels who are convinced of his strong faith, Ilya leads a crusade for justice and saves Waldima, the ruler of a town named Kib, from many troubles, and finally begs God to transform him into a stone. Like *Magana jari Ce, Iliya Dan Maikarfi* is another Hausa novel that may have been heavily inspired by European literary works. As Pilaszewicz observes:

> [*Iliya Dan Maikarfi*] is unusual not only because of its ending, so contrary to the Islamic spirit, but also because it drew certain themes from the Russian epic poem about Elias Muromcik. This was pointed out to me by Yu. K. Sceglov, who identified Waldima with Prince Vladimir and the mysterious town of Kib with Kiev. (1985: 224)

The other works written in the early 1950s are *Gogan Naka* (Your Hero) by Garba Funtunwa, *Shirtacen Gari* (The Enchanted Town) by Amadu Katsina, *Da'u Fataken Dare* (Da'u, the Night Raider) by Tanko Zango, the longest novel ever in the Hausa language, and *Bayan Wuya Sai Dadi* (After Pain Comes Pleasure) by Abdulmalik Mani, all produced in 1954.

The late fifties and post-independence period saw the rise of a new kind of novella writing influenced by the convergence of Islamic religious beliefs, western science fiction and Indian cinema. *Tauraruwa Hamada* (1965) (The Sahara Star) by Sa'idu Ahmed relays the story of the kidnapping of a princess by a thief, Danye, and his accomplice named Dabo. The two thieves are gifted with magical powers embodied in a talking snake that enables them to avoid their entrapments. *Tauraru Mai Wutsiya* (1969) (The Comet) by Umaru Dembo tells of the extraterrestrial journey of a boy named Kilba who is befriended by a creature from outer space, Kolin Koliyo. *Dare Daya* (One Night) is a novella written in 1973 which draws on the rift within a royal family.

Jabiru Abdullahi wrote *Gari Na Kowa* (1968) (Good to Everyone), which recounts the plight of an orphan, Salihi, who was wrongly accused of and imprisoned for the loss of his patron's money. However, because of his devotion to God, his kindness, and honesty, Salihi, like Tafawa Balewa's Shaihu Umar, rises to become a leader whose miraculous powers and integrity assist him in restoring stability and justice to the people who have been taken advantage of.

Common to virtually all these Hausa novellas is the interplay between the "real" and the fantastic, the human and the divine. There is a recurrence of the quest theme as well as that of the struggle between good and evil in relation to the moral concept of crime and punishment. Moreover, they are structurally framed in episodic journeys of a hero or trickster whose deeds lead naturally to a reward or retribution and punishment.

In addition to the novellas, Pilaszewicz reports the existence of a few essays that could be classified as travel diaries written in Hausa (and some in English) by some of the first western-trained northern intellectuals who played a significant role in the struggle for Nigerian independence from British rule. Most of these essays present a comparative and contrasting analysis between the Islamic background of the authors and the culture of their European colonizers. For example, on Aminu Kano's *Motsi Ya Fi Zama* (Moving is Better than Sitting), which provides an account of his European tour, Pilaszewicz comments that

> Aminu Kano was struck by the individualism, bordering on egoism, of the people of the big European societies. Straightforwardness, openness and a

> desire to get to know other societies are the Hausa characteristics as presented by Aminu Kano, and these traits make it easier for him to establish contact with foreign civilizations. (Pilaszewicz 1985: 226)

On the other hand Malam Haruna, a Hausa of Christian background, provided in his *Yawo a Turai* (A Journey to Europe) important information regarding the political atmosphere of northern Nigeria during the pre-independence period.

Here again, it is important to draw attention to the dearth of Hausa women's contribution to the emerging modern Hausa literature in the Roman script, from the arrival of the Europeans in Hausaland to the late 1960s. This is in sharp contrast with what Hausa–Fulani Muslim women intellectuals had achieved in the Hausa *ajami* writing during the precolonial era. Part of the explanation lies in colonial British attitudes: while the British might not have opposed women's education, neither did they actively promote their recruitment into colonial schools. To this extent, they acquiesced with the sentiments of northern leaders who, though opposed to the spreading of the European form of schooling in the north in general, were more especially fearful of women's assimilation to European values.

Hausa literature during Nigeria's post-independent era

The late 1970s and 1980s, which mark Nigeria's era of economic abundance brought about by the oil boom, inspired the production of the type of prose fiction that Furniss (1996) identifies as the "Boomtown Novels." A 1979 competition organized by the Northern Nigeria Publishing Company resulted in the publication of three novels in 1980: Sulaiman Ibrahim Katsina's novel *Mallakin Zuciya* (Power over my Heart), which won the first prize, is a didactic love story about the struggle of young western-educated people against arranged marriages and the confrontation between a supporting father of the girl and her opposing conservative mother. The second prize won by Hafsatu Abdulwahid's novel *So Aljannar Duniya* (Love is Heaven on Earth) marks the emergence of female writers of modern Hausa prose fiction. It is the story of love between a young Fulani couple shaken by the intervention of a female *jinn*. The novel is framed within magical realism. The third novel, Magaji Dambatta's *Amadi Na Malam Amah* (Malam Amah's Amadi), also constructed within magical realism, depicts a hero's successful struggles against evil spirits.

These three prize-winning novels from a competition of twenty-two registered stories show a departure from the early novels in that they draw on fantasy and realism to present themes involving the trials and tribulations of individuals whose lives are interwoven in the complexities and contradictions of modern life. The quest theme is extended to the question of love in monogamous and polygamous marriages and to women's struggles for freedom from the confines of both traditional and modern values. And it is no longer the corruption of traditional *malams* that is in focus, but that of the new comprador bourgeoisie born out of the oil boom and their exploitation of commoners. The stories also have a didactic ending centered on contemporary sociopolitical and religious issues (Furniss 1996: 38).

Kitsen Rogo (literally "The Fatness of Cassava," but better translated as "Illusion") by Abdulkadir Dangambo, published two years before the aforementioned three novels by the NNPC, is a didactic story about the negative consequences of rural–urban migration. The story focuses on the life of its main character, Ibrahim, who left his village in search of fortune in the city, only to be caught up in the life of banditry and thievery, which sends him to prison. Upon release, however, he is rehabilitated with the help of his father by returning to their rural roots.

Another prose-fiction competition organized in 1980 by the Nigerian Federal Department of Culture in collaboration with the Gaskiya Corporation produced four new novels that appeared in 1982. The overt political tone in these novels is in sharp contrast to all the previously published novels. These include *Turmin Danya* (The Strong Man) by Sulaiman I. Katsina, *Tsumangiyar Kan Hanya* (The Driving Whip) by Musa Mohammed Bello, *Karshen Alewa Kasa* (The Discarded Left-Over) by Bature Gagare, and *Zabi Naka* (Choose Yours) by Munir Muhammed Katsina. The last two novels more clearly portray life in the aftermath of the Nigerian civil war where the proliferation of weapons in the society and their control by demobilized, but non-rehabilitated ex-soldiers leads to all sorts of banditry (from drug trafficking to armed robbery). This creates a new reign of terror that is counteracted, finally, by the restoration of a strong leadership and new social order. In *Karshen Alewa Kasa*, peace and order are restored in the society as the result of the death of the main characters, who represent the villains, one the victim of a snake bite, and the other of a fatal bullet shot.

Turmin Danya is a more politically committed novel than *Mallakin Zuciya* to which it is thematically similar. It graphically treats the theme of corruption, but in a more complex way and exposes all the sociopolitical ills that erupted in Nigeria as a result of the oil boom from the late 1970s to mid-1980s. It exposes the conspiracy between the administrative leaders of government and the new incompetent entrepreneurial class of corrupt *Alhajis*, who appropriate all federal construction contracts, but fail to deliver or end up with cheap and substandard constructions.

Tura Ta Kai Bango, Sulaiman I. Katsina's third novel, published in 1983, is perhaps the most radical of all the modern Hausa novels for its critical depiction of how the corrupt machinery of party politics takes advantage of the impoverished and manipulable marginalized masses in northern Nigeria. It also effectively exposes the repression of oppositional voices by conservative forces in power. The novel ends with a note of optimism by showing that with perseverance, and mass cooperation, progressive politics can mobilize the grassroots to overthrow corrupt dictatorial regimes. The portrayal of women characters as active agents in this process is another positive departure from most Hausa novels, which often offer a stereotypical characterization of modern Muslim women as passive agents in society.

For most of the novels produced during the oil-boom era, the modern setting symbolized by products of western material culture – the structure of the houses, cars, and modern roads, etc. – reflects the impact of European culture on Hausa society. The interaction of Hausa–Fulani Muslim characters with non-Muslim Hausa characters in these novels, as in Bello's *Karshen Alewa Kasa*, seems to indicate how Hausaness is being reinterpreted within a larger heterogeneous postcolonial political entity called Nigeria, which is different from the identity constructed and depicted in the *jihad* literature.

The overwhelming emergence of love stories in the Hausa language is another trend in the development of imaginative prose fiction in modern Hausa popular culture resulting from the growth of literacy and formal education in northern Nigeria in the 1980s. This genre represents an important outlet for a number of young Muslim Hausa–Fulani-women writers whose works, in theme and language, often deal with the interplay between womanhood, culture, religion, and national identity.[2]

"Stepping outside gender" in Muslim Hausa–Fulani culture

The attraction of contemporary western-educated Hausa–Fulani women to the writing of love novellas and their predominance as authors in the production of such a genre merits special attention. This phenomenon is due, in part, to the interconnectedness of gendered space, language, religion, and literacy / literature. The mainstream patriarchal Islamic sociopolitical praxis in most Islamic cultures, among which are the Hausa–Fulani, produces a set of dichotomies along gender lines which accounts, to a large extent, for the variant forms of literature produced by male and female literati. For example, masculinity is linked to public space, to access to classical religious training, and to authorized public voices for representing and interpreting cultural identity. This contrasts with the expected mute feminine voices confined in domesticity and the denial of the authority to define themselves and beyond. While men accede to religion through the written word, women accede to religion through a patriarchal interpretation that is mediated in most cases through orality. And it is through this process that males and females develop different literacies. Consequently, for most women, the language of literary expression becomes the oral and its form is nonclassical, except for a minority of women from the privileged class who have access to classical literacy. The works of women writers from the latter category are often formulated within a discursive framework that reflects their entrapment within patriarchy. Moreover, since they write in classical modes and in conformity with cultural expectations, their works are given greater prominence, as opposed to the novellas written in colloquial language, a register that subversively challenges the status quo.

Hausa–Fulani women's access to the western form of education has altered the cultural understanding of the relationship between gender, space, and expressive voice. By writing about their lives, making public women's struggles in the private space of domesticity, these women writers in Hausa language have broken the cultural taboo. This female act of challenging the status quo by making public the private, that is, domesticity, offers a feminine perspective on the issue of Hausa–Fulani-Islamic identity and suggests also an "act of stepping outside" the cultural construct of gender, gendered space, and voice.

The art of love-story writing by contemporary Hausa–Fulani women in the Hausa language fulfills the same purpose as that of the writing of autobiographies by contemporary Muslim-Arab women writers (see Faqir 1999). Thus, by painting their lives through biographies or through fiction, Muslim women are crossculturally interrogating patriarchal Islam, the broader sociopolitical realities, at the same time as they provide a response to the voices of outsiders speaking for or about them.

Considering the above, then, the lack of serious study of Hausa–Fulani women's love novellas by both native and western scholars implies a lack of appreciation of the revolutionary potential embodied in these works. In using a form and language usually regarded as unworthy of serious study, these Hausa–Fulani women writers are, in fact, calling for a social transformation of gender relations and a re-examination of both implicit and explicit power relations at different levels of the social hierarchy.

To continue classifying such writings in the realm of popular culture therefore – as is often done by literary critics – is at once to undermine Muslim women's contribution to, and to reinforce the marginalization of, the female voice in literature. The attraction of literary critics to Hausa literature produced in classical form suggests a class bias whose consequence is a dismissal of the largest proportion of the literature in colloquial Hausa that falls predominantly within the domain of women's writing and orality. The categories employed in literary criticism – of what is "popular" and "excellent" and what is not, for example – are themselves products of cultural construction that betray a patriarchal framing. This is an ideological context that continues to both undermine and marginalize women's contribution in literature virtually throughout the world (see Showalter 1985).

Playwriting in Hausa

Although dramatic performances were part of Hausa traditional culture, the writing of drama into play scripts was a product of European influence. Just as they reacted to the introduction of the novel, the Hausa *ajami* literati resisted this new genre as well. Its reliance on humor, and its playfulness, and the dramatic representation of a false reality were regarded as incompatible with the theme of religious morality and seriousness promoted by *ajami* Islamic writing.

The first Hausa play, *Wasannin Kwaikwayo Shida* (Six Hausa Plays) published in Lagos, was written by Rupert East in 1930. By the late 1930s, the politically militant Aminu Kano produced several plays that were never published because of their radical tone. *Kai Wane a Kasuwa Kano Da Ba Za a Cuce Ka Ba* (Whoever You Might Be, You Will Be Cheated at Kano Market), *Karya Fure Ta Ke Ba Ta'Ya'Ya* (A Lie Blossoms but Yields No Fruit), and *Gundumar Dukan Y'en Kano* (A Hammer with Which to Beat the Kano Native Administration) are among his best-known plays performed on stage. The three plays treat the theme of exploitation of the masses by either the crooked merchants (as seen in the first play) or colonial administrators who collected heavy taxes from the impoverished masses with the help of the local authority (as shown in the second play). The third play focuses on the relationship between an abusive native authority backed by a colonial power and the reaction of an exploited local population.

From 1954 to 1979, there were thirteen more play scripts published mainly in Zaria by the North Regional Literature Agency (NORLA) and the Northern Nigeria Publishing Company. These publications include *Wasan Marafa* (1954)

(Marafa's Play) by Abubakar Tunau; *Malam Inkuntum* (1954) (Mr. Inkuntum) by Dogondaji; and Shaibu Makarfi's two famous plays, *Zamanin nan Namu* (1959) (These Times of Ours) and *Jatau Na Kyallu* (1960) (Kyallu's Jatau), which deal with the theme of conflict between tradition and modernity arising from the impact of European education and how this conflict affects other important aspects of Hausa life (marriage and divorce, alcoholism, prostitution, materialism). These plays set the foundation for modern drama in the Hausa language.

The decade 1970 to 1980 seems to have been the most prolific for the publication of play scripts with the production of ten plays by NNPC alone. Among these one can cite Umar Dembo's famous play *Wasannin Yara* (1971) (Children's Games); *Uwar Gulma* (1971) (Mother of Mischievous Tale-Telling) by A. Moh Sada Malam; *Malam Muhamman*, by Bello Muhamed (1974), and *Zaman Duniya* (1980) (The Way of Life) by Yusuf Ladan. Of note also is Umaru Ladan and Dexter Lyndersy's *Shaihu Umar* (1975), which is a dramatic adaptation of Tafawa Balewa's novel by the same title.

In addition to original works in Hausa, there were also attempts to produce translations and adaptations of foreign plays. Ibrahim Yaro Yahaya's adaptation of Shakespeare's *Twelfth Night* as *Daren Sha Biyu* (1971) is one such example. Ten years later, another work by Shakespeare, *The Merchant of Venice*, was produced by Dahiru Idris under the title *Matsolon Attajiri* (1981). Translated works that figure among the thirteen plays produced in the decade of the 1970s include *Mutanen Kogo* (1976) translated by Ahmed Sabir, which is a dramatized Hausa rendering of the famous Arabic *Tawfiq al-Hakim* (The People of the Cave).

Although the traditional Hausa clerics opposed the promotion of imaginative prose writing of any sort in the Hausa language, modern teachers in Islamic schools have begun to produce plays in *ajami* pamphlet forms intended for religious celebrations such as *Maulidi*. These pamphlets are mainly handwritten and circulate in mosques and the market place and, like radio and TV drama, remain unpublished (see Yahaya 1978: 253; Gérard 1981a; Pilaszewicz 1985; and Furniss 1996).

Developments in poetry

Modern Hausa poetry is characteristically distinguishable from its classical counterpart by its strong inclination to secular thematic content. Abdulahia Dan Fodio's war poetry dedicated to his warriors in celebration of victory against the growing tyranny of the *jihad* leadership marks the beginning of the secularization of Hausa *ajami* poetry.

British invasion of Hausaland also had a major impact on *ajami* poetry produced during the early twentieth century. Two poets provide some insight into the state of Hausa society in the wake of European colonization. The first is Malam Shi'itu, known as the founder of the *Tijaniyya* brotherhood of Zaria whose poetry gained fame in the 1930s. The other is Imam Umaru Salaga (1858–1934), the great Hausa poet whose poetry offers an excellent picture of various aspects of Hausa culture while also including religious, political, and moral themes. In *Zuwan Nasara* (The Coming of the Christians), for example, a poem of 197 verses, Imam Umaru Salaga presents his ambivalence about British colonization in Hausaland as shown in the following excerpt:

Anna Attahiru, jikan Atik'u
Wliyyu-l-Lahi? Sun tasai Nasara.
Dad'a kuma ya shiri, ya bar k'asarsa:
Shina tafiya, shina tsoron Nasara.
K'asar kuma tai ciri – birnin da k'auye,
Ana ci: Ba mu son malakan Nasara
Dad'a Sarkin Musulmi ya yin tawaga:
Abin ga da firgita – ku, an – Nasara!
Suna bi shi awa ya d'auki bashi
Fa ko ya zagi sarkin an-Nasara

Where is Attahiru, grandson of Atik'u
And the Saint of God? They drove him away, the Christians
So he made preparations to leave his country:
He was travelling fearful of the Christians.
And the country became deserted – town and village,
They were saying: "we do not want the Christians' rule"
Then the Head of the Muslims removed his folk and property:
All this is terrible – oh you, Christians!

Fa babu sina bugin shrai'an Nasara.
Ka bar komi – da kurd'I, ko sarauta.
Da malantarka babu ruwan Nasara.
Fa halin Ingilishi shina da tafshi:
Suna tausai mutum – manyan Nasara.
Fa ni dai ko Allah zamininsu,
Zama dai sun rik'e ni da kew, Nasara!
Fa domina zamansu tutur shi dure,
Zama na mori mulkin Nasara.

It is not wise to fight the Christians' law.
Leave everything – the money and the chieftancy.
As for your learning, it is no concern of Christians.

The character of the English people is soft:
They have mercy on people, the big Christians.
As for me, I thank God for their times because
They have treated me kindly, the Christians.
For me their rule may last for ever
Because I feel enjoyment under the rule of the Christians.
(in Furniss 1996: 206–07)

Aliyu Na Mangi (born 1895) is one of the poets who reinvented Hausa *ajami* poetry by combining religious writing with a more secular style of social commentary and satire. He is best known for his famous poem *Wak'ar Imfiraji*, a poetic composition of 1,000 verses built on both patterns inherent in Hausa classical poetic didacticism and popular song structure. *Wak'ar Keke* (The Song of the Bicycle) was written in *ajami* under Aliyu Na Mangi's dictation. It is a satire of *malams* who embrace modernity without knowing its ways. More importantly, Aliyu Na Mangi posed new questions about the boundaries between *wak'ar baka* (song) and *rubuciyar wak'a* (written song or poem). Hitherto, oral verse was categorized as song while written verse was classified as poetry. Himself a blind person, Aliyu Na Mangi could only compose orally, and what appeared in writing was only a transcription of his oral transmissions. But his poetic brilliance defied this modal classification of song and poetry.

In addition, the romanization of Hausa script influenced the emergence of Hausa modern poetry in Roman script, existing side by side with its *ajami* modern counterpart. The Second World War inspired the thematic production of new poetry in Hausaland that continued to be structurally informed by Hausa-Islamic poetic versification. As Pilaszewicz (1985) observes, the emergent Hausa poets of the Second World War period combine members of the traditional *ajami* literati, the westernized elite, as well as members of other social categories who subscribed as readers and writers to the only newspaper of the time, *Gaskiya Ta Fi Kwabo*.

Unlike the Hausa novel or the plays of the 1930s, which stayed away from any political radicalism (except those written by Aminu Kano which were never published), Hausa modern poetry in *ajami* or *boko* was very political and more reflective of the political dynamism of the historical events shaping the new identity of Hausaland as European colonialism drew it into the politics of Nigerian nationhood. For example, *Wak'ar Maraba da Soja* (Song of Welcome to the Soldiers) is a praise poem written by the militant Sa'adu Zungur (1915–58) in celebration of the return of African soldiers who fought during the Second World War.

The struggle for independence inspired a different kind of concern. Sa'adu Zungur, for example, composed *Arewa Jumhuriya ko Mulkiya* (Is the North to be a Republic or a Constitutional Oligarchy?), a poem that overtly debates the place of the north in Nigerian nationhood. In *Mulukiya*, he calls for the retention of the northern oligarchy in order for the north to preserve its Islamic identity. A reply to Sa'adu's political position was offered by Mudi Sipikin, a supporter of the Republic, in his poem *Arewa Jumhuriya Kawai* (The North, a Republic Pure and Simple).

In the postcolonial period, Hausa poetry has continued to express the dynamics and counter-dynamics of contemporary issues – from corruption to spousal abuse, from personal love to military coups. The conflicts between the urban and rural, and the foreign (usually western) and the indigenous have been particularly prevalent. There has also been a poetry of sensitization about agriculture, public health, and formal education. Here again, women have been keen contributors to this new poetic trend.

Conclusion

In conclusion: this chapter does not claim to be a comprehensive study of Hausa literary traditions. However, it offers a critical appraisal of the crucial aspects of the historical development of Hausa written literature. We began with a discussion on the complexity of Hausaness as an identity construct that refers to people that are ethnically Hausa as well as other ethnic groups such as the Fulani who have been culturally and linguistically assimilated to Hausaness. Secondly, we showed through an analysis of the historical development of the Hausa literary tradition, that what is currently identified as Hausa written literature evolved as a derivative of Hausa-Arabic literature with a religious thrust. Furthermore, with the advent of European colonization in Hausaland, Hausa-Islamic literature began to show a split into various trajectories that reflect the language and cultural policies adopted by the given colonial administrations as well as a gradual shift into secularist formulation. Within both the religious and secular frameworks, Hausa-Islamic women have made and continue to make a contribution in spite of the marginalization of their works by literary critics. Because most of the mainstream scholarship on Hausa literature largely focuses on northern Nigeria's experience, there is a big gap that needs to be filled with regard to the Hausa literary traditions in other parts of Hausaland within the African continent as well as in the diaspora, in the Middle East and the western hemisphere, where the Hausa-speaking people migrated and forged new subcultural identities.

Notes

1. Alamin Mazrui, personal communication.
2. In an attempt to address the exclusion of the contribution of Muslim northern Nigerian women in the study of African literature and popular culture, Margaret Hauwa Kassam presents a bibliography of the works of nineteen contemporary female writers in northern Nigeria, among which fifteen are in Hausa (Newell 1997: 125). These include the works in three volumes of Wada Talatu Ahmed's *Rabin Raina I* (1986, 1987, 1988) (Half of My Life, or My Half Life); Gwaram Hauwa and Hajiya 'Yar Shehu's *Alkalami a Hannun Mata* (1983) (A Pen in Women's Hands); Hadiza Sidi Aliyu's *Salatar Tsiya* (1994); Ramat Balaraba Yakubu's *Budurwar Zuciya* (1989), and more recently Isa Zuwaira's *Labarin So* (1995) (The Story of Love).

Bibliography

Abu-Manga, Al-Amin. 1999. *Hausa in the Sudan: Process of Adaptation to Arabic.* Cologne: Rüdiger Köppe.

Achebe, Chinua. 1958. *Things Fall Apart*. London: Heinemann.

Alkali, Hamidu. 1967. "A Note on Arabic Teaching in Northern Nigeria." *Kano Studies* 3. 6: 10–11.

Al-Nagar, Umar. 1972. *The Pilgrimage Tradition in West Africa*. Khartoum: Khartoum University Press.

Andrzejewski, B. W., Stansilaw Pilaszewicz, and W. Tyloch, eds. 1985. *Literatures in African Languages: Theoretical Issues and Sample Surveys*. Cambridge: Cambridge University Press.

Boyd, Jean. 1989. *The Caliph's Sister: Nana Asma'u 1793–1865, Teacher, Poet and Islamic Leader.* London: Frank Cass.

Cosentino, Donald J. 1978. "An Experiment in Introducing the Novel among the Hausa." *Research in African Literatures* 9. 1: 19–30.

Dan Sidi, Aliyu. 1980. *Wakokin Aliyu Dan Sidi, Sarkin Zazzau*. Zaria: Northern Nigeria Publishing Company.

Faqir, Fadia. 1999. *In the House of Silence: Autobiographical Essays by Arab Women Writers.* Reading: Garnet.

Furniss, Graham. 1996. *Poetry, Prose, and Popular Culture in Hausa.* Edinburgh: Edinburgh University Press for the International African Institute.

Gérard, Albert, ed. 1981a. *African Language Literatures: An Introduction to the Literary History of Sub-Saharan Africa*. Washington, DC: Three Continents Press.

Gérard, Albert. 1981b. "West Africa: Arabic Writing." In Gérard 1981a: 27–40.

1981c. "West Africa: *Ajami* Tradition." In Gérard 1981a: 47–74.

Harrow, W. Kenneth, ed. 1996. *Studies in African Literature: The Marabout and the Muse: New Approaches to Islam in African Literature*. Portsmouth, NH: Heinemann.

Hiskett, Mervyn. 1975. *A History of Hausa Islamic Verse*. London: School of Oriental and African Studies.

Hodgkin, E. C. 1966. *The Arabs*. London: Oxford University Press.

Mack, Beverly, and Jean Boyd. 1997. *The Collected Works of Nana Asma'u, Daughter of Usman Dan Fodiyo*. East Lansing: Michigan State University.

2000. *One Woman's Jihad: Nana Asma'u, Scholar and Scribe*. Bloomington: Indiana University Press.

Mazrui, Ali A. 1986. "Examining the Triple Heritage." In *The Africans: A Reader*. Ed. Ali A. Mazrui and Toby Kleban Levine. New York: Praeger.

Newell, Stephanie, ed. 1997. *Writing African Women: Gender, Popular Culture and Literature in West Africa*. New Jersey: Zed.

Pilaszewicz, Stanislaw. 1985. "Literature in Hausa Language." In *Literatures in African Languages: Theoretical Issues and Sample Surveys*. Ed. B. W. Andrzejewski, Stanislaw Pilaszewicz, and W. Tyloch. Cambridge: Cambridge University Press: 190–254.

1988. "In the Service of the Nation and State: A Study of Novel Writings of the Hausa Author Sulaiman Ibrahim Katsina." *Studies on the Developing Countries* 1: 39–56.

Showalter, Elaine, ed. 1985. *The New Feminist Criticism: Essays on Women and Literature Theory*. New York: Pantheon.

Starratt, Priscilla. 1996. "Islamic Influences on Oral Traditions in Hausa Literature." In *Studies in African Literature. The Marabout and the Muse: New Approaches to Islam in African Literature*. Ed. Kenneth W. Harrow. Portsmouth: Heinemann: 161–75.

Yahaya, Ibrahim Yaro. 1978. "Nazarin Kan Yanayin Wasan Kwaikwayon Hausa." In *Studies in Hausa Language, Literature and Culture. The First Hausa International Conference*. Ed. Dr. Yahaya and Dr. Abba Rufa'i. Kano: Bayero University, 7–10 July: 244–55.

Yamba, Ch. B. 1990. "Permanent Pilgrims: An Anthropological Study of the Role of Pilgrimage in the Lives of West African Muslims in Sudan." PhD diss. University of Stockholm.

19

Literature in Yorùbá: poetry and prose; traveling theater and modern drama*

KARIN BARBER

Yorùbá verbal art is one of Africa's most remarkable fields of creativity, both in its variety and its extent. Oral traditions, some of them of great antiquity, continue to flourish and evolve; written literature constitutes one of the largest, longest-established, and liveliest traditions in Africa; there are also numerous new popular genres on the interface between written and oral modes. Supported by a public of about 30 million Yoruba-speakers, mostly in southwestern Nigeria, Yoruba literature plays a central role in many dimensions of ordinary life, ranging from lessons in school to life cycle ceremonies such as naming, marriage, and burial; from contact with ancestors to commentary on the contemporary national situation. Yoruba literary culture is also one of the few in Africa to be supported by an extensive, long-standing, and sophisticated local critical scholarship in the same language as the literature itself.

Oral genres

Oral genres constitute a vast field of expression with much intertextuality and cross-genre borrowing. Terminology for genres varies. Some genres are widely recognized, their key features agreed upon. But there is also much local specificity and much contextual variation in the use of terms even within a single locality. Some of the principal categories widely used in Yorubaland (though with variations) are the following:

(i) *Oríkì* ("praise poetry"), the appellations or attributive epithets saluting the intrinsic qualities of individual human beings, kin groups, towns, *òrìṣà* ("gods"), animals, material objects, and immaterial forces. They are vocative in address and name-like in form; disjunctive; and often condensed and allusive in reference. A performance of *oriki* is a fluid assemblage of textual units held together by their common application to a subject, with whose social and moral being

*Except in quoted texts, Yorùbá words will be tone-marked on first use only.

they are held to have a deep connection. The most treasured *oriki* are *oríkì orílẹ̀*, the "*oriki* of origin," which link individuals to an extended kin group through common origin in a named town or region. These *oriki* often contain long, coherent, patterned passages, making much use of structural parallelism and tonal play. Distinctive features of the place and community of origin are singled out and turned into emblems of identity. Thus people claiming common origin in ancient Ìrè-Èkìtì, reputedly the home of Ògún the god of war and iron, are saluted for their skills as blacksmiths: "Without Ire people, we would not be able to hoe the farm; without Ire people, we would not be able to clear the path." Common origin in Ìjẹ̀ṣà is celebrated in terms of the land's natural produce: "I am an Ijẹṣa, of the land of kola." The people called Òpómúléró, originating in Ìwàtá, have *oriki orilẹ* that refer to a funeral ceremony distinctive of this kin group: "The post wears a wrapper, the post ties a baby-sash" – a ceremony that in turn commemorates a historical incident when an ancestor of the kin-group was commissioned by the Aláàfin to carve two hundred house-posts in the image of his dead mother. These emblematic appellations can be greatly elaborated, though their meaning is not always self-evident from the text alone. They form the bedrock of social identity and can arouse profound emotions of pride and gratification when performed.

Individuals also acquire personal *oriki* in the course of their lives, in recognition of their actions and personalities as these take shape. Some may be drawn from a common stock – for example, any dark-complexioned person could be saluted with the attribution "The forest's darkness brings it honour, The hill's roundness gives it joy" – while others are highly idiosyncratic, and may commemorate obscure and even shameful or embarrassing incidents in the person's life, like the epithet "One who marries his wife with a ladder," commemorating a certain reckless lover's nocturnal abduction of another man's bride. *Oriki* remark on what is distinctive in a person rather than simply flattering him or her. Men tend to acquire more *oriki* than women, and prominent people in the community acquire more than obscure ones. Profusion and variety are of great importance in a performance, for the more prolonged and intense the salutation, the more the aura of the subject is enhanced.

One of the most important bodies of *oriki* in the past was the praises of the deities, for it was through *oriki*-salutations that devotees established the typically intense dyadic communication with their own *oriṣa*. The reciprocity and mutual identification of devotee and deity was often enacted through the merging of *oriki*, so that the *oriṣa* could be saluted through the *oriki* of a prominent devotee while the devotee's collection of *oriki* could absorb some lines from his or her deity's praises. *Orișa* with exceptionally impressive bodies of *oriki* include Ṣàngó, Ògún, and Ṣọ̀pọ̀nnọ́n, where the poetry attains a remarkable intensity and grandeur.

Oriki are recognizable from the high degree of nominalization (e.g., Òbùmubùmuṣàgbálóńgbólóńgbó, "One-who-dips-and-drinks-dips-and-drinks-making-the-liquor-barrel-slosh"); the frequent use of phrases such as "Child of . . ." "Father of . . ." "Native of . . ."; and the frequent incidence of cryptic, condensed, and deliberately obscure phrases, such that a single word may turn out to be a repository of extensive fields of meaning. For example, the epithet *Àbú*, found in the *oriki* of ancient Ifẹ̀, is said to encapsulate the entire narrative of the episode in the reign of Ọ̀rànmíyàn in which this Ọba went on a journey leaving the kingdom in the care of a slave (*àbú* = "one who is abused," i.e., because of his servile status), who in due course founded the next dynasty in Ifẹ. In many cases, even the kin group that "owns" the *oriki* may entertain divergent interpretations of certain phrases or may have no explanation for them, beyond the statement that "It's *oriki*."

(ii) *Ẹsẹ Ifá* (Ifá divination verses) are the vast corpus of sacred verses associated with Ifá, the most prestigious form of divination in Yoruba culture. The divination system operates through 256 *odù* or "signatures," to each of which is attached an indefinitely large corpus of verses, learnt over many years of rigorous training before an apprentice diviner is deemed competent to practice professionally. The verses are all modeled on a single format, involving a narrative of a previous divination carried out by a legendary or primordial diviner. In a consultation session, the diviner operates the divining instruments (either sixteen palm-nuts or a divining chain strung with eight identical two-sided symbols) in order to produce an *odu*. He then selects a verse from this *odu* and expounds it to the client, often chanting all or part of it in the process. The verse thus functions as a precedent for the present situation and a model for action that will shape the future. Most verses include an account of a sacrifice made (or foolishly not made) by the protagonist in the narrative; the diviner adapts this to prescribe a sacrifice for the current client. The parts into which each verse can be divided have been variously analyzed but almost always follow the same order. The opening sections, which state the name of the legendary diviner(s) and the client, and the reason for the consultation, are memorized by a meticulous system of rote-learning and held to be incapable of change. They are often gnomic and evocative phrases of great poetic beauty, for example: "When fire dies, it covers itself with ashes; When the moon dies, it leaves the stars behind; Few are the stars who shine with the moon" (Abimbola

1977: 72–73). In some cases, this textual slot conventionally understood as the "names" of the diviners may balloon out and encompass elaborate proverbial sequences many lines long. Thus one verse opens:

> "Excess of wisdom turns a person mad
> Medicine, if it is over-abundant
> Turns a person insane
> If a woman is excessively clever
> Her husband's clothes will always remain skimpy"
> Did divination for the rich man of Ifẹ
> On the day that he was bewailing his lack of children.

Here the first five lines stand for the names of legendary or primordial diviners, but also constitute a poetic proverbial statement that is the main content of the verse.

The central narrative portions of each verse, telling the story of what happened to the client after the divination had been performed and the sacrifice prescribed, tend to be more fluid and may be greatly elaborated. The verse usually closes with a summary statement and a recapitulation of the opening lines. Although these distinctive formal features make the genre easily recognizable, they do not limit its scope. Historically, it would seem that the corpus was built up through the absorption of numerous already existing narrative and poetic materials, which were captured into the Ifa format without being fully reduced to it. The Ifa corpus thus plays host to a great diversity of genres. The verse structure can be enormously extended to encompass a sequence of linked mythological narratives, in verses known as "Ifá ńlá" or "great Ifa"; it can be truncated to display a single, condensed idea; it can accommodate "quotations" of proverbs, *oriki*, and historical narrative. Because of its sacred status and its all-encompassing inclusiveness, the Ifa corpus of verses is widely considered to be the authoritative repository of all Yoruba wisdom, and is highly regarded by most Yoruba people whatever their religious affiliation.

(iii) *Àlọ́* are subdivided into *àlọ́ àpamọ̀* (*àlọ́* that are told to be known, i.e., riddles) and *àlọ́ àpagbè* (*àlọ́* that are told to be supported with a chorus, i.e., folktales defined by the fact that they contain integral songs with choruses). Folktales and riddles, traditionally recounted on moonlit nights in the compounds of large extended-family groups, are no longer widely performed in this manner. However, they are still transmitted through school readers and radio programs, and through incorporation into other genres such as the Yorùbá novel and popular drama (see below). Among the best-known and most popular types of folktale were those that dealt with Ìjàpá, the tortoise trickster famous for his greed, deceitfulness, and wit. Styles and names of narrative types varied according to locality. One popular narrative form was *àrọ̀*, a chain-type story in which one thing inexorably leads to another so that huge consequences follow from a small initial trigger; *arọ* were often formulated as a chant or recitation and performed by children as a feat of memory.

(iv) *Ìtàn*: narratives held to be true, which include myths of gods and heroes, as well as historical narratives pertaining to towns, lineages, and individuals. Part of every town's identity is its *itan* of origin, the story of how it came to be founded – often by a named hero, a hunter or prince who left his home and traveled into an uninhabited territory before receiving a supernatural sign that he should settle there. The history of every town is subsumed into the history of its *ọba* (kings) and the events in their reigns. Each *ilé* (compound/lineage) in a town likewise has its own *itan* recounting the reasons its founding ancestor left his town of origin and journeyed to settle down in a new place, and recalling the deeds of the most prominent of the lineage's "big men" of the past. Numerous *itan* revolve around the activities of prominent figures in the nineteenth-century wars, and indeed much of Samuel Johnson's great work, *The History of the Yorubas*, is based upon oral narratives of this kind. *Itan* may be elicited in disputes, for instance over inheritance, land boundaries, or claims to chieftaincy titles, and in the colonial period enormous numbers of lineage and town *itan* were collected by the courts in the course of litigation following the colonial authorities' attempts to fix political relations within and between towns; these provide a source that has been noted by historians but has yet to be fully investigated by textual scholars. *Itan* exist in a symbiotic relationship with *oriki*: *itan* are told to explain obscure lines of *oriki*, while *oriki* in turn provide the mnemonic pegs onto which extended narratives are hung.

(v) *Òwe*: proverbs or sayings, ranging from brief memorable expressions, often involving punning or tonal play, such as "Iṣẹ́ loògùn ìṣẹ́" (Work is the medicine for poverty), to sayings that expand into extensive parables. *Owe* are regarded as the jewels of the language; command of them is indispensable to eloquence, and knowledge of them is widely disseminated. Often, an artful speaker will quote only the first half of a proverb, or drop the merest allusion to it; since "ààbọ ọ̀rọ̀ làá sọ fọ́mọlúwàbí" (half a word is enough for the wise), the listener can be relied on to complete the meaning and apply it appropriately. Many *owe* are associated with explanatory narratives that locate the proverb's origin in a concrete historical incident: for example, S. O. Bada in his *Òwe Yorùbá àti ìṣẹ̀dálẹ̀ wọn* (1979, Yoruba Proverbs and their Origins) explains even apparently quite general proverbs like "Ènìyàn-án ṣòro" (People are difficult) by relating them to a detailed narrative, in this case the story of a man who settled in a village called Ayé-lála near Ìsẹ́yìn and prospered there until the day that the townspeople needed a stranger as human sacrifice, when they seized him and buried him alive. His last words were "Ènìyàn-án ṣòro, ayé mà lála o!" (People are difficult, the world is tough), and thus the saying allegedly originated. Although *owe* gain their authority from the fact that they are distillations of past experience, tested by repeated reapplication over time, they still belong to a growing tradition and new *owe* can be seen coming into being. The saying "Ó le kú – ìjà Ọ̀rẹ̀ (It's terribly hard – like the battle of Ọ̀rè) refers to an episode in the Nigerian civil war of 1967–70, but by now is well on its way to being accepted as an established proverb. In changing economic and political circumstances, old sayings may be inverted and new variants may be generated precisely to convey a sense of how things have changed. In "Olówó ń sọ̀rọ̀: tálíkà lóun ní *idea*" (The rich man speaks; the poor man says he has an *idea*), the use of the English loan word serves to underscore the hollowness of the dreams of the poor.

Narratives – encompassing historical *itan*, *alọ apagbe*, extended *owe*, and *arọ* – may all in certain circumstances be referred to generically as "itan," i.e., as narrated sequences of action. And other modalities, crosscutting the named categories, can be identified. Deirdre LaPin, in a 1977 study that traverses a range of Yoruba local culture-areas including Èkìtì, Ìbàdàn, Ẹ̀gbá, Oǹdó, Ọ̀yọ́, Ìjẹ̀ṣà, and Ìgbómìnà, has proposed six "modes" of narrative, defined according to form, theme, and use, crosscutting the common genre-categories: charters (narratives of past events held to be true and used as a basis for claims in real life); romances (extended narratives of human heroism and quest, in imaginary but plausible circumstances); parables (abstract and hypothetical stories demonstrating a truth, often through parallel sequences of events); formulaic tales (fantasy sequences of highly schematic and regular exchanges, leading from small beginnings to great outcomes); fables (humorous and dramatic exemplification of a general truth); and song-stories (postulating an extreme imaginary scenario in which the consequences of the worst imaginable human behavior are acted out). This proposal has the advantage of focusing attention on certain kinds of narrative that could easily be missed because they lack distinguishing names in local typologies – such as the romance type, which could well have fed into the work of the great pioneer of Yorùbá written fiction, D. O. Fágúnwà.

(vi) *Ọfọ̀* or *ògèdè*: incantations. An extremely powerful poetic genre, regarded as intensely efficacious and downright dangerous, used by knowledgeable people (especially medicine-men) to realign the balance of spiritual forces. *Ọfọ* work through a system of verbal correspondences. For example, "Ohun tí a wí fọ́gbọ́ lọgbọ́ gbọ́ / Ohun tí a wí fọ́gbà lọgbàá gbà" (What we say to the *ọgbọ́* leaf the *ọgbọ́* leaf hears / What we say to the garden enclosure, the garden enclosure accepts) works through similarity of sound: the second syllable of the name of a type of leaf, *ọgbọ́*, is identical to the sound of the verb "to hear," *gbọ́*. This correspondence is felt to activate an inner relationship of necessity, and by analogy to bring about a necessary consequence – in this case, the addressee's hearing and obeying the speaker's commands. There are a number of related types of incantations, including a type associated with Ifa verses, called *àyájọ́*, and a type used only for bringing about blessings and good fortune, called *àwúre*.

(vii) *Orin*: songs, most often processional and recreational, associated with major festivals and life cycle ceremonies. Although generally the least prestigious and least studied of Yoruba oral genres, these are probably also the most ubiquitous. Every funeral features great parties of lineage co-wives, dressed in the same patterned cloth (aṣọ ẹbí or "Aǹkóò," from the English "and Co." – company), singing well-known processional songs, often in competition with *oriki* of lamentation performed by the bereaved or by professional praise singers. Every *oriṣa* has songs that are performed at its shrine by devotees on its sacred day in the four-day week. People sing as they work; mothers sing lullabies to their babies; young girls have whole repertoires of pre-wedding songs, many of them salacious; while the devotees of the *egúngún* masquerade cult may go from house to house, singing defamatory songs about those householders who fail to acknowledge them with gifts of money.

*

These textual types – *oriki, ẹsẹ Ifa, alọ apamọ, alọ apagbe, owe, itan, arọ, ọfọ* and *orin* – can be differentiated on formal grounds. But one genre may constitute the material out of which another is composed. Thus proverbs are very frequently incorporated both into *oriki* and into Ifa verses, while Ifa verses may be incorporated into *oriki* and vice versa, and numerous *alọ apagbe* are to be found in Ifa verses, minus their characteristic songs. In addition, and crosscutting these distinctions, numerous named performance modes can be identified that mobilize genres such as *oriki* and *ẹsẹ Ifa* for specific purposes. *Ìyẹ̀rẹ̀ Ifá*, for example, are a specialized mode of chanting *ẹsẹ Ifa* as a public display of skill, reserved for particular occasions, notably the all-night vigil that opens the annual Ifa festival. This has led Ọlátúndé Ọlátúnjí to adopt a two-pronged classification of oral poetry, in which genres identified on formal grounds ("feature types") intersect with genres identified according to style of performance ("chanting modes") (Ọlatunji 1984). There are numerous chanting modes based on *oriki*, some very localized and others widely found in the Yoruba-speaking area. Among the most widespread and best known are *ìjálá* (hunters' chants), *iwì egúngún* (ancestral masquerade chants), *Ṣàngó pípè* (literally "the calling of Ṣàngó"), and *ẹkún ìyàwó* (bridal chants). Localized modes include *àṣamọ̀* (Èkìtì), *alámọ̀* (Èkìtì), *àdàmọ̀* (Ifẹ̀, Ìjẹ̀ṣà, and Èkìtì each have their own versions), *olele* (Ìjẹ̀ṣà), *ọ̀wẹ̀wẹ̀* (Oǹdó), *ẹ̀fẹ̀* (Ẹ̀gbádò), and *àjàgbó* (Àkókó). Chanting modes are distinguished by intonation and voice-quality; by the focus of the address (thus in *ijala*, the subjects are often animals, while in *iwi egungun* there are usually long passages addressing the legendary founder of the ancestral masquerade cult, and in *ẹkun iyawo* the focus is on the performer herself, who is the bride); by the nature of the additional textual materials that supplement the *oriki* (thus in *ijala*, philosophical reflections and witty topical commentary may be added, while in *ẹkun iyawo* there are extensive passages of reflection upon the bride's impending change of status); and by the people who perform the chant and the contexts in which they do so (see Babalọlá 1966; Olatunji 1984; and Olúkòjú 1978).

Oral genres typically attract a range of performers of different levels of competence, and with the exception of *ẹsẹ Ifa* are usually learnt informally, by habituation and participation. Some performances are predominantly the preserve of men (e.g., *ijala* and *ẹsẹ Ifa*, since hunters and most diviners are male) or of women (*ẹkun iyawo*, publicly performed only by brides). Some are predominantly performed by the young (*alọ*, *ẹkun iyawo*), some by the old (proverbs, *itan*). In general, however, performance in Yorubaland is characterized by a practical and existential belief that competence determines entitlement. In many genres there are specialists who may make their living or supplement their income from public performances, but also ordinary household members who perform only in family ceremonies but whose expertise may nonetheless in some respects surpass that of the professionals.

Oral genres in Yorubaland are held to be empowering and effectual. Proverbs are rules of thumb, only fully meaningful when brought to bear on an actual situation. *Itan* are the means by which the past is reactivated in the present. Ifa verses come into play in the course of divination consultations where models from the past are used to shape the future. The performance of *oriki* heightens a human subject's social well-being, spurs a masquerade into action, and inspires the *oriṣa* to make their presence felt among the human community.

Many traditional oral genres in Yoruba are constituted in such a way that their meaning is not self-evident, but requires active exegesis or "deriddling" by knowledgeable audiences. Any audience is likely to contain rings or layers of listeners differentiated by their degree of prior knowledge. This suggests that the interpretation of Yoruba oral texts is not something that can simply be assured on the basis of common, publicly available linguistic competence, but is rather a genre or a series of genres in itself with its own techniques and styles of verbal linkage and unpacking. This is an aspect of Yoruba orature that still remains to be systematically studied.

In the present day, these oral traditions continue to serve old functions such as the establishment of communication with the spiritual world, the celebration of individual and group identity, the inculcation of shared values, or the affirmation of individual uniqueness. But they have also been collected, broadcast, discussed, and staged as "Yoruba heritage" by colonial and postcolonial cultural nationalists. They have entered into the constitution of numerous new genres, both written and semi-oral. They are the linguistic basis of neotraditional chanted poetry; they are frequently incorporated into written literary texts; they are the focus of continual commentary and redeployment in the Yoruba-language press; and they are staged within the format of contemporary popular theater, film, and video drama (see below).

Written literature

Though some Yoruba texts may have been written in Arabic script as early as the eighteenth century, surviving literature written in Yoruba dates from the mid-nineteenth century with the establishment of the Church Missionary Society (CMS) mission in Abẹ́òkúta and its program of translation and publication of religious texts for the edification of converts. The involvement of the bicultural "Saro" group – Yoruba repatriated slaves who had initially been deposited in Sierra Leone before making their way back to their homeland – facilitated the early and extensive production of Yoruba-language texts, including original compositions as well as translations. The principal effort went into Bible translation, and the Saro clergyman (later Bishop) Samuel Ajayi Crowther's pioneering efforts in this regard have influenced Yoruba literary language to this day. But there was also room for the publication of original compositions, in the shape of hymns and "native airs," and for renditions of local oral traditions. The *Ìwé Ìròhìn* ("Newspaper") of the Abẹokuta mission – which antedated by three years the first English-language newspaper, published in Lagos in 1862 – contained local and international news items, but also made room for verbal art forms such as renditions of folktales.

Yoruba-language writing was given a boost in the 1880s and 1890s by an upsurge of cultural nationalism among the Lagos elite, when numerous histories and collections of Yoruba proverbs and other oral texts were produced. Notable among these works were E. M. Líjàdù's pioneering collection of poems by the popular early nineteenth-century Ẹgba oral poet Aríbilóṣòó (1886), and his two scholarly works on the Ifa divination corpus, *Ifa* (1898) and *Orunmila* (1908). The series of school readers entitled *Ìwé Kíkà*, produced for the CMS between 1871 and 1915, also contained notable collections of folklore, proverbs, and historical narrative drawn from oral tradition. *Ìlọsíwájú Èrò Mímọ́*, a translation of Bunyan's *The Pilgrim's Progress* by the CMS missionary David Hinderer, first printed in the 1860s, was reissued in 1911 and thereafter widely distributed; it had a lasting influence on Yorùbá-language fiction, as will be seen below. In the early years of the twentieth century, numerous local histories were published, including *Ìwé Ìtàn Ìbàdàn àti díẹ̀ nínú àwọn ìlú agbègbè rẹ̀ bí Ìwó, Ọ̀ṣogbo àti Ìkìrun* (History of Ibadan and Some of Her Neighboring Towns Such as Iwo, Oṣogbo, and Ikirun) by I. B. Akínyẹlé (1911), *Ìwé Ìtàn Ekó* (History of Lagos) by J. B. O. Lòsì (1913), and *Ìwé Ìtàn Àjàsẹ́* (History of Ajasẹ) by A. Akínsọ̀wọ́n (1914). Akinyẹle's history of Ibadan was particularly influential and was subsequently published in an English version by Akinyẹle (*The Outlines of Ibadan History*, 1946) and in a three-volume revised version undertaken by Akínyẹlé's niece Kẹ́mi Morgan. The original Yoruba-language version is remarkable for the large number of personal *oriki* of Ibadan notables included in the text: *oriki* that were later extracted and republished with commentaries by other Yorùbá scholars.

These pioneering efforts in historiography were followed in the 1920s by a proliferation of Yoruba-language newspapers, at least six being founded between 1922 and 1929. It was through the press, rather than directly through the churches or the schools, that the first well-known and extensive work of fiction in Yoruba was published: I. B. Thomas's *Ìtàn Ìgbésí Aiyé Èmi Ṣẹ̀gilọlá* (The Life Story of Me, Ṣẹ̀gilọlá), which was serialized in Thomas's own newspaper, *Akéde Èkó*, and immediately afterwards published as a book (1930).[1] This narrative is the confessions, in epistolary form, of a Lagos prostitute who, stricken with disease in middle age, looks back over her life with a mixture of glee and repentance, and regales the readership with an arrestingly lifelike account of her past exploits and her present sufferings. This initiative was paralleled by that of a rival Lagos newspaper editor, E. A. Akintan, who began the serialization of *Ìgbẹ̀hìn-á-dùn tàbí Ìtàn Ọmọ Orukan* (All's Well That Ends Well, or The Story of an Orphan) in his paper *Elétí ọ̀fẹ́* before I. B. Thomas, but did not complete it or publish the episodes as a volume until the success of *Ṣẹgilọla* had shown the way. The Yoruba-language or bilingual newspapers also published recensions of oral poetry. In 1924, for example, *The Yoruba News* published the *oriki* of Oyèéwọlé, the new Baálẹ̀ of Ibadan, on his installation. Other publications of the period included A. K. Ajíṣafẹ́'s two short prose works, *Ènìà ṣòro* (People Are Hard), and *Tan' t' Ọ́lọ́run* (Who Is Equal to God?), both of which consist of a succession of brief narratives designed to exemplify a proverb or illustrate a moral lesson.

The most important early writer of Yoruba fiction was D. O. Fágúnwà, whose first novel, *Ògbójú Ọdẹ Nínú Igbó Irúnmalẹ̀* (The Intrepid Hunter in the Forest of Spirits) was published in 1938 and immediately became a popular classic, adopted into school curricula and widely read by adults as well. This story is written in majestic and memorable prose, reminiscent of the cadences of the Yoruba Bible, and deals with the adventures of a hunter who encounters a succession of spirits, some benign, some malign, some functioning as allegorical figures echoing Bunyan's *The Pilgrim's Progress*, others drawn from Yoruba folklore, Greek and Roman mythology, and English fiction. Fagunwa followed this novel with four others in a similar vein: *Igbó Olódùmarè* (1949a); *Ìrèké Oníbùdó* (1949b); *Ìrìnkèrindò Nínú Igbó Elégbèje* (1954); *Àdììtú Olódùmarè* (1961). All retained the episodic plot structure, organized round a journey or succession of journeys, and the theme of a human encountering a sequence of supernatural challenges. But the last of these novels moved into new ground, dealing with the experience of modernity (educated characters, motor cars, an epistolary romance), which might have heralded a new move toward realism in his work had Fagunwa not tragically drowned in 1963, at the age of sixty, while still working on his sixth novel.

The success of Fagunwa's novels led to a whole "school of Fagunwa," allegorical and adventure stories of spirits and ghosts in folkloric settings (see Ògúnṣínà 1992). This strand of Yoruba writing continued into the 1970s and took on many variant forms in the work of such writers as A. Oyèédélé (*Aiyé Rèé*, 1947; *Ìwọ ni*, 1970), J. O. Ògúndélé (*Èjìgbèdè l'ọ̀nà Ìsálú Ọrun*, 1956; *Ibú Olókun*, 1956), J. F. Ọdúnjọ (*Kúyẹ̀*, 1964), and Ọdúnjọ and A. B. Ọladipúpọ̀ (*Kàdárà àti Ẹ̀gbọ́n rẹ̀*, 1967). However, the dynamic center of fictional creativity had shifted even before Fagunwa's death. The realistic style pioneered by I. B. Thomas came to flower in the 1950s and early 1960s. In *Aiyé d'Aiyé Òyìnbó* (1955), Isaac Délànọ̀ depicted the experience of colonization from a local, uneducated woman's perspective. The story is remarkable for its detailed evocation of village life and attitudes, and for its ambivalence about the changes introduced by the colonial regime. His second novel, *L'ọ́jọ́ Ọjọ́ Un* (1963), is a historical narrative set in Abẹokuta, which, though presented as fiction, has extensive documentary components and toward the end turns into a teetotalers' tract. Fẹmi Jẹ́bọdà's prize-winning tale of the seamy side of life seen from the point of view of a rogue and vagabond, *Olówólaiyémọ̀*, published in 1964 but written for an Independence celebration competition in 1960, brings the "realist" strand in Yoruba writing to wonderfully ebullient realization.

In the late 1960s and throughout the 1970s there was an explosion of literary creativity, with many new authors emerging and pioneering new styles and themes. Among the most prominent were Adébáyọ̀ Fálétí, whose *Ọmọ Olókùn Ẹsin* (1969) is a historical novel dealing with a revolt against the overlordship of Ọyọ, and Ọládẹ̀jọ Òkédìjí, author of two brilliantly innovative crime thrillers (*Àjà ló lẹrù*, 1969, and *Àgbàlagbà Akàn*, 1971), as well as a more somber tragic novel of the destruction of a young boy who is relentlessly drawn into a life of crime in the underworld of Ifẹ (*Atótó Arére*, 1981). Notable also are Akínwùmí Ìṣọ̀lá, whose university campus novel *Ó le kú* (1974) broke new ground in social setting and ambience; Afọlábí Ọlábímtán, author of several novels, including *Kékeré Ẹkùn* (1967), which deals with the conflicts arising from early Christian conversion in a small village, and *Baba Rere!* (1978), a contemporary satire on a corrupt big man; and Kọ́lá Akínlàdé, prolific author of well-crafted detective stories such as *Ta ló pa Ọmọ Ọba?* (Who Killed the Prince's Child?). These authors were all verbal stylists of a high order; they transformed the literary language, moving away from Fagunwa's rolling cadences to a more demotic, supple prose that successfully caught the accents of everyday life (Okediji in particular excelled at this) while retaining the capacity of traditional orature to import other genres and to allude intertextually to the whole field of Yoruba verbal art. Thus Ládélé's *Ìgbì Ayéńyí* has a whole chapter made up of an Ifa verse narrating the story of Àlàbá who saw a living skeleton and made the mistake of boasting about it; Iṣọla's *O le ku* resorts to *oriki*-like poetry to convey the beauty of one of his heroines; Láwùyì Ògúnníran's *Eégún Aláré* (1972) moves continually between prose and poetry to develop a fascinating narrative about a traveling masquerade group. All these writers, furthermore, draw confidently on proverbs, sayings, anecdotes, and allusions shared by their knowledgeable public; as with the oral genres, the addressee is drawn into a collaborative role and is credited with the cultural resources to act as co-constitutor of the text's meaning.

In the 1980s and 90s a third generation of Yoruba authors emerged, and the themes and styles diversified further. Olú Owólabí, already published in the 1970s, became established in the 1980s as one of the most prolific writers in Yoruba, producing novels and plays on topics ranging from the experience of soldiers in the civil war (*Ẹni Ọlọ́run ò pa*, 1980; *Ìjà Ọ̀rẹ̀*, 1983) to bank robbery (*Ìsújú Ọ̀sanyìn*, 1983) and elections (*Ọ̀tẹ̀ n'ibò*, 1988). Humorous, topical, and realistic portrayals of everyday life extended into areas such as the experiences of a middle-class couple returning to Nigeria after fifteen years in Britain (Adébísí Thompson, *Bọsún Ọmọ Ọ̀dọ̀fin*, 1987 – a low-key but shrewdly observant novel by one of the few Yoruba women writers). The economic catastrophe of the 1980s and 90s delayed the publication of many manuscripts but did not entirely block the appearance of new work. By now there must be around two hundred Yoruba novels in print.

Written poetry and drama have also been very successful genres. Poetry is perhaps the earliest written literary genre to make its appearance in Western Nigeria, *oriki* and hymns both featuring in the earliest publications of the missionary and secular press. Ṣóbọ̀ Aróbíodù (J. S. Ṣówándé) was an Ẹgba poet whose long topical and didactic poems written in the style of traditional poetic chants – but dealing with contemporary issues, personal experiences, and reflections from a Christian perspective – were highly successful, even though they did not directly give rise to a tradition of imitators. In 1904 E. M. Lijadu published *Ìwé Kini ti Ṣóbọ̀ Aró-bí-odù* (Ṣobo Aro-bi-odu's First Book), soon to be followed by a second compilation, both of which were widely acclaimed. A. K. Ajiṣafẹ of Abẹokuta was best known for his long philosophical and topical poem *Aiyé Akámarà* (1921) (The Vicissitudes of the World). His model was adopted by other writers, including Gabriel Ibítóyè Òjó, whose narrative poem *Ọlọ́run Ẹ̀san* (1952) (Vengeance Is God's) became particularly well known after it was included in the primary-school curriculum. D. A. Ọbásá, founder of the Ibadan bilingual newspaper *Yorùbá News* in 1924, published several anthologies of poetry. *Ìwé Kinní ti Àwọn Akéwì* (1927) (First Book of Poets' Utterances) was followed by two sequels – the Second and Third Books of Poets' Utterances, in 1934 and 1945. The most successful early poetry derived its inspiration from oral genres and managed to overcome the limitations of the printed page. Other styles were painfully faithful copies of English poetic meter and structure, and never really made much headway since Yoruba is a tonal language whose indigenous poetry is neither metrical nor rhymed. Many writers, including J. F. Ọdunjọ, Akinwumi Iṣọla, and Afọlabi Ọlabimtan, have produced volumes of poetry as well as novels, though on the whole they are better known for the latter. New work is emerging – mostly in the form of long discursive and philosophical poems, probably influenced by popular media poetry (see below) – recent publications being *Ìjì Ayé*, by Ọlánipẹ̀kun Olúránkinṣẹ́ (1987) and *Orin Ewúro* (1998), by a poet using the name "Àtàrí Àjànàkú" (Elephant Head or Skull).

Written drama exists mainly as a literary form intended to be read, rather than as a script to be produced on a stage. Some plays, however, have successfully been performed – sometimes after adaptation – by university and popular theater companies, either on stage or on television. Adébáyọ̀ Fálétí was one of the first writers to produce distinguished literary dramas, among them *Nwọn rò pé wèrè ni* (1965) (They Thought She Was Mad), a contemporary moral tale revolving around forged/fake money; *Ìdààmú Pààdì Minkáílù* (1974) (Father Michael's Trouble), set in a church community; and his best play, *Baṣọ̀run Gáà* (1972) (Gáà the Kingmaker), set in eighteenth-century Ọyọ and showing the downfall of a notorious tyrant. Akinwumi Iṣọla has achieved an exceptional combination of popular and erudite success with his written dramas. His *Ẹfúnṣetán Aníwúrà* (1970), a verse drama about the nineteenth-century Ibadan woman chief of that name, was successfully performed by the popular theater group "I Show Pepper" (Ìṣọ̀lá Ògúnṣọlá), using a combination of scripted and improvised performance. When this play was subsequently made into a film, its premiere – in the Liberty Stadium, Ibadan – attracted an audience of over 14,000. He also oversaw the adaptation of his play *Kò Ṣe é Gbé*, about one man's struggle against corruption in the Customs Office, into a popular video drama: whereas the published play ends in despair after the hero is defeated, the video has him cleverly routing the evil-doers and surviving, injured but triumphant in his hospital bed.

Another written Yoruba-language play that has enjoyed great and repeated success as stage production is Okediji's *Rẹ́rẹ́ Rún* (1973), about a trade union strike that fails because of the fallibility of its leader. Okediji has also published *Ṣàngó*, a play about the legendary Ọyọ king of that name (1987), and *Aájò Ajé*, which follows the fortunes of three young men as they pursue, with increasing obsessiveness, their goal of winning the pools. Olú Dáramọ́lá's *Ilé tí a fi itọ́ mọ* (1970) (The House Built of Spit) is a literary drama about a middle-class couple whose marriage is threatened when the husband has an affair with his secretary. This play was taken up by a popular theater group, the Oyin Adéjọbí Theatre, and adapted to their own worldview and dramaturgical style, with great success; their version was also published in the popular "photoplay" magazine *Atọ́ka*, which presents stage dramas in strip-cartoon format using photographs and bubble captions. A rare woman playwright is Jọláadé Fáwálé, whose *Tẹni n'tẹni* (1982) is a conjugal melodrama about a man who, having fallen in love with a foreign woman while on business in Europe, deliberately wrecks his marriage to the faithful, pious Ẹkúndayọ̀ in order to be with his new love. Eventually, however, the homebreaker turns missionary and she is instrumental in reuniting the couple and promoting forgiveness all round.

Popular poetry and drama

Popular poetry and drama have received much less recognition by scholars than either the older oral traditions or the newer, print literature in Yoruba. Contemporary popular genres are products of the colonial period and after; they are produced by members of the intermediate classes, midway between the illiterate farming population and the salaried elites; they are innovative, rapidly changing, often ephemeral; they are not supported by educational or cultural establishments; and they tend to promulgate practical moral messages that are often conservative but are highly valued by their audiences.

In the sphere of neotraditional chanted and printed popular poetry (known generically as *ewì*), the work of Ọlátúnbọ̀sún Ọládàpọ̀ and Ọláńrewájú Adépọ̀jù is the best known. Both have published volumes of their poetry, which they also perform live and on radio, television, records, and cassettes. This poetry draws heavily on the idiom of older oral genres such as *oriki* and *ẹsẹ Ifa*, but also has a distinctive tone and form of address: it tends to be discursive and coherent rather than segmentary or fragmented; often reflective and philosophical, personal, and sometimes introspective in tone; but – like all other popular genres – ultimately the servant of a "moral lesson," which may be tinged with Christian (Ọladapọ) or Muslim (Adepọju) vocabularies, but which appeals to a broader, ecumenical popular common sense. Ọladapo's *Àròyé Akéwì*, volumes I (1973) and II (1975), and Adepọju's *Ìrònú Akéwì* (1972) are taught in schools as well as being widely read outside the educational context; in the 1980s, Ọladapọ also used to publish his poems in his own cultural magazine, *Ọ̀kín Ọlọ́jà*. This type of half-chanted, half-recited poetry has become extremely popular and there are now numerous "*ewi* exponents" developing their own styles.

The lyrics of popular *jùjú* music by stars such as Sunny Adé and Ebenezer Obey are also widely known and highly regarded for the "deep Yoruba" on which they draw, as they combine proverbs, old poetic idioms, neologisms, and slang to produce a richly varied texture. In the atmosphere of heightened religious competition characteristic of the late 1980s and the 1990s, Muslim and Christian singers have relayed rival didactic messages through the medium of gospel songs and Islamic *waka*. These often borrow eclectically from a range of textual genres: thus Wasiu Káyọ̀dé Sadeeq, a *waka* singer, in his audio cassette *Ẹni Ayé ń Yẹ*, combines quotations from the Qur'an, Yoruba proverbs, fragments of English-language songs ("If you are happy and you know it"), references to astronomy ("In all the solar systems that exist in the world, Jupiter is the biggest and it takes a little more than two hundred years, you Muslims, for

Jupiter to turn round the earth") interspersed with extended prose parables narrated in a speaking voice against a musical background.

The Yoruba Popular Travelling Theatre is impressive for the sheer scale of its textual creativity. Its origins lay in 1940s Lagos, though it drew on earlier antecedent performance styles that had been pioneered in the late nineteenth and early twentieth centuries by the Lagos elites and also by the more populist breakaway Independent churches. A crucial figure in this theater's development was Hubert Ògúndé, a policeman and primary-school teacher who in 1944 convened a group of amateur performers to stage "Native Air operas," a theatrical form that had been in existence for some time and involved the enactment of Bible stories through an entirely sung text – largely choral – accompanied by stylized gestures. Ogunde, however, revolutionized this form, enlivening it with styles of music that owed as much to highlife as to hymn tunes, and within two years of his first Native Air opera he was recruiting a professional paid cast to stage topical, folkloric, and satirical dramas. Other groups later took the same path of development: the theaters of Oyin Adejọbi, Kọ́lá Ògúnmọ́lá, and Dúró Ládiípọ all at first performed for the church and then gradually secularized, commercialized, and professionalized. As they did this they also developed styles of their own. Duro Ladiipọ, for example, became famous for his mythological plays that harnessed the talents of traditional oral performers of praise poetry and incantations. The most famous of these, *Ọba Kò So* (The King Did Not Hang), dealt with the apotheosis of the legendary Ọyọ king Ṣango. Kọla Ogunmọla specialized in social and moral satire, one of his most popular plays being *Ifẹ́ Owó* (Love of Money). At the same time most theater companies diversified, so that a single company could easily have within its repertoire a mythological play, a modern satire on sexual *mores* or corruption, a thriller set in the criminal underworld, a tale of occult practices revolving around money magic and human sacrifice, a folkloric play, and a play based on a written novel or drama – and they were likely also to explore other media such as television, print, the photoplay magazine *Atọ́ka*, records, and cassettes.

The popular theater found a vast audience, and expanded greatly during the oil-boom years. Whereas in the 1960s there had been not more than a dozen fully professional and commercial theater companies, by 1980 more than a hundred were in existence (see Jeyifo 1984). These theaters traveled the length and breadth of Yorubaland and into the north to play to Yoruba enclaves there. Each had a membership of fifteen or more permanent paid actors and actresses and its own exclusive repertoire of plays, which was continually adapted and expanded. Their plays were unscripted and improvised by the actors, under the guidance of the company's boss or manager. They varied greatly in style, but they almost all shared the following features. First, they represented an extended, worked-out narrative entirely through the actions of free-standing dramatic characters, without the intervention of a storyteller. This was a form unknown in Yoruba culture before the missionary and colonial interventions of the nineteenth century. Second, they shared an esthetic of intense impact, achieved by incorporating and juxtaposing dense, concentrated chunks or sequences of dramatic action and display. Third, they shared a love affair with the Yoruba language – its idioms, archaisms, innovations, slang, dialectal peculiarities, and its sacred and secret registers. Many plays boasted extensive and complex verbal texts which drew in a lifelike manner on the idioms of everyday life – but also condensed and heightened these verbal resources to generate memorable, sometimes polished, dialogue. And finally, they were all dedicated to the demonstration of a moral – and were met halfway by popular audiences who took upon themselves the task of self-edification by actively seeking out a moral lesson they could apply to their own lives. Most popular theater groups have steered clear of overt political commentary, though the theater's "founding father," Ogunde, was exceptional in giving voice to anti-colonial feeling (in *Worse Than Crime*, 1945; *Strike and Hunger* 1945; and *Bread and Bullet*, 1950) and the controversies of party politics in the period immediately after independence (in *Yorùbá Ronú*, 1964). Other theaters, though less explicit, nonetheless did articulate popular responses to the economic, political, and social situation of ordinary people, and were often sharply satirical of overbearing authority figures and social pretension.

Since the late 1980s the popular theater has been in decline. The actors have migrated into film and video production, where they mingle with another category of performer, the slightly higher-status English-language television-trained actor. Film is the most prestigious dramatic form at present; its production usually involves the creaming off of stars from a number of the old live theater companies to produce a composite super-company convened only for the duration of the shoot. Hubert Ogunde was again the key figure in the efflorescence of Yoruba-language film-making, which gathered momentum following the success of his *Aiyé* (1979) and *Jáiyésinmi* (1981), both of which used the technical possibilities of film to mount vivid and blood-curdling representations of witchcraft. Another notable popular star who became a film tycoon was "Bàbá Sàlá," the nickname of Moses Ọláìyá, a television and stage comedian very popular with audiences for his subversive and ambiguous lampoons of authority and respectability. Video dramas tend to be made as a substitute when funds cannot be raised to make a film. Video drama is now a booming concern, with more than twenty video-production houses in Lagos alone and more than 2,000 actors making a living from it. The plays deal very much with witchcraft, the occult, and extraordinary family coincidences. They are often of poor technical and artistic quality. Nonetheless the sheer profusion and variety means that a new arena for experimentation has been opened up, and some video dramas have been interesting and well put together – among them Tunde Kelani's *Ti Olúwa nilẹ̀* (The Land is God's).

The electronic media have played a significant role in the constitution and dissemination of new cultural forms in Yorubaland since their inception, and in the creation of a pan-Yoruba public arena. The Western State Television Service was inaugurated in Ibadan in 1959 – the first in sub-Saharan Africa – and from its inception the station sought out performance arts of all kinds for inclusion in its programming. It was partly through the influence of television that the popular theaters developed a naturalistic, speech-based drama out of the earlier choral style of the Biblical "native air opera." Weekly TV comedy serials by popular theater groups were among the favorite programs, and in turn stimulated increased public interest in these groups' live performances. TV fostered the rise of new genres such as neotraditional poetry (see above), and by screening documentary footage of "cultural events" such as traditional festivals, television also encouraged the process, which had already begun through the medium of print, of converting localized religious activities into "traditional heritage," part of "Yoruba culture" conceived as a generalized, diverse but ultimately unified field.

The Yoruba public that took shape in the colonial and postcolonial periods has been a key factor in the vitality of traditional genres and the efflorescence of new popular forms. Since the huge expansion of access to primary education in the late 1950s and 60s, a large potential readership has come into being, able to enjoy Yoruba-language texts, though not necessarily English-language ones, and with simultaneous access to radio, television, and live performance. The interaction among these different channels – whereby oral poetry is collected in booklets, neotraditional poets perform on television, radio, and records, but simultaneously publish their texts in books and magazines, *Atọka* publishes renditions of live improvised drama, popular theater companies dramatize novels and adapt published literary dramas – means that within the sphere of Yoruba-language creativity, the audience is being continually replenished and its cultural competence reinforced. This seamless interaction between oral performance and the prestigious world of print was one of the factors that helped to foster the great vitality and confidence of Yoruba verbal culture throughout the twentieth century. Unlike in many African contexts, there was no sharp divide between a domain of orality, indigenous language and the traditional past on the one hand, and literacy, English, and modernity on the other. Rather, there was a continuous circulation and appropriation of materials and modes of transmission, fostering an extraordinarily innovative, diverse, and satisfying verbal culture.

Both oral and written Yoruba literature form the subject matter of an extensive and thriving literary scholarship. Several degree programs in Yoruba language, literature, and culture are offered in the universities of western Nigeria, and numerous dissertations, including PhDs, have been written in Yoruba about oral and written Yoruba literature. A metalanguage suitable for critical discussion has been established. Yoruba scholarship is now at least four generations old, and boasts many luminaries. Among the university-based "founding fathers" are Adeboye Babalọla, whose work on oral praise poetry has set standards of scrupulous investigation yet to be surpassed; 'Wande Abimbọla, doyen of Ifa scholarship; Afọlabi Ọlabimtan, who combines critical scholarship with creative writing, and who has done much to establish a vocabulary for future literary scholars; Ọlabiyii Babalọla Yai, whose work on oral genres has provoked radical reconceptualization of the notion of "orality"; Akinwumi Iṣọla, who has brought not only a creative writer's experience, but also that of a practical producer of highly successful live and video drama, to his interpretation of Yoruba literary texts; and Ọlatunde Ọlatunji, a pioneer in the attempt to grasp and conceptualize the field of Yoruba oral literature as a whole, who has also contributed to the study of written poetry and other genres. Their work has been supported by steady advances in the field of Yoruba linguistics, by such scholars as Ayọ Bamgboṣe, O. Awobuluyi, and Ọlasope Oyelaran. The solid foundations laid down by these scholars, and the general levels of Yoruba literacy among the younger generation, suggest that the move towards Yoruba-language scholarship will not easily be reversed.

The formal scholarly literature coming from the universities is underpinned by a more widely diffused, local, and "unofficial" scholarship taking the form of booklets explaining the meaning of proverbs, collections of *oriki*, pamphlets on the interpretation of dreams and on herbal medicines and spells, local town histories, and religious tracts and handbooks of both Islamic and Christian orientation, as well as more substantial works on "Yoruba customs and traditions." The fact that there are a number of small printing presses specializing in the publication of Yoruba texts means that the unofficial sphere of Yoruba-language writing has the means to flourish without the intervention of official cultural or educational institutions. Activity in the sphere of Yoruba writing is also stimulated by the lively and flourishing Yoruba-language press; several newspapers regularly include features on Yoruba oral and written literature.

Aláròyé, for example, has a column dedicated to expounding proverbs and another on popular actors, singers, and media poets.

Although the Yoruba-language sphere of cultural production has by and large existed in parallel to English-language literature, there has also been some activity across the borders. Popular Yoruba genres such as the traveling theater show themselves to be highly conscious of the infiltration of the English language into local life, and they use it strategically for satirical and moral effect. Many Yoruba novelists drew ideas from English-language writers ranging from James Hadley Chase to Conan Doyle. In the sphere of literary drama, some writers have used both languages: notably Wálé Ògúnyẹmí, whose English-language and Yoruba-language plays have enjoyed equal success with university audiences. Yorubas writing in English draw much of their linguistic richness from a substratum of Yoruba. Actual translation, in both directions, has also been important. Ọlánipẹ̀kun Ẹ̀san, a classical scholar, translated into Yoruba, and substantially recast, a number of Latin and Greek works including Sophocles' *Oedipus Rex*, transformed into *Tẹlẹ́dalàṣẹ* (1965) (The Creator's Will must Prevail). More recently, Bọ̀dé Ṣówándé has published an adaptation of Molière's *L'avare*, under the title *Arédè Owó* (1990). Wọlé Ṣóyínká translated Fagunwa's *Ogboju Ọdẹ Ninu Igbo Irunmalẹ* into English, under the title *The Forest of a Thousand Daemons*; Akinwumi Iṣọla in turn has translated one of Ṣoyinka's greatest plays, *Death and the King's Horseman*, into Yoruba. Two years after the publication of his play *Aajo Aje*, Ọladejọ Okediji published his own English translation, *Running After Riches* (1999); and Wálé Ògúnyẹmí has translated Chinua Achebe's classic novel *Things Fall Apart* into Yoruba. Thus, though an intense enjoyment of the Yoruba language is what has sustained all aspects of Yoruba textual production for the last 150 years at least, Yoruba textuality is not a closed domain cut off from other cultural traditions, but an open field that continually grows and diversifies by interacting with others (see Irele 1981, especially "Tradition and the Yoruba Writer").

Present dire economic circumstances are inevitably affecting the output of all branches of Yoruba literary production. However, the signs are that the huge capacity of this culture for creative innovation is surviving and that new works are still being produced.

Note

1. However, this work was preceded at least thirty years earlier by an "obscene romantic fiction" published anonymously under the title *Dolápọ̀ Aṣẹ́wó Ọmọ Aṣẹ́wó* (Dolápọ̀ the Prostitute, Child of a Prostitute): see Fálọlá 1988: 26.

Bibliography

Abimbola, 'Wande. 1977. *Ifa Divination Poetry*. New York: NOK.

Adepoju, Olanrewaju. 1972. *Ironu Akewi*. Ibadan: Onibonoje.

Ajisafe, A. K. 1921a. *Aiye Akamara*. Lagos, Nigeria: Ife-Olu Printing Works.

1921b. *Enia soro*. Bungay, Suffolk: Richard Clay.

1921c. *Tan' t'Olorun?* Bungay, Suffolk: Richard Clay.

Akinlade, Kola. 1971. *Ta Lo Pa Omo oba?* Lagos: Macmillan Nigeria.

Akinsowon, A. 1914. *Iwe Itan Ajase ati oniruru asoro on ila aro*. Lagos: Tika Tore.

Akinyele, I. B. 1911. *Iwe Itan Ibadan ati die ninu awon ilu agbegbe re bi Iwo, Osogbo ati Ikirun*. Ibadan: Egbe Agba-O-Tan.

Atari Ajanaku [P. Adedotun Ogundeji]. 1998. *Orin Ewuro*. Ibadan: Sam Bookman.

Babalola, S. A. 1966. *The Content and Form of Yoruba Ijala*. Oxford: Oxford University Press.

Bada, S. O. 1979. *Owe Yoruba ati isedale won*. Ibadan: University Press.

Bunyan, John. 1911. *Ilosiwaju ero mimo lati aiye yi si eyi ti mbo*. Exeter: James Townsend for the Church Missionary Society.

Daramola, Olu. 1970. *Ile ti a fi ito mo*. Ibadan: University Press.

Delano, Isaac. 1955. *Aiye d'Aiye Oyinbo*. Lagos: Thomas Nelson.

1963. *L'ojo Ojo Un*. London: Thomas Nelson.

Esan, Olanipekun. [1965] 1981. *Teledalase*. Ibadan: University Press.

Fagunwa, D. O. [1938] 1950. *Ogboju Ode Ninu Igbo Irunmale*. London: Thomas Nelson.

1949a. *Igbo Olodumare*. Lagos: Thomas Nelson.

1949b. *Ireke Onibudo*. Lagos: Thomas Nelson.

1954. *Irinkerindo Ninu Igbo Elegbeje*. Lagos: Thomas Nelson.

1961. *Adiitu Olodumare*. Lagos: Thomas Nelson.

1968. *The Forest of a Thousand Daemons*. Trans. of *Ogboju Ode Ninu Igbo Irunmale* by Wole Soyinka. London: Thomas Nelson.

Faleti, Adebayo. 1965. *Nwon ro pe were ni*. Ibadan: Oxford University Press.

1969. *Omo Olokun Esin*. London: University of London Press.

1972. *Basorun Gaa*. Ibadan: Onibonoje.

1974. *Idaamu Paadi Minkailu*. Ibadan: Onibonoje.

Falola, Toyin. 1988. "Earliest Yoruba Writers." In *Perspectives on Nigerian Literature 1700 to the Present*. Ed. Yemi Ogunbiyi. Lagos: Guardian Books (Nigeria): vol. 1.

Fawale, Jolaade. 1982. *Teni n'teni*. Ibadan: Omoleye.

Irele, Abiola. [1981] 1990. *The African Experience in Literature and Ideology*. Bloomington: Indiana University Press.

Isola, Akinwumi. 1970. *Efunsetan Aniwura*. Ibadan: University Press.

1974. *O le ku*. Ibadan: Oxford University Press.

1994. *Iku Olokun-Esin*. Ibadan: Fountain.

Jeboda, Femi. 1964. *Olowolaiyemo*. Ibadan: Longman Nigeria.

Jeyifo, Biodun. 1984. *The Yoruba Popular Travelling Theatre of Nigeria*. Lagos: Nigeria Magazine Publications.

Johnson. Samuel. 1921. *The History of the Yorubas*. Lagos: Church Missionary Society.

Ladele, T. A. A. 1978. *Igbi Aye Nyi*. Ibadan: Longman Nigeria.

LaPin, Deirdre. 1977. "Story, Medium and Masque: The Idea and Art of Yoruba Story-Telling." Diss. University of Wisconsin, Madison.

Lijadu, E. M. 1886 [1910]. *Kekere Iwe Orin Aribilosoo*. Exeter: James Townsend.
1898. *Ifa*. Ado-Ekiti: Omolayo Standard Press.
1908. *Orunmila*. Ado-Ekiti: Omolayo Standard Press.
ed. 1904. *Iwe Kini ti Sobo Aro-bi-odu*. Lagos: n.p.
Losi, J. B. O. 1913. *Iwe Itan Eko*. Lagos: Tika Tore.
Morgan, Kemi. n.d. *Akinyele's Outline History of Ibadan*, vols. I, II, III. Ibadan: Caxton.
Obasa, D. A. 1927. *Iwe Kinni ti Awon Akewi*. Ibadan: Ilare Press for the Egbe Agba-O-Tan.
1934. *Iwe Keji ti Awon Akewi*. Ibadan: Ilare Press for the Egbe Agba-O-Tan.
1945. *Iwe Keta ti Awon Akewi*. Ibadan: Ilare Press for the Egbe Agba-O-Tan.
Odunjo, J. F. 1964. *Kuye*. Ibadan: African Universities Press.
Odunjo, J. J., and A. B. Oladipupo. 1967. *Kadara ati Egbon re*. Ibadan: Onibonoje.
Ogundele, J. O. 1956a. *Ejigbede lona Isalu Orun*. London: Longmans, Green.
1956b. *Ibu Olokun*. London: Hodder and Stoughton.
Ogunniran, Lawuyi. 1972. *Eegun Alare*. Lagos: Macmillan Nigeria.
Ogunsina, Bisi. 1992. *The Development of the Yoruba Novel 1930–1975*. Ibadan: Gospel Faith Mission Press.
Ojo, Gabriel Ibitoye. 1952. *Olorun Esan*. Ibadan: Ministry of Education (General Publications Section).
Okediji, Oladejo. 1969. *Aja lo leru*. Ibadan: Longman Nigeria.
1971. *Agbalagba Akan*. Ibadan: Longman Nigeria.
1973. *Rere Run*. Ibadan: Onibonoje.
1981. *Atoto Arere*. Ibadan: University Press.
n.d. *Aajo Aje*. Ife: Agbemem Nigeria.
1999. *Running after Riches* (trans. of *Aajo Aje*). Ibadan: Spectrum.
Olabimtan, Afolabi. 1967. *Kekere Ekun*. Ibadan: Macmillan Nigeria.
1977. *Baba Rere!* Ibadan: Macmillan Nigeria.
Oladapo, Tunbosun. 1973. *Aroye Akewi*, vol I. Ibadan: Onibonoje.
1975. *Aroye Akewi*, vol. II. Ibadan: Onibonoje.
Olatunji, Olatunde. 1984. *Features of Yoruba Oral Poetry*. Ibadan: University Press.
Olukoji, Ebenezer O. 1978. "The Place of Chants in Yoruba Traditional Oral Literature." PhD thesis, Ibadan University.
Olurankinse, Olanipekun. 1987. *Iji Aye*. Ibadan: Onibonoje.
Owolabi, Olu. 1980. *Eni Olorun o pa*. Ibadan: Evans Brothers Nigeria.
1983. *Ija Ore*. Ibadan: Evans Brothers Nigeria.
[1983] 1988. *Isuju Osanyin*. Ibadan: Vantage.
Oyedele, A. 1947. *Aiye Ree*. Ibadan: Ministry of Education (General Publications Section).
1970. *Iwo ni*. Lagos: Macmillan Nigeria.
Sowande, Bode. 1990. *Arede Owo*. Lagos: Kraft.
Thomas, I. B. 1930. *Itan Igbesi Aiye Emi Segilola*. Lagos: Church Missionary Society (Nigeria) Bookshops.
Thompson, Adebisi. 1987. *Bosun omo Odofin*. Ibadan: Paperback Publishers.

20

African literature and the colonial factor

SIMON GIKANDI

Modern African literature was produced in the crucible of colonialism. What this means, among other things, is that the men and women who founded the tradition of what we now call modern African writing, both in European and indigenous languages, were, without exception, products of the institutions that colonialism had introduced and developed in the continent, especially in the period beginning with the Berlin Conference of 1884–85 and decolonization in the late 1950s and early 1960s. African literature had, of course, been produced outside the institutions of colonialism: the existence of oral literature in all African languages and precolonial writing in Arabic, Amharic, Swahili, and other African languages is ample evidence of a thriving literary tradition in precolonial Africa. But what is now considered to be the heart of literary scholarship on the continent could not have acquired its current identity or function if the traumatic encounter between Africa and Europe had not taken place. Not only were the founders of modern African literature colonial subjects, but colonialism was also to be the most important and enduring theme in their works. From the eighteenth century onwards, the colonial situation shaped what it meant to be an African writer, shaped the language of African writing, and overdetermined the culture of letters in Africa.

In 1955, Georges Balandier began his influential theoretical study of the colonial situation by observing that despite the changes that had occurred in the era of decolonization, "the colonial problem remains one of the main issues with which specialists in the social sciences have to deal. Indeed, the pressures of a new nationalism and the reactions resulting from decolonization give this problem an immediacy and a topicality that cannot be treated with indifference" (1970: 21). The point Balandier made about the relationship between colonialism and the social sciences can be said about the conjunction between African literature and the colonial situation. Colonialism, especially in its radical transformation of African societies, remains one of the central problems with which writers and intellectuals in Africa have to deal; the tradition of African writing that has produced Nobel Prize laureates was built and consolidated when African writers began to take stock of the colonial situation and its impact on the African psyche. Even the African writing that emerged in the postcolonial era, a literature shaped by the pressures of "arrested decolonization" and the "pitfalls of national consciousness," can be said to have been driven by the same imperative as writing under colonialism – the desire to understand the consequences of the colonial moment (see Jeyifo 1990: 33–46; and Fanon 1968: 148–205). The purpose of this chapter, then, is to explore the paradigmatic and practical value of the colonial moment in the history of African literature. Our starting point is that the key to the development of modern African literature can be found in a number of institutions – the Christian mission, the colonial school, and the university – that were crucial to the emergence, nature, and function of African literature.

Colonial culture and African literature: an overview

A discussion of the relationship between colonialism and African literature should perhaps begin with a simple question: why has colonialism been the main subject of African literature and why do colonial institutions seem to be such a central component of a literature which was expressively produced as a critique of European domination? The most obvious answer, as we shall see in our discussion of several colonial institutions, is that the political and cultural force of colonialism in Africa was so enduring that writers concerned with the nature of African society could not avoid the trauma and drama that accompanied the imposition of European rule on the continent. As early as the end of the eighteenth century, Africans writing in European languages, most notably Olaudah Equiano, had appropriated dominant literary conventions to oppose slavery and to validate an African identity; but others, such as Johannes Capitein, had produced treatises arguing that slavery was not necessarily an affront to morality and Christianity. While the political interests of these early writers might now appear radically divergent, it is important to keep in mind that their writing was generated by a common desire to deploy writing both as the mark of the African's humanity and as a point of entry into the culture of modernity (see Gates 1985: 9–10).

If the late colonial period (1880–1935) seems to preoccupy the imagination even of writers who were born in the age of decolonization and after, it is because it is considered to be a period unlike any other in African history. Adu Boahen has remarked: "Never in the history of Africa did so many changes occur and with such speed as they did between 1880 and 1935 . . . The pace of this drama was truly astonishing, for as late as 1880 only very limited areas of Africa had come under the direct rule of Europeans" (1985a: 1). For almost four centuries Africans had endured traumas induced by the foreign encounter, most notably the transatlantic slave trade, but the European element had remained localized at the coast and no significant political entities had lost their sovereignty until the late colonial period. After the Conference of Berlin, however, the whole continent was divided among the major European powers and the nature of African society was rapidly transformed under the tutelage of foreign powers. And while the process of colonial rule might have appeared to the European powers to be a matter of military strategy and commercial interests, for many African societies it was tantamount to what F. Abbas has called "a veritable revolution, overthrowing a whole ancient world of beliefs and ideas and an immemorial way of life"; European conquest confronted local societies with the difficult choice "to adapt or perish" (quoted in Boahen 1985a: 3). Either way, what was at issue in the colonial encounter was the question of African autonomy, a major subject in early writing from the continent.

It is easy to underestimate the centrality of the ideology of sovereignty and the idea of autonomy to African debates on colonialism and decolonization and the literary texts they inspired. And yet, as Chinua Achebe was to note in an influential essay published in the early 1960s, one of the key motivations for producing an African literature was to restore the moral integrity and cultural autonomy of the African in the age of decolonization. The fundamental theme of African writing, noted Achebe, was that "African people did not hear of culture for the first time from Europeans; that their societies were not mindless but frequently had a philosophy of great depth and value and beauty, that they had poetry and, above all, they had dignity. It is this dignity that many African people all but lost during the colonial period and it is this they must regain now" (1973: 8). For many African writers in the age of decolonization, then, the loss of sovereignty was not simply the process by which older cultures and institutions were deprived of their authority under colonialism; it was also conceived, especially by members of the African elite, as the ultimate loss of agency and free will. Thus the narrative of colonialism came to be conceived as the unwilled evacuation of African subjects from the movement of time; for many African intellectuals in the nineteenth century and early twentieth century, to be colonized, as Walter Rodney noted aptly, was "to be removed from history" (1972: 245–56).

But the process of colonial rule was to appeal to African writers for something more than its drama and impact: for writers born between the cusp of European rule and decolonization, especially in the period between 1900 and

1945, colonialism was more than a period of loss and temporal dislocation; it also represented the challenges and opportunities of modernity. It is these opportunities that the authors of the Pan-African Conference held in London in 1900 had in mind when they reminded "the modern world" that colonized people, "by reason of sheer numbers and physical contact," were bound to have an immense effect upon the world: "If now the world of culture bends itself towards giving Negroes and other dark men the largest and broadest opportunity for education and self-development, then this contact and influence is bound to have a beneficial effect upon the world and hasten human progress" (see Langley 1979: 738). For the colonized African elite, colonialism was a challenge because its impact was evident throughout Africa and it had bound the destiny of the continent with other worlds.

At the same time, however, the colonial process presented an interpretative enigma: colonial culture had transformed many African societies through voluntary and enforced modernization, but as many observers of the African scene were quick to note, this process did not seem to penetrate too deeply into the fabric of local communities. Ostensibly, colonialism touched every aspect of social and political life on the continent, but its impact also seemed to be superficial because, in spite of the predominance and preponderance of colonial modernity, so-called traditional society seemed to function as if the colonial event was a mere interruption in the *longue durée* of African history. For the men and women who came to produce modern African literature, the subjects who were most affected by the colonial process, the simultaneous existence of a modern and traditional world could only be negotiated through works of the imagination. It is not accidental that the foundational texts of modern African literature in the European languages were concerned with the dialectic of modernity and tradition as it was played out on the continent under colonialism.

Nevertheless, this turn to writing as a way of accounting for the existence of the modern within what appeared to be traditional societies was the source of an important paradox: in order to oppose colonialism, and thus to assert indigenous interests and rights, African leaders and intellectuals had to turn to a recently discovered European language of tradition, nation, and race. This new language, which sought a synthesis between modernization and African autonomy, is evident in declarations by leaders such as Makombe Hanga, chief of the Barue, as he confronted the Portuguese in Central Mozambique in 1895: "I see how you white men advance more and more in Africa . . . My country will also have to take up these reforms and I am quite prepared to open it up . . . I should also like to have good roads and railways . . . But I will remain the Makombe my fathers have been" (quoted in Ranger 1985: 49). In his confrontation with the Germans in Namibia, the great Nama leader Hendrik Wittboi easily resorted to the language of the *Volksgeist* popularized by his European adversaries: "The Lord has established various kingdoms in the world. Therefore I know and believe that it is no sin or crime that I should wish to remain the independent chief of my land and people" (quoted in Ranger 1985: 49).

The emergence of African literatures in European language needs to be located within the crucial claim that colonized subjects had set out to use the instruments and grammar given to them by the colonizer to oppose foreign domination and assert their sovereignty. It should not hence come as a surprise that the pioneers of African literature and African cultural nationalism, writers like Sol Plaatje in South Africa or Caseley Hayford in West Africa, identified very closely with colonial culture and its institutions, even as they opposed the destructive practices of imperial rule and fought for African political rights. Indeed, a key axiom of African literary history is that the founders of African literature were the most Europeanized. What this meant was that African literature was not initially intended to provide a radical critique of European rule; rather, it was a discursive mode through which Africans could try to represent and mediate their location both inside and outside colonial culture.

But why did literature become one of the most important weapons of cultural resistance against European intervention in Africa in the late nineteenth century? Literature came to occupy a central place in colonial culture for three closely related reasons. First, one of the most attractive aspects of colonial culture, from the perspective of the colonized, was what came to be universally conceived as the gift of literacy. Even though many African subjects may have been ambivalent about many aspects of colonial modernity, they seemed unanimous about the power and enchantment of literacy and the culture of print that enabled it: "Literacy was for many African peoples a new magic, and was sought after as such and at all costs since it appeared to open the treasure house of the modern world. To know the amount of power, authority and influence which the first generation of African clerks, interpreters and teachers exercised is to have some idea of the spell which literacy cast over many African peoples" (Afigbo 1985: 496).

The literary history of Africa has often been written from the perspective of university-educated writers and intellectuals (see Wauthier 1979 and July 1968), but we need to foreground the significance of the first generation of literate Africans, many of them clerks, interpreters, and teachers with only a few years of education, in the establishment of an African tradition of letters.

Out of this class came not only the writers who produced the earlier works in European languages (Plaatje and Tutuola, for example), but even more influential writers working in African languages, including Thomas Mofolo (Sotho), H. I. E. Dlomo (Zulu), D. O. Fagunwa (Yoruba), and Shabaan Robert (Swahili). These writers were the great mediators between colonial culture and the newly literate African masses. Indeed, the subject, language, and form used in the most influential works of these writers was intended to simultaneously represent the bourgeois public sphere that colonialism had instituted and satisfy the reading desires of the newly literate African.

But there was a second reason why literature came to occupy such an important role in the mediation of the colonial relationship: in both the popular imagination and the annals of Africanism or Orientalism (see Miller 1985 and Said 1979), the process of colonization existed as both an unprecedented historical episode and a monumental literary event. While it is true that colonial conquest and rule were effected through violent military methods, aggressive diplomacy, and blatant economic exploitation, these processes ultimately came to acquire their authority and totality when they were represented in powerful narratives of conquest. Napoleon's invasion of Egypt (1789), to cite one of the most prominent examples, came to have a presence, a voice, and rationale when it was represented in *Description de l'Egypte*, the massive twenty-four volume account of the expedition. In this account, as Edward Said has noted, a diachronic and contested event was transformed into a synchronic narrative of European conquest and rule; Orientalism acquired its intellectual power through textualization, which brought together "a family of ideas and a unifying set of values proven in various ways to be effective" (1979: 41–42). Nevertheless, against the texts of European power produced during the process of conquest, there emerged powerful African texts produced in response; works written as a counterpoint to the Napoleonic narrative (the most famous example is 'Abd al-Rahman al-Jabarti's *'Ajaib al-Athar*) contested the terrain of culture as vigorously as the literature of conquest. Indeed, most of the African writing produced in the nineteenth century by writers as diverse as al-Jarbati and Edward Blyden simultaneously sought to take stock of the colonial situation and to challenge its philosophical and cultural assumptions on the nature of the colonized, their culture, and community.

The third reason why colonialism and literary culture came to be so closely associated in the history of African literature is one that has become central in postcolonial studies: this is the recognition that the idea of culture itself lay at the heart of the colonial project of conquest and rule. Colonial writers understood not only the obvious fact that culture and knowledge were used as instruments of control, but that the process of colonization produced new cultural formations and configurations, what Nicholas Dirks has described as "the allied network of processes" that spawned new subjects and nations (1992: 3). As Dirks has noted, the idea of culture, as an object and mode of knowledge, was formed out of colonial histories and spawned specific cultural forms; these cultural forms, he concludes, "became fundamental to the development of resistance against colonialism, most notably in the nationalist movements that used Western notions of national integrity and self-determination to justify claims for independence" (1992: 4). It was at this point – the point where western notions about nation, culture, and self were turned against the project of colonialism – that the largest body of work by African writers was produced.

African literature and the institutions of colonial modernity

The history of African literature has been so closely associated with the defense of an African tradition that it is not unusual for students and scholars of this literature to negate the colonial institutions that enabled this literature. These institutions – the Christian missions, the colonial school, and the university – were the places in which Africans were transformed into modern subjects and this process of transformation was in turn to become the condition of possibility of African writing itself. But before we examine the character of these institutions and the means by which they enabled African literature, we need to call attention to another factor that disappears only too easily in African literary history – the central role accorded literary texts in the project of colonial modernity by both the colonizer and the colonized. Let us remember, for a start, that colonialism was consolidated in Africa at a time when literature in Europe, especially in Britain, had acquired unprecedented cultural capital, both because of its association with the idea of the nation and because of the perceived opposition to the materialism generated by industrialization. The setting up of colonial missions and schools in Africa was concurrent with the expansion of public education in the major European countries, and with it the spread of literary culture.

The liberal ideas that had led to the expansion and reform of education in Britain thus found their way to Africa fairly quickly. Headmasters of colonial schools often fashioned themselves after Thomas Arnold of Rugby; many of their ideas about culture were influenced by his son Matthew Arnold, the chief inspector of schools in mid-Victorian England. One of the central ideas in the new thinking about education, which these men brought from the universities of Oxford and Cambridge and the newly founded one at London, was the centrality of culture – especially literary culture – in the work of civilization. Their philosophies were often echoes of Matthew Arnold's famous claim that culture, conceived as the corrective to materialism, represented a "spiritual standard of perfection" for modern culture ("Sweetness and Light," found in Buckler 1958: 464). Material progress and civilization were certainly central to the colonial mission, but to the men and women who ran the colonial schools, these were inconsequential in the absence of the higher spiritual standard promised by the mastery of culture. This position was to be eloquently expressed by E. Carey Francis, headmaster of Alliance High School in Kenya:

> The school is run on the lines of a grammar school in this country [i.e., England] but with everything simpler, no matrons and no frills. The boys wash their own clothes and keep the place clean. We engage in much the same activities: games, dramatics (we have produced a full Shakespeare play each year for the last three years), singing, Scouting and innumerable societies. Boys have a background poor in the things of European civilization: they know nothing of wireless and motor bicycles and little of money, and few of them come from homes where there is intelligent conversation or where books or even newspapers are regularly read. Yet they are essentially the same as English boys. They would bear comparison with those of the European schools in Kenya, or with a good school in this country, in intelligence, in athletic prowess, in industry, courtesy, courage and trustworthiness, and as gentlemen. (quoted in Sicherman 1990: 392)[1]

The invocation of Shakespeare in Francis's address was not incidental: increasingly, in the late colonial period, literature was seen as the depository of the values that defined civilization. Indeed, the canonical figure of Shakespeare was to have a lasting influence in anglophone African literary and political circles (see Johnson 1997) in the same way as Victor Hugo and the Cartesian system came to influence francophone literary culture and philosophy.

What is crucial to remember is that this influence was most marked in the work of writers with impeccable anticolonial credentials. By the 1930s, for example, Sol Plaatje had emerged as the voice of black nationalism in South Africa, but one of his most important cultural projects during this period was the translation of Shakespeare's *Comedy of Errors* into Tswana. The translation, aptly titled *Diphosho-phosho* (Mistake After Mistake), was welcomed by Tswana intellectuals, such as David Ramoshoana, as evidence that contrary to colonial beliefs, Shakespeare's "language and ideals" were not "an impenetrable mystery" to the African mind (see Willan 1984: 331). In his autobiography, the great Nigerian nationalist Chief Obafemi Awolowo had no doubt who his favorite author was – "Shakespeare is my favorite. Some of the mighty lines of Shakespeare must have influenced my outlook on life" (quoted in Mazrui 1993: 559). When Shakespeare's *Macbeth* was first performed at Makerere University College in 1949, the lead role was played by none other than A. Milton Obote, the future prime minister of Uganda. And as is well known, Julius Nyerere, one of Africa's leading and most respected nationalists, began his literary career translating Shakespeare into Swahili.

Why Shakespeare? Why literature? As we have already seen, Shakespeare was considered important in anglophone Africa because, like Hugo in the French colonies, he was associated with the language and ideals of the civilization the colonizers were trying to promote on the continent. In this case, the language of the colonizer had become the stand-in for more than a culture of letters; it was a code word for the modern life and moral consciousness that colonialism presented as a mark of its modernity. In the colonies, perhaps even more than the metropolitan centers, literary culture was privileged as the insignia of Englishness or Frenchness. And to the extent that African nationalism justified its political claims through the invocation of the essential humanity of the colonized, the production of a literary culture was conceived as an important step in sanctioning the case for African rights and freedom. Surprisingly though, while literary culture seemed to be valued by authors such as Matthew Arnold because of its ability to proffer a spiritual standard outside the tutelage of religion, in the colonial situation, education and culture were bound up with Christianity: "More than anything else," noted Carey Francis in regard to his African students at Alliance, "we long for them to get a genuine Christian faith" (quoted in Sicherman 1990: 392).

In retrospect, it should not surprise us that religion was one of the most important themes in African literature in the colonial period. There are several reasons for the close connection between Christianity, colonial culture, and literary production: the most obvious one is that the establishment of Christian missions was so closely associated with colonial conquest and rule that it was often difficult to differentiate the two processes. Quite often, especially in Central and Eastern Africa, Christian missions acted as a vanguard for colonial expansion; missions provided imperial powers with the alibi and justification for the imposition of colonial control; or, as happened in Buganda in the 1880s, religious conflicts functioned as effective masks for imperial rivalries. In addition, the journeys undertaken by missionaries into the heart of Africa in the mid-nineteenth century were often represented in the British press as the heroic adventures of heroic figures willing to give their lives for the cause of empire. There was thus tremendous pressure on European governments to sanction and protect the works of the missions.

Thus, the romantic myth surrounding David Livingstone's death in Central Africa in 1873 was enough to move British public opinion toward a more aggressive imperial policy: "The work of England for Africa," noted an 1873 *Daily Telegraph* editorial, "must henceforth begin in earnest where Livingstone left it off" (quoted in Oliver 1952: 35). Missionaries were frequently the first to designate certain areas as specific zones of influence for their respective European powers. This designation of regions and countries as belonging to certain imperial powers was important because missionaries had a moral force and authority that could never be matched by colonial administrators. They were, in the words of John and Jean Comaroff, both the most active ideological agents of empire, the conscience of colonialism, and "its moral commentator" (1992: 186). It was in their role as the ideological agents of empire, note the Comaroffs, that missionaries rehearsed "all the arguments of images and ideology, of dreams and schemes, voiced among the colonizers as they debated the manner in which natives should be ruled, their works reconstructed" (1992: 184).

In December 1857, Livingstone gave an impassioned appeal for greater commitment for evangelization to a gathering at Cambridge University. The immediate response to the appeal was the formation of the Foundation of English High Churchmen of the Universities Mission to Central Africa by evangelical and Christian groups; the committee's mission, it was stated, was to establish "centres of Christianity and civilisation for the promotion of true religion, agriculture and lawful commerce" (quoted in Oliver 1952: 13). Christianity went hand in hand with civilization, agriculture, and commerce, and wherever one went in colonial Africa the most successful missions were the ones that were able to function – and present themselves – as outposts of modernity.

But if European powers valued the Christian missions for their capacity to mark out territorial zones of influence, Africans increasingly came to see their association with missionaries as their conduit into the new global economy engendered by colonialism. The transformative moment in Chinua Achebe's *Things Fall Apart* (1958), one of the classic novels of colonialism in Africa, is when many men and women in Umuofia begin to rethink their attitude toward "the new dispensation": "The white man had indeed brought a lunatic religion, but he had also built a trading store and for the first time palm-oil and kernel became things of great price, and much money flowed in Umuofia"

(1958: 126). In *Une vie de boy* (*Boy!*), Ferdinand Oyono's novel of colonial brutality, Young Toundi abandons his family and community on the eve of his initiation intoxicated by the bright new things displayed by missionaries (1956a: 12–13). And if one of the most dominant themes in African literature concerns the rise of colonial modernity, the transformation of African societies from traditional to national or global cultures, then it is not difficult to see why missions came to occupy a central role in the making of the cultures and communities of modernity: Christianity was "regarded as containing the secret source of power of the white man" (Opoku 1985: 525).

More than as representatives of Christianity's assumed cabalistic powers, however, missionaries were often seen as the agents of modernity in its most secular sense. Indeed, within the ideologies of missionaries and evangelists working in Africa in the colonial period, the notion of conversion was barely distinguished from modernization and the idea of progress. When Livingstone spoke about the evils of African society, his concerns were more secular than ecclesiastical: African society was evil because it had not yet awakened to the virtues of European civilization that were, in his mind, the values associated with the bourgeois *Weltanschauung*, namely, utilitarian individualism, private property, and enlightened self-interest (see Comaroff and Comaroff 1992: 187). It was this modernity, rather than the ideologies of Christian conversion, that attracted Africans to the missionary enterprise. And one of the most powerful symbols of this modernity was the printing press, the instrument that enabled literacy and hence literature.

The coming of the printing press to many mission schools was to be surrounded by legends. When John Ross conveyed a printing press to the Lovedale Mission in South Africa in 1823, he saw it as an extension of the commission of the Christian Church to "the world of readers, who become the men of action, for evil as much as for good" (Shepherd 1941: 400). By 1910, the printing press at King's College, Budo, in Uganda was already surrounded by a venerable tradition: it had been brought to the school from Kampala, a distance of over ten miles, on the head of a porter, cheered by admiring crowds along the way (McGregor 1967: 22). The books printed by these presses were, in turn, to become legendary. The first Xhosa grammar and translation of the Bible was printed at Lovedale early in the nineteenth century; it was at this historic press that Tiyo Soga's famous translation of Bunyan's *The Pilgrim's Progress* was published in the 1860s; it was also here that Tengo Jabavu, the great South African nationalist, printed *Imvo*, a Xhosa weekly newspaper. The long-term effect of the arrival of the printing press was, however, in the emergence of African newspapers and literary texts. The story of Lovedale is exemplary in this regard: in addition to the production of Xhosa grammars and readers, the Lovedale Press was also to publish the works of the first generation of African writers in southern Africa, including H. I. E. Dhlomo, D. D. T. Jabavu, A. C. Jordan, and Sol Plaatje. This situation was repeated throughout the continent: the Christian missions provided the means of production of early African literature.

The Africans' attraction to the material things of European culture did not exclude the impact of Christianity on their lives and practices. On the contrary, the new Christian system challenged the *doxa* of many African societies, including the institutions of marriage and the definition of the family, and, in the process, provoked a series of social crises. Clearly, if the recovery and celebration of an African traditional culture has become a defining characteristic of African literature in the colonial period, it is because missionaries generally tended to abhor native customs and traditions, which they saw as a threat to the new morality. As A. J. Temu has noted, missionaries "saw nothing good in African dances, music or in such important African traditions as circumcisions and initiation ceremonies. They lumped them together as heathen and immoral without trying to understand them, what they were for and what significance they had in the life of the people to whom they had come to teach Christianity" (1972: 155). As exemplified in works such as Achebe's *Arrow of God* (1964), Ngugi wa Thiong'o's *The River Between* (1965), and Mongo Beti's *Le pauvre Christ de Bomba* (1956) (*The Poor Christ of Bomba*), missionaries and their new African protégés sought to uproot such customs and traditions ruthlessly and relentlessly.

In the end, however, it was the colonial schools set up by missionaries that were to have the most profound effect on the shaping of African society and literary culture. From the very beginning, there was a very close relationship between Christian conversion, literacy, and a modern identity. Missionaries considered the school to be the key to the recruitment of new members and for the social reproduction of the values of colonial modernity; indeed, many of the Protestant churches insisted on literacy as a prerequisite for conversion, and early African Christians were generally referred to as readers. The desire for education and literacy was propelled, as we have already seen, by the social and economic opportunities they offered African Christians: "Literacy gave the elite access to the scientific and social thought of the western world, equipped them to enter into dialogue with the colonial powers over the destiny of Africa, and familiarized them with the social fashions of Europe which made their life style an example to be emulated by their less fortunate countrymen" (Afigbo 1985: 496).

Education and literacy were, however, as much about epistemologies as they were about fashions and manners. In fact, we can explore the way education and literacy overdetermined literary production in Africa by reflecting on how the introduction of literacy affected the cultural life of colonial society and their transformation of key epistemological assumptions. The first point to note here is one that scholars of literacy, most notably Brian Stock, have made in regard to medieval European society: that the rapprochement between the oral and the written came to play "a decisive role in the organization of experience"; that it brought about a change in the means "by which one established personal identity, both with respect to the inner self and to external forces"; and that textuality shaped the nature and meaning of experience itself because "as texts informed experience, so men and women began to live texts" (1983: 3–4). The interface of the oral and the written has, of course, been a major area of research in African literature and major writers have narrated the process by which literacy came to invent modern identities (see Ricard and Swanepoel 1997). What has perhaps not been explored in great detail is the process by which literacy and textuality represented both cultural discontinuity and new epistemic possibilities. In this regard, Stock's conclusion on the effects of textuality on European medieval culture applies as well to colonial Africa: "When texts were introduced into communities hitherto unfamiliar with writing, they often gave rise to unprecedented perceptual and cognitive possibilities; they promised, if they did not always deliver, a new technology of the mind" (1983: 10).

Still, what were the values promoted by a new economy of discourse based on reading and writing? And how did the resulting practices lead to the development of a culture of letters in Africa? In regard to the first question, it is important to note the indispensability of writing to what has come to be known as the invention of tradition in colonial Africa (see Ranger 1983). For the products of the mission schools, people such as Plaatje and Mofolo in South Africa, or Samuel Johnson in Nigeria, the meaning and authority of an event depended on its textual representation. It was through writing that the histories of important events such as the *mfecane* in southern Africa, or the history of the Yorubas in Nigeria, were made central to discussions about the African past. Similarly, for the university men who founded some of the most famous colonial schools in Africa, schools such as King's College, Budo, in Uganda, the Lovedale Institute in South Africa, and the Lycée William Ponty in Senegal, the written text contained the most visible symbols of the bourgeois society they were asking their students to imagine and contemplate. Since there were few living examples of modernity in the colonial zone, models could only be found in books. At Alliance High School in Kenya, the headmaster, E. Carey Francis, determined that his charges should live up to the "inexorable moral rectitude" of the Victorian gentleman and a code of cleanliness to match, and wrote a book called *Hygiene for Africans* in which "he included caricature sketches of characters whose style of dress and personal appearance . . . he considered disgraceful" (Kipkorir 1980:120).

Literature and decolonization

If the period since the 1930s is now seen as "the era which witnessed the most extensive flowering of written literature in Africa" (Mazrui 1993: 553; see also Soyinka 1985), it was not simply because of the expansion in literary and educational opportunities that took place during this time period (although the emergence of the African university was crucial to the production of a literary culture), but also because it was during this period that colonial culture and its notions about the African were vigorously challenged and the idea of an autonomous African polis became a real alternative to imperial rule. This was the time when intellectuals and creative writers were called upon to imagine something that had never existed before – a modern African nation. The critique of colonialism in the literary works produced in the high nationalist period went hand in hand with the imagination of a national community (see Anderson 1991). And thus modern African literature, which began as an attempt to understand the shock of colonial conquest, came of age as an assertion of the illegitimacy of the colonial enterprise and the necessity of an autonomous African culture. Indeed, there is a way in which the most influential texts of the high nationalist period, works by Jomo Kenyatta, Peter Abrahams, Camara Laye, Ferdinand Oyono, and Chinua Achebe can be read as deliberate interventions in the "colonial situation debate" that opened this discussion.

At the heart of this debate were two questions that were to concern African intellectuals well into the 1970s: what had been the African response to colonialism? What were the real theoretical implications of imperialism for the nature of African societies and cultures and hence modes of literary expression? After several decades of African independence, the answers to these questions may appear simple, but in the period between the end of colonialism and decolonization, before the emergence of an African historiography and literary tradition, these issues were so much bound up with the politics of colonial rule that it was difficult to think of an autonomous African narrative on colonialism itself. Writers trying to imagine alternative stories to colonialism were caught between two inscrutable discourses. On one hand, there was the official colonial discourse, which insisted (in a familiar paternal language) that colonialism was good for Africa and that many Africans welcomed the colonial project. As Albert Sarraut, the French Minister for the Colonies put it in *La mise en valeur des colonies françaises*, the colonizer had the "sole right to protect the weak and to guarantee their economic and human development" (cited in Bretts 1985: 314). On the other hand, there was an influential liberal historiography that recognized many of the destructive aspects of colonialism, but insisted that, on balance, colonialism had uplifted the African's condition (see Boahen 1985b: 782–83).

It was not difficult for African writers and intellectuals to respond to the official view: colonial paternalism became the subject of irony and satire in novels such as Achebe's *Things Fall Apart* and *Arrow of God,* Mongo Beti's *Mission terminée* (1957), and Oyono's *Le vieux nègre et la médaille* (1956) and *Une vie de boy* (1956). Responding to liberal historiography, however, was to prove more difficult for two reasons. First, while they seemed eager to defend the imperial tradition at its moment of atrophy, liberal officials and historians were generally sympathetic to African nationalist aspirations; indeed, many of them had educated and patronized nationalist intellectuals and writers and provided the institutional spaces in which the African voice could be heard. White liberals could not simply be dismissed as apologists for colonialism. Secondly, the liberal defense of imperialism was premised on an assumption that many African nationalists shared: that colonialism had introduced modern structures to Africa and that these institutions – the church, the state, the school, and the market economy – were central to the project of decolonization itself.

In regard to the question of colonial modernity, then, African discourses in the nationalist period were compelled to draw a fine line between imperialism and modernity. Pan-Africanist manifestos in the early twentieth century were as unanimous in their critique of imperialism as they were enthusiastic in their endorsement of modernization. In his *Discourse on Colonialism*, Aimé Césaire summed up the spirit of these manifestos by claiming that colonialism had hindered the proper Europeanization or modernization of Africa:

> The proof is that at present it is the indigenous peoples of Africa and Asia who are demanding schools, and colonialist Europe which refuses them; that it is the African who is asking for ports and roads, and colonialist Europe which is niggardly on this score; that it is the colonized man who wants to move forward, and the colonizer who holds things back. (1972: 25)

This double perspective – the critique of colonialism and the sanctioning of European modernity – was expressed succinctly by Jomo Kenyatta at the end of *Facing Mount Kenya*:

> If Africans were left in peace on their own lands, Europeans would have to offer them the benefits of white civilisation in real earnest before they could obtain the African labour which they want so much. They would have to offer the African a way of life which was really superior to the one his father lived before him, and a share in the prosperity given them by their command of science. (1965: 305–06)

Emerging out of a nationalist discourse that wanted the African to be both free and modern, African literature came to champion what were seen as traditional values within the structures and institutions of colonial modernity. Not unexpectedly, then, works of literature committed to the recovery of the traditional African past were often written in European languages, as if to exhibit the African writer's mastery of the language and forms of the colonizer.

It is, of course, taken for granted that when the products of the mission schools went to university, they turned to writing as a self-conscious revolt against the culture of colonialism. This is true up to a point: major African writers began their careers when they went to university. But in order to show how imaginative literature came to function as a powerful critique of colonial culture and its institutions, it is important to note the hold this ideology had on even the most anti-colonial writers in the African literary tradition. When Ngugi wa Thiong'o arrived at Makerere University College from Alliance High School, he was a true devotee of the missionary ideology, working against African backwardness with evangelical zeal (see Sicherman 1990: 390). At University College, Ibadan, as Robert Wren's research has shown, many students were devout Christians who rejected their native cultures and traditions (see Wren 1991). African undergraduates in the few African universities established in the last days of colonial rule had become, by virtue of their education, some of the most privileged African subjects in the imperial realm, and they tended to be ignorant of, or skeptical toward, African cultures; they were more comfortable with European things. These students were steeped in all the major traditions of European literature and culture, but as Abiola Irele was to recall, "in terms of concrete knowledge of the African background [they] knew next to nothing" (quoted in Wren 1991: 119). But herein lies the great irony of the colonial moment in Africa: it was these students, the most privileged colonial subjects, the masters of European culture, who were to lead the literary revolt against the institutions of colonialism; and it was through the awareness of their alienation within the institutions of European literature and culture that they sought to produce a literature of their own.

Note

1. Note parallel with Lord Macauley in India. "Minute on Indian Education." In *Selected Writings: Thomas Babington Macauley*. Ed. John Clive and Thomas Pinney. Chicago: University of Chicago Press, 1972: 237–51.

Bibliography

Achebe, Chinua. 1964. *Arrow of God*. London: Heinemann.

1973. "The Role of the Writer in a New Nation." In *African Writers on African Writing*. Ed. G. D. Killam. London: Heinemann: 7–13.

[1958] 1996. *Things Fall Apart*. Expanded edition with notes. London: Heinemann.

Afigbo, A. E. 1985. "The Social Repercussions of Colonial Rule: the New Social Structures." In *The UNESCO General History of Africa*, vol. VII: *Africa under Colonial Domination 1880–1935*. Ed. A. Adu Boahen. Berkeley: University of California Press: 487–507.

Al-Jabarti, 'Abd al-Rahman. 1994. *'Abd al-Rahman al-Jabarti's History of Egypt* [*Ajaib al-Athar fi 'l-tarajim wa-'l-akhbar*]. Ed. Thomas Philipp and Moshe Perlmann. Stuttgart: Franz Steiner.

Anderson, Benedict. 1991. *Imagined Communities: Reflections on the Origin and Spread of Nationalism*. Rev. edn. London: Verso.

Balandier, Georges. [1955] 1970. *The Sociology of Black Africa: Social Dynamics in Central Africa*. Trans. Douglas Garman. New York: Praeger.

Boahen, A. Adu. 1985a. "Africa and the Colonial Challenge." In *The UNESCO General History of Africa*, vol. VII: *Africa under Colonial Domination 1880–1935*. Ed. A. Adu Boahen. Berkeley: University of California Press: 1–18.

1985b. "Colonialism in Africa: Its Impact and Significance." In *The UNESCO General History of Africa*, vol. VII: *Africa under Colonial Domination 1880–1935*. Ed. A. Adu Boahen. Berkeley: University of California Press: 782–809.

Bretts, R. F. 1985. "Methods and Institutions of European domination." In *The UNESCO General History of Africa*, vol. VII: *Africa under Colonial Domination 1880–1935*. Ed. A. Adu Boahen. Berkeley: University of California Press: 312–32.

Buckler, William E., ed. 1958. *Prose of the Victorian Period*. Boston: Houghton Mifflin.

Césaire, Aimé. 1972. *Discourse on Colonialism*. Trans. Joan Pinkham. New York, Monthly Review Press.

Comaroff, John L. and Jean Comaroff. 1992. *Ethnography and the Historical Imagination*. Boulder, CO: Westview.

Dirks, Nicholas B. "Introduction: Colonialism and Culture." In *Colonialism and Culture*. Ann Arbor: University of Michigan Press: 1–26.

Fanon, Frantz. [1963] 1968. *The Wretched of the Earth*. Trans. Constance Farrington. New York: Grove.

Gates, Jr., Henry Louis. 1985. "Editor's Introduction: Writing 'Race' and the Difference It Makes." *Critical Inquiry* 12. 1: 1–20.

Jeyifo, Biodun. 1990. "The Nature of Things: Arrested Decolonization and Critical Theory." *Research in African Literature* 21. 1: 33–46.

Johnson, Lemuel. 1997. *Shakespeare in Africa*. Trenton: Africa World.

July, Robert William. 1968. *The Origins of Modern African Thought: Its Development in West Africa during the Nineteenth and Twentieth Centuries*. London: Faber and Faber.

Kenyatta, Jomo. [1938] 1965. *Facing Mount Kenya*. New York: Random House.

Kipkorir, B. E. 1980. "Carey Francis at the A. H. S., Kikuyu – 1940–62." In *Biographical Essays on Imperialism and Collaboration in Colonial Kenya*. Ed. B. E. Kipkorir. Nairobi: Kenya Literature Bureau: 112–59.

Langley, J. Ayo. 1979. *Ideologies of Liberation in Black Africa 1856–1970: Documents on Modern Political Thought from Colonial Times to the Present*. London: Rex Collings.

Mazrui, Ali A. 1993. "The Development of Modern Literature Since 1935." In *The UNESCO General History of Africa*, vol. VIII: *Africa since 1935*. Ed. Ali A. Mazrui. Berkeley: University of California Press: 553–81.

McGregor, G. P. 1967. *King's College, Budo: The First Sixty Years*. Nairobi: Oxford University Press.

Miller, Christopher. 1985. *Blank Darkness: Africanist Discourse in French*. Chicago: University of Chicago Press.

Mongo, Beti. 1956. *Le pauvre Christ de Bomba*. Paris: Laffont.

1957. *Mission terminée*. Paris: Buchet-Chastel.

Ngugi wa Thiong'o. 1965. *The River Between*. London: Heinemann.

Oliver, Roland. 1952. *The Missionary Factor in East Africa*. London: Longman.

Opoku, K. Asare. 1985. "Religion in Africa during the Colonial era." In *The UNESCO General History of Africa*, vol. VII: *Africa under Colonial Domination 1880–1935*. Ed. A. Adu Boahen. London: Heinemann: 508–38.

Oyono, Ferdinand. 1956a. *Une vie de boy*. Paris: Julliard.

1956b. *Le vieux nègre et la médaille*. Paris: Julliard.

1975. *Boy!*. Trans. John Reed. London: Heinemann.

Ranger, T. O. 1985. "African Initiative and Resistance in the Face of Partition and Conquest." In *The UNESCO General History of Africa*, vol. VII: *Africa under Colonial Domination 1880–1935*. Ed. A. Adu Boahen. Berkeley: University of California Press: 45–62.

1983. "The Invention of Tradition in Colonial Africa." In *The Invention of Tradition*. Ed. Eric Hobsbawm and Terence Ranger. Cambridge: Cambridge University Press: 211–62.

Ricard, Alain, and C. F. Swanepoel, eds. 1997. *The Oral-Written Interface*. Special issue of *Research in African Literatures* 28.1.

Rodney, Walter. 1972. *How Europe Underdeveloped Africa*. Dar es Salaam: Tanzania Publishing House.

Said, Edward W. 1979. *Orientalism*. New York: Vintage.

Shepherd, Robert H. W. 1941. *Lovedale, South Africa: The Story of a Century 1841–1941*. Lovedale: Lovedale Press.

Sicherman, Carol. 1990. *Ngugi wa Thiong'o: The Making of a Rebel*. London: Hans Zell.

Soyinka, Wole. 1985. "The Arts in Africa During the Period of Colonial Rule." In *The UNESCO General History of Africa*, vol. VII: *Africa under Colonial Domination 1880–1935*. Ed. A. Adu Boahen. Berkeley: University of California Press: 539–64.

Stock, Brian. 1983. *The Implications of Literacy: Written Language and Models of Interpretation in the Eleventh and Twentieth Centuries*. Princeton: Princeton University Press.

Temu, A. J. 1972. *British Protestant Missions*. London: Longman.
Wauthier, Claude. 1979. *The Literature and Thought of Modern Africa*. 2nd English edn. Washington, DC: Three Continents Press.
Willan, Brian. 1984. *Sol Plaatje: A Biography*. Johannesburg: Ravan.
Wren, Robert. 1991. *Those Magical Years: The Making of Nigerian Literature at Ibadan, 1948–1966*. Washington, DC: Three Continents Press.

21

The formative journals and institutions

MILTON KRIEGER

A long prehistory brings the story of journals voicing and connecting the expressive cultures of Africa and the Caribbean from the early nineteenth century through the twentieth, to *Présence Africaine*, a distinctive model and influential force by mid-century, and beyond. This chapter surveys their sources, examines some major texts, links these periodicals to the black world's urgent public issues, and assesses the genre's condition as the twenty-first century begins.

The early African precursors came from European mission churches that published oral narratives and some secular poetry and prose as adjuncts to religious texts. These were most notable from the Xhosa when a press opened at Lovedale in 1823 and the Yoruba as Samuel Crowther's similar evangelism emerged in the 1840s and generated a print culture of some diversity. The next phase, more secular, included newspapers created by publishing writers like Edward Wilmot Blyden and John Tengo Jabavu. Then came twentieth-century works like *Nigeria Magazine*, regularly funded and produced by colonial authorities with a scholarly style, "finished" look, and commercial appeal; there were 40,000 copies of its 1960 independence issue.

"Independents," however, dominated twentieth-century periodical literature. Secular and nonofficial reviews with creative and critical writing in diverse formats from small presses, these were started by individual or collaborating writers themselves, drawing on local practices and interests. Site by site, genre by genre, adding nonprint idioms, they privileged indigenous voices. Their composite role after the First World War (whether or not by conscious policy) was of great historic magnitude, spreading multiethnic, multinational, Negritude, and pan-African works, feeding and sometimes leading the politics of self-determination that emerged on the continent and in the diaspora by mid-century. Most pioneers would concur with the British Guyana poet and *Kyk-Over-Al*'s founder, A. J. Seymour, citing the desire for a "little review" to provide the new writers from his emerging literary community a forum for challenges to orthodox forms and content (Seymour 1986: 3).

Trinidad (1929–30) and *The Beacon* (1931–33, 1939), for instance, with Albert Gomes, C. L. R. James, and Alfred Mendes at the helm, printed the island's writers from every background, including militant works on its identity and tensions, and on the nationalist and labor politics that produced the oilfield strike of 1937. In lusophone Africa, following earlier journals in Angola, Baltasar Lopes made *Claridade*'s nine issues (1936–60) Cape Verde's distinctive voice of cultural (if not yet political) affirmation, with a poem in Crioulo rather than Portuguese on its first cover. Peter Abrahams registered in *Tell Freedom* the impact of such sources when writing about Johannesburg's *The Bantu World* and its circle in the late 1930s; though funded by whites, its content and reach were pan-African, and it published his own early poems (Abrahams 1981: 188–202, 227). These were exemplary pioneers, in significant local as well as European languages.

Francophone circumstances extended the genre, in a way that straddled two categories that Michael Echeruo later identified, the "journal for Africans" with an operational base, patrons, and brokers "abroad," and the "African journal" more exclusively the product of indigenous creativity (1993: 724). Colonial policy brought soldiers, workers, and students to France, in numbers unmatched elsewhere. They framed debates on empire and liberation, culture, race and class, national and social struggle, in periodicals with distinctive literary and political cultures, expressed theoretically, critically, and creatively. Guyana's René Maran, a colonial administrator in Africa and a Prix Goncourt novelist (*Batouala*, 1921), made *Les Continents* (twelve numbers, 1924) a short-lived prototype. Its successors voiced issues of culture and politics raised in France and abroad, as Marcus Garvey, Claude McKay, W. E. B. Du Bois, the French Communist Party, and others contested the black world's immediate allegiances and visions of the future. La Comité de Défense de la Race Nègre from 1926 rallied those who perceived race and culture more than class as the salient bonds between Old and New World Africans, reflected in *La Dépêche Africaine* (1928–32) and *La Revue du Monde Noir* (1931–32). Those more critical of empire and committed to class analysis formed La Ligue de Défense de la Race Nègre in 1927 to channel this wing of migrant opinion, variously attached to and distanced from, first, the Communist International, then France's United and Common Front movements. The Senegalese war veteran Lamine Senghor made *La Voix des Nègres* (1927) its voice, picked up despite schisms after his death into the 1930s in *La Race Nègre* and *Le Cri des Nègres*, with 3,000 copies per issue, produced by Sudanese and Senegalese successors.

Many forces in France during the 1930s divided the black worker, middle-class, and intelligentsia elements, including Old and New World Africans with their different territorial bases, skin colors, and degrees of assimilation, and disparate views about the French cultural avant-garde, political left, and imperial politics. But *Légitime Défense* (one issue, 1932) proclaimed commonalities among France's black peoples, recognizing alienation and the need to resist further assimilation. Aimé Césaire (Martinique), Léon Damas (Guyana), and Léopold Senghor (Senegal) used its successor, *L'Etudiant Noir* (1935), to advocate Negritude, a civilizational view with African roots, diasporic branches, and universal possibilities. This quest for indigenous cultural patrimonies and black world linkages engaged periodicals in the homelands as well. Haiti's turn of the century, belletristic *Le Jeune Haïti* and *La Ronde* gave way under the pressures of poverty, violence, and American occupation (1915–34) to the more politically conscious *La Nouvelle Ronde* (1925) and its successors into the 1930s, *La Trouée*, *La Revue Indigène*, and *Le Petit Impartial*, then *La Ruche* after the war, all influenced by Jacques Roumain's contacts and career in France and at home. It was much the same in Martinique, where Césaire made *Tropiques* (1941–45) a modernist, anti-Vichy landmark in literary and political culture.

Such were the seminal sources for *Présence Africaine*, founded in 1947 by Senegal's Alioune Diop. Its first decade fitted Echeruo's later "journal for Africans" rubric, for the Cold War and a heavily metropolitan patronage (André Gide wrote the first issue's foreword; Jean-Paul Sartre's and French anthropologists' circles helped create its niche) muted some of its precursors' global Left influences. Thereafter, moving away from Negritude's (by then) ambiguous "self-other" texture, shifting the orientation from ecumenical humanism to nonalignment and Third World initiatives in the spirit of the 1955 Bandoeng Conference, key writers of color made the journal more confrontational. Previously featured as creative writers, black authors' criticism and commentary also flourished in *Présence Africaine*'s second series, begun in 1955. They developed Echeruo's "African journal" role and influence through writer and artist congresses still held in Paris (1956) and Rome (1959), but with a more assertive agenda, and after 1960 used the journal's apprenticeship ground, publishing imprint, and other auspices to expand this repertoire.

"Spin-off" impacts spread to Africa when *Présence Africaine* collaborators, now familiar with publishing conventions and production techniques, returned to independent homelands, started journals, and organized festivals of culture in Dakar (1966), Algiers (1969), and Lagos (1977).[1] They expanded local print opportunities and fostered experimental cultures and resistance politics. *Présence*

Africaine, francophone at its roots but also influential on other terrain where colonization was challenged, moved writers and artists across boundaries of ethnicity, language, and culture, and of age and class (if less so gender) in late colonial and early independence years. Not so vigorous as in 1950, or 1975, the journal has remained a literary and cultural influence in 2000.

Among its prominent heirs in Africa were Nigeria's *Black Orpheus: A Journal of African and Afro-American Literature* (1957–82, but sporadic after 1970) and *Abbia: Cameroon Cultural Review* (1963–82, likewise less frequent in its later years). *Black Orpheus*'s title came from Sartre's vision of the search for identity and freedom while traversing (colonial) hell. Its founder-broker-patron was Ulli Beier, a German transplanted to Ibadan in 1950, present at the Paris congress in 1956, inspired to transmit that experience to Nigeria and the larger anglophone African community. A tireless promoter, linking entrepreneurial, academic, and creative venues based in Lagos, Ibadan, and Oshogbo respectively, using his experience and contacts on campus and in extramural clinics and workshops, Beier made *Black Orpheus* far more active and influential than its circulation of 3,500 suggests. Its contributing scholars and writers were formidable: expatriates like Martin Esslin, both Janheinz Jahn and Gerald Moore as early co-editors, and Paul Theroux; Nigerians like John Pepper Clark, Duro Ladipo, Christopher Okigbo, and Wole Soyinka; continental and diasporic Africans like Ama Ata Aidoo, Nicolás Guillén, Langston Hughes, Vincent Kofi, Ezekiel Mphahlele, Agostinho Neto, Grace Ogot, Jean-Joseph Rabéarivelo, and Tchicaya U Tam'si.

The journal offered critical debate and both verbal and visual creativity, contributed to every facet of global discourse on the African condition, and built a domestic readership. Funded primarily by Nigeria's Western Region government and the Rockefeller Foundation, Beier published *Black Orpheus* at least twice a year in its first decade, created links with similar ventures like South Africa's *Drum* and Uganda's *Transition*, and issued through Mbari Publications some twenty books of creative writing that the journal had printed in preliminary stages. After 1966, with Beier gone and civil war raging, with John Pepper Clark and Abiola Irele as editors until 1975 in conditions lacking Beier's foreign and domestic support, *Black Orpheus* sustained its high critical content and standard but lost some of its creative writing force, partly because deaths and exiles mounted. Still, *Black Orpheus* published Okigbo's "Path of Thunder." It lapsed until two issues in 1982, but it was no longer edited by John Pepper Clark and Abiola Irele and it came out of the University of Lagos. Those two last issues were parochial and academic when compared to its best and better days, and it went dormant.

Abbia was more domestically focused than *Black Orpheus*. Its readers were student advocates for African culture and nationalism during the 1950s who came home after independence in 1960–61 as ministers, civil servants, and independent professionals. Including the anglophone Bernard Fonlon, editor for its entire history, they started *Abbia* with patronage and funds from President Ahidjo and UNESCO among other sources, reaching a press run of 20,000. In many genres, using French, English, and indigenous languages, *Abbia* engaged Cameroon's intelligentsia, its regional and local cultures, and issues like language policy and educational models that were debated in all new nations. *Abbia* served Cameroon's culture as a vigorous journal of record and commentary through twenty years, forty volumes, and 5,500 pages. It faltered as its founders aged and their successors lost interest in *Abbia* as both a nation-building project celebrating Cameroon's unity and a voice for its diverse critics. Like *Black Orpheus*, its early success and subsequent limits reflected generic problems for late twentieth-century African periodicals, as political tension and fiscal duress made most countries uneasy homes for writers and artists.

Black Orpheus and *Abbia* typified larger-scale periodicals, with public as well as private subsidies, sustained for many years. Attention is also due smaller ventures that published young writers emerging in their homelands after the Second World War. Two student journals at university colleges in anglophone Africa were exemplary, *The Horn* (Ibadan, Nigeria, 1958–64) and *Penpoint* (Makerere, Uganda, 1958- , replaced in about 1970 by *Dhana*, *Busara*, *Joliso*, etc., from new East African campuses and publishers). *The Horn* drew on both the formal British literature syllabus and on modernist, international tastes within Ibadan's English department faculty. The staple fare of poems with some reviews, from Zaria and Nsukka campuses as well as Ibadan, helped shape the use of English and Nigeria's literary sensibility at independence and beyond. It gave the poet John Pepper Clark and the critics Abiola Irele and Omolara Ogundipe-Leslie their first productive settings, and added to Christopher Okigbo's and Wole Soyinka's earlier voicings abroad. *Penpoint* lasted longer, as an English department product each school term. More varied than *The Horn*, it included puzzles, prizes, and sturdier fare like essays on Luganda language and literature, reports from Makerere students at conferences abroad, and debates on African issues of the day. Peter Nazareth, James Ngugi, and David Rubadiri in its early issues, then by 1963 (following a writers' conference in Kampala) Dennis Brutus, Ezekiel Mphahlele, and Richard Rive from southern Africa, attested *Penpoint*'s apprenticeship and interlocutor roles. As *The Horn* nurtured talent for *Black Orpheus* at Ibadan, so *Penpoint* prepared writers who made Rajat Neogy's *Transition*, founded in 1961, one of the continent's literary and cultural arbiters from Kampala, which Wole Soyinka turned into *Ch'indaba* (1975–76) and then resumed as *Transition* (1991–).

Simultaneously in the anglophone Caribbean, as federation politics and universities with branch campuses emerged, periodicals shaped literary and public culture. The argument can be made, even if they drew on expatriates and their resources, like those we have seen in late colonial and early independent Africa, that British Caribbean journals were more autonomous in Echeruo's sense than Africa's. Europeans locally active in schools and in social and sport clubs started *Bim* (1942– ; the word signified "inhabitant of Barbados" in colonial times), but the earlier, very diverse Trinidad journals were more the longtime editor Frank Collymore's model. He published writers of color from Barbados and the anglophone Caribbean (including Derek Walcott in his teens), arranged British Council and British Broadcasting Corporation access that spread their work in print and nonprint channels between the colonies and abroad, and used teachers posted among branches of the University College of the West Indies to discover talent and circulate *Bim* – all on a shoestring, soliciting advertisements as well as manuscripts. A. J. Seymour's *Kyk-Over-Al* (founded in 1945) similarly tapped scarce resources to bring writers into prominence in a British Guyana much changed by radical Second World War and postwar political aspirations. It fostered a national literature from the varied local roots of popular, experimental, less-established writing, then widened its geographic network and added visual to verbal arts. Edna Manley's talent and patronage made *Focus* (1946–60) a similar force in Jamaica. *Bim* and *Kyk-Over-Al*, despite times in abeyance, survived their founders into the 1990s, publishing authors from most of the major Caribbean cultures and languages and exerting influence far beyond their sites of origin.

Cuba and Haiti were important but different, more island- or country-specific Caribbean settings, because the region's Spanish- and French-speaking lands lacked the regionwide connections of British territory before 1960, and because of their distinctive experiences thereafter. The culture and arts "revista" thrived in republican Cuba (1902–58); *Bohemia* (founded in 1910) circulated 200,000 copies by the 1950s, and a vigorous provincial culture produced 205 of that era's 558 journals outside Havana. These periodicals produced both a modernist esthetic in *Revista de Avance* (1927–30) and *Orígenes* (1944–56), and the more directly political engagement of *Ciclón* (1955–58). Fidel Castro's victory and Nicolás Guillén's return from exile in 1959 then allied insurgent politics and culture. A weekly newspaper supplement *Lunes de Revolución* (1959–61) published the revolution's early, free experiments, with a print run of 250,000, until security concerns after the Bay of Pigs invasion led to official control of and orthodoxy in *Casas de las Américas* (founded in 1960), the Spanish world's most widely circulated journal and a global model of state-sponsored culture, literature, ideology, and scholarship (see Ellis 1983). In the Duvaliers' Haiti, where the populist *La Ruche*'s editor, Jacques Stephen Alexis, took up arms in 1961 but was captured and executed, periodicals struggled for expressive and critical space. Journals like *Nouvelle Optique* (1971–74) from Canadian exile and *Le Petit Samedi Soir* (intermittent since 1972) at home challenged the harsh conditions the regime imposed on writers, artists, and the population at large.

There was an anti-regime lusophone African counterpart in *Mensagem* (1951–52), started by students like Agostinho Neto in Lisbon, shifted to Luanda, short-lived, but the model for other journals as Portugal's African subjects took new cultural and political bearings, revolted, and seized independence. But South Africans created the continent's most ambitious and militant periodicals. Jim Bailey, a mining magnate's son, started *African Drum* against apartheid's grain in 1950, moved it from Cape Town to Johannesburg, brought Anthony Sampson from London as the first of several professional expatriate editors, and hired a young African staff. A journal remarkable for its content and mass audience emerged by mid-1951, renamed *Drum*. Investigative photographic exposés under a "Mr. Drum" byline (most notably by Henry Nxumalo, before his murder while working for the journal) about convict farm labor, prisons, and township life gave its journalism a unique political edge and popular appeal. It covered resistance politics through Sharpeville and the Rivonia trials at home, and nationalist movements abroad. Its literary pages were equally notable. Todd Matshikiza, Bloke Modisane, Casey Motsisi, Ezekiel Mphahlele, Nat Nakasa, Lewis Nkosi, and Can Themba were *Drum* editors and writers. Peter Abrahams's and Alan Paton's novels in serial form, Peter Magubane's photographs, and major writers from Africa at large were part of the mix. So were popular elements like opinion polls, an African heroes series, cooking and farming tips, comics and cartoons, sports, show business, and "soft" sex texts and photographs (observing racial bars). *Drum* was international for anglophones, with distribution in Africa, the Caribbean and the USA, and editions published by 1960 in Ghana, Kenya, and Nigeria. *Drum*'s impact can be gauged in Peter Nazareth's account of its "slangy" influence on English spoken in East Africa.[2] Formal bans and informal pressures in the 1960s scaled down its coverage and frequency; *Drum* lost militancy, quality, and finally autonomy when Bailey sold it in 1979. With populist, insurgent township cultures like Sophiatown's suppressed, and most of the 1950s' vanguard dead or publishing abroad while banned at home, *Drum* became a "pulp" magazine.

From this vacuum emerged a number of small new South African journals, short on funds and dodging apartheid bans, most notably for black writers *The Classic* and *The New African* in the 1960s and *New Classic* and *S'ketsh'* in the 1970s, involving Nat Nakasa, Lewis Nkosi, Mongane Serote, and Sipho Sepamla. Then Soweto in 1976 called forth *Drum*'s major successor and a new generation of talents, in *Staffrider* (founded in 1978), published by anti-apartheid whites at Ravan Press. The title was apt, referring to a risky, illegal, creative performance art by young blacks riding trains open-air between townships and Johannesburg. Skirting censors, with a 7,000 press run by 1980 and probably more hand-to-hand circulation than Africa's norm, much of its text came from readings and art displays mounted, then chosen for *Staffrider*, by local collectives. Women and youths in factories, bars, gangs, and the streets were substantial sources; accounts of funerals as political actions, Miriam Tlali's "Soweto Speaking" column, and workers' testimonies were staple fare. From 1979, a "Staffrider Series" expanded *Staffrider* texts into low-priced book-length prose, poetry, drama, and anthologies. This comprehensive post-1976 project, tapping popular rage and its cultural product, circulated resistance works calling for and leading to the end of apartheid. Township editorial direction lapsed as banning orders mounted in the 1980s, but *Staffrider* conducted vital debates between black consciousness and "one nation, one culture" viewpoints, and on Albie Sachs's call in "Preparing Ourselves for Freedom" for the African National Congress to give artistic autonomy precedence over a politicized esthetic. The Congress of South African Writers took over *Staffrider* in 1991 and its force diminished, but *Current Writing* (1989), *Rixaka* (1990), and others picked up the slack and maintained these exchanges. Parallels with the tensions of revolutionary politics and culture in Castro's Cuba, faced by so many vigorous twentieth-century journals, were clear. And recalling Echeruo, whoever paid the bills and published it, *Staffrider* was, like *Drum*, decisively an "African journal."

This, then, at the threshold of the twenty-first century, was the foundation periodical literature for Africa and the Caribbean. More specialized or scholarly journals continued to appear, sharing or competing for the acclaimed writers and artists, seeking their successors, engaging debates in local, transnational, and transcontinental circles, sustaining critical and creative networks as politics and funds allowed. Nigeria illustrated the range, risks, and hopes: *Odu* was characteristic, with its starts, stops, "New Series" revivals, and (at times tenuous) survival since 1955, moving from an early Yoruba to West African and then all-African coverage, combining scholars and nonscholars, Nigerians and foreigners, as editors and contributors, shifting venues between Ibadan and Ife campuses. Many newer Nigerian universities started similar journals of humane letters, but few survived. By contrast, *Okike* (published at Nsukka since 1972) retained Chinua Achebe's tight original focus as "An African Journal of New Writing" and appeared close to schedule.

In 1995, the year Ken Saro-Wiwa was executed, a new Nigerian periodical appeared. *Glendora Review: African Quarterly on the Arts* renewed *Black Orpheus*'s quest for identity and freedom, with fresh cultural and commercial bearings. Beyond previously established themes, idioms, and debates, it covered music, films, videos, photography, the publishing industry, and censorship. The design and colors were bold, and it used e-mail and distributors in Europe and North America. Editor Dapo Adeniyi's first column recalled Nigeria's once "luxuriant hub of assorted art and literary activities," recounted their decline, departure abroad, or death, then stated his hope and purpose: "to amplify the voices of those creative people of Nigeria and of Africa wanting to speak to the rest of the world" (1995: 4). Echoing here the pioneers of African and Caribbean periodical literature, he faced conditions in the domestic economy and polity and new technologies more fully developed and controlled abroad that made the entire genre's maintenance, and *Glendora Review*'s, a formidable task. But the indigenous sources traced here are deeply and tenaciously creative. Ways to graft and endure will surely emerge and persist, and carry African and Caribbean voices further into the new century, at their local roots and in the global culture.

Notes

1. The Paris and Rome congresses, and African journals including *Black Orpheus*, received funds from the Congress for Cultural Freedom, which also financed periodicals published in Cuba. This was found to be a USA Central Intelligence Agency conduit in the mid-1960s, a subtext to Echeruo's concern for autonomy.
2. Kenya in fact had a version of *Drum* in *Joe* (1973–79), founded by Hilary Ng'weno and Terry Hirst, keyed to city life, full of cartoons and comics, satiric, didactic, mildly political, with a peak press run of 30,000.

Bibliography

Abraham, Peter. 1981. *Tell Freedom*. London: Faber and Faber.

Adeniyi, Dapo. 1995. "Editor's Wishes." *Glendora Review* 1. 1: 4.

Alao, George. 1999. "The Development of Lusophone Africa's Literary Magazine." *Research in African Literatures* 30. 1: 169–83.

Antoine, Régis. 1992. *La littérature franco-antillaise*. 2nd edn. Paris: Karthala.

Arnold, A. James, ed. 1994. *A History of Literature in the Caribbean*, vol. 1: *Hispanic and Francophone Regions*. Amsterdam: John Benjamins.

Benson, Peter. 1986. *Black Orpheus, Transition, and Modern Cultural Awakening in Africa.* Berkeley: University of California Press.

Burness, Donald. 1977. *Fire: Six Writers from Angola, Mozambique, and Cape Verde.* Washington, DC: Three Continents Press.

Dash, J. Michael. 1981. *Literature and Ideology in Haiti, 1915–1961.* Totowa, NJ: Barnes and Noble.

Echeruo, Michael. 1993. Review of *The Surreptitious Speech: "Présence Africaine" and the Politics of Otherness* by V. Y. Mudimbe. *The Journal of Modern African Studies* 31. 4: 719–24.

Ellis, Keith. 1983. *Cuba's Nicolás Guillén: Poetry and Ideology.* Toronto: University of Toronto Press.

Eskenazi-Mayo, Roberto. 1993. *A Survey of Cuban Revistas, 1902–1958.* Washington, DC: Library of Congress.

Hassan, Salah D. 1999. "Inaugural Issues: The Cultural Politics of the Early *Présence Africaine*, 1947–55." *Research in African Literatures* 30. 2: 194–221.

Kirkwood, Mike. 1980. "Staffrider: An Informal Discussion." *English in Africa* 7. 2: 22–31.

Krieger, Milton. 1996. "Building the Republic through Letters: *Abbia: Cameroon Cultural Review*, 1963–82, and its Legacy." *Research in African Literatures* 27. 2: 155–77.

Maugham-Brown, David. 1989. "The Anthology as Reliquary? *Ten Years of Staffrider* and *The Drum Decade.*" *Current Writing* 1: 3–21.

Mudimbe, V. Y., ed. *The Surreptitious Speech: "Présence Africaine" and the Politics of Otherness, 1947–1987.* Chicago: University of Chicago Press.

Nazareth, Peter. 1961. "The Language of *Drum.*" *Penpoint* 10: 15–20.

Seymour, Arthur J. 1986. "Literature in the Making: The Contribution of *Kyk-Over-Al.*" *Kyk-Over-Al* 33–34: 3–8.

Steins, Martin. 1986. "Black Migrants in Paris." In *European-Language Writing in Sub-Saharan Africa.* Ed. Albert Gérard, vol. 1. Budapest: Akadémiai Kiadó: 354–78.

Stevenson, W. H. 1975. "The Horn: What It Was and What It Did." *Research in African Literatures* 6. 1: 5–31.

Weiss, Judith. 1977. *Casa de las Américas: An Intellectual Review in the Cuban Revolution.* Estudios de Hispanófila 44. Chapel Hill: University of North Carolina.

Woodson, Dorothy C. 1980. *Drum: An Index to "Africa's Leading Magazine," 1951–1965.* Madison: University of Wisconsin African Studies Program.

22

Literature in Afrikaans

AMPIE COETZEE

This chapter will not be strictly chronological and teleological. It is not an attempt to begin at a "beginning" and indicate a "development" to an ever-shifting present. It utilizes the concept of the "discursive formation," where these formations were created within the political, social, and material conditions in South Africa. These broadly historical formations, identified by the distribution of "statements" within discourses, from approximately the sixteenth to the twentieth centuries, can be identified as follows: Europe meets Africa; the indigenization of language; colonization; literature as discourse; the phenomenon of a "minor literature"; modernism and postmodernism.

Europe meets Africa

The creation of a written literature in South Africa – literature as a nineteenth-century European construct – does not begin with the canonical "literary" text. It will take its representations from the navigation texts and travel journals of those who documented the first meetings and confrontations in the contact zone between the indigene, the Portuguese and Dutch seamen and explorers. The travel discourses of the first Portuguese and Dutch navigators who sailed around the southernmost point of Africa, Bartolomeu Dias (1487–88), Vasco da Gama (1497–99), and Jan Huygen van Linschoten (1579–92) (see Axelson 1988: 1–8; *Itinerario Voyage* 1934), which record what seems to be the first significant impressions of the people and landscape of southern Africa, have to be read not only for their content as texts describing what they saw and experienced. They are also representations in language, limited as instruments of representation; but also powerful as textual creations constructing images of the other people as wild, barbaric, dirty, stupid, and untrustworthy. These perceptions persisted into the nineteenth century in Europe, for instance in Friedrich Hegel's lectures on the philosophy of world history. His divisions of Africa are similar to those of the navigator Van Linschoten, and his typification of the indigenes have the elements common to all early travel journals: they are wild, childlike, without god, ruled by passion, full of witchcraft (Hegel 1975: 173–90).

These texts not only established the preconceptions of the settlers and colonists even before they arrived, they also intruded into the new worlds by appropriation: the naming of places, the setting up of signposts and beacons were all indicative of conquest. Places became signifiers – such as Dias's name for the Cape of Good Hope (Cabo de Boa Esperança), because it promised the discovery of India. Or it stood for the end of Africa, according to Pacheco Pereira (Axelson 1988: 3, 11). Because this cape was on a route somewhere the Dutch built a fort here, a post of refreshment for the navigators to India, a halfway station where the instruments of the Dutch East India Company (the VOC) would plant fresh vegetables and obtain cattle from the Khoi living there and inland.

This transitory station did, however, alter. Bartering and unequal exchanges led to conflict with the Khoi, but also to the enrichment of the company's servants, and ultimately to the desire for their own land to produce supplies for the company.[1] In 1657 it was decided to settle "free people" here, who with their freedom from the company's service would qualify for plots of land of their own choice. There are records of contracts made with two Khoi captains for the purchase of land; but they did not understand the contracts, as they were written in legal Dutch. What was exchanged for the land is unknown, and the Khoi had no concept of the written text, even though these texts had been the agents depriving them of their land and, ultimately, bringing to them an awareness of ownership, from whence most of the conflicts of the future would arise. From being a signifier of the sea route to India, the cape had now become a signified; and historians speculate that when the settlers began cultivating what they perceived as their own land the seeds were sown for the beginnings of a nation, the "Afrikaner nation" (February 1991).

Literary genres that have become part of what is now called Afrikaans literature, and which are essentially a continuation of certain discourses originating in the contact zone, are the travel journal, anthropological fiction, and the farm novel. Travel discourse with descriptions of landscapes and people can be traced from François Valentyn's descriptions of the Cape of Good Hope, the travel journals of Olaf Bergh, Isaq Schrijfer, Hendrik Wikar, Jacobus Coetsé, and Willem van Reenen in the seventeenth and eighteenth centuries, to Breyten Breytenbach's *Paradise* books at the end of the twentieth century, with their descriptions of this land and its landscape. But they are also virulent in their protest against the political ideology of the Afrikaner. Writing about the "natives," their customs and character, which had definite scientific pretensions in the work of Peter Kolb and Olfertus Dapper, was part of the colonial reconnaissance since the seventeenth century. This became a tradition in early Afrikaans literature, categorized in the major literary histories as "Animal, Native and Folklore in the Narrative," represented in the work of the writers Sangiro (A. A. Pienaar), G. C. and S. B. Hobson, P. J. Schoeman, G. H. Franz, Mikro (C. H. Kühn), and to a certain extent the "first" recognized poet, Eugène Marais (see Kannemeyer 1984). This "anthropological" writing has never really ceased – see, for example, the recent novels of Piet van Rooyen. It remains an integral part of the Afrikaans writer's awareness of his / her physical environment. The farm novel (the "plaasroman" in Afrikaans), another genre growing from the representations at the beginnings of colonization, became canonized since the novels of D. F. Malherbe. The first of this genre, according to J. C. Kannemeyer, was his *Die Meulenaar* (1926) (The Miller). This genre – growing out of the need for finding the meaning of the farm and of land – has created various statements within the discourse. In it there have been celebrations of labor, the idealization of nature, and significant creations of relationships between master and worker in the works of Malherbe and C. M. van den Heever (*Somer*, 1935, Summer; *Laat Vrugte*, 1939, Late Fruits). The farm novel is still being written, but modern farm writing is often satirical, as in the work of Etienne Leroux, where the farm has become the site of a Bacchanalia and a decaying Foundation (*Sewe dae by die Silbersteins*, 1962, Seven Days at the Silbersteins; *Een vir Azazel*, 1964, One for the Devil), and postmodern, with an apocalyptic burning of the farm, such as in a novel by Eben Venter, *Foxtrot van die Vleiseters* (1993) (Foxtrot of the Meat Eaters). The dark past is narrated by a dying survivor in a book by Karel Schoeman, *Hierdie Lewe* (1993) (This Life). Then it also becomes a holiday resort: the farm merely a memory in a work by Etienne van Heerden *Kikoejoe* (1996) (Kikuyu). With the Restitution of Lands Act 1994, land rights that people lost because of racially discriminatory laws passed by previous governments since 1913 can now be restored or compensated for. Changes in the ownership of land could bring about changes in the meaning of the farm. The discourse may remain, although the statements may differ.

The indigenization of language

When Jan van Riebeeck, the first Dutch East India Company official who became commander at the Cape of Good Hope in 1652, began his settlement, the language of the indigene had been Khoi for many centuries (Van Rensburg 1997: 2). Soon a heterogeneous community developed here, consisting of the indigenous Khoi, the liberated new Dutch settlers (known as "freeburghers"), sailors of various nationalities, and slaves who had been arriving since 1658 from India, Madagascar, Indonesia, and various parts of Africa. In learning Dutch these slaves started speaking a language differing from Dutch, eventually becoming established, and named Cape Afrikaans. This variety of early Afrikaans is recorded in the Arabic script of the successors of the Muslim slaves, specifically the *Bayaan-ud-dijn*, the "Explanation of the Faith" written by Abu Bakr in 1869 (Van Rensburg 1997: 13).

The freeburghers of necessity had to become acquainted with the Khoi cattle suppliers. They, however, as was the case with colonizers throughout the world, did not learn the Khoi language; but the Khoi began learning theirs, and examples of Khoi Afrikaans have been recorded since 1671 (Van Rensburg 1997: 25). The pasture-seeking freeburghers moved inland and made more contact with the Khoi. Their language also changed until they no longer spoke Dutch, and the Khoi no longer spoke their own language. Several linguistic groupings – the Dutch-speaking freeburghers, Malay slaves from the east, the indigenous Khoi, and various Portuguese, French, and German soldiers of fortune and sailors – mingled the language of the colonizer. All these learners of Dutch spoke an "acquisition language," a form of language normally not learnt to perfection, and not in this case learnt from the Dutch East India Company officials, but from the ordinary people. A kind of "acquisition Dutch" developed, which became the lingua franca, and eventually it supplanted Dutch and Khoi (Van Rensburg 1997: 23).[2]

The written language, such as the language of the Bible, remained Dutch, however. For persons involved with the conversion of the indigene to Christianity, it was a matter of grave concern that these people could not read the word of God. This led to the creation of an organization for the translation of the Bible into Afrikaans. They called themselves the "Genootskap vir Regte Afrikaners" (GRA: Fellowship of Real Afrikaners). Although their attempts were not successful at convincing the British Bible Society to undertake a translation (the language according to the society was still too dialectic) they inaugurated a written language by starting a newspaper in Afrikaans and translating well-known passages from the Bible. In spite of opposition from Dutch and English speakers (there were various official attempts to discourage the use of this "kitchen-dialect" and "patois") they succeeded; but the language, because of this opposition and because of a developing "Africanized" white identity, became a vehicle for a national identity – a white national identity. The language created by slaves and the Khoi was ultimately being appropriated for white nationalism, i.e., Afrikaner, in opposition to the English.

At the same time persons with poetic inclination began writing creatively in Afrikaans. The land, the landscape, historical events such as the Anglo-Boer War of 1899–1902 entered into the poetic expression of the work of Eugène Marais, C. Louis Leipoldt, Totius, and Jan Celliers. The writings of these first poets were significant statements within the discourse on language.

The coupling of language and white nationalism would ultimately bring about an ideological burden for Afrikaans. The landmarks of disaster were: 1925, when it was given official status, and standardization of the language became a project; 1948, when an Afrikaans-speaking political party ruled the country and institutionalized apartheid; 1976, the Soweto uprising and nationwide protest against the government, incited by the enforcement of Afrikaans at schools; 1994, when the political power was taken away from the Afrikaner. Now Afrikaans is, democratically, only one of eleven official languages. It has lost its privileged status, and English has become the language of the ruler, although Afrikaans, Zulu, and Xhosa have the most speakers (Van Rensburg 1997: 78).

On the other hand, a liberation of the language has taken place. During the era of apartheid it had developed as a medium of struggle. Although it was the language of institutional power, it was also the language of the oppressed, especially in provinces such as the Western Cape. Protest poetry and protest theater prevailed and an "alternative Afrikaans" became prominent. Since democratization, the writing and canonization of literature is becoming less and less confined to standardized, white, Afrikaans; the previously marginalized "coloured" writers have since the beginning of the 1990s produced significant poetry and prose from the world of the historically oppressed and the poor. The following writers have recently been published: Abraham Phillips, A. H. M. Scholtz, S. P. Benjamin, Patrick Petersen, André Boezak, Eugene Beukes, Isak Theunissen, and an anthology of poetry, *Nuwe Stemme* (New Voices), has been launched. The interest of creative writers (such as Thomas Deacon and Hans du Plessis) is revived by historic variations of Afrikaans in the oral tradition (such as Orange River and Khoi Afrikaans).

Colonization

Because South Africa only really became decolonized in 1994, with the first democratic election, colonization is a necessary discourse in South African literature. There is much of Afrikaans literature of the past that can be considered colonial, and there is much that has developed from an unconscious but definite anticolonial attitude by writers.[3] An example is the novel *'n Ander Land* by Karel Schoeman (1984) (Another Country), where a visitor from Europe comes to South Africa towards the end of the nineteenth century and experiences Africa while at the same time journeying inward into his own life and thoughts.

The well-known kind of colonization, the control by a far-away power over an "uncivilized" part of the world for mostly mercantile reasons, has been inflicted four times on South Africa: first by the Dutch, almost imperceptibly since 1652, then by the British from 1795, by the Dutch again, 1803–06, and finally by the British from 1806 (Davenport 1987: 40–43). From the colonial powers came the concept "literature." When the Fellowship of Real Afrikaners began encouraging and creating its own "literature," they knew what they were up to: beginning to create a culture of reading.

Britain's imperialist onslaught at the end of the nineteenth century on the gold of South Africa (which ended in the Anglo-Boer War) was the momentum for some of the most memorable war poetry in Afrikaans. The "triumvirate" of Celliers, Totius, and Leipoldt, publishing their first poems from 1908 to 1911, expressed the suffering and grief of people in tender and bitter verses – Celliers's *Die Vlakte en ander Gedigte* (The Plain and Other Poems) appeared in 1908. Leipoldt's poem "Oom Gert Vertel" (Uncle Gert's Tale, in his *Versamelde Gedigte* 1980, Collected Poems) is the remarkable poetic narrative of an old man's sorrow and guilt after the war. Totius will remain known for his "Forgive and Forget" (in his *Versamelde Werke*, 1977, Collected Works).

The most vicious form of colonialism, and the kind of control that was perpetuated until 1993, was, however, "colonialism of a special type" (Bundy 1989: 3), or "internal colonialism," which "corresponds to a structure of social relations based on domination and exploitation among culturally heterogeneous, distinct groups. South Africa combined the worst of imperialism and colonialism, so that 'Non-white South Africa' was the colony of 'White South Africa'" (Casanova 1975: 231). This lineage of power had developed from the seventeenth century, and the Afrikaner nationalists, when they came into power in 1948, institutionalized internal colonialism. The farmer and Afrikaner proletariat of the 1930s strove toward capitalist accumulation, and in the economic boom of the 1960s "capital found that apartheid worked" (Saul and Gelb 1981: 16).

Almost simultaneously with the strengthening of Afrikaner hegemony resistance grew among a younger group of writers, called the "Sestigers" (writers of the sixties). Although an awareness of injustice and alienation was beginning to be reflected in the thus far largely realistic Afrikaans prose, symbolic solutions for the growing contradictions in the country were not yet perceived. Writers such as Mikro, F. A. Venter, and later Chris Barnard engaged the "question of race," but they were unable to break away from the false consciousness into which they had grown. Certain (white) poets, before the advent of the "Sestigers," had already in their poetry addressed race and class: Barend Toerien, but particularly Peter Blum, who satirized white bourgeois values, in the language ("coloured Afrikaans") and from the perspective of a black oppressed proletariat; and Ingrid Jonker, whose fame was established by a poem (published in 1963) on the protest of the black child. Toerien's poem "Orlando Landskap" (Orlando Landscape) voices the oppression of the workers of the township Orlando (see the selection published later, entitled *Aanvange*, 1984). The satirical sonnets of Blum are collected in *Steenbok tot Poolsee* (1956) (Capricorn to Polar Sea) and *Enklaves van die Lig* (1958) (Enclaves of Light). "Die kind" (The Little Child) by Jonker was published in her first book of poetry, *Rook en Oker* (1963) (Smoke and Ochre).

The most productive "Sestigers" were André P. Brink, Breyten Breytenbach, Etienne Leroux, Jan Rabie, Bartho Smit, and later, but writing within the same discourses, Elsa Joubert. Most of them left the mother country at some stage and traveled or lived in France (Breytenbach became a French citizen). From this decolonized space their writing became liberated from the essentially realist and esthetic tradition that had developed in Afrikaans literature. They came into contact with Surrealism, the absurd, protest literature, and a completely different literary landscape.[4] Not only did they introduce different techniques, styles, and metaphors in prose and poetry, but they contested the hegemony into which they had been born. The protest was of such a serious nature that it led to imprisonment (of seven years for Breytenbach on charges of terrorism against the state), and the banning of their books. Brink's novel *Kennis van die aand* (1973) (*Looking on Darkness*, 1974), a novel about a sexual and political relationship between a coloured man and a white woman, was the first Afrikaans novel to be banned by the Publications Control Board. This censorship board was instituted in 1963 and became a powerful instrument toward the colonization of thought and creativity. Breytenbach's volume of poetry, *Skryt* (1972), was also banned, ostensibly for a poem about the atrocities committed under the regime of Prime Minister Balthazar John Vorster (the head of state at the time of Soweto 1976, and the death in police detention of Black Consciousness activist Steve Biko in 1977).[5]

Breytenbach and Brink are still the most prolific writers in Afrikaans (for wider consumption both are now writing in English as well), and it is difficult to assess in a few words their value to the literature and culture in the country. In general, however, Brink's prose has varied from realistic commitment to stream of consciousness, to magical realism, to postmodern deconstructions.

He is an innovator and an excellent storyteller: a literary specialist. Breytenbach is a master of metaphor (probably the greatest in Afrikaans) and of the poeticization of reality, but also a deconstructor of his own creations, postmodern, a nonlinear thinker – and politically and socially an unreconstructed anarchist.

Short-story writers who have written within the critical and contesting mode of the "Sestigers," transforming the Afrikaans short story are Abraham H. de Vries and Hennie Aucamp. The poet Antjie Krog, beginning her career as poet with adolescent and romantic verses in 1970, developed her original themes into powerful gender and political verses in such works as *Dogter van Jefta* (1970) (Daughter of Jephta) and *Gedigte 1989–1995* (1995) (Poems). Elsa Joubert began writing traditional travel novels, then exploited moments in the liberation of Africa. But her most significant work has been the documentary novel of the life of a black housemaid, Poppie Nongena, whose suffering under the bureaucracy of apartheid is painstakingly recorded in *Die swerfjare van Poppie Nongena* (1962) (The Wandering Years of Poppie Nongena).

The awareness of the cultural and esthetic power of literature, of its contribution to knowledge, of the writer as prophet and intellectual, which the "Sestigers" exploited, came not only from their exposure to the outside world. It was a consciousness constructed since the "beginning" of Afrikaans by the GRA in 1875: of the meaning of "literature," "writing," and "culture."

Literature as discourse

In 1905, the journalist and historian Gustav Preller utilized the nature poem "Winternag" (Winter's Night) by Eugène Marais to prove how suitable "our mother tongue" is for the expression of our most intimate experiences (Opperman 1961: 100). Preller also argued for the professionalization of Afrikaans in journalism and literature. The conscious manufacturing of Afrikaans literature had seriously begun (see Hofmeyr 1987).

The production of poetry increased in quantity and in quality, and by the 1930s there was a new generation of poets, critical of their predecessors, striving towards greater maturity – away from the national and patriotic and from the panegyrics of nature. The leading figure was the poet, critic, and philosopher N. P. van Wyk Louw, who in his *Berigte te Velde* (1941) (Dispatches) formulated the ideals of a new generation, the idea of an Afrikaans national literature, where every human experience could be reflected in literature, without inhibition. Poetry would not be in service of the local and the typical, but of all humanity; poetic creation is therefore a high and compelling task, and the poet consistently has to strive toward perfection. At the beginning of these essays he states: "I wanted to show you how great the task is to create a new civilization in this country – the destiny of our nation" (Louw 1941: 16).

Van Wyk Louw expresses a constant concern with the esthetic, the aristocratic, and the attainment of knowledge (the poet as intellectual, the poet as the guardian of the beautiful). His long poem *Raka* (1951) is a Beowulf-like heroic epic where an evil force (Raka) disrupts the idyllic existence of a tribe in Africa. He threatens their culture, their knowledge, and their art. The beautiful and pure protagonist, Koki, dies in the conflict to save his people from Raka. In powerful rhythms and impressive metaphors this poem is a symbolic representation of the persistent threat of the base, the barbaric, and the evil to the ethical and the esthetic.

Van Wyk Louw's poetry, up to his last volume *Tristia* (1962), with its echo of Ovid, strives to confirm poetry as the practice of the beautiful and the expressive word. This does not necessarily mean the elevated and the individualistic, as he also transforms the language and expressions of farm workers into folk poetry in the series "klipwerk" ("Stone work") in his *Nuwe Verse* (1954) (New Verse). The significance of Van Wyk Louw is that he saw poetry as a specific discourse – and it is still venerated as such, as a separate field of creative culture in the Afrikaans letters of today. These poetic adaptations of the language of working-class rural people would later reach perfection in the work of the poet who called himself "Boerneef" (I. W. van der Merwe), literally, "farm cousin."

Elisabeth Eybers, of the same generation, is seen as the "poetic voice of the woman." She began by expressing the world of the young woman, then the mother, then the cynicism of middle age and the ironic distance of old age. Hers is a poetry that changed from romanticism to irony. Uys Krige remained the romantic and the nomad of his generation, the traveler who brought the Mediterranean world into Afrikaans poetry: a renaissance person. The poets of the decade after the 1930s, specifically D. J. Opperman and Ernst van Heerden, consolidated poetry as a craft, to the extent that Opperman started creative classes in poetry at the University of Stellenbosch, where he taught literature. Many of the younger poets were taught much of their craft by him, often inheriting his type of metaphor and the meticulously constructed poetry he practiced. His epic *Joernaal van Jorik* (1949) is a richly metaphorical, poetically dense history of the Afrikaners: of their achievement and of their guilt.

As literature became a serious matter in the 1930s, literary criticism sought its theoretical foundation in the work of the Russian Formalists, in the autonomy of the "woordkunswerk" ("verbal art") and in close reading as means of analysis. The relationship of literature to society, and its effect on society was seen as of peripheral importance. Various literary theoretical conflicts arose in apartheid South Africa between those who wished to construct a *littèrature engagée*, and those who perceived literature as an autonomous discourse.

The phenomenon of a "minor literature"

Although Afrikaans writers since the 1960s have undoubtedly been instrumental in awakening the consciousness of their readers to the political and social system they had inherited – and have often been at the forefront in protesting – the role of the so-called "brown" (coloured, *métise*) poets and novelists in Afrikaans cannot be underestimated. The predecessor of the younger black writers mentioned earlier was the poet and thinker Adam Small. Often using Cape Afrikaans – the unstandardized version of Afrikaans spoken by city workers, rural people, and fisher folk – his poetry is lyrical, straightforward, and addresses political suppression directly. This can be called people's poetry. His versatile, popular play, alternating dialogue, song, music, with an achronological, modernist construction of scenes, *Kanna hy ko hystoe* (1965) (Kanna, He's Coming Home), tells of the coming to town of an impoverished family, and of the disasters they experience. They are awaiting the return of their "savior," the talented son (Kanna) studying overseas; but he returns too late. This play is to a certain extent reminiscent of earlier Afrikaans plays by J. F. W. Grosskopf, recreating similar situations when Afrikaners were poor. Examples of social realist plays by Grosskopf are *As die tuig skawe* (1926a) (When the Harness Chafes) and *In die wagkamer* (1926b) (In the Waiting Room).

There was writing by black/coloured writers in Afrikaans before Small, specifically poetry, by S. V. Petersen (from 1940) and P. J. Philander (from 1955). In the work of Petersen the subaltern position of the black person is also expressed. They did not, however, deterritorialize Afrikaans from its standard, white, form and create a new literary language, a new venue for writers who came from an oppressed minority: a minor literature within an established, canonical one – such as Franz Kafka had created in German in Prague according to Gilles Deleuze and Félix Guattari (1993).

Small's creation of an alternative means of expression, identifiable by the language of the oppressed, has given impetus to a discourse by "Black Afrikaans writers," who have now clearly identified themselves as such.[6] The advent of prose writing by those who had previously been marginalized, especially since the 1980s – Abraham Phillips, A. H. M. Scholtz, S. P. Benjamin, Patrick Petersen,

Boezak, Beukes, and Theunissen – has strengthened the production of the literature of the Other, particularly in terms of a new narrative voice. Probably the most significant of these voices, also because of the oral nature of his narrative and its loose structure, is that of A. H. M. Scholtz, who introduced his first book, *Vatmaar. 'n Lewendagge verhaal van 'n tyd wat nie meer is nie* (1995) (Take it. An Alive Story of a Time that is no More), as the "story of the brown people of South Africa. They didn't come from the North, neither from over the sea. They originated here, true South Africans . . ."

Those writers who are still "marginalized" are rapidly becoming part of canonical, "major," Afrikaans literature. But in this process they are widening the fields of experience created and expressed in this literature. Although the prose writers are using standardized Afrikaans, and although the memory of the evils of apartheid will fade, poverty and class discrimination still remain. New poetry is still being produced in the street language of Adam Small, in the tradition of the "minor literature," for instance, *My Straat* (1998) (My Street), by Loit Sols: "Die ghetto's wiemel van creativity, mense wat moet praat: / as ekkie gan praatie, gan my bek stink" / "The ghettoes are swarming with creativity, with people who have to talk: / if I don't talk my mouth is going to smell."

Modernism and postmodernism

Whereas "modernism" should be seen as a more or less natural development in specifically Afrikaans prose since the 1960s, from the meaningful contact of the "Sestigers" with Europe, "postmodernism" will here mean, in the first place, writing trends after modernism. Although it may have been in reaction to modernism, or part of a cosmopolitan mindset, it does not in Afrikaans literature refer to any kind of organized movement.

While poetry was being instituted as a specific kind of discourse in the thirties, Breyten Breytenbach, in self-exile in Paris, had already since 1964 been writing a disjunctive, deconstructive, surrealist kind of verse – for example, in *Die Ysterkoei moet Sweet* (1964) (The Iron Cow Has to Sweat). The self-consciousness of his texts and their inherent deconstruction, even in erotic poetry and political protest, remain the only constant throughout a prolific career as poet. His *ars poetica* is spelt out, even in his prose writing: a rejection of the idea that language can represent reality, and an insistence on the mere signifying (sign-ness) nature of representation. As a painter of international standing, Breytenbach also manifested this poetic conviction in his drawings and paintings.

One can probably pinpoint the beginning of an awareness of the benefits of intertextual writing from the short stories of Koos Prinsloo, specifically his volume *Jonkmanskas* (1982).[7] His writing is also anarchistic in the sense that it subverts the father figure, is openly homosexual (whereas the earlier short-story writer, Hennie Aucamp, had treated this matter with care), and denigrates the political leaders of the time. Writing within the time of the militarization of South Africa, he creates the border, young men who have to fight battles in which they do not believe, and have to adapt to civil life afterwards. The "Grensverhaal" (Border Narrative), written from the traumatic experiences of young, protesting, soldiers became a brief genre in the early eighties, especially among short-story writers – for example, Etienne van Heerden's *My Kubaan* (1983) (My Cuban) and Alexander Strachan's *'n Wêreld Sonder Grense* (1984) (World without Borders). The novel of John Miles, *Blaaskans* (1983) (Half-Time), a novel with militarization as background, is postmodern in its conscious misreading of Afrikaner history, anarchistic in its belief that history is no more than faulty memory.

The involvement of the writer with his text, and with the writing process, is significant in Abraham H. de Vries's volume of short stories, *Nag van die Clown* (1989) (Night of the Clown), of which a postmodern analysis has been made by Van Heerden in his study entitled *Postmodernisme en Prosa* (1993 and 1995). The writer as memory, recreating memory, is the main character in Van Heerden's previously mentioned farm novel *Kikoejoe.* John Miles problematizes the task of the writer as chronicler in *Kroniek uit die Doofpot* (1991) (trans. as *Deafening Silence*, 1997), his history of the black policeman whose quest for justice led to his and his family's death by a hit squad in 1987. How does the writer – the white writer – use documents to create a life and a history? How can he do so, being part of a morally unacceptable hegemony?

Present-day Afrikaans novelists who do not quite fit into a "postmodernist" label, but who work from a preoccupation with history, of South Africa and of the Afrikaner, are Marlene van Niekerk and particularly Karel Schoeman. Van Niekerk's novel *Triomf* (1994) (trans. in English with same title) takes the reader back to the proletariat Afrikaner, the "poor white" of the 1920s, although in this novel they have now become "white trash." The suburb where they live was built on the ruins of the old black township Sophiatown. The current political situation stemming from the first democratic election of April 1994, their racism and their incestuous relations recreate a cynical present from an imagined past. Karel Schoeman's farm novels *Hierdie Lewe* (1993) (This Life) and *Die Uur van die Engel* (1995) (The Hour of the Angel) are subtitled "Voices," and in both novels his search is for the voices of the past, the voices of the marginalized – to tell their story of this country. This calling-up of the unheard voices from the past is substituted for – and probably inspired by – his factual historical work, of which a recent example is the history of the (land) exploitation of the Griqua people by the British and the Boers (*Griqua Records*, 1996).

Conclusion

In Afrikaans, which had indigenized itself in Africa, a literature was constructed by black and white writers. In the process of affirming a language, this literature has become part of the creation of a hegemony, but ultimately and ethically also part of its necessary destruction, still retaining its esthetic status as literature. The tendencies of the most recent Afrikaans texts – to attempt memorizing and writing the past, and to open up the language dialogically to many voices – will give it the strength to create another, broader, future for what remains of the construct "the Afrikaner."

Notes

1. The importance of exchange, also as the means of representation of the westerner to the Other, has to be emphasized. See the attention given to it by Greenblatt 1992: 197.
2. According to linguists it was already difficult to find a fluent speaker of the Khoi language in the nineteenth century (Van Rensburg 1997: 23).
3. Only recently Afrikaans literary theorists have taken note of the discourse of postcolonialism. See Viljoen 1996.
4. Brink's collection of essays, *Mapmakers* (1983), is a particularly significant indicator of a growing consciousness. See the beginning of the introduction, "A Background to Dissidence": "I was born on a bench in the Luxembourg Gardens in Paris, in the early spring of 1960 . . ." (1983: 29).
5. The title of the volume is untranslatable, probably a combination of the Afrikaans word "skryf" (to write) and "skyt" (shit). The title of the specific poem is "Letter to butcher from abroad."
6. In 1985, they had their first symposium, published as *Swart Afrikaanse Skrywers* (Black Afrikaans Writers) (ed. Smith, Gensen and Willemse); in 1995, a second symposium was held, leading to the publication in 1997 of *Die Reis na Paternoster* (The Journey to Paternoster) (ed. Willemse, Hattingh, Wyk and Conradie).
7. "Jonkmanskas" is an untranslatable word for an antique clothes' cupboard, specifically designed for a young man.

Bibliography

Axelson, Eric, ed. 1988. *Dias and His Successors*. Cape Town: Saayman and Weber.
Benjamin, S. P. 1997. *Die Reuk van Steenkool*. Pretoria: Queillerie.

Blum, Peter. 1956. *Steenbok tot Poolsee*. Cape Town: Nasionale Boekhandel.
1958. *Enklaves van die Lig*. Cape Town: Human and Rousseau.
Breytenbach, Breyten. 1964. *Die Ysterkoei moet Sweet*. Johannesburg: Afrikaanse Pers Boekhandel.
1972. *Skryt. Om 'n sinkende skip blou te verf*. Poetry International Series. Amsterdam: Meulenhoff.
1980. *A Season in Paradise*. London: Jonathan Cape.
1993. *Return to Paradise*. Cape Town: David Philip.
Brink, André P. 1973. *Kennis van die Aand*. Cape Town: Buren.
1974. *Looking on Darkness*. London: W. H. Allen.
1983. *Mapmakers: Writing in a State of Siege*. London: Faber and Faber.
Bundy, Colin. 1989. "Around Which Corner: Revolutionary Theory and Contemporary South Africa." *Transformation* 8: 1–23.
Casanova, Gonzalez. 1975. *Beyond the Sociology of Development*. London and Boston: Routledge and Kegan Paul.
Celliers, Jan F. E. 1974. *Die Vlakte en ander Gedigte*. Cape Town: Tafelberg.
Davenport, T. R. H. 1987. *South Africa: A Modern History*. 3rd edn. Braamfontein: Macmillan.
Deacon, Thomas. 1993. *Die preikasies van Jacob Oerson*. Cape Town: Tafelberg.
Deleuze, Gilles, and Félix Guattari. 1993. *Kafka: Toward a Minor Literature*. Trans. Dana Polan. Foreword by Réda Bensmaïa. Theory and History of Literature, vol. 30. Minneapolis: University of Minnesota Press.
De Vries, Abraham H. 1989. *Nag van die Clown*. Cape Town: Human and Rousseau.
Du Plessis, Hans. 1984. *Gewete van Glas*. Cape Town: Human and Rousseau.
February, Vernon. 1991. *The Afrikaners of South Africa*. London: Kegan Paul.
Franz, G. H. 1946. *Moeder Poulin*. Cape Town: Nasionale Boekhandel.
1954. *Rabodutu*. Cape Town: Nasionale Boekhandel.
Greenblatt, Stephen. 1992. *Marvellous Possessions*. Oxford: Clarendon Press.
Grosskopf, J. F. W. 1926a. *As die tuig skawe*. Cape Town: Nasionale Pers.
1926b. *In die wagkamer*. Cape Town: Nasionale Pers.
Hegel, G. W. F. 1975. *Lectures on the Philosophy of World History*. Cambridge: Cambridge University Press.
Hobson, G. C. and S. B. 1929. *Kees*. Pretoria: J. L. van Schaik.
1930. *Skankwan van die duine*. Pretoria: J. L. van Schaik.
1933. *Buks*. Pretoria: J. L. van Schaik.
Hofmeyr, Isabel. 1987. "Building a Nation from Words: Afrikaans Language, Literature and Ethnic Identity, 1920–1924." In *The Politics of Race, Class and Nationalism in Twentieth Century South Africa*. Ed. Shula Marks and Stanley Trapido. London: Longman: 96–123.
Itinerario Voyage ofte Schipvaert van Jan Huygen van Linschoten near Oost often Portugaels Indien, 1579–1592. 1934. 's Gravenhage: Marthinus Nijhoff.
Jonker, Ingrid B. 1963. *Rook en Oker*. Johannesburg: Afrikaanse Pers-Boekhandel.
Joubert, Elsa. 1978. *Die Swerfjare van Poppie Nongena*. Cape Town: Tafelberg.
Kannemeyer, J. C. 1983. *Geskiedenis van die Afrikaanse Literatuur*. Part 1. Pretoria: Academica.
1984. *Geskiedenis van die Afrikaanse Literatuur*. Part 2. Pretoria: Academica.
Kobe, Peter. 1762. *Naaukeurige en uitvoerige beschryving van de Kaap de Goede Hoop*. Amsterdam: Balthazar Lakeman.

Krog, Antjie. 1970. *Dogter van Jefta*. Cape Town: Human and Rousseau.
1995. *Gedigte 1989–1995*. Pretoria: Hond.
Leipoldt, C. Louis. 1980. *Versamelde Gedigte*. Cape Town: Human and Rousseau.
Leroux, Etienne. 1962. *Sewe dae by die Silbersteins*. Cape Town: Human and Rousseau.
1964. *Een vir Azazel*. Cape Town: Human and Rousseau.
Louw, N. P. van Wyk. 1941. *Berigte te Velde*. Cape Town: Nasionale Boekhandel.
1951. *Raka*. Cape Town: Nasionale Boekhandel.
1954. *Nuewe Verse*. Cape Town: Nasionale Boekhandel.
1962. *Tristia*. Cape Town: Human and Rousseau.
Malherbe, D. F. 1926. *Die Meulenaar*. Cape Town: Nasionale Pers.
Mikro [C. H. Kühn]. 1934. *Toiings*. Pretoria: J. L. van Schaik.
1935. *Pelgrims*. Pretoria: J. L. van Schaik.
1940. *Huurlinge*. Cape Town: Nasionale Boekhandel.
1942. *Huisies teen die heuwel*. Cape Town: Nasionale Boekhandel.
Miles, John. 1983. *Blaaskans. Die bewegings van Flip Nel*. Emmarentia: Taurus.
1991. *Kroniek uit die Doofpot*. Emmarentia: Taurus.
1996. *Deafening Silence*. Cape Town: Human and Rousseau.
Mossop, E. E., ed. 1931. *Journals of the Expedition of the Honourable Olaf Bergh (1682–1683) and the Ensign Isaq Schrijfer (1689)*. Cape Town: Van Riebeeck Society.
1935. *The Journal of Hendrik Jacob Wikar (1779) and The Journal of Jacobus Coetsé Jansz (1760) and Willem van Reenen (1791)*. Cape Town: Van Riebeeck Society.
Opperman, D. J. 1941. *Joernaal van Jorik*. Cape Town: Nasionale Boekhandel.
1961. *Eerstelinge*. Cape Town: Human and Rousseau.
Petersen, Patrick. 1993. *Vergenoeg*. Vredenburg: Prog.
Phillips, Abraham. 1992. *Verdwaalde Land*. Strand: Queillerie.
1993. *Erfenis van die Noodlot*. Groenkloof: Queillerie.
1997. *Die Messiasbende*. Cape Town: Queillerie.
Prinsloo, Koos. 1982. *Jonkmanskas*. Cape Town: Tafelberg.
Sangiro [A. A. Pienaar]. 1921. *Uit Oerwoud en Vlakte*. Cape Town: Nasionale Boekhandel.
1944. *Simba*. Johannesburg: Voortrekkerpers.
Saul, John S., and Stephen Gelb. 1981. "The Crisis in South Africa: Class Defense, Class Revolution." *Monthly Review Press* 33. 3: 1–156.
Schaperia, I., ed. 1933. *The Early Cape Hottentots Described in the Writing of Olfert Dapper (1668), Willem ten Rhyne (1686) and Johannes Gulielmus de Grevenbroek (1685)*. Cape Town: Van Riebeeck Society.
Schoeman, Karel. 1984. *'n Ander Land*. Cape Town: Human and Rousseau.
1993. *Hierdie Lewe*. Cape Town: Human and Rousseau.
1995. *Die Uur van die Engel*. Cape Town: Human and Rousseau.
1996. *Griqua Records. The Philippolis Captaincy 1825–1861*. Cape Town: Van Riebeeck Society.
Schoeman, P. J. 1949. *Op ver paaie*. Cape Town: Nasionale Boekhandel.
1972a. *Jagters van die Woestynland*. Cape Town: Nasionale Boekhandel.
1972b. *Jabulani die Zoeloe*. Johannesburg: Perskor.
Scholz, A. H. M. 1995. *Vatmaar. 'n Lewendagge verhaal van 'n tyd wat nie meer is nie*. Cape Town: Kwela.

Small, Adam. 1962. *Kitaar my Kruis*. Cape Town: HAUM.

1965. *Kanna hy ko hystoe*. Cape Town: Tafelberg.

Smith, Julian, Alwyn van Gensen, and Hein Willemse, eds. 1985. *Swart Afrikaanse Skrywers*. Bellville: University of the Western Cape.

Strachan, Alexander. 1984. *'n Wêreld Sonder Grense*. Cape Town: Tafelberg.

Toerien, Barend. 1984. *Aanvange*. Cape Town: Tafelberg.

Totius (J. D. du Toit). 1977. *Versamelde Werke*. Cape Town: Tafelberg.

Valentyn, François. 1971. *Description of the Cape of Good Hope with the Matters Concerning It. 1762*. Cape Town: Van Riebeeck Society.

Van den Heever, C. M. 1935. *Somer*. Pretoria: J. L. van Schaik.

1939. *Laat Vrugte*. Pretoria: J. L. van Schaik.

Van Heerden, Etienne. 1983. *My Kubaan*. Cape Town: Tafelberg.

1996. *Kikoejoe*. Cape Town: Human and Rousseau.

1997. *Postmodernisme en Prosa. Vertelstrategieë in vyf verhale van Abraham H. de Vries*. Cape Town: Human and Rousseau.

Van Niekerk, Marlene. 1994. *Triomf*. Cape Town: Queillerie.

Van Rensburg, Christo, Achmat Davids, Jeannette Ferreira, Tony Links, and Karel Prinsloo, eds. 1997. *Afrikaans in Afrika*. Pretoria: J. L. van Schaik.

Van Rooyen, Piet. 1993. *Die Spoorsnyer*. Cape Town: Tafelberg.

1995. *Agter 'n Eland aan*. Cape Town: Queillerie.

1997. *Die Olifantjagters*. Cape Town: Tafelberg.

Venter, Eben. 1993. *Foxtrot van die Vleiseters*. Cape Town: Tafelberg.

Viljoen, Louise. 1996. "Postkolonialisme en die Afrikaanse Letterkunde: 'n verkenning van die rol van enkele gemarginaliseerde diskoerse." *Tydskrif vir Nederlands en Afrikaans* 3. 2: 158–75.

Willemse, Hein, Mairon Hattingh, Steward van Wyk, and Pieter Conradie, eds. 1997. *Die Reis na Paternoster*. Bellville: University of the Western Cape.